SEVENTH BOOK OF

Junior Authors
& Illustrators

Biographical Reference Books from
The H. W. Wilson Company

American Reformers

Greek and Latin Authors 800 B.C.–A.D. 1000
European Authors 1000–1900
British Authors Before 1800
British Authors of the Nineteenth Century
American Authors 1600–1900
Twentieth Century Authors
Twentieth Century Authors: First Supplement
World Authors 1950–1970
World Authors 1970–1975
World Authors 1975–1980
World Authors 1980–1985
World Authors 1985–1990
Spanish American Authors: The Twentieth Century

The Junior Book of Authors
More Junior Authors
Third Book of Junior Authors
Fourth Book of Junior Authors and Illustrators
Fifth Book of Junior Authors and Illustrators
Sixth Book of Junior Authors and Illustrators

Great Composers: 1300–1900
Composers Since 1900
Composers Since 1900: First Supplement
Musicians Since 1900
American Songwriters

Facts About the Presidents
Facts About British Prime Ministers
Nobel Prize Winners
World Artists 1950–1980
World Artists 1980–1990
World Film Directors: Volumes I, II

SEVENTH BOOK OF
Junior Authors
& Illustrators

EDITED BY SALLY HOLMES HOLTZE

THE H. W. WILSON COMPANY • NEW YORK • DUBLIN • 1996

Library of Congress Cataloging in Publication Data
Main entry under title:
Seventh book of junior authors & illustrators / edited by Sally Holmes Holtze.
p.   cm.   Continues: Sixth book of junior authors & illustrators.
    Summary: Contains more than two hundred sketches of authors, illustrators, and a translator of children's books who have come to prominence since the publication of the previous book.
    ISBN 0-8242-0873-0
    1. Children's literature—Bio-bibliography.   2. Children's literature—Illustrations—Bio-bibliography. [1. Authors. 2. Illustrators.] I. Holtze, Sally Holmes.   II. Seventh book of junior authors & illustartors.
PN1009.A1S3936   1996
809'.89282—dc20   95-47983
                                                                                          CIP
                                                                                          AC

Preface

HOW DOES ONE BECOME AN AUTHOR? An illustrator? Surely, one is born with the talent, or not. Yet that talent may fail to flourish, in many instances, due to many factors: the lack of opportunities, such as the time, space, or materials, to develop it; or simply because of the ignorance of possibilities. In their autobiographical sketches, many of the artists and authors in this book describe remarkable ways in which they have been encouraged in their unique talents by teachers, parents, and others along the way.

"We always had paper, crayons, glue, glitter, and scissors in the house," writes Loreen Leedy, "ready for the next burst of creativity." The parents of Peter Catalanotto kept one wall in the basement for their children to draw on: "When every inchwas covered with drawings . . . ," he writes, "my father would paint it white and we'd start anew." Crucial to Lois Ehlert's creativity was a table that her parents earmarked for her use, so she could always return to her art projects easily. And Susan L. Roth describes the family philosophy: you could only do your best work if you used good papers, good paints, good tools; the rule was upheld even for the creations of her four-year-old brother. These are inspiring and admirable stories, and perhaps none found here are more moving than the story of how Gennady Spirin was able to attend art school in Moscow.

While many readers may pick up this book to learn about a favorite author, they may find that the experiences these other authors and illustrators relate can open their eyes to possibilities and help them to shape their own stories or art.

This is the seventh book in a series that affords authors and illustrators a unique method of reaching their readers: through their autobiographical sketches. The first book of this series, *The Junior Book of Authors*, was published in 1935. A revised edition came out in 1951. *More Junior Authors* followed in 1963. The *Third Book of Junior Authors*, which contained the first cumulative index to the volumes, was published in 1972. The next three volumes appeared in 1978, 1983, and 1989.

The *Seventh Book of Junior Authors and Illustrators* contains 235 sketches of authors, illustrators, and a translator of children's books who have come to prominence since the publication of the *Sixth Book of Junior Authors*. Over a period of several years, the editor compiled a list of a thousand authors and illustrators who might be considered for inclusion in the volume. Several factors were considered in placing a name on the list: the recommendations of reviews and critics and the appearance of book titles on various lists of recommended books; awards and honors voted upon by professionals in the field of literature for children and young adults; and popularity. An advisory committee of children's and young adult literature specialists from across the country was chosen to vote on names from the preliminary list and invited to suggest additional names. The committee and the editor vote for approximately 135 names.

The committee for the *Seventh Book* consisted of Jane Botham, Coordinator of Children's Services, Milwaukee Public Library; Mary Mehlman Burns, Senior Librarian Emerita, Framingham State College; Betty Carter, Associate Professor, School of Library and Information Studies, Texas Women's University; Barbara Elleman, Editor, *Book Links*; Barbara Fischer, Central Branch Manager, Chesterfield County Public Library; Linda Perkins, Library Services Manager, Children's Services, Berkeley Public Library; and Roger Sutton, Editor-in-Chief, *Bulletin of the Center for Children's Books*.

The sketches appear in alphabetical order by that form of a person's name that appears most often on the title pages of his or her books. The index provides cross references for all names and pen names, not only in this volume but in all six previous volumes in the series. Phonetic pronunciations are supplied when necessary. When authors and illustrators have omitted from their sketches important information about themselves, such as biographical information or awards, editorial additions follow their autobiographical sketches. When biographical sources disclosed contradictory information, every possible attempt was made to obtain the correct information.

There are many awards and prizes given to children's books and their authors and illustrators every year, so editorial decisions have been made to include certain ones consistently. In particular, awards voted upon by children are omitted. The popularity of the books with children is not taken lightly; however, the dates of eligibility and other rules governing some of these awards result in the judgment of books by unusual comparisons.

The Selected Works section does not include the complete works of most authors and illustrators; we have tried to select books that have received particularly favorable reviews or that are important to an author or illustrator's career, or that are representative of their work. That the title may be out of print is not considered. Books published by adult book departments or those never published in the U.S. are not listed in Selected Works, but important books in this category are mentioned in the biographical data following the autobiographical sketch. The About sections provide references to books and articles that are likely to be generally available and that are in English. Articles of criticism have not been included, though they may be mentioned in the biographical details of the sketch.

When it has been impossible to obtain autobiographical material, biographical sketches have been compiled. When a sketch has been written by someone who knew the subject personally, credit is given to the writer in the heading of the sketch. Other biographical sketches were written anonymously by the editor and by Nandi Rodrigo and Karen Gray Ruelle, to both of whom the editor gives her thanks.

The editor would also like to acknowledge those who have helped to prepare this book, especially Bruce R. Carrick, Vice President of General Publications of The H. W. Wilson Company. Thanks are also due to Judith O'Malley, Associate Editor, and Elisa Ann Ferraro, Managing Editor, of General Publications. The editor also thanks the library promotion departments and publicity departments of the companies that publish the children's books and young adult books. As always, the Children's Book Council is much appreciated, for maintaining a collection of contemporary books that is available to researchers for examination. The editor is also thankful for the dedication and thoughtfulness of the advisory committee.

Most of all, we are grateful to the authors and illustrators who took the time and energy away from their important work to complete what is often a difficult task—to write about one's self; and we are especially grateful to those writers and illustrators who expressed their pleasure in participating in the process.
SALLY HOLMES HOLTZE
November 1995

Contents

SEVENTH BOOK OF
Junior Authors
& Illustrators

JON AGEE

April 19, 1960–

AUTHOR AND ILLUSTRATOR OF *The Incredible Painting of Felix Clousseau*, etc.

Biographical sketch of Jon Agee:

JON AGEE was born in Philadelphia, Pennsylvania, and grew up in Nyack, New York. As far back as he can remember, he was amusing himself by creating books. He studied painting and filmmaking at The Cooper Union in New York City and, upon graduating in 1981, he was showing his picture-book ideas to publishers.

Pantheon Books picked up his first story, *If Snow Falls*, in 1981. It was followed by *Ellsworth* and *Ludlow Laughs*. He is probably best known for his fourth book, *The Incredible Painting of Felix Clousseau*. Writing in a *Horn Book Magazine* review, critic Mary M. Burns stated: "Every so often a work appears that expands the limits of the picture storybook genre as it piques the imagination with unexpected possibilities. Jon Agee's witty tale of the iconoclastic painter who befuddles the art cognoscenti of Paris is just such a book." She admired the economy of the text and stated that the book "delights the eye, promotes laughter, and stimulates the intellect."

Agee has also written and illustrated several unusual books that invite readers to puzzle out answers. Two of these are books of palindromes, which are words or phrases that, when read forward and backward, say the same thing. For example, the title of the first book is a palindrome: *GO HANG A SALAMI! IM A LASAGNA HOG!*. *Flapstick*, in contrast, is a book in which the readers lifts a flap to reveal a hidden object that is the last word of a humorous poem. Edward Sorel, writing in *The New York Times Book Review*, so enjoyed it that he stated, "In my book [Agee] can do no wrong."

When writing or illustrating a book, Agee is basically entertaining himself. He never consciously sets out to make his books appeal to children. In fact, he believes, the best picture books are created by authors who are simply, by no fault of their own, connected to some anarchic, childlike spirit, and simultaneously gifted in narrative and artistic talent. He speaks of the book artists Tomi Ungerer, Hans Fischer and Ludwig Bemelmans (to name just a few) as being "naturals"; innovating with apparent ease within the format of around thirty-two pages. He also shares with Ungerer a sense of the ironic, double-meaning in things. And like Ungerer, his books are always driven by a droll sense of humor.

Agee's pictures are usually limned in bold black line. It's no wonder he borrowed generously from Ferdinand Léger when working on *Ludlow Laughs*. Henri Matisse and Raoul Dufy influenced *Flapstick*. For his latest book, he looked at the work of André François and Margot Zemach, and "rediscovered" the wonderfully expressive books of British author and illustrator John Burningham.

Agee's most recent projects are theatrical as well bibliographic. He wrote both the story and lyrics for a the musical

B.O.T.C.H., performed at the TADA! theater company in New York City in 1991. TADA! will present his second musical, *Flies in the Soup*, in the winter of 1995. Concurrently, he's finished a picture book with Michael di Capua Books, called *Dmitri the Astronaut*.

The Incredible Painting of Felix Clousseau was named a Notable Book of the Year by the American Library Association. *Ludlow Laughs* was a Reading Rainbow Book.

SELECTED WORKS: If Snow Falls, 1981; Ellsworth, 1983; Ludlow Laughs, 1985; The Incredible Painting of Felix Clousseau, 1988; GO HANG A SALAMI! IM A LASAGNA HOG! and Other Palindromes, 1992; The Return of Freddy LeGrand, 1992; Flapstick: 10 Ridiculous Rhymes with Flaps, 1993; So Many Dynamos!, 1994.

JEZ ALBOROUGH

JEZ ALBOROUGH

November 13, 1959–

AUTHOR AND ILLUSTRATOR OF *Where's My Teddy?*, etc.

Autobiographical sketch of Jez Alborough:

I WAS BORN in Kingston upon Thames, Surrey, on the thirteenth of November 1959. I have always believed that we make our own luck so making an entrance on such a traditionally unlucky day was perhaps a gesture of defiance.

I did, however, suffer from asthma, but I regard this illness as more of a teacher than a random blow of bad luck. In some ways I could say that it has taught me everything I know about myself.

During long absences from school, like many other asthmatics I have heard about, I practiced my drawing and writing—occasionally combining the two by making little dummy books.

I remember once a guest coming to our house who seemed taken by my enthusiatic creativity. On a subsequent visit he brought me a gift; a box of crisp white paper, some pencils and a rubber [eraser]. It was an act of support and encouragement which I have never forgotten. (The identity of this guest remains to this day a mystery. I like to think he was my guardian angel.)

I did not enjoy my secondary school—a place where art and the imagination were regarded as less important attributes than the ability to cram the memory with facts, figures and quotations which at that age meant very little to me. I find in myself now a great desire to learn and sometimes feel that those dull physics lessons could have been wonderful, stimulating teachings if I had attended a school which held imagination and inventiveness in higher regard. The art of good teaching must be finding a way to make any subject interesting to any student. A seven-year sentence dragged on until I was released into the freedom of Art School in Norwich—three years in which I could draw, explore and grow up around other artists. It was like having all the best bits of your childhood during your adolescence.

After college I spent two years chasing after editorial illustration commissions along with countless other art school graduates until I found that being able to write as well as draw gave me a head start in the equally competitive world of children's books. In 1984, one of my dummy books, called *Bare Bear*, was actually printed and bound and turned into a 'real' book. I found the experience so thrilling that I have continued submitting dummy books to my publisher to this very day—and so far, they have let me go on playing with my paper and pencils rather than go out and get a 'proper' job.

———

Jez Alborough has written and illustrated over thirty picture books for children, many of which have not yet been published in the United States. He is a popular speaker for storytelling events for children, and also gives talks about his work to librarians and teachers. In 1993 he appeared on *Playdays*, a British Broadcasting Corporation children's television program, explaining how a picture book is created.

With his brother, the playwright Graham Alborough, he has written a children's musical, *The Great Alphonso*, and a humorous play, *Murder at Teatime*, which was televised in the series "Murder Most Horrid." He is currently developing a children's television series.

Jez Alborough and his wife live in London.

Bare Bear, which was published in England in 1984, was a runnerup for the 1985 Mother Goose Award presented by the British book club, "Books for Children." Alborough was a contributor to *The Great Games Book*, a collection of illustrations of fourteen board games that was illustrated by various artists and published in England in 1985. It won a 1987 Bologna Children's Book Fair Graphics for Children prize in 1987.

SELECTED WORKS: Beaky, 1990; Where's My Teddy?, 1992; Bear Hugs, 1993; Cuddly Dudley, 1993; Clothesline, 1994; Hide-and-Seek, 1994; It's the Bear!, 1994.

ABOUT: Contemporary Authors, Vol. 131.

THOMAS B. ALLEN

January 23, 1928–

ILLUSTRATOR OF *In Coal Country*, etc.

Autobiographical sketch of Thomas B. Allen:

THINGS I'VE DONE: Grew up in middle Tennessee during The Great Depression. Played in woods and creeks. Started art lessons when I was nine. Beat up the class bully when I was twelve. Rode my bike to grandaddy's farm. Played football at Vanderbilt. Studied painting at The Art Institute of Chicago, B.F.A. Served as an officer in The U.S. Marine Corps. Produced a whole lot of pictures. Illustrated for *The New Yorker*, *Gourmet*, the *Atlantic*, *Esquire*, *Sports Illustrated*, *Life*, *Fortune*, CBS, NBC, Columbia Records, The Franklin Library, etc. Won some awards. Caught a whole lot of fish. Played golf with Arnold Palmer. Taught at the School of Visual Arts, Parsons School of Design, Syracuse University, Southampton College, and the University of Kansas. Found my calling as an illustrator of books for children.

PLACES I'VE BEEN: Cuba (I was twelve), Yucatan, Belize, Nicaragua, Costa Rica, Panama, Columbia, Puerto Rico, Nova Scotia, England, Scotland, Belgium, France, Holland, and all over the United States. While doing these things and traveling to these places, I've met many wonderful people: artists, writers, editors, art directors, musicians, designers, photographers, actors, producers, directors, teachers, lawyers, carpenters, sailors, fishermen, equestriennes, philosophers and students.

The sum of all the aforementioned defines, I think, who I am . . . my Being and my character.

My first serious quest for the answers to "who am I?" and "why am I here?" came in the early 1970's, at the age of forty-three. I spent three summers and three winters living a Spartan life in a drafty cabin on a pond near Cold Spring, New York. It was a time of both quiet despair and rejuvena-

Thomas B. Allen [signature]

tion. I gave up old values and searched for new ones. I drew, painted, illustrated and wrote poetry. I think of it as my Thoreau period.

My work table was by a window that overlooked the pond. I spent many hours observing life in, on and around that pond. A pair of Canadian geese came to visit every spring and dazzled me with their mating ritual. A busy family of muskrats lived in the opposite banks. Deer came out of the woods to drink from the pond. Raccoon washed their food at the water's edge. Tree frogs laid their thousands of eggs in the shallows. I saw a bullfrog catch and swallow a bird. There were rabbits and squirrels and bass and perch and sunfish and dragonflies and mayflies and waterbugs. A flock of exotic evening grossbeaks swarmed over the sumac trees each fall. There were the birds I fed in winter and one huge owl that appeared as a silhouette against the night sky in the leafless walnut tree.

Those three years formed the beginning of a journey that has continued to unfold before me as I have learned and grown through teaching, illustrating books for children, and sharing myself with youngsters. T. S. Eliot said it, "We shall not cease

from exploration/ And the end of all our exploring/ Will be to arrive where we started/ And know the place for the first time." I feel as though I'm getting close.

I have become an illustrator of Americana, a label I resisted for a long time. Though I'm very pleased with the results of my efforts in illustrating earlier periods of history—the pilgrims and the Civil War, for example, I am much more at home with the children of *In Coal Country* and *On Granddaddy's Farm.* I was one of them. It's like coming home. It's authentic. I "know the place for the first time."

I now live and work far from my cabin on the pond, in a city of fountains and lights, right in the middle of the United States. From my perch on the top floor of a 1920's building, I watch pigeons fly in a landscape of domed towers and spired steeples, while metal cranes and giant, insect-like machines are making a narrow creek into a Venetian canal. Cars and trucks and buses flow by like minnows. When my daughter Hilary is home from the North Carolina School of the Arts, flute music fills the air.

I have so many books to illustrate that I've retired from teaching. Yet, I love to leave my busy studio to visit with school children, teachers and librarians and talk about my books. I have three children, Melissa, Ivo and Hilary, and two grandchildren, Jake and Victoria, and I like to visit with them too. Sometimes I go to Birdsong Creek in Tennessee to spend time with nature as I did on the pond some twenty years ago.

Thomas B. Allen was born in Nashville. He graduated from the Art Institute of Chicago in 1952. He has been married twice, and is now single. *Blackberries in the Dark* was named a Notable Children's Book of the Year by the American Library Association. It was also named a Notable Children's Trade Book in the Field of Social Studies by a joint committee of the Children's Book Council and the National Council on the

Social Studies. *In Coal Country* was named an Honor Book for Illustration in the 1987 *Boston Globe-Horn Book* awards. It was also named a Best Illustrated Book of 1987 by the *New York Times*, an ALA Notable Book, and an NCSS/CBC Notable Book. *The Chalk Box Kid, On Granddaddy's Farm*, and *Littlejim* were all named NCSS/CBC Notable Books. *The Most Beautiful Place in the World* was the 1989 Younger Fiction winner of the Jane Addams Children's Book Award. *The Secret Garden* was named a Children's Choice Book by a joint committee of the International Reading Association and the Children's Book Council.

SELECTED WORKS WRITTEN AND ILLUSTRATED: On Granddaddy's Farm, 1989.

SELECTED WORKS ILLUSTRATED: Blackberries in the Dark, by Mavis Jukes, 1985; The Chalk Box Kid, by Clyde Robert Bulla, 1987; In Coal Country, by Judith Hendershot, 1987; The Secret Garden, by Frances Hodgson Burnett, adapted by James Howe, 1987; The Most Beautiful Place in the World, by Ann Cameron, 1988; Littlejim, by Gloria Houston, 1990; Climbing Kansas Mountains, by George Shannon, 1993; The Days Before Now, by Margaret Wise Brown, 1994; Littlejim's Gift: An Appalachian Christmas Story, by Gloria Houston, 1994; Sewing Quilts, by Ann Turner, 1994.

ABOUT: Cummings, Pat, comp. and ed. Talking with Artists II; Cummins, Julie, comp. and ed. Children's Book Illustration and Design; Heller, Steven. Innovators of American Illustration; Kansas Alumni Magazine June 1988.

MARGOT APPLE

March 9, 1946–

ILLUSTRATOR OF *Sheep in a Jeep*, etc.

Autobiographical sketch of Margot Hubicki Apple:

MY MOTHER used to tell me . . . "You're so stubborn . . . you just won't take NO for an answer." I'm sure she found me to be very trying at times, but I now realize that without that very same stubbornness and

determination to get what I wanted, I would never have stuck with children's book illustration. My struggle for acceptance and recognition in this field has been long and at times very painful. And I still call upon my old determination to get me going again each time one of my favorite books slips into out-of-print status.

Often authors and illustrators begin their biographies saying, "Oh, I always wanted to write . . . or . . . illustrate books for children." But I truly didn't have a clue I would end up illustrating children's books. I knew only that I would have to work at some sort of art because drawing was the only thing I excelled in as a child. I also knew, even if it wasn't on a conscious level, that my parents expected me to be an artist . . . preferably a rich and famous one, an expectation that still comes back to haunt me, especially at the time children's book awards are handed out each year.

As a child living in our old house in inner-city Detroit I was surrounded by an atmosphere rich both in culture and old-fashioned ideas. I missed out on the wild childhood adventures less protected children experience. Instead I heard music at home every day and visited backstage after symphony concerts. On very special occasions, I met famous conductors and performers, like Sir John Barberolli and Victor Borge, when they were guests in our home. All this came about because my father was a violist with the Detroit Symphony Orchestra. He was also a choir master, music teacher, and conductor. I think my proudest moment was watching him conduct one hundred members of the orchestra in a concert of Tchaikovsky compositions. He was never appreciated enough by those who make one's career, a talent unrecognized and sadly underused. I often wonder if I will share his lot in life.

From my mother, who was a commercial artist before turning homemaker, I learned to love animals of all kinds—even spiders. We talked to the one that lived on the windowsill above the kitchen sink. We had two dogs and three birds. But I always longed to live in the country, on a farm, so I could have a big dog and a horse. Instead we fed the birds and the squirrels and took pony rides in the park. Mother also taught me craftsmanship and attention to detail. She made the best Halloween costumes, doll accoutrements and stick horses you ever saw. Today I am compulsively neat about detail in whatever I knit, sew, or illustrate. "Don't do a half-baked job. Do it well or don't do it at all," she told me.

What my environment lacked in terms of being close to nature, it made up in places that inspired imaginative thinking and learning. My two most favorite places were the main public library and the Detroit Institute of the Arts. Both were housed in magnificent buildings that spoke of a grander era. They inspired in me a sort of reverent behavior reserved for sacred places. I will always cherish the hours I spent there. The museum carried me visually through history. There was the Egyptian room full of amulets, sculpture, hieroglyphics, and the mummy. And then the armor collection and medieval chapel with its circular stone staircase led me past paintings depicting life around the world

and through the ages. You could go to the museum and leave your own boring little life behind.

At the library my love of books was hatched and nurtured. The children's room was huge to me and wonderful. And although I was a very poor reader, a disability that hindered me throughout my school years, I delighted in gathering stacks of books and taking them home, only to return them mostly unfinished because I ran out of time. I guess it was the feel, shape, and smell, and the illustrations that fascinated me. I took out books by my favorite illustrators over and over again. I remember especially the work of Paul Brown, Kate Seredy, Marguerite Henry, and Wesley Dennis.

My fascination with beautiful books followed me through my school years. At Pratt Institute I majored in the Book Arts Division of the Department of Graphic Design and Illustration. During those years I collected books by Maurice Sendak, who has been one of my heroes ever since. It gives me great pleasure whenever my work is compared to his. I feel it's an honor that my work would remind someone of an artist I admire.

After graduation I fled the city in search of the country life I longed for as a child. It was the long distance from New York, the mecca of freelance artwork, that pointed me in the direction of book illustration. In those days, before the fax and express mail, only book publishers used artists that far away from New York. It had also been made painfully clear to me in art school that I would never make the grade as a "Fine Artist."

Now as I sit in my little house in the country paid for by "Sheep in a Jeep" books and built by my ingenious husband (whom I believe can figure out anything but knitting), I feel pretty lucky. And I'm doing some of the same things I did as the lonesome child who spent hours amusing herself illustrating the characters in her made-up world. I guess those hours spent with my pencils and crayons and at the library started me on an inevitable path, one which I find natural and comfortable. This work allows me to spend the time at home that is required to take care of our cats and horses. And the time alone that I find I need to hatch those ideas and scribble those pictures. It is my most sincere hope that my work will touch many, many children and bring them the love of books and reading that our world so desperately needs now.

_____

Margot Apple was born in Detroit. She studied commercial art at Cass Technical High School, graduating in 1964. She received a B.F.A. degree from Pratt Institute in 1969. She also has studied ceramics, weaving, and knitting in the arts field; and she has studied the Chinese language at the University of Massachusetts. She was married to James A. Smith in 1982. Apple's work has appeared in magazines such as *Country Journal* and *Horticulture*, and in the children's magazines *Cricket*, *Spider*, *Ladybug*, and *Babybug*. She has also exhibited work in several group shows and one-person shows. In the fall of 1994 the artwork for *Just Like My Dad* was shown at the Frederic Remington Art Museum in Ogdensburg, New York.

Apple is a member of the Society of Children's Book Writers and Illustrators, Authors Guild, The Western Massachusetts Illustrators Guild, and several associations concerned with raising horses.

Critic Ruth K. MacDonald, writing in *School Library Journal*, stated that *Blanket*, "with pictures of nighttime rumpussing and carrying on in the dark . . . is reminiscent of Sendak's *Wild Things* in its final wordless spread." Her books have received many awards voted upon by children and have appeared on several "best books" lists. *The Scariest Witch in Wellington Tower* was a 1981 Junior Literary Guild selection.

SELECTED WORKS WRITTEN AND ILLUSTRATED: Blanket, 1990; Brave Martha, 1995.

SELECTED WORKS ILLUSTRATED: The Chocolate Touch, by Patrick Catling, 1979; Yours 'Til Niagara Falls, Abby, by Jane O'Connor, 1979; The Scariest Witch in Wellington Towers, by Joyce Segal, 1981; The Great Rescue Operation, by Jean Van Leeuwen, 1982; Angel's Mother's Boyfriend, by Judy Delton, 1985; Sheep in a Jeep, by Nancy Shaw, 1986; Bunny's Night Out, by Roni Schotter, 1989; Sheep on a Ship, by Nancy Shaw, 1989; Sheep in a Shop, by Nancy Shaw, 1991; Sheep Out to Eat, by Nancy Shaw, 1992; Just Like My Daddy, by Tricia Gardella, 1993; Sheep Take a Hike, by Nancy Shaw, 1994.

ABOUT: Something About the Author, Vol. 42, 64.

CAROLINE ARNOLD

May 16, 1944–

AUTHOR OF *Trapped in Tar: Fossils of the Ice Age*, etc.

Autobiographical sketch of Caroline Arnold:

I GREW UP in Minneapolis, Minnesota, and among my earliest memories are trips to the library with my parents and three younger brothers on Saturday mornings. When I grew older I was allowed to go to the library by myself, riding my bicycle and filling the basket with as many books as would fit. In fifth grade I met a girl who loved to read as much as I did. We often spent whole days reading and talking about books, especially during the long, lazy days of summer when we lay on blankets under the apple tree in my backyard or took our books and a picnic lunch to one of the lakes nearby.

Part of each summer was spent in northern Wisconsin at a camp that was owned by the settlement home that my father directed. I learned to love nature in those north woods and stories we told around the campfire at night became the basis for one of my few fiction books, *The Terrible Hodag*. If you drove from the city to the camp directly it took about three hours, but for our family it was always an all-day expedition. My father was an avid amateur naturalist and stopped for anything that looked inter-

Caroline Arnold

esting. Then my brothers and I would tumble out of the car to search for wildflowers, chase a butterfly or to look through the binoculars at a meadowlark or a hawk. When my cousins, who were rock hounds, came with us, we also stopped to hunt for agates and other kinds of stones. The excitement that we shared when we spied a deer or uncovered the fossil of an ancient sea creature continues to influence my writing today. As I write about animals, dinosaur bones and other scientific subjects, my goal is to convey that same sense of discovery.

As a child, I had no idea that I would be a writer when I grew up. I liked to draw and at Grinnell College and the University of Iowa I studied art, intending to become a professional artist and art teacher. In the meanwhile I got married and as my husband, Art, pursued his graduate work in biology, I became exposed to the fascinating world of animal behavior. In 1971 Art did a research project in western Uganda for four months. We lived literally in the midst of lions, elephants, zebras, hippos and other African wildlife. Many of these animals later became subjects for my books.

Beginning in 1976, I decided to use my training in art to try book illustration. My favorite subjects were plants and animals, and as I wrote stories to provide the text for my drawings, I found myself becoming a science writer. My first book, *Five Nests,* was published in 1980, but I was just the author. I did not get the chance to do my own illustrations until my fifth book, a project book about solar energy called *Sun Fun.* I discovered that for every page I had to do a separate drawing for each color. Techniques have changed since then, but after illustrating three books I decided to stop drawing and devote all of my energy to writing.

I began working with photographer Richard Hewett in 1982. When we go to a museum or zoo to research one of our books I function both as a writer and as a photographer's assistant. The firsthand experience of seeing animals close-up, going behind the scenes in a museum or climbing up ancient ruins also helps me to bring my subjects to life when I write my manuscript. I also hold film, adjust lights and, when necessary, act as a model. All of our projects are true collaborative efforts with my text providing a guide for the photos and the photos exerting an influence over my final text.

I enjoy the opportunity to explore different formats in my writing. I have also written books illustrated by artists and worked with other photographers including my husband. With each of my ninety-five books for children, it has been a challenge to find the best way to present the information I have collected in my research. I like writing because I like to find out things and with every new book I discover things I never knew before.

———

Caroline Arnold was born in Pittsburgh, Pennsylvania. She graduated from Grinnell College with a B.A. degree in 1966 and received her M.A. degree from the University of Iowa in 1968. She was married in 1967 and has two children. She has been an art teacher, a laboratory assistant, a secretary, and a writing teacher in addition to being a writer and illustrator.

Arnold wrote a script for a television drama for children, *Fire for Hire*, which was produced by META-4 and first broadcast on KCET in Los Angeles in 1984. She also wrote the text for part of a CD-ROM multimedia news program, *The Secret Life of Animals*, produced by Newsweek Interactive in 1994. She has been a contributor to numerous magazines for children including *Highlights for Children*, *Cricket*, and *Humpty Dumpty*.

She is a member of the Authors Guild, the Society of Children's Book Writers and Illustrators and the Southern California Council on Literature for Children and Young People.

Animals That Migrate was named an Honor Book in the 1983 New York Academy of Sciences Children's Science Book Awards. *Trapped in Tar* won the same honor in 1988. Twenty of Arnold's books have been named Outstanding Science Trade Books for Children by a joint committee of the National Science Teachers Association and the Children's Book Council. They include *Cheetah*, *Dinosaur Mountain*, and *Pets Without Homes*.

Two of her books have been named Notable Books of the Year by the American Library Association: *Dinosaur Mountain* and *Saving the Peregrine Falcon*.

SELECTED WORKS WRITTEN: Animals That Migrate, 1982; Pets Without Homes, 1983; Saving the Peregrine Falcon, 1985; Trapped in Tar: Fossils from the Ice Age, 1987; Cheetah, 1989; Dinosaur Mountain: Graveyard of the Past, 1989; The Terrible Hodag, 1989; Killer Whale, 1994; The Ancient Cliff Dwellers of Mesa Verde, 1992; On the Brink of Extinction, 1993; Watching Desert Wildlife, 1994.

ABOUT: Contemporary Authors, Vol. 107; (New Revision Series), Vol. 24; Grinnell Magazine Winter 1994; Roginski, Jim. Behind the Covers Vol. II; Something About the Author, Vol. 34, 36.

SANDY ASHER

October 16, 1942–

AUTHOR OF *Out of Here*, etc.

Autobiographical sketch of Sandra Fenichel Asher, who writes children's books under the name Sandy Asher:

ON SUNDAY afternoons, my parents often visited friends. I was dropped off at the Children's Reading Room in the basement of the mammoth Free Library of Philadelphia. That was where I visited *my* friends, the characters in beloved books: Peter and Wendy, Dorothy and the Scarecrow, and especially Jo March.

I can remember thinking, as I breathed in the exotic smells of leather bindings and old paper, that nothing in the world could possibly be better than to write a story someone would love as much as I loved those books. Wouldn't it be wonderful, I thought, to come back to this library when I'm all grown up and see one of *my* books, on these shelves, tucked in among my favorites?

The first writing I can remember doing was in second grade. I took popular songs and made up skits about them. I also directed—that is, I bossed my friends around and told them where to stand and what to say and when to sing, dance, and take a bow. Our teacher, Mrs. Lomozoff, let us perform for the class.

We were such a hit, she sent us on a tour of the whole school. We did fine performing for the elementary classes. But when we lined up in front of our first junior high audience, they looked so huge to us, we broke out in nervous giggles. "Please begin your play," we were told. And we tried—several times!—but we couldn't stop laughing. Finally we were asked to leave the room.

That was the end of my touring company, but it was the start of my writing career. Throughout my school years, I was fortunate to have teachers like Mrs. Lomozoff who encouraged me to write. I will always be grateful to them.

The first time I tried to write a novel, I had no idea what I was doing. How could I fill up so many pages with words? Perhaps, I thought, if I put in lots of characters and let them all run around having adventures, it will somehow add up to a novel.

It didn't. Ten years passed as I mailed that manuscript off to publishers and collected seventeen rejection letters. I also rewrote the book several times, dropping characters and eventually concentrating on two: Ruthie and Denise, who were finally featured as *Daughters of the Law*.

Writing is a series of "firsts." Each story is different, and so are the challenges of getting it told. Every bit of a writer's life, good or bad, comes in handy.

Out of Here draws on my memories of high school in Philadelphia.

Princess Bee and the Royal Goodnight Story goes back even farther, to the weekend my mother went off to a meeting and left me all alone—except for my father, brother, grandparents, aunt, and uncle. Well, it felt as if she'd left me all alone, and that feeling went into Bee's story.

Where Do You Get Your Ideas?, grew out of the writing workshops I've taught all over the country. And *A Woman Called Truth* required months of research at the library.

Speaking of libraries, I was recently invited back to Philadelphia to speak at a conference. I glanced down from my hotel window and discovered the Free Library looming across the street! I hurried over and found the Children's Reading Room, right where I'd left it in the basement. And there on the shelf were my books, beside those of my favorite authors.

It was every bit as wonderful as I'd dreamed it would be.

———

Sandy Asher was born in Philadelphia. She attended the University of Pennsylvania from 1960 to 1962 and earned her B.A. degree from Indiana University in 1964. She did graduate study at the University of Connecticut and received an elementary education certificate from Drury College in Springfield, Missouri.

She was married in 1965 and has two children. She began her career as a scriptwriter for radio in 1963, and was a copywriter for an advertising agency and a drama critic. She taught creative writing at Drury College from 1978 to 1985, where she has been writer-in-residence since 1985. She frequently speaks at conferences, such as the annual Institute for Publishing and Writing Children's Books sponsored by Rhodes College.

Her professional memberships include The International Association of Theatre for Children and Young People, the Dramatists Guild, the Society of Children's Book Writers and Illustrators (where she has been a Director of the Board since 1989), and the Missouri Center for the Book.

She received a creative writing fellowship grant in playwriting from the National Endowment for the Arts in 1978. Among her other honors for her playwriting is the 1994 Distinguished Play Award from the American Alliance for Theater and Education for *A Woman Called Truth*. She is a contributor to many magazines, such as *The ALAN Review* and *Writers Digest*.

Three of her books have been named Junior Library Guild books: *Just Like Jenny*, *Things Are Seldom What They Seem*, and *Everything Is Not Enough*. Her books have also won awards chosen by children.

SELECTED WORKS: Summer Begins, 1980; Daughters of the Law, 1980; Just Like Jenny, 1982; Things Are Seldom What They Seem, 1983; Missing Pieces, 1984; Teddy Teabury's Fabulous Fact, 1985; Everything Is Not Enough, 1987; Best Friends Get Better, 1989; Princess Bee and the Royal Good-Night Story, 1989; Out of Here: A Senior Class Yearbook, 1993.

ABOUT: Contemporary Authors, Vol. 105; Gallo, Donald R. Speaking for Ourselves; Journal of Reading February 1990; McElmeel, Sharron L. Bookpeople: Vol. II; Something About the Author, Vol. 34, 46, 71; Something About the Author Autobiography Series, Vol. 13. PRONUNCIATION: FENN uh shell

JIM AYLESWORTH

February 21, 1943–

AUTHOR OF *Old Black Fly*, etc.

Autobiographical sketch of Jim Aylesworth:

WHEN PEOPLE ASK me about my life as a children's author, the first thing I always tell them is that I am a teacher.

"I'm a first grade teacher!" I say. And at this writing, I've been one for almost twenty-five years.

In that time, I've read hundreds and hundreds of books to my kids, and I've seen how very much they like them. *"Read it again, Mr. Aylesworth! Read it again!"* they say. As often as not, I do read it again. And to be honest, I'm glad to do it because I like those read-aloud picture books just as much as they do.

I like them because they are so much fun, but also because they help me to be a good teacher. My kids like books so much that they don't mind working hard to learn how to read. They have a fun reason for working and learning, and of course, that makes school a much happier place, and my job as a teacher all the easier.

It was as a teacher that I first began writing. It was in the mid seventies, but I don't remember exactly when. I do remember the great joy I felt when I heard that my first book, *HUSH UP!*, had been accepted for publication. And I remember how

proud I was to read it to my class when it was ready. That was in 1980. *"Why don't you write another one?"* one of my kids suggested, and not being really sure that I could write another one, I decided to try. One after another, I now have more than twenty books! It's hard for me to believe, like a dream come true. Now other teachers and other children from all over America write letters telling me that they like my books, and of course that makes me proud too.

I'd like to keep on writing books. It's fun being an author. I get to go to so many interesting places, and people are so nice to me and all. I can't be sure that I can do it, but as I tell my kids at school to do, I'm going to try my very best.

———

Jim Aylesworth was raised in Alabama and Indiana. He earned a B.A. degree in English from Miami University in Oxford, Ohio, in 1965. He received an M.A. degree from Concordia University in River Forest, Illinois, in 1978. He has been a teacher since 1971, and has been a college professor in children's literature at Concordia University, at The College of DuPage, and at The

Aylesworth: *ALES worth*

University of Chicago. He received the "Those Who Excel" honor from the Illinois State Board of Education in 1975 and was named Alumnus of the Year by Concordia in 1985. He is a guest speaker at many book events.

SELECTED WORKS: Hush Up!, 1980; Shenandoah Noah, 1985; Two Terrible Frights, 1987; Hannah's Hog, 1988; The Completed Hickory Dickory Dock, 1990; One Crow: A Counting Rhyme, 1988; The Cat & the Fiddle & More, 1992; Old Black Fly, 1992; My Son John, 1994; McGraw's Emporium, 1995.

ABOUT: Contemporary Authors, Vol. 106; (New Revision Series), Vol. 22; McElmeel, Sharron L. Bookpeople: A Multicultural Album; Something About the Author, Vol. 38. PRONUNCIATION: The first syllable of Aylesworth is pronounced like "ale".

JEANNIE BAKER

November 2, 1950–

AUTHOR AND ILLUSTRATOR OF *Where the Forest Meets the Sea*, etc.

Autobiographical sketch of Jeannie Baker:

MY FATHER died when I was young and after that, life at home became unhappy and frustrating. I left home at seventeen, when I started at Art College, being by this time determinedly independent and paying my way by waitressing jobs.

Brighton College of Art was agreeably unstructured and within my time at college I managed to find the main ingredients of my work which I have since been able to evolve and refine.

The first ingredient was an obsession with textures, and with the careful depiction of these textures my work developed into its "illusion of being three dimensional".

The second ingredient was the "Children's Picture Book" format which allowed enormous scope for me to stretch myself. I could produce personally satisfying artwork, have it published, share it with others, and gain some kudos and a little money.

Still being determinedly independent, I persisted in doing essentially my own projects so that I could conceive my own ideas, illustrate them and be in control as much as possible.

In recent years, I have developed a passion for the natural environment and the more I see and learn the more I find there is yet to see and learn. And with this passion, one sees the unthinking and unnecessary waste of the natural environment . . . so my work now tends to include an educative environmental element.

As I write I am making my second animated film where I am working with much of the same and additional artwork from my new picture book. I am working with a small crew using the method of 'stop motion animation' to make a film version of the project.

My work tends to take up most of my time as a consequence of the detail involved in my artwork and the effort needed to maintain the clarity of this detail. . . . So, apart from my husband, my work is a big part of my life but I wouldn't have it any other way. Starting new projects provides the perfect occasion for travel and exploration.

My work has allowed me to travel widely. I have climbed mountains in Tasmania . . . slept with dingoes in the central Australian desert . . . backpacked for days alone in the North Queensland jungle . . . gone exploring in Jordan and Syria and travelled almost every mile of the New York subways.

———

Jeannie Baker received her B.A. degree with honors in Art and Design. She also attended Croyden College of Art in Surrey, from 1967 to 1969. Since then she has created "collage constructions." She has had numerous one-person exhibitions, including a 1992 show in Brisbane City Hall Art Gallery and Museum; a 1992 show at The Museum of Victoria, Melbourne; and a 1991 exhibition at the Royal Botanic Gardens in Sydney. Her work has appeared in many group shows, and is represented in collections in museums such as The Powerhouse Museum in Sydney and The State Gallery of West Australia. Her illustrations have appeared in such publications as *Nova*, *The London Times*, and *The Sunday Times*.

Baker has twice been Invited Resident of the New York Studio by the Visual Arts Board of the Australia Council, in 1983 and 1980. She has received special arts grants from several organizations. A ten-minute animated film, *Where the Forest Meets the Sea*, was produced by Film Australia and directed by Baker. It won several awards, such as the Australian Film Institute Award for best Australian Animated Film in 1988. Baker directed another film, *The Story of Rosy Dock*, also produced by Film Australia.

Home in the Sky was named a 1985 Commended Book in the Children's Book Council of Australia Book of the Year Awards. It was named a Notable Book of 1984 by the American Library Association.

Where the Forest Meets the Sea received from the same organization a 1988 Picture Book of the Year Honour Award. It was named a 1989 "Fanfare" book by *The Horn Book Magazine*, and was also named an Honor Book in the *Boston Globe-Horn Book* awards in the picture book category. It was placed on the 1990 International Board on Books for Young People list for Illustration, and an Outstanding Science Trade Book for Children by a joint committee of the National Science Teachers Association and the Children's Book Council.

Window was named 1992 Picture Book of the Year by The Children's Book Council of Australia. It was also named a Notable Trade Book in the Field of Social Studies by a joint committee of the National Council on the Social Studies and the CBC.

SELECTED WORKS WRITTEN AND ILLUSTRATED: Grandfather, 1977; Grandmother, 1978; Millicent, 1980; One Hungry Spider, 1982; Home in the Sky, 1984; Where the Forest Meets the Sea, 1988; Window, 1991; The Story of Rosy Dock, 1995.

SELECTED WORKS ILLUSTRATED: Polar, by Elaine Moss, 1990.

ABOUT: Contemporary Authors (First Revision), Vol. 97-100; Horn Book March/April 1985; Something About the Author, Vol. 23.

KEITH BAKER

March 17, 1953–

AUTHOR AND ILLUSTRATOR OF *Who Is the Beast?*, etc.

Autobiographical sketch of Keith Baker:

ONCE a kindergarten student asked me, "Have you been dead?"

"No," I answered. "Why did you ask me that?"

"Well," he said, "Whenever our class talks about authors, they're dead!"

I have never been dead. If I had, there are many things I would have missed. Like spaghetti, which is my favorite food—it doesn't have bones. And green, which is my favorite color—I'm Irish. And 17, which is my lucky number—I was born on March 17, St. Patrick's Day, and this makes me very Irish.

My favorite sports are tennis and swimming, although I don't do them at the same time. I also like to bike and ski. My favorite T.V. show is "The Simpsons," and my favorite Simpson is Lisa. My favorite cartoon strip is "Calvin and Hobbes" (Hobbes is the tiger, I think). My favorite book is *The Cat in the Hat*. I don't have a cat—I'm allergic to them. But I do have a hat. My favorite author is Dr. Seuss, although he isn't my doctor. And my favorite ice cream is chocolate fudge, no—raspberry ripple, no—mocha chip, no—oh! I like them all.

I could tell you some of my most unfavorite things, too—like vacuuming, traffic, and mosquitoes. I wouldn't have missed those things at all if I had been dead.

But I would have missed my family and friends the most. And I would have missed my job, which is writing and illustrating picture books. My favorite part of making books is painting. I love mixing colors and smooshing paint on paper. I almost always use acrylic paint. It dries quickly, and then I can paint on top of it to fix my mistakes. Sometimes I cut and glue shapes from patterned paper onto my paintings. I have never tried gluing spaghetti onto a painting.

I also like writing books. It can be hard at times, though, like when I can't think of an ending for a story. For instance, I have an idea about a turtle who swims to the bottom of the sea. He hears a voice say, "Way down deep," over and over again. The turtle finally gets to the bottom of the sea, but what does he find? I don't know! If you have any ideas to end this story, send them to me.

Now to end this letter let me tell you that we might meet someday because I am not now—nor ever have been—dead.

Keith Baker grew up in La Grande, a small town in Northeastern Oregon. He graduated from Eastern Oregon State College in 1976 and Art Center, College of Design in 1986. He names as influences on his work Eric Carle, Leo Lionni, Brian Wildsmith, and Ezra Jack Keats.

A video about Keith Baker, *Get to Know Keith Baker*, was produced by Harcourt Brace Jovanovich in 1994.

Big Fat Hen won a 1994 Golden Kite Award from the Society of Children's Book Writers and Illustrators. *The Magic Fan* won the 1989 UNICEF-Ezra Jack Keats National Award for Children's Book Illustration.

Who Is the Beast? was included in the American Institute of Graphic Arts Book Show. It was also named a Children's Choice Book by a joint committee of the International Reading Association and the Children's Book Council.

SELECTED WORKS WRITTEN AND ILLUSTRATED: The Dove's Letter, 1988; The Magic Fan,1989; Who Is the Beast?, 1990; Hide and Snake, 1991; Big Fat Hen, 1994.

SELECTED WORKS ILLUSTRATED: Elephants Aloft, by Kathi Appelt, 1993.

LESLIE BAKER

June 17, 1949–

AUTHOR AND ILLUSTRATOR OF *The Third-Story Cat*, etc.

Autobiographical sketch of Leslie Baker:

I WAS BORN on June 17, 1949 in Baltimore, Maryland. My mother was a nurse who used her talents rescuing orphaned animals. As a result, I grew up surrounded by cats, dogs, tailess squirrels and even a mallard duck named Dolly who lived with us for twelve years. My father was a businessman with a huge laugh and an even bigger sense of humor, which was helpful in dealing with this constant parade of animals. Next to my pets, my best playmate was my big brother Ken. We spent a lot of time together building forts, swimming in the ocean and playing with the other kids on the block. But what I liked best was sitting on the floor on Saturday mornings painting with my watercolors or drawing on the shirt cardboards my Dad saved for us. Drawing was my passion, second only to reading and horses. We moved around when I was young but we always considered home our big old house in Maryland where my grandmother lived.

But for a brief time in seventh grade when I considered becoming a veterinarian, I always wanted to be an artist. So after high school, I went on to college where I studied fine arts and art history. Although I dabbled briefly in commercial art after graduation, I was always painting. Later I went back to school to get an M.Ed. and certification and began teaching.

For the next decade after grad school, I taught art while painting and exhibiting my work. Several visual arts grants during this time allowed me extra time to travel and paint. Later, I went on to teach fine arts at various colleges around Philadelphia and during this time I married my husband David.

It was shortly before I gave birth to my daughter that I turned my attention to children's books. For my first effort I wrote and illustrated a simple tale starring my cat Nellie, a fiesty calico, who was always escaping from my third floor studio. By the time *The Third-Story Cat* was published I was already illustrating a book for another author. I felt as if I had found a medium of expression that perfectly merged my love of art and literature. Plus, I was able to work at home and be with my child.

For the past ten years and many books later I've continued to work in a field I find challenging with its complex and varied work. I enjoy being part of a process that allows me to develop an idea into story and art to a finished book. Even working on another author's story I always try to find the connection the words make in me to use as a focal point in my paintings. In addition stories often require extensive research. I like nothing better than spending hours in the library poring over books to get accurate information for my illustrations.

But perhaps best of all, is meeting the countless children I've spoken to at schools everywhere. In turn, they have shared their stories and art with me through letters and school writing programs. I've made many new friends. Although I continue to paint today, I find my art now has reached a wider audience through my books.

———

Leslie Baker earned a B.F.A. degree with honors from Beaver College in Glenside, Pennsylvania. She received her M.Ed. from Tyler School of Art of Temple University in Philadelphia in 1973. She also studied at Tyler School of Art in Rome in 1970 and at Pratt Institute in Brooklyn, New York in 1967. She has been an Instructor at many arts institutions from 1973 to the present, including at the University of Arts in Philadelphia and at Beaver College. She has also been a staff artist at publishing and advertising companies. She wrote a book for adults, *The Art Teacher's Resource Book*, in 1979.

Baker was married in 1981 and her daughter Emma was born in 1985. Her art has been shown in one-person shows such as the Rosenfeld Gallery in Philadelphia in 1981 and in 1983. She has also been represented in group shows like the Original Art Annual exhibition at the Society of Illustrators in New York City, in which her art has appeared from 1988 to 1994.

She received a Visual Arts Grant from the Pennsylvania Council for the Arts in 1979 and a 1975 Irwin Grant for travel and study in France. She also won the 1975 Purchase Prize from the Pennsylvania Council for the Arts. *The Third-Story Cat* won a 1988 International Reading Association Children's Book Award.

SELECTED WORKS WRITTEN AND ILLUSTRATED: The Third-Story Cat, 1987; Morning Beach, 1990; The Antique Store Cat, 1992.

SELECTED WORKS ILLUSTRATED: Winter Harvest, by Jane Aragon, 1988; All Those Secrets of the World, by Jane Yolen, 1991; Honkers, by Jane Yolen, 1993; Looking for Angels, by Valiska Gregory, 1995.

DEBRA BARRACCA

December 24, 1953–

CO-AUTHOR OF *The Adventures of Taxi Dog*, etc.

Biographical sketch of Debra Ann Barracca:

DEBRA BARRACCA was born in New York City, on Manhattan's Lower East Side, where she took accordion lessons and dreamed of becoming a veterinarian. She loved dogs with a passion, and she spent her time making up books about dogs and reading about dogs. "Kids used to make fun of me because that's all I was interested in," she says. Barracca attended the High School of Music and Art, where her specialty was art, and, realizing she didn't have the stomach to become a vet, she went into graphic design instead. She received a B.A. from the City University of New York, where she studied English Literature, Sociology and Art.

Her first job was in the Art Department of Metropolitan Life, an insurance company. Following that, she worked as a freelance graphic designer for many years in advertising and publishing. It was in 1983, while she was working at Bantam Books, that she met her husband, Sal Barracca. He was also freelancing at Bantam. They had actually met ten years earlier at Bantam, but only briefly. They were married in 1985.

In 1988, Debra and Sal Barracca formed Halcyon Books to package children's books. They both were interested in creating, designing and directing children's book projects, and the company has packaged several books (a Bible and a lullaby book) besides the Maxi books that were bought by Dial Books. The Barraccas feel that it is very important "to give something back" to society, so a portion of the proceeds of Halcyon Books goes to various charities. Appropriately enough, most of the charities are animal organizations, such as the Save-a-Stray Program of the Associated Humane Societies.

The idea for *The Adventures of Taxi Dog* came from a real-life taxi ride with a dog in the front seat. This rhyming picture book about a dog named Maxi who rides in a taxi with the driver, Jim, was published in 1990. *Booklist* called it a "memorable picture-book excursion" with "an indelible canine character" written in "snappy, rhymed lines." The book was illustrated by Mark Buehner. Barracca says that she and her co-author, Sal Barracca, originally wrote the book in prose, but that didn't work well, so they switched to rhyme "and it clicked." The book was selected for an American Institute of Graphic Artists show. They have continued the adventures of Maxi with *Maxi, the Hero*, also illustrated by Buehner. *Maxi, the Star* and *A Taxi Dog Christmas*, both illustrated by Alan Ayers, came next.

The Barraccas lived in New York City until 1986, when they moved to Westchester County in upstate New York. It was Barracca's first time living in a house, and she claims, as a "city person," she couldn't sleep for a whole year because of the noise of all the little animals running across the roof. They've since moved several times—"a different address for each Maxi book"—and she says she's now used to living in a house and wouldn't want to move back to a city apartment.

In 1991, their daughter Samantha was born. They moved Halcyon Books to their home and are working on new book projects all the time. Meantime, there is talk of a television show based on Maxi's adventures, and Samantha is now old enough to accompany the Barraccas to their various book-signings and readings, "She knows all the words and recites them along with us!" says Barracca. In addition, Barracca continues to freelance as a graphic designer, which she says she loves to do.

SELECTED WORKS WRITTEN WITH SAL BARRACCA: The Adventures of Taxi Dog, 1990; Maxi, the Hero, 1991; Maxi, the Star, 1993; A Taxi Dog Christmas, 1994.

SAL BARRACCA

November 10, 1947–

CO-AUTHOR OF *The Adventures of Taxi Dog*, etc.

Biographical sketch of Salvatore James Barracca:

SAL BARRACCA was born in Brooklyn, New York. Although his father, an engineer, wanted him to be an engineer as well, Barracca was an artist right from the start. "In elementary school I did all the artwork for our plays. I was the school artist," he says. When he was twelve years old, the family moved to Long Island, where he continued to excel at art, and then in his junior year of high school, they moved to Connecticut, where he graduated from Norwich Free Academy High School in 1966. "It was a great school with its own art building. It had wonderful reproductions of famous sculptures."

Barracca studied illustration at New York City's School of Visual Arts, graduating in 1970. While he was at art school, he lived with his grandmother in Brooklyn. Among his anecdotes from that time is the one about the nude sculptures he was working on. He would come home to work on them and discover that parts had been broken off of them; this grandmother always claimed it was an accident! Barracca planned to become an illustrator, and he pursued that goal for ten years. But lack of income forced him to moved in a different direction, so he became an art director, working for various companies over the years.

In 1983, he met Debra Miller at Bantam Books, where they were both freelancing. (They had met briefly at the same company ten years before.) They were married in 1985. In 1986, Barracca formed Sal Barracca and Associates, a company representing about twenty-five illustrators who work in both advertising and publishing. The company is located in New York. In 1988, Barracca and his wife formed Halcyon Books to package children's books. In addition to the Maxi books, Halcyon has packaged several books which were bought by Dial Books, including a Bible and a lullaby book.

Both Sal and Debra Barracca love dogs and children, and they both wanted to create their own books. The idea of the Maxi books came from a ride they took in a taxi that had a dog in the front seat. *The Adventures of Taxi Dog*, illustrated by Mark Buehner, was published in 1990. It was selected to be in an American Institute of Graphic Arts show. Sal and Debra Barracca went on to write *Maxi, the Hero*, also illustrated by Mark Buehner, and *Maxi, the Star* and *A Taxi Dog Christmas*, both illustrated by Alan Ayers. They all feature Maxi, a dog who rides in a taxi with the driver, Jim, and they are written in rhyme.

The Maxi books are written by Sal and Debra Barracca as a team. The first was originally written in prose, but they felt it wasn't working, so they tried rhyme instead. For their first book, they worked together on the same piece, passing words back and forth until they found the right combination. They've continued working as a team, but now they come up with an outline, and each of them works separately

on the same piece. Then they sit down together to finish, picking the best of each one's writing to create the text. They use the same meter, and have the same formula, so this method works well for them.

Barracca still dreams of being an illustrator and the Barracca team continues working to come up with a new character or story that he might illustrate.

In 1986, the Barraccas moved from New York City to Westchester County in New York. In 1991, their daughter Samantha was born. She now accompanies her parents to their book signings and readings, and often will recite along with them, since she knows all the Maxi stories by heart.

SELECTED WORKS WRITTEN WITH DEBRA BARRACCA: The Adventures of Taxi Dog, 1990; Maxi, the Hero, 1991; Maxi, the Star, 1993; A Taxi Dog Christmas, 1994.

GRAEME BASE

April 6, 1958–

AUTHOR AND ILLUSTRATOR OF *The Eleventh Hour*, etc.

Biographical sketch of Graeme Rowland Base:

GRAEME BASE was born in Amersham, England. He immigrated to Australia in 1966 and became an Australian citizen. He was impressed by the variety of plant and animal life and often went on nature and bird-watching expeditions.

By the age of twelve, he had decided to become a commercial artist. He studied graphic design, earning a diploma of art in 1978 from the Swinburne Institute of Technology. However, he did not enjoy the work he did in advertising at several design studios from 1979 to 1980. He did learn from the experience, though; for example, about how a picture looks when it's reproduced in the printing process, elements of design, and working on deadlines. He found that he did like drawing book jackets and record

GRAEME BASE

covers, and then realized that he wanted to be an illustrator.

He began his career as a book illustrator by doing the artwork for other people's stories, but because he could not, of course, change the text to work more closely with the pictures, he felt frustrated.

The first book he wrote and illustrated was *My Grandma Lived in Gooligulch*, which is in verse. His second book, *Animalia*, an alphabet book with hundreds of hidden objects inside the pictures, was a great success, selling over a million and a quarter copies.

During his travels to promote *Animalia*, he worked for ten months sketching and writing for his next major book, *The Eleventh Hour: A Curious Mystery*. The book, first published in Australia in 1988, includes many images that are the result of ideas that influenced him on his travels in India, Egypt, Africa, and Europe. It contains a mystery that readers may try to solve; and the clues and answers are provided in the book in case the reader wants to give up. The book has sold over nine hundred thousand copies.

A *Publishers Weekly* review said of this book: "The fun of poring over the pictures for hidden messages and significant particulars is, happily, matched by the enjoyment derived from the text—witty, ingenious verses that ably skirt the singsong or mundane." *People Weekly* refers to Base as having "the eye of a Renaissance painter and the ear of Dr. Seuss."

Base's most recent major book, *The Sign of the Seahorse*, is an ecological tale of intrigue set in the Seahorse Café, a sort of underwater rock club for fish. It has sold half a million copies.

After he produces his finished artwork, Base supervises every stage of the reproduction of the art, and even of the printing and binding of the books.

He counts among his influences the illustrators John Tenniel and Ernest Shepard, as well as Maxfield Parrish and Base's contemporary, Robert Ingpen. He also admires the work of Michael Hague.

Graeme Base married artist Robyn Anne Paterson in 1991. He and his wife were born on the same day of the year. They played in a band from 1980 to 1985, an experience that may have informed his creation of the Seahorse Café. He plays clarinet, piano, guitar and drums. He also writes instrumental music and is co-author, with Craig Christie, of a contemporary opera based on Tutenkamen.

His other world travels include South America and the Galápagos Islands. He is a member of the Australian Society of Book Illustrators.

Base was commissioned to create a poster commemorating UNESCO's 1990 International Literacy Year.

Animalia, which was first published in Australia in 1986, was named an honor book in the 1987 Children's Book Council of Australia Book of the Year Awards. *The Eleventh Hour* was named a Picture Book of the Year in the 1989 Children's Book Council of Australia Book of the Year Awards. It also won a high commendation in the book design awards of the Australian Book Publishers' Association in 1988.

SELECTED WORKS WRITTEN AND ILLUSTRATED: My
Grandma Lived in Gooligulch, 1983; Animalia, 1987;
The Eleventh Hour: A Curious Mystery, 1989; The
Sign of the Seahorse: A Tale of Greed and High Ad-
venture in Two Acts, 1992; My Grandma Lived in
Gooligulch: A Pop-up Book, 1995.

SELECTED WORKS ILLUSTRATED: Adventures with
My Best Worst Friend, by Max Dann, 1982; Jabber-
wocky: From Through the Looking Glass, by Lewis
Carroll, 1987.

ABOUT: Booklist January 1, 1990; Contemporary
Authors, Vol. 134; People Weekly December 18, 1989;
Something About the Author, Vol. 67.

BARBARA BASH

October 20, 1948–

AUTHOR AND ILLUSTRATOR OF *Urban Roosts*,
etc.

Autobiographical sketch of Barbara Bash:

MY FIRST CONNECTION to art and creativity was through the alphabet. I loved to
draw the twenty-six letters. All through elementary school I experimented with their
forms constantly, often in the margins of
my math notebooks. In high school I always
volunteered for the job of making posters—
getting the chance to write really BIG was
thrilling! During art class I liked to include
the name of the object as part of the drawing—for me, word and image needed to go
together. After intensively studying dance
and ceramics in college, I took this understanding of movement and form and began
to apply it to the study of calligraphy—the
art of beautiful writing. I was living in the
San Francisco Bay Area at the time. I set
myself up in a little storefront and hung out
my shingle as a calligrapher and graphic
designer. My palette of colors was the alphabets of the Roman Empire, the Middle
Ages, and the Renaissance—the period of
history when calligraphy was the sole form
of written communication. I loved studying
the old manuscripts in the Rare Book Room
of the university library. The color of the

ink, the texture of the vellum skins, the little
mistakes of the scribes—it was all so alive
and human! The alphabets were like windows into their times (just as one's hand-
writing is a window into one's own
personality). They expressed the openness,
the tensions, and the lively energy of humanity striving to become "civilized".
Looking back now, I realize that my interest in illustration followed the same path as
the medieval scribes. At first I loved the
simple beauty of the letterforms, then I began to ornament and illuminate—my letters sprouted flowers and vines! Eventually
I found myself genuinely curious about the
natural world and wanting to know more.

By this time, around 1980, I was living at
the edge of the Rocky Mountains in Boulder, Colorado, with the natural world at my
doorstep. I met a wonderful naturalist
named Audrey Benedict who took me up
into the mountains and out to the grass-
lands. She showed me the interconnected-
ness with each ecosystem. I looked and
listened and sketched and wrote. I began to
see the world with a naturalist's eye.

The inspiration to make children's books
came out of my fascination with the natural
world, my affection for books as containers

of our culture, and my appreciation of beautiful letters strung together into words as carriers of our thoughts. I write and illustrate for children because I love the process of gathering all this information and then distilling it down to its essence. That's what children see.

In researching my books, I use books and photographs and films to help me become familiar with the topic. Then I go and see it for myself. I traveled to Arizona to see the saguaro cactus, to East Africa to sketch the baobab tree, and to the Pacific Northwest to sit in the cathedral of an old growth forest. For *Urban Roosts*, I walked all over New York City, finding bird's nests on skyscraper ledges and deep in the train tunnels below Grand Central Station. For *Shadows of Night*, I watched a twilight emergence of 100,000 bats coming out of an abandoned mineshaft in southern Colorado. It's fun to travel and explore like this. It's also essential to my work that I take it all in with my own senses. Then something alive and personal can be communicated through my books.

Now I live with my husband and four-year-old son on a small farm in upstate New York. In the summers our farm is like an island surrounded by an ocean of corn. Sometimes I look out my studio window and see a hawk gliding by.

Barbara Bash grew up in Barrington, Illinois. She attended Wheaton College in Norton, Massachusetts, the Unversity of Michigan in Ann Arbor, and Antioch College in Yellow Springs, Ohio. She was married in 1988 and has a son. She has been working as a calligrapher and illustrator since 1972. She began teaching calligraphy and book arts in 1979 at The Naropa Institute, a Buddhist contemplative college, in Boulder, Colorado. For seven years, she collaborated and performed with storytellers, musicians, dancers, and poets, exploring Buddhist principles and the artistic process. She studied Dharma Art with Chogyam

Trungpa Rinpoche and Chinese pictograms with Ed Young.

She now lives outside of Kingston, New York, writing and illustrating books on natural history and doing expressive calligraphic performance art.

Four of her books were named Outstanding Science Trade Books for Children by a joint committee of the National Science Teachers Association and the Children's Book Council: *Shadows of Night, Desert Giant, Urban Roosts*, and *Ancient Ones. Desert Giant* and *Urban Roosts* were also named Reading Rainbow Books. *Ancient Ones* was named a Children's Book of Distinction by the Hungry Mind Review.

SELECTED WORKS WRITTEN AND ILLUSTRATED: Desert Giant: The World of the Saguaro Cactus, 1988; Tree of Life: The World of the African Baobab, 1989; Urban Roosts: Where Birds Nest in the City, 1990; Shadows of Night: The Hidden World of the Little Brown Bat, 1992; Ancient Ones: The World of the Old Growth Douglas Fir, 1994.

SELECTED WORKS ILLUSTRATED: Tiger Lilies & Other Beastly Plants, by Elisabeth Ring, 1984; What Makes the Crops Rejoice, by Robert Howard and Eric Skjei, 1986; Discover My World: Forest, Ocean, Desert, Mountain, by Ron Hirschi, 1990; A Naturalist's Guide to the Southern Rocky Mountains, by Audrey Benedict, 1991.

MICHAEL BEDARD

June 26, 1949–

AUTHOR OF *Emily*, etc.

Autobiographical sketch of Michael Bedard:

ONE OF THE earliest memories I have is of sitting as a four-year-old, poring over the pages of a collection of Currier and Ives prints: a hunter confronted by a great bear, a ship tossed upon a raging sea, the great Crystal Palace of New York ablaze. These images imprinted themselves on my mind and are as clear now in memory as they were to that child then.

My father was a butcher when I was growing up. I remember the sawdusted floors of the shop, the freezer hung with waxen sides of beef, the smell of the pickling barrels. We lived in a series of store-top apartments then, moving as the family grew, settling finally in a bungalow bursting at the seams with children.

I remember roving the dirt lanes behind the places where we lived and the ravines to which those lanes invariably led. For my friends and I these remnants of wilderness were the sites of wonder, an inexhaustible source of delight edged with danger that shaped our imaginations. When I write now it is to this world that I often return and to the fear and wonder that walked hand in hand with us then.

Books were a rare commodity around our house when I was growing up, and my earliest reading was relegated to the pages of comic books, which I loved with a passion. Apart from these there were perhaps half a dozen books, inherited from a dead uncle, which I could call my own. It was in the pages of these books that I first encountered Tom Sawyer, Huck Finn, Long John Silver, and Tarzan, and through them was initiated into the magic of books. It is a magic which time has not dulled; each time I begin a book now it is with the same sense of opening a way into another world, of embarking on an adventure into uncharted territory.

I certainly had no thought of becoming a writer when I was young. It was enough then simply to be a kid. It was not until I was seventeen or so and fell under the spell of poetry that I first began to write. We had a teacher that year with a passion for poetry that proved infectious. It was then I first met William Blake, John Keats, T. S. Eliot, Emily Dickinson. I came to love the taste of words on the tongue. By the end of that year I had begun to write. I knew right then what I wanted to do with the rest of my life.

I studied Philosophy and English at the University of Toronto, graduating in 1971. I spent the next several years working at a university library. During this time I married, and my wife and I began raising a family. Later, I took a job as a pressman at a small printing shop and while working there published two collections of original fairy tales for children.

Since 1982 I have worked at home full-time, writing and helping to manage a busy household of six. I work in a small room in the basement of the house. I write longhand first, then type later. I tend to be very superstitious about writing and will rarely talk about a piece until it is nearly complete.

A large part of the delight in writing lies in exploring new areas of knowledge. For the novel *Painted Devil* I spent a good deal of time researching the history of puppetry and in particular the Punch and Judy play which stands at the center of the story. I also had the opportunity to delve more deeply into the life of Emily Dickinson, since there was a character in the book who was like her in many ways. As a result of this research the idea for the picture book *Emily* came to me, as I imagined what it might be like for a young child to move in across the street from this remarkable woman.

I always say that writing a book is more

like having a baby than building a house. Much of the work goes on secretly while the piece unfolds organically from within and takes on its own shape. At the heart of every book there lies a silence, a core of mystery from which the work springs. At the heart of the reader the same mystery moves. Where mystery meets mystery, imagination opens. I have been writing for many years now, yet the act fills me still with awe, the same awe that four-year-old child had, poring over the colored prints in the Currier and Ives.

———

Author and storyteller Sarah Ellis, writing in the *Horn Book Magazine*, refers to Michael Bedard's style as "a real storyteller's voice." And *Publishers Weekly* states that *Emily* is "like a Dickinson sonnet, a quiet gem . . . unassuming upon first glance . . . in fact deeply lustrous, with new facets becoming apparent the longer one looks." *Redwork* won the 1991 National Chapter of Canada IODE Violet Downey Book Award. It also won the 1991 National Chapter of Canada IODE Violet Downey Book Award. It also received the Canadian Governor General's Award and was named a Best Book for Young Adults by the Canadian Library Association.

SELECTED WORKS: The Lightning Bolt, 1989; Redwork, 1990; Emily, 1992; (reteller) The Nightingale, by Hans Christian Andersen, 1992; Painted Devil, 1994.

"ERIC BEDDOWS"

November 29, 1951–

ILLUSTRATOR OF *Joyful Noise*, etc.

Autobiographical sketch of Ken Nutt, who illustrates under his own name and under the name "Eric Beddows":

I GREW UP in a small town in Ontario, Canada. My parents did not have a lot of

money or many books. Each Friday was grocery shopping day at our house. I remember that, in my early years, I would anxiously await our return home from the A & P supermarket because, included in the week's groceries would be one volume from an encyclopedia. It took twenty-nine weeks, if you counted the index, atlas and gazetteer, to get a full set. By then the A & P would be offering a different set for sale at the check-out.

Once home, I would sit at the kitchen table and, while I kneaded the little button of colour in the pasty-white oleomargarine sac (it was illegal back then to sell margarine pre-coloured), I would look through that week's volume. To save on copyright fees these particular encyclopedias had lifted their illustrations from the works of great artists of children's literature. I was in awe of those pictures. They were my introduction to the works of Arthur Rackham, Walter Crane, Gustave Doré and Rockwell Kent. Even William Blake was there, illustrating the Holy Bible.

As I grew up and school started me down the rocky road of social integration, I became 'the kid who drew'. I made the posters for the candidates for students council. I planned the overly ambitious decorations for the school dances.

After high school, I enrolled in a university Fine Arts program. The core of this university's philosophy was to teach you to believe in yourself. After two years, wisely or unwisely, I believed in myself so much that I quit. I was now an artist.

A number of years later, a writer friend who was familiar with my artwork, showed me a manuscript for a children's book he had written. He asked me to illustrate it. Oddly, for all my love of the great illustrators of the past, I had never thought of drawing pictures for a book myself. I illustrated my friend's manuscript and enjoyed doing it very much. It was published and people enjoyed the book enough to offer me more manuscripts. I was now an illustrator.

I still paint and draw for myself and am interested in lots of other things as well. I like math and physics and building mathematical models. I like paleontology and I collect fossils. No dinosaurs, though. My specialty is invertebrates. I would like to illustrate a 'no dinosaurs' fossil book.

One of my favourite parts of making illustrations for books is the research. Sometimes I do research in a library and sometimes I do it by traveling. To illustrated a book about a kitten who visits an Egyptian civilization entirely populated by cats, I flew to Egypt and crawled through tombs and inside the pyramids. I drew my roughs while floating down the Nile.

I have enjoyed these last dozen years of being an illustrator, but I feel that I am really just learning how to do it. I think that the activities in life that you enjoy for a long time are those that you continue to learn from. Children's books, like children, still have a lot to teach me.

———

Eric Beddows studied painting and drawing at York University in Toronto from 1970 to 1972. He received a writer's grant for book illustration from the Ontario Arts Council in 1981 and another in 1985.

He has had exhibitions of his work by Gallery Stratford in 1990 and by the Vancouver Art Gallery from 1988 to 1990. His work is represented in the Osborn Collection in Toronto and in the National Library of Canada in Ottawa.

Joyful Noise won the 1989 John Newbery Medal, given by the American Library Association. It was also named an Honor Book in the 1988 *Boston Globe-Horn Book Awards*.

Night Cars was a runner-up in the 1989 Amelia Frances Howard-Gibbon Awards; it won the 1988 International Order of the Daughters of the Empire (IODE) Award for Children's Book of the Year; and it won the 1989 Elizabeth Mrazik-Cleaver Picture Book Award from the Canadian Children's Book Centre.

The Emperor's Panda was a runner-up for the 1987 Canadian Library Association Book of the Year for Children Award. It also appeared on the 1988 International Board on Books for Young People Honour List for Illustration.

Eric Beddows illustrated a trilogy written by Tim Wynne-Jones, which includes *Zoom at Sea* and *Zoom Away*, which he illustrated under the name Ken Nutt; and *Zoom Upstream*, which he illustrated as Eric Beddows. *Zoom at Sea* and *Zoom Away* both won the Howard-Gibbon Award, in 1984 and 1986 respectively. *Zoom at Sea* also won the 1983 IODE Award and the 1984 Ruth Schwartz Children's Book Award, given by the Ontario Arts Council.

Joyful Noise and *Who Shrank My Grandmother's House?* were both named Notable Books of the Year by the ALA.

SELECTED WORKS ILLUSTRATED AS ERIC BEDDOWS: The Emperor's Panda, by David Day, 1986; The Cave of Snores, by Dennis Hasely, 1987; Joyful Noise: Poems for Two Voices, by Paul Fleischman, 1988; Night Cars, by Teddy Jam, 1989; Shadow Play, by Paul Fleischman, 1990; Who Shrank My Grandmother's House?: Poems of Discovery, by Barbara Juster Esbensen, 1992; Zoom Upstream, 1994.

SELECTED WORKS ILLUSTRATED AS KEN NUTT: I Am Phoenix, by Paul Fleischman, 1985; Zoom at Sea, 1986.

ABOUT: Canadian Children's Literature 1987; Emergency Librarian May 1993; Quill and Quire October 1985.

SHONTO BEGAY

February 7, 1954–

AUTHOR AND ILLUSTRATOR OF *The Mud Pony*, etc.

Biographical sketch of Shonto Begay:

SHONTO BEGAY, a Native American, was born near Shonto, Arizona, one of a family of eight boys and eight girls. His father was a traditional guardian of Navajo healing—a medicine man; and his mother was a weaver who created rugs. His aunt and his grandparents were strong forces in his upbringing. The family lived near a small trading post and a Bureau of Indian Affairs boarding school, where a few teachers and traders lived in sandstone and concrete buildings. There Begay started school at age four, and he encountered electricity and modern plumbing for the first time.

From an early age, he loved the natural world where he lived in Klethla Valley—the red mesas, the plants, the rocks and juniper trees. He was brought up to understand the land was sacred and that the people belonged to the land, rather than the other way around. The places he knew "harbored the ancient Gods and animal beings that were so alive," he writes, in the stories of his people. As a child, he loved to draw and to create clay statues of people on horses. Materials for the horses' manes and coloring were all collected from nature. He later spent some of his time herding sheep and driving cattle.

Begay graduated from Monument Valley High School in Kayenta, Arizona. He studied fine arts at the Institute of American Indian Arts in Santa Fe, New Mexico, earning an Associate of Fine Arts degree. He then studied at the California College of Arts and Crafts in Oakland, California, earning a B.F.A. degree in 1980.

SHONTO BEGAY

In a departure from his drawing and painting, he worked as a National Park Service Ranger from 1976 to 1981 in Grand Teton National Park, and at the Navajo National Monument from 1981 to 1986. Since 1981 he has been an artist, illustrator, poet, and speaker.

Begay's illustrations are created with a mixture of watercolor and colored pencils. His acrylic paintings are made up of a series of small brush strokes that, he writes, are "like the words of prayers." He thinks of his artwork as "personal visions shared." His paintings have been shown in over thirty exhibitions and are represented in museum collections.

The Mud Pony was Begay's first book for children. It was named a Reading Rainbow selection. *The Mud Pony* has also been published in Spanish as *El Poni del Barro*.

Ma'ii and Cousin Horned Toad was a story that Begay's grandmother used to tell him. He remembers her telling it in the firelight of their home, with shadows flickering on the walls as she used gestures and different voices to relate the tale of greedy Coyote.

Native People, Native Ways is a series of four books that detail the traditional dress, art, and architecture of many different tribes in the vaious regions of the Americas throughout history. *The Native American Book of Change* debunks stereotypes of Native Americans and describes the clashes between American Indian tribes and those seeking to exploit them and their resources. *The Native American Book of Knowledge* and *The Native American Book of Life* describe the origins and history of Native Americans and day-to-day pastimes, socialization, and food practices and feasts. *The Native American Book of Wisdom* is about the belief system of Native Americans, in which a tribal medicine man visits a contemporary classroom to tell the children of the traditions of his people.

Navajo is a collection of paintings and poems that explore aspects of Navajo life that are not often described in Western literature. Begay's intent is to allow readers to feel "the echoes and reverbations of the way things were . . . on the mesa many hundreds of years before Columbus."

Shonto Begay lives in Kayenta, Arizona, with his wife and their four children.

SELECTED WORKS WRITTEN OR ADAPTED AND ILLUSTRATED: Ma'ii and Cousin Horned Toad: A Traditional Navajo Story, 1992; Navajo: Visions and Voices Across the Mesa, 1995.

SELECTED WORKS ILLUSTRATED: The Mud Pony: A Traditional Skidi Pawnee Tale, by Caron Lee Cohen, 1988.

SELECTED WORKS WRITTEN BY WHITE DEER OF AUTUMN AND ILLUSTRATED: Native American Book of Change, 1994; Native American Book of Knowledge, 1994; Native American Book of Life, 1994; Native American Book of Wisdom, 1994.

ABOUT: Book Links July 1992; Instructor March 1995.

ANTHEA BELL

May 10, 1936–

TRANSLATOR OF *Konrad*, etc.

Biographical sketch of Anthea Bell:

ANTHEA BELL was born in Suffolk, England. As she lived in a rather isolated place, in farming country, the children's books she read were sent to her by friends of the family who were able to shop in Cambridge book shops. She remembers particularly receiving and reading *Puck of Pook's Hill*, *The Sword in the Stone*, and *The Hobbit*. As a student, Bell learned French first, in school. Later she chose to learn German as a second foreign language. Her enthusiasm was sparked by a German volume of fairy tales available at her school library. When she learned enough of the grammar, she began to read the stories with the aid of a dictionary. She was educated at Talbot Heath School, Bournemouth, and at Somerville College at the University of Oxford. She holds the degree of M.A., Oxon. During her college years, she attended lectures by C.S. Lewis, who was then Professor of Poetry, and by J.R.R. Tolkein.

After she graduated, a friend asked her to write a report on some German children's stories. She evaluated the stories as to their suitability for publication, and has since evaluated hundreds of books in this manner, a responsibility she takes very seriously.

When she finds a book adequate, but not outstanding, she does not receommend that the publisher go to the added expense of translating a work. Therefore, she states, it is only the best of foreign children's literature that does get published in English.

The first children's book Bell translated was *The Little Water-Sprite* by Otfried Preussler, which was his first book. Bell has since translated almost all of his works.

Bell has translated around two hundred titles, including books for adults and books for children. Among her titles from the German are *My Life in Politics* by Willy Brandt and *Reading Psychosis* by Evelyne Keitel. From the French, she has translated six noveles by Henri Troyat, including the trilogy beginning with *Sylvie*, and Franqise Sagan's *Painting in Blood*.

Her name is well-known name among children's librarians because of her contribution to some of the finest children's books available in translation. She has translated several novels by the Austrian writer Christine Nöstlinger, who won the 1984 Hans Christian Andersen award from the International Board on Books for Young People. She has also translated classic books by the Brothers Grimm, E.T.A. Hoffmann, Clemens Brentano, and Wilhelm Hauff. From the French, she has translated the Little Nicholas series by René Goscinny, *Mr Bingley's Bears* by Gabrielle Vincent, and two novels in a trilogy by Claude Gutman, *The Empty House* and *Fighting Back*. She is also the co-translator of the Asterix series by René Goscinny and Albert Uderzo.

Anthea Bell has also translated children's books from the Danish, including *Buster's World*, *The Sheikh of Hope Street*, and *The Boys from St. Petri* by Bjarne Reuter. She is serving a third term on the committee of the Translators' Association of the UK.

Bell lives in Cambridge, England. She is divorced and has two grown sons. She has six Birman cats and breeds cats as a hobby.

The American Library Association has awarded the Mildred L. Batchelder Award to Bell three times: in 1979 for *Konrad*, in 1990 for *Buster's World*, and in 1995 for *The Boys from St. Petri*.

Anthea Bell won a 1990 FIT Astrid Lindgren Translation Prize, awarded by the International Federation of Teachers of Belgium. Her translation of *The Big Janosch Book of Fun and Verse* was honored by being placed on the 1982 International Board on Books for Young People Honour List. She received the same honor in 1978 for *The Cucumber King*.

Bell was also awarded the 1987 Schlegel-Tieck Prize administered by the Translators' Association of the UK with the support of the German government, for *The Stone and the Flute* by Hans Bemmann. Many of the books Bell has translated have been named Notable Books of the Year by the ALA, including *The Boys from St. Petri*.

SELECTED WORKS TRANSLATED: The Satanic Mill, by Otfried Preussler, 1973; The Cat and the Mouse Who Shared a House, by Ruth Hürlimann, 1974; The Cucumber King: A Story with a Beginning, a Middle and an End, by Christine Nöstlinger, 1975; Konrad, by Christine Nöstlinger, 1977; The Big Janosch Book of Fun and Verse, by Janosch, 1980; The Swineherd, by Hans Christian Andersen, 1982; Buster's World, by Bjarne Reuter, 1989; Elephant and Crocodile, by Max Velthuijs, 1990; Aesop's Fables, 1994; Dwarf Nose, by Wilhelm Hauff, 1994.

ABOUT: Horn Book October 1978.

JAMES BERRY

1925–

AUTHOR OF *A Thief in the Village and Other Stories*, etc.

Biographical sketch of James Berry:

JAMES BERRY was born in colonial Jamaica. From the age of about ten, he writes that "through my school books, through the white family of my village and my own village people—I began to pick up certain established attitudes and beliefs that frightened and troubled me." He realized that there was a prevailing understanding that the life of black people was "irreversibly and unquestioningly inferior." This alarmed him then and now, and he has expressed himself in his writing in order to "struggle, to find, to claim and to celebrate and establish my humanity," according to a statement in a British Book Trust publication.

Berry went to Britain in 1948. In 1971 he received a C. Day Lewis Fellowship and was writer-in-residence at Vauxhall Manor Comprehensive School in London. He was concerned about the lack of material on the Caribbean that was available to British schools. His first book, *Bluefoot Traveller*, was published in England in 1976. It is an anthology of Anglo-Caribbean poetry for young adults. He wrote poetry for adults as well, such as *Fractured Circles* and *Chain of Days*, and edited the anthology *News for Babylon: the Chatto Book of Westindian-British Poetry*, which was published in 1984 in Britain. His poem "Fantasy of an African Boy" won the 1981 National Poetry Competition, and his concern for Africa and his use and adaptation of Caribbean forms has established him as a poet and, as university lecturer and poet Stewart Brown wrote, a "cultural activist".

A Thief in the Village is a collection of stories told with the setting of Berry's childhood in Jamaica. A *Horn Book* reviewer stated, "Stirring and elemental, eloquent in their depiction of the brilliant, poverty-stricken splendor of Jamaica, these stories almost sing." His book of historical fiction, *Ajeemah and His Son*, is a story of a father and son kidnapped into slavery. It was praised by Betsy Hearne in the *Chicago Bulletin on Books for Children*: "Intense scenes and rhythmic dialogue punctuate the narrative and focus the characters as singular individuals pinioned by history." He also produced a collection of tall tales, *Anancy Spiderman*, which was retitled *Spiderman-Anancy* when it was published in the United States.

When I Dance is a collection of poetry for children that contains proverbs, folk wis-

dom, and Creole language. Critic Mary M. Burns, writing in the *Horn Book*, calls "exciting, honest, well-crafted, [a book to] read, remember, and cherish."

Berry has conducted workshops for children in the British school system since 1977, with a special interest in multicultural education and in the development of black writers. He was awarded the Order of the British Empire in 1990 and the Cholmondeley Award for Poets in 1991. His 1995 collection for adults, *Hot Earth Cold Earth*, was called his "most impressive collection" by a writer in the British newspaper *The Independent*. It includes both poems in English and poems in Creole in a voice of "mature passion," according to the reviewer.

Ajeemah and His Son won the 1993 *Boston Globe-Horn Book* Award for fiction. *A Thief in the Village* was an honor book in the 1989 Coretta Scott King Awards.

The Future-Telling Lady and Other Stories was named a Notable Children's Trade Book in the Field of Social Studies by a joint committee of the National Council on the Social Studies and the Children's Book Council. *When I Dance* won the 1989 Signal Poetry Award from the British journal *Signal: Approaches to Children's Books*.

SELECTED WORKS: A Thief in the Village and Other Stories, 1988; Spiderman-Anancy, 1989; When I Dance, 1991; Ajeemah and His Son, 1992; The Future-Telling Lady and Other Stories, 1993.

ABOUT: Contemporary Authors, Vol. 135; Publishers Weekly December 23, 1988; Something About the Author, Vol. 67.

CAROLINE BINCH

June 5, 1947–

ILLUSTRATOR OF *Amazing Grace*, etc.

Autobiographical sketch of Caroline Binch:

HORSES WERE my first inspiration to draw and paint. I adored them and any sto-

ry I read was usually about a horse or pony—preferably wild. They would not be tamed by anybody but formed a close friendship with a boy (it was always a boy back then!). I remember some black-and-white drawings in one of the books that greatly impressed me by being lifelike yet sensitive—I've never forgotten those images. My first "good" work was done in pencil. I once took ten days to draw every detail of the aged poet W. H. Auden's face. I was nineteen years old and the drawing still impresses me.

But before that came art college. I was encouraged to go there by my art and English teacher when I was sixteen. It opened up the world for me, not only in showing me all kinds of ways of making images, but music became very important. I discovered the exciting sounds of jazz and blues and the photographic images that were irresistable to draw. Even though I secretly purchased my lifelong dream, a big dapple-grey horse, with most of my grant money, I was bowled over and inspired by Afro-American sounds and images, and my work headed in that direction.

My Mum had spent her first twenty years living on the edge of the Kalahari desert in what was then S. W. Africa—now Namibia. Her father was a guard on the railways, and she told me stories throughout my childhood of the desert and the wild animals. I was delighted when I found a book filled with photographs of the people of Namibia, they were the most beautiful people I had ever seen! The wonderful beadwork necklaces, the inventiveness of their garments, plus the great dignity and joy that shone out of the pages, set me off trying to get more onto my page than was in the photo. That fascination with details has preoccupied me ever since. I love the light flow and suggestion of a quick water-colour wash, but it cannot grip me like spending a week or two on trying to capture, more than a camera can, an aged face. I love what time does to people and nature, and I love to put down all the tiny wrinkles, twists, and curls of fading. Light plays a very important part in my work too. Like most people I adore the sun and how it lights—especially early or late in the day. And then there are shadows. They are very special to show form and heat.

This obsession with detail results in a very lengthy process when it comes to illustrating children's books, however. It takes such a long time to find my models, photograph and process film, sort through hundreds of photos, draw and then painstakingly paint the way I do. I hate it at times as much as I love it! When it's cold outside, and wind and rain lash my windows, I can easily lose myself painting sun-shadows on a group of brightly wrapped African figures. On the other hand, when the sun's bright and warm outside my door, it can be so difficult to stay in when the day hails me and the dogs whine to "come on out and get down to the beach." My discipline has to be iron-hard at times.

Some years ago I spent a year travelling around South and Central America. That trip and my shorter, more numerous ones, to the Caribbean are special high spots in my life. Time becomes so different when you are away from schedules and telephones—it extends. I love to sketch and photograph all the different ways of being and looking in cultures and countries that are still far away from our materialistic and organised lives.

I live now with my thirteen-year-old son, whose father is an Afro-American musician who has never made it up to the empty, Celtic corner at the foot of England called Cornwall. It's so windswept, hardly any trees live—yet there are tremendous rocks that have been piled upon each other or "planted" in circles by ancient peoples. We live here with two dogs, three cats, and the wild wind and sea.

Caroline Binch was born in Manchester, England. She studied graphic design for two years, but left to work on her own. Since 1969, she has made a career as an artist and photographer. She began in children's book illustration by illustrating the covers to Rosa Guy's novels. Her publisher, Puffin, persuaded her to try a picture book. She also had done a cover for a book by Mary Hoffman, who liked it and recommended her work to her editors at Dial Books for Young Readers in the U.S., which led to her illustrating several of Hoffman's books. Caroline Binch travels with her son to many of the countries where she does research for her artwork, including Tobago, Gambia, and West Africa. *Amazing Grace* was named a Commended Book in the 1991 Kate Greenaway Medal Awards, given by the British Library Association. It was also a Book-of-the-Month Club selection. *Hue Boy* was also Commended in the Kate Greenaway Awards, in 1993. It was named a Best Illustrated Book of the Year 1993 by *The New York Times*. It was also named a Notable Children's Trade Book in the Field of Social Studies by a joint committee of the Children's Book Council and the National Council for the Social Studies.

SELECTED WORKS WRITTEN AND ILLUSTRATED: Gregory Cool, 1994.

SELECTED WORKS ILLUSTRATED: Paris, Pee Wee and Big Dog, by Rosa Guy, 1985; Amazing Grace, by Mary Hoffman, 1991; Billy the Great, by Rosa Guy, 1991; Hue Boy, by Rita Phillips Mitchell, 1993; Boundless Grace, 1995.

ABOUT: Publishers Weekly December 20, 1991; Something About the Author, Vol. 81.

FRANCESCA LIA BLOCK

December 3, 1962–

AUTHOR OF *Weetzie Bat*, etc.

Autobiographical sketch of Francesca Lia Block:

MY FATHER was a painter and my mother wrote poetry. They encouraged my writing from an early age, reading aloud to me and writing down things that I said. I feel fortunate to have been surrounded by love and books during my childhood years.

I continued writing while I was in school, taking various creative writing workshops and studying English literature. During my senior year at U.C. Berkeley I began *Weetzie Bat*, which was published by Charlotte Zolotow at HarperCollins in 1989.

Weetzie is about a dreamy young woman who literally sees the world through rose-colored sunglasses. To escape the reality of her life with an alcoholic mother and absent father, Weetzie wishes on a genie lamp for a "Duck" or boyfriend for her best friend Dirk, "My Secret Agent Lover Man for me" and a house for them all to live in happily ever after. Dirk meets a blonde surfer named Duck, Weetzie meets a mysterious filmmaker named My Secret Agent Lover Man, and they get a house and even babies, but the happily ever after part is more complicated than Weetzie expects. Still, love transcends pain and the characters are all reunited in the end as a loving, if untraditional, family. *Witch Baby*, the sequel that I wrote in response to the encouragement of my editors Charlotte Zolotow and Joannna Cotler, is about the angry changeling child

Francesca Lia Block

For me, the best part of being a writer is making a connection through my books with people I might otherwise never have met. I feel less alone in the world knowing that there are quite a few Witch Baby's, and some boys who love each other the way Dirk and Duck do; and more than one pixie girl who believes in magic like Weetzie Bat.

————

Francesca Lia Block was born in Los Angeles, California. She received her B.A. degree in English Literature from the University of California at Berkeley in 1986. She was elected to Phi Beta Kappa. While at Berkeley she was a recipient of the Shrout Short Stories Award and the Emily Chamberlin Cook Poetry Prize. She is the author of five novels in the Weetzie series, as well as *The Hanged Man* and two adult novels, *Ecstasia* and *Primavera*. Block has been a contributor to *The New York Times*, the *Los Angeles Times*, and *Spin* magazine. She is a member of the Authors Guild.

Weetzie Bat, Cherokee Bat and the Goat Guys, and *Missing Angel Juan* were named Best Books for Young Adults by the American Library Association.

SELECTED WORKS: Weetzie Bat, 1989; Witch Baby, 1990; Cherokee Bat and the Goat Guys, 1992; Missing Angel Juan, 1993; The Hanged Man, 1994; Baby Be-Bop, 1995.

ABOUT: Contemporary Author, Vol. 131; Gallo, Donald R. Speaking for Ourselves, Too; Horn Book January 1993; Publishers Weekly December 22, 1989; Something About the Author, Vol. 80.

with dark tangled hair and purple tilted eyes who appears in a basket on Weetzie's doorstep in the first book. On her cowboy boot roller skates, she goes off to discover "What time are we upon and where do I belong." Witch Baby is constantly revealing and expressing the pain of everyone around her, but it is through this struggle that she finds her identity. *Cherokee Bat and the Goat Guys* is the story of Weetzie's daughter Cherokee who, along with Witch Baby and their boyfriends, forms a band while their families are away. Cherokee weaves magic for her friends but is overwhelmed by the powers of nature and sexuality that are unleashed.

When I write a book it is a very personal experience, like writing a love letter or a message to a friend. I rarely have a large audience or genre in mind. For example, I did not intend *Weetzie Bat* for young adults but I am glad I have reached younger readers. I have written two contemporary fantasy novels published for adult readers, but some young adults may be interested in them as well. Because I do not like to limit myself by being overly concerned with genre, I feel fortunate to have an agent, Julie Fallow Field at McIntosh & Otis, and editors whom I can trust to place my work appropriately.

CANDY DAWSON BOYD

August 8, 1946–

AUTHOR OF *Circle of Gold*, etc.

Autobiographical sketch of Marguerite Dawson Boyd:

AS THE OLDEST of three children, born on August 8, 1946, I grew up on the south

Candy Dawson Boyd

side of Chicago in an African-American, segregated working-class community. Our brick row house was within walking distance of the lofty and medieval arches of the University of Chicago.

My life was occupied by my family and by the tiny, storefront public library next to the now-defunct El train station on 61st Street. The complex, often turbulent life in our home pushed me to that library. It was filled with the discarded books from white people's libraries, their names stamped on the title pages. No matter, there I found the world I yearned for—where good triumphed and evil lost; where one could be poor and unloved, but only temporarily; where love lived, even survived beyond the grave, and where adventure flourished.

But I never saw my face, nor the faces of my sister, Stephany; brother, Julian; my mother, Mary Ruth; or my father, Julian, on the pages of those books. It was as if African-Americans didn't exist, except as slaves.

From hundreds of conversations heard at the dinner table, family gatherings, parties, church, and in stores, I learned that I came from a remarkable people who had an amazing history of courage, defiance, endurance, and greatness. I knew these truths in my bones.

Where were our stories? I had plenty to tell: my daddy, forever reading, struggling to keep his family fed and housed and my mama, a school teacher, who loved the blues and made chicken and dumplings that made me holler with happiness during those freezing hawk-blowing Chicago winters.

What about my sister selling her paper bird cages at school; caring for her personally named one hundred dolls, as well as that stray cat she adored, Cleopatra, who had kittens all the time? And my brother, who vanished when he discovered the empty lot behind our house where the neighborhood boys played ball? He came home only for peanut-butter sandwiches and strawberry Kool-Aid.

Where was I with my solitary doll, Sally, missing an eye, most of her hair and an arm? How I loved her. And I loved the handsome boy down the street, jazz music, dancing, foreign movies, acting, art, and reading. Where could I read these stories? I found a few by African-American authors when I got much older.

Since school organized some of my inner turmoil and confusion about life, I kept on attending, earning one degree after another. In 1982 I graduated from the University of California-Berkeley with a Ph.D. Currently, I am a tenured professor at Saint Mary's College of California in the School of Education—the first African-American to achieve tenure and full professor. Being the first wasn't fun or easy, but necessary.

Moving from Chicago to California in my mid-twenties changed my life. For the first time, I taught fifth-graders from many ethnic groups. Finding literature that didn't distort and insult them was quite difficult. Well, to put it bluntly, I got mad. What could I do?

After reading every children's book in the Berkeley public library—a task that took two years—and taking two courses in writing for young people—I wrote. And I wrote and wrote and wrote.

Rejected for nine long, painful years, my

first book, *Circle of Gold*, was published in 1984.

In my own fitful way I have been writing ever since, working to tell ordinary stories about African-American children and their lives that reveal their extraordinary wonderfulness—the good and the sad; the beautiful and the painful; and the loved and the rejected. Here, in the private place I create when I write, I belong and I love my surprising characters, so much.

———

Candy Dawson Boyd received her B.A. degree in 1967 from Northeastern Illinois State University. She received her M.A. from the University of California at Berkeley in 1978. She was a teacher in several Chicago and California schools from 1968 to 1979. She then became district teacher trainer in reading and communication skills from 1973 to 1976. She taught language arts to college students, then went to St. Mary's College of California at Morgana, where she held several positions before her present one. She has reviewed children's books for the *Los Angeles Times* and the *San Francisco Chronicle*.

She is a member of the International Reading Association, the American Educational Research Association, and the California Reading Association. She has won many professional honors including the 1986 Outstanding Bay Area Woman Award, the Outstanding Person in Mount Diablo Unified School District, and the 1991 Celebrate Literacy Award for exemplary service in the promotion of literacy, given by the San Francisco Reading Association and the IRA.

Circle of Gold won an honorable mention in the 1985 Coretta Scott King Awards and also was named a Notable Children's Trade Book in the Field of Social Studies by a joint committee of the Children's Book Council and the International Reading Association. *Charlie Pippin* was named a Children's Choice Book by a joint committee of the IRA and the Children's Book Council.

SELECTED WORKS: Circle of Gold, 1984; Breadsticks and Blessing Places, 1985; Forever Friends (reissue of Breadsticks and Blessing Places), 1986; Charlie Pippin, 1987; Chevrolet Saturdays, 1993.

ABOUT: Contemporary Authors, Vol. 138; Rollock, Barbara. Black Authors and Illustrators of Children's Books; Something About the Author, Vol. 72.

NORMAN R. BRIDWELL

February 15, 1928–

AUTHOR AND ILLUSTRATOR OF *Clifford, the Big Red Dog*, etc.

Autobiographical sketch of Norman Ray Bridwell:

I WAS BORN in Kokomo, Indiana. My father was a factory worker. He brought home stacks of used work order forms, which I used for drawing paper. I loved to draw and spent all of my spare time creating drawings from my imagination.

I never thought of being a writer. I made up a lot of stories as I walked to and from school. I never wrote them down, but I did sketches to illustrate them.

I went to John Herron Art School in Indianapolis for four years. I couldn't find a commercial art job in Indiana, so I went to New York to work. I did many things. I designed necktie fabrics, I did lettering, and I designed cartoons for filmstrips and slides. I was never very successful.

1962 was a bad year for me. My freelance jobs were very scarce. I had a baby daughter to support. I had to find a new source of income. I made some sample illustrations and tried to be a children's book illustrator.

I was turned down by every editor who saw my samples. One young editor told me I wasn't very good. She suggested that I try writing a book of my own, since it was not likely that anybody would ask me to illustrate their books.

I took one of my sample pictures, a painting of a little girl with a horse-size red dog, and made up a story about them. I kept the

bright red color of the dog but I made him larger. I made him house-size. I was going to call him Tiny, but my wife named him Clifford, for her imaginary childhood friend.

I never expected the book to be accepted. I was shocked when Scholastic Books offered to publish *Clifford the Big Red Dog*. I was very lucky.

I now have had over sixty books published. I can't believe my good fortune. I have no desire to write for older readers.

I live on Martha's Vineyard with my wife, Norma. She is a fine artist. She does oils and watercolors. Our daughter, Emily Elizabeth, is a cermics artist. Our son, Tim, is a screenplay writer and director.

When I'm not working on a book, I enjoy reading history and humor. My taste in music runs to jazz or classical. I like to walk the beaches or the forest with a small camera. I photograph things that I think make interesting patterns.

On May 10, 1994, I was awarded an honorary degree, Doctor of Humane Letters, by Indiana University.

———

Norman Bridwell attended Cooper Union Art School in addition to his studies at the John Herron Art Institute. His books have been translated into Spanish, Danish, German, Chinese, French, Italian, and Greek. There are over 42 Clifford books in print.

Clifford and the Grouchy Neighbors was named a Children's Choice Book by a joint committee of the International Reading Association and the Children's Book Council.

SELECTED WORKS WRITTEN AND ILLUSTRATED: Clifford, the Big Red Dog, 1962; Zany Zoo, 1963; Bird in the Hat, 1964; Clifford Gets a Job, 1965; Clifford and the Grouchy Neighbors, 1986; Clifford's Good Deeds, 1975; Clifford's Neighborhood, 1985; Clifford's Bedtime, 1991; Clifford's Noisy Day, 1992; Clifford the Firehouse Dog, 1994.

ABOUT: Contemporary Authors (First Revision), Vol. 13-16; (New Revision Series), Vol. 5, 20; McElmeel, Sharron L. Bookpeople: a Multicultural Album; Something About the Author, Vol. 4, 68.

MARTHA BROOKS

July 15, 1944–

AUTHOR OF *Paradise Cafe*, etc.

Autobiographical sketch of Martha Brooks:

I DIDN'T ALWAYS want to be a writer. I used to want to be a singer. That happened because when I was eighteen I had surgery to correct a congenital problem with my chest. Ever since I could remember I had been plagued with illness. After the surgery my father, who was a doctor, decided singing lessons would be the thing to bring my health along. So, quite by accident, it was discovered I had a voice that could fly like crazy! I sang operatic arias. And I have fooled around with jazz.

But I never did become a singer by trade. In those early years I dibbled and dabbled at it while supporting myself as a typist. I did other things, too. I modelled, and I was a modelling instructor. I met my future husband, Brian. We got married. Our daughter, Kirsten, was born in 1972. I sang

MARTHA BROOKS

life-and-death struggles. At the sanatorium, patients were ill sometimes for years with tuberculosis. They got on the best way they knew how. They loved and laughed even as they grieved for lost opportunities, lost loves, and their lost place in the world. Those early influences profoundly affected my vision as a human being and an artist. I continued to dip into the well of my childhood for some of the stories in *Paradise Cafe and Other Stories* and, later, for *Two Moons in August.*

Sitting on the doorstep to the great heart of fiction is memory. Writing from that place, from those powerful life experiences that move us and forever change our perceptions, is where art begins. I mentor gifted young writing students in my home. I always tell them, "follow your hunches and pay attention to your memories." Or, as Susan Sontag advises, "you 'lend' your experiences to your characters."

———

to her. It was around this time that I discovered writing, and its suitability to my health and energy levels. I could pace myself. I could (with my husband's support) stay at home. Writing, I quickly decided, can also have a cadence that is quite like singing. The words, like black notes, travel on the breath, from the heart, onto white pages where they sing and sing and then lift off!

I loved this other voice. I guess that's what kept me going through the years I struggled to produce something that someone might actually want to publish. Finally, I wrote *A Hill for Looking* (published in Canada in 1982). You won't find that first book in American bookstores, as it was published only in Canada. But I can tell you that it is autobiographical. My older sister, Alice, and I were born and raised by our parents in an incongruously romantic but isolated setting—the estate-like grounds of a tuberculosis sanatorium in a lush, lake-filled valley in the middle of the Canadian prairies. The story concerns my eleventh summer, when I befriended one of my father's patients. She was a twenty-seven-year-old artist whose loneliness mirrored my own.

I grew up surrounded by the drama of

Martha Brooks was born and raised in Ninette, Manitoba, in the Pembina Valley of southwestern Manitoba. For most of her life, she has lived in Winnipeg. She is a creative writing teacher with the Artists in the Schools Program of the Manitoba Arts Council. She also tours other schools through programs such as the Canadian Children's Book Centre. She counts among her most recent influences Southern U.S. writers such as Ellen Gilchrist, Eudora Welty, and Kaye Gibbons, who wrote *Ellen Foster.*

Brooks is the co-author of a stage adaptation of William Kurelek's *A Prairie Boy's Winter,* produced by the Prairie Theatre Exchange in 1984. With her best friend Maureen Hunter, she co-wrote *I Met a Bully on a Hill,* produced at the same theater, before writing a play of her own, *Andrew's Tree,* which was commissioned by the Exchange in 1988. It won several honors, including the Chalmers Canadian Children's Play Award in 1991. She has recently completed another commissioned play, *Moonlight Sonata.*

Paradise Cafe was named an Honor Book in the 1991 *Boston Globe-Horn Book* awards. It was also nominated for the Governor General's Award for Children's Literature. The stories in the collection have been anthologized in several educational textbooks, as have others of her stories.

Her short story, "A Boy and His Dog," won the Canadian Authors Association's Vicky Metcalf Award for the best Canadian short story for children of the year 1989. It is included in the collection *Who Do You Think You Are?*

Two Moons in August, a novel, was also nominated for the Governor General's Award. It was named a Best Book for Young Adults by the American Library Association.

Her autobiography, *A Hill for Looking,* which was written for children and published in Canada, was short-listed for the Canadian Library Association's Children's Book of the Year Award in 1983.

Traveling On into the Light was also named a Best Book for Young Adults by the ALA. It was named a 1995 Book of Distinction by the *Hungry Mind Review.*

Her story "A Boy and His Dog" was included in *Who Do You Think You Are?*, a 1993 anthology edited by Hazel Rochman and Darlene Z. McCampbell. Her work is widely anthologized, and her books have been published in Spain, Germany, Italy, Australia, the U.K., Japan, and, soon, in China.

SELECTED WORKS: Paradise Cafe and Other Stories, 1990; Two Moons in August, 1992; Traveling On into the Light and Other Stories, 1994.

ABOUT: Brooks, Martha. A Hill for Looking; Contemporary Authors, Vol. 136; Something About the Author, Vol. 68.

POLLY SCHOYER BROOKS

August 11, 1912–

AUTHOR OF *Queen Eleanor, Independent Spirit of the Medieval World,* etc.

Polly S. Brooks

Biographical sketch of Polly Schoyer Brooks:

POLLY SCHOYER BROOKS was born in South Orleans, Massachusetts, and was brought up in Pittsburgh. She earned a B.A. degree from Radcliffe College in 1933, after which she did social work in a mill town outside of Pittsburgh. In 1934, she married Ernest Brooks, a lawyer and later President of The Old Dominion Foundation and Vice President of the Bollinger Foundation. They have four children

Brooks's interest in historical literature for children began when her children were exposed to the excellent history teaching at The Dalton School. She enjoyed reading aloud to them the Arthurian legends of Howard Pyle and his *Men of Iron,* about the Arthur legends, Conan Doyle's *The White Company,* and Olivia Coolidge's nonfiction book, *Roman People.*

She was asked to write a history of the Renaissance for junior high school students, which led her to write her first book, *The World Awakes: The Renaissance in Western Europe,* along with a co-author, Nancy Zinsser Walworth. Determined to make history come alive, she and her co-author researched their historical characters by travelling to the places they wrote about.

After writing three books with Walworth, she branched off on her own to write separate biographies of women she had found interesting in her research for the books on the Renaissance, the Midde Ages, and Rome. She states, "I feel strongly that real, historical characters can be just as interesting and exciting as fictionalized ones."

Writing in *The Horn Book Magazine* about *Queen Eleanor*, reviewer Mary M. Burns stated that "Legend is separated from known facts; gossip from evidence. . . . the book brings history to life, setting a multidimensional portrait of a fascinating woman against a magnificent panorama of events." The book was named a Notable Book of the Year by the American Library Association, and was an Honor Book in the nonfiction category of the 1984 *Boston Globe-Horn Book* awards. It was also named a Notable Children's Trade Book in the Field of Social Studies by a joint committee of the Children's Book Council and the National Council on the Social Studies.

The *Horn Book* also lauded Brooks' Joan of Arc story, calling it "carefully rendered and moving," a "marvelous story . . . undergirded . . . with smoothly incorporated explanations and details of people, time, and place." The book was named a Best Book of the Year for Young Adults by the ALA. Brooks is also a contributor to *Junior Encyclopedia Britannica*.

SELECTED WORKS: Queen Eleanor, Independent Spirit of the Medieval World: A Biography of Eleanor of Aquitaine, 1983; Beyond the Myth: The Story of Joan of Arc, 1990; Cleopatra, Goddess of Egypt, Enemy of Rome, 1995.

SELECTED WORKS WRITTEN WITH NANCY ZINSSER WALWORTH: The World Awakes: The Renaissance in Western Europe, 1962; The Middle Ages, 1966; The World of Walls, 1966; When the World Was Rome, 1972.

ABOUT: Contemporary Authors (First Revision), Vol. 1-4; (New Revision Series), Vol. 17; Something About the Author, Vol. 12.

ROBERT BURLEIGH

January 4, 1936–

AUTHOR OF *A Man Named Thoreau*, etc.

Autobiographical sketch of Robert Burleigh:

I GREW UP and have spent most of my adult life in Chicago, "that somber city." As a child and teenager, I was neither a particularly good or inquisitive student. By and large, my interests were in the area of sports. I do remember writing a little rhymed poem (about a cowboy!) as a very young child, which I still have. I also recall reading a number of novels for children about World War II heroes. Beyond that, I think my reading was largely confined to *The Sporting News*, which my father subscribed to and for which I waited eagerly each week.

Even in college, I was merely a kind of mental drifter. Then, rather by accident, I stumbled on Plato's *Apology* and at the same time, Edmund Wilson's *To the Finland Station*. Something in both moved me deeply, shook a bit of seriousness out of me—something in the portrayal of this courageously rational man (Socrates) and something about the history of a movement (socialism) that promised to change the lackluster world.

In graduate school for several years, I finally made the attempt to educate myself, reading books and looking at pictures and largely taking classes that I liked without any particular thought of graduating. I had no ambition but to be a poet, but since no jobs were available with that title, I later worked as a teacher, a timekeeper in a hotel, and a mental health caseworker, among other things. Finally I landed a job with an educational publishing company, where I worked until last year, writing hundreds of filmstrip, video, and videodisc scripts and helping to produce them. It was here, in fact, where I think I learned to write, with less fat and affectation and somewhat more pith. At present, I am writing children's books and painting full time.

Flight: The Journey of Charles Lindbergh won the 1992 Orbis Pictus Award for Outstanding Nonfiction for Children, presented by the National Council of Teachers of English.

SELECTED WORKS: A Man Named Thoreau, 1985; Flight: The Journey of Charles Lindbergh, 1991.

ABOUT: Something About the Author, Vol. 55.

Mainly for fun, I wrote a couple of would-be picture books (none as yet published) which got me a New York agent. I wrote the Thoreau book because I loved *Walden* and wanted to catch, if possible, its beautiful, witty simplicity in a quick stroke. The Lindbergh book was more on assignment. I'm not fond of his politics, but I am fetched by any loner making his way, so I could easily get into the drama of his flight across the sea, which is the entire focus of the book.

I still write, and will continue to do so, although for the past six years I have taken up, with a good deal of energy, painting and sculpture. For me, writing, art-making, and perhaps other things that I have not yet arrived at, are mainly part of a process of understanding and feeling one's way.

———

Robert Burleigh was born in Chicago, Illinois. He attended De Pauw University from 1953 to 1957 and the University of Chicago from 1958 to 1964. He was for many years a writer and producer for the Society For Visual Education in Chicago. He has written one poetry book for adults: *The Triumph of Mittens: Poems.*

CAROLE BYARD

July 22, 1941–

ILLUSTRATOR OF *Working Cotton*, etc.

Biographical sketch of Carole Marie Byard:

CAROLE BYARD was born in Atlantic City, New Jersey. Her mother died when Byard was very young, and her father and grandmother raised her. Her interest in art began as early as the fourth grade, when she remembers copying a drawing and enjoyed working on art outside of art class. During her high school years, a teacher noticed her talent and encouraged her to attend art school. She was awarded an art scholarship to the Columbus College of Art in Ohio, which she wasn't able to use at the time because she needed to earn money first.

When she was nineteen, Byard went to work, and attended the Fleisher Art Memorial in Philadephia, Pennsylvania as a part-time student from 1961 to 1963. She moved to New York City in 1964 as she was awarded a full tuition merit scholarship at the New York Phoenix School of Design, which later became Pratt Manhattan Center, and earned her diploma there. After graduation, she became assistant instructor and then full instructor at the school, teaching life drawing, pen-and-ink drawing, and painting from 1968 to 1971. Byard became a founding member of the Black Artists Guild in 1971. In 1972 she received a Ford Foundation travel grant and went to Africa.

Next, she taught at the Studio Museum in Harlem from 1972 to 1973. She was instruc-

CAROLE BYARD

tor of drawing and painting and department head of visual arts at the Baltimore School for the Arts in Maryland from 1980 to 1984. She taught foundation drawing in 1988 at the Maryland Institute College of Art in Baltimore, and since 1988 she has been a member of the faculty at Parsons School of Design in New York City.

Her sculpture, paintings, and prints have been widely exhibited. She has been represented in shows at the University of Rhode Island in 1971; at Studio Museum of Harlem in 1973, 1974, 1979, and 1985; and in Berlin, Germany in 1973, among many others. She has had one-person shows, including a show at the Reese Palley Gallery in Atlantic City in 1985. She has been an artist-in-residence at the Studio Museum of Harlem, the New York Foundation for the Arts, and the Blue Mountain Center. She attended the Festival of African Culture in Lagos, Nigeria, in 1977.

At Parsons, one of the courses she taught was an art history course, "A Closer Look at Three Artists During Troubled Times," which concentrated on the work of Kaethe Kollwitz, Charles White, and Valerie Maynard. She has also curated shows such as a national exhibit in 1990 for the Women's

Caucus of Art and the College Art Association Conference. She is a speaker at colleges such as the Minneapolis College of Art and Design.

In 1985 Carole Byard was awarded a Visual Arts Fellowship from the National Endowment for the Arts.

Working Cotton was named an Honor Book in the 1993 Randolph Caldecott Medal awards given by the American Library Association. Two of the books Byard has illustrated have won Coretta Scott King Awards: *Africa Dream* in 1978 and *Cornrows* in 1980. *Working Cotton* was named an Honor Book in the 1993 Coretta Scott King Awards.

SELECTED WORKS ILLUSTRATED: Willy, by Helen H. King, 1971; Nomi and the Magic Fish: A Story from Africa, 1972; Under Christopher's Hat, by Dorothy M. Callahan, 1972; The Sycamore Tree and Other African Tales, retold by Lee Po, 1974; Arthur Mitchell, by Tobi Tobias, 1975; Africa Dream, by Eloise Greenfield, 1977; Cornrows, by Camille Yarbrough, 1979; Grandmama's Joy, by Eloise Greenfield, 1980; The Black Snowman, by Phillip Mendez, 1989; Working Cotton, by Sherley Anne Williams, 1992.

ABOUT: Black Enterprise December 1975; Marantz, Sylvia and Kenneth M. Artists of the Page: Interviews with Children's Book Illustrators; Rollock, Barbara T. Black Authors and Illustrators of Children's Books: A Biographical Dictionary; Something About the Author, Vol. 57; Who's Who in American Art, 1984; Wilson Library Bulletin October 1976.

ANN CAMERON

October 21, 1943–

AUTHOR OF *The Stories Julian Tells*, etc.

Autobiographical sketch of Ann Cameron:

I WAS BORN and grew up in a small town of about seven thousand people, Rice Lake, Wisconsin. My favorite person was my grandfather, Oscar Lofgren, who taught me Swedish and told me stories. He was a blacksmith and on our land he had a shop where he made things for us out of iron. I loved watching him hammer the hot iron

Ann Cameron

on the anvil and watching the sparks fly. He died when I was six. I think because of my relationship with him, I grew up to be a friendly and warm person.

My dad was a small-town lawyer who handled all kinds of cases—sometimes cases of clients who didn't have any money: one family paid him in eggs that they delivered to his office every Saturday morning. My mother had been a high school English teacher before she married and admired writers tremendously. She used to say thought writing was "the most difficult job in the world." When I was in third grade, I decided I wanted to be a writer. I don't think the idea that it was "the most difficult job in the world" was a help to me!

From the time I was seven till I was ten, my inseparable playmate was a boy named Bradley whom I admired tremendously. My memories of that period of my life inform my stories about Julian. So does my relationship with my father, who was a showman like Julian's dad.

In the summers, my family lived at our cottage on a lake. My dad taught me how to swim, fish, water ski, hunt and run a motorboat. He bought me a horse—a wonderful pinto pony named Paint—and taught

me how to ride. One of the things I liked to do best on a hot summer day was to ride Paint bareback into the lake. He'd get in deep enough so he had to swim, and I'd start floating off his back.

By the time I was in high school, I was very interested in lots of things—skiing, acting, politics, science. I graduated valedictorian of my high school class and went East to the big, scary, and exhilarating world of Harvard College, where I got my B.A. with Honors in 1965. At Harvard, I studied writing with Robert Lowell and R.S. Fitzgerald. Both of them gave me confidence that I could indeed be a writer. From Lowell I learned how to go deeper into my imagination to visualize scenes and people before I wrote. From Fitzgerald, I learned to write as sparely as possible. When you use exactly the right words, and not a single unnecessary word, your writing has maximum impact.

At Lowell's recommendation, after college I moved to New York to work in publishing. I became an assistant editor in the adult trade department at Harcourt, Brace. I read lots of manuscripts submitted to the publishing house for consideration. I also read the editors' letters of advice that accompanied novels sent back to authors for revision. I hoped—not only hoped, really *believed* that by reading all these letters I'd learn to avoid all the mistakes the authors had made. No such luck! Occasionally I've written books in which the first draft was the final one and hardly a word was changed—*The Stories Julian Tells, More Stories Julian Tells,* and *The Most Beautiful Place in the World* were like that—but most often a book goes through three or more drafts.

I entered the Iowa Writers' Workshop at the University of Iowa, where I got an M. F.A. in 1972. I taught a literature course at Iowa and also was the first reader of all the manuscripts submitted to the Workshop by student applicants. I started two more adult novels and abandoned them when I couldn't see how to organize them. Then I started writing for children. My third try, *The Seed*, the story of a little seed that is afraid to grow, was published in 1974. Like most writers, I get lots of ideas but don't feel a story irresistibly bubbling up inside of me. I have to push and pull at my mind to make my initial idea fill out with details and meaning. The most important rule for writing is "apply seat of pants to bottom of chair." I don't really like to do this! Starting a new book is terribly hard. By the end, I've forgotten how hard the beginning was, am proud of myself and ready to tackle the next book right away. Then, I get involved in other things and much time passes . . .

My first book about Julian was inspired by stories a friend from South Africa, Julian DeWette, told me about his childhood. Julian was then writing an adult novel about his childhood. He was most interested in writing about the painful parts of the story—about living with apartheid, the three-way system of segregation by race—Whites, Blacks, and Coloreds—that, for forty years, forcibly kept people apart in South Africa. When I used Julian's stories, I moved the characters out of South Africa and set the stories in an imaginary country without racism—a country that represents the world we could have, someday.

After Iowa, I lived in Berkeley, California for a year and then returned to New York. In 1983, I moved to Guatemala. I had always wanted to immerse myself in another culture. To live in two (or more) countries makes one's life bigger, I think. The more we know, the better we can choose ways of living that suit us and make us happy.

In 1989, I met Bill Cherry, who was then working for the United States Congress in Washington, D.C., helping develop laws on agriculture. In 1990 we got married (in one short ceremony I got a husband; two grown daughters, Angela and Cristi; and a granddaughter, Jessica). Bill retired, and now we both live in Guatemala. We have a small house with a view of three volcanoes and a waterfall, and flowers growing over the roof. There's a lemon tree in the back yard, and almost every day we have fresh lemonade from the tree. (My book *The Most Beautiful Place in the World* is based on stories of Guatemalan children.

In 1993, the mayor and city council of Panajachel named me the unpaid supervisor of the municipal library—which had limited open hours, no budget for improvements and almost no children's books. Now, continuing donations from U.S. individuals, schools, libraries and civic organizations enable us to keep the library open six days a week—and buy new children's books in Spanish. Now the library is packed with children learning. One of the reasons I want to work harder and write more is to have more money for it. Back of pants, get on your way to that restaurant and sit down!

––––––

Ann Cameron was a guest at Yaddo in 1968 and a MacDowell Colony Fellow in 1968 and 1986. She received a grant from the National Endowment for the Arts in 1974.

The Stories Julian Tells received the 1981 Irma Simonton Black Award of the Bank Street College of Education. It was also named a Notable Children's Trade Book in the Field of Social Studies by a joint committee of the National Council on the Social Studies and the Children's Book Council. The American Library Association named it a Notable Book of 1981. *More Stories Julian Tells* was also named an ALA Notable Book.

The Most Beautiful Place in the World was a joint winner of the 1989 Jane Addams Children's Book Award and received a 1988 Child Study Children's Book Award, given by the Child Study Children's Book Committee at Bank Street College of Education. It was also selected as a Notable Children's Trade Book in the Field of Social Studies.

SELECTED WORKS: The Stories Julian Tells, 1981; More Stories Julian Tells, 1986; Julian's Glorious Summer, 1987; Julian, Secret Agent, 1988; The Most Beautiful Place in the World, 1988; Julian, Dream Doctor, 1990; The Secret Huey Tells, 1995.

SELECTED WORKS ADAPTED: The Kidnapped Prince: The Life of Olaudah Equiano by Olaudah Equiano, 1995.

ABOUT: Contemporary Authors, Vol. 101; McElmeel, Sharon L. Bookpeople: A Multicultural Album; Something About the Author, Vol. 27.

JOAN CARRIS

August 18, 1938–

AUTHOR OF *Pets, Vets, and Marty Howard*, etc.

Autobiographical sketch of Joan Davenport Carris:

I WAS BORN in Toledo, Ohio and was an adorable infant, but awfully independent. (My mother's euphemism for *difficult*, I'm sure.) In 1956 I enrolled at Iowa State University, which began a career of moving, something I never intended but have found most educational. At Christmas in 1960, I married, finished my first year of teaching high school English the following June, and moved to Des Moines.

The birth of our first daughter, Mindy, sent us from a tiny Des Moines apartment to a tiny house; from there we went to West Des Moines, two miles. That was easy, so we moved to Minneapolis a few years later, added Leigh Ann to the family, then trekked back to Des Moines, where we added Brad and said "Whoa!" to further additions, except for assorted cats, dogs, gerbils, hamsters, guinea pigs, rabbits, and fish. (No wonder there are animals in all my books.)

In 1972 we moved to Princeton, New Jersey, where we raised more gerbils than I care to remember, and where I had a perceptive and wonderful friend who said, "Joan, why don't you write a book for kids . . . maybe about a magic cat?"

Well, she had me there. Not only do I love cats, except when they're prying the lid off the gerbil cage, I also love fantasy. And so, a pile of hopeful paper grew into *Witch-Cat*, which was published two years

after *When the Boys Ran the House*. *Mirabile dictu* . . . I had become an author.

I prefer writing to teaching high school English, which I did for several years, because now I am my own boss. My commute is ten steps (bedroom to office) and I can go to work naked if I want. I'm free to move, usually in clothing, to interesting places like England (1983-1985), where I can soak up new material. The more I experience firsthand, the better I can depict other locations, lifestyles, and speech.

For example, the downeast North Carolina dialect, which I studied on repeated trips, flavors *A Ghost of a Chance*, a story of pirates, buried treasure, dolphins, and prejudice. In *Hedgehogs in the Closet*, set in England, Nick's friend Akbar lends his Indian-accented English to the story, the third in the Howard boys' series. Authentic dialogue, believable characters, and accurate, memorable settings are important to me. For *Pets, Vets, and Marty Howard*, I spent months in my vet's office; for *Stolen Bones*, I dug dinosaur fossils in Montana— and wow, is that fun!

Of course, you can always tell who a writer is by how she writes and what she writes about. I try to write funny books (even my four textbooks are full of humor) because humor is essential for happiness, in my opinion. So much of life is tragic, difficult, or just plain stupid, that we need comedy to keep us positive and sane.

Humor always has a point to make, of course, frequently a very serious one. (Remember Mark Twain, George Bernard Shaw, E. B. White, among others?) But humor is all too often dismissed as frivolous or unimportant. It almost never wins major awards. Even so, humorous books are the ones kids read with joy and recommend to each other.

If I Ran the School, to paraphrase Dr. Seuss, I would make the required reading mainly (not entirely) light-hearted books and engrossing nonfiction. By the end of fifth grade, all my kids would be proficient, dedicated readers, and in sixth grade we could begin considering the grimmer literature, focusing on the meaty topics that demand more mature understanding.

My books are meant as gifts to my readers. I want them to laugh, to love reading, and to learn along with my characters that people can achieve whatever they're determined to achieve—and smile while they're doing it!

———

Joan Carris received her B.S. degree from Iowa State University in Ames in 1960. She did graduate studies at Drake University in Des Moines, Iowa, from 1970 to 1972, and studied children's literature at Hofstra University on Long Island, New York, in 1980.

Her current work as an instructor is for the New Jersey Council on Children's Literature. In annual authors and illustrators symposiums since 1986, writers, agents, editors, and artists are mentors to students in one-on-one conferences. She is also active in numerous Society of Children's Book Writers and Illustrators conferences. She has written several textbooks: *S.A.T. Success, S.A.T. Word Flash,* and *Success with Words.* She is also a freelance editor of text-

books and novels and she has had a humor column in the *Trenton Times.*

Carris has contributed articles to such magazines as *THINK Magazine, The Princeton Magazine,* and *Better Homes & Gardens.* She has appeared on "The Today Show", "The Larry King Show", National Public Radio, and other television and radio programs. She is a member and past president of the Children's Book Guild of Washington, D.C., and among her professional memberships are the Authors Guild and the SCBWI.

The Revolt of 10-X and *Pets, Vets, and Marty Howard* were Junior Library Guild selections. *Witch-Cat* was made into a CBS Story Hour Special. *Pets, Vets, and Marty Howard* was named an Oustanding Science Trade Book for Children by a joint committee of the National Science Teachers Association and the Children's Book Council.

SELECTED WORKS: The Revolt of 10-X, 1980; When the Boys Ran the House, 1982; Pets, Vets, and Marty Howard, 1984; Witch-Cat, 1984; Hedgehogs in the Closet, 1988; Just a Little Ham, 1989; Aunt Morbelia and the Screaming Skulls, 1990; The Greatest Idea Ever, 1990; A Ghost of a Chance, 1992; Howling for Home, 1992; Stolen Bones, 1993; Beware the Ravens, Aunt Morbelia, 1995.

ABOUT: Contemporary Authors, Vol. 106; (New Revision Series), Vol. 27; McElmeel, Sharron L. Bookpeople: Vol. II; Something About the Author, Vol. 42, 44.

ALDEN R. CARTER

April 7, 1947–

AUTHOR OF *Up Country,* etc.

Autobiographical sketch of Alden Richardson Carter:

BOOKS AND RIVERS have always meant a lot to me. I have many good memories of growing up in Eau Claire, Wisconsin, a quietly prosperous community at the confluence of the Chippewa and Eau Claire rivers. I had toys, friends, a dog, Cub Scouts, good schools, caring parents, an old-

gree in English and humanities and an officer's commission. Altogether, I enjoyed the next five years. I saw a lot, did a lot, got the hell scared out of me a few times, and managed to accomplish some things that made me proud. And throughout, I dreamed of becoming a writer.

Carol and I got married the September after I left the navy. From 1976 to 1980, I taught English and journalism at the high school in Marshfield, Wisconsin. I wrote during the summers, but soon realized that I wasn't getting good enough fast enough. Fortunately, my social-worker wife understood my frustrated dreams, and in 1980, I quit teaching to devote full time to writing.

Most of my friends and family thought I was crazy. In my more lucid moments during the next two years, I could hardly blame them. But after a bushel of rejections letters and a ton of returned manuscripts, the mail finally brought the offer of a contract. Few days in my life have been so grand.

My young adult novel *Growing Season* made me a published writer in 1984 at the age of thirty-seven. An agent encouraged me to write nonfiction between novels, and over the next ten years, I wrote twenty books for young readers on a wide range of subjects including electronics, Shoshoni Indians, America's military history, and the People's Republic of China. Fiction, however, remained my major interest. I followed *Growing Season* with six more novels, and had the satisfaction of seeing several of them named American Library Association Best Books for Young Adults.

I write for and about young adults because I find myself constantly amazed with their courage. Despite all the problems— both traditional and recently invented— that fill the teenage years, the vast majority of young people reach the threshold of adulthood triumphant in the realization of their competence, resilience, and grit. Theirs are stories worth telling.

I'm a happy man. My wife, son, and daughter share my love of travel, canoeing, and the Wisconsin out-of-doors. I finally

er brother I could lean on, and a younger sister I could confide in. And lots and lots of books.

I'm glad I have those memories, because things were not always easy at home. My father was a kind and gentle man, but also a severe alcoholic, and his long battle with drinking was a central theme of my childhood. In the bad times, books were my salvation and, naturally enough, becoming a writer seemed the most wonderful dream imaginable.

My father died shortly before my seventeenth birthday, and I honestly don't know how I would have survived the next couple of years without books and rivers. I spent the summer after I graduated from high school at our family cottage on the Flambeau River. One beautiful June afternoon, I spotted a dark-haired girl on the bridge over the river. Tanned and hard-muscled from working in the sun, Carol Shadis was definitely a girl who could handle her end of the canoe. And, although it would take us nine years to tie the knot, she would eventually become my wife.

I left Wisconsin that fall to attend the University of Kansas on a Navy ROTC scholarship. I graduated in 1969 with a de-

write rather than just dream about writing. And I have books and rivers always.

———

Carter lives in Marshfield, Wisconsin, with his wife and their two children. He has travelled to forty countries. He has frequent speaking engagements at schools and conferences. His topics include the creative process, improving one's writing, and getting published.

RoboDad was published in paperback under the title *Dancing on Dark Water* in 1993. Carter has had short stories published in anthologies like *Join In*, edited by Donald R. Gallo.

Some of the novels named Best Books for Young Adults by the ALA include *Growing Season, Sheila's Dying*, and *Up Country*. The latter was also placed on the ALA list "The Best 100 Books for Young Adults."

Radio was named an Outstanding Science Trade Book for Children by a joint committee of the National Science Teachers Association and the Children's Book Council. The papers of Alden R. Carter are housed in the State Historical Society of Wisconsin's special collections section of the W.D. McIntyre Library at the University of Wisconsin in Eau Claire.

SELECTED WORKS: Growing Season, 1984; Wart, Son of Toad, 1985; Radio: From Marconi to the Space Age, 1987; Sheila's Dying, 1987; The Shoshoni, 1989; Up Country, 1989; The Battle of Gettysburg, 1990; Robo-Dad, 1990; The American Revolution: War for Independence, 1992; The Civil War: American Tragedy, 1992; Battle of the Ironclads: The Monitor and the Merrimack, 1993; Dogwolf, 1994; China Past—China Future, 1994; Between a Rock and a Hard Place, 1995.

ABOUT: Contemporary Authors, Vol. 135; Gallo, Donald R. Speaking For Ourselves, Too; North Carolina Libraries Winter 1991; Something About the Author, Vol. 67; Something About the Author Autobiography Series, Vol. 18.

JUDITH CASELEY

October 17, 1951–

AUTHOR AND ILLUSTRATOR OF *Priscilla Twice*, etc.

Autobiographical sketch of Judith Caseley:

I GREW UP surrounded by books. My parents kept a wall of them, first in our home in Winfield, New Jersey, and in their later houses in Cranford. My two sisters and brother and I thought my father, Lester Goldberg, was a strict stoic, and my mother, his taskmaster. No television during the school week, lots of exercise and hiking, fig newtons instead of chocolate covered doughnuts. In many ways, it worked. Every summer, we stayed in a cabin in Maine or New Hampshire and joined a local library for entertainment. I still remember the excitement of climbing those steps, and later, reading voraciously in bed by flashlight. I babysat a lot, to grab my share of television shows, and still watch guiltily.

My parents fostered our individuality, giving me private lessons in the viola although they could ill afford it. My father shuttled me back and forth to orchestra rehearsals, reading in the car or at the back of the auditorium while he waited. I loved the experience of playing, but felt like an outsider. I tried to play the flute, like a member of the "in" crowd would, but I pursed my lips without getting a single sound. Many of my books, like the picture book, *Ada Potato*, and *Kisses*, a young adult novel, feature music and draw on these feelings.

My high school artwork didn't make me feel like less of an outsider. I couldn't draw horses or fashion models or copy cartoons, like the kids I thought were the best artists. My pictures were bold, crude and colorful. Still, after a year of anguish studying English at Syracuse University, I changed my major from English to art and decided to become a painter. I never took a single course in illustration, and still struggle with the "imposter" syndrome. When are they

Caseley: *CASE lee*

Judith Caseley

going to figure out that I can't draw? Color is still my delight, and Ava Weiss, the wonderful art director at Greenwillow Books, still chides me about my subtle tones—fuschia and turquoise, canary yellow and scarlet, forest green and marigold orange!

After art school, I moved to London, England, got married, and lived there for seven years. Letter writing from sheer homesickness started honing my story skills. My friends and family told me they read them like novels, over a cup of coffee. I worked part-time at Sotheby's Fine Art Auctioneers, designed greeting cards, won some awards for miniature watercolors, moved back to the United States, and remarried.

Bored with greeting cards and broke from gallery work, I armed myself with a portfolio of cards and an idea for a picture book about stage fright. I met Susan Hirschman, who gave me a contract for *Molly Pink* and changed my life.

The stories she encouraged me to write were very personal nuggets from my early family life. Like Dorothy from the Kane family series, and Molly Pink, I got awful stage fright. My grandfather came to live with us, as in *When Grandpa Came to Stay*. And when my children, Jenna and Michael,

were born, a wealth of new family material emerged—Jenna's resistance to toilet training (*Annie's Potty*), her gardening with my father (*Grandpa's Garden Lunch*), letter writing between my father and Jenna (*Dear Annie*), her noisy friends (*The Noisemakers*), comparing Jenna with my sister Bara's child (*The Cousins*), a happy but harried life with two children (*Mama, Coming and Going*). I watch my children grow now, crying, laughing, shy with strangers, bold on the monkey bars, afraid of the dark, making stories of their own. There is still so much to write about.

A postscript: I spent the afternoon in the park with my ninety-three-year-old grandmother. An old man found us, and told us a long story about his marriage of seventy years and his poor dead wife. After he left, my grandmother turned to me with her finely etched face and deep brown eyes. "If only he would read," she said. "It would fill a big void in his life."

Judith Caseley was born in Rahway, New Jersey. She received her B.F.A. degree from Syracuse University in 1973. *Apple Pie and Onions* and *When Grandpa Came to Stay* both received the Child Study Children's Book Award given by the Child Study Children's Book Committee at Bank Street College of Education. Two of her books were named Best Books for Young Adults by the American Library Association: *Kisses* and *My Father, the Nutcase*. Caseley travels and lectures extensively at schools, colleges, and universities. She is a member of the Society of Children's Book Writers and Illustrators.

SELECTED WORKS: Molly Pink, 1985; When Grandpa Came to Stay, 1986; Apple Pie and Onions, 1987; Ada Potato, 1989; Annie's Potty, 1990; The Cousins, 1990; Grandpa's Garden Lunch, 1990; Kisses, 1990; Dear Annie, 1991; My Father, the Nutcase, 1992; The Noisemakers, 1992; Mama, Coming and Going, 1994.

PETER CATALANOTTO

March 21, 1959–

AUTHOR AND ILLUSTRATOR OF *Dylan's Day Out*, etc.

Autobiographical sketch of Peter Catalanotto:

I GREW UP on Long Island in a family of five children, four of whom went to art colleges. There was a wall in our basement my parents allowed us to draw on. When every inch of wall was covered with drawings of cartoon and comic-book characters (my favorite was Spider-Man), my father would paint it white and we'd start anew.

In second grade I decided I would work as an artist when I grew up. At that age, I thought that meant I would move into New York City, I would paint my entire life, I would starve to death, and then, after I was dead, people would start buying my paintings. Somehow this appealed to me. I guess it seemed noble and romantic.

In high school I applied to four art colleges and was rejected from three of them. Pratt Institute seemed the obvious choice and in 1977 I moved into New York City. After four years of drawing, painting, and basketball, I set out to work as an illustrator and a cartoonist. Since nobody found my cartoons funny, I concentrated completely on my illustration. I still do cartoons in my journal and hope to publish them someday.

The first five years of my career were painfully slow. To pay the rent I worked part-time as a bartender, a bicycle messenger, and a custodian. (I recently did an author visit at the school where I used to mop floors.) A lot of my early illustration jobs were for magazines like *Reader's Digest*, *Family Circle*, and *Woman's Day*. In 1987 I did the cover for Judy Blume's *Just as Long as We're Together*, after which the editor, Richard Jackson, offered me a picture book manuscript, *All I See* by Cynthia Rylant. I enjoyed painting *All I See* so much, I was inspired to write my own story, and by following my dog around my apartment I wrote *Dylan's Day Out*.

PETER CATALANOTTO

It surprised me to discover it was harder to illustrate my own text than one of another writer. When I write, there's a constant struggle in my head between words and pictures. For every thought, there's an image. I've got to decide which thought works best in words and which in pictures. With other writers' texts, I simply concentrate on the pictures, since the words are already there. However, to me, illustration isn't only painting attractive pictures. The paintings must speak and extend the text. Artists need to use their minds as well as their hands.

One of the aspects of making books I enjoy the most is the research. For *Dreamplace*, by George Ella Lyon, I spent four days in the Anasazi cliff dwellings in Mesa Verde, Colorado. *Mama Is a Miner*, also written by Lyon, took me into a working coal mine in eastern Kentucky. I do lots of sketching and photographing to recreate these incredible places in my watercolor paintings.

Another place my books have taken me is the inside of over five hundred elementary schools. I enjoy talking to the students about my work. I think it's important for them to know, if they love to write and draw, they can make it their career.

Peter Catalanotto was born in Brooklyn, New York and grew up in East Northport, Long Island. He earned a B.F.A. degree from Pratt Institute in 1977. He married Jo-Ann Maynard in 1989, and has a daughter, Chelsea. Catalanotto has visited over five hundred elementary schools in twenty-five states, where he has discussed and demonstrated the creative process for his books. His work has been exhibited with the Mazza Collection in Findlay, Ohio, and is represented at the Elizabeth Stone Gallery in Birmingham, Michigan.

Soda Jerk was named a Best Book For Young Adults by the American Library Association. *An Angel for Solomon Singer* was named a Notable Book of the Year by the ALA. *All I See* and *Dylan's Day Out* were named Junior Library Guild selections.

SELECTED WORKS WRITTEN AND ILLUSTRATED: Dylan's Day Out, 1989; Mr. Mumble, 1990; Christmas Always . . . , 1991; The Painter, 1995.

SELECTED WORKS ILLUSTRATED: All I See, by Cynthia Rylant, 1988; Soda Jerk, by Cynthia Rylant, 1990; An Angel for Solomon Singer, by Cynthia Rylant, 1992; Who Came Down That Road?, by George Ella Lyon, 1992; Dreamplace, by George Ella Lyon, 1993; Mama Is a Miner, by George Ella Lyon, 1994; Cecil's Story, by George Ella Lyon, 1995.

ABOUT: Contemporary Authors, Vol. 138; Something About the Author, Vol. 70.

DENYS CAZET

March 22, 1938–

ILLUSTRATOR OF *"Never Spit on Your Shoes"*, etc.

Autobiographical sketch of Denys Cazet:

SUPERMAN AND I were born the same year . . . 1938.

He landed on an old farm near the city of Metropolis. I landed in Oakland, California, surrounded by an extended family of great-aunts, uncles, grandmothers, and grandfathers, who all believed the sun rose and set in my favor. French was their first language. They never tired of talking, eating, arguing, laughing, or telling stories. I never tired of listening to them. I never tired of being with them.

Holiday dinners lasted five or six hours. My three best friends always showed up at dinner time. They were like seagulls at a beach picnic.

The four of us were inseparable. We listened to the radio together, swapped comics, and traded Captain Midnight decoders for atomic rings. We spent every Saturday afternoon at the movies and the rest of the week arguing about the latest battle between Flash Gordon and Emperor Ming.

We had a secret clubhouse where we kept our secret treasures and made secret promises.

We had a firehouse, too. We built it in the middle of an old pepper tree. When someone shouted fire, we'd scramble down the tree, jump on our bikes, and rush down the hill to an imaginary fire. Our fireman days ended when we all ran into a slow-moving Cadillac.

My mother always accepted our esca-

Cazet: rhymes with *gazette*

pades with a sly smile. My father always had that 'now what' look.

Early in elementary school, and for reasons that still remain a mystery, my parents took me out of public school and enrolled me in a Catholic school.

My friends cried.

I wasn't so happy about it myself.

The teacher wore dark, Darth Vader robes, and had the sense of humor of a wheelchair. I felt I was in a play without a part.

Every day, after school, I stopped at our local branch of the public library. I'd sit on the floor and surround myself with picture books, my walled fortress against the forces of oppression; sanctuary within the magic circle.

But then, at my new school, I discovered something about heroes.

I discovered that there are no heroes without adversaries. Superman had Lex Luther. Batman had The Joker. Flash Gordon had Emperor Ming the Merciless.

Denys Cazet had Sister Borgia.

Once, while I was in the middle of a daydream, Sister Borgia smashed her cane across my desk. She hit the desk so hard, she broke the cane in half and splinters flew across the room.

"Pay attention," she hissed. I did. But not to the squillon spelling words she was writing on the blackboard.

I paid attention to the human condition. I paid attention to character, and the unfolding daily dramas around me. I paid attention to the heroes and to their adversaries. Not giant heroes, like Superman. But to the little heroes and their giant adversaries.

And, I haven't forgotten.

I try to remember what it was like to be young.

When I was six, I hid my grandfather's shoes so he couldn't go to work. If he didn't have shoes, I reasoned, he would have to stay home and then we could continue playing together. That is the story of *Big Shoe, Little Shoe.*

I really did have a *Great-Uncle Felix,* and all the pictures in the book were drawn from the same places we used to walk together.

In *A Fish in His Pocket,* Russell's school book falls into a pond. It happened to me. My mother tried to dry out my book by putting it in the oven. When she took it out, it looked like a salad bowl.

The Grandfather in *December 24th* was my father. The grandparents in *Saturday* and *Sunday* were my own.

If I had to choose a book that was the most autobiographical, it would be *Frosted Glass.*

Like Gregory, the shy hero in the book, I love to draw. My father loved to draw, too. When he was in school in France, he would sneak into school early and draw funny pictures of the teacher on the teacher's ink blotter. He drew so much in school, and irritated so many teachers, that he had to go to school an extra day each week.

My father didn't have any formal training in illustration. Neither did I. Like Gregory, we just never stopped drawing.

Sometimes, I feel very sad knowing that so many of the wonderful people in my life have died, sad that my own children won't have known them as I did. I wrote *Christmas Moon* because I realized that, in one sense, they are still around. They are part of me. Their spirit is imprinted on mine.

Because I was a teacher and a school librarian for many years, there are many school characters that have been an important part of my life, too. It doesn't take much to reinvent them. They are already there, anxiously waiting to be cast in a new play, a new story.

The children in *Never Spit on Your Shoes, Are There Any Questions?* and *Born in the Gravy,* are very much like the students I remember as a teacher.

It's not easy being new, being young. Or being grown up, for that matter, watching our children step out into the world. We hope for heroes, but know there are no heroes without adversaries. Daydreams help. Being kissed goodnight is good. But what about that noise in the night?

Sister Borgia's footsteps?

Perhaps it is time to build another fortress. Time to write another story. Time to go to my studio and gather my paints and pencils. Time to draw the magic circle.

Sanctuary.

———

Denys Cazet received a B.A. degree in Economics from St. Mary's College in Moraga, California, in 1960. He earned an M.A. degree in Techniques and Psychology of Reading from California State University in Sonoma in 1971. He has attended various other California colleges. He taught elementary school for ten years and spent another three teaching junior high and high school students. He has also taught college courses. He was a media specialist and librarian and a director of elementary school media services for ten years. He has been a consultant for the California State Department of Education Library Resources and Media Programs.

Denys Cazet has been granted fellowships and grants through the U.S. government. His St. Helena Elementary Media Center was cited by the U.S. Department of Education. His programs have received achievement recognitions, and in 1976 his Media Center was one of four national finalists for the School Library Media Program of the Year Awards.

Frosted Glass was named a Notable Children's Trade Book in the Field of Social Studies by a joint committee of the National Council on the Social Studies and the Children's Book Council. *"Never Spit on Your Shoes"* and *December 24th* were named Children's Choice Books by a joint CBC-International Reading Association committee.

SELECTED WORKS WRITTEN AND ILLUSTRATED: Lucky Me, 1983; Big Shoe, Little Shoe, 1984; Christmas Moon, 1984; Saturday, 1985; December 24th, 1986; A Fish in His Pocket, 1987; Frosted Glass, 1987;

Great-Uncle Felix, 1988; Sunday, 1988; Good Morning, Maxine!, 1989; Mother Night, 1989; Daydreams, 1990; "Never Spit on Your Shoes", 1990; "Are There Any Questions?", 1992; "I'm Not Sleepy", 1992; Born in the Gravy, 1993; Nothing at All, 1994; Dancing, 1995.

SELECTED WORKS ILLUSTRATED: Annie, Bea, and Chichi Dolores, by Dorina Maurer, 1993; Where Can Daniel Be?, by Leah Komaiko, 1994.

ABOUT: Contemporary Authors, Vol. 108; Something About the Author, Vol. 41, 52.

LYNNE CHERRY

January 5, 1952–

AUTHOR OF *The Great Kapok Tree*, etc.

Autobiographical sketch of Lynne Cherry:

THE DEDICATION of my book *Chipmunk Song* reads "to dad, who taught me to love the critters and to mom, who encouraged me to draw them."

As my mother (Helen Cogancherry, now a children's book illustrator herself) painted portraits down in the basement, I (and all the neighborhood kids) would make little books and draw pictures. I'm certain that having a place to make a big mess helped develop my creativity.

My father took me walking in the woods and taught me about everything. I developed a deep, abiding love for the natural world. As a child growing up near Swarthmore, Pennsylvania, the woods and the creek were as much my community as the neighborhood of kids. Under rocks I would discover big orange salamanders with black spots—or black salamanders with orange spots. I would observe them and release them.

I wrote many little books stapled together at the binding. When I was ten years old, I wrote a book called *Kitty's Adventures.* Several years ago, I showed *Kitty's Adventures* to my editor. She said, "I love the story, but you're improved a lot as an illustrator since you were ten." I re-

illustrated the book and we renamed it *Archie, Follow Me*, but it is the same story! The story describes how the animals will come out and you can see them up close if you sit absolutely still in the woods. These woodland creatures were the friends who I visited when I wanted to let my mind wander. Many ideas came to me in quiet places and they still do. Nature has been an integral part of my life from my earliest days.

One day I came home from school and heard the roar of bulldozers. I ran to my woods, and only a fraction of it remained. Many people write to tell me how a woods, a field, or a beach they loved has been developed, and with it went a part of their soul. Often these natural places are developed with a fine green lawn that requires chemicals to stay fine and green. People are beginning to realize that these fine green lawns destroy the habitat of creatures that we like to have around, so many people are forgoing their fine green lawns for plantings of flowers that attract hummingbirds and berry bushes that feed migrating songbirds and provide nesting places for them and other creatures.

My concern for the destruction of beautiful and ecologically important places led to my concern about the destruction of the ancient forests and the tropical rain forests. As human populations burgeon, natural places become more and more threatened. So, in 1989 I traveled to the Amazon Rain Forest to research the illustrations for *The Great Kapok Tree: A Tale of the Amazon Rain Forest*. I wrote this book to teach about the importance of the rain forest ecosystems, to motivate children to try to save them and to teach that the values that we have inherited are not etched in stone.

The native peoples of North America had a very different attitude toward the land than the colonists who supplanted them. They thought of themselves as *part of nature*. In order to write *A River Ran Wild*, I went back to graduate school and got a degree in history from Yale. I then wrote this environmental history to help teachers convey a respect and stewardship for the natural world. *We are all part of nature.* I am an author and illustrator of children's books that purvey a respect and love for nature but I am also a living organism, part of the food chain and part of a web of life on our fragile Planet Earth.

———

Lynne Cherry earned a B.F.A. degree from Tyler School of Art in Elkins Park, Pennsylvania in 1973. She received her M.A. in History from Yale University in 1988. She has been an artist-in-residence at several organizations, including the Smithsonian Environmental Research Center in Maryland, acted as historical consultant, organized teacher-training conferences with The Center for Children's Environmental Literature (of which she is founder and director), and doing illustrations for the Java History Trail Project.

Through her books and a newsletter, *Nature's Course*, which is published by the Center for Environmental Literature, Cherry encourages teachers to involve their students in "participatory democracy." Cherry has also been a frequent lecturer at conferences and schools in the U.S. and

Canada, speaking about integrating enviromental children's books into school curricula, among other topics. She has been keynote speaker at such meetings as the Vancouver Reading Association in Canada in 1995, and the New England Library Association and the California Reading Association in 1993. Her work has been exhibited at galleries such as the New York Society of Illustrators and at The Children's Museum of Manhattan in New York City.

The Snail's Spell won a 1983 New York Academy of Sciences Children's Book Science Award. *The Great Kapok Tree* was a Reading Rainbow Book and was named an Outstanding Science Trade Book by a joint committee of the Children's Book Council and the National Science Teachers Association.

A River Ran Wild was a Reading Rainbow Book. It was named a Notable Children's Trade Book in the Field of Social Studies by a joint committee of the National Council on the Social Studies and the CBC. It was also named a Children's Choice Book by a CBC/International Reading Association committee.

Chipmunk Song was also a Reading Rainbow Book.

SELECTED WORKS WRITTEN AND ILLUSTRATED: Who's Sick Today?, 1988; Archie, Follow Me, 1990; The Great Kapok Tree: A Tale of the Amazon Rain Forest, 1990; A River Ran Wild, 1992; The Armadillo from Amarillo, 1994; The Dragon and the Unicorn, 1995.

SELECTED WORKS ILLUSTRATED: The Snail's Spell, by Joanne Ryder, 1982 (reissued, 1992); Harriet and William and the Terrible Creature, 1985; Chipmunk Song, by Joanne Ryder, 1990.

ABOUT: Something About the Author, Vol. 34.

GRACE CHETWIN

AUTHOR OF *The Riddle and the Rune*, etc.

Biographical sketch of Grace Chetwin:

MS. CHETWIN writes, "Born in Nottingham, England, I lived for five years in New Zealand after graduating from Southampton University, then I emigrated to the United States, and am now an American citizen. I have circled the world twice, taught school, designed and built many gardens and a wildlife refuge, created a modern dance company, run a marathon, and become an author. I love making things: clothes, pottery, gardens and lily ponds. Last year, I built a beautiful flower garden, and two ponds which support bass, goldfish, frogs, newts, and toads, dragonflies and many other kinds of insects, not to mention several varieties of water lilies and lotus. Each pond has a fountain made from hollow logs. I keep the fountains running all through the freeze so the animals always have water to drink. In my back garden I am making a tiny suburban woodland for birds, and this last winter we have had as regular visitors five kinds of woodpecker, chickadees, cardinals, juncoes, ruby-crowned kinglets, creepers, nuthatches, doves and jays (which I love, though people say I am crazy). Indoors, I am making candlesticks four, five, and six feet tall to stand on my hearth, carving on them flowers, vines, ferns, newts, rushes, and dragonflies: all the things I find in my garden.

In my family, I have a cat, two grown daughters and a husband who once played tennis for Great Britain.

In high school, I won a scholarship to art school, but at the last minute opted instead for university. Intending to study English, I graduated with an honors degree in philosophy with English and French. How come? I love seeking out those mysteries that lie beneath the surface. This is the stuff of fantasy, and I am a fantasy author. I never expected to write books of any kind for publication. I bumped into it by accident in the fall of 1983 and now I cannot stop. I've produced over twenty books in ten years: picture books, novels for children and young adults and grown-ups, and nonfiction books; and my work has been featured in newspapers, magazines, and textbooks. I cannot recall what life was like before I became an author. As for the future? On with the Grand Adventure!"

Whatever the subject or setting, all of Chetwin's heroes and heroines undergo strange and remarkable adventures. In her 1994 novel, *Jason's Seven Magical Night Rides*, the hero's lively imagination and curiosity prompt him to take a risk that wins him a week of amazing rides with various mythological beasts and heroes over land, sea, and air. Grace Chetwin's own real-life experiences have proven as diverse, challenging, and enriching as any undertaken by the heroes and heroines in her more than twelve novels published since 1984 for children and young adults.

As a child, she wrote and illustrated her own books in her attic den. She says, "I have been telling stories since I can remember." In elementary school, the teachers would "send me around the school to entertain their classes whilst they did essential paperwork." Since this was more fun than staying behind her desk, she made sure she thrived, learning to suit her tales to each particular class and grade, using cliffhangers to make them ask for more, and never telling the same story twice. While she loved telling stories and found it so easy, she did not always want to write. When she was eleven, her godfather, apparently recognizing her gift and wishing to encourage it, presented her with a handsome fountain pen. Another well-meaning adult then suggested she sit down and perform writing exercises such as describing in detail a brass doorknob that she was routinely required to clean. She feels that "had adults not interfered, I would have started writing naturally on my own and much sooner."

While Chetwin has taught English, French, and modern dance, produced operas, plays, and run her own dance company in addition to raising a family, she now considers herself a full-time writer. As an author, she spends a great deal of time giving presentations and lectures in grade schools, colleges, and libraries all over the country. And her earliest experience in spinning tales has stood her in good stead. As she once shaped her tales to fit her elementary schoolmates, so she can "instantly fit a presentation to a waiting audience," she says, "—en route to the podium, if need be!" Likewise, she has delivered speeches, even conducted day-long workshops, off the cuff, substituting at a moment's notice.

In addition to her writing, she also illustrates, often in pen and ink. But she created the pictures (including the full-color jacket) for *Jason* using Adobe Photoshop on a Macintosh IIsi, teaching herself on the wing. While for the most part, her pictures were drawn and painted freehand with the mouse ("painting with pixels"), she also incorporated into the pictures famous or historic images: a medieval woodcut of a unicorn, a bronze statue of the Chimera, a line portrait of Poseidon from an ancient Greek plate.

When asked how she develops her unique plots, she replied that they just happen, spontaneously and completely, and often overnight. The labor then consists in putting them down in the right order. To explain, she gave as an instance the way *Jason* happened. She was busy writing *The Chimes of Alyafaleyn*, her twelfth book, when she dreamed about Jason, the horses, and the idea of his taking the rides. The dream was so vivid, so complete, she even knew his name. Equally vivid was a sense of urgency. Jason wanted his story told, there and then, no matter that Chetwin was in the middle of another book. "Walk away from me now, and I won't be here when you come back," was the message. So Chetwin set aside *The Chimes* and wrote down Jason's story. The same urgent, galvanizing energy was what produced the pictures, and in that totally novel form. (Chetwin had to buy a new computer in order to do it.) "A certain energy within you emerges as you realize a character," she explains. "We comprise many different voices within, and our characters both manifest and embody these aspects of ourselves." Chetwin says "the book is written before I start. After I've pulled out the first draft, I have an idea of how the story goes, but I can't say what it's really about until the final draft."

She identifies three main levels to her books. On the surface is the plot, the story, which must tug the reader along as irresistibly as the Saturday matinee films she saw as a child. "After all," she says, "the prime directive of a storyteller is to keep the action moving. If it sags, the reader should close the book and put it back on the shelf." Under the plot level is the psychological level, a mesh of feeling and motivation, the web, the force that drives the tale. On the deepest level of the story lies metaphor, images and symbols revealing fundamental truths about ourselves the way dreams do. For instance, *Jason* is about a single-parent boy, Jason, winning a week of exciting and literally fabulous rides. Under that is his yearning for a father, and under that is a study or what a father is. "As the tale moves on, Jason experiences different aspects of the father's role and makeup, and this exposure expands his own awareness and understanding of those around him, especially his mother. At the end of the story, Jason has

undergone great growth and change within himself and in his feelings toward his parents."

Gom on Windy Mountain (subtitled *From Tales of Gom in the Legends of Ulm*) is the first in a series about a wizard born in a mythological world called Ulm. It is followed by *The Riddle and the Rune*, *The Crystal Stair*, and *The Starstone*. The American Library Association named *Collidescope* a Best Book of the Year for Young Adults. Grace Chetwin's work in progress is *Gerrad's Quest*, subtitled *From Tales of Ulm by Hester's Hearth*. This novel, while based on the Gom series, is not primarily about Gom himself, but the young son of a major character in the series who wants to meet Gom and be a hero just like him.

Chetwin's books have been translated into Danish, French, Italian, Hebrew, and Spanish, and several are already on tape. She lives in Glen Cove, New York.

SELECTED WORKS: On All Hallows' Eve, 1984; Out of the Dark World, 1985; Gom on Windy Mountain, 1986; The Riddle and the Rune, 1987; The Crystal Stair, 1988; The Starstone, 1989; Collidescope, 1990; Child of the Air, 1991; The Chimes of Alyafaleyn, 1993; Friends in Time, 1993; Jason's Seven Magical Night Rides, 1994.

ABOUT: Contemporary Authors, Vol. 123; Something About the Author, Vol. 50.

EILEEN CHRISTELOW

April 22, 1943–

AUTHOR AND ILLUSTRATOR OF, *The Robbery at the Diamond Dog Diner*, etc.

Autobiographical sketch of Eileen Christelow:

WHEN I WAS about three or four, I dreamed I could read. It was a recurring dream: turning page after page and reading all the words. But when I woke up, I could no longer read.

Finally, in the first grade, in spite of the

infamous red, blue and yellow Dick and Jane readers, I learned to read! Books were a part of life in my family. My parents read bedtime stories to me and my brother every night. The table by my father's red armchair always held a stack of books with markers in various places. He read history, economics, novels, and paperback mysteries with thrilling, lurid covers. He also read Donald Duck, Mickey Mouse and Pogo comic books, which he bought as soon as they hit the newsstand and which he allowed us to read only after he was finished.

My brother and I were given books on birthdays, at Christmas, and when we were sick. I saved them all, eventually shelved them alphabetically, catalogued them, loaned them to my friends and charged fines when they were overdue. Much of my early childhood was spent slouched in an armchair or up in a tree house with my nose in a book. . . . A good early education for a writer!

My parents didn't buy a television until I was eleven or twelve. We were allowed to watch an hour and a half a week. So we selected our shows carefully. I discovered, thanks to my father's enthusiasms: Laurel and Hardy, Abbot and Costello, the Marx brothers, Jackie Gleason and Art Carney, and British films, like the *Lavender Hill Mob*. All had wonderful slapstick humor which, in retrospect, I'm sure has influenced my picture books.

I wasn't much interested in writing until I had a dynamic and demanding English teacher in the eighth grade and another in high school. I wrote many stories for our high school magazine and planned to major in English in college. But freshman English was so tedious that I lost all enthusiasm for that idea. Instead, I took art history and some drawing and design courses—a pre-architecture major intended to lead to three years of graduate work in architecture. But, my senior year, I discovered photography!

My first years out of college, in Philadelphia, in the late 1960s, I photographed buildings for architects, and did photo essays for small magazines on urban life; subjects like skid row, Chinatown, inner city schools, political demonstrations.

While I was photographing, I was also looking at children's picture books in bookstores and at the library. I read picture books to any neighborhood child who wanted to listen. I started experimenting with my own stories, illustrating them with photographs or drawings.

By the mid-seventies, my husband and I were living in Berkeley, California, with a child of our own. She and I went to the library once or twice a week and borrowed piles of books to read at bedtime, nap time, and times in between. I decided, once again, that I was going to try writing and illustrating picture books. I started with an alphabet book, thinking it would take a few weeks. Two years later, I reached Z, having taught myself something about illustration and about the complexities of writing a "simple little picture book."

While earning my living as a photographer and graphic designer, I continued to experiment with picture books. One job I had was to design and illustrate a poster about animal camouflage for a science museum. The poster gave me the idea for what became my first published book, *Henry and the Red Stripes.*

In 1981, I sold my first two books and we moved to Vermont. Twelve years and twelve books later, picture books are still an exciting challenge. I have file folders filled with ideas for new stories: clippings from newpapers, stories heard on the radio, family stories, childhood memories, conversations overheard, and nursery rhymes, all waiting for me to find their beginnings, middles, and endings and to bring them alive in the space of a thirty-two page picture book.

———

Eileen Christelow was born in Washington, D.C. She received her B.A. degree from the University of Pennsylvania in 1965. She was a freelance photographer from 1965 to 1972, and lived in Cornwall, England, for a year during 1971 and 1972. Her daughter was born in England in 1972. She was a graphic designer and photographer from 1973 to 1981. Her photographs have appeared in publications such as *Progressive Architecture, Home,* and the *New York Times Book Review.*

Christelow is a member of the Society of Children's Book Writers and Illustrators and of Windham County Reads, a literacy advocacy group.

Many of her books have been named Children's Choice Books of the Year by a joint committee of the Children's Book Council and the International Reading Association. They include *Don't Wake Up Mama!, Five Little Monkeys Sitting in a Tree,* and *Henry and the Dragon. The Robbery at the Diamond Dog Diner* was a Reading Rainbow book, and many of her books have been named Junior Library Guild selections, including *Jerome and the Babysitter* and *The Five-Dog Night.*

SELECTED WORKS WRITTEN AND ILLUSTRATED: Henry and the Red Stripes, 1982; Henry and the Dragon, 1984; Jerome and the Babysitter, 1985; The Robbery at the Diamond Dog Diner, 1986; Five Little Monkeys Sitting in a Tree, 1991; Don't Wake Up Mama!: Anoth-

er Five Little Monkeys Story, 1992; The Five-Dog Night, 1993; What Do Authors Do?, 1995.

SELECTED WORKS ILLUSTRATED: Zucchini, by Barbara Dana, 1982.

ABOUT: Contemporary Authors, Vol. 111; McElmeel, Sharron L. Bookpeople: A Multicultural Album; Something About the Author, Vol. 35, 38.

EMMA CHICHESTER CLARK

October 15, 1955–

ILLUSTRATOR OF *Listen to This,* etc.

Biographical sketch of Emma Chichester Clark:

EMMA CHICHESTER CLARK was born in London, England. She graduated from the Chelsea School of Art with a B.A. degree with honors in 1978, and she received an M.A. degree from the Royal College of Art in 1983. Since 1983 she has been a freelance illustrator, designing magazine covers and working for book publishers. Clark was visiting lecturer at Middlesex Polytechnic and City and Guilds School of Art from 1984 to 1986.

Clark has had two exhibitions of her work at the Thumb Gallery in London. She also won First Prize in the Folio Society's awards at the Royal College of Art and received Second Prize in the Benson and Hedges Gold Awards.

In addition to illustrating books for children, she has also illustrated several books for adults. After illustrating others' books, she began to write and illustrate her own. *The Story of Horrible Hilda and Henry* is a "lively story," states reviewer Ann A. Flowers in *The Horn Book Magazine,* in which two children are so naughty— painting walls, being unpleasant to their parents, and acting up at the zoo—that the zoo keeper puts them in a cage with Brian, a lion. The remedy works so well that the parents take Brian home from the zoo to keep the children in line.

A more tranquil story is told in Clark's *Across the Blue Mountains.* A lady lives in a lovely house, enjoying her pets and flowers, but wonders if life isn't better on the other side of the nearby mountain. She sets off to find out, and readers can see that when she gets lost and stumbles across a house that is just perfect for her, it turns out to be her own.

Clark is a member of the Chelsea Arts Club. She lives in London with her husband and one cat.

Too Tired was named a Notable Book of the Year by the American Library Association. *Listen to This* received the 1988 Mother Goose Award given by the British book club "Books for Children."

SELECTED WORKS WRITTEN AND ILLUSTRATED: The Story of Horrible Hilda and Henry, 1989; The Bouncing Dinosaur, 1990; Catch That Hat!, 1990; I Never Saw a Purple Cow, 1991; Lunch with Aunt Augusta, 1992; Across the Blue Mountains, 1993.

SELECTED WORKS ILLUSTRATED: Listen to This, compiled by Laura Cecil, 1988; Cissy Lavender, by Primrose Lockwood, 1989; Stuff and Nonsense, compiled by Laura Cecil, 1989; Boo!: Stories to Make You Jump, compiled by Laura Cecil, 1990; The Queen's Goat, by Margaret Mahy, 1991; The Minstrel and the Dragon Pup, by Rosemary Sutcliff, 1993; Good Night, Stella, by Kate McMullan, 1994; Too Tired, by Ann Turnbull, 1994.

ABOUT: Contemporary Authors, Vol. 132; Something About the Author, Vol. 69.

SHIRLEY CLIMO

November 25, 1928–

AUTHOR OF *The Korean Cinderella*, etc.

Autobiographical sketch of Shirley Climo:

I WAS BORN in Cleveland, Ohio—the tardy tag-along in a family of three girls and a boy. I was certainly unexpected but probably not "completely unnecessary", as my brother and sisters insisted. My parents gave all four of us a great deal of attention and affection—with more than enough left

for each other. Theirs was an unusual union for 1919—a love match between a poor Pennsylvania Dutch farm boy and a gently-raised girl from the suburbs. The marriage worked—or perhaps my parents worked at it—and, despite the Depression, my early memories are of an outgoing and optimistic family. Then, when I was nine, my brother was killed in an accident, and, when I was thirteen, my father died from a heart attack. Suddenly, we were an all-female family, and, as head of the household, my mother went to work. She became, among numerous other writing jobs, a children's book author.

I inherited my love of writing from her. At least she passed it along by encouraging my efforts. Thanks to her help, I sold my first story—"The Witch's Cat's Kitten"—to a children's magazine when I was sixteen. When I saw that ten-dollar check with my name on it, I was determined to be an author.

For a while, I hoped to be an artist as well and took Saturday morning art classes at the Cleveland Institute of Art. But my older sister, Mary Alice, was already a published illustrator of five juvenile books. The competition on the homefront was too strong for me, so I continued telling my stories in words instead of pictures. My art training, however brief, gave me an appreciation of the illustrator's needs, and I still explore picture possibilities in every word I write.

In my junior year at De Pauw University in Indiana, my mother suddenly died. I was offered first chance at one of her jobs—writer for a children's program on CBS radio in Cleveland. I dropped out of college and scripted Fairytale Theater for the next three and a half years. Each week I faced a deadline dilemma and the challenge of developing characters and advancing the plot through dialog. Fairytale Theater gave me my real writing education and began my strong interest in folklore.

In the fifties, my job description changed. As radio drama faded from the airwaves, my three children took the leading roles. For the next couple of decades, I concentrated on keeping diaper pails empty and lunch boxes full and confined my writing to grocery lists and PTA newsletters. Then a trip to Cornwall provided both the information and inspiration for my first juvenile book. *Piskies, Spriggans, and Other Magical Beings*, a collection of Cornish folklore, was published in 1981. Fourteen other books followed in as many years and five more are scheduled.

Although my titles include three novels and three nonfiction books, I never stray too long or too far from folktales. Wilhelm Grimm said, "The fairytale flies, but the legend walks and knocks at your door."

My door is always open to any legend or myth, fable or folktale.

———

Shirley Climo attended De Pauw University from 1946 to 1949. She was married in 1950 and has three children and four grandchildren. She wrote for Fairytale Theater from 1949 to 1953. She is a contributor to many magazines and newspapers, including *The Writer, Cricket, Ranger Rick, Seventeen*, the *Chicago Tribune*, and the *Washington Post*. Her work is also represented in collections such as *Family Read-Aloud Christmas Treasury*. She is a member of Authors Guild and the Society of Children's Book Writers and Illustrators.

Four of her books were named Notable Children's Trade Books in the Field of Social Studies by a joint committee of the Children's Book Council and the National Council for the Social Studies: *Someone Saw a Spider, The Korean Cinderella The Egyptian Cinderella*, and *King of the Birds*. *Someone Saw a Spider* was also named an Outstanding Science Trade Book for Children by a joint committee of the CBC and the National Science Teachers Association.

SELECTED WORKS: The Cobweb Christmas, 1982; Someone Saw a Spider, 1985; King of the Birds, 1987; The Egyptian Cinderella, 1989; T.J.'s Ghost, 1989; City! Washington, D.C., 1991; The Korean Cinderella, 1993; Stolen Thunder, 1994; Atalanta's Race, 1995; The Little Red Ant and the Great Big Crumb, 1995.

ABOUT: Contemporary Authors, Vol. 107; (New Revision Series), Vol. 24; Something About the Author, Vol 35, 39, 77.

BABETTE COLE

September 10, 1949–

AUTHOR AND ILLUSTRATOR OF *Princess Smartypants*, etc.

Biographical sketch of Babette Cole:

BABETTE COLE was born in Jersey in the Channel Islands in 1949. After the Second World War, her parents wanted a fresh start and sailed for Africa. However, her mother had never been out of England, and she insisted on stopping in the Channel Islands, where they settled. Her father was a builder, but also a good draftsman and painter, and Cole was encouraged to draw while she was in school. She also loved animals, and had two dogs, some birds, Siamese cats, and a pony, which she called "Prom" for short, its name being Promise.

She attended convent school as a second-

BABETTE COLE

ary school when she was older, and she remembers being called upon to make posters and feast day cards by the nuns. She had a continuing passion for horses and read pony magazines.

The expectations for her were that she become a nun or a wife and mother. She wanted to be a veterinarian. However, she was told that she did not have the academic qualifications to pursue science as a career.

She was turned away from the first art school she tried to enter, and that was a difficult blow. She worked for an advertising agency for a while. She disliked the work, but learned a great deal, and eventually ran the department.

She was able to leave Jersey in 1970 to attend Canterbury College of Art in the south of England. The reason she chose the college was that she could keep her pony at school, and she had to have him flown off the island. There she found that her artwork was judged not commercial enough for the Graphic Design Department, but too commercial for the Fine Art Department. While at school, she took her artwork to publishers to try to get a children's book published.

When she did not succeed after many

tries, she invited two illustrators, Peter Firmin and Oliver Postgate, to attend an art show of her work, required for her degree. They then asked her to help with some children's television projects they were creating for the BBC. This gave her an entree into publishing, and her first book was published in 1976. Cole graduated in 1974 with a B.A. first class degreee with honors in illustration and film.

Cole travelled to Africa with an anthropologist friend. Near Rhodesia, they became caught in the crossfire of a war that they hadn't been aware of. Border guards held them captive until their papers could be verified. In Africa Cole wrote her three Nungu stories, which were later published. Since then, Cole has written about thirty books, which have been published in about twenty languages, including Urdu, Xosa, and Chinese.

As a child, Cole was strongly influenced by Edward Lear, Lewis Carroll, C.S. Lewis, and Kenneth Grahame. Later in life, she admired painters and draftsmen such as Phil May, Randolph Caldecott, George Stubbs, and Arthur Rackham—as well as the great artists Rubens, Durer, and Egon Schiller.

Her technique is difficult to reproduce in the printing process, so Cole now has her book contracts stipulate that she is in charge of the printing of her work.

As she has always loved horses and showed ponies from an early age, she realized a dream of owning a stud farm. She now lives in the country in Lincolnshire in a five-hundred-year-old house named Ivy Cottage, which she carefully restored. There she breeds show and event horses.

Cole loves to travel and see other cultures and other ways of living. She is a sailor and is skipper on trips around the Caribbean. Her ambition is to sail across the Atlantic Ocean.

Her artwork has been shown in exhibitions at the Bologna International Book Fair in Italy from 1985 to 1989 as well as the Salon International du Livre in Switzerland in 1988.

Princess Smartypants was named a Commended Book in the 1986 Kate Greenaway Medal Awards by the British Library Association. Several of her books have been named Children's Choice Books by a joint committee of the International Reading Association and the Children's Book Council: *The Slimy Book, The Trouble with Dad,* and *Cupid.*

SELECTED WORKS WRITTEN AND ILLUSTRATED: Nungu and the Elephant, 1980; Nungu and the Hippopotamus, 1980; The Trouble with Mom, 1984; The Hairy Book, 1985; The Slimy Book, 1986; The Trouble with Dad, 1986; Princess Smartypants, 1987; The Trouble with Gran, 1987; Prince Cinders, 1988; King Change-a-Lot, 1989; Cupid, 1990; Tarzanna, 1992; Supermool, 1993; Dr. Dog, 1994.

SELECTED WORKS ILLUSTRATED: Grasshopper and the Unwise Owl, by Jim Slater, 1980; The Wind in the Willows Pop-Up Book, by Kenneth Grahame, 1983.

ABOUT: Marantz, Sylvia S. and Kenneth M. Artists of the Page: Interviews with Children's Book Illustrators; Something About the Author, Vol. 61.

PETER COLLINGTON

April 2, 1948–

AUTHOR OF *The Coming of the Surfman,* etc.

Autobiographical sketch of Peter Collington:

WHEN I WAS fourteen years old I suddenly decided I had to have a surfboard. My friends all laughed at me. No one surfed in England. Surfing was American. Every beach had giant waves crashing down on them over there. They pointed out that the waves at our local beach were pathetically small by comparison. I wouldn't be deterred. I decided to build a surfboard myself. I planed away at bits of timber in woodwork class while arching my back away from the hoots of mockery coming from my classmates. I had a dream and I was following it. It didn't matter to me ei-

Peter Collington.

ther, that the day I chose for the launch of my completed board, the wind factor was zero. Sailboats were becalmed out in the bay. I looked out on the Atlantic and felt good. It was only a matter of time before big waves would be heading my way over the horizon. I would paddle my board out to meet them. They would be coming all the way over from America. I threw the board into the water and launched myself upon it. The board immediately nosedived to the bottom, where momentarily I lay clutching its smoothly contoured sides, thinking. Something about my design and construction was not meeting the minimum requirements needed for surfing; namely, that the board had to float. I came up for air to review the situation. My board reluctantly followed me. It could float quite well on its own, but it had trouble with the two of us together. I knew what I had to do to salvage some dignity. I got out of the suddenly freezing water, went home and chucked the surfboard in the garage. I never looked for it again.

About thirty or so years later I was writing *The Coming of the Surfman.* The story was about a guy who moves into a rundown urban neighbourhood and opens a surfing supply store. There is no-where around to surf. People think he's a nut. Then he builds a giant wave machine in an abandoned factory and for a time the two warring neighbourhood gangs put aside their violent behavior and learn to surf, live in harmony and eat good nutritional food. When I had finished writing the story, the incident that had happened when I was fourteen bobbed to the surface. It was suddenly obvious to me why I was writing this particular book.

So, if your present life is fraught with many difficulties and like me, you may have done many dumb things: look at it this way: you never know in the future how you might use your present experience.

As it turns out, fourteen was a crucial age for me. I bought a camera with some birthday money and fell in love with photography. I knew what I wanted to be. When I was sixteen I left school and did a three year photographic course at my local college. For a long while I was in seventh heaven. I even started to open books and read them cover to cover. But then an element of disenchantment set in. I was always searching for the perfect image, but I could never find it. It was only later when I had left college that I found out what the problem was. I wanted to photograph things that were in my head. It was then, in my early twenties, that I took up illustration. I had to support myself with numerous dead-end jobs for years to come, while I learnt my craft in my spare time. My first book wasn't published until I was in my late thirties. A long wait, I know, but before then I wasn't ready. The important thing in life, I think, is to find out what you want to do. This insight may come suddenly or it may come bubbling to the surface later on. You may have to take many detours to end up where you want to be. The main thing is to keep believing in yourself and trusting your own judgement. You'll get there in the end.

———

Peter Collington was born in England and grew up on the south coast, near the small town of Christchurch, in Dorset. He studied photography at Bournemouth College. He has lived in London, New York, and Madison, Wisconsin. He lives with his American wife, Bonnie, and their daughter Sasha in Blandford in Dorset. *The Angel and the Soldier Boy* and *On Christmas Eve* were both made into animated films produced by Grasshopper Productions Ltd., the former in 1989 and the latter in 1992. *The Angel and the Soldier Boy* won an ACE Award, given by The National Academy of Cable Programming in America. *The Coming of the Surfman* received the Bologna Book Fair Honor Book award in 1994.

SELECTED WORKS WRITTEN AND ILLUSTRATED: Little Pickle, 1986; The Angel and the Soldier Boy, 1987; (reissued, 1994); My Darling Kitten, 1988; On Christmas Eve, 1990; The Midnight Circus, 1993; The Coming of the Surfman, 1994.

ABOUT: Contemporary Authors, Vol. 127; Marantz, Sylvia and Kenneth M. Artists of the Page: Interviews with Children's Book Illustrators; Something About the Author, Vol. 59.

JANE LESLIE CONLY

1948–

AUTHOR OF *Crazy Lady*, etc.

Biographical sketch of Jane Leslie Conly:

JANE LESLIE CONLY was born in Virginia, one of four children of Robert Leslie Conly and Sally McCaslin Conly. She grew up on a farm adjacent to the Potomac River near Leesburg, Virginia, where they kept many animals—horses, a cow, sheep, chickens, dogs, and cats. She loved to fish in nearby ponds and in the river.

Both of Conly's parents were writers, and Conly herself began writing when she was in the first grade. They gave her advice on different aspects of writing. The family moved to Washington, D.C., in 1962. Conly graduated from Smith College in 1971, and from the Johns Hopkins Writing Seminar Program in 1974. Since 1973, she has lived in Baltimore.

JANE LESLIE CONLY

Her father was a journalist who worked for such publications as the Washington *Times-Herald* and the *National Geographic*. He was also a writer for children, under the pseudonym Robert C. O'Brien. His most famous work, *Mrs. Frisby and the Rats of NIMH*, was published in 1971. It won the 1972 John Newbery Medal from the American Library Association, as well as other distinctions; it was a finalist in the National Book Awards and was named an Honor Book in the 1971 *Boston Globe-Horn Book* Awards.

When her father became ill and realized he was going to die from heart failure, he asked Jane Leslie Conly to finish the novel he was working on, *Z for Zachariah*. The book is a science-fiction story of survival set after an atomic war. A sixteen-year-old girl finds that she and one man are the only human beings she knows of who are alive. She nurses him to health after he is injured, but when he recovers, he becomes a menace to her and she must use her wits to escape him, hoping to find other people.

Conly did finish her father's novel, a fact noted on the dust jacket of the book. Her mother edited it, and it was published in 1975. The book was named an Honor Book in the 1976 Jane Addams Children's Book Awards and won a 1976 Edgar Allan Poe Award from the Mystery Writers of America. It was also named a Notable Book of the Year and a Best Book for Young Adults by the ALA. Sally Conly, the sister of Jane Leslie Conly, later wrote a biographical piece about her father that appeared in the *Fourth Book of Junior Authors and Illustrators.*

Jane Leslie Conly went on to write more books in the series that her father began about the rats of NIMH. *Racso and the Rats of NIMH* was lauded by Ann A. Flowers in the *Horn Book* as "an outstanding success" as a sequel. In addition to being warmly received by critics, the book won awards and honors. It was named a Children's Choice Book by a joint committee of the International Reading Association and the Children's Book Council. It was also named a Notable Children's Trade Book in the Field of Social Studies by a joint committee of the CBC and the National Council on the Social Studies. Her follow-up novel, *R-T, Margaret, and the Rats of NIMH*, was an IRA-CBC Children's Choice Book.

The next book Conly wrote is independent of the series of NIMH books. *Crazy Lady* is the story of a seventh grader who is asked to do odd jobs for a reclusive, alcoholic woman who has a mentally retarded son named Ronald. He begins to help and support Ronald, and a *Horn Book* reviewer states that the boy's "instinctive ability to connect with Ronald has an authentic ring to it, as does the narrative's first-person voice and its description of the dilapidated but cohesive urban neighborhood." It was named a 1994 Newbery Honor Book, an ALA Notable Book, and an ALA Best Book for Young Adults.

In addition to her work as a writer, Conly has also been director of a community center, a camp director, and a mortgage counselor. She is married and has two children, the first of whom was born in 1985. Since his birth, she spends her work time on writing, which she describes as vital to her "overall sense of contentment."

Conly's hobbies are gardening, cooking, reading, fishing, and working on a log cabin that she and her husband own on a creek in southern Pennsylvania.

SELECTED WORKS: Racso and the Rats of NIMH, 1986; R-T, Margaret, and the Rats of NIMH, 1990; Crazy Lady!, 1993; Trout Summer, 1995.

ABOUT: Something About the Author, Vol. 80.

FLOYD COOPER

January 8, 1956–

ILLUSTRATOR OF *Grandpa's Face*, etc.

Biographical sketch of Floyd Cooper:

FLOYD COOPER was born in Tulsa, Oklahoma, the oldest of four children. He was raised in Tulsa, and although he wanted to move to New York, he remained in Oklahoma for school, attending the University of Oklahoma; he had received a four-year scholarship with the stipulation that he attend an in-state institution. He graduated with a B.F.A. degree in 1980.

Cooper had begun his illustration career with freelance work while he was still a student, but upon graduation, he moved to Kansas City, Missouri, to work at Hallmark. Although he had an established position at Hallmark doing greeting card illustration, Cooper had his sights set on New York and a career as a freelance illustrator. He says, "Hallmark was a great place to work . . . but it's hard to be around so many fuzzy bunnies without becoming one!" He apprenticed with illustrator Mark English, and the two of them held after-hours critiques to keep their portfolios updated and their work fresh. Cooper credits Mark English with helping him boost his confidence enough to make the move to New York. "He had a big impact on me," says Cooper, who felt lucky to "have the good fortune to work side by side with the master."

Moving to New York was not an easy step for Cooper. He had heard many things,

FLOYD COOPER

both good and bad, about the city. It was English who assured him it would be the best move for him and, says Cooper, "he was right!" Cooper finally made the big move in 1984.

When Cooper got to New York, he decided he'd like to go from advertising and corporate illustration to illustrating children's books. It was at this point that he and his mentor parted ways. English had shunned picture books, saying it was a very difficult area to break into. In the hierarchy of illustrators, "fine artists look down on illustrators, and illustrators look down on kiddie-book illustrators," says Cooper. However, he found it to be a stimulating outlet for his creativity, and so he pursued children's book illustration.

It was both an exciting time and a difficult time for Cooper. After many rejections, he decided to get an agent. His first book, *Grandpa's Face*, was written by Eloise Greenfield. A *Kirkus* review noted Cooper's "realistic, full-color double spreads . . . in rich earth tones and vibrant colors." The review further stated, "Cooper makes an outstanding debut." *Grandpa's Face* was named a Notable Book of the Year by the American Library Association. It was also named a Notable Children's Trade Book in the Field of Social Studies by a joint committee of the National Council on the Social Studies and the Children's Book Council.

Some of Cooper's other books include *Coming Home: From the Life of Langston Hughes*, of which a critic wrote in *The New York Times Book Review*, "This is a book that will no doubt touch many young readers, because in the text Mr. Cooper is honest about Hughes's difficult childhood." She also wrote that "the artist offers a vibrant picture of the community that surrounds Hughes's family."

Cooper moved to New Jersey in 1985. He says he left New York because his car kept getting broken into, and he didn't want to give it up. Friends helped him find a place in New Jersey, where he lives with his wife, Velma, and his young son Dayton Michael, who also wants to be an illustrator. "New Jersey's not bad," he says, "It's still accessible to New York."

Illustrating children's books gives Cooper great satisfaction; he feels it is very important work. "I feel children are at the frontline in improving society," he writes. "This might sound a little heavy, but it's true. I feel children's picture books play a role in counteracting all the violence and other negative images conveyed in the media." Cooper also tries to make time for his other interests, like playing basketball and tennis. He has also done some toy designing for Olmec, a corporation now owned by Hasbro. He designed an action figure called Sun-Man, a Black superhero. His wife has also designed some dolls for the company, which has a multicultural bent.

In addition, Cooper enjoys playing on his Macintosh computer. He and his wife now handle the agenting of his books themselves, keeping track of everything on their computer. He claims the past year was pretty hectic, but now they're "getting the hang of it." The Coopers also like to travel, and they make an annual trip to Jamaica.

Two of Floyd Cooper's books have been named Honor Books in the Coretta Scott King Awards, given by the American Library Association. *Brown Honey and Broomwheat Tea* won the honor in 1994 and *Meet Danitra Brown* won it in 1995. *Grandpa's Face*, which was published in a 1993 Spanish edition, *La Cara de Abuelito*, was named a Notable Children's Trade Book in the Field of Social Studies by a joint committee of the Children's Book Council and the National Council on the Social Studies. It also was named an American Library Association Notable Book of the Year, as was *Chita's Christmas Tree* and *Coming Home*. *Pass It On* was also named a CBC/NCSS Notable Book. Cooper is working on companion volume to *Brownwheat Tea*, called *Gingerbread Days*, also by Joyce Carol Thomas. He was the featured speaker at the University of Oklahoma's sixteenth annual Festival of Books conference held in October 1995.

SELECTED WORKS WRITTEN AND ILLUSTRATED: Coming Home: From the Life of Langston Hughes, 1994.

SELECTED WORKS ILLUSTRATED: Grandpa's Face, by Eloise Greenfield, 1988; Chita's Christmas Tree, by Elizabeth Fitzgerald Howard, 1989; Laura Charlotte, by Katherine O. Galbraith, 1990; The Girl Who Loved Caterpillars: A Twelfth-Century Tale from Japan, adapted by Jean Merrill, 1992; Be Good to Eddie Lee, by Virginia Fleming, 1993; Brown Honey in Broomwheat Tea, by Joyce Carol Thomas, 1993; From Miss Ida's Porch, by Sandra Belton, 1993; Pass It On: African-American Poetry for Children, selected by Wade Hudson, 1993; Meet Danitra Brown, by Nikki Grimes, 1994; Coyote Walks on Two Legs, by Gerald Hausman, 1995.

BRUCE COVILLE

May 16, 1950–

AUTHOR OF *Oddly Enough*, etc.

Autobiographical sketch of Bruce Coville:

I WAS BORN in Syracuse, New York. Except for one year that I spent at Duke University in North Carolina, I lived in and around central New York until September of 1990. Then I moved to New York City,

where I lived for two years. Now I am back in Syracuse.

I grew up around the corner from my grandparents' dairy farm, which was three miles outside of a small town called Phoenix. As a child I loved Mary Poppins and Dr. Dolittle, and I can remember getting up ahead of everyone else in the family so that I could huddle in a chair and read *The Voyages of Dr. Dolittle*. I also read lots of things that people consider junk (Nancy Drew, the Hardy Boys, Tom Swift, and zillions of comic books). My only real regret is the time I spent watching television, when I could have been reading instead. (After all, a mind is a terrible thing to waste!)

The first time I can remember thinking that I would like to be a writer came in sixth grade, when our teacher, Mrs. Crandall, gave us an extended period of time to write a long story. I loved doing it. I started working seriously at becoming a writer when I was seventeen.

Like most people, I was not able to start selling my stories right away. So I had many other jobs along the way to becoming a writer, including toy maker, gravedigger, cookware salesman, and assembly line worker. Eventually I became an elementa-

ry teacher, and worked with second and fourth graders.

When I was nineteen I married Katherine Dietz, who lived right around the corner from me. She was (and is) a wonderful artist, and we began trying to create books together. However, it was not until 1977 that we finally sold our first book, which was called *The Foolish Giant*. We did two more books together—*Sarah's Unicorn* and *The Monster's Ring*. We then worked separately for a long time. We began to collaborate again in 1992 with *Space Brat*.

Kathy and I have three children: a son, Orion, born in 1970; a daughter, Cara, born in 1975, and another son, Adam, born in 1981.

I feel like a very lucky person. From the time I was young, I had a dream of becoming a writer. Now that dream has come true, and I am able to make my living doing something that I really love.

———

Bruce Coville also attended the State University of New York at Binghamton, and received a B.A. degree from SUNY at Oswego in 1974. He taught at a Liverpool, New York, school from 1974 to 1981 and was co-host and co-producer of a cable program promoting local theater in 1983. He is a member of the Society of Children's Book Writers and Illustrators. He is a writer of books and lyrics for theatrical pieces; an editor of anthologies; and a writer of nonfiction, plays, short stories, picture-book texts, and novels for children and adults. He was the editor of *Seniority Magazine* and has contributed to *Wilson Library Bulletin*, *Disney's Big Time*, and other publications.

Many of Coville's books are in series, such as the "Camp Haunted Hills" stories and the "A.I. Gang" stories. *Oddly Enough* was named a Best Book for Young Adults by the American Library Association.

SELECTED WORKS: The Foolish Giant, 1978; Sarah's Unicorn, 1979; The Monster's Ring, 1982; The Eyes of the Tarot, 1983; The Ghost in the Third Row, 1987; My Teacher Is an Alien, 1989; Jeremy Thatcher, Dragon Hatcher, 1991; Jennifer Murdley's Toad, 1992; Space Brat, 1992; Aliens Ate My Homework, 1993; Into the Land of the Unicorns, 1994; Oddly Enough, 1994; Fortune's Journey, 1995.

SELECTED WORKS COMPILED AND EDITED: *The Unicorn Treasury*, 1988; Herds of Thunder, Manes of Gold: A Collection of Horse Stories and Poems, 1989; Bruce Coville's Book of Monsters, 1993.

ABOUT: Contemporary Authors, Vol. 97-100; (New Revision Series), Vol. 22; McElmeel, Sharron L. Bookpeople: A Second Album; Something About the Author, Vol. 32, 77.

HELEN COWCHER

1957–

AUTHOR AND ILLUSTRATOR OF *Tigress*, etc.

Biographical sketch of Helen Cowcher:

HELEN COWCHER was born and grew up in Cheltenham, England. She grew up in the countryside, with all sorts of animals around—cats, chickens, sheep, cows, and more. There was a big garden, too, and she felt "very much part of the natural world."

She attended a small private school and later went to Cheltenham Ladies College. After college, she enrolled in a one-year art course at Bournemouth Art College, then went to the Chelsea School of Art in London for three years, obtaining a degree in Graphic Design. She worked as a natural history illustrator, specializing in fine, detailed black-and-white botanical illustration. She taught illustration at Bath Academy of Art once day a week for several years, illustrated gardening books, and did commercial artwork; however, she wanted to do her own children's book. She wrote to a school child in 1994, "I decided to become an author so that I could do books, which I have always loved. I like the feel of holding a book, that in this small object is the whole world. I write words in order to do the picture I most want to do. And books are better in a way, than paintings, because you can reach so many people in many different countries from doing one book."

While her main interest was painting, her inspiration was nature. She had for some time supported groups like Greenpeace or Friends of the Earth, but she wanted to do more. Around 1984, she learned more about the destruction of the rain forest. As she began research on the subject, she was concerned that there was little media attention about the problem at the time. She began painting on that theme. Her interest led to the publication of her book *Rain Forest*, which was published in 1988. The book is from the point of view of the birds and animals that live there.

Cowcher wrote the picture book *Antarctica* because it is the story of the world's "last great wilderness". She states that the continent, which is the size of Europe, is vulnerable to exploitation by countries asserting their rights to scientific and mineral exploitation; and yet Cowcher believes that, since the wildlife depends on the sea for food, upsetting the balance of the Antarctic food chain must be avoided. She conveyed these observations in an article, "Green Guide to Children's Books" that appearead in a British magazine, *Books for Keeps*, which recommends all of her picture books. Critics praised *Antarctica* with its expressive, sometimes stylized art, calling it "spectacular."

Cowcher has travelled to India several times; her first trip was in 1983. When she visited in 1989, she went to the Rathambhore Tiger Sanctuary in Rajasthan. The sanctuary encompasses an area of about two hundred square miles. Her third book, *Tigress*, was based on her experiences there. She described creating its illustrations, with the book's design inspired by the abstract designs of Tiger Rugs of Tibet, and how she executes close-ups of the view of the tiger's eye, peering out from under a leaf, conveying the tigress half-hidden in the undergrowth as if to say, "Just a peek at me, then I'm gone." When she worked on the book, she played Indian music, looked at photographs of her trip, and even burned incense to bring back memories of the time she was there.

She donates half the proceeds of the book to Living Earth charity, to work for the improvement of environmental education in Venezuelan schools. She has visited Venezuela several times with other British artists to paint the natural environment there. Living Earth sent them, and funds are raised by the sale of their paintings to aid the charity's work in the schools.

Her most recent book is *Whistling Thorn*, a book about giraffes, ants, and acacia bushes in Africa.

She has been successful in her work to the extent that she is able to do her own painting, to create picture books, and to raise money for Friends of the Earth, Living Earth, and other wildlife charities. She is pleased that 150,000 people visited a Natural History Rainforest Art Exhibition, helping to raise money that went to wildlife charities; and an auction at Bonhams Fine Art raised 40,000 British pounds in an evening, with the proceeds going to Arts for the Earth and the rain forest campaign.

Her plans for future work include more picture books, painting and exhibitions, and creating design images based on her books and on the natural world, to be used for objects such as ceramics. She is also interested in working with a dance choreographer to develop costume and stage design. Helen Cowcher lives in London and is married to Paul Wakefield, a landscape photographer.

Antarctica, *Rain Forest*, and *Tigress* were all named Outstanding Science Trade Books for Children by a joint committee of the National Science Teachers Association and the Children's Book Council. *Rain Forest* was also named a Notable Children's Trade Book in the Field of Social Studies by a joint committee of the CBC and the National Council on the Social Studies.

Cowcher's first three books have been published in Spanish-language editions in the U.S.

SELECTED WORKS: Rain Forest, 1988; Antarctica, 1990; Tigress, 1991; Whistling Thorn, 1993.

ABOUT: Nettell, Stephanie, Meet the Authors and Illustrators.

SHARON CREECH

July 29, 1945–

AUTHOR OF *Walk Two Moons*, etc.

Autobiographical sketch of Sharon Creech Rigg, who also writes under the name "Sharon Rigg":

I GREW UP in a big, noisy family in a Cleveland suburb, with hordes of relatives telling stories around the kitchen table. Here I learned to exaggerate and embellish, because if you didn't, your story was drowned out by someone else's more exciting one.

I'm not sure whether I was naturally inclined toward writing or whether I had great teachers who loaded me with skills and inspiration. It's probably a combination of the two, but I do know that I was always intrigued by the instruments of writing: paper, pens, pencils, books. I hoarded them. The grandest day of the year was the first day of school when I got all those new books and clutched new pencils and pristine notebook paper.

I don't remember the titles of books I read as a child, but I do remember the *experience* of reading—of drifting into the pages and living in someone else's world, the excitement of never knowing what lay ahead. I loved myths—American Indian myths, Greek myths, and the King Arthur legends—and I remember the lightning jolt of exhilaration when I read *Ivanhoe* as a teenager. These were all magical worlds, full of mystery and imagination: anything could happen, anything at all.

To be a novelist: oh! That seemed the most thrilling aspiration. To be able to create other worlds, to be able to explore mystery and myth—I couldn't imagine any better way to live—except, perhaps, to be a teacher, because teachers got to handle books all day long.

In college I took my first writing course, though I spent most of my time sitting in front of the typewriter feeling very proud of myself, and balling up sheets of paper

SHARON CREECH

and tossing them on the floor, which is what writers in movies did. Later, in graduate school, I was fired with new enthusiasm when I took a writing course with John Gardner, and attended workshops with James Dickey, John Irving, and others. This was serious business. They were blunt with their criticism, and reserved with their praise, but when you got their praise, you knew you had deserved it.

During graduate school, I worked at the Federal Theatre Project Archives and longed to write plays. Next I worked at *Congressional Quarterly*, as an editorial assistant, but this was not pleasant work for me, for it was all politics and facts, and these are not two of my loves.

Longing to teach, and wanting to show my children that there was a larger world out there, I applied for a job at an American school in England. At the time I was divorced, with two children. The headmaster was reluctant to hire a single parent, but he took a chance, and in 1979 my children and I moved to England, to work at an amazing school called TASIS, nestled in a Surrey village.

Three years later, I remarried, and my new husband was appointed headmaster of the Swiss branch of TASIS, so off we all moved to Lugano, cradled in the foothills of the Alps. After two years there, we returned to England, where I have taught American and British literature, and where we have lived (in a cottage built before America was founded!) ever since.

In many ways, teaching and travelling offered the perfect training ground for writing. I had to study classical literature in order to teach it. Our students read Shakespeare and then traipse off to Stratford to clomp through his house. We read Chaucer's *Canterbury Tales* and then take the train down to Canterbury and follow in his pilgrims' steps. It all comes alive in this way.

Most of our students are Americans, but we also have students from thirty other countries, and this contact, as well as travelling throughout Europe, has also helped me as a writer. I've learned that our cultures shape us differently, but in many ways we are all the same.

The idea and title for *Walk Two Moons* came out of a fortune cookie: "Don't judge a man until you've walked two moons in his moccasins." You just never know where inspiration will surface! Buried in that proverb is the key to what both readers and writers do: slip into others' moccasins to imagine what their lives are like. I look forward to wearing many, many moccasins in the years ahead.

My two grown children now live in the States. My husband and I return to Chautauqua Lake, N.Y., each summer to reunite with them and to reacquaint ourselves with our home country.

———

Sharon Creech grew up in Cleveland, Ohio. She received a B.A. degree from Hiram College and an M.A. from George Mason University. Her work with the Federal Theatre Project Archives was based at George Mason University in Fairfax, Virginia.

Creech's first three novels were published

in England, where she now lives nine months of the year. Her first two books, published for adults under the name Sharon Rigg, are *The Recital* in 1990 and *Nickel Malley* in 1991. Her third novel, which is for children, is *Absolutely Normal Chaos.* Published in 1990 in England and in 1995 in the U.S., the book is based on her own "rowdy and noisy" family.

Creech's first book to be published in the U.S. is the novel *Walk Two Moons*, which won the 1995 Newbery Award given by the American Library Association. It was also named a Notable Book of the Year by the ALA.

Sharon Creech has had poetry and short stories published. She also had a play produced in New York City in 1992, *The Center of the Universe: Waiting for the Girl.*

SELECTED WORKS: Walk Two Moons, 1994; Perfectly Normal Chaos, 1995.

ABOUT: Horn Book July 1995.

LINDA CREW

April 8, 1951–

AUTHOR OF *Children of the River*, etc.

Autobiographical sketch of Linda Crew:

A SENSE OF PLACE is important to me in my life and in my writing. Three of my grandparents were born in Oregon, and one great-great-grandmother arrived with a wagon train travelling the Oregon Trail in the 1860's. I was born and raised in Corvallis, as was my mother. My oldest son now walks the halls of the same high school where I struggled through my own angst-filled adolescence, and he daily passes the drinking fountain by the gym where his grandfather and grandmother first set eyes on each other at a dance in the wartime fall of 1942. Some people might find this small town history stifling, but I'm glad to have roots.

I can't claim I always wanted to be a writ-

er. Looking back, though, I'm struck by how often I presented my school assignments in fictional form—a short, *Gone with the Wind* rip-off for a Civil War unit, a sort of Ann Frank-in-a-bomb-shelter play for a high school political science class. But when a teacher once suggested I send a children's story I'd written to a publisher, I remember feeling a bit baffled. Why would I want to publish it?

In the eighth grade I won a city-wide essay contest on the topic "What My Country Means to Me." I don't recall what I thought my country meant to me at that point, but I remember my mother's surprised whoop of joy when she picked up the local paper and read this small headline: Linda Welch Wins Jaycee Essay Event. I also remember how I concocted the piece. First I played all my folk music records, analyzing the lyrics, jotting down what I considered to be the most ringing phrases. Then I strung them together! That sounds terrible, but beginners have to start somewhere. And I still feel that studying the writing of others is a good way to learn.

I've always enjoyed being creative. I started whipping up doll clothes on my mother's sewing machine when I was six, and recently I've admitted to myself that I still like doing this. It must go back to one of my favorite books, *A Little Princess*, by Frances Hodgson Burnett. Remember Sara Crewe's doll with her trunk of lavish clothes? The little girl in me still longs for that. . . . Wouldn't you know my own daughter prefers snakes!

Anyway, in junior high I thought of myself as an artist and was thrilled when a teacher insisted on buying my first oil painting. And of course I also wanted to be a folk singer. In the eighth grade I marched over and sang at the high school "hootenanny". My musical talents were definitely borderline, but I guess I had a fair amount of nerve.

During high school the theater bug bit me, and for several years I was absolutely determined to become an actress. At the start of my sophomore year at the University of Oregon, however, this ambition suddenly and mysteriously evaporated, leaving me totally clueless as to what I should do instead.

"Well," said my mother, "you've always been a good writer. How about journalism?"

For lack of a better idea I tried it and, luckily, loved my new major—interviewing, researching, saying what needed saying without a lot of fuss. But my assignments always ended up full of dialogue, and I was constantly betrayed by the fiction writer's urge to improve on real life for the sake of a better story.

I received my B.A. in journalism in 1973, and the next year I married Herb Crew in the front yard of the farmhouse where we still live, now with our three children. At this writing Miles is fifteen and our twins, Mary and William, are almost nine. These twenty years have been rich and full, and while farming, house remodelling, and raising kids have limited my actual time for writing, I can't imagine what I'd have written about without the inspiration of my family and this busy life here at Wake Robin Farm.

———

Linda Crew attended Lewis and Clark College in the 1969-1970 school year, and received her B.A. degree from the University of Oregon in 1973. She has written a novel for adults, *Ordinary Miracles*, published in 1993.

She is a member of Authors Guild, the Society of Children's Book Writers and Illustrators, and Phi Beta Kappa. *Children of the River* won the Children's Book Award of the International Reading Association and was named an honor book in the 1989 Golden Kite Awards by the Society of Children's Book Writers and Illustrators. It was named a Best Book for Young Adults by the American Library Association and was also named to the "Best of the Best" list of the hundred best Young Adult novels to be published in the last twenty-five years. *Nekomah Creek* was also named a ALA Notable Children's Book of the Year.

SELECTED WORKS: Children of the River, 1989; Someday I'll Laugh About This, 1990; Nekomah Creek, 1991; Nekomah Creek Christmas, 1994; Fire on the Wind, 1995.

ABOUT: Contemporary Authors, Vol. 130; Gallo, Donald R. Speaking for Ourselves, Too; Something About the Author, Vol. 71.

CHRIS CRUTCHER

July 17, 1946–

AUTHOR OF *Staying Fat for Sarah Byrnes*, etc.

Biographical sketch of Chris Crutcher:

IN CHRIS CRUTCHER'S book *Running Loose*, the setting is Trout, Idaho. The inspiration for that setting was Cascade, Idaho, a small lumber and logging town in the mountains of Idaho where Crutcher grew up. His high school was so small that those who played sports played them all, so Crutcher played football, basketball and ran track, out of necessity rather than ability, he says. His father loved the classics as well as

CHRIS CRUTCHER

popular fiction, and his mother wrote poems for birthdays and anniversaries and enjoyed any and all word games. Crutcher was not a great reader himself, finishing only one book of fiction in high school, but that book had a great impact on him. It was Harper Lee's *To Kill a Mockingbird*. He sees it as a "real" book about justice and injustice told with a perfect storyteller's voice; the kind of story he would like to someday tell.

Crutcher studied sociology and psychology in college where he was also a competitive swimmer. He received his B.A. degree from Eastern Washington State College in 1968. He began teaching in 1970. He taught from 1973 to 1976 at Lakeside School in Oakland, California, a K-12 alternative school for students who couldn't make it in the public school system. He then became Director of the school, and served from 1976 to 1981. He began writing fiction after leaving Lakeside School. Tired of urban life, Crutcher returned to the Northwest, where he took a job as a child and family therapist at Spokane Community Health Center from 1982 to 1995. Through that same period he served as chairperson for the Spokane Child Protection Team, a position he continues to hold.

Having finished his first book, *Running Loose*, before moving to Spokane, Crutcher continued to write seriously. His books receive critical praise in addition to awards, and reviewer Anita Silvey, writing in *The Horn Book Magazine*, stated that *Stotan!* is "part of a growing body of books, which includes Bruce Brooks's *The Moves Make the Man* . . . and, historically, the novels of John Tunis, that use a sports setting and competition to discuss the greater issues of being young and alive." Crutcher enjoys running, swimming, biking and playing basketball.

Crutcher has contributed articles to *The Signal Journal* and *Spokane Magazine*. He has had short stories published in the anthologies *Connections* and *Ultimate Sports: Short Stories by Outstanding Writers for Young Adults*, both edited by Donald R. Gallo. In addition to his young adult books, he has also written an adult suspense novel, *The Deep End*, which is currently being adapted as a major motion picture, and he is currently working on a screenplay for his young adult novel, *Staying Fat for Sarah Byrnes*, and another adult novel.

The American Library Association has named each of his young adult books, to date, as Best Books for Young Adults, and two of his books appeared on the Best of the Best list, chosen from twenty-five years of the Best Books list. They are *Stotan!* and *Athletic Shorts*.

SELECTED WORKS: Running Loose, 1983; Stotan!, 1986; The Crazy Horse Electric Game, 1987; Chinese Handcuffs, 1989; Athletic Shorts: Six Short Stories, 1991; Staying Fat for Sarah Byrnes, 1993; Ironman, 1995.

ABOUT: Contemporary Authors, Vol. 113; (New Revision Series), Vol. 36; Emergency Librarian January/ February 1991; Donald R. Gallo. Speaking for Ourselves; Horn Book May 1988; Publishers Weekly February 20, 1995; Something About the Author, Vol. 52; Teaching PreK-8 February 1990.

KAREN CUSHMAN

October 4, 1941–

AUTHOR OF *Catherine, Called Birdy*, etc.

Autobiographical sketch of Karen Lipski Cushman:

I'VE ALWAYS BEEN a late bloomer—but I always eventually bloom. Here I am making a new career late in life and having a wonderful time.

I was born in a suburb of Chicago in October, 1941, and moved with my family to Los Angeles in 1952. In my own mind, I was always a writer, even though I didn't write much. The first thing I remember writing was a plea for brotherhood, understanding, and multiculturalism—I was obviously ahead of my time—called "Jingle Bagels," a play about Santa Claus going down the wrong chimney and landing in a Jewish house during Hanukah. When I matured to thirteen or so, I started an epic poem cycle based on the life of Elvis. Some parts remain; some, alas, are lost to the world.

Coming, as I did, from an ethnic working-class Chicago family, I didn't know writing was a job, something that real people did with their lives. Secretary, maybe, or salesman, or school crossing guard, like my Grandpa.

A fortuitous scholarship got me to Stanford University, where I excelled at writing depressing poems and irreverent parodies of school songs, but college creative writing class sent me screaming into the night looking for something else to do.

I graduated in 1963 with a degree in English and Greek. I wanted to dig for treasures on the Acropolis by moonlight. Instead I found myself at the telephone company in Beverly Hills. I quit. I found other jobs. Quit them all.

Several jobs into the 1960s, I was working at the Hebrew Union College in Los Angeles, where I met Philip, then a rabbinical student. We married and moved to Oregon, where Philip taught and I wove and made blackberry jam and had a daughter, Leah.

Back in California, Philip and I earned Master's degrees in counseling and human behavior, respectively. Philip then got his doctorate in psychology and has been a psychotherapist and teacher for nearly twenty years.

I earned a second Master's, in Museum Studies, and for ten years have been at the graduate department of Museum Studies at John F. Kennedy University. I have edited the *Museum Studies Journal*, taught classes in museology and material culture, and shepherded reluctant students through their Master's projects.

Leah graduated with a degree in biology from the Unversity of California, Santa Cruz. Her career plans include reading, sleeping, and working in a bookstore.

Catherine, Called Birdy is my first book. Over the years I've had lots of book ideas. I'd tell my husband and that would be that. This time when I said, "Listen, I have this great idea for a book," he refused to listen. He said, "Don't tell me. Write it down." So I did, and the rest is history. Now I use that story as a metaphor for living when I speak to school classes: It's not enough to have an idea. You have to make a commitment, take a stand, write it down.

Birdy grew from my interest in children and history. I wondered what the lot of children might have been in the Middle Ages when they had no power and little value. Especially girl children. Birdy's plight was that she couldn't do much about her situation. So what could she do? That's what the book is about.

Being from California, I am sometimes asked if I "channeled" the book, it being easier for some to imagine psychically communicating with a long-dead British teenager than to imagine research and writing, I suppose. But I did it the hard way. I made it up.

The made-up parts are based on extensive research, which I loved doing. I learned all about bee-keeping, shearing sheep, ointments and remedies, superstitions and fears, clothing, food, language, table manners, bathing habits, privies. It took three years to research and write. Information on battles, kings, and cathedrals was easy to find. Domestic history was harder to uncover, but I felt a responsibility to offer young people the most accurate picture possible of the times.

The Midwife's Apprentice began with the title and an image of a homeless girl sleeping on a dung heap, longing for a name, a full belly, and a place in the world. *The Ballad of Lucy Whipple* follows a girl dragged unhappily across the country to search for gold. I think Catherine, Alyce, and Lucy are all me. I know myself better now than before I began to write. Now you do, too.

———

Karen Cushman earned her first M.A. degree from the United States International University in San Diego. Her second, in Museum Studies, was from John F. Kennedy University in Orinda, California. She is currently adjunct professor in the Museum Studies Department at the university. She and her husband live in the Rockridge area of Oakland, California, with their two cats and their dog.

Catherine, Called Birdy was named an Honor Book in the 1995 John Newbery Medal awards, given by the American Library Association. *School Library Journal* called it "superb historical fiction." It won the Carl Sandburg Award for Children's Literature from the Friends of the Chicago Public Library, and a 1994 Golden Kite Award from the Society of Children's Writers and Illustrators. It also was named a Best Book for Young Adults and a Notable Book of the Year by the ALA.

SELECTED WORKS: Catherine, Called Birdy, 1994; The Midwife's Apprentice, 1995.

ABOUT: Publishers Weekly July 4, 1994.

MARGERY CUYLER

December 31, 1948–

AUTHOR OF *Weird Wolf*, etc.

Biographical sketch of Margery Stuyvesant Cuyler, who also edits poetry collections under the pen name "Daisy Wallace":

MARGERY CUYLER was born in Princeton, New Jersey. Her grandfather was an artist, and he lost a lot of money. This affected her father greatly, and he went into business. There were five children in her family, and her father discouraged careers in art for his children, since he had had such a negative experience. Yet, all of her siblings ended up as artists of one sort or another, she says.

She told interviewer Jim Roginski that she was "very bad" as a child, getting thrown out of several schools. She thinks of herself as like her character Soap in her novel *The Trouble with Soap*. What interested her particularly about writing about the relationship between her character Soap and the "goody-goody" character in the book, Laurie, is that "the whole key to life is to break through the walls that parents and society build all around you, to be an individual, to express yourself."

MARGERY CUYLER

Cuyler graduated from Sarah Lawrence College in Bronxville, New York, in 1970. She went into editing and considered it as a stable profession. She began her career at Atlantic Monthly Press in Boston, working for the late Emilie McLeod, who was Editor-in-Chief. She went to Walker & Company in New York next, and was editor there from 1972 to 1974. Then she was at Holiday House in New York until 1995 when she moved to Henry Holt, also in New York, as Vice President and Editor-in-Chief of their Books for Young Readers division.

She edited some poetry collections for her own Holiday list at one time, because she wanted to employ the artists who illustrated the books. She also saw a need for the material she collected, which is poetry for children ages five to eight. She declined to take a royalty on the books. She liked writing, so she wrote her first book under her own name, on the subject of Jewish holidays, a book she thought the market lacked. She realized that an advantage of being an editor is knowing what kind of books are needed on the market.

Cuyler writes nonfiction as well as fiction, and finds the research process time-consuming, but she enjoys learning about her subject as she goes along. The ideas must be made clear, in a simple fashion, to a young reader. She functions differently in the two different roles of editor and writer. She told Roginski that she feels confident as an editor, but that as a writer she feels insecure. When you write, she says, "You're sharing a private part of yourself, your imagination, with the world. It's a humbling experience." However, she feels that the act of expressing one's talent in an art form is very important, and one that is not taken seriously in our culture. She believes people have a "duty" to honor any artistic talent they have, and finds that it is a necessity for her to do so.

Margery Cuyler is married and lives in Princeton, New Jersey. She is a lecturer on children's book editing, speaking at institutions such as Rutgers University, Vassar College, and the New School for Social Research. She is a member of the Women's National Book Association and the Children's Book Council, and is a library trustee and member of the alumnae board of Sarah Lawrence College.

Both *The Trouble with Soap* and *Witch Poems* were named Children's Choice Books by a joint committee of the International Reading Association and the Children's Book Council. *Fat Santa* won a 1988 New Jersey Institute of Technology New Jersey Authors Award.

SELECTED WORKS: Jewish Holidays, 1978; The All-Around Pumpkin Book, 1980; Fairy Poems, 1980; The All-Around Christmas Book, 1982; The Trouble with Soap, 1982; Sir William and the Pumpkin Monster, 1984; Fat Santa, 1987; Shadow's Baby, 1988; Freckles and Jane, 1989; Weird Wolf, 1989; Baby Dot: A Dinosaur Story, 1990; Daisy's Crazy Thanksgiving, 1990; That's Good! That's Bad!, 1991; Buddy Bear and the Bad Guys, 1993; Invisible in the Third Grade, 1995.

SELECTED WORKS EDITED AS DAISY WALLACE: Monster Poems, 1976; Witch Poems, 1976; Giant Poems, 1978; Ghost Poems, 1979; Fairy Poems, 1980.

ABOUT: Contemporary Authors, Vol. 117; Roginski, Jim. Behind the Covers; Something About the Author, Vol. 39.

BARBARA DANA

December 28, 1940–

AUTHOR OF *Zucchini*, etc.

Biographical sketch of Barbara Dana:

BARBARA DANA was born in New York City. Her father was a writer, director, and teacher, and her mother was an actress and teacher. Dana wanted to be either a cowgirl or an actress, and she chose actress, starting her acting career while she was still in high school. She received her diploma from Quintano's School for Young Professionals.

Dana starred and played in roles in film, television, and the theater. In Broadway theaters, she appeared in *Who's Afraid of Virginia Woolf?*, *Where's Daddy?*, *Room Service*, and *Enter Laughing*.

Her television credits include *As the World Turns*, *The Fugitive*, *Sesame Street*, and a production of *The Effect of Gamma Rays on Man-in-the-Moon Marigolds*. She has appeared in films such as *The In-laws*, *P.J.*, and *Popi*.

Her husband suggested that she try writing for children when he read some of her stories. Dana has written stories for middle-grade children as well as for young adults. In *Zucchini*, a boy takes on as a pet a ferret that was born in the Bronx Zoo. For the older audience, *Crazy Eights* depicts a fourteen-year-old who writes a stream-of-conciousness account of her thoughts, as she heads toward a mental collapse.

Necessary Parties is the story of a fifteen-year-old boy who is bewildered by his parents' decision to divorce; so he sues to stop them. The book was adapted for television.

A role in her acting career led Dana to write one of her books. She starred in *Joan of Lorraine* on stage, playing Joan of Arc; the experience informs her novel *Young Joan*, which tells the saint's story from the point of view of the child, before the events surrounding her death for which she is most famous. Critic Ilene Cooper, writing in a starred *Booklist* review, says that Dana shows a Joan "whose goodness is shown through her relationships with family, friends, and, most especially, the animals she intuitively understands. . . . The heart of the story is that a simple person can be touched by majesty."

In addition to her books for children, she wrote the screenplay for *Chu Chu and the Philly Flash*, which was produced by Melvin Simon in 1981. It starred her husband, Alan Arkin, and Carol Burnett.

Barbara Dana lives in upstate New York. She enjoys writing, singing, acting, and horseback riding. She and her husband have three sons.

Necessary Parties was named a Best Book of the Year for Young Adults by the American Library Association.

Zucchini won a 1984 Washington Irving Children's Book Choice Award given by the New York Westchester Library Association and has won several awards voted upon by children. The book was illustrated by Eileen Christelow.

SELECTED WORKS: Spencer and His Friends, 1966; Rutgers and the Water-Snouts, 1969; Crazy Eights, 1978; Zucchini, 1982; Necessary Parties, 1986; Young Joan, 1991.

ABOUT: Contemporary Authors, (First Revision), Vol. 17-20; (New Revision Series), Vol. 8; Something About the Author, Vol. 22.

JENNY DAVIS

June 29, 1953–

AUTHOR OF *Good-Bye and Keep Cold*, etc.

Biographical sketch of Jenny Davis:

JENNY DAVIS was born in Louisville, Kentucky, and when she was a child, her family moved to Pittsburgh, Pennsylvania. She remembers, growing up in the 1960's, the famous toys associated with that time, such as Hula Hoops; and she remembers air raid drills where schoolchildren were trained to take cover in the event of a Cold War attack by the Russians. Her whole family participated in marches for equal rights during the civil rights movement of that time.

The music and entertainment of the time colors her memories, as does the time when the Vietnam War entered her conciousness, and she worked to hand out leaflets and work against the war at the Friends Meeting House. Her writing efforts as a young person were disappointing, in one instance. She worked very hard on a short story and read it to family and friends; yet a teacher gave her a bad grade for misplaced commas. As a teacher herself now, she has learned from that experience to take care with the responses she gives to her students.

When she entered high school she found it to be a place filled with gangs, race riots, and growling dogs, she says. She made a habit of cutting class, spending her time in museums, libraries, and parks instead. She educated herself—haphazardly, she says, but she found that she could teach herself, a lesson she has found valuable throughout her life.

Like her character Livvie in her novel *Sex Education*, Davis wrote in a piece for Donald R. Gallo's *Speaking for Ourselves*, she spent her fifteenth year in a university psychiatric hospital. She is "still figuring out" the reason she was there, but, she says, "it had to do with pain and caring."

She attended Allegheny Community College and was gratified to find there the "diversity of high school without the violence." She graduated with a B.A. degree from the University of Kentucky in 1976, and earned her M.A. degree from the university in 1981.

Davis worked as a child advocate in Appalachian Regional Hospitals in Hazard, Kentucky, from 1973 to 1975. She was employed by the Fayette County Health Department in Lexington, Kentucky, as a sex educator from 1983 to 1985. Since 1985 she has worked as a teacher of reading and writing to fifth and sixth graders at the Lexington School, in addition to writing books.

Hanna B. Zieger, writing in a *Horn Book Magazine* review, describes the difficult adolescence of protagonist Edda Combs, who must be mature, as her widowed and disturbed mother is not; she is a character that prompts Zieger to write that there are "caring, serious children in our society who are trapped in a similar inversion of the usual pattern of responsibility and nurturing. This book provides a moving portrait of such a child."

Davis was a speaker at the 1989 Assembly on Literature for Adolescents worshop sponsored by the National Council of Teachers of English held in Baltimore, Maryland.

Checking on the Moon was named a Best Book for Young Adults by the American Library Association. *Good-Bye and Keep Cold* received the same honor, and was also named a Notable Children's Trade Book in the Field of Social Studies by a joint committee of the Children's Book Council and the National Council on the Social Studies.

The Michigan Library Association named *Sex Education* Young Adult novel of the Year in 1989.

She was married in 1975 and divorced in 1981, and she has two sons.

SELECTED WORKS: Good-Bye and Keep Cold, 1987; Sex Education, 1988; Checking on the Moon, 1991.

ABOUT: Contemporary Authors, Vol. 128; Gallo, Donald R. Speaking for Ourselves; Something About the Author, Vol 74.

"ALEXANDRA DAY"

September 7, 1941–

Author and Illustrator of *Good Dog, Carl*, etc.

Autobiographical sketch of Sandra Woodward Darling, who writes under the pen name "Alexandra Day":

I WAS BORN in Cincinnati, Ohio. My father, with difficulty, earned his living as an artist.

My family was very inclined to the arts, and their allied branches. One of my grandfathers was an architect, and the other a printer. Two of my uncles earned their living as painters, two others were architects. Painting was a popular hobby among my relatives of both sexes, and it was a rare family excursion in which at least one easel wasn't carried along.

My mother excelled in the arts of the house. She cooked and baked and gardened and canned and sewed and decorated and ordered with knowledge, precision, and grace. She taught me these things, which helped me to grow up with a realization that I could, by my actions, make the home and the world more orderly and beautiful.

My home, through the double influences of my parents, was always fully stocked with the materials necessary for action and art—glue, paint, twine, nails, thread, pencils, wire, tools, brushes, and paper. Best of all, my sisters and I were encouraged to use these things freely.

Another important influence in my childhood was nature. We frequently stayed in a family vacation cottage on a remote island in Ontario, and from the age of nine to age thirteen we lived on a farm in Kentucky.

Here my mind was filled with the lights, shadows, scents, and forms of the country.

I attended Swarthmore College, a small Pennsylvania liberal arts school. Its atmosphere of idealistic perfectionism and relentless striving after excellence has had a powerful influence on my life. When I am tempted to drowse through life, or accept small compromises in the pursuit of a goal, I am renewed by the brisk wind of Swarthmore striving.

Inasmuch as Swarthmore had no art department, I have had very little formal training in painting. After college, I did take two courses at New York's Art Students League, one in painting (from Will Barnet), and another in figure drawing.

In 1967 I married Harold Darling. His lifelong interests in old books, publishing, children's literature and cinema converged with my artistic heritage and produced, after due gestation, The Green Tiger Press. This, which started as a very small operation in our small bedroom, was devoted, at first, to the publication of pictures from old children's books on notecards and calendars. We soon began to publish books and, in a few years, expanded to include material created freshly for us by living authors and artists. Finally, in 1982, we decided to make a book based on the old song, "The Teddy Bears' Picnic", and having no illustrator, I decided to try it myself. It was a popular success, and since then I have been busy illustrating more than a book a year.

My role in The Green Tiger Press was art and production director. This experience, plus the larger awareness that owning a publishing company involves, gave me great advantages as a book creator. I, unlike most of thos who write and illustrate, could see exactly how books came into being, were promoted, sold and returned. I absorbed the mistakes and successes of other book makers, and when my turn came I had a head start.

In 1986 we sold The Green Tiger Press and founded The Blue Lantern Studio, a firm that created visual books for many publishers. In 1992 The Blue Lantern started publishing its own books, and as before, I learn daily how better to use that marvelous invention, the printed book, to speak the language of pictures.

————

Alexandra Day graduated from Swarthmore College with a B.A. degree in 1963. She founded The Green Tiger Press with her husband in 1970, and they ran it until 1986.

Alexandra Day lives in Seattle. She is a member of the "Our Best Friends" Therapy Dog Program, Inc., a nonprofit, volunteer group of trained and registered dogs and their owners, whose goals are to create a caring and supportive atmosphere that aids healing in fifty-seven health care facilities in San Diego County, California. She also enjoys gardening and fashion design.

The Teddy Bears' Picnic was named a Children's Choice Book by a joint committee of the Children's Book Council and the International Reading Association. It was also a runnerup of the Critici in Erba Award at the Bologna Children's Book Fair. A Spanish version of *Carl's Afternoon in the Park, Carlito en el parque una tarde*, was published in 1992. There are over two million Carl books in print, with board-book versions published of several of the book titles.

SELECTED WORKS WRITTEN AND ILLUSTRATED: Good Dog, Carl, 1985; Frank and Ernest, 1988; Carl Goes Shopping, 1989; Paddy's Pay-Day, 1989; Carl's Christmas, 1990; River Parade, 1990; Carl's Afternoon in the Park, 1991; Carl's Masquerade, 1992; Carl Goes to Daycare, 1993; Carl Makes a Scrapbook, 1994; My Puppy's Record Book, 1994; Carl's Birthday, 1995.

SELECTED WORKS ILLUSTRATED: Teddy Bears' Picnic, by Jimmy Kennedy, 1983; The Blue Faience Hippopotamus, 1984.

ABOUT: Contemporary Authors, Vol. 136; People Weekly September 23, 1991; Something About the Author, Vol. 67.

CYNTHIA DeFELICE

December 28, 1951–

AUTHOR OF *Weasel*, etc.

Autobiographical sketch of Cynthia DeFelice:

WHEN I WAS A CHILD I didn't write much, and never dreamed of becoming a writer. I kept a diary from time to time, wrote poetry in short, furious bursts of emotion and, of course, I wrote when asked by my teachers to do so. But I was always reading. My parents read to me, bought me books, and took me to the library. Summer vacations began with a trip to the bookstore, where my sister, brothers, and I were allowed to pick out books for our summer reading. To me, those trips to the bookstore were even better than the rare occasions when we were given a quarter and turned loose at the penny candy store on the boardwalk. I loved choosing the books I wanted, taking them home, putting my name plate inside, and taking my time deciding which one to read first.

I read everything: "good books" and "junk," including all the Nancy Drew and Hardy Boys books, comic books and, my favorite, *MAD* magazine. The books I liked best were the ones that made me feel as if I was right in the story, part of what was happening. The story became my story. In that way, I was able to have exciting adventures and experience life from the point of view of people very different from myself.

My childhood was a happy one. I felt safe, secure, and loved. But, like everyone, I had my secret joys and sorrows, confusions, embarrassments, and terrors, many of which I can recall vividly. What solace it was to discover in books characters who shared the emotions I was unable to explain, even to myself, but which I felt so intensely. Reading made me feel connected to the big world outside my nice, safe suburban neighborhood in Pennsylvania.

I had many different, interesting jobs before deciding to attend graduate school to

DeFelice: *DEE fa LEESE*

become a school librarian. I was pretty sure I would love my new career, and I did, because it combined two of my favorite things: kids and books.

My library work led me to become fascinated with the oral tradition of storytelling. Soon my best friend and I were telling stories together—just for fun at first, at the school where we taught together, and later, professionally. Soon I knew that I wanted to write stories as well as tell them. My first book, *The Strange Night Writing of Jessamine Colter*, soon followed. Much as I loved my job, I began writing full-time and never looked back.

Three of my books, *Dancing Skeleton*, *Mule Eggs*, and *Three Perfect Peaches* (which is co-authored by my storytelling partner, Mary DeMarsh) grew naturally from stories that I tell. *Weasel* and *Lostman's River* both deal with incidents in history that captured my imagination. *Devil's Bridge* and *The Light on Hogback Hill* are based more on experiences I have had, either as an adult or as a child. In *When Grampa Kissed His Elbow* I was able to create a grandfather, since I never knew either of mine.

Kids ask me, "What is the best thing about being an author?" There are so many "best things!" I like being able to work when I want to, at my own pace. I enjoy the opportunity to meet my readers, young and old, at conferences, schools and festivals. I love the feeling of being caught up in the lives of the characters I am writing about. I enjoy the challenge of trying to write as honestly as I can, and I find enormous satisfaction in hearing from readers that something I wrote touched them, delighted them, made them shiver with fear or shake with laughter, or think about something new.

Cynthia DeFelice was born in Philadelphia, Pennsylvania. She received her B.A. degree from William Smith College in 1973 and her M.L.S. degree from Syracuse University in 1980. She was married in 1974. She was an elementary school media specialist in the Newark, New York, public schools from 1980 to 1987. She is a member of the Authors Guild, the Society of Children's Book Writers and Illustrators, and several associations of storytellers.

The Dancing Skeleton, which was illustrated by Robert Andrew Parker, was named a *New York Times* Best Illustrated Children's Book of the Year. *Weasel* was named a Notable Children's Book of the Year by the American Library Association and a Notable Children's Trade Book in the Field of Social Studies by a joint committee of the National Council on the Social Studies and the Children's Book Council.

SELECTED WORKS: The Strange Night Writing of Jessamine Colter, 1988; The Dancing Skeleton, 1989; Devil's Bridge, 1992; The Light on Hogback Hill, 1993; When Grandpa Kissed His Elbow, 1992; Lostman's River, 1994; Mule Eggs, 1994; (with Mary DeMarsh) Three Perfect Peaches, 1995.

ABOUT: Booklist May 15, 1990; Something About the Author, Vol. 79.

LISA DESIMINI

March 21, 1964–

AUTHOR AND ILLUSTRATOR OF *My House*, etc.

Autobiographical sketch of Lisa Desimini:

I STARTED DRAWING on my own when I was ten years old. I used flattened boxes from department stores and copied cartoons and pictures on greeting cards.

I got out of a lot of classes, doing decorations for school dances and working on the yearbook committee. I drew all the time. My teachers, friends and parents told me that I should be an artist. I thought it was a good idea. It was either an artist or a marine biologist.

I went to the career advisor when I was in tenth grade and we discussed which college I should go to, should it be large or small, in the country or the city. She had index cards describing different types of careers in art, and I chose an illustrator. I wanted to paint images for book covers, magazines and newspapers.

I decided to go to the School of Visual Arts in New York City. It took a while to get used to the city, but I knew I had made the right decision. It was good to be in the heart of everything, not to be sheltered, to be around teachers who were successful artists as well.

After graduating, I waitressed at a nearby restaurant and went on interviews at magazines and publishing companies. I was out of school for six months when I went to see an editor at Harper & Row. During the appointment I discovered she was an editor of children's books. At first I thought I was wasting my time, but she was interested in my work, so I started to get excited. There was a story that she had been holding onto for a year, looking for the right artist. She asked me to do a couple of paintings. I had never considered illustrating a children's book, but I couldn't turn down the opportunity.

I did two paintings for the book and wait-

ed about a month for an answer. I promised myself that if I got the book, I would quit my waitressing job. I did get the book, *Heron Street* by Ann Turner, and have been illustrating children's books ever since.

I love working at home and I love working at my own pace. I do feel isolated at times, so I have to make sure I get out of the house. I teach a class in illustration at School of Visual Arts and take kick-boxing classes, and I'm interested in becoming a natural foods chef. I can also take little trips and bring my work with me.

I certainly never thought of writing anything, but after illustrating the sixth book it seemed only natural to write my own. I worked hard on my writing for a couple of years. I enjoyed it so much it didn't feel like work at all. Since then I have written three books and illustrated over a dozen books for other authors.

There is nothing like starting from scratch, to come up with your own idea, design the layout of the book and bring your idea to life. I even help with choosing the type and picking the color of the endpapers. It is also interesting to be handed a story and have to search inside myself for images that make the words feel like my own. I have many more ideas and love the excitement of not knowing what kind of projects will come my way, so I think I'll be doing children's books for a long time.

———

Lisa Desimini was born in Brooklyn. She graduated from the School of Visual Arts in 1986.

A *New York Times Book Review* writer stated that the art in *My House* "smashes adult patterns of visual connection and cliche." Lisa Desimini's artwork has been exhibited in shows at the Society of Illustrators and at the Society of Publishing Designers.

Heron Street was named a Notable Children's Trade Book in the Field of Social Studies by a joint committee of the National Council on the Social Studies and the Children's Book Council.

Poem-Making was named a Notable Book of the Year by the American Library Association. *My House* was named a 1994 Best Illustrated Book of the Year by *The New York Times*.

SELECTED WORKS WRITTEN AND ILLUSTRATED: I Am Running Away Today, 1992; Moon Soup, 1993; My House, 1994.

SELECTED WORKS ILLUSTRATED: Adelaide and the Night Train, by Liz Rosenberg, 1989; Heron Street, by Ann Turner, 1989; Light: Stories of a Small Bright Kindness, by Nancy White Carlstrom, 1990; The Thieves' Market, by Dennis Haseley, 1991; How the Stars Fell into the Sky: A Navajo Legend, by Jerrie Oughton, 1992; Poem-Making: Ways to Begin Writing Poetry, by Myra Cohn Livingston, 1992; Fish and Flamingo, by Nancy White Carlstrom, 1993; The Passerby, by Liliane Atlan, 1993; The Magic Weaver of Rugs, by Jerrie Oughton, 1994.

ABOUT: Publishers Weekly December 22, 1989.

.

ALEXIS De VEAUX

September 24, 1948–

AUTHOR OF *An Enchanted Hair Tale*, etc.

Biographical sketch of Alexis De Veaux:

De Veaux: *De Voe*

BORN AND RAISED in Harlem, New York, Alexis De Veaux is a poet, children's book author, essayist, playwright, editor, fiction writer, and lecturer.

De Veaux earned her B.A. degree from Empire State College of the State University of New York in New York City in 1976. She earned an M.A. degree in American Studies at SUNY in Buffalo in 1989 and her Ph.D. degree, also in American Studies, at the same university in 1992.

Her career began in 1972, with the publication of a prize-winning short story, "Remember Him A Outlaw." In 1974, she was a master artist with the New Haven, Connecticut, board of education for a year. After graduation from college, she became Adjunct Lecturer in the writing department of Sarah Lawrence College in Bronxville, New York from 1979 to 1980. She was on the faculty of the writing program at Vermont College of Montpelier University in Vermont from 1984 to 1985, and she was Owen Dutson Visiting Scholar at the departments of English and Theater at Wabash College in Crawfordsville, Indiana, in 1987.

From 1978 through 1990, De Veaux was contributing editor and editor-at-large at *Essence* magazine. A few of the articles she has written for that publication are "Black Women Scholars," in 1995; "Walking Into Freedom with Winnie and Nelson Mandela," in 1990; and "Forty Fine, a Writer Reflects on Turning Forty," in 1990. She is also a contributor of articles to publications such as *The New York Village Voice*. Her short stories have appeared in anthologies and in magazines such as *Memory of Kin: Stories About Family by Black Writers*, and *The Utne Reader*.

After she left her position at *Essence*, Alexis De Veaux became Visiting Assistant Professor in Women's Studies, the Department of American Studies, at SUNY in Buffalo. After holding this position for a year, she became Assistant Professor in Women's Studies there, a position she continues to hold.

As a poet, De Veaux has been published in anthologies such as *Soul Looks Back in Wonder*, compiled and illustrated by Tom Feelings, and the journal *The Black Scholar*. Her plays have been published and have been produced by various theatrical companies, including *The Tapestry*, produced by Genesis Arts Company in San Diego, California, in 1991 and *A Season to Unravel*, by the Negro Ensemble Company in New York City in 1979. Her play *Circles* was produced on Visions, a KCET-TV television show in California in 1976, along with *Tapestry*.

Her books for adults include *Spirits in the Street*, which is an experimental memoir published in 1973, and *Blue Heat: Poems and Drawings*, which was published in 1985. Her works have been published in Spanish, Dutch, Japanese, and Serbo-Croatian.

De Veaux has taught creative writing and has worked for the Urban League and the Neighborhood Youth Corps. She considers herself an activist who recognizes the impact of history on the present, and is an advocate of reading and writing, particularly, she points out, to the development of African-American children, "who are the descendants of a people to whom education and literacy were once denied."

She has given readings and presented lectures at many institutions, including the Brooklyn Academy of Music, Riverside Church in New York City, Folger Shakespeare Library in Washington, D.C., UNEAC Writers Union in Havana, Cuba, as well as many libraries, colleges and universities.

The Lorraine Hansberry Award for Excellence in African American Children's Literature was presented to Alexis De Veaux in Los Angeles, California, in 1991. She received the Fannie Lou Hamer Award for Excellence in the Arts from Medgar Evans College in 1984 and, twice, a Unity in Media Award, in 1982 and 1983, from Lincoln University in Pennsylvania for Reporting.

She received a National Endowment for the Arts Creative Writing Fellowship, a Creative Artists Public Service Grant from the New York State Council on the Arts in 1981, and a Research and Script Development Grant, Public Broadcasting Service, in 1989, among other grants and honors.

Don't Explain was named a Best Book of the Year for Young Adults by the American Library Association. *An Enchanted Hair Tale*, which was illustrated by Cheryl Hanna, was named an Honor Book in the 1988 Coretta Scott King Awards. It was also a Reading Rainbow Book.

SELECTED WORK: Na-ni, 1973; Don't Explain: A Song of Billie Holiday, 1980; An Enchanted Hair Tale, 1987; The Woolu Hat, 1995.

ABOUT: Contemporary Authors, Vol. 65-68; (New Revision Series), Vol. 26; Essence June 1988; Rollock, Barbara. Black Authors and Illustrators of Children's Books; Black Women in America, an Historical Encyclopedia, Vol. 1.

DAVID DIAZ

ILLUSTRATOR OF *Smoky Night*, etc.

Biographical sketch of David Diaz:

DAVID DIAZ is an illustrator who had worked for magazines and for corporate clients for about fifteen years before he illustrated his first picture book, *Neighborhood Odes* by Gary Soto. For his second, *Smoky Night* by Eve Bunting, he won the prestigious Randolph Caldecott Medal, presented by the American Library Association in 1995.

David Diaz met his future wife in the eleventh grade, in art class. Although he already had a girlfriend, Cecelia was not deterred, and began a "daily sarcasm session" to catch his attention. Eventually, the banter increased to the point where Diaz says that the focus of his time in art class was to see how much he could distract her from

DAVID DIAZ

her weavings and batik work. This friendship and romance led to the marriage of the two artists. "Cecelia opened my eyes to vivid color, and I began to use it," Diaz stated in the Caldecott Medal acceptance speech he presented to an American Library Association audience in 1995.

Diaz had a wonderful high-school art teacher, Sandra Tobe, who motivated her students. She encouraged them to enter competitions with their work, and in this way planted the idea that one could be successful and make money from doing art. She introduced Diaz to Duane Hanson, described by Diaz as a "hyperrealist sculptor." Diaz became Hanson's apprentice for four years, time spent both in high school and, later, at a school of advertising and design. While working for Hanson, Diaz was exposed to superrealist movement in art and felt himself drawn to it. At one point he worked with a technique of drawing tiny circles with a sharp pencil to create a gradual tonal quality; however, one of the pieces, a drawing six inches square, took sixty to eighty hours to complete. Diaz began to look for another method of artwork, and experimented with many.

In 1980, Diaz saw a show of German Ex-

pressionist art at the Guggenheim Museum. He considers this artwork an influence upon his own, and he also credits William Steig's work. He was impressed by "the depth of characterization he conveyed in so few lines," and as Diaz studied his work and followed the course of it over Steig's career, he noticed how Steig moved from "tightly rendered pieces toward a looser line." This is a course Diaz then developed in his own artwork.

It was in 1979 that Diaz began to show his portfolio in order to get work. He and his wife moved from Florida to California, and while he went to work as a clerk in a film-processing business, he sold his first illustration. He received twenty-five dollars for a piece for the *San Diego Reader*. Money and food were scarce, and the automobile the couple drove was so decrepit, they made it a practice never to park it in front of a client's office. The early years of his career and the variety of the assignments allowed Diaz to experiment with many mediums, including oils, pen and ink, watercolor paints, and woodcuts. When he finished a job for a client, he often created a small work of art from the leftover materials, and presented it to his employer as a gift. They were so well received that Diaz realized that they were effective promotional pieces, and he and his wife began to expand them into limited-edition books that they collaborated upon at the end of each year.

Persistent in pursuing work, the design and art jobs that Diaz procured totalled over five thousand over time. In 1989, he began to work with what he calls "a series of bold, loose, brush-stroke faces." He worked on the style for about three years and then made a trip to the Amazon River in Brazil in 1992. The loose sketches he created on this trip led him to create a style and a collage technique he used in the Diaz' next year-end book, *Sweet Peas*.

His first book for children came about when Harcourt Brace editor Diane D'Andrade asked him to illustrate *Neighborhood Odes*. When Diaz gave her a copy of *Sweet Peas*, she asked him to look at Eve Bunting's manuscript about the Los Angeles riots. The story of *Smoky Night* concerns a child who is a witness, in his own neighborhood, to the breaking glass, the looters, and the destruction of that event. Two families—African-American and Korean—end up in a shelter after they are evacuated from their building; and their two cats are brought in by a fire fighter, safe from harm. The families in the story take a step towards friendship in the realistic, thought-provoking book. *Horn Book* reviewer Ellen Fader compared Diaz's work to that of Georges Rouault and of the early work of the late picture-book artist John Steptoe in her review. She stated, "Because each double-page spread is so carefully designed, because the pictorial elements work together harmoniously, the overall effect is that of urban energy, rather than cacophony." The chairperson of the Caldecott Award selection committee, Grace W. Ruth, called the book "dramatic and ground-breaking."

Diaz's illustrations have appeared in such publications as *Atlantic Monthly* and *The Washington Post*. Among his corporate clients are American Express, Perrier, Pepsi Cola, and Benetton. Diaz lives in Rancho La Costa, California, with his wife and three children.

Smoky Night was also named an ALA Notable Book. *Neighborhood Odes* was named a 1993 *Hungry Mind Review* Children's Book of Distinction and was named a Notable Children's Trade Book in the Field of Social Studies by a joint committee of the Children's Book Council and the National Council on the Social Studies. He has also won recognition for his work from the New York Art Directors Club and the American Institute of Graphic Arts.

SELECTED WORKS: Neighborhood Odes, by Gary Soto, 1992; Smoky Night, by Eve Bunting, 1994.

ABOUT: Horn Book July 1995.

BERLIE DOHERTY

November 6, 1943–

AUTHOR OF *Dear Nobody*, etc.

Autobiographical sketch of Berlie Doherty:

WE LIVED near the sea. Liverpool, where I was born, was an exciting journey away by train and ferry. I was four when we moved. My favourite haunt was a bay called Red Rocks. I would go there on my own to watch the sunset, write poetry, and daydream. I inherited daydreams from my mother.

From my father I inherited stories. He always told me a bedtime story. And although he had no personal success as a writer, he had a passion for it. To me there was nothing unusual or special about sitting at a typewriter in the corner of the room. It was just what my dad did.

When I was ten a teacher noticed that I never wrote stories when I was asked to, but spent hours deep in thought until the right idea came, and then wrote, whatever else I was expected to be doing. It annoyed other teachers but it interested him. "One day," this teacher told me, "you'll be a writer."

I wrote openly until I was seventeen, and then my writing became secretive and experimental. I despaired of my ability. Again it was a teacher who led me on. She encouraged me to do an English degree at Durham University. I loved every minute of it, yet I was not doing what I wanted to do. I was not writing. I left with a degree in English Literature but had no idea what to do with it. I decided to become a social worker. I was totally absorbed in the lives of the people I was working with, children and families whose emotional problems seemed insurmountable. But soon I married and had three children: Janna, Tim and Sally. In those early years I felt very fulfilled, in a very loving marriage. And yet there was that ghost, waiting in the wings. Part of me stood on one side and watched and waited, and I was aware of her all the time.

When I did come to write, it was by

Doherty: *DOH er ty*

Are! and *The Making of Fingers Finnigan*, reading them chapter by chapter to one of my classes. I clung on to this writing; it was keeping me afloat. All I wanted to do now was to write. With no doubts at all in my mind I gave up my secure teaching job to make my living as a writer. I was supporting my three children and paying my mortgage. It had to work. I was writing day and night.

Sometimes children say to me, "What would you do if you didn't write?" and the answer, now, is that I don't know. I can't imagine doing anything else. It's lovely to know that I can earn a living by doing what I most enjoy, and that I caught it from my parents, too.

———

Berlie Doherty received her B.A. degree with honors in 1964. She was married in 1966. She earned a postgraduate certificate in education in 1978, and was an English teacher in Sheffield from 1980 to 1982. Since 1989, she has been a full-time writer. She has been a writer-in-residence at several schools and libraries, and has been Chair of Arvon Foundation at Lumb Bank since 1989. She is a member of Yorkshire Arts Literature Panel, Writers Guild of Britain, and Northern Association of Writers in Education.

Doherty has written many television and radio plays broadcast on the BBC-TV and radio in England, including a serial based upon *White Peak Farm*. She has written many stage plays, which have been produced in England. She is a contributor to magazines such as the *Times Educational Supplement*.

Dear Nobody won the 1991 Carnegie Medal, given by the British Library Association. It was published in England that year.

Granny Was a Buffer Girl also received a Carnegie Medal, in 1986. It was named an Honor Book in the 1988 *Boston Globe-Horn Book* awards.

White Peak Farm was named both a No-

chance. Sally was starting school. I needed a career to fit in with my children's school hours. I applied for a teaching course at Sheffield University. The tutor asked us to write a short story. I wrote as if I were in a dream, the way I had written when I was a child. It was as if it had already existed, and was only waiting to be written down. It meant more to me than anything I had ever written, and it still does.

Writing it had unlocked something in me, and it was a kind of emotional truth. I called it "Requiem". It was indeed a way of laying to rest one part of my life, and discovering a new kind of peace. Twelve years later it became a full-length novel for adults, but a great deal was to happen before then.

The tutor recommended I should try to sell it. I got eight pounds for it. Nothing, in the whole of my writing career, seeing my work on television and on the stage, winning awards, nothing has given me more joy than that first letter of acceptance gave me.

I started teaching, but it was short-lived. I couldn't cope with the breakdown of my marriage and with the stresses of teaching at the same time. I taught for two years, during which time I wrote *How Green You*

table Book of the Year and a Best Book for Young Adults by the American Library Association.

How Green You Are! and *The Making of Fingers Finnigan* were published in England, in 1982 and 1983 respectively. *Walking on Air* is a book of poetry.

SELECTED WORKS: Paddiwak and Cosy, 1989; Granny Was a Buffer Girl, 1988; White Peak Farm, 1990; Dear Nobody, 1992; Snowy, 1993; Walking on Air, 1993; Willa and Old Miss Annie, 1994.

ABOUT: Contemporary Authors, Vol. 131; Gallo, Donald R. Speaking for Ourselves, Too; Something About the Author, Vol. 72; Something About the Author Autobiography Series, Vol. 16.

MICHAEL DORRIS

January 30, 1945–

AUTHOR OF *Morning Girl*, etc.

Biographical sketch of Michael Dorris:

MICHAEL DORRIS was born in Louisville, Kentucky. He majored in English and classics at Georgetown University, receiving his B.A. degree cum laude in 1967. He went on to earn a M.Phil. degree at Yale University, studying in the Department of History of the Theatre from 1967 to 1968, and in the Department of Anthropology from 1968 to 1971.

Dorris married Louise Erdrich, a writer, in 1981. One of their children, Reynold Abel, whom Dorris had adopted previous to their marriage, suffered from fetal alcohol syndrome, an affliction that Dorris calls an "insult" in the "manner in which he entered the world." After the boy's death, Dorris wrote *The Broken Cord: A Family's Ongoing Struggle with Fetal Alcohol Syndrome*. The book was a *New York Times* bestseller and a Book-of-the-Month Club selection. It was made into a motion picture by Universal Television and ABC-TV in 1992. The National Book Critics Circle named it the best nonfiction book of 1989. It also re-

ceived a Christopher Award and was named a Notable Book by the American Library Association.

Dorris has remained active in organizations dealing with the subject, such as the National Organization for Fetal Alcohol Syndrome and the Research Society on Alcoholism. He has also been active in Native American organizations such as Native American Rights Fund, National Congress of American Indians, and National Indian Education Association. These associations only scratch the surface of the interests and endeavors of Dorris, however. He is a teacher, an anthropologist, a songwriter, and a writer of novels, short stories, and poetry for adults as well as novels for children.

After serving as an Assistant Professor of Anthopology at several colleges, he was Visiting Senior Lecturer in Anthropology and Maori Studies at Auckland University in New Zealand in 1980. He founded the Native American Studies Program and Department of Anthropology at Dartmouth College and was a full professor there from 1972 to 1989. He is an Adjunct Full Professor there, and was Chair of the Master of Arts in Liberal Studies Program from 1982 to 1985.

He has been a consultant on many editorial boards for publications, for theater and film productions; for endowments and fellowships; for foundations and for educational institutions. His novels include *A Yellow Raft in Blue Water*. With his wife, he has co-written several books, such as *Route Two and Back* and *The Crown of Columbus*. His book of short stories, *Working Men*, was published in 1993, and in 1994 he had published a book of essays, *Paper Trail*, which contains an essay on writing for children about Native American children, as well as one interpreting the "Little House" series by Laura Ingalls Wilder.

Dorris explains in the essay that when he and his wife were researching their book on Columbus, they found that the Taino tribe encountered by Columbus was "virtually [anonymous]." Among the first people Columbus met was one "very young girl," and Dorris wondered what she was like prior to the encounter. This led him to write *Morning Girl*, his first book for children. The girl and her brother alternately narrate chapters that reveal their lives—their rivalry, their sadness over a baby's death, their spirituality. Betsy Hearne states, in her review of the book in *The Chicago Bulletin of the Center for Children's Books*, "it is the subtle complexity of these developments that underscores the irony of Columbus' journal [excerpt]," in which Columbus refers to them as "a people poor in everything" who should be "good and intelligent servants." The novel won the 1992 Scott O'Dell Award for Historical Fiction. It was placed on the *Horn Book* "Fanfare" list as well as many recommended reading lists.

Guests, his second novel for children, was published two years later. It is a coming-of-age story that centers on a Native American boy who runs away from his people at the time when strangers are about to join their traditional harvest feast. Alongside his story is one of a girl who is also questioning the mores of her people. *The Horn Book*

Magazine called it "an introspective novel," told in language that comes "close to poetry," "short and powerful." A third novel for children is forthcoming, *Amory Goes Wild*.

Among his memberships are Phi Beta Kappa, P.E.N. (American Center), The Writer's Guild, Author's Guild, American Anthropological Association, and Modern Language Association. Dorris has appeared on Bill Moyers' PBS special "A World of Ideas," along with Louise Erdrich, and has been interviewed on many television and radio programs. He lives in New Hampshire with his wife and three daughters.

SELECTED WORKS: Morning Girl, 1992; Guests, 1994.

ABOUT: Contemporary Authors, Vol. 102; (New Revision Series), Vol. 19; Chavkin, Allan and Nancy Feyl Chavkin, editors. Conversations with Louise Erdrich and Michael Dorris; Ladies' Home Journal May 1993; Mother Jones May/June 1991; The New York Times Magazine April 21, 1991; Parents November 1992; Publishers Weekly August 4, 1989; Something About the Author, Vol. 75.

ARTHUR DORROS

May 19, 1950–

AUTHOR AND ILLUSTRATOR OF *Abuela*, etc.

Biographical sketch of Arthur M. Dorros:

ARTHUR DORROS was born in Washington, D.C. and grew up in and around that city. He was the oldest of four children. He had many pets—frogs, cats, and dogs. He once had thirteen box turtles, and he gave them all the name "Bobby" since they all looked alike. He remembers being an avid learner, though he didn't always like school; but in high school he enjoyed biology and English, and sociology. He loved reading and remembers that until he was about sixteen, he read a book every day. He liked adventure stories and when he read *Kon-Tiki* by Thor Heyerdahl, he wrote to the author, hoping to join his next expedition.

Dorros: *DOH rohs*

Arthur Dorros always loved to draw. There were several adults who influenced him in different ways when he was a child. His grandfather would write letters to him, with the same drawing of a bird on them. A neighbor made sculptures out of tree roots he found. And the mother of Arthur Dorros kept oil pastels in a drawer and would readily provide her children with art supplies. Also, his father was a great storyteller. However, Dorros stopped drawing in fifth grade, as he didn't think his drawings were done as well as they should be. He took it up again at sixteen, drawing for his biology class, and never gave it up again.

Dorros studied English in college, receiving his B.A. degree from the University of Wisconsin in Madison in 1972. He received teaching certificates from Pacific Oaks College in Pasadena, California in 1979. Though he has worked as a builder, draftsman, and longshoreman, he became a teacher in elementary and junior high schools and in adult education programs in Seattle and New York City. He has been a director of children's writing workshops, and has taught courses on writing. He has also been an artist in residence in New York City public schools.

In addition to his books written and illustrated for children, he has been a scriptwriter for filmstrips, such as *Teaching Reading: A Search for the Right Combination*, produced by the National School Public Relations Association. He has also been photographer for several filmstrips, as well as directing and writing a video called *Portrait of a Neighborhood*.

His interests have led Dorros to travel to South America, Central America, Asia, Europe, and Australia. He continues to conduct writing and bookmaking workshops. He lives in Seattle, Washington, with his wife and his son Alex. Dorros is a member of the Authors Guild.

His book *Tonight Is Carnaval* is also published with a Spanish translation by his wife, under the title *Por Fin es Carnaval*. Three of the books Arthur Dorros wrote and illustrated have been named Outstanding Science Trade Books for Children by a joint committee of the National Science Teachers Association and the Children's Book Council. They are *Feel the Wind, Rain Forest Secrets*, and *Ant Cities*. The latter was also named a Reading Rainbow book, as was *Alligator Shoes*. *Tonight Is Carnaval* was named a Notable Children's Trade Book in the Field of Social Studies by a joint committee of the National Council on the Social Studies and the CBC. *Abuela* was named a 1992 Fanfare Book by *The Horn Book Magazine*, as well as a Notable Book of 1991 by the American Library Association, and a Reading Rainbow Book.

SELECTED WORKS WRITTEN AND ILLUSTRATED: Alligator Shoes, 1982; Ant Cities, 1987; Feel the Wind, 1989; Rain Forest Secrets, 1990; Follow the Water from Brook to Ocean, 1991; This Is My House, 1992; Radio Man, 1993; Elephant Families, 1994.

SELECTED WORKS WRITTEN: Abuela, 1991; Tonight Is Carnaval, 1991.

SELECTED WORKS ILLUSTRATED: What Makes Day and Night (rev. ed.), by Franklyn M. Branley, 1987; Magic Secrets, by Rose Wyler and Gerald Ames (rev. ed.), 1991.

ABOUT: Something About the Author, Vol. 78.

TESSA DUDER

November 13, 1940–

AUTHOR OF *Alex*, etc.

Autobiographical sketch of Tessa Duder:

UNTIL around twelve I was besotted with ballet and wanted to spend my life dancing. Somewhere around thirteen, common sense prevailed—I had weak feet and broad shoulders, and in the 1950s, Auckland, New Zealand, wasn't a good place for aspiring ballerinas to start. The dream of Covent Garden faded. I decided to become a journalist.

So, at seventeen, I began as a cadet with a major evening newspaper. I have always loved words and the elegance and power of language, whether the forum be journalism or literature. But if anyone had told me then that in my early fifties I would be established as a writer of fiction for the young, as an editor, and newly exploring my skills as an actor, television scriptwriter and playwright, I would have laughed in disbelief.

My early life, with a doctor father and 1950s career mother, was secure, loving, ordered—and protected. I shone at butterfly and medley swimming, and at 17 won an Empire Games silver medal for my country, but I knew a life-long marriage, not a life-long career, was considered my real goal.

Marriage did come early, at 23, followed by fifteen years rearing four daughters. All my considerable energies went into my husband's career and growing family, apart from the hour or so a day I spent at my piano, practising Bach and Chopin.

Then one summer night in February 1978 a story chose me to write it. That may sound precious, but it is exactly what happened. The story of a family's near-disaster competing in a yacht race hit me ready-made, heaven knows from where. Two and a half years of obsessive, clandestine writing later, I had a manuscript; after much skillful editing, that overwritten beginner's

manuscript became my first novel *Night Race to Kawau*, published in 1982.

Twelve years later, I have some seventeen books published, and I have known much joy and hard work as a writer. My journalistic training instilled in me a respect for research, accuracy and deadlines. I've written six novels, including the Alex quartet for which I'm best known; several books of non-fiction for both adults and children; 'school readers' (as we call literacy learning material) and short stories. Currently I'm writing scripts for children's television, a full-length play for high school performance and short plays to perform as a member of Metaphor, an established drama quartet of writer/actors. I travel regularly all over New Zealand visiting schools, and in the last five years have been privileged with invitations to speak at literacy and writers' gatherings in Stockholm, Florida, Sydney, Melbourne, Rotorua and Auckland. I cannot think of any better or more challenging way of earning a living. A recent and associated professional pleasure is acting, in both classes and productions.

Our daughters are grown now. The eldest is qualified both as a teacher and speaker of Maori, the third is trained in graphic arts and the youngest is studying for a career as an actor and singer. Our second daughter Clare died suddenly in 1992 from an undiagnosed heart condition, aged 24. My work, especially the collaborative aspect of it, continues to help me grow through the tragedy of a young life cut too short. All my daughters, but especially Clare, were inspiration for my four books and the 1993 movie about my fictional "fifth daughter" Alex. In 1995 I expect to be ready for the hard solitary work of another novel.

I've been very lucky to develop my career during a decade in which New Zealand children's literature came of age. For me and my colleagues, Margaret Mahy has been our mentor, guru and friend. Through her genius, through the achievement of Joy Cowley as a world-acclaimed writer of 'school readers', and through the growing number of us also published in the USA and elsewhere, New Zealand has been put up on the literary map.

———

Tessa Duder was born in Auckland. She attended the University of Auckland from 1958 to 1959 and 1982 to 1984.

She worked as a journalist in Auckland and London for six years before marrying in 1964. A period of travel followed, with four daughters born in England, Pakistan, and New Zealand. Her writing career began in 1982 with the publication of *Night Race to Kawau*.

Tessa Duder serves on the boards of the New Zealand Children's Book Foundation and the Spirit of Adventure Trust, an organization that operates two sailing ships to take young people to sea. Since 1985, she has won several major writing and travel bursaries from the QEII Arts Council, including the 1991 Writer-in-Residence Fellowship at Waikato University and the 1993 Australia-New Zealand Literary Exchange Travel Fellowship. She's an Associate Editor for *Viewpoint* magazine on young adult books (published in Melbourne, Australia), and columnist for the literary magazine *Quote Unquote*. Since 1992 she has been vice-president of the NZ Society of Authors (PEN NZ Inc.) and in 1994 was named a member of the Order of the British Empire for services to literature.

There are four books in the Alex series; with their New Zealand titles and publication dates, they are: *Alex*, 1987; *Alex in Winter*, 1988; *Alessandra: Alex in Rome*, 1991; and *Songs for Alex*, 1992. *Alex* was published in the U.S. as *In Lane Three, Alex Archer* and *Alessandra: Alex in Rome* was published as *Alex in Rome* in the U.S.

Alex was named New Zealand Book of the Year in 1988. The New Zealand Library Association awarded the Esther Glen Medal to *Alex* in 1989; to *Alex in Winter* in 1990; and to *Alessandra: Alex in Rome* in 1992. Duder was a script consultant for *Alex*, a film produced by Isambard Productions and Total Film in 1993.

Duder is the editor of several anthologies. *Nearly Seventeen* includes short stories and plays, including her one-act play, *The Runaway*. *Falling in Love* is contains romantic stories for young adults, and *Crossing*, co-edited with Agnes Nieuwenhuizen, is an anthology of Australia and New Zealand short stories. None of the three have been published in the U.S. to date. She has also contributed a short story to *Ultimate Sports*, edited by Donald R. Gallo.

The American Library Association named *Jellybean* and *In Lane Three, Alex Archer* Notable Books of the Year, and *In Lane Three, Alex Archer* a Best Book of the Year for Young Adults.

SELECTED WORKS: Jellybean, 1986; In Lane Three, Alex Archer, 1989; Alex in Rome, 1992; Journey to Olympia: The Story of the Ancient Olympics, 1992; The Making of Alex: The Movie, 1993.

ABOUT: Fitzgibbon, Tom and Barbara Spiers. Beneath Southern Skies: New Zealand Children's Book Authors and Illustrators; Kirkpatrick, D.L. , 3rd ed. Twentieth-Century Children's Writers; Something About the Author, Vol. 80.

OLIVIER DUNREA

September 22, 1953–

AUTHOR AND ILLUSTRATOR OF *The Painter Who Loved Chickens*, etc.

Biographical sketch of Olivier Jean-Paul Dominique Dunrea:

OLIVIER DUNREA was born in Virginia Beach, Virginia. When he was a child, his family lived on a homestead with farm animals, and his favorite books were animal stories like *Charlotte's Web*, *Big Red* and *Lad: a Dog*. He liked to draw animals and make up stories about them.

He attended the University of Delaware from 1971 to 1973. At that time, he travelled to London and Paris on a scholarship. He earned a B.A. degree from Chester State College in 1975, majoring in theater arts and music. He received an M.A. degree from Washington State University in 1976. In 1978 he spent six weeks in Scotland sketching and painting ancient monuments.

Dunrea was a teaching fellow for a year at Washington State. He worked as an administrative assistant at several Philadelphia, Pennsylvania, companies from 1977 to 1981. He was able to return to Scotland in 1981 on a travel grant from the English-Speaking Union, in order to study archaeology and Scottish folklore. He was artist-in-residence at the Delaware State Arts Council in Wilmington from 1981 to 1983.

Dunrea likes to write stories set in prehistoric times, with stone dwellings that have secret passageways and tunnels. He has five dogs: four springers and his old Scottie, "Little Bridey" from *Fergus and Bridey*. He travels a lot and spends three to four months a year in Belgium.

Always experimenting with new art techniques, he has begun to work with oils. He took a materials and techniques course in oils at the Pennsylvania Academy of Fine Arts that was so helpful, he now takes a class there each fall. He has also started to work in egg tempera. He now makes handmade paper, after studying papermaking in Switzerland. He creates six- and ten-foot-long wall hangings that, he says, "look like bark." His carved, life-size hens with individual feathers made from paper adorn his house.

Dunrea conducts graduate courses in writing such as "The Writing Process: One Writer's Approach to Writing for Children." His work concentrates on "whole language," a system by which one learns to read by reading and learns to write by writing. One of the places he has taught the subject is the Regis University Whole Language Institute in Denver, Colorado. He also runs workshops for children, such as "What Can You Do With a Piece of Paper."

The Los Angeles gallery Every Picture Tells a Story represents his work, and he had a sculpture commissioned by Mazza Collection at Findlay University in Findlay, Ohio. Some of his sketches and watercolors are also at Mazza Collection.

He is a member of the English-Speaking Union and the Philadelphia Children's Reading Round Table. Olivier Dunrea lives in Philadelphia and has nine nephews and nieces.

His awards include a travel grant from the Philadelphia branch of the English-Speaking Union in 1980. He was named Outstanding Pennsylvania Children's Author in 1985. *Deep Down Underground* was named an Outstanding Science Trade Book for Children by a joint committee of the Children's Book Council and the National Science Teachers Association.

SELECTED WORKS WRITTEN AND ILLUSTRATED: Eddy B, Pigboy, 1983; Ravena, 1984; Fergus and Bridey, 1985; Mogwogs on the March!, 1985; Skara Brae: The Story of a Prehistoric Village, 1986; Deep Down Underground, 1989; Eppie M. Says . . . ; 1990; The Broody Hen, 1992; The Painter Who Loved Chickens, 1995.

SELECTED WORKS ILLUSTRATED: The Star of Melvin, by Nathan Zimelman, 1987.

ABOUT: Contemporary Authors, Vol. 124; Something About the Author, Vol. 46, 59.

Dunrea: *Dun ray*

JANE DYER

ILLUSTRATOR OF *Talking Like the Rain*, etc.

Biographical sketch of Jane Dyer:

JANE DYER grew up in New Jersey and Pennsylvania. As a child she enjoyed being inside the house, reading, drawing, playing piano, or daydreaming. She brought her artwork home from school and her mother saved it, but she wasn't the best artist in school, she says.

Dyer always wanted to be a teacher, and she used to play school with her cat and dog, pretending to teach them to how to write. She also assembled pet animals to stage wedding scenes. She once placed rose petals on a turtle's back, so that when it crawled forward, the petals were dispersed down the make-believe wedding aisle. This activity was surely the precursor for the book *Piggins and the Royal Wedding*.

Dyer studied elementary education and fine art in college. She began her career as a teacher and writer, and worked as a textbook illustrator for years before she began illustrating picture books on a full-time basis, which she has done since 1984.

In *The Three Bears Rhyme Book*, she modelled Goldilocks after her youngest daughter, who has curly, strawberry-blonde hair. She used photographs of bears to draw the pictures for the book, and also drew upon memories of her childhood, when her mother sewed clothes and household furnishings, saving scraps of material that would end up as quilts. Dyer portrays such recycled fabrics in the artwork of the book, for example in the quilt of Baby Bear.

Original art from Jane Dyer's books has been exhibited at galleries, and several of her paintings have been reproduced as greeting cards. A piece of her artwork from *The Three Bears Rhyme Book* was chosen for the National Year of the Younger Reader poster.

Time for Bed, written by Mem Fox, is described in a review in *The New York Times*

JANE DYER

Book Review as "a gorgeous lap book" by the writer, Lisa Shea. She states, "Jane Dyer's exquisite watercolors enhance the lullaby's sense of nighttime beauty and mystery, with close-up portraits of large-eyed, reposing mother-and-baby pairs of mice, cats, cows, sheep, deer, dogs, birds and geese. Even the mother and child honeybees working on the sticky centers of lush pink and white flowers bend their sleepy heads to their task in the day's last light."

Her book *Piggins*, written by Jane Yolen, introduces a very proper butler who solves a mystery in addition to his duties. The book is set in Edwardian England. Its sequel, *Picnic with Piggins* tells the story of how Piggins unravels the clues to a second mystery. Both books were named Book-of-the-Month Club selections and Junior Library Guild selections.

Dyer lives with her husband and two daughters in Northampton, Massachusetts, in a 150-year-old house overlooking a garden with a lily pond. They have two Himalayan cats and a Wheaten terrier.

SELECTED WORKS ILLUSTRATED: Piggins, by Jane Yolen, 1987; The Three Bears Rhyme Book, by Jane Yolen, 1987; Picnic with Piggins, by Jane Yolen, 1988;

Piggins and the Royal Wedding, by Jane Yolen, 1989; Baby Bear's Bedtime Book, 1990; The Patchwork Lady, by Mary K. Whittington, 1991; The Snow Speaks, by Nancy White Carlstrom, 1992; Talking Like the Rain: A First Book of Poems, by X.J. and Dorothy Kennedy, 1992; If Anything Ever Goes Wrong at the Zoo, by Mary Jean Hendrick, 1993; Time for Bed, by Mem Fox, 1993; The Girl in the Golden Bower, by Jane Yolen, 1994.

LOIS EHLERT

November 9, 1934–

AUTHOR AND ILLUSTRATOR OF *Color Zoo*, etc.

Autobiographical sketch of Lois Jane Ehlert:

MY MOTHER recently found a list of books I read in first grade that included *Art Stories, Book 1* and *What'll You Do When You Grow Up?* So it seems that art and books were already playing a part in my life. My family had a habit of going to the library. I remember getting my first library card, and how exciting it was to select books to take home. I have a younger brother and sister, and each week the three of us would go, each selecting five books (the limit), reading them all and going back the following week for more. Now that I am writing and illustrating my own books, I remember that excitement, trying to make my books as fine as I can so someone will get excited when they see my books.

It is difficult for me to remember a time when I wasn't writing or making something. I think being creative is something that is within us, but just like planting a seed in a garden, if you don't tend it, it won't bloom.

I grew up in Beaver Dam, a small city in Wisconsin. My mother and dad both worked, but still found time to make things. My dad had a basement workshop where he built things of wood, and my mother was a good seamstress. She taught me to sew when I was about eight years old. Both of their

LOIS EHLERT

hobbies produced great scraps for me to use on my projects. There was no art supply store in Beaver Dam, so cloth scraps, pieces of wood, wire and ribbons were my supplies, along with a big box of crayons purchased at the dime store. My crayons always wore out fast. I liked to color heavily to make the colors bright. Later, when I had my own spending money, I bought a tin box of watercolors, with the brush included. If you look closely at my books, you will see that I still use simple art materials and combine them with scraps of "good stuff" which I still save.

I worked on a card table, next to the piano. My mom and dad allowed me to leave my projects spread out on this table so I could return to it when I had free time. They must have known, even then, that art was important to me.

I continued using the card table all through high school. By that time I knew I wanted to be an artist. I didn't know any artist personally, but somehow I knew that was what I wanted to be. I babysat with the art teacher's children, and after they were in bed I read all of his art books.

During my senior year, I made art samples on the card table, and filled out an application for a scholarship to Layton School of Art in Milwaukee. I was lucky. I got the scholarship and moved to Milwaukee. I spent four wonderful years learning about art, still using my card table. But now it was a "drawing board", because I propped up a bread board at an angle with a tin can. This is where I did all of my art projects.

I got my first job in an art studio and continued working on ideas for books at night on, you guessed, the card table. After working for other people for a number of years, I began to freelance and now have my own studio with a real drawing board. Although my dad is gone, I still have the card table. The wooden top is scratched, splattered with paint, and the legs are wobbly. I still use it for wrapping packages and cutting boards. I think it reminds me that if you want to do creative work, you need a spot to do it. You won't do much writing or drawing if you have to hunt for a pencil each time you get an idea.

Now when I get an idea for a book, I leave things out where I can see them as I'm working. My ideas evolve. I start with a subject and then the text and pictures walk through the books, hand in hand. If I run out of space to spread things out, I even use the floor. None of the books are easy; I try not to repeat myself. When I complete the story in rough form, I make pencil sketches of what I want to illustrate. I continue reading and doing research on the subject. Then I make a "dummy" book, binding it and making a cover. I sit down and page through it, looking for weak ideas or words before I do any sketches in color. I am happiest when I finally get to the point of doing sketches in color, because I love color. When I complete color sketches, I will present it to a publisher for the first time. If they are interested, then the book goes through many more changes in both text and art before I make the final illustrations and submit the final text. My wastebasket generally overflows. What you see when you choose one of my books to read is probably version number fourteen or fifteen or sixteen. It looks simple though, doesn't it? And you know what? I can't think of anything I'd rather do.

———

Lois Ehlert was born in Beaver Dam, Wisconsin. She graduated from art school in 1957. She earned a B.F.A. degree from the University of Wisconsin in 1959. She has been a teacher in a children's art education program at the Layton School of Art, she has worked in layout and design, and she has been a freelance designer in a variety of mediums—books, toys, clothes, games, posters, and packaging, for example. She is a member of the American Institute of Graphic Arts.

Lois Ehlert has won many awards in design, illustration, and related work since 1961. A brief list includes a National Endowment for the Arts grant in 1984; American Institute for the Graphic Arts honors for her books for children; the Gold Award from Dimensional Illustrators Awards Show, and inclusion of her work in a Biennale of Illustration Exhibition in Bratislava in 1991.

Color Zoo was named an Honor Book in the 1990 Caldecott Awards presented by the American Library Association. It was also named a Notable Book by the ALA. *Moon Rope* was also named an ALA Notable. *Chicka Chicka Boom Boom* was named an Honor Book in the 1990 *Boston Globe-Horn Book* Awards. *Red Leaf, Yellow Leaf* won the same honor in 1992.

Among her many other awards for specific children's books, *Fish Eyes* was named a *New York Times* Best Illustrated Book of the Year. *Color Farm* and *Planting a Rainbow* were named Oustanding Science Trade Books for Children by a joint committee of the Children's Book Council and the National Science Teachers Association. Her work is represented in the Kerlan Collection at the University of Minnesota.

SELECTED WORKS WRITTEN AND ILLUSTRATED: Growing Vegetable Soup, 1987; Planting a Rainbow, 1988; Color Zoo, 1989; Eating the Alphabet, 1989; Color Farm, 1990; Color Zoo, 1990; Feathers for Lunch, 1990; Fish Eyes, 1990; Red Leaf, Yellow Leaf, 1991; Circus, 1992; Moon Rope: A Peruvian Folktale/Un laso a la luna, 1992; Nuts to You!, 1993; Mole's Hill, 1994; Snowballs, 1995.

SELECTED WORKS ILLUSTRATED: Chicka Chicka Boom Boom, by John Archambault and Bill Martin, Jr., 1989; Thump, Thump, Rat-a-Tat-Tat, by Gene Baer, 1989; Crocodile Smile, by Sarah Weeks, 1994.

ABOUT: Contemporary Authors, Vol. 137; Cummings, Pat, comp. and ed. Talking with Artists; Horn Book November 1991; Kingman, Lee and others, comps. Illustrators of Children's Books: 1957-1966; Kingman, Lee and others, comps. Illustrators of Children's Books: 1967-1976; Library Talk March 1992; Publishers Weekly February 12, 1992; Something About the Author, Vol. 35, 69.

AMY EHRLICH

AMY EHRLICH

July 24, 1942–

AUTHOR OF *Where It Stops, Nobody Knows*, etc.

Biographical sketch of Amy Ehrlich:

AMY EHRLICH was born in New York City and grew up there and in Connecticut. Her father was a writer of television scripts and novels, and worked at home. When her parents eventually divorced, her mother started a travel agency.

When she was a child, some of Ehrlich's favorite books were the Babar picture books and books by Laura Ingalls Wilder and P.L. Travers. She was a great reader, and the first book for adults that she enjoyed was *A Tree Grows in Brooklyn*. She began to make up stories of her own, and in the ninth grade, she won a prize for a short story.

She asked her mother if she could attend a boarding school, and went to one in Poughkeepsie, New York. She attended Bennington College, from 1960 to 1962 and later from 1963 to 1965, but she did not graduate. She took a job teaching in a daycare center, and worked as a fabric colorist and a receptionist. She also worked as a copy writer and as an editorial assistant at publishing houses, living in a commune in Vermont in the summers and returning to New York to earn money in freelance jobs.

She lived in Jamaica, for a time, and when she returned in 1973 she had a son. She worked as a roving editor for *Family Circle* magazine in New York from 1976 to 1977, and began working at Delacorte Press in 1977. In 1978 she became Senior Editor at Dial Books for Young Readers, a job she held until 1982. She then became an Executive Editor at Dial until 1984.

Ehrlich was living in a house in Brooklyn and raising her son when she heard that her sister in Vermont was very ill. She moved there, at first temporarily, and settled there, marrying Henry Ingraham, a college professor, in 1985.

Her first book, *Zeek Silver Moon* was written for a friend who had a child. It was illustrated by Robert Andrew Parker. Since then she has written and adapted thirty books for young readers, and adapted Dee Brown's book for adults, *Bury My Heart at Wounded Knee*, for children. She is also the editor of *The Random House Book of Fairy Tales*, which came out in 1985.

Her novel *Where It Stops, Nobody Knows* was named a Book of the Decade by

Booklist magazine. Two of her books, *The Everyday Train* and *Thumbelina*, were named Children's Choice Books by a joint committee of the Children's Book Council and the International Reading Association.

Ehrlich lives on her Vermont farm, where she keeps horses, cows, chickens, cats, and dogs.

SELECTED WORKS: Zeek Silver Moon, 1972; Leo, Zack, and Emmie, 1981; Annie Finds a Home, 1982; Bunnies at Christmastime, 1986; The Everyday Train, 1987; Emma's New Pony, 1988; Where It Stops, Nobody Knows, 1988; The Story of Hanukkah, 1989; The Dark Card, 1991; Lucy's Winter Tale, 1992; Parents in the Pigpen, Pigs in the Tub, 1994.

SELECTED WORKS ADAPTED OR RETOLD: Dee Brown's Wounded Knee: An Indian History of the American West, 1974; Thumbelina, by Hans Christian Andersen, 1979; The Wild Swans, by Hans Christian Andersen, 1981; The Snow Queen, by Hans Christian Andersen, 1982; Cinderella, 1985; Pome and Peel, 1989.

ABOUT: Contemporary Author, Vol. 37-40; (New Revision Series), Vol. 14; Something About the Author, Vol. 65.

SARAH ELLIS

May 19, 1952–

AUTHOR OF *The Family Project*, etc.

Autobiographical sketch of Sarah Ellis:

WHEN I READ about people who wrote their first book at age nine, I'm envious. I was a later bloomer. But looking back, I realize that although I wasn't a child writer, my childhood gave me good training for writing because I was a reader and I played a lot. Reading and playing are a lot like writing, losing yourself in another world when you read, creating characters and settings and conflict as you play. Sometimes I combined the two activities by playing at being a character in a book. Heidi was a favourite. I ate bread and cheese and pretended that the family cat was a goat. I also grew up in a good house for a future writer,

a big old house with a trapdoor and a back staircase and lots of cubbyholes. I could make an attic room into an animal hospital or a haunted house and I didn't have to tidy it up for days. And I grew up surrounded by stories, by stories of the olden days, my father's childhood in London and my mother's on the prairie, by Bible stories, by my older brothers' anecdotes of their glamorous high school life, and by bedtime readalouds, *The Adventures of Tom Sawyer* and *Winnie-the-Pooh* and *The Rootabaga Stories*.

When I look back, it seems inevitable that I would have become a writer. But it took me a while to make that discovery. I played violin and piano as a child and French horn in high school (music helped me survive adolescence), and for a while I considered music as a career. But university offered too many other things to study. I ended up in library school, rather by chance, but being a librarian turned out to be the second most perfect job for me. Being a children's librarian gave me a chance to read like crazy, to talk to kids about books and to indulge the performer in me, to tell stories and do puppet shows, to dress up as Mary Poppins and Paddington Bear and a buttercup.

One year I took time off from the library and went to Simmons College in Boston to study children's literature. Here I made a whole new set of friends and realized how much I liked writing *about* children's books. When I came back to Vancouver I started, very slowly and privately, to write stories for children and discovered how much fun it is. I was then faced with a dilemma that has plagued me all my life—there are too many things that I want to do. So I did some rearranging to accommodate writing, and five books later it seems to have been the right choice. My life at the moment is a patchwork with the two biggest pieces being writing and working at the library. I fit in smaller patches of critical writing, university teaching, speech-giving, and a bit of storytelling. Being a writer has given me lots of opportunities for travel, and I love the feeling of having an airline ticket in my desk drawer at all times. The freedom to work at my own pace, the satisfaction of creating something new and the sense of connection and community with other writers and readers—I'm glad that I've finally figured out what I want to be when I grow up.

————

Sarah Ellis was born in Vancouver, British Columbia. She earned a B.A. degree with honors from the University of British Columbia in 1973, and her M.L.S. degree in 1975. She also received an M.A. degree from Simmons College in Boston in 1980. She has been a librarian in such libraries as the Toronto Public Library and the Vancouver Public Library, and is currently with the North Vancouver District Library.

Sarah Ellis writes the "News from the North" column in *The Horn Book Magazine*. She is a member of the Canadian Society of Children's Authors, Illustrators and Performers, the Writers Union of Canada, and the Vancouver Storytelling Circle.

The Baby Project, published in the U.S. as *The Family Project*, won the 1987 Sheila A. Egoff Children's Prize administered by the West Coast Book Prizes Society in Vancouver. *Pick-up Sticks* won a 1991 Governor General Literary Award for Children's Literature from the Canada Council in Ottawa.

SELECTED WORKS: A Family Project, 1988; Next-Door Neighbors, 1990; Pick-up Sticks, 1992; Out of the Blue, 1995.

ABOUT: Contemporary Authors, Vol. 123; Something About the Author, Vol. 68.

LISA CAMPBELL ERNST

March 13, 1957–

AUTHOR AND ILLUSTRATOR OF *Sam Johnson and the Blue Ribbon Quilt*, etc.

Biographical sketch of Lisa Campbell Ernst:

LISA CAMPBELL ERNST was born in Bartlesville, Oklahoma. She loved to draw from a very young age. When she was a child, her mother would give her a list of items, such as a mouse, a shoe box, and a bell, and invite her to create a story about the items. She was also encouraged in art projects and given art lessons. Some of her favorite books were A.A. Milne's *Winnie-the-Pooh* and books by H.A. Rey and Dr. Seuss.

As she began her studies at the University of Oklahoma, she had planned to study journalism; but just before classes started, she changed her major to art. She earned her B.F.A. degree from the university in 1978. She went to New York City for a *Mademoiselle* magazine guest editorship and stayed, working as an assistant advertising director at Ogilvy & Mather, an agency in New York, for a year in 1978. She decided she didn't want to continue in advertising, however, and thought that if she could do anything she wanted, it would be to illustrate children's books.

She decided to set herself a time limit, after which, if she were unsuccessful, she

LISA CAMPBELL ERNST

would reevaluate her plans. She showed her portfolio to publishers on her lunch hour, and began to get assignments. After just six months, she quit her job and became a full-time author and illustrator.

Her books frequently focus on animals, which she loves. Her pet rabbit Penny keeps her company in the studio where she works, and she chose her little Scottie Terrier from her affection for Margery Flack's *Angus* books, which Ernst had as a child. She made a trip to England in 1986, and was amused to find that, when she got home, all the photographs she took on her trip were not of the usual tourists' favorite sights, but of sheep from the Cotswolds and Holstein cows.

The sheep she saw made their way into *Nattie Parsons' Good-Luck Lamb*, and the cows appeared in *When Bluebell Sang*.

Lisa Campbell Ernst married Lee R. Ernst, an art director in advertising, in 1978. They lived in New York for years, but eventually moved to a place where they could be closer to their families, and decided upon Kansas City, Missouri, where they live with their daughter.

Ernst uses pastel chalk and pencil to create her artwork. She sometimes thinks

about a book for two years, then spends nine months writing it and drawing the pictures.

The Frog on Robert's Head was named a Children's Choice Book by a joint committee of the International Reading Association and the Children's Book Council. *Mirror Magic* was included in the American Institute of Graphic Arts Book Show in 1981.

Several of her books have been named Junior Library Guild selections: *Sam Johnson and the Blue Ribbon Quilt, Nattie Parsons' Good-Luck Lamb*, and *Mirror Magic*.

SELECTED WORKS WRITTEN AND ILLUSTRATED: Nattie Parsons' Good-Luck Lamb, 1987; When Bluebell Sang, 1989; Ginger Jumps, 1990; Sam Johnson and the Blue Ribbon Quilt, 1992; Walter's Tail, 1992; Zinnia and Dot, 1992; The Luckiest Kid on the Planet, 1994.

SELECTED WORKS ILLUSTRATED: Kites for Kids, by Burton and Rita Marks, 1980; Mirror Magic, by Seymour Simon, 1980; The Frog on Robert's Head, by David Cleveland, 1981; Dress Little Bunny, by Harriet Ziefert, 1986; Gumshoe Goose, Private Eye, by Mary DeBall Kwitz, 1988; Who Says Moo, by Ruth Young, 1994.

ABOUT: Contemporary Authors, Vol. 114; Cummings, Pat, comp. and ed. Talking with Artists; Kansas City Star Magazine December 13, 1992; Something About the Author, Vol. 44, 55.

NANCY FARMER

JULY 9, 1941–

AUTHOR OF *The Ear, the Eye and the Arm*, etc.

Autobiographical sketch of Nancy Forsythe Farmer:

I GREW UP in a hotel on the Arizona/ Mexico border. The guests included retired railroad men, rodeo riders and the circus crowd. I remember cages of lions and wolves in the parking lot. Once, when I was nine, the circus vet invited me to attend an elephant autopsy and he discovered that the animal had two hearts.

Nancy Farmer

Life there was a wonderful preparation for writing. I worked at the desk from age nine, renting rooms and listening to the stories the patrons told each other. One man, who only had one eye, told me he lost the other in a fight with a grizzly bear. He had a picture of the stuffed grizzly in front of a trading post.

The only writer in the hotel was a man who wrote a western every month and was paid $300, a decent salary in those days. He lived on egg sandwiches and whiskey. One of my jobs was to make sure he got enough sandwiches to dilute the whiskey. Seeing him slumped over the typewriter day after day made me decide that writing was a lousy job.

After finishing college, I joined the Peace Corps and went to India. I was trained to speak Hindi and to teach English. Due to an administrative error I was sent to an area where they threw rocks atanyone who spoke Hindi. They wanted a chemistry teacher. I taught chemistry because I could read the textbooks faster than they could. Back in the U.S. I got a job as an insect pathology technician. I had never taken entomology. All I knew was that bugs had more legs than cows, but my boss wanted some-

one who wouldn't talk back to him. He wanted to supply all the information. This was fine with me. He was an excellent teacher.

If one is interested in bugs, the natural place to visit is Africa, which has the biggest and meanest bugs in the world. I bought a ticket and $500 worth of traveler's checks. I wound up running a lab on Lake Cabora Bassa in Mozambique. This was an absolutely wonderful job. I spent two weeks every month sailing around the lake in a little boat in the wildest country that exists on the planet. One of my chores was to visit remote villages, to be sure their water supplies were safe. I saw a lot of things that were completely mysterious. African culture is extremely complicated, and I don't consider myself an expert even after twenty years.

When this contract ran out, I went to Zimbabwe. Someone introduced me to Harold Farmer, who taught English at the University. He proposed after about a week and we have been happily married for eighteen years. We have one son, Daniel.

Oh, yes. How did I decide writing wasn't a lousy job? When Daniel was four, while I was reading a novel, the feeling came over me that I could create the same kind of thing. I sat down almost in a trance and produced a short story. It wasn't good, but it was *fun*. I was forty years old.

Since that time I have been absolutely possessed with the desire to write. I can't explain it, only that everything up to then was a preparation for my real vocation.

———

Nancy Farmer was born in Phoenix, Arizona. She received a B.A. degree from Reed College in Oregon in 1963. She served in the Peace Corps in India from 1963 to 1965. She studied chemistry at Merritt College in Oakland and the University of California at Berkeley from 1969 to 1971. She worked as a lab technician, in Zimbabwe, from 1975 to 1978. She married in 1976 and her son was born in 1978. She then became a freelance writer. She returned to scientific work at Stanford University Medical School, from 1991 to 1992.

Farmer has had several books for children published in Africa. *Lorelei* was published in 1988. *Tapiwa's Uncle*, a former version of *Do You Know Me*, was published in 1992. A shorter version of *The Ear, the Eye and the Arm* was published in Zimbabwe in 1989. Farmer also wrote a picture book called *Tsitsi's Skirt*, published in Zimbabwe in 1988, and she wrote stories for many readers for the fourth, fifth, and seventh grades that were published in Zimbabwe.

In 1987 she won the Gold Award for a short story submitted to the Writers of the Future Contest held by Bridge Publications. The prize money allowed her and her family to move to California. She received a National Endowment for the Arts grant for 1992. Farmer has had her stories anthologized in *Writers of the Future Anthology #4* and *Best Horror and Fantasy of 1992*. She is also working on a children's novel, several picture books, and a book of adult science fiction. She is a member of the Society of Children's Book Writers and Illustrators.

The Ear, the Eye and the Arm was named an Honor Book in the 1995 Newbery Awards by the American Library Association. The book was also named a Notable Book and a Best Book for Young Adults by the ALA. It was named an Honor Book in the Golden Kite Awards, given by the Society of Children's Writers and Illustrators.

SELECTED WORKS: Do You Know Me, 1993; The Ear, the Eye and the Arm, 1994; The Warm Place, 1995.

ABOUT: Something About the Author, Vol. 79.

ANNE FINE

December 7, 1947–

AUTHOR OF *Alias Madame Doubtfire*, etc.

Autobiographical sketch of Anne Fine:

I WAS BORN in the Midlands of England two years after the end of the Second World War. When my elder sister and I were six and three, my mother gave birth to triplets—three more girls. The head teacher of the school next door took pity on her, and let me in two years early. As a result, I can't remember a time when I couldn't read, and books have always been a passion. I made pretend ones for all my stuffed animals. I haunted everyone's bookshelves. And I can remember every library I've ever used, especially the American ones, where, for the first time in my life, instead of being allowed to take out two, or four, or six at the most, I was permitted armfuls. Oh, blessed land! So, if I have a hero, it's Andrew Carnegie, the great philanthropist who founded so many of the free public libraries in Britain and the States.

It never occurred to me, though, that I might be a writer. I think I thought that books were born on the shelves. But I was good at writing stories, and had a lot of practice. My primary school teacher came in each Monday in the worst of moods. "We'll have a bit of peace till break-time," he'd say. "I know. You can all write an essay." He'd chalk three titles on the board. A Day in the Life of a Lost Umbrella. My Best Friend. The Worst Advice I Ever Took. Anything like that. Then, "No talking," he'd say. "Just settle down and get on with it."

I loved those lessons more than anything in the world (apart from reading). I covered acres of paper. I wrote fast. And I learned to judge the form and the length of a story. I look back, and reckon it was excellent training. After all, I still work the same way—with a pencil and an eraser, in absolute silence. I still hide my work with my arms when people walk in, and I hate discussing what I'm writing, or showing it to anyone until it's finished.

And I still prefer reading to writing. The only reason I got started at all was that, trapped home one day by a blizzard, I couldn't get to the library to change my books. My baby daughter took her usual nap. And, desperate for fresh print, I started writing, then typing up. It was the coldest winter, so I chose a glorious summer's day as the book's setting: proof, if any were needed, of fiction's power to sweep the willing off and away.

I've written thirty books now, over twenty years, for both adults and children. I've written in Scotland, California, Canada, Arizona and Michigan—wherever my academic husband took us to live. I've been back in England for some years, but still I draw on the experiences of living far and wide. It was only after comparing the way in which my American friends responded to the challenge of divorce with what I saw in Scotland that I was prompted to write what has since become the best known of my novels for older children, *Alias Madame Doubtfire*. And the idea for *Flour Babies* came from a magazine cutting about an experiment in a real California High School.

A lot of my work, even for fairly young readers, raises quite serious issues. I suppose I believe that many personal decisions have a social or political resonance. In *The Chicken Gave It to Me*, for example, Gemma and Andrew have to think hard about their attitude to factory farming. And the way people pick their way through tricky family situations has always interested me. I won't deny the *The Book of the Banshee* owes quite a lot to the experience of having tempestuous teenagers in the house!

The greatest compliment (after "It's perfect! Don't change a word!") is "It made me laugh out loud." I'm proud to write comedies. Technically, they're the hardest, and I adore them. So, since I write always for the reader in myself, I always end up with the kind of book I'd have enjoyed most as a child. And if only someone else had written them first, I'd have been left with what I'd always prefer—more time to read.

———

Anne Fine received a B.A. degree with honors from the University of Warwick in 1968. She married in 1968. She was an English teacher at a secondary school from 1968 to 1970. She worked for the Oxford Committee for Famine Relief from 1970 to 1971. Since 1973 she has been a freelance writer, and she is a volunteer for Amnesty International.

Anne Fine has written a play, a radio play, and several novels for adults, of which *The Killjoy*, was published in the U.S. in 1987.

Alias Madame Doubtfire was produced into a motion picture, *Mrs. Doubtfire*, by Twentieth Century Fox.

My War with Goggle-eyes, published as *Goggle-Eyes* in Britain, was made into a four-part BBC Television series.

Anne Fine has twice been named the British Book Awards Children's Author of the Year, in 1990 and in 1993.

My War with Goggle-eyes won the 1990 Carnegie Medal presented by the British Library Association as well as the 1990 Guardian Award. *Flour Babies* won the 1992 Carnegie Medal. It was named an Honor Book in the 1994 *Boston Globe Horn Book* Awards and a Notable Book of the Year by the American Library Association.

It also won the Whitbread Children's Novel Award in 1993.

The Book of the Banshee was a Junior Library Guild selection. *Bill's New Frock* was named a Highly Commended Book in the 1990 Carnegie Medal Awards. *Alias Madame Doubtfire*, which was published as *Madame Doubtfire* in Britain, was a runner-up for a 1988 Guardian Award. Sixteen of Fine's books for older children, available in Britain, have not yet been published in the U.S.

SELECTED WORKS: The Summer-House Loon, 1979; The Granny Project, 1983; Alias Madame Doubtfire, 1988; My War with Goggle-eyes, 1989; Bill's New Frock, 1990; Poor Monty, 1991; The Book of the Banshee, 1992; Flour Babies, 1994.

ABOUT: Contemporary Authors, Vol. 105; (New Revision Series), Vol. 38; Kirkpatrick, D.L. Twentieth-Century Children's Writers; Publishers Weekly November 22, 1993; Something About the Author, Vol. 29, 72; Something About the Author Autobiography Series, Vol. 15.

DENISE FLEMING

January 31, 1950–

AUTHOR AND ILLUSTRATOR OF *In the Small, Small Pond*, etc.

Biographical sketch of Denise Fleming:

DENISE FLEMING was born in Toledo, Ohio. She attended Kendall College of Art and Design, graduating in 1970. She married David Powers in 1971 and has a teenage daughter.

Fleming began her children's book career in the early 1980s, after she was encouraged by author illustrator Wendy Watson. She approached New York publishers with her portfolio, and began her career by illustrating books by other authors. She also drew illustrations for series books such as Care Bears, but this is not what she really wanted to do. She enrolled in a papermaking class, which piqued her interest and led her to take a more advanced course, "Handmade

DENISE FLEMING

Paper for the Painter," at the Arrowmont craft school in Gatlinburg, Tennessee. This course taught her all about pulp, pigment, and chemicals, and her art supplies now include five-gallon pails of white cotton pulp, small bottles of colored pulp, and hand-cut stencils. Instead of a canvas, she employs a structure made of large wire screen to create her handmade paper.

The new materials and techniques led Fleming to develop her unique style of collage. She took a new portfolio to New York, where an editor at Henry Holt and Company, Laura Godwin, liked her work so much that she was offered a contract immediately.

Her love of gardening and her interest in natural habitats inspires her books, the first of which is *In the Tall, Tall Grass*. The book shows a small boy observing a caterpillar as it moves through the grass and meets many other creatures. The book was named an Honor Book in the picture book category of the 1992 *Boston Globe-Horn Book* awards, and was a Junior Library Guild selection.

In the same vein, *In the Small, Small Pond* shows, in "eye-catching compositions," according to a *Horn Book* review, all the animals of a small pond throughout the seasons. "Belying the adjectives in the title," the reviewer writes, "this large attractive book is open and expansive; and it discloses more information than might appear at first glance, though the art alone is excuse enough for repeated visits." The book was named a 1994 Caldecott Honor Book by the American Library Association.

Barnyard Banter is a catalog of barnyard animals and their sounds. A *Horn Book* reviewer stated, "The imaginative illumination of a very basic and familiar scheme is masterful." The book was named a Notable Book by the ALA. *Lunch* was also an ALA Notable Book.

SELECTED WORKS: In the Tall, Tall, Grass, 1991; Count!, 1992; Lunch, 1992; In the Small, Small Pond, 1993; Barnyard Banter, 1994.

SELECTED WORKS ILLUSTRATED: All Through the Town, by Alice Low, 1984; This Little Pig Went to Market, 1985; This Is the House, by Linda Hayward, 1988; D Is For Doll, by Linda Hayward, 1988; Tea Party Manners, by Linda Hayward, 1988; Dollhouse Mouse, by Natalie Standiford, 1989.

ABOUT: Publishers Weekly December 20, 1991; Something About the Author, Vol. 81.

FIONA FRENCH

June 27, 1944–

AUTHOR AND ILLUSTRATOR OF *Snow White in New York*, etc.

Autobiographical sketch of Fiona French:

I WAS BORN near a city called Bath in Somerset (Avon now) on 27th June 1944. My main education was in a convent in Devon. Then to art school—Croydon College of Art, until 1966.

I enjoyed history and geography in school but most of all I could lose all sense of time and place in the art classes. So when the time came to choose a career, I chose art. I left a strict convent school and went to art school during the 1960's. I studied painting

and printmaking and for my final exhibition included a book of short stories which I had written and illustrated and this small book pointed the way into the future.

Charles Keeping, the well-known children's book illustrator, had been one of my tutors at art school and he encouraged me to show my folder of work to various publishers in London.

I had a successful interview with a marvellous editor called Mabel George at Oxford Unversity Press, and the idea for my first picture book was accepted in late 1968, but much work was done before it could be published in 1970. The pattern of all my future books grew out of this book; 'research' being the key word. Only by reading and studying; looking at paintings and other visual sources can I create a story and then the illustrations for a picture-book.

This year in 1994, I was a guest speaker at the Keene State College 'Children's Book Festival' Oct. 22nd .'94 and it was my first visit to America.

America lived up to all my expectations, it was wonderful. I have returned home with lots of new ideas!

———

After she received her N.D.D. degree at art school in 1966, Fiona French worked as a children's art therapy teacher. She then worked as an assistant to Bridget Riley, a painter. She taught part-time at Wimbledon School of Art and at Brighton and Leicester Polytechnic schools, from 1970 to 1974. French has had at least one book published in Britain each year since 1970. *Junior Bookshelf* called her "the ultimate designer among today's picture-book makers."

Her paintings were exhibited at Bacon's Bookshop and Gallery, Norwich, England, in 1994.

Snow White in New York won the 1986 Kate Greenaway Medal, awarded by the British Library Association. It was named a Children's Choice Book by a joint committee of the International Reading Association and the Children's Book Council. *King Tree* was named a Commended Book in the 1973 Greenaway Awards.

The Blue Bird received the 1973 Children's Book Showcase award from the Children's Book Council. *Anancy and Mr. Dry-Bone* received an honourable mention citation from the International Graphic Prize "Fiera di Bologna". *Rise & Shine* was published as *Rise, Shine!* in England.

SELECTED WORKS WRITTEN AND ILLUSTRATED: Anancy and Mr. Dry-Bone, 1991; The Blue Bird, 1972; King Tree, 1973; City of Gold, 1974; Snow White in New York, 1987; Rise & Shine, 1989; The Magic Vase, 1991; King of Another Country, 1993.

SELECTED WORKS RETOLD AND ILLUSTRATED: Cinderella, 1988; Little Inchkin, 1994.

ABOUT: Contemporary Authors (First Revision), Vol. 29-32; (New Revision Series), Vol. 40; Kirkpatrick, D.L. Twentieth-Century Children's Writers, 3rd ed.; Kingman, Lee and others, comps. Illustrators of Children's Books: 1967-1976; Peppin, Brigid and Lucy Micklethwait. Book Illustrators of the Twentieth Century; Something About the Author, Vol. 6.

SHERRY GARLAND

July 24, 1948–

AUTHOR OF *The Lotus Seed*, etc.

Autobiographical sketch of Sherry Garland:

WHILE I was growing up in small Texas towns, my family was very poor and could not afford many children's books. So, instead of asking my mother to read me bedtime stories, I would make up stories for her. Our large family of nine children was always moving from one rent-house to another and I had a physical defect for many years, so I often felt like an outsider. I was painfully shy, making it difficult for me to form friendships. Instead, I created a bevy of "make-believe" friends who shared fantastic adventures with me and my favorite dog while exploring the woods and mountains, rivers and fields of Texas. I preferred playing with animals and climbing trees to

SHERRY GARLAND

the company of other children. Most of the characters in my novels are like that— loners who love nature, who are shy or different and who don't fit in.

My first taste of being an author came at the age of seventeen. My high school English teacher made her class enter a statewide essay contest called "Why I Love Texas." To my surprise I won first place! The thrill of being on local TV and in newspapers, along with the $100 prize money, made me think that being an author would be glorious. I dreamed of this, but to me books were written by greats like William Shakespeare or Mark Twain, not by ordinary people like me who led ordinary lives. I wrote poetry and stories for years, but I hid them under my mattress and never showed anyone.

One day I woke up from a vivid dream and quickly began typing it out. The story developed into a 350,000-word manuscript for an historical novel. I never sold that novel, but the experience I gained helped me learn to write. The next novel sold immediately, thus launching my writing career in 1982.

My first books were adult paperbacks written under a pseudonym. But I was not happy. I wanted to write books with more meaning and depth. I had been working with Vietnamese families since 1981 and had grown to love the people and culture. I wanted to write about their experiences and to show their side of the war and the hardships they suffered. But none of the publishers of my adult books were interested in this subject. They told me Americans wanted to forget the Vietnam War and did not want to read about Vietnamese. I was so frustrated that for several years I didn't write any more books.

Then, in 1988, I saw an educational publisher's ad wanting someone to write a children's nonfiction book about Vietnam. I accepted the contract, even though I didn't receive much money. It took me two years to research that book. All the while I was studying about Vietnam, ideas for fictional stories kept popping into my head, so I wrote some picture books and young adult novels set in Vietnam. When I submitted them, I soon learned that children's book publishers welcomed stories about other cultures. I also sold books set in Texas, like *The Silent Storm* and *Letters from the Mountain*, which reflect my personal experiences more closely.

Even though several of my books focus on the Vietnamese, it is my belief that all humans share similar loves, fears, and dreams, no matter what the culture. Today I continue to write about loners who are different, who don't fit in, but who triumph over adversity. Whether my books are set in the mountains of Vietnam or the cotton fields of Texas, writing for children is satisfying— it's like telling my mother a story.

———

Sherry Garland was born in McAllen, Texas and grew up in the town of Weatherford. She received a B.A. degree in French from the University of Arlington in 1970 and did graduate study in linguistics and English from 1970 to 1971. She was married in 1971. She worked in the university library while in school, and was a librarian at the Texas A. and M. University Departments of Oceanography and Meteorology Libraries from 1972 to 1975. She has also written two books for adults.

Garland lives in Houston and currently is a full-time author. She also makes appearances at schools and conferences. She is a member of the Society of Children's Book Writers and Illustrators and other professional organizations.

The Lotus Seed was named a Notable Book of the Year by the American Library Association. It was a Reading Rainbow Book and a selection of the Book-of-the-Month Club. Both *Shadow of the Dragon* and *Song of Buffalo Boy* were named ALA Best Books for Young Adults. The latter was also named a Notable Children's Trade Book in the Field of Social Studies by a joint committee of the National Council on the Social Studies and the Children's Book Council, and received the 1993 Rita Award for best young adult novel from the Romance Writers of America. *The Silent Storm* was named a Junior Library Guild selection. Her books have been nominated for state awards in nine states.

SELECTED WORKS: Vietnam: Building a Nation, 1990; Best Horse on the Force, 1991; Song of the Buffalo, 1992; The Lotus Seed, 1993; Shadow of the Dragon, 1993; The Silent Storm, 1993; Why Ducks Sleep on One Leg, 1993; I Never Knew Your Name, 1994; Cabin 102, 1995; Indio, 1995; The Summer Sands, 1995.

ABOUT: Something About the Author, Vol. 73.

ARTHUR GEISERT

September 20, 1941–

AUTHOR AND ILLUSTRATOR OF *After the Flood*, etc.

Autobiographical sketch of Arthur Geisert:

I THINK etching is the most beautiful way of putting ink on paper. I've always admired the great etchers—Callot, Piranesi, Rembrandt, and Whistler—and try to emu-

late them in my work. I try to combine a classical etching style with narrative and humor. All of my book illustrations are copper-plate etchings etched with Dutch mordant in a traditional manner.

I grew up in Lakewood, California, a suburb of Los Angeles. My mother was a homemaker; my father was an aerospace engineer. I have one brother, Stephen, who is four years younger.

I made my first etching at the Otis Art Institute, Los Angeles. The press was an ancient star-wheeled ornate cast iron press that arrived in Los Angeles in the nineteenth century via a clipper ship around Cape Horn. Besides a short stay at the Otis Art Institute, I've attended Concordia College in Seward, Nebraska, B.S. 1963; the University of California at Davis, M.A., 1965; and short stays at the old Chouinard Art Institute in Los Angeles and the Art Institute of Chicago.

After teaching five years at Concordia College, River Forest, Illinois, and one year at Concordia College, Seward, Nebraska, I moved to Galena, Illinois, with my wife, Bonnie and son, Noah.

After moving to Galena, we built two houses from scratch. This construction ex-

perience has been used in my books, particularly *Pigs from A to Z* and *Pigs from 1 to 10*, and to a lesser extent, *The Ark* and *After the Flood.* We've lived in Galena since 1971, and other than building houses, I've done little else except make etchings. For the first ten years in Galena, publishers rejected my work. It was to the point where I told myself that I would give up when the rejection letters equalled my body weight.

That happened during our eighth year in Galena. I gained two more years by burning all the envelopes and doubling my beer intake. Then one day an editor in the adult division of Houghton Mifflin called me and said that he had seen some of my etchings at a Boston Printmakers exhibit. He asked if I had more work similar to that in the exhibit and if I did would I mind sending it to him and he would show it to the children's book department. Within an hour, the biggest package of etchings in postal history was on its way to Boston.

Ten years later I'm working on my tenth picture book, illustrated with etchings, for Houghton Mifflin. The working title is *A Real Hard Counting Book/ Liber de difficillimo computando numerum/ Numeabilia Romana ab Uno ad Duo Mila/ Roman Numerals from One to Two Thousand.* My etching studio is the first floor of our house. The house is on a hilltop in an abandoned stone quarry. Behind the house and around its sides are fifty-foot high stone ledges. The front of the four-story house faces southwest with panoramic views of Galena and thedistant Mississippi River and Dubuque, Iowa. I've used these views for backgrounds in the illustrations. *Aesop & Company,* written by Barbara Bader, is a good example.

I collaborated with Bonnie on *Haystack.* She used to help her family make haystacks in rural South Dakota where she grew up. After building two houses together, collaboration holds no fears. Once in a while, in the thick of things when trying to meet a deadline, the etching goes into a twenty-four-hour schedule. The fumes from the Dutch mordant have killed some of Bonnie's plants up to and including the fourth floor. Other than that, it is a pretty idyllic existence.

———

The artwork of Arthur Geisert has been exhibited in many shows in the U.S. and around the world. These include the International Print Biennial in Krakow, Poland, where he won the Purchase Award in 1978; the National Museum of American Art in Washington, D.C. in 1982; the International Impact Art Festival at the Kyoto Municipal Museum of Art in Japan; the American Academy and Institute of Arts and Letters; and the 13th Biennale of Graphic Design in Brno, Czechoslovakia, in 1988.

He is a member of the National Artist's Equity Association, Los Angeles Printmaking Society, Boston Printmakers, the Society of American Graphic Artists, and the Society of Children's Book Writers and Illustrators. He received the Illinois Art Council Artist's Fellowship award in 1986. Geisert has been invited to present lectures at Findlay University in Ohio, the Kerlan Collection at the University of Minnesota inMinneapolis, and at The Smithsonian in Washington, D.C., to name a few.

Pigs From A to Z was named a *New York Times* Best Illustrated Book of 1986. *Oink* was a Reading Rainbow book. *The Ark* was named a Notable Children's Book by the American Library Association, and was also named a Notable Children's Trade Book in the Field of Social Studies by a joint committee of the Children's Book Council and the National Council on the Social Studies.

His books have been translated into Japanese, French, Spanish, and German. As the word "Oink" is the same in English, Spanish, and German, Geisert was able to read one of his works in three languages simultaneously for an audience at the Clarence Mitchell Library of Highland Community College in Galena, Illinois, in 1994.

SELECTED WORKS WRITTEN AND ILLUSTRATED: Pa's

Balloon and Other Pig Tales, 1984; Pigs from A to Z, 1986; The Ark, 1988; Oink, 1991; Pigs from 1 to 10, 1992; Oink Oink, 1993; After the Flood, 1994.

SELECTED WORKS ILLUSTRATED: Aesop & Company, by Barbara Bader, 1991; Haystack, by Bonnie Geisert, 1995.

ABOUT: Contemporary Authors, Vol. 120; Julie Cummins, ed. Children's Book Illustration and Design; Galena, Illinois Gazette December 15, 1994; Something About the Author, Vol. 52; 56.

ROY GERRARD

January 25, 1935–

AUTHOR AND ILLUSTRATOR OF *The Favershams*, etc.

Autobiographical sketch of Roy Gerrard:

I WAS BORN in a working-class family in Lancashire, England in 1935. My father encouraged my reading and through him I developed a love of books generally, and of verse in particular. He was also fond of doing lengthy bicycle tours on which I accompanied him enthusiastically. Our trips to the England/Wales border country with its rugged hills and ruined castles sparked off my sense of history, which later bore fruition in my book *Sir Cedric.*

My sense of history (a grand-sounding phrase) was of the blood-and-thunder variety; a romanticised view of ancient battles and vanished kingdoms. This attitude became slightly more sophisticated when I acquired some awareness of medieval art, but it still is basically childlike.

Also in childhood I developed a love of Victorian buildings—I was fascinated (and still am) by their rich ornamentation and often-unconscious humour. The nearby city of Manchester was a good example of a Victorian city—someone once described it as "like a gray engraving of Venice"—now alas, the old buildings are being replaced by multi-story brutalism. God preserve us from such progress!

After an idyllic period at art school I

Roy Gerrard [signature]

spent fifteen uneventful years as an art teacher. I painted intermittently during this period but during the early 1970's, whilst convalescing from a climbing accident, I rediscovered the beauty of water-colour and began to work obsessively in this medium. English artists, it seems, are prone to water-colour; something to do with the gray softness of English light. We certainly produced a fine crop of water-colourists over the years, particularly so in the nineteenth century.

I left teaching in 1980 to concentrate fully on writing, illustrating children's books and painting.

Having been around for so long I have absorbed many artistic influences, some of which I have forgotten but which are still twitching my strings. The comic strip illustrators of my childhood were certainly formative, as were the adult-oriented graphic artists, André François, Emmett, Steinberg etc. The later French Impressionists and the English Landscape School are in there somewhere, too. Rather a hotchpotch of influences but I recognise occasional faint echoes of these people in my work; I like to think my own style puts in an appearance also.

At the time of writing I'm sixty years old. Over the years I have acquired a much-loved wife and two children, plus several beautiful and exhausting grandchildren. Producing a book every two years or so and painting between books, I still work obsessively and regard picture-making as the best thing life can offer.

I live on the Cheshire/Derbyshire border, surrounded by a green landscape which is a joy to behold. I continue to potter around the countryside on my bicycle, telling myself that I am absorbing rural images and storing them in my head for future use, but I think what I'm really doing is just pottering around the countryside on my bicycle.

———

Roy Gerrard was born in Atherton, Lancashire, in England. He attended Salford School of Art from 1950 to 1954. He trained as an illustrator and studied textile design for one year. He was married in 1958. He taught art and eventually became department head at Egerton Park County Secondary School in Denton, England from 1956 to 1966. He held similar positions at Hyde Grammar School, Hyde, England from 1966 to 1980.

His work has been exhibited in one-person shows at the SEEN Gallery in London from 1978 to 1985. Gerrard enjoys poetry and American jazz.

The Favershams won the Graphics for Children Award in the 1983 Bologna Children's Book Fair. Three of Gerrard's books have been named *New York Times* Best Illustrated Books of the Year: *The Favershams*, *Sir Cedric*, and *Sir Frances Drake*. *Sir Cedric* was named a Notable Children's Trade Book in the Field of Social Studies by a joint committee of the Children's Book Council and the National Council for the Social Studies.

SELECTED WORKS WRITTEN AND ILLUSTRATED: The Favershams, 1983; Sir Cedric, 1984; Sir Cedric Rides Again, 1986; Sir Frances Drake: His Daring Deeds, 1988; Rosie and the Rustlers, 1989; Mik's Mammoth, 1990; A Pocket Full of Posies, 1991; Jocasta Carr, Movie Star, 1992; Croco'nile, 1994.

SELECTED WORKS ILLUSTRATED: Matilda Jane, by Jean Gerrard, 1983.

ABOUT: Contemporary Authors, Vol. 110; Marantz, Sylvia and Kenneth M. Artists of the Page: Interviews with Book Illustrators; Something About the Author, Vol. 45, 47.

JAN SPIVEY GILCHRIST

February 15 1949–

ILLUSTRATOR OF *Nathaniel Talking*, etc.

Biographical sketch of Jan Spivey Gilchrist:

JAN SPIVEY GILCHRIST was born in Chicago, Illinois, and raised in a warm community on the south side. She remembers playing games on the sidewalks while parents watched from front porches. However, she became ill with a bone disease that kept her from physically joining in on the fun. So she began to draw the scene she saw. She also copied pictures from an illustrated family Bible. She loved to draw babies. Her parents encouraged her and she felt support from her school and classmates. But then she made a visit to the Art Institute of Chicago where she discovered that there was no African American art represented. She was profoundly affected by this discovery and vowed to place African Americans in paintings. She also wanted to depict black families as she knew them, with a mother and a father, and a warm family life.

Gilchrist's parents stressed that she had to study something in school that would allow her to support herself. She studied art and planned to teach as well. She married in 1970 and received her B.S. degree from Eastern Illinois University in 1973, then worked as a substitute teacher from 1973 to 1976 for the Chicago Board of Education. She was an art teacher from 1976 to 1979 at Harvey Schools in Harvey, Illinois. Gilcrest earned her M.A. degree from the University of Northern Iowa in 1979. She was an art teacher in the early 1980's at Cambridge School Department, Cambridge,

JAN SPIVEY GILCHRIST

Massachusetts, and at the Joliet Public Schools in Illinois. She was divorced in 1980 and remarried in 1983. She has two children.

Gilchrist is a fine artist who shows her work in the United States and in Canada, and she has won many awards for her work. Portraits of children and families are her specialty. Her first foray into children's books came about when she met Eloise Greenfield at a gathering and showed her some slides of her artwork. Greenfield put her in touch with her own publisher, Philomel, and Gilchrist travelled to New York to present her work to the publisher. This led to her first book, *Children of Long Ago*. She has had commissions for her fine art from Eastern Illinois University in 1974 and from the State of Illinois Families with a Future campaign in 1986 and 1987. She also won the Distinguished Alumni Award from Eastern Illinois University in 1992. She is a member of Phi Delta Kappa. Alpha Kappa Alpha selected Gilchrist to be an Honorary Member, a distinction also bestowed upon Coretta Scott King and Maya Angelou.

Nathaniel Talking won a 1990 Coretta Scott King Award. *Night on Neighborhood Street* was an Honor Book in the Coretta Scott King Awards, in 1992.

SELECTED WORKS WRITTEN AND ILLUSTRATED: Indigo and Moonlight Gold, 1992.

SELECTED WORKS ILLUSTRATED: Children of Long Ago: Poems, by Lessie Jones Little, 1988; Nathaniel Talking, by Eloise Greenfield, 1988; Big Friend, Little Friend, by Eloise Greenfield, 1991; Everett Anderson's Christmas Coming, by Lucille Clifton, 1991; First Pink Light, by Eloise Greenfield, 1991; Night on Neighborhood Street, by Eloise Greenfield, 1991; Red Dog Blue Fly, by Sharon Bell Mathis, 1991; William and the Good Old Days, by Eloise Greenfield, 1993; Lift Ev'ry Voice and Sing, by James Weldon Johnson, 1995.

ABOUT: Something About the Author, Vol. 72.

MEL GLENN

May 10, 1943–

MEL GLENN

AUTHOR OF *Class Dismissed*, etc.

Autobiographical sketch of Mel Glenn:

I ONCE WROTE a poem, "Mr. Robert Winograd, English, Period 1, Room 102." It's about an English teacher who is told he looks like an English teacher. "How does an English teacher look?", the poem asks, "Wouldn't it be a novel experience / If, just once, I met someone who said, / 'Hey, you look like a big league ballplayer'?"

Robert Winograd, my literary alter ego, says he would like to be a big league ballplayer, but he is unalterably trapped in the body of an English teacher.

And that's who I am, plain and simple, a teacher.

I teach English, not a very popular subject where "yo, man," is considered a compound sentence and you really get questions like, "Mr. Glenn, when you double space for a term paper, does that mean between the words?"

I teach in the same school I went to as a kid. I teach in some of the same rooms I sat in when I went to Lincoln High School in Brooklyn.

And yes, I write poetry, an avocation that is as popular in America as selling snowshoes in the desert. I say it loudly and proudly. I ponder the perfect phrase, etch out the exact word and toss out more drafts than an open window. So the question becomes—why?

I write because I remember. I remember how it felt not to make the basketball team, how it felt to worry about tests, how it felt finding my way through the teenage social labyrinth.

I write because I want to say to that scared kid in the third row, fourth seat, "you're not alone and with luck and some work you'll actually live through your adolescence and become an important member of society." I write because feelings deserve respect and questions deserve answers and in some small way if my poems suggest that high school is the one universal experience we all share and survive, I will have accomplished something, taught something to students both in and out of my classroom.

I write poetry, specifically, because I hear the words in my head, sometimes more easily than I hear prose. The images, metaphors and even the bad puns tumble out at sometimes an alarming rate. So persistent are the words that everything, papers to grade, errands to run, takes a back seat to frenzied scribbling. I have always written, a genetic predisposition, if you will, from grade school on up. It's what I can do.

When you grow up you realize the adult world is just composed of everyone you went to high school with. To a large extent we are who we were and high school plays a large part in defining ourselves. If, as it has happened, a kid says to me after reading one of my poems, "I've felt just like that," I know that I have succeeded as both a poet and a teacher. There are few joys that come close.

————

Mel Glenn was born in Zurich, Switzerland. He received his B.A. degree from New York University in 1964 and his M.S. from Yeshiva University in 1967. He served in the Peace Corps in Sierra Leone, West Africa, from 1964 to 1966, taught junior high school from 1967 to 1970 and since then has been a high school English teacher in Brooklyn, New York. He writes both poetry and novels for children and is a member of the Society of Children's Book Writers and Illustrators. Glenn was married in 1970 and has two grown children.

My Friend's Got This Problem, Mr. Candler was named a Notable Book of the Year by the American Library Association and a Notable Children's Trade Book in the Field of Social Studies by a joint committee of the National Council on the Social Studies and the Children's Book Council.

Class Dismissed was named an Honor Book in the 1982 Golden Kite Awards presented by the Society of Children's Book Writers and Illustrators. The book was also named a Best Book for Young Adults by the ALA and an ALA "Best Books of the Best Books, 1970-1982." *Class Dismissed II* won a 1987 Christopher Award.

SELECTED WORKS: Class Dismissed: High School Poems, 1982; One Order To Go, 1984; Class Dismissed II: More High School Poems, 1986; Play-by-Play, 1986; Back to Class: Poems, 1988; Squeeze Play, 1989; My Friend's Got This Problem, Mr. Candler: High School Poems, 1991.

ABOUT: Contemporary Authors, Vol. 123; Copeland, Jeffrey S. Speaking of Poets; Something About the Author, Vol. 45, 51.

NANCY GOOR

March 27, 1944–

RON GOOR

May 31, 1940–

AUTHORS AND ILLUSTRATORS OF *Insect Metamorphosis*, etc.

Autobiographical sketch of Nancy and Ron Goor by Ron Goor:

WE ARE a team. Our collaboration began in 1967 when we met on a blind date and got married fifteen days later. Our first professional project together was the development of the Insect Zoo at the Smithsonian's Natural History Museum in Washington, D.C. While I was working as Assistant to the Director of the Natural History Museum, Nancy became the first director of the first live insect zoo in the U.S. The zoo has since become a permanent exhibit at the Smithsonian.

I began taking photos of insects and soon had built quite a large collection. Frustrated that these photos were just sitting unseen in a drawer, I wrote a children's book about insects to serve as a vehicle for the photos. I made every mistake possible in this first attempt. The most egregious error was to fictionalize a nonfiction topic. One publisher after another rejected the manuscript, but they all commented on how good the photos were. Finally, Scholastic urged me to rewrite it as nonfiction. In rewriting it I increased the grade level to that of high school/college. The Scholastic editors were horrified. Their audience was elementary school children. They suggested bringing in an experienced writer, Millicent Selsam, and the result was *Backyard Insects*.

Nancy watched the rewriting process and decided that if Millicent Selsam could do it, so could she. Little did she know that this would start her on a whole new career. Nancy does the writing, and I do the photography for our children's books, but the division of labor has never been too finely drawn. We map out a plan for a book together, establishing major themes and a point of view, and then I begin to take pictures as Nancy starts on the text. Research plays an important and often fun part in the project. It was no hardship to have to go to Pompeii several times to take the photos and explore the ruins and the artifacts in the museums. While working on *In the Driver's Seat*, we got to ride in an army tank, Nancy got to ride in an Amtrak electric engine, and I took a three-day trip in an eighteen-wheel trailer truck and even got to sleep in the bed behind the cab. With each book, as the project develops, the text begins to influence the choice of photographs, just as the photography in turn influences the text. Obviously it is most helpful to have the writer and photographer work so closely together. Besides, it's more fun that way.

Our aim in doing nonfiction books is to open children's (and adults') eyes to the wonder and beauty of our world. Some of the books are an outgrowth of my background in biology. For instance, in *Heads* and in *All Kinds of Feet*, we wanted readers to look at animals in new and fresh ways and to think about the way they are put together. Why do hippos have eyes so high on top of their heads? Why do camels have such long, thick lashes? Why do giraffes have prehensile tongues? Why do polar bears have large feet with fur on the bottom while wading birds have long toes?

Our two children (now grown up and taller than either of us) were our collaborators on all the books. They helped us by finding insects, posing for pictures, and even suggesting topics for books. For instance, *Signs* was inspired by our youngest son's remark, "I like to read signs!" We saw how he and his friends had first learned how to read—and later sharpened their reading skills—by looking at signs around the neighborhood.

———

Both Ron and Nancy Goor were born and raised in Washington, D.C. Ron graduated from Swarthmore College in 1962 and was awarded a Masters in Public Health and a Ph.D. in biochemistry from Harvard University in 1967. Nancy graduated from the University of Pennsylvania in 1965 and received an M.F.A. degree from Boston University in 1966.

The Goors have produced two books for adults on healthy eating. The fourth edition of *Eater's Choice* and the revised edition of *Choose to Lose* were both published in 1995.

Shadows: Here, There, and Everywhere was named a Notable Book of the Year by the American Library Association. *Shadows, Heads*, and *All Kinds of Feet* were named Outstanding Science Trade Books for Children by a joint committee of the National Science Teachers Association and the Children's Book Council. *In the Driver's Seat* was a Junior Library Guild selection.

Pompeii: Exploring a Ghost Town was named a Notable Children's Trade Book in the Field of Social Studies by a joint committee of the National Council on the Social Studies and the CBC. *Insect Metamorphosis* was named an Honor Book in the 1990 *Boston Globe-Horn Book* Awards, as well as an ALA Notable Book.

SELECTED WORKS WRITTEN AND ILLUSTRATED: Shadows: Here, There, and Everywhere, 1981; In the Driver's Seat, 1982; Signs, 1983; All Kinds of Feet, 1984; Pompeii: Exploring a Roman Ghost Town, 1986; Heads, 1988; Insect Metamorphosis: From Egg to Adult, 1990; Williamsburg: Cradle of the Revolution, 1994.

SELECTED WORKS WRITTEN BY MILLICENT SELSAM AND ILLUSTRATED BY RON GOOR: Backyard Insects, 1981.

ABOUT: Contemporary Authors, Vol. 113; Something About the Author, Vol. 34, 39.

SHEILA GORDON

SHEILA GORDON

January 22, 1927–

AUTHOR OF *Waiting for the Rain*, etc.

Autobiographical sketch of Sheila Gordon:

FROM THE TIME I first learned to read, reading became my consuming passion and the public library an enchanted trove stacked with treasure. Even today, I cannot walk past my local branch library, or a bookshop—especially a second-hand bookshop—without going in. I am compelled to range the shelves, just in case some wonderful treat of a book is there for me, to engage, delight, to illuminate my reading hours and my experience of this intriguing, confounding world we live in.

In all the writing I have done for children, the book is almost an icon, an object treasured for its power to transform and enrich our everyday lives.

Love of reading, of the potency of words, seemed to lead naturally to writing. On the day our youngest child went off to primary

school, I found myself at my desk writing a novel.

Growing up in South Africa, my earliest remembered impressions were of the manifest injustice of the system of apartheid. Even a young child could see that black children went barefoot, lived in hovels—hungry, without the schools or the joy of libraries which were taken for granted by children in a white society which lived in comfort and privilege. Later, I came to see that black people were also without civil rights or the most fundamental human rights, and my moral awareness was shaped by the injustice and cruelty I saw all around me.

As a university student I became involved in anti-apartheid activism, but by the time we had our own children we decided we did not want to raise them in a totalitarian society, and we came to live in New York.

Even at this distance, the struggle against apartheid remained a part of my being. The release of Nelson Mandela from twenty-seven years of imprisonment came as I was finishing *The Middle of Somewhere*, and it was gratifying to be able to end my story on a note of hope.

The books I have written about children

living under apartheid have dwelled on the deep concern I feel for children in any society, where the politics of the 'grownups' has failed them; deprived them of a safe, orderly life and the richness and rewards of books, education, and that satisfying of the curiosity and wonderment about life that is the joy and marvel of childhood.

———

Sheila Gordon was born in Johannesburg, South Africa. She received her B.A. degree in English Literature from the University of Witwatersrand in Johannesburg. She is married and has three children; her two sons are writers, and her daughter a physician.

Waiting for the Rain won the 1988 Jane Addams Children's Book Award. It was named a Notable Book of the Year and a Best Book for Young Adults by the American Library Association, as well as a Notable Children's Trade Book in the Field of Social Studies, by a joint committee of the National Council on the Social Studies and the Children's Book Council. *The Middle of Somewhere* was named an Honor Book in the same awards, in 1991.

SELECTED WORKS: A Monster in the Mailbox, 1978; Waiting for the Rain: A Novel of South Africa, 1987; The Middle of Somewhere: A Story of South Africa, 1990.

JUDITH GOROG

December 16, 1938–

AUTHOR OF *A Taste for Quiet and Other Disquieting Tales*, etc.

Autobiographical sketch of Judith Gorog:

ALTHOUGH I love to read about the lives of others, I hate writing about myself. What sort of heroine is a boring, easily discouraged kid? Called clumsy, I retreated in misery from sports until I was in college. I quit drawing in sixth grade when a teacher criti-

cized my work. Giving up on everything else gave me lots of time to daydream and to read, which I did, making heavy use of the San Leandro Public Library, and later the libraries in San Lorenzo, and in Wiesbaden, Germany, where we moved when I was sixteen. I read and I babysat, saving money for college, which I was sure would be the life of books, ideas, and friendship that I sought. (It was.) Wiesbaden, which was a spa even in Roman times, was a small and beautiful city, with gardens (some of the fountains froze into ice cascades in winter), tree-lined streets on which to walk, shop windows, a huge library, a museum. There was a new language, cafes and coffee houses, parks, music, dance, and dancing at Fasching. There were three nights of parties every year before the beginning of the Lenten fast. Normally exceedingly thrifty, I used a portion of my college savings to take horseback riding (Dressage) lessons. Public transportation, both local and to other cities, was cheap and convenient. Also, I explored on a motor scooter piloted by a classmate, Carole, who had lived in Paris for three years. Her French was excellent, my German pretty good. Across the river, in Mainz, there was real jazz, played by Americans who had stayed after WWII.

I graduated from high school, then went to work, taking some college classes at night. Wiesbaden was headquarters for the U.S. Air Force in Europe, with many low-paying clerical jobs, some reserved for U.S. citizens. During that year, someone running programs for the American community decided it would be a fine thing to have a homecoming queen for a Football game (American football, not soccer, played by athletes serving in the military. This was the olden days). Not one girl or woman signed up to be a contestant for the queen, but someone working in a nearby office put in my name, and so I "won" the position. It was embarrassing beyond belief. After that, the director of a small English language theatre group asked me to read for a part. I did, and performed in *Picnic*. The play even had some kissing scenes, which, because I thought the hero was old, I found pretty gross. The director and the other actors, some of whom had been professionals in the theatre, taught me all they could about makeup, about how to move on stage, and how a person five feet and eleven inches tall might move more or less gracefully when not on stage. It cannot be claimed that I acted in the part, though I did memorize my lines and move about on the stage.

I returned to California, planning to get a degree in English, teach, and write. I also thought that eventually I would get married and have children and that I would give my children such a perfect childhood and so much encouragement that they would never ever fail, never feel bad about themselves. Wow.

Well, I worked my way through college as a lifeguard/swimming instructor, a playground director in Alameda, California, and as a scanner/librarian in the Lawrence Radiation Laboratory in Berkeley. After my M.A., I worked as a science and technical writer and editor. I am married, and have written some books, and do have three children, who say, "Ease up on the encouragement, mom; it is so much PRESSURE!!"

At this point in life I have concluded (1) that for some of us being an adult is a whole lot more fun than being a child was; (2) that most European cities are more fun for children and adults (rich or poor) than suburbs are anywhere; and (3) that aside from democratic ideals, the U.S.A. has given two outstanding gifts to the world: Public Libraries—especially the children's sections, and jeans in all incarnations.

Among the first readers of my books were a number of storytellers. They have drawn readers to the books, and have enriched my life with their other stories, so that the telling of the stories is very much in my mind when I write. For my readers I hope the stories make them laugh, tickle their curiosity, and open some doors within their own imaginations.

———

Judith Gorog was born in Madison, Wisconsin. She attended San Jose State College from 1957 to 1959, and received her B.A. degree from the University of California at Berkeley in 1961. She earned an M.A. degree from Mills College in 1963. She has worked as a writer and editor, as a production editor and writer at RCA-Astro Electronics, and has also worked as a park director.

Gorog's stories appear in many anthologies, including *100 Great Fantasy Short Short Stories* edited by Isaac Asimov. She is a member of PEN, the Authors Guild, and the Society of Children's Book Writers and Illustrators.

SELECTED WORKS: A Taste for Quiet and Other Disquieting Tales, 1982; Caught in the Turtle, 1983; No Swimming in Dark Pond and Other Chilling Tales, 1987; Three Dreams and a Nightmare and Other Tales of the Dark, 1988; In a Messy, Messy Room, 1990; On Meeting Witches at Wells, 1991.

ABOUT: Contemporary Authors, Vol. 114; Something About the Author, Vol. 39.

HOWARD GREENFELD

August 1, 1928–

AUTHOR OF *Books: From Writer to Reader*, etc.

Autobiographical sketch of Howard Greenfeld:

I SPENT my childhood in New Rochelle, New York and moved to New York City at the age of thirteen. After graduation from high school, I felt the need for a change and headed west for the University of Kansas. Restless after a year there, I moved on to the University of Chicago, where I also remained for just one year. Finally, I completed my M.A. at Columbia University. Throughout these years, the one thing that remained constant was my fascination with the written word; and more specifically with the world of books.

Upon graduation from Columbia, I spent almost a year in Rome, Italy, where I taught English at a Berlitz school. After returning to New York, I went to work in the editorial department of Random House, learning from some of the greatest of all editors and publishers—Bennett Cerf, Donald Klopfer, and Saxe Commins. After a few years, however, my restlessness returned. I wanted to strike out on my own—and away from New York. So I moved to Florence, Italy, where, in partnership with a young Italian editor I had met through my work, I founded a small publishing house, The Orion Press. Our goal was an ambitious one: to publish English-language translations of serious works of European literature, beautifully produced at reasonable prices. (At that time, printing, binding, and overhead expenses were considerably lower in Europe than they were in the United States.)

Though we were badly undercapitalized, we managed to remain in business for eight years, and I remain very proud of the books we published. Among these were the first translation into English of Primo Levi's *If This Is a Man* (also known as *Survival in Auschwitz*), Italo Calvino's *Italian Fables*, several works by the great Tunisian-French sociologist Albert Memmi, screenplays by Federico Fellini, Jean Cocteau, and René Clair, and several works by Jean Piaget. (During this time, I myself translated Memmi's *The Colonizer and the Colonized* from the French and Fellini's *Juliet of the Spirits* from the Italian.)

In the end, out of financial necessity, Orion was sold—first to a small house and then to a larger one. I worked as editor for both and for another publishing house, but I did so with little enthusiasm; I wanted to retain my independence. Because of this, I was very grateful to be offered the chance to write a book of my own—a biography of Marc Chagall for young adults. I had worked with the painter on the publication of his early autobiography in the United States, we had become friends, and he had frequently suggested that I write a book

about him. Though I was apprehensive about my ability to write such a book—or any book, for that matter, for I was an editor and publisher and not an author—I accepted the challenge.

I never dreamed that this would be merely the first of nearly twenty-five books that I have written—over the next twenty-five years, during which I lived in Paris, in a small village in Tuscany, Italy, and, finally, in Princeton, New Jersey, where I now live with my wife Paola and our son, Daniel. A number of these books were written for young adults. They include biographies of Picasso, Gertrude Stein, F. Scott Fitzgerald, and the Impressionist painters; a book about Gypsies, and a series of short books about the Jewish holidays; a study of the many phases of book publishing, *Books: From Writer to Reader*; and *The Hidden Children*, first-hand accounts of Jewish children who had to go into hiding in order to save their lives during the Holocaust. Over the past ten years, I have written three adult biographies: Puccini, based largely on hundreds of previously unpublished letters to and from the composer which I discovered in Italy; Caruso, written with the encouragement of the great tenor's son; and *The Devil and Dr. Barnes*, a controversial biography of a brilliant eccentric Philadelphia art collector.

Howard Greenfeld received his B.A. degree in 1951 and his M.A. in 1952. *Gertrude Stein* was selected for the Children's Book Showcase in 1974. *Books: From Writer to Reader* appeared in the 1976 American Institute of Graphic Arts Show and was named a Junior Library Guild selection.

SELECTED WORKS: Marc Chagall, 1967 (rev. ed., 1981); Pablo Picasso: An Introduction, 1971; Gertrude Stein: A Biography, 1973; F. Scott Fitzgerald, 1974; They Came to Paris, 1975; Books: From Writer to Reader, 1976; Gypsies, 1977; Passover, 1978; Rosh Hashanah and Yom Kippur, 1979; The Hidden Children, 1993; Paul Gauguin, 1993.

ABOUT: Contemporary Authors, Vol. 81-84; (New

Revision Series), Vol. 19; Publishers Weekly September 3, 1973; Something About the Author, Vol. 19.

HELEN V. GRIFFITH

October 31, 1934–

AUTHOR OF *Georgia Music*, etc.

Autobiographical sketch of Helen Virginia Griffith:

WHEN I was little, I used to like to play office. I had an old adding machine, a broken telephone, and a tablet of colored sheets of paper. It was fun to speak on the phone and jot down notes.

I used to jot down stories, too, and poems, and in second grade I produced and directed a play that my teacher let us perform for the class. I never took writing seriously though, and when I grew up I got a job in an office. A real office was as much fun as my play office—more, because the equipment really worked.

After about twenty years of clerical work in various offices I began to feel the urge to do something more creative, something that came from inside myself. I had always been a compulsive course taker, and now the courses I chose were concerned with artistic expression—painting, pottery, and finally a course called Writing for Magazines. The course didn't teach you how to write, as I had expected. Rather, it focused on marketing. Until then, I hadn't the vaguest idea how manuscripts got into magazines. Everything the teacher told us was a revelation to me. I followed his directions and sold an article. It wasn't long before I found that I preferred writing fiction, as I had when I was a child, so that's what I started doing.

My writing was a hobby at first. I would write things on my lunch hour and mail them out. If they came back, it didn't matter. I read them over and, if I still liked them, I sent them out again.

I sold some things to magazines and then

Susan Hirschman at Greenwillow Books bought my first book, *Mine Will, Said John*. That was in 1980 and the manuscript had been on the road for three years. All of the books that I have had published since have been by Greenwillow Books.

I still work in an office. My occupation is still officially clerk or secretary. The fact that there are books out there with my name on the cover is amazing to me. I feel very lucky.

———

Helen Griffith was born in Wilmington, Delaware, and has lived there all her life. She works in the family business, a distributor of roofing and siding. She and her brother raise alpacas and now have a herd of twenty-five. She is a member of the Authors Guild.

Mine Will, Said John was named a Children's Choice Book by a joint committee of the International Reading Association and the Children's Book Council. *Georgia Music* was a Reading Rainbow Book and was an Honor Book in the 1987 *Boston Globe-Horn Book* Awards. Her three books about Alex were all named Junior Library Guild selections.

SELECTED WORKS: Mine Will, Said John, 1980; Alex and the Cat, 1982; More Alex and the Cat, 1983; Foxy, 1984; Georgia Music, 1986; Grandaddy's Place, 1987; Caitlin's Holiday, 1990; Grandaddy and Janetta, 1993; Dream Meadow, 1994; Grandaddy's Stars, 1995.

ABOUT: Contemporary Authors, Vol. 105; (New Revision Series), Vol. 22; McElmeel, Sharron. Bookpeople: A Multicultural Album; Something About the Author, Vol. 39; Teaching Pre-K January 1990.

"MWENYE HADITHI"

September 21, 1950–

AUTHOR OF *Crafty Chameleon*, etc.

Autobiographical sketch of Bruce Hobson, who writes under the pen name "Mwenye Hadithi":

I WAS BORN in Nairobi in a rambling brick and wood house surrounded by ten acres, one of which was garden, the other nine just wild bush and forest leading down to the river. It was a child's paradise for exploration; impala and dik-dik were often startled out of the bushes late in the evening, and porcupines and wart-hog were regular visitors.

A crocodile wandered up to the house early one morning and we had to call the park wardens to come and take it away, since my father wanted his breakfast and my mother refused to cross the main courtyard to the kitchen because the animal was asleep by the ironing board. My most vivid animal memory of that time was having been read *Winnie-the-Pooh* in the evening , then waking up to go to the bathroom late at night and seeing a Heffalump stuck in the courtyard entrance. I woke my elder brother and together we crept up on it in terrified excitement. It was a hippopotamus, which had been scratching itself on the rough brick of the gate pillars, and then had got itself stuck in the gateway!

My early life was full of animals. Even when I was sent off to boarding school when I was seven, the school grounds were a ha-

ven for all sorts of beasts. We would coax huge fat tarantula-like spiders out of their holes by tickling them with bits of grass, and keep them in our desks as pets. Once a huge troop of marauding baboons ventured across the hockey pitch, snarling and screaming. It was a fairly terrifying sight, but in no time there was a counter attack from small boys armed with hockey sticks and stones, and the attack-and-retreat war lasted much of the afternoon. Now the city has spread and most of the bush is gone, but still monkeys invade the gardens, porcupines and mongooses make nocturnal raids on city gardens, and recently we had the unnerving experience of one night finding the mouse-trap had disappeared altogether with a mouse in it, and the next night hearing the piano being played in the middle of the night *all by itself!* It turned out that the keyboard was on a genet cat's route into the kitchen, where we watched the perfectly beautiful animal flowing like water over the shelves and tables, completely unafraid, looking for more of those easy-to-catch mice!

At thirteen I went to Rugby School in England, where there wasn't a lot in the way of animals except us boys, and the freezing

Mwenye Hadithi: *Ma WEN yeh Ha DEE thee*

cold soon had me longing to be home. From there I attended London University, studying languages and uncertain what I was going to do with myself. The study of foreign literature was the one school subject in which I found genuine pleasure, and when my first attempts at short stories and radio plays were sold immediately I decided to be the next great African Writer. I soon found out that even if you have some measure of success, writing doesn't pay the bills.

Back to Kenya, where I reluctantly took a job in an office to show my parents how all that education had not been wasted, but office work soon palled, so I gave up my job as a Conference Coordinator after two years, and moved with my future wife to her family's house on the coast, which had been built by Denis Finch-Hatton miles from anywhere, in absolute paradise. It was the sort of place where all the most exciting children's adventures have taken place since the beginning of time: private beach, the only neighbour for miles a snake-collector, basking sharks jumping in the giant swimming-pool of a creek, eerie happenings almost every night, with an extensive slave-village ruins behind the house buildings, and secret tunnels, now mostly filled with sand, running from the beach under the cliffs to the ruins themselves.

Of course, it wasn't the place to do any actual work. So a year or so later we moved back to Nairobi, where I started a gardening business and wrote for fun. As soon as I had given up on being a writer and the business was becoming successful, *Greedy Zebra* was published, and that was the start of the Mwenye Hadithi (which simply means a story-teller in Swahili) animal series.

Between writing novels, I had begun the animal studies primarily as a vehicle for the pictures of the artist Adrienne Kennaway, whose vivid drawings seemed ideal for children's illustrations. It also seemed that the children of Africa were being won over by imported lifestyles, by popstars and fizzy drinks, and none of them listened any more to the old stories which would traditionally have been told round a fire or at celebration. The telling of such a story was a great art, and in the story well-known characters of the village with a particular weakness might appear, thinly disguised as animals, and the story would take the form of a moral lesson. I read through many collections of oral literature and at first tried to present these African stories in a way which would appeal to Western children, but editors would unfailingly reject the traditional stories as they stood. So I began to make up my own myths, borrowing here and there from the old stories, and these were immediately successful. Of all the books, *Hot Hippo* is the closest to a traditional story (and incidentally my favourite). I still get very excited when letters arrive from children worldwide who have enjoyed one of my stories enough to tell me about it.

Now my daughter is eight I have begun to write for an older age-group, adventure stories and the like, but I hope the Hadithi stories continue to appear.

———

Mwenye Hadithi received a B.A. degree with honors from Queen Mary College in London in 1973. He was married in 1979 and has one daughter.

Crafty Chameleon won the 1987 Kate Greenaway Medal awarded by the British Library Association. *Hot Hippo* was named a Children's Choice Book by a joint committee of the International Reading Association and the Children's Book Council.

Greedy Zebra was made into an audio recording in 1985, produced by Revallee Studios. *Hot Hippo* was made into a filmstrip in 1987 by Weston Woods.

SELECTED WORKS: Greedy Zebra, 1984; Hot Hippo, 1986; Crafty Chameleon, 1987; Tricky Tortoise, 1988; Lazy Lion, 1990; Baby Baboon, 1993; Hungry Hyena, 1994.

ABOUT: Something About the Author, Vol. 62.

MARTIN HANDFORD

September 27, 1956–

AUTHOR AND ILLUSTRATOR OF *Where's Waldo?*, etc.

Biographical sketch of Martin John Handford:

MARTIN HANDFORD was born in London, England. He was an only child and lived with his mother, who was a nurse. He drew pictures everywhere they went—even while riding on buses and trains. When he drew a picture of an army of thousands of soldiers, he drew *all* of them. He worked on crowd scenes and battlefield sketches, drawing his inspiration from the books and comics he liked.

As an adult, he learned that the artists of the comics he liked to read in the 1960's are Ronald and Jerry Embleton. He also liked history books and historical films, one favorite of which is *The Alamo*. He admired several illustrators, H. Charles McBarron, who illlustrated military subjects, and Cornelius De Witt, who illustrated a children's book called *The History of the World*. He also admired Norman Rockwell.

After graduating from school, Handford worked for three years for an insurance office. This allowed him to obtain a full state grant for college course work. He then attended the Maidstone College of Art, and received a B.A. degree in 1980. Around this time he also spent some time in a punk rock band, as a singer and dancer.

After graduating, he began a career as a freelance illustrator. He did magazine illustration and book jackets, and worked for advertising agencies. His famous and successful book illustrating career came about when David Bennett, an art director at Walker Books in England, called him in after seeing Handford's artwork in magazines. They sat down with his portfolio of crowd scenes and developed the idea of placing a recognizable figure within the scenes.

In all of the Waldo books, a somewhat goofy figure can be found among the hundreds of tiny figures in a huge crowd scene. The enjoyment of the book is to find the figure in each large double-page spread.

The character is Waldo in America, but he is named Wally in England, Walter in Germany, Charlie in France, and Holger in Denmark. Over thirteen million copies of the books have been sold worldwide. The popularity of the series has resulted in spin-off books such as miniature books and books of Waldo posters; and hundreds of products, such as dolls and lunchboxes with the Waldo figure, have been licensed. An animated television show was created for the CBS television network.

Handford creates the books in his home studio, where he listens to reruns of his favorite old television show, Sergeant Bilko, or his beloved tapes by the BeeGees. He awakes about one o'clock in the afternoon, and once he starts to work, he works until about five o'clock in the morning. He creates a drawing by starting to draw with pen on the left side of an empty sheet of paper. With minimal preliminiary drawing, he inks in an area, then fills in the color with watercolor on a paintbrush. Then he outlines the next segment. It takes him a month to complete each of the twelve spreads in a book.

Among the children's book illustrators he admires are Richard Scarry and Mitsumasa Anno. Handford lives in England.

Where's Waldo? (as *Where's Wally?*) was a runnerup for the 1988 Mother Goose Award given by the British book club "Books for Children."

SELECTED WORKS: Where's Waldo?, 1987; Find Waldo Now!, 1988; The Great Waldo Search, 1989; Where's Waldo?: The Ultimate Fun Book, 1990; Where's Waldo?: The Magnificent Poster Book, 1991; Where's Waldo? in Hollywood, 1993.

ABOUT: Biography Today January 1992; Contemporary Authors, Vol. 137; Newsweek August 13, 1990; People Weekly November 11, 1991; Something About the Author, Vol. 64.

DENNIS HASELEY

June 28, 1950–

AUTHOR OF *The Old Banjo*, etc.

Autobiographical sketch of Dennis Haseley:

I WAS brought up in Broadview Heights, Ohio, an area that changed during my childhood from a rural township to a suburb of Cleveland. My father was always doing clever woodworking or carpentry projects; and my mother read a lot to us when we were young, even adult authors like J.D. Salinger and Thomas Wolfe, that she edited as she went along. In part because of the examples of my parents, I became interested in not just the regular boyhood things like bicycling and baseball, but also creative projects. My brother and I performed our own radio plays on our reel-to-reel tape recorder, and did skits for the family 8 mm movie camera.

I wrote my first poem when I was seven or eight. It was about a cuckoo clock (I don't know why—we didn't have one), and I knew it was a poem because every other line rhymed. I found it a couple of years ago, on the top of a closet in the same home where I spent my childhood. It's printed out in these big block letters that slant down the page, and I can almost remember writing it and showing it to my parents, these ordinary words I had put together that actually made a rhyme, and became something that was new.

I read a lot throughout school. There was great magic in going into fictional worlds, as well as sadness when the book was ending, and I knew I would have to say goodbye to the characters I had to come to know so well.

I began writing poetry and prose with some seriousness at Oberlin College, where I was a literature major and a student in creative writing seminars. I had the opportunity junior year to live in New York City for a semester as an apprentice to an established novelist and screenwriter. It was a great way to learn: I had a lot of time to

DENNIS HASELEY

write, and the opportunity for my work to be read and critiqued regularly by a professional author.

Following graduation from Oberlin, my poetry was published in a number of small magazines. I noticed that although my poems used "poetic" images and devices, my real interest seemed to be in using this form to tell stories. At about the same time, I happened upon a number of terrific picture books for children, and I began to feel that there were intriguing possibilities in this form to use both narration and the suggestion of images that could be expanded upon by illustrators.

Happily, several editors liked my work. *The Pirate Who Tried to Capture the Moon* and *The Old Banjo* were my first books published. I continued (and continue) to write the stories for picture books, and about nine years ago, began writing novels.

In addition to my writing, I have a career as a psychotherapist, with an M.S.W. from New York University, as well as postmaster's training. It's no accident that I'm very drawn to understanding and expressing the inner worlds of my characters. I feel very much that the two fields I have chosen for my life's work have many parallel elements, and serve to enhance one another.

Haseley: *HASE ley*

I often start a story—whether for a picture book or a novel—with an image or a metaphor that captures me. For instance, for a recent novel, *Dr. Gravity*, it was the idea of a town that could float. Another novel, *Shadows*, began when I came upon a reprinted 19th-century book instructing the reader how to make various hand shadows. My upcoming picture book, called *Crosby*, came out of the single image of a boy flying a rather bedraggled kite. Starting with one key, evocative image, I try to reach in some way into my own experiences and emotions and build a story that becomes for the reader—and for me—something that's new.

———

Dennis Haseley received his A.B. degree from Oberlin College in Ohio in 1972 and his M.S.W. degree from New York University in 1982. He is a psychotherapist and has been writing since 1982. He was married in 1986. He has also worked as a professional fund raiser and a community organizer. His work is represented in the De Grummond Collection at the University of Southern Mississippi.

The Old Banjo was a Junior Library Guild selection and a Reading Rainbow Book. It was adapted into an audio tape and filmstrip by Random House in 1986. *The Cave of Snores* was adapted for television; it was an episode of TV Ontario's series for children, "Return to the Magic Library."

Kite Flier was named a Notable Children's Trade Book in the Field of Social Studies by a joint committee of the National Council on the Social Studies and the Children's Book Council. Haseley was a speaker at the Northern California Children's Booksellers Association in 1991.

SELECTED WORKS: The Counterfeiter, 1982; The Old Banjo, 1983; The Pirate Who Tried to Capture the Moon, 1983; Kite Flier, 1986; The Cave of Snores, 1987; My Father Doesn't Know About the Woods and Me, 1988; Ghost Catcher, 1991; The Thieves' Market, 1991; Shadows, 1992; Dr. Gravity, 1992; Horses with Wings, 1993; Getting Him, 1994.

ABOUT: Something About the Author, Vol. 44, 57.

JUANITA HAVILL

May 11, 1949–

AUTHOR OF *Jamaica's Find*, etc.

Autobiographical sketch of Juanita Havill:

I GREW UP in a small town in Southern Illinois. I didn't know that there had been a writer in my family until long after I had made the decision to become one. At first, I wanted to be a poet. I wrote poems that rhymed in grade school, happy poems and poems about the seasons and holidays and animals. In high school and college I wrote blank and free verse that helped me get through difficult times. I still write poetry.

Around eighth grade I started to write a novel about a girl who achieved her dream of traveling to England. It didn't matter to me that I had never been to England. Going to the country where my mother's family came from was one of my dreams and therefore as likely a setting as any for my first novel. I never finished it. By the time I got to high school I had turned my attention to journalism. Journalism has changed a great deal since then. It was "just the facts" at the time, and I learned how difficult it is to write objectively and how important accuracy is. As editor-in-chief of the high school paper, I enjoyed writing opinion pieces as well. The local newspaper even hired me, but not to report the news of the day. My first duty was to collect money from newspaper carriers every Saturday morning. Then I was promoted to editing the "counties," which were reports of happenings in the smaller towns around the county: weddings and family reunions for the most part, handwritten in indecipherable ink scrawls that I had to type very cautiously. I knew that putting the wrong-colored sash on a bridesmaid's gown would result in an angry complaint by the "reporter," as well as the readers who were present for the wedding.

While riffling through old newspapers, I came across a column that my great-grandfather Frank W. Havill had written.

Juanita Havill

Although I knew that he had been publisher of the town newspaper and a prominent citizen, I had no idea that he had spent his younger years writing stories about his hometown under the pen name "Bourbon." Perhaps that is where my need to put words on paper came from.

Love of books came from my mother and her family. I cannot remember a time when books were not piled high on the marble-topped coffee table in her living room, volumes and volumes, from book clubs and the local library. The library was a second home to me, especially in summer when the air conditioning afforded relief from the sultry, oppressive days, and the drinking fountain offered the coldest water fountain water in town—so cold it hurt your teeth. Once I made a vow to myself to read every book in the library, which was frustrating for two reasons. Children weren't allowed to check out books from the adult section, and the library kept acquiring new books. I tried anyway. I had read in a Robert Browning poem that "man's goal is always higher than his reach/or what's a heaven for?" and I figured that the library with all of its books came very close to being my unattainable goal of heaven.

Reading and writing became a part of my life, and I naturally chose English as a major in college. On the way to getting a B. A., I managed to achieve my dream of traveling to England, by way of France, where I studied for a year. Later, I returned to France, and married, and my daughter was born there. Just before my son's birth in 1978, we returned to Southern Illinois and a year later moved to Minnesota.

In Minnesota I became a writer, a working writer, and I began to submit my poems and stories for publication. Small press publications accepted my poems and large publishing houses sent me pleasant rejection letters. Then I took the first writing course I had ever taken, "Writing for children," taught by Emilie Buchwald, author, editor, publisher, professor, and friend, who made writing books for young readers seem possible. I will always be grateful. I believe, as a writer, that it is the element of the possible that frees us even as we set impossible goals.

From that time, I believe it was the spring of 1981, I have not stopped writing for young readers. Houghton Mifflin published my first book *Jamaica's Find* in 1986 and Crown brought out my first middle-grade novel in 1989, *It Always Happens to Leona*. Both books are about contemporary children in the U. S., children I hope my readers will recognize.

I love writing. I can't imagine doing anything else. In fact, when I drive or go on walks with my dog Victor, when I cook or iron or travel, I am writing. I am looking at landscapes, meeting people, noticing details, or simply remembering things that will appear in my stories. A writer's mind is not like a camera or a tape recorder or for that matter, a TV. You can't switch it off. Thank heavens!

———

Juanita Havill was born in Evansville, Indiana. She grew up in Mt. Carmel, a small Southern Illinois town on the Wabash River. She studied English at the University of Illinois at Urbana-Champaign, earning a

B.A. degree in 1971. She earned an M.A. degree in French there in 1973, and went to Paris to live. She attended the Universite de Rouen from 1969 to 1970. There she taught English and did translations and worked in the personnel department of the Organisation for Economic Co-operation and Development.

She is a member of the Writers' Guild and the Society of Children's Book Writers and Illustrators. She has written stories and articles for numerous children's magazines such as *Cricket*, and her poetry has been published by small presses. She also teaches writing courses to adults and children and lectures on children's literature.

Jamaica's Find won the 1987 Ezra Jack Keats New Writer Award and was a Reading Rainbow Book. It was named a Children's Choice Book by a joint committee of the Children's Book Council and the International Reading Association.

Sato and the Elephants was named a Notable Children's Trade Book in the Field of Social Studies by a joint committee of the National Council on the Social Studies and the CBC. The American Library Association named it a Notable Book of the Year.

SELECTED WORKS: Jamaica's Find, 1986; Leroy and the Clock, 1988; It Always Happens to Leona, 1989; Jamaica Tag-Along, 1989; Leona and Ike, 1990; The Magic Fort, 1991; The Treasure Nap, 1992; Jamaica and Brianna, 1993; Kentucky Troll, 1993; Sato and the Elephants, 1993; Jennifer, Too, 1994; Saving Owen's Toad, 1994; Jamaica's Blue Marker, 1995.

ABOUT: Something About the Author, Vol. 74.

KEVIN HAWKES

August 28, 1959–

ILLUSTRATOR OF *By the Light of the Halloween Moon*, etc.

Autobiographical sketch of Kevin Hawkes:

SOMETIMES I have trouble remembering when I first wanted to become an artist. It

must have been in the third grade, when I realized that my career goal of becoming a cowboy was in serious trouble. I think I won an art contest that year. Monster of the month or something. At any rate, it was about then that I started thinking that I really liked drawing and painting. I was big on paper-mâché too. The things I used to cart home on the bus. One time I made a life-size figure of a mountaineer, complete with cardboard climbing axe. I made him sitting down. He sat next to me on the bus when I brought him home. My mother and father were very supportive of my artistic efforts. My mother kept a folder of all my art projects, except the large sculptures that ended up in closets, under beds and in the garage. She bought me a set of oil paints when I was twelve and signed me up for painting lessons with a neighbor. I still remember that first oil painting of a tree, a lake, and some mountains. Boy, was it awful, but I did have a lot of fun using the paint. I still do, as a matter of fact.

Pretty soon I was painting and drawing a lot of things that I felt strongly about. The woods, rivers, wildlife, castles. My father had been stationed in France as an Air Force officer and so I had this thing about castles. Stairways in particular. I remember climbing the leaning tower of Pisa with my father and my three brothers. That was a set of stairs! Circular all the way to the top. I loved not knowing what was around the next curve.

I guess you could say that I had a well-rounded childhood. None of us specialized right away. Mom and Dad made sure we had exposure to a lot of things; music, sports, art, camping, travelling. I think this interest in everything contributed to my wanting to become an illustrator. I couldn't see drawing or painting the same thing all the time as very interesting, which is probably why I ended up illustrating picture books. There is always something different happening. One day I'm illustrating ghosts and trolls and the next day it's camels and Greek temples.

I graduated from Utah State University with a degree in illustration, then moved to Boston, where I visited publishing houses and told editors that I wanted to illustrate children's books. "What kind of children's books?" they asked. I gave them blank stares in response. So I went to work at a bookstore and spent a lot of time looking at picture books. I also started to paint in a completely different way than I had at college. After many trips to New York City, I got a wonderful break and found a publisher who loved my work.

Ever since, things have been busy. I love color, rich, dense, beautiful color. Light and shadow are a big part of my work as well as movement. It seems that all of my characters come from places where the lampposts are never straight, the hills impossibly steep and the skies impossibly blue. I love to tell stories through my artwork and transport young readers to new and unusual places.

———

Kevin Hawkes was born in Sherman, Texas. He received a B.A. degree from Utah State University in 1985. Married in 1982, he has three children. The family now lives in Maine. He is a member of the Society of Children's Writers and Illustrators.

By the Light of the Halloween Moon won a 1993 Golden Kite Award from the Society of Children's Writers and Illustrators. Four books by Kevin Hawkes have been shown at exhibitions at the Society of Illustrators, including *The Nose* and *The Turnip.* Hawkes contributed an illustration to *The Greatest Table* by Michael J. Rosen, a compilation created to benefit the hunger relief organization Share Our Strength. It was a Book-of-the-Month Club selection.

SELECTED WORKS WRITTEN AND ILLUSTRATED: Then the Troll Heard the Squeak, 1991; His Royal Buckliness, 1992.

SELECTED WORKS ILLUSTRATED: Lady Bugatti, by Joyce Maxner, 1991; The Turnip, by Walter de la Mare, 1992; By the Light of the Halloween Moon, by Caroline Stutson, 1993; The Librarian Who Measured the Earth, by Kathryn Lasky, 1994; The Nose, by Nicholai Gogal, retold by Catherine Cowan, 1994; The Enormous Snore, by M.L. Miller, 1995.

ABOUT: Contemporary Authors, Vol. 135; Publishers Weekly July 5, 1991; Something About the Author, Vol. 78.

RUTH HELLER

April 2, 1924–

AUTHOR AND ILLUSTRATOR OF *Chickens Aren't the Only Ones*, etc.

Biographical sketch of Ruth M. Heller:

RUTH HELLER was born in Winnipeg, Manitoba in Canada. She moved to San Francisco at the age of eleven. Artistic as a child, she copied comic strips from the newspaper, and added "illustrations" to her school reports. However, she was not able to study art until she was in the upper grades.

She received her B.A. degree from the University of California at Berkeley in Fine Arts in 1946. She worked as a medical secre-

RUTH HELLER

tary from 1949 to 1953, and was married in 1951. She raised two sons, and later attended the California College of Arts and Crafts in Oakland, from 1963 to 1965. She began her career as a designer and illustrator in 1967, creating designs for products such as wrapping paper, cocktail napkins, kites, and greeting cards. Then she designed posters for Creative Playthings. She moved on to create coloring books for several publishers. While at an aquarium doing research for a coloring book, she noticed in the tank the egg sac of a dogfish shark. This discovery intrigued her, and led her to do research into other egg-laying animals. She then wrote her first book for children, *Chickens Aren't the Only Ones.* Heller believes that children enjoy and understand books of substance, but it wasn't easy for her to sell her book to publishers. It took her five years and many rejections. Her book was written in rhyme, and some publishers thought that if children were old enough to understand the information, they would be too old for the picture-book approach. However, she remembers reading Dr. Seuss books to her sons when they were children, and thinks that rhyme can help children remember what they read. She also thinks it adds en-

joyment. A *Horn Book* reviewer agrees, stating that Heller treats her subject "with elaborate playfulness." Several other writers who have influenced her writing are Ogden Nash, Gilbert and Sullivan, Edward Lear, and Hilaire Belloc.

She revised the book in 1980 at Yaddo, a writers' retreat in Saratoga Springs, New York. It was published in 1981, and was named a 1983 Younger Honor Book in the New York Academy of Sciences Children's Science Book Awards. Her publisher also has had it translated into Spanish, as *Las gallinas no son las únicas.*

She wrote a sequel to the book, called *Animals Born Alive and Well,* which was published the next year. Illustrations from the book were exhibited at the Bologna International Children's Book Fair in 1983. Her next book, *The Reason for a Flower,* was about plants that have seeds and flowers; she then wrote *Plants that Never Ever Bloom,* about plants that do not have seeds or flowers. *Reason . . .* was a Reading Rainbow selection, as was her *A Cache of Jewels,* a book in a series written about the parts of speech.

She has illustrated several books written by Shirley Climo, *The Egyptian Cinderella* and *The Korean Cinderella,* the latter of which she researched by travelling to Korea. Both books were named Notable Children's Trade Books in the Field of Social Studies by a joint committee of the National Council for the Social Studies and the Children's Book Council, in 1990 and 1994 respectively. *King of the Birds,* which she illustrated, was also NCSS/CBC book, in 1989.

It takes Heller a year to produce a book. She loves to work hard. Many days, she leaves her home on Russian Hill in San Francisco and spends the entire day in her studio, which is at the bottom of Telegraph Hill, with a view of the bay. She may begin at 6:30 in the morning and not leave until 9:00 at night. Because she doesn't have a scientific background, she works diligently on her research for her books about science.

She takes photographs at the zoo, and keeps files of photographs, making her drawings of animals from them. She consults with scientific advisors to check the accuracy of her work. She is a member of Authors Guild, The Society of Children's Book Writers and Illustrators, the San Francisco Society of Illustrators, and the New York Society of Illustrators.

She lives with her husband and travels, among other places, to Marbella, Spain, where she bought a condominium. She enjoys tennis, swimming, and cooking, and keeps a journal for ideas, which she thinks is very important. She speaks at children's literature conferences, such as the 1989 19th Children's Literature Institute at the College of Education and Allied Professions at the University of Toledo.

SELECTED WORKS WRITTEN AND ILLUSTRATED: Chickens Aren't the Only Ones, 1981; Animals Born Alive and Well, 1982; The Reason for a Flower, 1983; Plants That Never Ever Bloom, 1984; How to Hide a Polar Bear and Other Mammals, 1985; A Cache of Jewels and Other Collective Nouns, 1987; Kites Sail High: A Book About Verbs, 1988; Many Luscious Lollipops: A Book About Adjectives, 1989; Merry-Go-Round: A Book About Nouns, 1990; Color, Color, Color, Color, 1995.

SELECTED WORKS ILLUSTRATED: King of the Birds, by Shirley Climo, 1987; The Egyptian Cinderella, by Shirley Climo, 1989; The Korean Cinderella, by Shirley Climo, 1993; Blue Potatoes, Orange Tomatoes by Rosalind Creasy, 1993; King Solomon and the Bee by Dalia Hardof Renberg, 1994.

ABOUT: Contemporary Authors, Vol. 130; Something About the Author, Vol. 66.

B.G. HENNESSEY

March 10, 1951–

AUTHOR OF *Jake Baked the Cake*, etc.

Biographical sketch of Barbara Gulbrandsen Hennessey:

B.G. HENNESSEY was born in New York City and grew up in Long Island, New

B. G. Hennessey

York. She has always loved books, and wrote her first one, *Patsy and the Turtle*, when she was five years old.

She attended St. Lawrence University and graduated from the University of Wisconsin in Madison in 1973. She was a fine arts major, and while at school, she ran a small private press, designing and printing broadsides. She also took children's literature courses. She was married in 1971.

After she graduated, she and her husband went to New York City, where she worked for seventeen years as a book designer and an art director of children's books. She worked at Dial Books for Young Readers, at Crown Books, and at Viking. She was also art director of Puffin Books and of Frederick Warne from time to time. Some of the authors and illustrators whom she worked with are Don Freeman, Robert McCloskey, Barbara Cooney, and James Marshall.

Hennessey is married and has three sons. She began writing books when her first child was learning language. The first was *A, B, C, D, Tummy, Toes, Hands, Knees*; however, several of her other manuscripts were published first. As an art director, she was interested to see which manuscripts were intriguing to the artists who illustrated them. As a writer, she composes her stories from a visual point of view, trying to give the illustrator material to work with.

In 1990, the family moved first to California, and then to Arizona. She occasionally visits classrooms in the area and reads from the book she wrote when she was five, which she still has.

The Dinosaur Who Lived in My Backyard was named a Children's Choice Book by a joint committee of the Children's Book Council and the International Reading Association.

SELECTED WORKS: The Dinosaur Who Lived in My Backyard, 1988; The Missing Tarts, 1989; A, B, C, D, Tummy, Toes, Hands, Knees, 1990; Eeny, Meeney, Miney, Mo, 1990; Jake Baked the Cake, 1990; School Days, 1990; When You Were Just a Little Girl, 1991; Sleep Tight, 1992; The First Night, 1993; Meet Winslow Whale, 1994; Road Builders, 1994; Corduroy's Halloween, 1995.

CHARLOTTE HERMAN

June 10, 1937–

AUTHOR OF *My Mother Didn't Kiss Me Goodnight*, etc.

Autobiographical sketch of Charlotte Herman:

WHEN I WAS in the fourth grade I had to write my autobiography. I was doing fine until I came to the part, *What I Want to Be When I Grow Up.*

I had no idea what I wanted to be, and because I couldn't think of anything else, I wrote, "When I grow up I want to be a secretary so I can work in a big office and type."

I think now that I always wanted to be a writer and just never knew it. I loved to write. Poetry, mostly. I wrote poems about fire engines racing through the streets at midnight, and poems about the Four Freedoms, and farewell poems to teachers.

I loved fountain pens, and paper, and pencils, and paper clips, and all kinds of of-

fice supplies that my father brought home from work. I loved the card game of Authors. And books—even though I didn't read lots of them.

There was a library right across the street from my school, but I found it overwhelming. There were so many books I didn't know where to begin. And nobody showed me.

But I loved the books I *did* read. I owned a copy of Robert Louis Stevenson's *A Child's Garden of Verses*, and read the poems over and over again until I had memorized every single one of them. My mother always wanted me to recite them in front of guests, but I never would.

Another book stands out in my mind. There used to be a storyteller named Malcolm Claire, affectionately known as Uncle Mal, who read his original stories over the radio. The program was called *Tune-In Tales*, and I always listened to it.

One day my mother came home from the Marshall Field's department store with Malcolm Claire's book, also called, *Tune-In Tales*. And it was autographed: To Charlotte, from Malcolm Claire, Uncle Mal. When I saw the autograph I thought, "Oh my God, he knows me!" I still have the book. And the autograph is as clear as ever.

When I was in college I studied to be a teacher because I didn't know what else to do. It was one of the best decisions I've ever made. I loved being with the kids. And it was there, in the classroom, while reading to my students, that I really discovered children's books. I knew then that I, too, wanted to write for children.

For me, writing is like having a time machine. I can visit my childhood whenever I want to. And I visit often in my books, *A Summer on Thirteenth Street* and the *Millie Cooper* series.

I am back there in the old neighborhood, in our four-room apartment. I can be with my mother while she's cooking or sewing, I can reach into my father's jacket pocket at any time and come up with a piece of Wrigley's Doublemint gum, and plead with my brother, Irv, to release me from a hammerlock.

My friends are still there, and we're all collecting newspapers and tin cans and singing patriotic songs while we plant our Victory gardens. All this in the belief that we would bring an end to World War II. My cat is there, too.

All the sights and sounds of my childhood come back to me and find their way into my books.

But it's not just my own childhood that I visit. Memories related to me by my mother, and an old family photograph taken in 1913 helped me make the journey to Russia; to a one-room house on Walenska Street where I visit my mother as a small girl. She and her sisters, along with their mother and father, still live in my book, *The House on Walenska Street.*

I also like to write contemporary stories— stories about children living today. And there's one thing I've learned. The problems and concerns, the hopes and dreams of all children are much the same. No matter where or when they live.

Charlotte Herman was born in Chicago, Illinois. She received a B.A. degree in Edu-cation from Roosevelt University in Chicago in 1960, and has taught in the Chicago Public Schools. She was married in 1957 and has four children.

She has conducted biannual workshops for the Children's Reading Round Table Children's Literature Conference at Kendall College in Evanston, Illinois, and Mundelein College in Chicago. She also makes author appearances in schools and libraries. She is a member of the Children's Reading Round Table in Chicago, the Society of Midland Authors, and the Society of Children's Book Writers and Illustrators.

The House on Walenska Street won the 1990 Carl Sandburg Award from the Friends of the Chicago Public Library. *Our Snowman Had Olive Eyes* won the Grand Pris Des Treize in France and a 1978 Society of Midland Authors Award. Her books have been translated into French, Danish, German, Chinese, Dutch, and Afrikaans.

My Mother Didn't Kiss Me Goodnight was named a Children's Choice Book by a joint committee of the International Reading Association and the Children's Book Council.

SELECTED WORKS: Our Snowman Had Olive Eyes, 1977; My Mother Didn't Kiss Me Goodnight, 1980; Millie Cooper, 3B, 1985; Millie Cooper, Take a Chance, 1988; The House on Walenska Street, 1990; Max Malone Makes a Million, 1991; A Summer on Thirteenth Street, 1991; Max Malone, Superstar, 1992; Millie Cooper and Friends, 1995.

ABOUT: Contemporary Authors (First Revision), Vol. 41-44; (New Revision Series), Vol. 15, 34; Something About the Author, Vol. 20.

AMY HEST

April 28, 1950–

AUTHOR OF *The Purple Coat*, etc.

Autobiographical sketch of Amy Hest:

I GREW UP in a small suburban community about an hour from New York City. My favorite things were biking, reading, and

Amy hest ♡

spying. I spied on everyone, and still do. Coffee shops, I find, make an excellent backdrop for this particular activity. I may *look* as though I'm minding my own business, sipping coffee, eating cheese Danish, but in fact I am really doing spy work. Listening to conversations at the tables nearby. Watching, amazingly discreet for someone who never went to spy school, to see who is saying what to whom. As I pick up bits and pieces of true life stories, I quietly weave in my own ideas, create new stories with my very own endings. Spy work is a lot of fun.

My parents took me to the city often. I loved the commotion and whirl on the streets, and the screeching subway underground. I loved the hot dogs and crunchy donuts at Chock Full O' Nuts, and the way mustard came on a tiny rippled paper. By the time I was seven, I was certain of one thing, that I would one day live in New York. Many years later, after graduating from library school, I moved to the Upper West Side of Manhattan, and I live here still, with my husband and two children, Sam and Kate.

I was a lucky child, really. I was so close with my grandparents, it was as if I had two sets of parents all the time I was growing up. They lived in New York, but came out to our house on weekends. Nana was my weekend roommate; Grampa slept in the den downstairs. Fridays Nana cooked up a storm and arrived laden with shopping bags filled with homemade Jewish delicacies. She lit Sabbath candles and told wonderful family stories. I was privy to the best gossip. Grampa and I played checkers. We took early morning walks. My goal: to get out of the house before my brother woke up, to be alone for once with Grampa. Destination: hot chocolate and a buttered roll.

I suppose I have to tell the truth about the kind of child I was. The best word to describe me: boring. I can't believe what a goody-goody I was. I rarely disobeyed my parents, although I do remember hurling certain vitamin tablets down the kitchen sink. I rarely got a bad grade in school, although I did fail art one time, in eighth grade, I think. I never once did anything extraordinarily wonderful, or extraordinarily terrible, and to make matters worse, nothing EVER happened. I was boring. Rugby Road was boring. I knew in my heart I wanted to be a writer when I grew up, but there was this nasty little voice in the back of my head and it was laughing at me. "You must be kidding, Amy! Why in the world would anyone want to read what YOU write? Remember who you are . . . THE most boring person in the universe . . . nothing ever happens to you . . . what NERVE you have, thinking you can do something wonderful and clever like write. . . . "

I worked for several years as a children's librarian, and later, in the children's book departments of several major publishing houses. I had a lot of good jobs. I had a secret, too. I wanted to write. And what I wanted to write, always, was children's books. It took me a long time to get over a kind of fear of writing, to start to believe I could do it. It took me a long time to realize all those boring days of my childhood may not have been so empty, after all.

My books are about real people—often

people in my own family, with new names but familiar personality traits. The setting is more often than not New York City. Family, home. Running themes in my life, and in my stories, too.

Amy Hest received a B.A. degree from Hunter College of the City University of New York in 1971. She earned an M.L.S. degree from C.W. Post College of Long Island University in 1972. She was a children's librarian at the New York Public Library from 1972 to 1975. She has been a full-time writer since 1971. She was married in 1977 and has two children. Hest is a member of the Society of Children's Book Writers and Illustrators.

The Purple Coat won a 1987 Christopher Award. *Pete and Lily* received a 1987 Child Study Children's Book Award from the Child Study Children's Book Committee at Bank Street College of Education. *The Purple Coat* was a Reading Rainbow Book.

SELECTED WORKS: Maybe Next Year, 1982; The Crack-of-Dawn Walkers, 1984; Pete & Lily, 1986; The Purple Coat, 1986; The Mommy Exchange, 1988; Where in the World Is the Perfect Family?, 1989; The Ring and the Window Seat, 1990; Love You, Soldier, 1991; Pajama Party, 1992; Nana's Birthday Party, 1994; Nannies for Hire, 1994; Rosie's Fishing Trip, 1994; In the Rain with Baby Duck, 1995; Party on Ice, 1995; The Private Notebook of Katie Roberts, Age 11, 1995.

ABOUT: Contemporary Authors, Vol. 115; Something About the Author, Vol. 55; Vol. 82.

MINFONG HO

January 7, 1951–

AUTHOR OF *Rice Without Rain*, etc.

Autobiographical sketch of Minfong Ho:

THE VOICES of my earliest childhood speak to me in Chinese. My father, in his deep quiet monotone, would tell me wonderful bedtime stories in Cantonese that he made up, about giants and turtles and emperors. My grandmother, my aunts, my

Minfong: ryhmes with *ping-pong*

MINFONG HO

amahs too, spoke in Cantonese, teasing or scolding me, or laughing and whispering among themselves, in an easy conspiracy. My mother's voice was cooler, more aloof, as she taught us T'ang Dynasty poems in Mandarin, evoking through them images of an exquisite but remote China. With her own friends and relatives she would speak in rapid-fire Hunanese or sibilant Shanghaiese, as I eavesdropped to pick up the latest gossip. As naturally and unquestioningly as I absorbed the basic feelings of love and anger, praise and blame that my family poured over me, so I also absorbed these four Chinese dialects. As my first language, Chinese is the language with the deepest emotional resonance for me. Throughout my childhood, it was the only language which mattered. I heard it, spoke it, whispered it, screamed it, dreamed in it and cried in it. Even now, when I cry, I cry in Chinese. Perhaps that's why I think of Chinese as the language of my heart.

If Chinese is the language of my heart, then Thai is the language of my hands, a functional language which connected me to the wide world outside my family. Growing up on the outskirts of Bangkok in Thailand, I absorbed the simple Thai spoken by peddlers of fried bananas or pickled mangoes as they walked down our lane, swinging their baskets of fruit from their shoulder poles. It was in Thai that I would ask for a ripe guava or rose-apple, mixed with sugar or salt or chili sauce. At the Sunday market at Sanam Luang, it was Thai that I bargained in, picking out a potted orchid or a caged rabbit. And within the gleaming Emerald Buddha Temple, it was Thai that the saffron-robed monks chanted, their faces hidden behind the stiff fans they each held.

Our house was an airy wooden building on stilts over a "klong", or small pond. I could lie on my stomach in our dining room, and push rice through the cracks of the floorboards down to the fish below. We seeded the pond with tiny fish, and once a year, the water from the "klong" would be drained, and we would be allowed to wade thigh-deep in mud next to fishermen to net the fish wallowing in the mud. This busy, beautiful world, of fruits and fish, of monks and marketwomen, swirled with the light, nuanced sounds of Thai, and I had only to reach out to touch it, connect with it. I taste and touch in Thai, so that I think of Thai as the language of my hands.

English came only much later, when I started learning it in school, in about the third or fourth grade. For a long time it remained a school language, separate from the Chinese or Thai of my immediate world. Learning English was a form of intellectual exercise, crammed with rules and regulations which were rigidly enforced by strict teachers. Thus I might know the difference between the present and past participle, yet be unable to jump-rope or play hopscotch in English. English was confined to the stark, alien world of textbooks and examinations, devoid of feelings or sense of taste and touch. No wonder then that English is for me a language of the head.

What happens when you have a different language for your heart, your hands, your head? When your head cannot express what your heart feels, or what your hands touch?

Fragmentation.

I felt a strange split, a kind of linguistic schizophrenia.

In school, I was made to recite Wordsworth's poem on the daffodils, without ever having laid eyes on that flower. Yet I did not know the English names of the common flowers growing all around me. (Years later, I discovered that the little purple blossom that grew wild everywhere in Thailand was called, "Madagascar periwinkle", which made it sound impossibly exotic.) Or, conversely, Thai words for everyday things, once I translated them into English—like my favorite foods "pomelo" or "minced fish patty"—sounded odd and unfamiliar.

Growing up is hard enough to do, without having to feel that one's head can't communicate with one's heart or hands. In an effort to piece together the bits and pieces of my life, I tried to write—strictly for myself, and at first in an awkward jumble of Chinese, Thai, English. Gradually, because English—through all those years of formal education—has become the language that I am most adept in, I wrote more and more in English. Despite the frustrations involved, I kept on writing, because writing was becoming a way to integrate the different experiences and languages of my head, my hands and my heart.

It is ironic that the language that I've become most proficient in, is the one which means the least in me, evoking very little feeling or memories. I have no easy English words for them, these Chinese voices lodged in my heart, or the Thai things I touched with my hands. And when, through some tedious processing of translation in my head, the Chinese and Thai comes out in English, the original experience becomes distorted.

Yes, it was frustrating for me to write in English. How do I, for instance, write convincing dialogue when my characters don't even speak English? How do I translate local idioms without making them sound quaint? How can I portray complex traditions without resorting to tedious explanations? It wasn't easy. It doesn't help, either, that sometimes I am made to feel like a kind of cultural Frankenstein, when those who speak only English look upon my fluency in 'their' language as freakish, an interesting but somewhat grotesque mimicry of their own language which they had somehow bequeathed me.

It was in the depth of my first winter in America that I really started to write. As a freshman at Cornell University, when it was snowing and bleak outside, I used to go to one of the greenhouses on campus, and just stand next to a potted banana tree growing inside. I missed the tropical sun, and the green leaves and naked brown babies splashing in the ponds. By standing near that banana tree, I felt a little more connected with home. But one day some biology class must have chopped up my banana tree for an experiment, because only its spongy trunk was left. That afternoon, I went back to my dorm room and started writing what would become my first book, about a village girl in Thailand.

In a way, I still write for the same reason: to bring back what is gone, to relive what is lost, to make a mosaic out of fragments. And to feel—head, hands and heart— whole again.

———

Minfong Ho was born in Rangoon, Burma. She grew up in Bangkok, Thailand, where she attended the Bangkok Patana School and later the International School of Bangkok. From 1967 to 1969, she studied at Tunghai University, then earned a B.A. degree with honors from Cornell University in 1973 and an M.F.A. from Cornell in 1980. She has been a teaching assistant at Cornell, and a journalist at a daily newspaper in Singapore. She was a lecturer in the English department of Chiengmai University in Thailand in 1975 and 1976 and a Writer-in-Residence at Singapore University in 1983. She currently lives in New York State with her husband and three children.

Her novels have been published in Singapore and England, and have also been translated and published in Thailand, France, Japan, and the Philippines. She won First Prize from the National Book Development Council of Singapore for *Rice Without Rain* in 1988. She also won the annual short story contest for *Asiaweek* magazine in Hong Kong in 1983.

Her first book, *Sing to the Dawn*, won first prize from the Council of Interracial Books for Children. *Rice Without Rain* was named a Best Book of the Year for Young Adults by the American Library Association. *The Clay Marble* was named a Notable Children's Trade Book in the Field of Social Studies by a joint committee of the Children's Book Council and the International Reading Association.

SELECTED WORKS: Sing to the Dawn, 1975; Rice Without Rain, 1990; The Clay Marble, 1991; Maples in the Mist: Tang Poems in Translation, 1995.

SELECTED WORKS WITH SAPHAN ROSS: The Two Brothers, 1995.

ABOUT: Contemporary Authors, Vol. 77-80; Something About the Author, Vol. 15.

WILL HOBBS

August 22, 1947–

AUTHOR OF *Bearstone*, etc.

Autobiographical sketch of Will Hobbs:

I WAS A READER. I grew up in an Air Force family, in Panama, Virginia, Alaska, California, and Texas. In Alaska, along about fourth grade, I fell in love with stories. Reading made it a little easier to move through a dozen schools. We were a close family, and that helped too. I have a sister and three brothers.

In Alaska, I came under the spell of mountains and rivers. I started backpacking at eleven and have kept at it ever since. When my wife Jean and I came to live in southwestern Colorado in 1973, we started hiking in the San Juan Mountains where,

Will Hobbs

years later, I would set *Bearstone* and *Beardance*.

By high school I was dreaming that one day I would become a writer. In college I studied literature. I became, naturally enough, an English and reading teacher; I liked kids and books, so it was a perfect match. Yet something was missing. By 1980 I couldn't stand NOT WRITING any longer, and made myself sit down and work. A grizzly had recently been killed in the San Juans, and grizzlies were supposed to be extinct in Colorado. I began to imagine a Native American boy meeting the last grizzly. *Bearstone* was published in its sixth draft in 1989.

Of my five novels, the one I revised least was the first published—*Changes in Latitudes*. It grew out of my childhood love of turtles and began with the image of swimming underwater with a sea turtle.

For my third novel, I turned to the Grand Canyon and my whitewater rafting experiences there. When I started *Downriver*, I'd rowed the Grand Canyon four times (at the time of this writing we've done nine trips and have spent six months on the river in the Canyon). In addition to wanting to give readers a sense of the Canyon's spirit of place, I wanted to write about the tough choices my young characters were making about their lives.

I had in mind these words of Aldo Leopold's as I began *The Big Wander*: "I am glad I shall never be young without wild places to be young in. Of what avail are forty freedoms without a blank spot on the map?" I set it in the canyon country of Utah, between Monument Valley and Escalante, Utah. When Clay Lancaster waves good-bye to his Navajo friends, he's on what the Navajos call the "Trail of Beauty," and I hope readers are too.

In 1990 a mother grizzly and three cubs were sighted in the San Juan Mountains. I began to imagine a sequel for *Bearstone*: Cloyd would meet up with the mate and cubs of the "last" grizzly. Writing *Beardance* was a marvelous experience. After being stuck for months, I threw away the first seven chapters and began with Cloyd and his old friend Walter riding back into the mountains. Once I began with Cloyd asking, "Do you think there could still be any grizzlies in the mountains?" I had to hold onto my hat. I wrote the story in a sort of trance, much like the boy's trance as it was turning winter at 11,800 feet and he was trying to keep those two grizzly cubs alive. His sensations were pouring through my fingers. I wrote this draft in less than a month.

In the beginning there's only the blank page or blank screen, and it can be very intimidating. I start by reading for a couple of months, gathering ideas, adding to a "compost pile" that may have started in my childhood. If I have faith, and make myself sit down and work, the "compost" will eventually heat up enough to burst into flames.

Will Hobbs was born in Pittsburgh, Pennsylvania. A Phi Beta Kappa graduate of Stanford University, he received his B.A. degree in 1969 and his M.A. in 1971. He was married in 1972. He taught reading and English for seventeen years, mostly in southwestern Colorado, including three years at the high school level, and the rest in seventh grade. He began writing full-time in 1990 and is a member of the Authors Guild.

Hobbs has written articles about writing and about his books for such publications as *The ALAN Review* and *The California Reader.* Critical articles about his works have appeared in *Signal, Book Links,* and *The Virginia English Bulletin,* to name a few. His future books will include an illustrated picture book, *Beardream.* Will Hobbs lives in Durango, Colorado.

Four of his novels—*Bearstone, Downriver, The Big Wander,* and *Beardance,* were named Best Books for Young Adults by the American Library Association. *Bearstone* and *Changes in Latitudes* were named Notable Children's Trade Books in the Field of Social Studies by a joint committee of the National Council on the Social Studies and the Children's Book Council. *Beardance* won the Western Writers of America Spur Award in 1993.

SELECTED WORKS: Changes in Latitudes, 1988; Bearstone, 1989; Downriver, 1991; The Big Wander, 1992; Beardance, 1993; Kokopelli's Flute, 1995.

ABOUT: The ALAN Review Fall 1994; Gallo, Donald R. Speaking for Ourselves, Too; Something About the Author, Vol. 72; Wilson Library Bulletin May 1991.

MARY HOFFMAN

April 20, 1945–

AUTHOR OF *Amazing Grace*, etc.

Autobiographical sketch of Mary Margaret Lassiter Hoffman:

I THINK I WAS always going to be a writer. When I was small, I made up stories and dialogue in my head all the time; it is only relatively recently that I discovered that not everyone does this. At my primary school in

England, my friends used to put on little plays that I had written, all now lost and forgotten. I also used to love dressing up and acting out traditional stories with my big sister. These were called Potted Pantomimes, later corrupted to Potty Pantomimes, and I enjoyed them much more than she did, as I was always Cinderella, Aladdin, Sleeping Beauty etc. and she had to be a supporting cast of Ugly Sisters, wicked stepmothers or handsome princes as the plot required.

Reading English Literature at Cambridge University held me back for many years and it was not until 1970 that I decided to write a complete book. I gave myself a year and it took eighteen months. I tried many British publishers before it was accepted and it was eventually published in 1975 as *White Magic* by a small firm called Rex Collings, who had previously brought out *Watership Down.* I wish I could say the rest is History but in fact it is more a case of hard slog and obstinacy.

Why I chose children's books in the first case is hard to remember. Maybe I thought they would be easier; maybe I thought that adult fiction had grown too distant from the art of storytelling, which is really what interested me. But I've stuck with them and had another fifty published since that first novel.

But they have mainly been picturebooks and junior fiction. Only now do I feel ready to venture back into full length novels. American readers may know my *Nancy No-Size* (Oxford University Press), *My Grandma Has Black Hair* (Dial) and Henry's Baby (Dorling Kindersley Inc.). But undoubtedly the book that made my name in the States was *Amazing Grace*, published by Dial in 1991, with superb illustrations by Caroline Binch.

My books reflect a second interest which strengthened my desire to write for children. When I joined a women's group in the early 70s, we specialised in the study of picturebooks. Pretty soon we found that the images of women and girls, where present, were much more limited and stereotyped than even their lives were at the time. As for Blacks or other minority groups, they were hardly there at all. And, most insidious, there was a dreary and limiting consensus about what constituted a real family and acceptable way of life. I'm talking about stories ostensibly set in the real world of recognisable domestic life, not fantasies.

If you believe something very passionately about society, you have to avoid the temptation of writing propaganda. I try very hard never to write something that isn't in itself a real story to catch the reader, but I think all of my books do have a message, for those who are ready and willing to listen. So *Amazing Grace* is a book about racial and sexual prejudice and also the simple story of a girl who is in love with narrative. *Henry's Baby* is also about sex-stereotyping, this time of boys, but is also the story of a boy's wish to belong.

I have a lot of contact with children, in schools and libraries and love receiving their letters, all of which I try to answer.

Mary Hoffman was born in Eastleigh, Hampshire, in England. she moved to London in 1948, where she has lived ever since. She went to Cambridge University in 1964 to read English, graduating in 1967, and she went on to University College, London, in 1968 for a postgraduate course in Linguistics. She worked for the Open University from 1975 to 1980, writing courses for teachers on the teaching of reading and language developement, and children's literature. She has been Reading Consultant to the BBC Schools TV series "Look and Read" since 1977.

She married in 1972 and she has three daughters. She is a member of the Society of Authors, the National Union of Journalists, and the International Board on Books for Young People.

Mary Hoffman is the author of several books for adults: *Reading, Writing and Relevance* and, under name Lassiter, *Our Names, Our Selves.* Both were published in Britain. She is a reviewer for the *Daily Telegraph*, the *Guardian*, and *School Librarian.*

Hoffman has written over fifty books for children, including a series of sixteen books in the "Animals in the Wild" series, which she calls "sharply conservationist."

She was nominated for the Eleanor Farjeon Medal for services to children's literature in 1994. *Amazing Grace* was named a Commended Book in the 1991 Kate Greenaway Medal Awards presented for illustration by the British Library Associaton. It was also a Book-of-the-Month Club selection.

SELECTED WORKS: Clothes for Sale, 1986; A Fine Picnic, 1986; Animal Hide and Seek, 1987; Nancy No-Size, 1987; My Grandma Has Black Hair, 1988; Amazing Grace, 1991; The Four-Legged Ghosts, 1993; Henry's Baby, 1993; Boundless Grace, 1995; Earth, Fire, Water, Air, 1995.

ABOUT: Contemporary Authors, Vol. 131; (New Revision Series), Vol. 15; Something About the Author, Vol. 15, 59.

ROSEKRANS HOFFMAN

January 7, 1926–

ILLUSTRATOR OF *Walter in Love*, etc.

Biographical sketch of Rosekrans Hoffman:

ROSEKRANS HOFFMAN was born in Denton, Nebraska. She and her brother were both artistic; he went on to become an architect, and she became first a painter, and later an illustrator and writer of children's books.

When she was seven years old, Hoffman was confined to her bed. She was incapacitated by osteomyelitis, and nearly died. She says she became an artist because "it was the one thing I could do" while restricted to her bed. Her parents were supportive of her art and often told her what a good artist she was. "They always referred to me as The Artist," she says, "although my mother didn't hang my things on the wall."

Hoffman graduated with a B.F.A. degree from the University of Nebraska in 1949, the same year she was first married. The marriage ended in divorce. She later married Robert Hoffman, in 1955.

Within weeks of graduating, Rosekrans Hoffman moved away from Nebraska, first to California for a year, then to New York, where she lived for many years. She has also lived in Connecticut and New Jersey. She was a painter, an abstract expressionist, and she painted in the evenings. During the day, she worked, in order to support herself. She says, "I had a lot of jobs in order to feed myself. They all had 'art' in the title. But they didn't involve much art." Her paintings were exhibited in New York City, in the Whitney Museum and in the Brooklyn Museum.

Hoffman decided she wanted to illustrate children's books as a way of filling in a missing part of her childhood. She believes it had been in the back of her mind all the time to become a children's book illustrator. "I did frescoes of children's stories at school," she says, "and I never really knew why. But one thing leads to another," and creating children's books, she says, was a way for her "to become whole," to put the fun in childhood.

Walter in Love, written by Alicen White, came out in 1973. It was the first book Hoffman illustrated. The story of two dogs in New York, it was reviewed favorably on television by Gene Shalit, and Hoffman laughingly says she then expected him to review all her subsequent books as well. She has since illustrated a number of books, including many textbooks. All her work has been for younger children.

Two of her favorite books to work on were *Jane Yolen's Mother Goose Songbook* and *Jane Yolen's Old MacDonald Songbook*. A *Horn Book Guide* reviewer stated, "Hoffman's rich, decorative borders are a unifying element throughout the book, tying the pages together and framing her humorous and fanciful illustrations and the words and music." The *Guide* also provides compliments on her work in *Where Do Little Girls Go*, calling the illustrations "beautifully detailed, subtle paintings."

Although she doesn't think of herself as a writer, Hoffman has written two books, which she also illustrated: *Anna Banana* and *Sister Sweet Ella*. She says she enjoyed writing them and hopes to write more, but still considers herself to be primarily an artist.

As an artist, Hoffman feels that her strength is her use of color. "I think I've always been very good with color," she says. In fact, she is writing a book about pieces of her life and her particular ideas about color. "Colors are born," she believes. "They have birth places. You remember something very vividly because of the color." She adds, "Color is probably the only thing I know anything about, and that is a mystery."

Hoffman and her husband, who is now retired, moved back to Nebraska in 1990. She is nourished by working on her illustrations. She describes her work as "sitting at her desk drawing," as opposed to when she used to paint: "always standing up, moving back and forth." If she had the time, she'd like to paint again.

"The process of illustration is very interesting," she says, "how you just go to the drawing board to work and let it happen." Hoffman doesn't use models, because the work "has to do with the drawing, not the model." She says, "I never took commercial art in school, and wouldn't I try to be honest on paper. It is simply my approach."

Hoffman began drawing in pen and ink, but she now uses pencil, and in place of watercolors, she uses colored ink. She claims that she really enjoys drawing pigs, the subject of a forthcoming textbook, *Pignic*, about pigs on a picnic. "I do hilarious pigs," she says, and then tells the story of an editor who once told her, "I got a manuscript with pigs in it, and I thought of you immediately!"

SELECTED WORKS WRITTEN AND ILLUSTRATED: Anna Banana, 1975; Sister Sweet Ella, 1982.

SELECTED WORKS ILLUSTRATED: Walter in Love, by Alicen White, 1973; Go to Bed!: A Book of Poems, by Lee Bennett Hopkins, 1979; My Mother Sends Her Wisdom, by Louise McClenathan, 1979; The Truth About the Moon, by Clayton Bess, 1983; Three Sisters, by Audrey Wood, 1986; The Horrible Holidays, by Audrey Wood, 1988; The Best Cat Suit of All, by Syl-

via Cassedy, 1991; Jane Yolen's Mother Goose Songbook, edited by Jane Yolen, 1992; Where Do Little Girls Grow?, by Milly Jane Limmer, 1993; Jane Yolen's Old MacDonald Songbook, edited by Jane Yolen, 1994.

ABOUT: Something About the Author, Vol. 15.

SOLLACE HOTZE

November 28, 1932–

AUTHOR OF *A Circle Unbroken*, etc.

Biographical sketch of Sollace K. Hotze:

SOLLACE HOTZE is a writer of books for children and young adults. She was born and raised in the small Western Reserve village of Gates Mills, Ohio, part of the Chagrin Valley, just east of Cleveland. Because it is a rural area, she remembers having few friends to play with, so books became her "constant companions", and she became a passionate reader.

She attended Sarah Lawrence College in Bronxville, New York, where she had a double major of English and Theater Arts. She received her B.A. degree in 1954. She later studied at the University of Chicago, earning an M.A.T. degree in the Teaching of English in 1974.

From 1974 to 1984, Hotze taught English to high-school students. She taught a summer writing workshop for teachers through the Barrington District 220 in the years 1988 through 1990. She also taught a writing workshop for parents from 1989 to 1991, and in 1991 she taught "Writing from the Right Brain," a writing workshop for teachers. In addition, she taught a student education course through the same school district, "Gifted English/Language Arts", for the first through the seventh grades, from 1989 to 1990. She has since retired from teaching and is a full-time writer.

Hotze wrote a student self-directed reading and writing text, called *Peer Voices: Book Four*, which was published in 1991.

She was not, she states, "one of those writ-

Sollace Hotze: SOL luss Hōtz

Oollace Hotze

ers who knows from age eight or ten that writing will become one's life." It was trying to help students become better writers, as well as her early love of reading, she says, that finally brought her to attempt writing, herself. "Now I can't imagine *not* being a writer," she says. "I have discovered that creating stories for others to read is even more pleasurable than reading stories others have written."

In addition to her books for children and young adults, Hotze writes short stories for adults. She has been published in *Whetstone, Family Circle*, and *Great River Review*. She has also served as co-editor of a literary journal, *Whetstone*, which she founded. She was co-editor from 1985 to 1988. She was also co-editor of the Tenth Anniversary Issue of *Story Quarterly*, another literary journal.

A Circle Unbroken is the story of Rachel, a child who is captured in 1838 by a band of renegade Indians, and recaptured years later by her minister father.

Summer Endings is set in 1945, and its protagonist is twelve-year-old Christine Kosinski, who sees several changes in her life at the end of World War II.

A ghost based on a real woman who lived

in New England is one of the characters of *Acquainted with the Night,* a novel set in 1970, wherein Molly and her cousin Caleb are romantically attracted after he returns from the Vietnam War. The *Bulletin of the Center for Children's Books* called it a "sad and touching love story, full of longing for the dead and the living . . . [that will] strike enjoyably bittersweet chords with new readers as well as old fans."

A Circle Unbroken and *Acquainted with the Night* were named Best Books of the Year for Young Adults by the American Library Association. *A Circle Unbroken* won a 1989 Carl Sandburg Award, given by the Friends of the Chicago Public Library.

SELECTED WORKS: A Circle Unbroken, 1988; Summer Endings, 1991; Acquainted with the Night, 1992.

GLORIA HOUSTON

AUTHOR OF *My Great Aunt Arizona*, etc.

Biographical sketch of Gloria Houston:

GLORIA HOUSTON was born in Marion, North Carolina. She grew up in Avery County near Spruce Pine, North Carolina, where her family had a country store, and she encountered all kinds of people from an early age. Among her favorite childhood reading were the "Little House" books of Laura Ingalls Wilder, and biographies in a series called "Lives of Great Americans"; but when she read *Little Women* at the age of seven, she knew she wanted to be a writer. She invented stories to tell to her parents. She was a serious student of the piano, but she also wrote stories and plays, which won awards.

She received her B.S. degree in Music Education from Appalachian State University in Boone in 1963. After she married, she lived for a time in Dallas and New Orleans, and she adopted two daughters. It wasn't until 1976 that she decided to submit her

work for publication. She received fifty-four rejections of her first novel, *My Brother Joey Died*, and it was published the same year she earned a Masters of Education degree in Curriculum and Instruction from the Univerity of South Florida in Tampa, in 1983. She earned a Ph.D. degree in Curriculum and Instruction from the same University in 1989. She has taught language arts and writing techniques, composition, and literature for young readers. She was Author-in-Residence and Visiting Assistant Professor at the College of Education, University of South Florida from 1983 to 1994. She is currently Author-in-Residence and Visiting Assistant Professor at the College of Education, Western Carolina University, in Cullowhee, North Carolina.

Gloria Houston writes primarily picture books and young adult novels, which are historical and contemporary realistic fiction. Her childhood memories of a growing up in an Appalachian mountain town influence her writing, especially concerning the language of the culture. She also credits family storytelling as an influence on her career in language and writing. She sets some of her books in the locale where she grew up, sometimes consulting *Our South-*

ern Highlanders by Horace Kephart, a book describing the geographical and climatic conditions and their influence on a culture that remained a seventeenth-century culture well into the 1900's. She also employs as a valued resource her father, who was the local historian and storyteller; and her mother, who has a "sensory memory" of colors, odors, and details that cannot be found in any published book.

Her wide range of interests includes folklore, psychology, travel, the writing process, reading, how children learn, collecting music boxes, attending plays and concerts, working out at the gym, hiking, and horseback riding.

Houston was a member of a national Blue Ribbon Committee of Language Arts Specialists to evaluate IBM's "Writing to Write" curriculum project and wrote the academic support paper for the curriculum. She was Associate Producer of the film adaptation of one of her books, entitled *The Perfect Christmas Tree*, produced by Sanmar Productions for release in 1996. She received the 1990 Distinguished Alumni Award from Appalachian State University. She presented a Dissertation Study, "Comparing Three Strategies of Vocabulary Learning," at the World Congress of the International Reading Association in 1990.

My Great Aunt Arizona was named a Notable Book by the American Library Association and to the Children's Choices list by a joint committee of the Children's Book Council and the International Reading Association. It was also named a Notable Children's Trade Book in the Field of Social Studies by a joint committee of the CBC and the National Council on the Social Studies. It has been on the nominations lists for many awards that are voted upon by children.

Littlejim was also named a NCSS-CBC Notable Children's Trade Book in the Field of Social Studies.

Among Houston's memberships are the Author's Guild, The Society of Children's

Book Writers and Illustrators, The National Council of Teachers of English, and Phi Kappa Phi. She often makes author appearances at various conferences, such as those held by the American Library Association and the National Council of Teachers of English. She appears in a biographical video produced by the Muses Bookstore of Morganton, North Carolina, "Going Home with Gloria Houston," in which she discusses each of her books, their inspiration, and their connection to her own family.

Gloria Houston is divorced and has two grown daughters.

SELECTED WORKS: My Brother Joey Died, 1982; The Year of the Perfect Christmas Tree, 1988; Littlejim, 1990; But No Candy, 1992; My Great Aunt Arizona, 1992; Littlejim's Gift: An Appalachian Christmas Story, 1994; Mountain Valor, 1994.

ABOUT: Publishers Weekly December 23, 1988; Something About the Author, Vol. 81.

ELIZABETH FITZGERALD HOWARD

December 28, 1927–

AUTHOR OF *Chita's Christmas Tree*, etc.

Autobiographical sketch of Elizabeth Fitzgerald Howard:

BOOKS HAVE ALWAYS been central in my life, but writing children's books is a happy recent development. Perhaps my childhood experiences were pointing me in this direction.

I have early memories of my mother, a former teacher, reading to us. I learned to read before starting school. After two weeks in kindergarten I was sent to first grade; after Christmas I went into second. My third grade teacher let us choose from her wonderful bookshelf. Our Boston Public Library branch yielded treasures. Books were the best Christmas presents. I relished rainy days when I didn't have to play outside, but could curl up with the *Understood Betsy*, *The Orange Fairy Book*, *Little Women*.

Elizabeth Fitzgerald Howard

I was born in Baltimore. My father, after a stint of teaching high school, decided to return to Boston (he had graduated from Harvard). My sister Babs arrived. Times became hard. Money was tight. We moved to Mrs. Ford's rooming house in the Allston section of Boston. The second floor housed solemn, serious African-American graduate students attending local universities. But our attic aerie was a magic place, the tower of a castle, the perfect setting for endless pretend games. My parents were the king and queen, Babs and I were princesses, Mrs. Ford was a wicked witch. Did we worry about Witch Ford's be-quiet-on-the-stairs rules, her be-quick-in-the-kitchen commands? Hardly. Pale playmates from the neighborhood came. Even Ruth and Muriel, despite their parents' admonition, "never play with those colored children." From our tower we princesses looked over the city, watching for Bluebeard or Robin Hood. I had a pretend grandmother in Sudbury. I had nine pretend brothers. I could see things: fairies in the dust flecks floating in the sunshine. Goblins in the leafy dell outside the dining room. I heard Santa Claus on the roof.

We had another special place, not pretend. The summer I was seven and Babs was four, we went on our first train trip by ourselves, from Boston to Baltimore. Joy! Five summers at great-Aunt Lulu's, where there were chickens, a dog named Toodles, potato bugs to pick, a shady spring with a tin dipper. Other relatives shared in loving and showing us off. How lucky we were—the only children in our family! Of course, we still played "Let's Pretend": we were at summer camp. I wrote a book of poetry, forever lost. But memories were being stored.

When I was eleven, Lulu retired from teaching and came to Boston. We all moved into an apartment in Roxbury, a black neighborhood where at last I had lots of African-American friends. We were too old for "Let's Pretend", but I organized and wrote plays for our "Little Women's Dramatic Club." When Lulu bought a house in Brookline, a major minor crisis erupted, since I had to leave Girls' Latin School in Boston for Brookline High. My father, a gentle visionary in fragile health, continued to suffer disappointment in career ventures, including writing; my mother, cheery realist, clerked for the Commonwealth. And we all lived happily ever after—at Lulu's house.

After majoring in history at Radcliffe I began working at the Boston Public Library, soon qualifying as a Children's Librarian. It was like coming home! I plunged with informed appreciation into old favorites, new classics. When I moved with my husband's teaching job to Hofstra College, I did not leave children's books. I did some freelance editing while taking school librarianship courses. We moved back to Boston, to the Philippines with the Peace Corps, to Milwaukee, to St. Louis, to Pittsburgh. Meanwhile we produced three beautiful daughters to read to: I volunteered in their school libraries. I acquired an M.L.S. and a Ph.D. at the University of Pittsburgh, and for fifteen years taught library science at West Virginia University, mostly children's literature. As I read more books and met more authors I wondered: Could I write for children?

Inspired by Pitt professor/author Margaret Hodges, I tried retelling folktales, and will try again. But when I read Cynthia Rylant's *When I Was Young in the Mountains*, which portrays the richness in ordinary family life, I decided to try writing about my own childhood and the ordinary extraordinary people in it. In the year that my first grandchild was born, so, also, was my first book, *The Train to Lulu's*. Other books about my family describe Cousin Chita's reminiscences of special times with Papa; Aunt Flossie's house full of history and hats; Mac, my father, who loved trains. Ordinary people who happen to be African American. We have long needed stories that reveal that black experience is also American experience. Particular stories remind us that our uniqueness can be celebrated while we realize that we are all so much alike. We all can rejoice in everybody's family stories. Hurray!

———

Elizabeth Fitzgerald Howard received her B.A. degree from Radcliffe in 1948. She earned her M.L.S. degree from the University of Pittsburgh in 1971 and her Ph.D. in 1977. She was married in 1953. In addition to her library work, she was a research assistant at Hofstra College, a resource director at the Episcopal Diocese of Pittsburgh in Pennsylvania, and a visiting lecturer in library science at the University of Pittsburgh. She became professor of library science at West Virginia University in 1991, after working as assistant and associate professor there since 1978.

She has been a board member of several civic organizations and of the American Library Association's Association for Library Services to Children Division. She is also a member of the Society of Children's Writers and Illustrators and the National Council of Teachers of English. She wrote a book for adults, *America as Story: Historical Fiction for Secondary Schools*, which was published in 1988.

The Train to Lulu's was a Reading Rainbow Book. *Chita's Christmas Tree* was named a Notable Book by the ALA.

SELECTED WORKS: The Train to Lulu's, 1988; Chita's Christmas Tree, 1989; Aunt Flossie's Hats (and Crab Cakes Later), 1991; Mac and Marie and the Train Toss Surprise, 1993.

ABOUT: Contemporary Authors, Vol. 128; Something About the Author, Vol. 74.

ELLEN HOWARD

May 8, 1943–

AUTHOR OF *Her Own Song*, etc.

Autobiographical sketch of Ellen Howard:

CHILDREN sometimes ask, "Do you write about your own life?"

I have to answer that I do not. The reason, I tell them, is simple: my own life is boring. Yet I would not trade it for anyone else's.

I grew up in a large and loving family— parents, grandparents, and three children all under the same roof, a big white house in Portland, Oregon. At school, I was an able and obedient student, but not, I think, a brilliant one. I liked to draw. I liked to play pretend, dressed up in cast-off clothes as a gypsy, a harem girl, an Indian maiden. I liked to play with dolls too, right through eighth grade, and only fear of what others would say made me give them up then.

Most of all, I was a child who loved to read. I read getting dressed in the morning. I read on the way to school. I read at lunch time, at recess, hiding under the bleachers so the playground monitors wouldn't force me into a game. I read in bed at night, forgetting to listen for the opening of the door at the foot of the stairs that warned of an adult's approach. The crime I was most frequently punished for was reading!

I also made up stories, first to tell to my captive sibling audience, later to write down. And I dreamed of the time when, a grown-up-married-lady with thirteen children, I would write books.

But childhood dreams have a way of getting lost. Grown-ups, many of them, seemed to think that writing was an impractical ambition. So, because I wanted to please the grown-ups, eventually I thought of a different answer to the question, "What do you want to be when you grow up?" I began to say I wanted to be a librarian and, as can happen to an unvoiced dream, by and by mine was forgotten.

After high school graduation, I went to college for two years. Then I married my high school sweetheart, and we had a baby girl. When Beth was four years old, my husband and I divorced, and I went to work in an office. I was very busy, a little unhappy, but . . . . How could I feel tragic when I had such a wonderful child, such a warmly supportive family and friends and employment and health and a home?

Prince Charming arrived in my life with three daughters of his own. When Chuck Howard and I were married in 1975, Cynthia, Laurie, Beth and Shaley took part in the ceremony. My family had grown overnight, it seemed. Not thirteen children, it is true, but four were plenty!

In the late 1970's, I returned to college (Cynthia went too!) and there an important thing happened. I rediscovered stories and remembered my dream of writing them.

I wrote all kinds of things at first—articles, short stories, poems, and a very bad novel. I found I was better at some kinds of writing than at others. Almost invariably, my best writing came from somewhere within me deeper than my conscious thoughts, a place where my essential self laughed and cried and tried to make sense of life. I stumbled into that place only occasionally. I still cannot go there at will, though I have learned some ways to help myself find it. What I found out when I entered that place was that I am a writer of stories for children.

And so my first published book was a story for children, *Circle of Giving.*

Since then, our daughters have grown up. Now we have grandchildren too. Now I no longer work in an office, but in my own home, writing books for children. Sometimes I speak in schools. Sometimes I give speeches to teachers, librarians, and others interested in books for children. But most of the time, I stay at home, gardening, cooking, washing and ironing... and writing. Writing is a work of challenge and satisfaction and joy. I believe that all the ordinary events of my life prepared me to do it.

I know my life sounds boring to others. But for me, it is filled with all the adventure and excitement and drama that I can find and make in books. To me it is the best kind of life!

———

Ellen Howard was born in New Bern, North Carolina. She lived most of her life in Oregon until moving to Kalamazoo, Michigan, in 1990. She attended the University of Oregon and received her B.A. degree from Portland State University in 1979. She has worked in business and medical offices, in libraries, and most recently, from 1980 to 1988, in the office of The Collins Foundation, a charitable trust.

She is a member of The Authors Guild and has served in both Oregon and Michi-

gan as a Regional Advisor of the Society of Children's Book Writers and Illustrators. She taught Writing for Children at Portland Community College and has spoken in Oregon, Washington, California, Colorado, Michigan, and Missouri to audiences of students, educators, librarians, and writers.

Circle of Giving was named an honor book in the 1984 Society of Children's Book Writers Golden Kite Awards. *Her Own Song* received the International P.E.N. USA Center West Children's Middle Grade Award in 1989. Three of her books have been named Notable Children's Trade Books in the Field of Social Studies by a joint committee of the National Council on the Social Studies and the Children's Book Council: *When Daylight Comes, Gillyflower,* and *Her Own Song. Sister* was named a Notable Book of the Year by the American Library Association. Her books have been translated into six foreign languages and published in seven foreign countries.

SELECTED WORKS: Circle of Giving, 1984; When Daylight Comes, 1985; Gillyflower, 1986; Edith Herself, 1987; Her Own Song, 1988; Sister, 1990; The Chickenhouse House, 1991; The Cellar, 1992; The Big Seed, 1993; Gilly's Secret (a reissue, retitled, of Gillyflower), 1993; The Tower Room, 1993; Murphy and Kate, 1995.

ABOUT: Contemporary Authors, Vol. 130; Hopscotch October 1992; Something About the Author, Vol. 67.

DIANE HOYT-GOLDSMITH

July 1, 1950–

AUTHOR OF *Mardi Gras: A Cajun Country Celebration,* etc.

Autobiographical sketch of Diane Hoyt-Goldsmith:

BEFORE I WAS six years old, my family moved many times, following my father's promotions from one army post to another. From Colorado to Illinois where I was born,

Diane Hoyt-Goldsmith

you held them in your hands. I liked the quality of paper and the magic of the illustrations. I marveled at the way photographs could transport you to far-away places and bring you close to experiences you could only imagine.

To me, type and letterforms were fascinating inventions. My older sister Jackie and I spent many hours tracing the capital letters of the English alphabet from the introductory pages of the World Book Encyclopedia. We used thin paper and a sharp pencil, carefully outlining every curve. I'm sure that these hours were the beginnings of my interest in book design.

I entered the University of Washington in Seattle as a pre-medicine student, but after two years there, I changed both my major and my location. I moved to New York City to study Fine Art.

At first, I thought I would be a painter. But my love of books inspired me to take classes in graphic design and typography as well. When I graduated from Pratt Institute, I found a job in publishing. I worked for nine years in New York as a book designer, specializing in books for children.

In 1979, my husband David and I moved to the San Francisco Bay area where I started my own design company. I began to create "packages" for publishers, combining the talents of a writer with those of an illustrator. Soon I got an idea for a book of my own.

My husband and I had been collecting carvings by Northwest Coast Indian artists for many years. We bought masks, bowls, chests, and even a nine-foot totem pole. I began to learn what these beautifully crafted objects meant to the culture that had produced them.

One day at a gallery opening in Portland, I met a Tsimshian carver named David Boxley. He was busy making a tiny eagle out of wood and mother-of-pearl for his son's headdress. Through the friendship that developed between us, I learned how important tradition is to the Native Americans of today. David is an active participant

to Missouri, then California, and finally to West Germany, we never stayed in one place very long. When my father left the service, we moved to Troutdale, Oregon. I remember well the adventure of those early years with all the changes they brought—new friends, different houses to live in, even a new language to learn.

I grew up in a beautiful part of the United States. Troutdale was a small farming community in Oregon when I was a child, famous for green beans and berries of every variety. Located at the mouth of the Columbia River Gorge with its high cliffs, waterfalls, and forests of cedar and fir, it was a magnificent landscape. My first permanent home gave me a love of nature that has stayed with me ever since.

During my childhood, books were a constant companion. Once I learned to read, my mother told me I was always "lost" in one story or another. Perhaps because we moved so often, books were my most dependable allies against loneliness. Books let me escape to other worlds and other times, visit exotic locations, and meet the most interesting people.

I loved the stories in books, but I also loved the way books looked and felt when

in the cultural renaissance that has been taking place among Native American tribes. He is teaching his traditions and values to his two young sons, passing on what he had been taught of the ways of his people. This remarkable artist and his eloquent expressions of culture were the inspiration for my first book, *Totem Pole*.

Because of my friendship with David, I realized that there were many stories, like his, that needed telling. This led to a series of books about Native American children and became a new career for me.

I soon discovered that creating these books has been a way for me to use all the skills that I have acquired in my life. Taking a book project from the idea stage through to production has been a rewarding and challenging experience. The research for my books gives me the opportunity to travel to new places and develop new friendships. My love of a good story helps me recreate the experiences of an individual child for my readers. My skills as a designer help me to put all the elements together, text and pictures, to tell the whole story.

I love writing nonfiction because I enjoy learning about the world we live in. I like to meet new people and learn about their lives. We are lucky to live in a country with such a rich and diverse cultural heritage. It is a privilege, as an author, to be able to share some of these wonderful people and their stories.

———

Diane Hoyt-Goldsmith was born in Peoria, Illinois. She received her B.F.A. degree from Pratt Institute in Brooklyn, New York, in 1973. She worked as a book designer for Macmillan Publishing Company and Harcourt Brace & Jovanovich in New York before starting her company, Square Moon Productions.

Her first book, *Totem Pole*, won a design prize from the 1990 Bookbinder's Guild of New York. *Pueblo Storyteller* was named an Outstanding Merit book in the 1992 Car-

ter G. Woodson Awards presented by the National Council for the Social Studies. *Celebrating Kwanzaa* won the same citation in 1994.

Four of her books have been named Notable Children's Trade Books in the Field of Social Studies by a joint committee of the Children's Book Council and the National Council on the Social Studies: *Totem Pole, Pueblo Storyteller, Hoang Anh: A Vietnamese-American Boy*, and *Arctic Hunter*.

SELECTED WORKS: Totem Pole, 1990; Pueblo Storyteller, 1991; Arctic Hunter, 1992; Hoang Anh: A Vietnamese American Boy, 1992; Cherokee Summer, 1993; Celebrating Kwanzaa, 1993; Day of the Dead: A Mexican-American Celebration, 1994; Apache Rodeo, 1995; Mardi Gras: A Cajun Country Celebration, 1995.

JAN HUDSON

April 27, 1954–April 1990

AUTHOR OF *Sweetgrass*, etc.

Biographical sketch of Jan Hudson:

JAN HUDSON was a Canadian novelist who had only two novels published at the time of her death at the age of thiry-five. They were published to great acclaim, and she was working on a third when she died.

She was born in Calgary, Alberta, in Canada. Her father was a professor and school librarian. Her mother was a teacher. With that background, it is perhaps no surprise that Jan Hudson loved words, books, and writing. At only ten years old, she read *The Rubaiyat of Omar Khayyam*.

Hudson received her B. A. degree from the University of Calgary in 1978. She went on to earn her L.L.B. degree in 1983 from the University of Alberta. She was a legal editor, writer, and researcher. She worked as an editor for the attorney general of British Columbia. In 1977 Hudson was married to a Blackfoot Native American man, and adopted his daughter. In order to familiarize herself with her husband's heritage, she began reading Blackfoot history. She read about a smallpox epidemic that killed half the tribe in 1837, and made this chapter of history the basis for a novel that she dedicated to her daughter.

Hudson completed the first draft of her book *Sweetgrass* in 1979. In the novel, a fifteen-year-old Blackfoot girl prospers in her community in the summer of 1937. However, smallpox breaks out when winter comes, leaving Sweetgrass to care for her sick mother and siblings in her father's absence. Sarah Ellis, in a *Horn Book Magazine* "News from the North" column, calls Hudson's use of history "fresh and integrated" and her story told with "clear descriptions of the details of Blackfoot life." She writes, "We . . . experience the . . . complex satisfaction of having genuinely entered another time and the lives of another people." *Booklist* called it "an unusually fine first novel," and *Language Arts* called it a "powerful" book, "a splendid mix of dialogue and narrative."

As good as the novel was, however, it was difficult for Hudson to get it published. She sent it to different publishers for years, rewriting it and resubmitting it. In 1984, a small Canadian publisher, Tree Frog Press, published the book. The book was not published in the U.S. until 1989. It won the 1984 Canadian Library Association's Book of the Year for Children Award. It also won the Governor General's Literary Award for an author, given by the Canada Council. It was named a 1989 Notable Book and a Best Book for Young Adults by the American Library Association. It was also cited by the International Board of Books for Young People in 1986. *Sweetgrass* has been translated into many languages.

Her second novel, *Dawn Rider*, was published in the U.S. in 1990. It has another independent protagonist, sixteen-year-old Kit Fox, who dreams of becoming the first to ride a horse that has come to the tribe, challenging a ban against women riders. *Booklist* states that "Hudson excels at portraying the changing consciousness of young women as they move into adulthood." The book was awarded the 1991 R. Ross Annett Award from the Writers Guild of Alberta and received an honorable mention in the 1991 Young Adult Canadian Book Awards. It was named a Best Book for Young Adults by the ALA.

Hudson was a member of the Writers Union of Canada, the Canadian Bar Association, the Free-Lance Editors Association, and the Canadian Society of Composers, Authors, Illustrators, and Performers.

SELECTED WORKS: Sweetgrass, 1989; Dawn Rider, 1990.

ABOUT: Contemporary Authors, Vol. 136; The Horn Book Magazine, September/October, 1986; Publishers Weekly, June 29, 1990; Something About the Author, Vol. 77.

SATOMI ICHIKAWA

January 15, 1949–

AUTHOR AND ILLUSTRATOR OF *Nora's Castle*, etc.

Autobiographical sketch of Satomi Ichikawa:

I WAS BORN in a traditional Japanese home in Gifu. It was a small village, probably beautiful in its way, but I could not see with my artist's eye then. Since I was a child, I dreamed of faraway countries, and at my twenty first birthday I set out to see the world.

First I went to Italy and learned to speak Italian, then I moved to Paris. I was alone there and did not speak French at all, but Paris captured me profoundly. Paris was just what I dreamed it would be. I decided to stay and live there.

It was sometime in my early years in Paris that all by chance I came across the books of French painter-illustrator Maurice Boutet de Monvel. I was not particularly interested in children's books at that time, but this one attracted me immediately. Mon-

Satomi Ichikawa

vel's drawings were so vivid, exquisite and subtle; I had never seen such art before. I fell in love with his work, and started to collect his books.

At that period, I was a student at a French language school, and worked as an au pair in a family. I often took the children out to the Luxembourg garden and watched them playing. There were many children playing, and I suddenly realized that Monvel's little people were there! They were everywhere in real life, as if they popped out of his drawings: vivid, exquisite, just the same. And when I started to watch closely around me, it was not only children, but also trees, leaves, flowers, birds, animals—all creatures were so expressive in their shapes and colors, just as they were in Monvel's drawings. This opened my eyes. I too wanted to draw. Some friend said to me long after: Satomi was born as an artist in Paris.

Although I'd never had art training in my life, I started to draw. My first attempt was a picture book for children! I was innocent; therefore I was bold. It did not matter if I was good or not, for I knew this was the only direction I wanted to take, and that I would give it my best self.

I tried to sketch from real life as much as

I could; at a nursery, a zoo, a farm, dance studio, and everywhere I travelled—to Southern France, in England, in America and Puerto Rico. Seeing many countries and different lives was often the source of the inspirations to create my stories. This was certainly true in the Nora books; they were based on my visits to France and England, and in *Isabela's Ribbons*, which was inspired by my trip to Puerto Rico.

I have only thanks for all my friends who so generously invited me into their lives. I am also grateful for all my editors: Judith Elliot of Heinemann in England, who discovered me; Ann Beneduce of Philomel and Mr. Imamura of Kaiseisha in Japan who supported me for these long years; and Patricia Lee Gauch, present editor of Philomel and author of the Tanya stories. And I am grateful to all the other people who work for books for children, and all the readers; these are the people who make it possible for me to continue my creations.

———

Satomi Ichikawa's work was exhibited at the Gallery Printemps Ginza in Japan in 1984. She received special mention in the Prix Critica in Erba at the 1978 Bologna Children's Book Fair for *Suzanne and Nicholas at the Market*. She received the Kodansha Prize in Japan in 1978 for *Sun Through Small Leaves*, which was written by Robina Beckles Wilson and published in England in 1980. She also won the Sankei Prize in Japan in 1981 for *Keep Running, Allan!*

Nora's Castle was named a Children's Choice Book by a joint committee of the Children's Book Council and the International Reading Association. *Dance, Tanya* was named a Notable Book of the Year by the American Library Association. *Rosy's Garden* has been translated into six languages.

SELECTED WORKS WRITTEN AND ILLUSTRATED: Suzanne and Nicholas at the Market, 1977; Nora's Castle, 1984; Nora's Stars, 1989; Nora's Duck, 1991; Fickle Barbara, 1993; Nora's Surprise, 1994; Isabela's Ribbons, 1995.

SELECTED WORKS ILLUSTRATED: Keep Running, Allen!, by Clyde R. Bulla, 1978; Here a Little Child I Stand: Poems and Prayers for Children, selected by Cynthia Mitchell, 1985; Dance, Tanya, by Patricia Lee Gauch, 1989; Rosy's Garden, by Elizabeth Laird, 1990; Bravo, Tanya, by Patricia Lee Gauch, 1992; Tanya and Emily in a Dance for Two, by Patricia Lee Gauch, 1994.

ABOUT: Contemporary Authors, Vol. 116, 126; Publishers Weekly June 7, 1993; Something About the Author, Vol. 36, 47, 78.

ROBERT INGPEN

ROBERT INGPEN

ILLUSTRATOR OF *Treasure Island*, etc.

Biographical sketch of Robert R. Ingpen:

ROBERT INGPEN was born in Geelong, Australia. His family, which originally came from England, has a long history in Australia. His great-grandfather, Thomas Lane Ingpen, arrived in Australia sometime before 1872, and one of his great-grand-uncles was a pioneer in the Australian gold fields in the 1840's. In addition to being an author-illustrator and an illustrator of books for children, Ingpen is an environmentalist, scientific illustrator and speaker. Most of his life's work has been dedicated to conveying information about his native Australia.

Ingpen's first work as an artist was in designing brochures and preparing diagrams to illustrate scientific writing. This work, states G.L. Kesteven, writing in the Australian journal *Orana*, was the beginning of the thread of realism in his work. Ingpen would work with a scientist, learning what the work was about, and sketching as it was explained to him. The sketches were later refined into diagrams that showed the natural object being studied as well as the laboratory instruments, the process of analysis, the data, and the theory being presented.

This work led naturally to the commission of a number of murals that Ingpen created on scientific and historical subjects. In 1966 his first mural was completed at the Clunies Ross Memorial Hall, and in 1969 he created a historical mural in Geelong City Hall. He created others, including the Conservation Mural in the Arthur Rylah Institute for Environmental Research, the Computer Services Mural for ACI Computer Services, and the Geelong Water Trust Mural.

With co-author Stuart Hawkins, Ingpen prepared a brochure explaining conservational measures for saving the Western Rock Lobster. In 1966 he designed and illustrated a brochure for the Marine Sciences Association. Its information on biotic systems and analysis of fishery industrial systems was published in Australian scientific journals and presented at conferences in Venezuela and Mexico.

Ingpen continued his scientific work in travels to Mexico and Peru, where he worked on problems of communication and extension services for fisheries. He was a contributor to a guidebook for the Melbourne Zoological Gardens as well as to a journal for the Fisheries Branch of the Federal Department of Primary Industry.

In addition to his work in the sciences and the natural world, Ingpen's interest in history led him to write a number of books on

Australian history. They include *Pioneer Settlement* and *Pioneers of Wool* in 1972; *Australia's Heritage Watch* in 1981; and *Australian Inventions and Innovations* in 1982. He also illustrated several historical books written by Michael Page, including *Turning Points in the Making of Australia* in 1981 and *Colonial South Australia* in 1985.

Concurrently with his writing for adults, Robert Ingpen began illustrating books for children. In 1974, he illustrated Colin Thiele's *Storm Boy*. It was named an Australian Children's Book of the Year 1975 by the Children's Book Council of Australia. He illustrated *The Runaway Punt* by Michael F. Page, which was published in Australia in 1976, and it was named to the International Board on Books for Young People Honour List in 1978.

Many of his books for children and adults have not been published in the United States. Of those that have been, his illustrations for *Treasure Island*, published in the U.S. in 1992, has artwork that "rivals Wyeth's," according to reviewer Anita Silvey, writing in *The Horn Book Magazine*. And Karen Jameyson, writing in her *Horn Book Magazine* column "News from Down Under," calls his full-page portraits for *The Great Deeds of Heroic Women* and *The Great Deeds of Superheroes* "haunting."

Robert Ingpen received the Hans Christian Andersen Medal for Illustration in 1986 from the International Board on Books for Young People. In 1989 he won the Dromkeen Medal from the Dromkeen Children's Literature Foundation in Australia. He lives in the town in which he was born.

Peace Begins with You was named a Children's Choice Book by a joint committee of the International Reading Association and the Children's Book Council as well as a Notable Children's Trade Book in the Field of Social Studies by a joint committee of the CBC and the National Council on the Social Studies.

SELECTED WORKS WRITTEN AND ILLUSTRATED: The Age of Acorns, 1990.

SELECTED WORKS ILLUSTRATED: Storm Boy, by Colin Thiele, 1978; The Great Bullocky Race, by Michael Page, 1988; The Great Deeds of Superheroes, retold by Maurice Saxby, 1990; Peace Begins with You, by Katherine Scholes, 1990; The Great Deeds of Heroic Women, retold by Maurice Saxby, 1992; Treasure Island, by Robert Louis Stevenson, 1992; River Through the Ages, by Philip Steele, 1993.

ABOUT: Orana August 1986.

BRIAN JACQUES

June 15, 1939–

AUTHOR OF *Redwall*, etc.

Biographical sketch of Brian Jacques:

AFTER ATTENDING Roman Catholic school in Liverpool, England, where he was born, Brian Jacques began work as a seaman. He then went on to work as a railway fireman and a longshoreman before becoming a long-distance truck driver for ten years. After a five-year stint as a docks representative, he became a free-lance radio broadcaster in 1980. He now broadcasts music programs and children's shows as well as quizzes, lectures, and documentaries at the BBC-Radio Merseyside.

Of his varied career before beginning to write children's books, Brian Jacques writes, "I sometimes think it ironic for an ex-seaman, longshoreman, truck driver, policeman and truck driver to find success writing children's novels." He did not write his first novel with publication in mind, but as a story to read to blind children at a home where he is a patron, the Royal Liverpool school in Wavertree. *Redwall* is the story of a battle between good and evil in the animal world. A gentle brotherhood of mice must react to the attacks of a terrifying horde of malicious rats. Brian Jacques had the novel typed out on thick recycled paper. When he met a writer friend of his, Alan Durband, who is known for his Shake-

speare books for young readers, he casually
showed him a shopping bag with the thick
paper manuscript inside. Durband took the
manuscript away with him to read while on
vacation. He loved it and sent it to his publisher, Century Hutchinson. The book was
first published in England in 1986.

The book was well-received and popular.
Writing in *The Horn Book Magazine*, Ann
Flowers calls the book "beautifully written"
and "exciting." She states, "The scenes of
combat are quite fascinating, with the strategy and counter strategy cleverly worked
out. The book offers an immense cast of distinctive characters. . . . " The author has
continued writing about the battle of good
and evil in the animal world he has created.
His second book, *Mossflower*, is a prequel
to *Redwall*, and there have been several
more books in the series.

Brian Jacques grew up reading
"old-fashioned romantic adventure novels"
by Sir Henry Ryder Haggard; works by Sir
Arthur Conan Doyle; and works by Robert
Louis Stevenson. He considers himself a storyteller and scoffs at critics who want to
find literary influences or see parallels with
books like Malory's *Childe Roland to the
Dark Tower Come*. Disliking comparisons

also to books like *Lord of the Rings* and
Watership Down, he points out that when
he grew up, in a fairly poor district in Liverpool, his "big, tough" dad gave him books
by R. M. Ballantine, Edgar Rice Burroughs,
and Zane Grey.

The author also rejects the characterization of his works as "fantasy." "I don't like
that name," he told Sally Estes in *Booklist*,
because "it seems to me to smack too much
of science fiction, which I hate—dungeons
and dragons and swords and sorcery and all
that kind of malarkey." He feels that in
writing books for children, a "good yarn" is
essential, keeping in mind a strong sense of
values for children; and he prefers the
phrase for describing his work.

Brian Jacques chose a long-ago era in
which to set his tales of struggle against evil
invaders. He feels that most of the adventure and romance has gone from today's
world. He also thinks that he
"unconsciously" was writing a movie serial
when he wrote *Redwall* with short, punchy
chapters and cliff-hanger endings.

Plans are now underway to bring the
mice heroes of *Mossflower*, to the screen as
either a film or a video production.
Redwall, *Mattimeo*, and *Mossflower* have
received awards that are voted upon by
children in England and in West Australia.
In addition to the *Redwall* series, Brian
Jacques has also written a book of ghost stories for children.

He has written numerous documentaries
and plays for television, radio, and the
stage. Several of his radio programs have
concentrated on film history, including
"The Hollywood Musicals," a six-part series.
He has received honors and commenda-
tions for his radio programs.

SELECTED WORKS: Redwall, 1987; Mossflower, 1988;
Mattimeo, 1990; Seven Strange and Ghostly Tales,
1991; Mariel of Redwall, 1992; Salamandrastron, 1993;
Martin the Warrior, 1994; The Bellmaker, 1995.

ABOUT: Booklist, November 1, 1991; Contemporary
Authors, Vol. 127; Something About the Author, Vol.
62.

WILLIAM JASPERSOHN

October 4, 1947–

AUTHOR AND ILLUSTRATOR OF *The Ballpark: One Day Behind the Scenes at a Major League Game*, etc.

Biographical sketch of William Jaspersohn:

WILLIAM JASPERSOHN was born in New Haven, Connecticut, and grew up in the Connecticut towns of Guilford and Branford. The son of a nursery school teacher and an engineer, he attended Guilford's public schools, then went on to Dartmouth College. He graduated in 1969 with an A.B. degree, majoring in English with a minor in French. After graduation, Jaspersohn taught at Waterville High School in Maine for two years. Then, he embarked on his writing career.

Jaspersohn didn't start out thinking of being a writer. "I went to college thinking I'd become a doctor," he says. "I did write a lot as a child and I enjoyed it, but I wasn't always rushing off to write a story." There were no writers in his family, so Jaspersohn had no writer role models until college. There, he met real writers for the first time and discovered that books were "things created by people—they didn't just drop out of the sky!" He credits meeting writers and having an influential creative writing teacher, Alexander Laing, with encouraging his shift in interest from science to the arts. He also became interested in films and made one while in college.

When he first began to write, Jaspersohn worked at various odd jobs including newspaper work, to support himself. He feels his journalism helped improve his writing skills. "I came to realize that my interest in writing and in film could be satisfied by doing books with photos," he says. For his first book, he approached Little, Brown and Company with a proposal to do a book on veterinarians. "They said yes to the proposal and that launched things." His first book for young readers, *A Day in the Life of a Veterinarian*, was published in 1978.

Jaspersohn enjoys writing about "real working people and their lives . . . real places where things happen." He says, "I realize I could use writing as a way to open doors to people I wanted to meet. It's given me a backstage glimpse at different places not afforded to most people. It's gotten me out into the world." Most of his books—around twenty nonfiction books—are illustrated with his own photographs. However, Jaspersohn doesn't really consider himself to be a photographer. "It's a tool," he says. "I've learned as I've gone on . . . my photography has been an evolutionary process."

Because he was a Red Sox fan—"since I was four years old!", he says—Jaspersohn's second book was *The Ballpark: One Day Behind the Scenes at a Major League Game*. He spent the whole second half of the 1978 baseball season taking notes and photographs at Fenway Park in Boston to put together the material for the book. "It was a hard but sublime experience," he says. For his book *Senator*, he spent eighteen months researching the life and career of Senator Bill Bradley. He flew to India and back to write *A Week in the Life of an Airplane Pilot*, and he spent time at the factory observing the industrial process for the making of Harley-Davidsons in *Motorcycle*. Jaspersohn's *How the Forest Grew*, one of the few books he didn't illustrate, was named an Honor Book in the 1980 *Boston Globe-Horn Book* Awards. *Cranberries* was named an Outstanding Science Trade Book for Children by a joint committee of the Children's Book Council and the National Science Teachers Association. *Magazine: Behind the Scenes at Sports Illustrated* was named a Notable Children's Trade Book in the Field of Social Studies by a joint committee of the Children's Book Council and the National Council on the Social Studies.

In addition to his nonfiction books, Jaspersohn has written a young adult novel, *Grounded*, and has created a package of four books for children: *My Soccer Book*, *My Baseball Book*, *My Ballet Book*, and *My Riding Book*. This set includes space for readers to write down their thoughts and feelings about various aspects of their chosen activity and is intended to encourage them to "gain a little more control over it," says the author. The set is illustrated with photos taken by Jaspersohn and Tom Ettinger. He has also written a mystery for adults called *Native Angels*, and is working on another called *Lake Effect*. He says he plans to concentrate more on this area of writing in the future.

Jaspersohn lives with his wife and two sons in Vermont. His wife is a flower farmer and his sons have posed for many of his photographs, most notably the cover photo on his book *Ice Cream*. Jaspersohn works on his books virtually every day in an office in his house. He says it takes him about two years from the time he thinks of an idea for a book to the time it's published, sometimes longer. "I'm interested in the texture of day-to-day events," he says. "I try not to prejudge my subjects. I try to keep an open mind . . . and see how it develops and go with that . . . Generally speaking, I think of myself as casting a net and pulling in all sorts of stuff and trying to make it into a book." He says that he has a real "sense of

responsibility to bring back the news in an accurate way." Jaspersohn adds, "when I talk to students one of the things I find myself saying is that writing is a power passed on to them by their parents and teachers, a power kids can use right now to open doors for them. . . . to gain control or gain understanding of who we are, what our experience has been and how the world works." He feels that, as a writer, "I find I can communicate with almost anyone. . . . young people have the same legitimate right to call themselves writers and open doors to what they're interested in." He adds, "whatever I'm working on, I'm satisfying my own interests first and hoping that it will be of interest to my readers."

SELECTED WORKS WRITTEN AND ILLUSTRATED: A Day in the Life of a Veterinarian, 1978; The Ballpark: One Day Behind the Scenes at a Major League Game, 1980; Magazine: Behind the Scenes at Sports Illustrated, 1983; Motorcycle: The Making of a Harley-Davidson, 1984; Ice Cream, 1988; Bat, Ball, Glove, 1989; Cranberries, 1991; A Week in the Life of an Airline Pilot, 1991; Senator: A Profile of Bill Bradley in the U.S. Senate, 1992; Cookies,1993; My Hometown Library, 1994.

SELECTED WORKS WRITTEN: How the Forest Grew, 1980; Grounded, 1989.

ABOUT: Contemporary Authors, Vol. 102.

LYLL BECERRA DE JENKINS

AUTHOR OF *The Honorable Prison*, etc.

Biographical sketch of Lyll Becerra de Jenkins:

LYLL BECERRA DE JENKINS was born in the state of Santander, Colombia, and grew up during a difficult period in Colombia's history. Her father, Luis Becerra López, was a journalist and a judge. Because of his outspoken views on General Gustavo Rojas Pinilla, the dictator who was in power during the 1950s, he faced impris-

Lyll Becerra de Jenkins: *leel ba SERA day jen kins*

onment and exile. The family travelled to many places including Panama, Costa Rica, and the Islands of San Andres and Providencia. Jenkins was educated in a convent school and attended Colombian universities in Cartagena and Bogotá.

Her first book, *The Honorable Prison*, describes the travails of a family placed under arrest in the Colombian mountains. While she wrote it as fiction, it includes many of the events of her own life. In the book, the father, a journalist, finds himself in disfavor with the reigning regime because of the opinions expressed in his writings. The action is set in the increasingly violent 1950s in an unnamed Latin American country. Before the family can flee the country, they are stopped and forced to live in a ramshackle house on an army base in the mountains. Reviewer Mary M. Burns writes in *The Horn Book Magazine*, "The characters who emerge through the first-person narrative are unique and unforgettable. . . . Described by the author as 'a fusion of personal experience and invention,' the book achieves its stunning effects not through sensationalism but through control; the reader is drawn into the story so that the events become immediate." The story is told by the daughter and is also the story of a teenage girl coming of age, trapped in a dangerous and confining "prison." Jenkins says that the character of the father in her book is based on her own father, and that her mother, Teresa Bretón, "is exactly like the mother in *The Honorable Prison*, courageous, proud and loving. . . . I had to say everything I could about my father in order to get to [the point where I could write about] my mother. My father inspired me in all my life's accomplishments, and yet without my mother I wouldn't have had any inspiration at all." The novel grew out of a story called "Tyranny" that originally appeared in *The New Yorker*. It was selected for the anthology *The Best American Short Stories of 1975* and was published in anthologies in Japan, Germany, and Sweden. After Jenkins rewrote it as a novel, *The Honorable Prison* won the 1989 Scott O'Dell Award for historical fiction for children and young adults, awarded by the Scott O'Dell Foundation. It was named a "Best Book of the Decade" by *Booklist* magazine and won Holland's Silver Pencil Award for best foreign novel of the year 1991. It was translated into ten languages.

Jenkins describes the kind of life she led in Colombia as "superficial." She was expected to "grow up, find a husband, and have tea parties." Indeed, she met and married John Joseph Jenkins, a lawyer and electrical engineer who was working for an American engineering company in Colombia. He travelled all over the world while she stayed home to raise their five children. At this time, Jenkins was very interested in dancing, and she became an accomplished flamenco dancer.

At the end of the 1960s, when their children were still young, the Jenkins family moved to the U.S. They settled in New Canaan, Connecticut, and Jenkins taught flamenco to children and adults. In Connecticut, she says, "I was lonely and missed Colombia. I didn't know who I was."

It was during a trip to Colombia that she first began to write. While at her sister's house, she entered a room where her late father's typewriter was kept; it had been preserved by her sister. She sat down and began to write. She wrote a story about the U.S., but she wrote it in Spanish; and she finds that when she writes about her own country—"the ironies and injustices inherent in my continent"—she automatically writes in English. This is a process that is a mystery to her.

It was not easy to write in her second language. "Why am I torturing myself with this?" she sometimes asked herself. She realized, however, that she was writing for the reader. Wanting to share her homeland and her experiences there with English readers, she writes in English. Yet, when writing about her experiences in the U.S., she wrote in Spanish.

Currently, she has not been able to write in Spanish. She has come to feel that "I may be depriving my writing of a richness that is in my subconscious—recently I've felt a sense of loss. I do believe I would have been a writer of more significance had I been writing in my own language. The flavor of my country, of growing up is missing in English. . . . I lament the rejection of my own language, but at the same time, I've acquired a double understanding of things, I understand with a dual perception because how things are said in English is different when translated into Spanish. I keep translating my country for the U.S. and the U.S. for Colombia. This is a privilege."

Jenkins cites the Argentinian writer Jorge Luis Borges as an inspiration for her writing. When she conducted an interview with him some years ago, he told her how lucky she was to live in the U.S. and "made some wonderful comments about English, its simplicity, its precision. He spoke with love about English. I agree. I characterize English as a wonderful, clear, precise language" as compared with Spanish, in which a sentence must be longer to convey the same meaning.

When *The Honorable Prison* was accepted for publication, Jenkins was originally a bit disappointed that it was seen as a book for young adults. She said, "Why a young adult book? I've written this book for everybody." But, she quickly became pleased at the outcome. "It might have gotten lost if it had not been marketed as a young adult book." She has received many letters from teachers at schools and universities who use her book to teach about Latin American politics.

Celebrating the Hero, her second book for young adults, tells the story of an American teenager who travels to South America to represent her family at a ceremony honoring her grandfather. A review in *The New York Times Book Review* states that it "gives a new perspective to the traditional coming-of-age novel." The *Horn Book Guide* calls it "insightful in its portrayal of family relationships and of Latin-American society." The book has been translated into Dutch, German, and French. Jenkins is working on a third book for young adults, and calls it a love story.

In addition to her novels, Jenkins has written many short stories that have been published in numerous Latin American and American magazines and newspapers, such as *La Nacion* and *La Prensa* in Buenos Aires; *El Tiempo* in Bogota; and *The Boston Globe* and *The New York Times*. She also teaches short fiction as an adjunct professor and lecturer at Fairfield University in Connecticut. Of her five children, three are writers. She and her husband also have three grandchildren.

SELECTED WORKS: The Honorable Prison, 1988; Celebrating the Hero, 1993.

ABOUT: Horn Book November 1990; New York Times March 12, 1989.

ANGELA JOHNSON

June 18, 1961–

AUTHOR OF *When I Am Old with You*, etc.

Autobiographical sketch of Angela Johnson:

WHEN I WAS a baby, my parents say that I would lie in my crib, awake through the entire night and tell myself stories. They'd hear whispers in the middle of the night for years to come, as this was a habit I'd keep through my childhood. When my brothers were finally born I had more of an audience. I didn't have to whisper my stories anymore.

I grew up in a small village in eastern Ohio. I loved it. No locked doors and access to Lawsons (a convenience store), comic books and later, underground New York City music magazines. The only literature I read in earnest while growing up was the Beat Poets.

The rest of the time was set aside for 1970s sitcoms.

In high school I wrote, but thought I wanted to be a social worker or teacher. I told myself from an early age that these two careers were noble and for me. It wasn't to be.

University life changed my life. I didn't write the entire time I was at college. All through high school I'd written punk poetry and kept a diary. It all disappeared at university. The day I decided not to go back to school, the muse came back.

I started writing vignettes and short stories while I took jobs as a babysitter. This would allow me more freedom to write.

A good friend encouraged me. Her second book for children had been published. I was on my way.

My first book, *Tell Me a Story, Mama* was written for all the times I'd begged my father for stories he'd told a thousand times. Childhood stories were the best. I could listen to them over and over. The child in *Tell Me a Story, Mama* can listen over and over, too. It's reassuring to children to know the stories won't change.

My books are primarily family stories, picture books. *When I am Old with You* epitomized this. It was written because my mother told me she somehow believed when she was a young married woman that she would be able to grow old with my grandparents, whom she adored. She thought they would all retire together. They were forty years older than her then. Some parts of our childhood visions never change.

After a few books with loving family themes, *Do Like Kyla*, *One of Three*, I thought it was time for comedy. *Julius* was born. *Julius* is a picture book about a fun-loving pig who comes to live with an unsuspecting family. I believe that *Julius* is the first book I've done that children are immediately drawn to, it's so fun and ridiculous.

My first novel, *Toning the Sweep*, was written as a valentine to the California desert. It is about coming of age and change. It's also about forgiveness, which is something I'm constantly working on myself. I try to work through these feelings in the story.

Sometimes I wake in the morning and can't believe that I write for a living. I periodically feel removed from the rest of the world. Writing can be lonely, but maybe twice a year I reread a line of a story that I've just written, and I know everything will be just fine.

Angela Johnson was born in Tuskegee, Alabama. She attended Kent State University from 1979 to 1982. She worked for Volunteers in Service to America (Vista) in Ravenna, Ohio, as a child development worker from 1981 to 1982. She has been a freelance writer since 1989. She is a member of the Authors Guild.

Toning the Sweep won a 1994 Coretta Scott King Award. *When I Am Old with You* was named an Honor Book in the 1991 Coretta Scott King Awards. It was also named a Notable Book of the Year by the American Library Association and a Notable Children's Trade Book in the Field of Social Studies by a joint committee of the National Council on the Social Studies and the Children's Book Council.

SELECTED WORKS: Tell Me a Story, Mama, 1989; Do Like Kyla, 1990; When I Am Old with You, 1990; One of Three, 1991; The Leaving Morning, 1992; The Girl Who Wore Snakes, 1993; Julius, 1993; Toning the Sweep, 1993; Shoes Like Miss Alice's, 1995.

ABOUT: Contemporary Authors, Vol. 138; Something About the Author, Vol. 69.

ANN JONAS

January 28, 1932–

AUTHOR AND ILLUSTRATOR OF *Round Trip*, etc.

Autobiographical sketch of Ann Jonas:

MY CHILDHOOD was an extremely normal one, spent in the suburbs of New York City. The only unusual thing about life in Great Neck was my parents' refusal to buy anything that they could make themselves. As a result, we built furniture, reupholstered furniture, made our clothes, painted the car, etc. In their spare time both parents sketched and painted.

With all these activities going on, books and reading were neglected. But then I discovered our local library. I became a compulsive reader and quickly worked my way

through the children's collection. Forbidden by the librarian from taking out any adult books until I was older, I was saved by a neighbor who gave me a big box of books from her cellar. They were Victorian children's novels, with a moral on every page, and very musty. I remember them, and their smell, fondly.

Living within a thirty minute train ride of New York, I couldn't wait to be allowed to make the trip alone. The city excited me and I determined to live there as an adult. Right out of high school I found a job there and became a commuter. After five years of typing and filing I found a job in the advertising department of a department store, first posing for the fashion illustrators and then working as a trainee in the art production department. I was occasionally given small illustration assignments, which made me think more seriously about my future.

I applied to Cooper Union, a free art and architecture school and was accepted! It was a wonderful experience—not only was I learning almost more than I could absorb, but I found I had some ability in graphic design. And, as a bonus, I met my future husband, Donald Crews, there.

After Cooper Union, I worked for my design instructor for a couple of years. After Don and I were married and had returned from Germany where he did a term in the army, we decided to freelance. We had our first child by then, but since we worked out of our home, I was able to remain active even after our second daughter was born. Our daughters grew up surrounded by art materials, which they used liberally. Most of our work was for the publishing industry: many book jackets, occasional packages, brochures and posters.

Don had started writing and illustrating children's books in the late 1960s. He, and his editor, Susan Hirschman, suggested that I try writing one. It wasn't until 1981 that I did. *When You Were a Baby* was the result. I had a great time planning it and doing the sketches. Much to my surprise, Don's editor, and now my editor too, liked it and offered me a contract. Working on that first book seemed like the best of worlds; for once I had complete control over the finished product. Both writing and illustrating gave me the freedom to change and manipulate the material in a way I never could when designing book jackets for someone else's manuscript. In fact, in some cases, such as *Round Trip*, I've reversed the procedure and worked out the illustrations before I have developed the story line.

It has been a very satisfying experience. I've drawn on my own children's lives for some of my books, and on others I've created a design problem for myself and let it develop into a book, always with the hope that if I have had fun writing and illustrating it in a way that amuses me, it will also entertain others.

Ann Jonas was born in New York City. She received her certificate from Cooper Union in 1959. She now lives in upstate New York.

Round Trip was named a *New York Times* Best Illustrated Book of the Year. *The Trek* was named an Honor Book in the 1986 *Boston Globe-Horn Book* Awards.

Both books were named Notable Books of the Year by the American Library Association and were Reading Rainbow Books.

Color Dance and *Reflections* were both named Outstanding Science Trade Books for Children by a joint committee of the National Science Teachers Association and the Children's Book Council. *The Trek* was named a Children's Choice Book by a joint committee of the International Reading Association and the CBC.

Holes and Peeks, *The Quilt*, and *Aardvarks, Disembark!* were all named ALA Notable Books of the Year. *Aardvarks* was named an Honor Book in the 1991 *Boston Globe-Horn Book* Awards.

SELECTED WORKS: Two Bear Cubs, 1982; When You Were a Baby, 1982; Round Trip, 1983; Holes and Peeks, 1984; The Quilt, 1984; The Trek, 1985; Now We Can Go, 1986; Where Can It Be?, 1986; Reflections, 1987; Color Dance, 1989; Aardvarks, Disembark!, 1990; The 13th Clue, 1992; Splash!, 1995.

ABOUT: Contemporary Authors, Vol. 118; 136; Horn Book May 1987; Marantz, Sylvia S. and Kenneth A. Marantz. Artists of the Page; Roginski, Jim. Behind the Covers II; Something About the Author, Vol. 42, 50; Teaching Pre-K November 1987.

REBECCA C. JONES

September 10, 1947–

AUTHOR OF *Germy Blew It*, etc.

Autobiographical sketch of Rebecca Castaldi Jones:

I HAD SEVEN DOLLS when I was a kid, and I considered them my children. I did not just feed and dress my children, the way other little girls did; I rescued them from kidnappers, pushed them out of the way of speeding trucks, caught them as they fell from helicopters, and used them as cover for my spying activities in the Korean Embassy.

The danger and excitement continued until I was in the sixth grade and a girl in my class discovered I still "played with

REBECCA C. JONES

dolls." When she told everyone at school, I was embarrassed. So I dressed my children in their best clothes and buried them in a box in the basement.

They would have died about that time anyway. I started getting terrible headaches and spent months at a time in hospitals and my bedroom—where the striped wallpaper came to look like prison bars. When the headaches disappeared (just as mysteriously as they came), I was tired of being alone with my own imaginings. I wanted real life.

So I majored in journalism and set out to find—and tell—the true stories of the world. I worked as a reporter for a couple of magazines, a couple of newspapers, and a television station. Then I began teaching journalism.

Along the way, I married my husband, and we had two kids. My daughter wasn't much interested in dolls, but my son developed a collection of stuffed animals with personalities and adventures that reminded me of my dolls. I began to write books—first about a girl stuck in the hospital and then about other kids in other situations. (I never wrote about dolls or stuffed animals, though.)

When my daughter was in high school,

she started getting terrible headaches. By now doctors had lots of fancy gadgets so they could look inside her head. They found she had a knot of tangled blood vessels in her brain. The tests showed I had some, too, but my knots were old and quiet; hers was raw and bleeding. Doctors removed her knot in an eleven-hour operation.

Amanda is still recovering from the complications that followed surgery. It has been very hard for her, and she has been very brave. But her struggle has been a little too exciting for me. I no longer feel like making up stories about other kids.

So I've stopped writing fiction. I still tell stories—but only true ones—in magazine articles and in my new nonfiction book, *The President Has Been Shot.*

Every once in a while, though, I see a doll or a stuffed animal that seems to call out to me. I expect I will return to writing fiction soon.

———

Rebecca C. Jones was born in Evergreen Park, Illinois. The third of four children, she grew up in Oak Lawn, Illinois, and Warsaw, Indiana. She went to Northwestern University, where she received a B.S. in journalism in 1969 and an M.S. in 1970.

She worked as a reporter for several midwestern newspapers, some New York magazines, and an Ohio television station. She taught journalism at Ohio State University and the University of Maryland. In 1992 she received the Excellence in Teaching Award from the University of Maryland University College, and in 1993 she received the Outstanding Faculty Award from the National Universities Continuing Education Association. She is now senior editor of *The American School Board Journal* and *The Executive Educator.* She is a member of the Children's Book Guild of Washington, D.C.

Jones is married to software engineer Christopher Jones. They live in Annapolis with their dog, Clifford. They have two grown children, Amanda and David.

SELECTED WORKS: Angie and Me, 1981; The Biggest, Meanest, Ugliest Dog in the Whole Wide World, 1982; Madeline and the Great (Old) Escape Artist, 1983; I Am Not Afraid, 1985; Germy Blew It, 1987; The Believers, 1989; Germy Blew the Bugle, 1990; Matthew and Tilly, 1991; Down at the Bottom of the Deep Dark Sea, 1991; Germy in Charge, 1993; Great-Aunt Martha, 1995.

ABOUT: Contemporary Authors, Vol. 106; (New Revision Series), Vol. 22; Something About the Author, Vol. 33.

BARBARA M. JOOSSE

February 18, 1949–

AUTHOR OF *Mama, Do You Love Me?*, etc.

Autobiographical sketch of Barbara Monnot Joosse:

I OWE my writing career to Tex. At twelve, I figured there were three careers for women: nurse, nun or teacher. I couldn't be a teacher because I couldn't spell. Between nun and nurse I chose "nun" because they had better outfits. It seemed exotic and mysterious to wear a veil and long, swirly skirts. But when I was thirteen, nuns began to wear street clothes. So I decided to be a nurse. Nurses, I knew, smiled through disgusting tasks, so I tested the authenticity of my calling with my pony, Tex, and my job of shovelling wet horse apples over the fence. When I couldn't shovel the muck high enough and it slid into my shirt, and I couldn't smile through *that*, I knew I couldn't be a nurse. Years later, I discovered writing, beginning with advertising copy and poetry.

I'm unsuccessful and slightly bored with most adult activities, so when my first child was born I had an excuse to hang out with the folks I liked best—kids. Writing for children became a natural next step.

I grew up in a small town, Grafton, Wisconsin. We lived in Sunset Court, a neighborhood where Mike Port was king and I was queen. We mixed wildly disgusting concoctions, glop. We made rafts and launched them on the Milwaukee River. We had forts and hideouts and apple fights. It was heaven. Two of my favorite characters, Wild Willie and Lucky Lucy, live in Sunset Court. Willie is my son, Robby, and the Wild Willie series is a blending of Robby's childhood and my own. In these books I put a fun boy and a rowdy girl together and let them go crazy. This blending of my childhood and my children's is typical of my stories.

I love watching people and wondering about them. That wondering is often the start of a story. I treat my characters with tenderness and respect . . . and humor. Fiction is really a combination of real and pretend. I begin with real people and places. I add a bit of my own life and my children's, a dash of imagination, and then something magic happens: a story.

I live in an old stone house beside a river with my husband, three children and an outrageous parrot. My house was built during the Civil War and has a very colorful history (including a resident ghost). There, I became interested in the real lives of people who lived before me, and have begun writing historical fiction. Historical fiction allows me to fulfill my curiosity and stretch my imagination. I can write about travellers on the Santa Fe trail, Maori of New Zealand, Inuit of the Arctic, children at the WW II Nazi camp in my hometown and my husband's family in the Dutch Resistance in WW II.

My writing studio overlooks the main street in Cedarburg, Wisconsin. From there I can watch school children and fire trucks and listen to bangy music coming out of convertibles. It feels like I'm smack in the middle of life itself, and that is exactly the place to write. I write every day (except weekends). Writing is not a labor for me, though it is a challenge. I revise extensively (twenty to two hundred revisions per story). I write picture books and novels for children.

I can't imagine my life without writing. I write as I eat or drink or breathe. It's as natural and necessary as that.

———

Barbara Joosse received her B.A. degree from the University of Wisconsin in Madison in 1970. She did graduate study at the University in Milwaukee in 1977. She has contributed articles and stories to such publications as *Cricket, Instructor*, the Authors Guild *Bulletin*, and the *Chicago Tribune*. She is a member of the Society of Children's Book Writers and Illustrators.

Mama, Do You Love Me?, which was illustrated by Barbara Lavallee, won a 1991 Golden Kite Award, given by the SCBWI. *Fourth of July*, which was illustrated by Emily Arnold McCully, was exhibited at the 1985 Bologna Book Fair in Italy.

SELECTED WORKS: The Thinking Place, 1982; Spiders in the Fruit Cellar, 1983; Fourth of July, 1985; Jam Day, 1987; Better with Two, 1988; Dinah's Mad, Bad Wishes, 1989; Mama, Do You Love Me?, 1991; Nobody's Cat, 1992; Wild Willie and King Kyle, Detectives, 1993; The Losers Fight Back, 1994; The Morning Chair, 1995; Snow Day, 1995.

ABOUT: Contemporary Authors, Vol. 109; Milwau-

kee May 1994; Milwaukee Journal October 23, 1994; Northshore Lifestyles March 1995; Something About the Author, Vol. 52.

MAIRA KALMAN

1949–

AUTHOR AND ILLUSTRATOR OF *Ooh-la-la (Max in Love)*, etc.

Biographical sketch of Maira Kalman:

MAIRA KALMAN was born in Tel Aviv, Israel. When she was four years old, her family moved to New York. She grew up in the Riverdale section of the Bronx, and her mother saw to it that she had piano lessons and dance lessons. She was often taken to concerts and museums. She attended the High School of Music and Art in order to study piano, and studied literature at New York University.

She had always wanted to be a writer, and she tried writing poetry, but wasn't satisfied with it, and decided to be an illustrator. She worked for magazines, including *The National Lampoon*. Beginning in 1979, she also worked as a designer for her husband, Tibor Kalman. He had his own graphic design company at the time, M & Company. He created designs for films, for restaurants, and for the music business, to name a few of the areas in which he worked. *The New York Times* referred to him in 1993 as "one of the most influential graphic designers of his generation." For the company, she created textiles designs, album covers, and movie titles. The clothing designer Isaac Mizrahi has used some of her designs in his clothes.

She began to write and illustrate books for children in 1986, and sees the form as without limits. Her first book was *Stay Up Late*, in which she illustrated the lyrics to the song by David Byrne of the musical group The Talking Heads. Her aim from the beginning was to produce books that would be intended for both children and

Maira: rhymes with *Ira*

MAIRA KALMAN

adults, so she chose to illustrate a song that was popular with adults.

The first two books that she wrote and illustrated featured her two children, who are now nine and twelve years old. She then created her character Max, a dog that first appears in *Hey Willy, See the Pyramids*, and becomes a full-fledged star in three later books.

For *Roarr: Calder's Circus*, Kalman wrote a text for the photographs of Donatella Brun, illustrating artist and sculptor Alexander Calder's whimsical creation. He fashioned an entire circus in miniature using wire, wood, cloth, and other materials. The figures were on exhibit for a long period by the Whitney Museum in New York City, accompanied by a film showing Calder manipulating the movable figures. The book was published by the Whitney Museum in 1991.

Architecture and fine art influence Kalman's work, and she is particularly fond of the work of Matisse and Chagall, whom she sees as her strongest influences. Her work is described by a *Booklist* magazine reviewer as "zesty" artwork that is "a totally new wave . . . filled with humorous asides that parents and kids will find amusing, each on their own level." A writer in *Parents Magazine* stated, "Kalman's extravagantly inventive artwork is bursting with the kind of outrageous detail children adore."

She always carries a sketchbook with her, and usually a small automatic camera light enough to keep in her pocket. She takes hundreds of photographs and cuts out images from magazines, and these become a reference for her. Some of the pictures she collects are of fashion, architecture, cinema, and food. She also collects postcards, labels, leaves, and fabrics.

While Kalman lived in New York, she spent time in cafes and at the Museum of Modern Art, sketching and writing, drawing from the influence of urban life. She and her family lived in Greenwich Village in Manhattan.

In 1993, Tibor and Maira Kalman decided to sell most of their belongings and move their family to Italy. Although Tibor Kalman folded his design company, he continued his work as Editor-in-Chief of *Colors*, a magazine published by the Benetton clothing company. Maira Kalman began to produce books from their new locale in Rome. The Italian influence can readily be seen in an article she wrote and illustrated on children's fashion for the March 6, 1994, *New York Times Magazine*. The Kalmans have since returned to New York. There, Kalman spends time in cafes and at the Museum of Modern Art, sketching and writing, drawing from the influence of urban life.

Ooh-la-la (Max in Love) was named a Best Illustrated Book of 1991 by *The New York Times*.

SELECTED WORKS WRITTEN AND ILLUSTRATED: Hey Willy, See the Pyramids, 1988; Sayonara, Mrs. Kackleman, 1989; Max Makes a Million, 1990; Ooh-la-la (Max in Love), 1991; Max in Hollywood, Baby, 1992; Chicken Soup, Boots, 1993; Swami on Rye: Max in India, 1995.

SELECTED WORKS ILLUSTRATED: Stay Up Late, by David Bryne, 1987.

SELECTED WORKS WRITTEN: Roarr: Calder's Circus, 1993.

ABOUT: Harpers Bazaar March 1992; House and Garden October 1992; New York Times January 9, 1992; September 26, 1993; Publishers Weekly September 27, 1991.

KEIKO KASZA

December 23, 1951–

AUTHOR AND ILLUSTRATOR OF *The Wolf's Chicken Stew*, etc.

Autobiographical sketch of Keiko Kasza:

I WAS BORN on a small island in the Inland Sea of Japan. Our house was five minutes away from the island's port, which was the only door to the rest of the world. I grew up in a typical Japanese extended family, living with my grandparents, parents, and two brothers. Uncles, aunts, and cousins living nearby dropped in constantly.

I wish I could relate some extraordinary stories from my childhood, but all the steps I took growing up were pretty typical. As was true of most Japanese children, my brothers and I found most of our toys in nature: sticks, rocks, and insects. Japanese kids are still inveterate collectors of insects, dead or alive! The family put great emphasis on education. Talking back to one's elders was unthinkable. It was a happy childhood, nothing out of the ordinary.

My life left the beaten path, however, when I decided to go to college in the United States. After graduating from California State University at Northridge with a B.A. in graphic design, I married an American, and the U.S. suddenly became my home. When I think back, it seems to me that my eyes were always looking beyond that little island's dock with tremendous curiosity. Still, I never imagined I would end up in a foreign country.

I became an authoress and illustrator of children's books more by accident than on purpose. There was no master plan. When my husband was working for his Ph.D., we moved around a lot. Everywhere we went

I was able to find work as a graphic designer, until we spent a year in Ecuador. Not knowing Spanish, I didn't even bother to look for a job there. But as I enjoyed my leisure, I received two children's books from a friend. One was Leo Leonni's *Frederick*, and the other was Anno Mitsumasa's *Journey*. Until that time, I had no idea how wonderful and creative picture books could be. Since I was temporarily free of design work and had a great desire to write, I immediately began to work on my own stories. My first efforts were pretty corny and far from publishable, but they still have a place of honor in the attic.

Finally, after four years of work, my first book, *The Parrot's Trick*, was published in Japan. My excitement at that moment is beyond words (or pictures!), but I didn't yet think of myself as a picture book writer. I was still making my living in graphic design. It was only after seven more years, and the publication of seven more books, that I quit my design work and decided to devote myself to picture books. The burden of two jobs and two children finally forced me to choose one career. I might have made the move sooner, but I lacked confidence in my ability as a writer/illustrator.

During the process of making a book, I feel like I'm on stage, acting under the lights. I become the character I am illustrating that day. I pretend I'm a bird looking for a mother, or a pig trying to impress his girlfriend. I jump, run, laugh, and cry in my basement studio. (It's a good thing I work alone!) Many of my stories come from my own childhood, and when I'm working, I become a child again. In a way, I haven't grown up since I left that warm house on a small Japanese island.

———

Keiko Kasza graduated magna cum laude from California State University in 1976. She lives in Indiana with her husband and two sons.

SELECTED WORKS WRITTEN AND ILLUSTRATED: The Wolf's Chicken Stew, 1987; The Pigs' Picnic, 1988; When the Elephant Walks, 1990; A Mother for Choco, 1992; The Rat and the Tiger, 1993; Grandpa Toad's Secrets, 1995.

MARILYN KAYE

July 19, 1949–

AUTHOR OF *Wrong Kind of Boy*, etc.

Autobiographical sketch of Marilyn Kaye, who also writes under the pen name "Shannon Blair":

I CAN'T REMEMBER a time when I wasn't writing. From the moment I learned to print the letters of the alphabet, I wanted to bring the letters together to form words. Then the words became sentences, the sentences grew into paragraphs, and a story began.

Unfortunately, that was usually where the story ended too. Somewhere, in a basement or an attic or stuffed in the back of a closet, there's a box filled with spiral notebooks, each containing the first chapter of a would-be novel. I had no problem coming up with ideas, concepts, situations, and characters—what I couldn't figure out was what to do with them.

So I didn't really entertain any notions of becoming a professional writer. I channeled my creative writing into personal letters and private journals. And I read incessantly. Fortunately, I discovered a career in which I could indulge my love for books—I became a children's librarian. I enjoyed this work, and found myself becoming increasingly intrigued with children's literature. I pursued additional study in this area, and ultimately became a teacher of children's and young adult literature. But as pleasant as my career was, I still felt something was missing. I wasn't writing—not the way I wanted to write.

Then, one day, I had one of my story ideas—a situation, a character. But this time, something happened; I asked myself 'what if'? What if the character responded to the situation in a certain way, where would that lead her? What sort of problem would her reaction create for her? How would she deal with this? And suddenly, I had a story, with a beginning, a middle, and an end. That happened in the autumn of 1981, and I've been asking myself 'what if' ever since.

I wrote my first four books under a pseudonym—Shannon Blair. Looking back,

I'm not sure why. I wasn't ashamed of my writing; I think maybe I was simply intimidated by the fact that I dared to write at all, and decided to hide behind another name.

I'm not sure how to describe my books. I've written books for young children, middle-graders, young adults; I've written series with continuing characters of my own invention, series with licensed characters, romances, fantasies, funny stories, sad stories. I think all my books are personal, but I can't say that my work is autobiographical. I do write from memory—not the memory of specific people and actual events, but the memory of feelings.

And although the only feelings I can truly remember are my own, I don't think I write for myself; I write to communicate, and I believe it's the memory of feelings that allows me to reach readers. No matter what kind of situation I'm writing about, I want my stories to have an emotional reality, a believable way in which characters respond and react to what's happening to them and around them. The situation can be improbable, implausible, even incredible—but as long as the emotions of my characters are honest and natural and real, I think—I hope—I'll be able to connect with readers.

Marilyn Kaye was born in New Britain, Connecticut, and grew up in Atlanta, Georgia. She received her B.A. and Master's in Librarianship from Emory University, and a Ph.D. from the University of Chicago. She has been a librarian in school and public libraries, a children's reviewer for *Booklist*, *School Library Journal*, and *The New York Times Book Review*, among other publications. She has been chair of the American Library Association Notable Children's Book Comittee. She is the author of over sixty-five books for children and adults, including the "Sisters," "Camp Sunnyside Friends," and "Video High" series books. She was also co-editor of *Celebrating Children's Books: Essays on Children's Literature in Honor of Zena Sutherland*, published in 1981.

Wrong Kind of Boy was named a Children's Choice Book by a joint committee of the International Reading Association and the Children's Book Council. *Daphne* was a Junior Literary Guild selection.

Kaye is a member of the ALA and Beta Phi Mu. She is currently Associate Professor in the Division of Library and Information Science, St. John's University in New York City.

SELECTED WORKS: Will You Cross Me?, 1985; Wrong Kind of Boy, 1985; Cassie, 1987; Daphne, 1987; Lydia, 1987; Phoebe, 1987; The Real Tooth Fairy, 1990; The Atonement of Mindy Wise, 1991; Real Heroes, 1993; Dream Lover, 1995.

ABOUT: Contemporary Authors, Vol. 107; (New Revision Series), Vol. 24; Roginski, Jim. Behind the Covers Vol. II; Something About the Author, Vol. 56.

BEVERLY KELLER

AUTHOR OF *Desdemona, Twelve Going on Desperate*, etc.

Autobiographical sketch of Beverly Keller:

AS A CHILD, I didn't live anywhere, but travelled with my parents. Wherever we stayed, my father let it slip that he was really Lawrence Tibbett, the great Metropolitan Opera star, secretly married to my mother, who was really Gertrude Ederle, the first woman to swim the English Channel. My mother weighed ninety pounds and was terrified of any body of water larger than a bathtub, but fortunately nobody pressed her to demonstrate a few strokes.

I knew what it was to be treated like a star. We had flowers and fruit baskets and prime tables. Now and then the band leader in a hotel dining room would beg my father to honor the guests with an aria. Now and then my father obliged.

So we changed hotels often. By the time I was in high school, I'd attended thirteen schools, and in the process missed learning

English grammar entirely. One compensates.

Graduated from the University of California at Berkeley, I wrote a column for The Hayward Review, and sold a humor piece to the *Atlantic* and a short story to *Women's Home Companion.*

I lived for two years in the Middle East, got caught in a camel migration where the Tigris and Euphrates Rivers join, and arrived in Lebanon in time for the Suez Crisis. At its height, I drove from Beirut to Europe in a Fiat 600. It threw a wheel in Turkey, but I pressed on, sleeping in abandoned villas on the Aegean, arriving in Rome at the outbreak of the Hungarian Revolution.

I lived in a penthouse that had belonged to Count Ciano, Mussolini's son-in-law. It wound around the building—vast terraces, marble floors, walls studded with assegais, spears, shields, guns, two kitchens...and there were rooms I never cared to enter.

Afterward, I travelled third class by rail through Europe with my two small children, which explains why I have looked my age for many years.

I wrote articles for the *San Francisco Chronicle, Rome Daily American,* and *Women's News Service* during the time abroad.

My third daughter was born when we returned to the states, and I returned to being your perfect television wife and mother. I was widowed at thirty-seven, and started writing again.

My short stories have been published in *The Magazine of Fantasy and Science Fiction,* Doubleday's *The Best from Fantasy and Science Fiction,* and in *Cosmopolitan.* When my first novel, *The Baghdad Defections,* was published, the *New York Times* called it "sensitive, penetrating and exciting", *Library Journal* called it "tremendously effective", and I assumed it would be a long-time annuity. A year later, the publisher offered me the overstock at substantial discount.

I've been writing children's books since, with something close to thirty published.

Almost all have done better than that tremendously effective first novel.

I've written one poem, which appeared in *The American Voice,* and have no idea when I'll think of another.

My eldest daughter is a physician and surgeon, my middle daughter a county prosecutor, and my youngest a student. Until my middle daughter married a judge this year, I had five grandchildren. Now I have nine.

If you have ever seen the Booth cartoon "Write about dogs", you may have some inkling of my working conditions. My dogs, which are large and many, all rescued from streets and shelters, doze and shed on bills, correspondence, and work in progress. I also knock myself out for any creatures in trouble, rescue spiders from the sink, and fed the house ants until the wretches started biting me. I can't say my friends understand, but they're fond of me.

I fear that, as a species, we endure the pain of others with astonishing equanimity. A life worth living, I think, is one devoted to preventing the suffering and preserving the lives of all sentient beings.

———

Beverly Keller was born in San Francisco. She earned a B.A. degree from the University of California at Berkeley in 1950. She has been a director and officer of a county humane society, and founded an emergency animal rescue service. She has been a speaker at children's literature conferences, such as the San Joaquin County Authors' Symposium in 1988.

The Sea Watch was named a Notable Book of the Year by the American Library Association. Many of her books have been named Junior Library Guild selections, including *The Beetle Bush, Pimm's Place,* and *Fiona's Bee. Fiona's Bee* was produced as an audio recording by Listening Library in 1976.

SELECTED WORKS: Fiona's Bee, 1975; The Sea Watch, 1981; No Beasts! No Children!, 1983; A Small, Elderly Dragon, 1984; Rosebud, with Fangs, 1985;

Desdemona, Twelve Going on Desperate, 1986; Only Fiona, 1988; Fowl Play, Desdemona, 1989; Desdemona Moves On, 1992; Camp Trouble, 1993; The Night the Babysitter Didn't Come, 1994.

ABOUT: Contemporary Authors, Vol. 49-52; (New Revision Series), Vol. 1, 17, 38; Something About the Author, Vol. 13.

ADRIENNE KENNAWAY

May 25, 1945–

ILLUSTRATOR OF *Hot Hippo*, etc.

Biographical sketch of Adrienne Kennaway:

ADRIENNE KENNAWAY was born in Christchurch, New Zealand. Her father was an electrical engineer, and when she was three years old, the family moved to Kenya, Africa. She describes the beauty of the land as "captivating" and fell in love with its forests, lakes, savannahs, and the tropical Indian Ocean coast. She and her brother were raised by a nanny called an *ayah*, and they spoke Swahili as well as English. Kennaway's mother was an art teacher and illustrator, and encouraged Kennaway in her talent for art. She took her daughter to draw animals in a game park a few miles away from Nairobi.

In 1951, Kennaway attended the first multiracial school in Kenya, along with her brother. The importance of art was emphasized, so Kennaway recalls spending a lot of time drawing and painting. She continued on to boarding school, which had more formal courses. In 1959, the family moved to England, where she was attended Ealing Art School in London. She studied fashion design and drawing, and then went to Italy to study at L'Academia de Belle Arte in Rome.

When her father was working in Malasia in 1963, she spent a year with him, painting, before taking a cargo ship back to Kenya. She began working as an illustrator for a publishing company there, and met the naturalist Leslie Brown. He was writing *Coral Reefs*, a book on tropical marine fish, and she was asked to illustrate it. To produce the illustrations, she had to learn to scuba dive, so that she could observe the fish swimming off Indian Ocean reefs in order to sketch them and photograph them for her work. She and Brown discovered unknown species of fish while doing the work.

Kennaway designed many series of postage stamps for the Kenya Post Office. The subjects were East African game fish, marine life, the "origins of mankind" based on the work of Richard Leakey, and ceremonial costumes of African tribes.

In addition to her work as an illustrator, Kennaway is a fine artist, in the impressionist and abstract forms, and has had many exhibitions in Africa and England. They include shows at the Gallery Watatu in Nairobi in 1975; at the New Stanley Gallery in Nairobi in 1983; and at the James Gallery in London in 1987. She has also created a series of paintings of birds of prey. She had an exhibition of the paintings in Dubai, and the Interior Minister purchased all of the paintings to present to the Sultan as a gift.

Her children's book career was begun with a conversation with a friend, Bruce Hobson, who writes under the pen name Mwenye Hadithi, which means "storyteller" in the Kikuyu language. He wrote a story of how the zebra got its stripes, called *Greedy Zebra*. An agent took the story, along with sketches by Kennaway, to a London publisher, and their collaboration on a series of successful animal stories was begun. Adrienne Kennaway lives in England.

Greedy Zebra was made into an audio recording in 1985, produced by Revallee Studios. *Hot Hippo* was made into a filmstrip in 1987 by Weston Woods.

Crafty Chameleon won the 1987 Kate Greenaway Medal presented by the British Library Association. *Hot Hippo* was named a Children's Choice Book by a joint committee of the International Reading Association and the Children's Book Council.

SELECTED WORKS WRITTEN BY MWENYE HADITHI AND ILLUSTRATED: Greedy Zebra, 1984; Hot Hippo, 1986; Crafty Chameleon, 1987; Tricky Tortoise, 1988; Lazy Lion, 1990; Baby Baboon, 1993; Hungry Hyena, 1994.

SELECTED WORKS ILLUSTRATED: Awful Aardvark, by Mwalimu, 1990.

ABOUT: Something About the Author, Vol. 60.

DAYAL KAUR KHALSA

April 17, 1943–July 17, 1989

AUTHOR AND ILLUSTRATOR OF *Tales of a Gambling Grandma*, etc.

Biographical Sketch of Dayal Kaur Khalsa by Barbara B. Yoffee:

"IN THE END, I'm really a writer," Dayal told a close friend at the end of her life.

Born in New York City, Dayal was the second child of Ruth and Daniel Schonfeld. Her father was a businessman. Her mother was determined to provide the kind of educational environment that would take both children to academic and creative heights.

Bright and witty, Dayal went through childhood with an insatiable curiosity, fantastic dreams and a charismatic personality that drew people to her.

She excelled in creative writing and doodled on everything from an early age. Art activities and art classes were part of her childhood. Dayal and her mother took an art class together in New York, but they found it more interesting to see a Broadway show and shop, so their outings together took a different turn.

When her Grandmother died in 1951, Dayal lost her best friend. She affectionately recalled a childhood story in *Tales of a Gambling Grandma*. Her grandma, then three years old, jumped into a cart full of hay and covered herself. Somewhere, she lost her shoe and so she escaped from Russia to America wearing only one little black shoe, hiding in a hay cart drawn by a tired

DAYAL KAUR KHALSA

white horse all the way across the wide slate-green Atlantic Ocean. At least that's how Dayal remembers the story told to her.

Dayal remembers spending most of her early childhood under a great weeping willow tree in her front yard in Queens, New York. Her grandma sat "like a flowering mountain in her big green garden chair." She told Dayal stories of her life and gave two important pieces of advice. "One: Never, ever go into the woods alone because the gypsies will get you or, should you escape that cruel fate, you'll fall into a hole. Two: Just in case the Cossacks come to Queens, learn to say 'Da' and always keep plenty of borscht in the refrigerator."

Dayal wrote *Tales* to honor her, as she felt her grandmother gave her the strength and courage to write and illustrate seven children's books, especially during the times of her illness with breast cancer, which occurred about the time *Tales* was published. Dayal was in her early forties and knew she had a limited time in which to produce books.

At a young age, she developed a keen understanding of and interest in literature and read "all the books in her local library." She majored in English literature and received her B. A. degree from City College of New York in 1963. Her interest in books and art led 'her to travel to Mexico, throughout the United States, and eventually to Canada, where she settled.

In 1969, her mother died. This was the second great loss of a loved one. Dayal's books would have made her grandmother and her mother proud of her. According to May Cutler, her publisher at Tundra Books in Canada, "the five [books] published before she died moved her to the ranks of those rare and precious creators of children's books who can both tell a good story and illustrate it spectacularly. You can count on two hands their number throughout the world."

As an example of her enchanting books, *I Want a Dog* is a hilarious tale of ingenuity in which May, trying to get her parents to get her a dog, pretends that she has one: a roller skate on a leash. When other children follow her lead, there is a wonderful parade of real and imagined dogs. Her artwork contains details that allude to famous paintings, such as Seurat's "Sunday Afternoon on the Island of Grand Jatte," in a whimsical manner.

Dayal's books were published in Canada by Tundra Books and, thanks to May Cutler, in the U.S. by Clarkson S. Potter. As with most children's authors and illustrators, Dayal Kaur Khalsa retold her childhood experiences. She had virtually total recall. She created her illustrations first and then the story followed. This was her way of creating a feeling and expressing it.

For the last ten years of her life, Dayal studied and became a member of the Sikh community. She found the love and discipline of the "family life" enriching and fulfilling. She studied children she knew at the Sikh Ashram in Montreal, and used this study to create a series of "Baabee Books" published in Canada in 1983 and 1984. She also taught yoga and co-edited an Indian vegetarian cookbook, *Taste of India*.

In 1990, shortly after Dayal's death, a longtime friend and fellow artist found the illustrations for a book Dayal had been working on, entitled *The Snow Cat*. The Canadian Library Association called it "a farewell treasure to read again and again."

Tales of a Gambling Grandma was named by the Canada Council to be an Honorable Mention in the Children's Literature Prize for Illustration in 1987. It also was a 1987 Amelia Frances Howard-Gibbon Award Finalist in Canada and was named a Notable Book of 1986 by the American Library Association. *How Pizza Came to Queens* was named a 1989 New York Times Best Illustrated Book.

Her books appeal to children and adults because of the sophisticated humor, a quality that kept the author laughing even while fighting her illness. Her original artwork may be found in the National Library in Ottawa, as she wanted to give a gift to the country that had been so good to her.

SELECTED WORKS: Tales of a Gambling Grandma, 1986; I Want a Dog, 1987; Sleepers, 1988; My Family Vacation, 1988; How Pizza Came to Queens, 1989; Julian, 1989; Cowboy Dreams, 1990; Snow Cat, 1992.

ABOUT: CM: A Reviewing Journal of Canadian Materials for Young People, December 1984; Horn Book Magazine, May/June 1989; Something About the Author, Vol. 62.

ERIC A. KIMMEL

October 30, 1946–

AUTHOR OF *Hershel and the Hanukkah Goblins*, etc.

Autobiographical sketch of Eric A. Kimmel:

The question I'm most often asked is, "What made you decide to become a writer?" The truth is, I had nothing to do with that decision, any more than I consciously decided to grow slightly less than six feet tall or to have brown eyes. I was born to be a writer. I never wanted to be anything else. Everything in my life pointed me in this direction.

Eric A. Kimmel

I clearly remember the moment when I became aware of my destiny. And I remember the book that did it. It was Dr. Seuss' *Horton Hatches the Egg.* I adored that book. I wanted to hear it over and over until I could say the words by heart. I was in kindergarten then, and since I didn't know where books came from or how they were made, I thought that the words, "by Dr. Seuss" were part of the title. "HortonHatchestheEggbyDr.Seuss."   I would say it all together, as if it were one word.

Then, towards the end of kindergarten, I experienced a revelation. Books don't drop out of the sky. People write them. A person who sits down and writes a book is called an author, and that's whose name is on the front of the book. The author. So those three mysterious words "by Dr. Seuss" meant there was a man named Dr. Seuss (Was he a doctor like my Uncle Milton or Uncle Abe?) and he created this wonderful story. When you do that, you get to put your name on the cover.

I felt electrified. I wanted that. I wanted to have my name on the cover of a book. It was the most wonderful thing I could imagine. I still get a shiver of excitement when-

ever I take a new book out of the envelope and hold it for the first time. Wow, I did that! I wrote a book! It never fails to amaze me.

Most of my books are based on storytelling and folktales. Again, this is no accident or anything I consciously chose to do. It was a gift given to me by my grandmother.

I had a wonderful grandmother. She spoke five languages besides English: German, Polish, Ukrainian, Yiddish, and Russian, and she could tell stories. Wild, wonderful, swirling tales that went on and on for days. There was a witch named Bubba Haw who lived in a house that walked on chicken feet; little elves called *kapelyushniki*, who lurked in the forest and lured travelers to their doom; and the wonder-working rabbis of Drohobych, my ancestors, who could raise the dead and fly to Jerusalem in a single night. There were kings and princesses in these stories too, real ones—Empress Elizabeth of Austria and her husband, Kaiser Franz Josef II, the German Kaiser Wilhelm, and Nicholas II, the Russian czar, whom Nana hated and never called by name. He was always "Fonya Chazar,"—Jack the Pig.

This story world of peasant tales, Biblical lore, and nineteenth century memories was far more interesting than the one I actually lived in—Brooklyn, New York, during the Eisenhower 1950's. My parents were less than pleased, since by the time I started school I believed in ghosts and fairies, had no interest in the Brooklyn Dodgers, and decided, for a time, to stop speaking English. So Nana and I had to cool it. We went underground, and I would root for "dose bums!", salute the flag and recite the Pledge of Allegiance, pretending to be normal as could be, even though I was wildly superstitious and, like my Nana, a staunch Austro-Hungarian monarchist at heart.

I never forgot those stories, and how endlessly fascinating they were. I've worked as a teacher, and as a teacher of teachers, but I always came back to my first love, stories and storytelling. As a writer, I see myself primarily as a storyteller, recreating on the printed page the experience of hearing and seeing a tale unfold. A reviewer once said of my books, "Kimmel writes with a storyteller's voice." That is exactly what I strive to do, since that is where I began, sitting with my grandmother under the lilac bush in our back yard, listening to stories.

———

Eric A. Kimmel was born in Brooklyn, New York. He received his B.A. degree from Lafayette College in 1967 and his M.A. from New York University in 1969. He earned a Ph.D. degree from the University of Illinois in 1973. He was assistant and associate professor of education at Indiana University in South Bend from 1973 to 1978. He was professor of education at Portland State University in Oregon from 1978 to 1994 and is now a full-time writer. He is a member of the International Reading Association, the Authors Guild, PEN Northwest, the National Storytelling Association, Phi Beta Kappa, and the Society of Children's Writers and Illustrators, among other professional organizations. He is a contributor to such publications as *Horn Book, Cricket, Spider,* and *The New Advocate.*

Hershel and the Hanukkah Goblins, illustrated by Trina Schart Hyman, was named an Honor Book in the 1990 Randolph Caldecott Medal Awards given by the American Library Association. *The Three Princes* was named an ALA Notable Book.

Kimmel received a 1991 Sydney Taylor Book Award from the Association of Jewish Libraries for *The Chanukkah Guest*. He won the 1991 Evelyn Sibley Lampman Award, given by the Oregon Library Association to honor an Oregon author. The American Folklore Society presented him with the 1993 Aesop Prize for *Days of Awe*. Two of his books, *The Greatest of All* and *Days of Awe*, have been named Notable Children's Trade Books in the Field of Social Studies by a joint committee of the National Council on the Social Studies and the Children's Book Council.

Three Sacks of Truth won the 1993 Irma Simonton and James H. Black Award presented by the Bank Street College of Education. A short story he wrote for *Cricket* magazine, "Four Dollars and Fifty Cents," won the 1990 Paul A. Witty Short Story Award from the International Reading Association.

SELECTED WORKS: The Tartar's Sword, 1974; Hershel and the Hanukkah Goblins, 1989; The Chanukkah Guest, 1990; Four Dollars and Fifty Cents, 1990; One Good Tern Deserves Another, 1994; Bar Mitzvah, 1995.

SELECTED WORKS RETOLD OR ADAPTED: Days of Awe: Stories for Rosh Hashanah and Yom Kippur, 1991; The Four Gallant Sisters, 1992; Three Sacks of Truth: A Story from France, 1993; The Three Princes: A Tale from the Middle East, 1994; The Adventures of Hershel of Ostropol, 1995; The Valiant Red Rooster, 1995.

BERT KITCHEN

April 24, 1940–

AUTHOR AND ILLUSTRATOR OF *Animal Alphabet,* etc.

Autobiographical sketch of Herbert Thomas Kitchen:

MY FULL NAME is Herbert Thomas Kitchen (Bert Kitchen). I was born in 1940 in Liverpool, England, just after the beginning of the Second World War. In 1942 the Merchant Navy Ship with my father on board, which was sailing between England and New York, was torpedoed by a German submarine just outside New York harbour. There were no survivors. He was twenty-one years of age.

To escape the heavy bombing of Liverpool, my mother and I and other relatives moved inland to Rochdale, Lancashire. My mother later remarried. In Rochdale, I went to the local Grammar School and then at the age of sixteen attended the Rochdale School of Art where I studied a wide range of Art subjects. At the end of that two-year

BERT KITCHEN

course I moved to London as a student at the Central School of Arts and Crafts, where I studied Textile Design and Drawing and Painting. In the second year of this three year course I married Muriel, my childhood girl-friend from Rochdale, and we settled in London.

Graduating from the Central in July 1961 I began teaching at the same College as a part-time Lecturer in Drawing and Design.

After leaving College I began painting and drawing in a committed way, supplementing my teaching salary by illustration and by doing other various types of commercial art-work. I also had exhibitions of my work on the way.

In 1967 and 1970 our two daughters, Corinna and Saskia, were born and apart from the occasional cats, a tortoise, a rabbit, goldfish, frogs and a newt, this completed our family as it stands today.

In 1983 I met Patrick Hardy, a publisher. This was to be an important meeting because Patrick introduced me to the world of children's books. Unfortunately Patrick is no longer with us, but I owe him my gratitude.

Now, in 1994, I have nine children's books to my credit as author and illustrator.

All of my books are very much connected to the world of nature and I enjoy this work very much.

I no longer teach but still do other art projects when I feel I can make a useful contribution. Most of the time, however, is spent on the books I produce and on my own drawing and painting.

In 1988 I made my first trip to New York with my family and visited other parts of the Eastern United States from Washington to Maine. Since then I have had a strong affection for America and visit whenever I get the opportunity.

I have many letters from young readers in the United States and these tell me that I have many friends there, all arising out of my work in children's books, and this makes me very happy.

————

Bert Kitchen has had many exhibitions of his work since 1961. They include a two-man show in 1963 in St. Martin's Gallery, London; a one-man show in 1973 at the Archer Gallery in London; the Portsmouth Art Festival in 1975; a one-man show in 1979 at the J.P.L. Gallery in London, and a one-man show that was a retrospective exhibition at Smith's Gallery, Covent Garden, London, in 1991. His paintings are represented in private collections in England, Germany, the United States, Canada, and Japan.

Kitchen has received the Chicago and Illinois Cassandra Foundation Award in 1969. He was included in the Honours list of the Critici in Erba prize in Bologna in 1988. He received the Gold Medal for Illustration from the New York Society of Illustrators in 1991. He is a member of the Society of Authors.

Animal Alphabet was named a Best Illustrated Book of the Year by the *New York Times. Animal Numbers* was awarded the 1988 Graphic Prize for Children in the Bologna Book Fair.

SELECTED WORKS WRITTEN AND ILLUSTRATED: Animal Alphabet, 1984; Mythical Creatures, 1984; Animal Numbers, 1987; Tenrec's Twigs, 1989; Gorilla-Chinchilla and Other Animal Rhymes, 1990; Pig in a Barrow, 1991; Somewhere Today . . . , 1992; And So They Build, 1993; When Hunger Calls, 1994.

ABOUT: Something About the Author, Vol. 70.

ANNETTE CURTIS KLAUSE

June 20, 1953–

AUTHOR OF *The Silver Kiss*, etc.

Autobiographical sketch of Annette Curtis Klause:

I WAS BORN in Bristol, in the Southwest of England on June 20, 1953. When I was small, my mother read and sang to me, and my father sat me on his lap and told me the plots to gangster and monster movies, so I learned at an early age to love stories.

Years later, in my own stories, I found that many of the odds and ends of my life, even those from when I was very small, found their way into my work: such as the abandoned car on the weed-infested, World War II bomb site behind my grandparents' house that I used to stop and explore on my way to school, even though I wasn't supposed to. It surfaced again in *The Silver Kiss* as the old car my vampire, Simon, inscribes with the blood of a young thug.

When I was seven, we moved up north to Newcastle upon Tyne. My father took my sister Julie and me to the library every Saturday. It was a special treat, and I could hardly wait to get home and start on the giant pile of books. I usually had them all read before the weekend was over.

Growing up, I wrote poetry, stories, and plays, on all sorts of topics, but the first books I wrote were about cats. Number one in the series was called *Gypsy Cat*. It contained illustrations in thick, unwieldy felt pen. At the end the title character had kittens, so I planned a book about each and every one of them, and wrote the titles on the

back of the carefully taped together volume. Only *Pie: Son of Gypsy* was ever written, but I outlined the plot of *Padpaws All Alone* to my sister, Julie, one night as we lay in bed, and she burst into tears. I guess that was all the affirmation I needed, because the story was never written down. It must have been heart rending; maybe I couldn't face it again.

The library wasn't my only source of reading. In the spare room were boxes and boxes of old science fiction magazines and paperbacks. The covers fascinated me long before I could decipher the stories. I read short stories at first, the Americanness of them just as alien as the future settings. Then, one day, I actually finished a novel. I was twelve at the time. I remember putting the book down on my pillow with a huge sigh of success. It was those first wonderful explorations of space I paid tribute to when I wrote *Alien Secrets*.

As a teenager, I became boy mad, and my poetry centered more and more on one topic—unrequited love. A new library opened right in our own neighborhood, and I would meet my girlfriend there on Saturdays and talk about boys as well as books. It was there, when I was fourteen years old, that

I read my first vampire book. I became mesmerized with the whole concept of vampires and wrote a dreadful, overwritten sequence of poems and prose called *The Saga of the Vampire* which years later I used as the starting point for *The Silver Kiss.* The final book only has a few elements similar to that original story, but I have to admit, the poem toward the end of *The Silver Kiss* is a slightly revised version of one of those old poems. I couldn't resist.

When I was fifteen, my father's career as a radiologist brought us to the United States. We were only going to be in Washington, D.C., for a year, but we stayed. I have a brother who was born our second year in this country. I suggested the name Simon. I hope he doesn't think I named the vampire after him. The vampire came first.

In high school I continued to write poetry, and in college I stopped writing soppy love poems and enjoyed shocking people with irreverence, but it wasn't until after I graduated with my Master's degree in Library Science and had married Mark, that I became serious about writing prose again. I wrote fantasy and science fiction stories and began submitting my work to magazines. I only managed to get a few poems published in small magazines here and there, however, but it kept me going.

When I began working as a children's librarian I tried writing children's stories, too. I didn't have any more luck with these than with the short stories, except every so often I would get an encouraging personal rejection instead of a form letter.

It took over ten years of writing and learning before I became a published novelist. I needed the help of workshops, the honest colleagues in my Tuesday night writing group, and lots and lots of books. And I'm still learning to this day.

———

Annette Curtis Klause attended the University of Maryland, receiving her B.A. degree in 1976 and her M.L.S. in 1978. She was married in 1979. She has worked for many Montgomery County, Maryland, libraries including the Olney Community Library, and Kensington Park Community Library where she was Head of Children's Services. She is currently Head of Children's Services at the Aspen Hill Community Library in Rockville. She is a member of the American Library Association.

Klause has had a short story published in *The U°n°a°b°a°s°h°e°d° Librarian* and is a contributor to *Short Circuits,* a 1992 collection edited by Donald R. Gallo. She has also had poetry published in various journals, and was a reviewer for *School Library Journal* from 1982 to 1994.

The Silver Kiss appeared on many "best book" lists and was named a Best Book for Young Adults by the American Library Association. *Alien Secrets* was named an ALA Notable Book for Children.

SELECTED WORKS: The Silver Kiss, 1990; Alien Secrets, 1993.

ABOUT: Donald R. Gallo Speaking for Ourselves, Too; Something About the Author, Vol. 79; Voice of Youth Advocates April 1991.

ELISA KLEVEN

October 14, 1958–

Author and Illustrator of The Paper Princess, etc.

Autobiographical sketch of Elisa Kleven, who also writes under the name "Elisa Schneider":

THE WAY I create picture books is closely connected to the way I played as a child. Like many children, I loved to create imaginary worlds, much different from the world I lived in. In Los Angeles, where I grew up, I used to look at a landscape of freeways and scrubby brown hills and wish it were more like the enchanted, rural landscapes in the books I loved: Hans Christian Andersen's and Grimms' fairy tales, the Little House books, *The Secret Garden,*

Kleven: *CLAY ven*

Charlotte's Web. Since the world outside wasn't as peaceful or enchanted as I wanted it to be, I made my own world, with dolls and with art. I cleared all the clothes out of my closet, and on the shelves and in empty fruit crates I created a miniature house, for dolls of every description (many of them handmade), and for all sorts of animals, as well. I'd lose myself in this house for hours, making up stories about its small inhabitants, making them treasures from scraps of this and that: a paper doily would become a lace tablecloth, a tattered sock would become a wooly rug, a postage stamp would become a portrait, half a walnut shell would become a baby's cradle.

The dollhouse had a garden, the lawn of which was made from the cast-off hem off a flowered dress. Around the garden I painted a mural, an intricate landscape of forests and fields, farms and villages, rivers and hills rolling on forever. There was infinite magic and infinity itself for me inside that closet.

I no longer have a dollhouse, but I'm still creating miniature worlds inside my books. Like a child breathing life into dolls and toys, I try to breathe life into the characters I draw, the adventures I give them, the landscapes and cityscapes and skies I place them in.

I work in collage, a malleable, forgiving medium that allows me great freedom to arrange and rearrange, discovering surprises as I go. As I did in childhood, I snip and glue old scraps into new shapes: a doily, cut to bits, becomes a snowstorm; a snippet of lambswool becomes a lion's mane; a piece cut out of a quilt calendar becomes a geometrically-patterned skyscraper. In addition to collage materials, I use watercolor, gouache, ink, colored pencils, pastels, magic markers—anything that works—to create my pictures.

I feel a real kinship with the characters in my books. Ernst the crocodile, in *Ernst*, is a dreamer, always imagining other worlds. The lion in *The Lion and the Little Red Bird* paints a private world on the walls of his cave (a world that is best when shared, of course.) Abuela, her granddaughter Rosalba, and the paper princess fly, fulfilling my own childhood dreams of flying.

Making books can be hard. It can be lonely. It requires patience and discipline. But it is deeply satisfying work, work that allows me to play. I hope that children will recognize in my books their own wonderful impulses to imagine, to create, and to play.

———

Elisa Kleven was born in Los Angeles, the youngest of four children. Her mother, Lorraine Art Schneider, was an etcher and printmaker, and her grandmother, Eva Art, was a sculptor. Although Kleven received no formal art training, she was influenced and inspired by the artists in her family.

Kleven received a B.A. degree in English from the University of California at Berkeley, where she was a Phi Beta Kappa. She received a teaching credential from U.C. Berkeley, as well. She taught in nursery and elementary schools, and was also a weaver and toymaker, before turning to picture books.

She married Paul Kleven in 1984 and their daughter, Mia, was born in 1991. She is a member of the Society of Children's Book Writers and Illustrators.

The Merry-Go-Round Dog was featured in the International Children's Book Art Exhibition in Tokyo in 1989. *B Is for Bethlehem* won a Child Study Children's Book Award from the Child Study Children's Book Committee at Bank Street College of Education. *Abuela* was named a Notable Book of the Year by the American Library Association, and *The Paper Princess* was a Book-of-the-Month Club selection. *De Colores* was an ALA Notable Book and also was exhibited in the American Institute of Graphic Artists show.

SELECTED WORKS WRITTEN AND ILLUSTRATED: Ernst, 1989; The Lion and the Little Red Bird, 1992; The Paper Princess, 1994.

SELECTED WORKS ILLUSTRATED: B Is for Bethlehem, by Isabel Wilner, 1990; Abuela, by Arthur Dorros, 1991; The City by the Bay, by Tricia Brown, 1993; Snowsong Whistling, by Karen Lotz, 1993; De Colores, and Other Latin American Folksongs for Children, by José Luis Orozco, 1994; Isla, by Arthur Dorros, 1995.

SELECTED WORKS WRITTEN AND ILLUSTRATED AS ELISA SCHNEIDER: The Merry-Go-Round Dog, 1988.

ABOUT: Something About the Author, Vol. 76.

SUZY KLINE

August 27, 1943–

AUTHOR OF *Herbie Jones*, etc.

Autobiographical sketch of Suzy Kline:

IF BOOK TITLES were on a menu, my selections would be under the Children's Special. Right between the spaghetti and meatballs and the hot dog plates.

Dessert would be a dish of rainbow sherbet. I write for the reluctant reader, the beginning reader, and the reader who wants to laugh out loud.

I write about simple things like a pencil stub, Monster Ball, green slime, a secret, a first kiss, an ash tray, and a basketball game.

My books are about everyday problems young people have-like being in the lowest reading group, striking out in baseball, being afraid of the dark, wanting to get married at seven, what to do on your birthday that's fun but doesn't cost money, hating your name, having two girlfriends, fibbing, going to a new school, stuttering, having no partner on a field trip, not getting to be ant monitor, and being shy and cheating.

My writing is inspired by my class, my family life, and my childhood. A few of my books reflect my faith, as when Herbie Jones needs help and turns to prayer.

When I was growing up, I didn't read many books. There was a park behind the bushes in our backyard. Mom would call for me just before dark, "SUZY! TIME TO COME HOME!"

I loved Terrace Park. That's where I made friendships and played baseball, tether ball, and basketball. When it rained, we went inside the old shed and played checkers, chess, and ping pong.

During the summer, my family would go on a few weekend fishing trips to Clear Lake. I loved sitting on that wooden pier with Dad, watching the red bobber, and asking him questions about his childhood while we waited for a bluegill to nibble on our lines.

I named a character, Horrible Harry, after my dad. He liked to do mischievous things too. Once my dad put cow manure in my granddad's mailbox.

I wrote lots of letters to my granddad about Dad. My grandparents lived in Indiana and we lived in California. Dad never got around to writing, so I did. I wrote about the everyday things Dad did. All those letters got me in the habit of writing about a male character.

Mom? She was my best friend. She always made me feel that I could do lots of things. When I went to bed, she would rub my back and sing me Brahms' "Lullaby". When I was in second grade and seeing a speech therapist for a stuttering problem, mom always said, "You'll get over it, Suzy." My books about Mary Marony are inspired by that part of my life.

Terry and Kathy were my childhood best friends who took me on their family camping trips. That was when I discovered starlit skies, lightning bugs, caverns, icy lakes, and campfires. I always packed *Betty and Veronica* comic books. Especially the 24-cent giant summer editions with over a hundred pages.

I loved romance.

I married Randy when I was ten. It was a simple ceremony in the tennis courts at Terrace Park. I wrote about my true feelings in a diary and kept fat scrapbooks. *Horrible Harry and the Kickball Wedding* was an inevitable book on my list.

I made the decision to be a writer when I was in fifth grade and wrote "The Mystery of The Missing Ink Blotter."

My teacher, Mr. Teague, had us read our work aloud on a microphone. When it was my turn, my classmates stopped talking and listened. You could hear a pin drop. That's when I told myself, "Someday, I'm going to be a writer."

A few things happened, though, before I got that first book published. I graduated from the University of California at Berke-

ley, became a teacher, got married, and had two daughters.

My husband has been a great source of inspiration for my writing. Herbie Jones was modeled after him.

I met Rufus in Psychology 1A when I spent a year at the Davis campus. He sat behind us and I thought he was brilliant and funny. His one-liners even made the professor laugh.

Our lifetime romance continues to be my greatest source of inspiration. We just recently celebrated our twenty-fifth anniversary.

Rufus reads all my manuscripts. His comments help shape many of my stories. His one-liners are often the words for Uncle Gus, Uncle Dwight, Mr. Jones, and Raymond.

Ruf teaches sociology at the University of Connecticut. Our oldest daughter Jennifer recently got married and is teaching math in high school. Emily, Phi Beta Kappa, just graduated summa cum laude from UConn with a major in literature. She wants to teach in college. It looks as though there will be four teachers in our family!

I've been teaching for twenty-three years. And writing for the past twelve. The reason I dedicate so many books to my students is because they have inspired me to write so many stories! We start each day with a morning conversation, a read aloud and then a chunk of writing time. I write, too. Then we share what we wrote. (Even when it's terrible!)

Each day is inspired by events in our lives and literature. My favorite moments in the classroom? When we observe our classroom hamster, fish, guinea pig, butterflies, ants, gerbil, and African water frogs; wave our hands like conductors to Tchaikovsky and Mozart; act scenes out from *Horrible Harry* and *Frog and Toad*; read *The Herbie Jones Reader's Theater*; square dance in the gym; and discover new friends like Lyle, and George and Martha.

Now that I have written thirty books, I feel as if my family has grown. Herbie

Jones, Horrible Harry, Song Lee, Orp, Mary Marony, and Marvin Higgins have come to live at our house. I hope I keep writing about these characters for a long long time. And I also hope the children who choose to read about them think of them as friends.

———

Suzy Kline was born in Berkeley, California. She was married in 1968. She attended Columbia University and earned a B.A. degree from the University of California at Berkeley in 1966. She studied further at California State College. She was named School District Teacher of the Year by the State of Connecticut in 1987 and Probus Educator of the Year in Torrington, Connecticut, in 1988. Among her professional memberships are the Society of Children's Book Writers and Illustrators, PEN, and the New England Reading Association.

Six of her books were named Children's Choice Books by a joint committee of the Children's Book Council and the International Reading Association. They include *Herbie Jones, What's the Matter with Herbie Jones?*, and *Orp and the Chop Suey Burgers*. Four of her books have been named Junior Library Guild selections: *Orp, What's the Matter with Herbie Jones?*, *Herbie Jones and the Class Gift*, and *Herbie Jones and the Monster Ball*.

SELECTED WORKS: Herbie Jones, 1985; What's the Matter with Herbie Jones?, 1986; Herbie Jones and the Class Gift, 1987; Herbie Jones and the Monster Ball, 1988; Orp, 1989; Orp and the Chop Suey Burgers, 1990; The Herbie Jones Reader's Theatre, 1992; Horrible Harry and the Kickball Wedding, 1992; Mary Marony Mummy Girl, 1994; Orp and the FBI, 1995.

ABOUT: Contemporary Authors, Vol. 120; Something About the Author, Vol. 48,

RON KOERTGE

April 22, 1940–

AUTHOR OF *Where the Kissing Never Stops*, etc.

Autobiographical sketch of Ron Koertge:

I WAS BORN in 1940 and lived in the midwest until I graduated the University of Illinois and went to Tucson and the university there. I'm married to Bianca Richards and we have no children. I teach at Pasadena City College.

It's easy to say now that I planned to be a writer or was even likely to be one, but I sure wouldn't have said that forty years ago. I wrote things in high school (*things* in the midnight-movie sense of the word) and took creative writing classes in college, but I was pretty much a pinball in those days—bouncing from one brightly-lit thing to another.

Using the lottery approach to life, in 1962 I applied to three graduate schools and—when only the University of Arizona offered a teaching assistantship—bought a map and went there. Never much of a student, the U. of A. was hard for me; but some of the other grad students met at a bar called the Green Dolphin to talk and to play pool. These guys took poetry—the kind you wrote, not the kind you studied—seriously. They knew which independent magazines to send poems to and which to avoid. They were doing and making literature, not just studying what somebody else had done.

When I left Arizona to come to Pasadena, I brought my interest in poetry with me and continued to publish in the so-called literary underground. But late in the 1980's, a friendly strain of restlessness made me write my first Young Adult novel, *Where the Kissing Never Stops*. Since then I've written six others.

Why did I turn to YA writing? Where do my ideas come from?

Around 1986, a friend of mind said that since I'd never bothered to grow up, I might like writing for teenagers. When I sampled

Koertge: *KUR chee*

half a dozen YA books from my local library, they were so chaste and polite. Each presented the years between thirteen and nineteen as incomplete blueprints of adolescence: no bathroom, no bedroom. I knew I couldn't lie about the way I'd felt as a young person, so I figured that I would write a book that told the truth about kids.

I agree with the French author Flaubert when he says that a writer doesn't choose subjects; they impose themselves. At the moment I'm waiting for an idea willing to take the form of another novel. What I can do is be available: read a fair amount, steal vocabulary for my word-book, be patient. In short, make regular payments to the Muse on the installment plan.

I suppose I write about my life (I like to bet on horses and two of my books have racetracks in them), but my mother was never a stripper (*Where the Kissing Never Stops*), I never had a gay relative (*The Arizona Kid*) or a father who embarrassed me with his hand puppet (*The Harmony Arms*). It's fun for me to make up people, get them in trouble, and then let them work themselves out while I record how that happens—the journalism of the imagination.

I'd like to keep writing for young people,

but I'm not sure that the books want to be written. The older I get, the less I know about myself and everything else. And for all I know, that's wisdom.

———

Ron Koertge was born in Olney, Illinois. He received his B.A. degree from the University of Illinois in 1962 and his M.A. from the University of Arizona in 1965. He has taught at Pasadena City College in Pasadena since 1965 and is Professor of English. He has written many books of poetry including *Sex Object, Twelve Photographs of Yellowstone*, and *High School Dirty Poems*. He wrote a novel for adults, *The Boogeyman*, which was published in 1980. He also wrote a college textbook for remedial readers called *100 Things to Write About*, published in 1990. Koertge was featured on Tom Vitale's "All Things Considered" segment on National Public Radio. He has been a visiting author in schools. He received a National Endowment for the Arts fellowship in poetry in 1990 and a 1993 California Arts Council grant.

Tiger, Tiger, Burning Bright and *The Harmony Arms* were named both Notable Books for Children and Best Books for Young Adults by the American Library Association. *The Arizona Kid, The Boy in the Moon*, and *Where the Kissing Never Stops* were named ALA Best Books for Young Adults. *Tiger, Tiger* won the 1994 Child Study Children's Book Award, given by the Child Study Children's Book Committee at Bank Street College of Education, as well as the 1995 Judy Lopez Memorial Award from the Women's National Book Association.

SELECTED WORKS: Where the Kissing Never Stops, 1986; The Arizona Kid, 1988; The Boy in the Moon, 1990; Mariposa Blues, 1991; The Harmony Arms, 1992; Tiger, Tiger, Burning Bright: A Novel, 1994.

ABOUT: Contemporary Authors, Vol. 65-68; (New Revision Series), Vol. 9, 25; Dictionary of Literary Biography, Vol. 105; Gallo, Donald R. Speaking for Ourselves, Too; Poet's Market, 1991; Something About the Author, Vol. 53.

GORDON KORMAN

October 23, 1963–

AUTHOR OF *Something Fishy at Macdonald Hall*, etc.

Autobiographical sketch of Gordon Richard Korman:

HUMOR HAS ALWAYS been an important part of my life. The way some families have conversations over meals, my parents and I used to crack jokes back and forth across the dinner table. Even when I was two and my big ambition in life was to be a dog when I grew up, the TV cartoons that were my favorites were the funny ones. If I hadn't become a writer, I'm sure that laughter would be a large part of my life. I just wouldn't be getting paid for it.

I was only twelve when my career started. My seventh-grade English teacher, who was actually a track and field coach, gave us four months to work on a single writing project. Mine was called *This Can't Be Happening at Macdonald Hall*, my first novel.

It was my fellow students, not my teacher, who suggested that the book might have a future (although he did offer to laminate it—not bad; laminating machines were pretty rare in public schools back then). Unfortunately, I knew of no publishers, but I *was* class monitor for the Scholastic book club, which, I reasoned, made me practically an employee. I had a corporate responsibility to mail my manuscript to the address on the book club sheets.

In retrospect, I was pretty confident, probably because my understanding of the publishing industry was zilch. If I had known then what I know now, I would have been terrified. I might never have sent the book in. But I don't think I truly appreciated what was happening a few days after my thirteenth birthday when I signed the contract for *This Can't Be Happening at Macdonald Hall*—although it almost killed me to wait over a year for the book to come out.

It launched the *Bruno and Boots* series

about two private boarding schools, one for boys and one for girls, located right across the street from each other. There are now seven books in the series, which has been translated into French, Swedish, Danish, Norwegian, and Cantonese. I never went to boarding school, or even private school, but it was a terrific ploy for getting my characters away from their parents. Actual experience finds its way into my books in more subtle ways. For instance, my three semester washout in film school manifested itself in *Macdonald Hall Goes Hollywood*, about a movie crew filming on location at Macdonald Hall. *The Zucchini Warriors*, about football, closely followed a Superbowl win by my beloved New York Giants; my baseball novel, *The Toilet Paper Tigers*, came after the Toronto Blue Jays finally won the World Series. My writing seems to follow my enthusiasm; I could have dozens of sports book if only my teams would perform a little better.

Because my career started in the classroom, I belive it should never stray too far from there. To that end, I put in about forty thousand miles each year visiting schools, and talking with students about reading and writing. It's important to stay plugged in, not to mentionthat some of the best ideas come from meeting my readers. Need a good name? Go to the source. Armando "Commando" Rivera from *The Twinkie Squad* came from an author visit, as did the inspiration for the three Z's (Justin Zeckenforf, Margaret Zachary, and Jessica Zander) in *Why Did the Underwear Cross the Road?*

Spending time in schools is also a great reminder that the true purpose of this job is to provide kids with the best novels we can come up with. I still don't know a feeling that compares with the knowledge that, at almost any given moment, someone is out there reading one of my books and laughing in all the right places.

———

Gordon Korman was born in Montreal, Quebec in Canada. He earned a B.F.A. degree from New York University in 1985, first studying film and television production, but later switching to dramatic writing. He has been a full-time writer since 1975. He is a member of the Writers Union of Canada, the Canadian Society of Children's Autors, Illustrators, and Performers, the Candian Authors' Association, and the Society of Children's Book Writers and Illustrators. He enjoys music, travel, and sports.

Several of Korman's books have been named Best Books for Young Adults by the American Library Association. They include *Losing Joe's Place*, *A Semester in the Life of a Garbage Bag*, and *Son of Interflux*. *I Want to Go Home!* was named a Children's Choice Book by a joint committee of the Children's Book Council and the International Reading Association. *The Twinkie Squad* was a Junior Library Guild selection, and *Why Did the Underwear Cross the Road?* was a Book-of-the-Month Club selection.

SELECTED WORKS: This Can't Be Happening at Macdonald Hall!, 1977; I Want to Go Home!, 1981; Don't Care High, 1985; Son of Interflux, 1986; A Semester in the Life of a Garbage Bag, 1987; The Zucchi-

ni Warriors, 1988; Losing Joe's Place, 1990; Macdonald Hall Goes Hollywood, 1991; The Twinkie Squad, 1992; The Toilet Paper Tigers, 1993; Why Did the Underwear Cross the Road?, 1994; Something Fishy at Macdonald Hall, 1995.

ABOUT: Canadian Children's Literature 1985; Contemporary Authors, Vol. 112; (New Revision Series), Vol. 34; Emergency Librarian January 1993; Gallo, Donald R. Speaking for Ourselves; New York Times July 24, 1985; Something About the Author, Vol. 41, 49, 81.

KATHLEEN KRULL

July 29, 1952–

AUTHOR OF *Lives of the Musicians*, etc.

Autobiographical sketch of Kathleen Krull:

MY EARLIEST WORKS include "A Garden Book" (second grade), "Hairdos and People I Know" (fifth), "The History of Queersville" (sixth), and "Death Waits Until After Dark" (eighth)—about a teacher who jumps out the window.

I grew up reading and writing. My mother got me (and my three brothers) started on weekly trips to the public library in Wilmette, Illinois. I'm one of those library-fiends who checked out six books a week or more. In the summers I raced the brother closest to me in age to see who could read the most mysteries by Enid Blyton. One day I stubbed my toe on the library door and ignored it—deeply immersed in books by Edward Eager or Betty Cavanna or Mary Stolz or Daphne Du Maurier—until several nauseated librarians pointed to the trail of blood I was leaving everywhere. But they forgave me and, when I got to high school, hired me to work there as a shelver. My dream job! I lasted several years but, alas, was eventually fired for—what else?—reading too much on the job. In school, my teachers in third and eighth grades (Sister de Maria and Sister Della) stand out as being particularly encouraging of my writing.

On the day after graduating from college with an English major and a music minor,

Kathleen Krull

I began my first job in children's book publishing. I was working as an editor at Western Publishing/Golden Books, in Racine, Wisconsin, when I got my first two books published there: *The Bugs Bunny Book*, an auspicious debut to be sure, and a Little Golden Book called *What Will I Be?: A Wish Book*. I also worked extensively on the Trixie Belden mystery series. I was about twenty-two. My last publishing job ended ten years later in 1984, in San Diego, California, where I had moved to help establish the children's book department at Harcourt Brace Jovanovich. I learned a lot during my publishing career—working with terrific authors and artists and writing numerous books of my own—but eventually left the corporate world and eased into writing full-time.

The ideas for my books have come to me in assorted amazing ways. *Songs of Praise* arrived in a dream (but derived ultimately from my years as a church organist, starting when I was twelve). *Gonna Sing My Head Off* grew out of my love for the folk music our parents raised us on. *Alex Fitzgerald's Cure for Nightmares* combined my stepdaughter's insomnia with my own experience as a California transplant; the idea for

its sequel, *Alex Fitzgerald, TV Star*, came from a newspaper article. Besides a lifelong passion for music (I grew up playing several musical instruments), *Lives of the Musicians* was also inspired by the trademark caricatures of the artist Kathryn Hewitt; the point of view (and "What the Neighbors Thought") comes from my fascination with the lives of neighbors—which is common, I think, though I did go to extremes and marry one of mine. The companion, *Lives of the Writers*, comes from my own passion for books and reading, of course. Especially miraculous is the way people have suggested book ideas to me, and the way some of those ideas have taken hold.

I seem to write several different kinds of books and I hope to do even more in the future. I am still interested in gardens, hairdos, people, history, and mysterious deaths, and have numerous other obsessions. I aim for making my books as fresh as I can—using ideas and combinations of words only I would use. I try to be clear and funny and relevant to what is going on in children's lives today, as well as true to my own memories of childhood. The "hidden agenda" to all my works is to create books that will mean as much to readers as books have meant to me.

Kathleen Krull was born in Fort Leonard Wood, Missouri, grew up in Wilmette, Illinois, and received her B.A. degree magna cum laude from Lawrence University in Appleton, Wisconsin. From 1973 to 1974 she was an Editorial Assistant in the textbook department of Harper & Row, in Evanston, Illinois. For five years after that she worked on mass-market books as an Associate Editor for Western Publishing/Golden Books, in Racine, Wisconsin. From 1979 to 1982 she was Managing Editor at Raintree Publishers, Milwaukee, Wisconsin, editing supplemental books for the school and library market. Then followed two years as Senior Editor at Harcourt

Brace Jovanovich, San Diego, California, where her authors included Tomie dePaola, Anne Lindbergh, Eve Bunting, and Jane Yolen. Since 1984 she has been a freelance book writer, also writing reviews and articles for such publications as the *New York Times Book Review*, the *Los Angeles Times Book Review*, and *Publishers Weekly*. She is a frequent speaker at conferences, workshops, and university classes. She is married with two stepdaughters.

Lives of the Musicians: Good Times, Bad Times (and What the Neighbors Thought) was named an Honor Book in the 1993 *Boston Globe-Horn Book* Awards. It also won the 1994 PEN West Children's Literature Award, and an Honor Book citation in the Society of Children's Book Writers' Golden Kite Awards. It was named a Notable Book in the Field of Social Studies by a joint committee of the National Council on the Social Studies and the Children's Book Council. It was also named a Notable Book of the Year by the American Library Association, as was *Gonna Sing My Head Off.* In 1994, Krull was awarded a "Celebrate Literacy" Award from the Greater San Diego Reading Association. In 1995 she was elected to the Board of Directors for the Society of Children's Book Writers and Illustrators.

SELECTED WORKS: Songs of Praise, 1989; Alex Fitzgerald's Cure for Nightmares, 1990; Alex Fitzgerald, TV Star, 1991; It's My Earth Too, 1992; Gonna Sing My Head Off: American Folk Songs for Children, 1992; Lives of the Musicians" Good Times, Bad Times (and What the Neighbors Thought), 1993; Lives of the Writers: Comedies, Tragedies, (and What the Neighbors Thought), 1994; Maria Molina and the Days of the Dead, 1994; The Other Side, 1994; V Is for Victory: America Remembers World War II, 1995; Lives of the Artists: Masterpieces, Messes (and What the Neighbors Thought), 1995; Presenting Paula Danziger, 1995.

ABOUT: Contemporary Authors, Vol. 106; Nonfiction Authors for Children; Something About the Author, Vol. 39, 52, 80; Who's Who in America, 50th ed. Pronunciation: Krull rhymes with "lull"

SUSAN KUKLIN

September 6, 1941–

AUTHOR AND PHOTOGRAPHER OF *Thinking Big*, etc.

Autobiographical sketch of Susan Kuklin:

MY MOTHER recently found the only copy of my first book. It was a photo essay about my grandparents written when I was in nursery school. The cover was made from purple construction paper, still my favorite color if you don't count black. I pasted photographs on the facing page of each spread. Perhaps it was fated that I become an author of photo essays.

When I was in school, books were my best friends. They disclosed a complex, exasperating, wondrous world. Afternoons spent researching a subject for a school report at the library were never a chore. I still remember the feel of the frayed edges of the catalog cards. My fingers would hunt for subjects that were fascinating just as my fingers now click the camera's shutter, looking for what's fascinating in a subject.

My hometown, Philadelphia, had marvelous museums, concerts, dance, and theater. As an only child not prone toward baby sitters, I'd tag along with family when they went to concerts and opera.

Once I became a teenager I was passionately involved in the theater. Summers were spent as an apprentice at the local summer theater, Playhouse in the Park. New York was Oz, a magical place where my dreams of becoming a stage actress would come true. When it came time to apply to college, I chose only schools in the New York City area. My family worried that I would go to the theater every night and forgo my studies. They were half right.

I majored in theater at New York University and studied acting at the Herbert Berghof Studio. Yes, I went to the theater almost every night with my pals in the drama department. No, I did not forgo other subjects.

While in graduate school, I began to di-

Kuklin: *COOK lyn*

Susan Kuklin

rect plays. Directing enabled me to look at the big picture, including the visual aspects of the art. Framing the actors, lighting, and pacing later became integral parts of my approach to photography and nonfiction writing.

Once out of school, I taught English and wrote curricula for the New York City Board of Education. During the summer I traveled as much as I could. For kicks, I photographed my trips, as well as friends, weddings, and children. It was fun for me to see photographically. My theater background helped me to understand the fundamentals of composition and lighting. I loved photography, but never thought about doing it professionally.

In 1970, I met my future husband on the beach on Fire Island. We married in '74 and moved to Knoxville, Tennessee, where we both taught at the University of Tennessee. While in Knoxville, I became intrigued with the rugged individuality of the people of Appalachia. Planned Parenthood of the Southern Mountains arranged for me to accompany their out-reach workers to families in remote parts of the mountains. The result was my first photo essay, called "Appalachian Families." Parts of this essay were published in a number of journals.

When we moved back to New York, I showed my Tennessee photographs to magazines and publishers. Following months of slammed doors and rejections, I began getting a few assignments that were unusual and varied. One day I'd ride with undercover cops in the South Bronx. Another, I'd cover George Balanchine's rehearsals at the New York City Ballet. It wasn't always glamorous. There was one year, for example, when almost every magazine that hired me folded. I lived on "kill" fees.

Dr. Herbert Terrace at Columbia University was working on a project for teaching language to a young chimpanzee called Nim Chimpsky. I became the photographer on the project and from it came my first children's illustration, *The Story of Nim: A Chimp Who Learned Language.*

The fascinating process of cummunicating with Nim and then turning the communication into a book for children inspired an entirely new direction for my work. At that time, I made the decision to work on complex—at time controversial—social issues that affect young people. Why such a decision? Because the issues are here, will not go away, and must be addressed.

When I begin a book I never know what the story line will be. Most of the people portrayed in my books face challenging predicaments. For example, how does a young dwarf cope with living independently in a world designed for people between five and six feet tall? (*Thinking Big*) How does a young person seek a quality life when told he or she is diagnosed with AIDS? (*Fighting Back: What Some People Are Doing About AIDS*)

My subjects are my partners and we become very close confidants as our book progresses. I try to describe in a very personal way, their thoughts, feelings, and reasoning. As far as I'm concerned my role is to portray who they are, not what I want them to be. I must confess that ridding myself of preconceived ideas can be a challenge. We go over and over the material until we are all convinced that everything said is accurate and consistent.

The preschool and intermediate level books that I do use the same photojournalism techniques that I use in my young adult books. In my "Going To . . . " series, a real life event in the life of a young child, such as going to the doctor, is examined strictly from the child's point of view.

Looking back, my work as a writer and photo-journalist has gone full circle. Authoring photo essays, like my first little purple book, is what I want to do.

———

Susan Kuklin earned her B.S. degree in 1963, and her M.A. in 1966. She was an English teacher from 1965 to 1974, and worked as a curriculum developer from 1970 to 1974. She taught film studies at the University of Tennessee at Knoxville from 1974 to 1976. She has contributed photo essays and photographs to numerous magazines, including *Time*, *Newsweek*, *New York*, the *New York Times*, and *Travel and Leisure*. Her work has appeared on *Dance in America*, *Nova*, and other television programs; and has been exhibited in shows such as "Fifty Years at the New York City Ballet" at the Lincoln Center Library in New York. Susan Kuklin is a member of PEN, the Authors Guild, and The Society of Children's Book Writers.

The Story of Nim was named an Outstanding Science Trade Book by a joint committee of the National Science Teachers Association and the Children's Book Council. *Mine for a Year* was named a Notable Children's Trade Book in the Field of Social Studies by the CBC and the National Council on the Social Studies. It was also a Junior Literary Guild selection. *Thinking Big* was named a 1986 honor book by the International Board on Books for Young People, and also received a Child Study Children's Book Award by the Child Study Children's Book Committee at Bank Street College of Education.

Several of Kuklin's books were named Best Books of the Year for Young Adults by the American Library Association, includ-ing *Reaching for Dreams*, *Fighting Back*, *What Do I Do Now*, and *After a Suicide*.

SELECTED WORKS: Mine for a Year, 1984; Thinking Big, 1986; Reaching for Dreams: A Ballet from Rehearsal to Opening Night, 1987; When I See My Doctor, 1988; Fighting Back: What Some People Are Doing About AIDS, 1988; What Do I Do Now? Teenagers Talk About Sex and Pregnancy, 1991; Speaking Out: Teeangers Take on Race, Sex and Identity, 1993; After a Suicide: Young People Speak Up, 1994; From Head to Toe: How a Doll Is Made, 1995; Komodo: Children of Japan, 1995.

SELECTED WORKS ILLUSTRATED: Nim, by Herbert Terrace, 1979; The Story of Nim, the Chimp Who Learned Language, by Anna Michel, 1980.

ABOUT: Contemporary Authors, Vol. 130; Something About the Author, Vol. 63.

DEBORAH NOURSE LATTIMORE

AUTHOR AND ILLUSTRATOR OF *The Dragon's Robe*, etc.

Biographical sketch of Deborah Nourse Lattimore:

DEBORAH NOURSE LATTIMORE was born and raised in the Los Angeles, California, area. She began writing and illustrating books while she was in grade school. When she went to college, she studied the art history of Egypt, Greece, Rome, and pre-Columbian America, and earned a degree in Egyptology.

An art historian and writer of academic articles and archaeological publications, she combines her interest in archaeology and classical art with storytelling skills to produce her books. Lattimore lives in Los Angeles with her children.

In *Why There Is No Arguing in Heaven*, Lattimore retells a Mayan creation myth. Critic Mary M. Burns, writing in *The Horn Book Magazine*, calls the illustrations "bold and dynamic," capturing the earthy humor of the tale. She writes, "This version of an ancient myth once again emphasizes the

DEBORAH NOURSE LATTIMORE

unversal tendency to infuse cosmology with
an enlarged vision of oneself."

The Dragon's Robe is a tale set in China
in the thirteenth century. A *School Library
Journal* reviewer called the artwork
"stunning." *The Flame of Peace* explores
the world of the Aztec civilization, and *The
Prince and the Golden Ax* is a Minoan tale.
Ninth-century Ireland is the setting for Lattimore's *The Sailor Who Captured the Sea*,
and *Punga* is a tale of the Maori people of
New Zealand.

The Dragon's Robe won the 1991 PEN
Center USA West Literary Award in Children's Literature. It also won a 1991 Southern California Council on Literature for
Children and Young People Award. *The
Flame of Peace* was honored in the same
awards in 1988.

The Flame of Peace and *The Sailor Who
Captured the Sea*, *Punga*, and *Why There
Is No Arguing in Heaven* were all named
Notable Children's Trade Books in the
Field of Social Studies by a joint committee
of the Children's Book Council and the Na-
tional Council on the Social Studies.

The Lady with the Ship on Her Head was
a Reading Rainbow Book.

SELECTED WORKS WRITTEN AND ILLUSTRATED: The

Flame of Peace: A Tale of the Aztecs, 1987; The Prince
and the Golden Axe: A Minoan Tale, 1988; Why There
Is No Arguing in Heaven: A Mayan Myth, 1989; The
Dragon's Robe, 1990; The Lady with the Ship on Her
Head, 1990; The Sailor Who Captured the Sea: A Story
of the Book of Kells, 1991; The Winged Cat: A Tale
of Ancient Egypt, 1992; Punga: The Goddess of Ugly,
1993; Frida Maria: A Story of the Old Southwest, 1994;
Arabian Nights: Three Tales, 1995.

SELECTED WORKS ILLUSTRATED: Zekmet, the Stone
Carver: A Tale of Ancient Egypt, by Mary Stolz, 1988.

ABOUT: Instructor March 1994.

BIANCA LAVIES

AUTHOR AND PHOTOGRAPHER OF *Tree Trunk
Traffic*, etc.

Biographical sketch of Bianca Lavies:

BIANCA LAVIES was born in The Hague,
Holland. She emigrated to New Zealand in
1953 and worked on farms there. She travelled to South Africa in 1958. In 1969 she
crossed the Atlantic Ocean, sailing from
South Africa via St. Helena and the West
Indies to the United States in a thirty-foot
sailboat named Apogee, with one other person and four cats. The boat was the first fi-
berglass boat to circumnavigate the world,
and upon her arrival in January 1969, the
news media, including *Time* magazine,
covered the story with her picture.

Lavies began her career as a journalist in
South Africa. From 1962 to 1969 she was a
freelance photojournalist, covering yachting. She covered the Durban, South Africa,
scene for the *Natal Mercury* and for magazines such as *South African Yachting* and
Yachting World. She also worked for magazines in Australia and New Zealand. When
she arrived in the U.S., she found that the
publicity of her journey helped her to find
a market for her work in publications in the
United States.

She began working for *The National
Geographic*, but as a writer. She spent eigh-

BIANCA LAVIES

teen years at the magazine, becoming a staff photographer in 1974. During her career she has crawled in snake pits and been attacked by killer bees. She illlustrated stories for the magazine and also became a natural history photographer. For her story "Mangrove Trees" in the May 1977 issue, one of her photographs was featured on the cover. Many of the books she wrote for children had their origins in articles for *The National Geographic* and other publications.

Bianca Lavies has won many awards for her work, including First in Feature Story, in the National Press Photographers Pictures of the Year Competition; Second in Feature Story, from the White House News Photographers Association, an honor she won twice; and the Award of Excellence in Science and Natural History, from the National Press Photographers. She also won an award for work published in *Ranger Rick* magazine.

She has contributed photographs to books such as The National Geographic's *Vanishing Wildlife* and *Our Continent*. She is represented in the *Time-Life* Library of Photography book *Photography as a Tool* and she has given lectures at workshops at the International Center of Photography in New York City in 1983; at West Virginia University in 1981; and at Shenandoah University in Virginia in 1995. She lives in Annapolis, Maryland, in a house where she has taken photographs for many of her books.

Ellen Fader, writing in *The Horn Book Magazine*, states in a review of *Lily Pad Pond* and *Tree Trunk Traffic* that "[T]he quality of the pictures is overwhelmingly excellent, offering perspectives seldom seen in books for children." She praises the "stunning" photographs and the concise and logical organization of information.

Tree Trunk Traffic was named an honor book in the 1989 New York Academy of Sciences Children's Book Science Awards. It was also named a Children's Choice Book by a joint committee of the International Reading Association and the Children's Book Council. *It's an Armadillo!* and *A Gathering of Garter Snakes* were named Notable Books of the Year by the American Library Association.

Many of her books have been named Outstanding Science Trade Books for Children by a joint committee of the Children's Book Council and the National Science Teachers Association. They include: *Backyard Hunter, The Secretive Timber Rattlesnake, Tree Trunk Traffic, Wasps at Home, A Gathering of Garter Snakes,* and *Compost Critters.*

SELECTED WORKS: It's an Armadillo!, 1989; Lilly Pad Pond, 1989; Tree Trunk Traffic, 1989; Backyard Hunter: The Praying Mantis, 1990; The Secretive Timber Rattlesnake, 1990; Wasps at Home, 1991; The Atlantic Salmon, 1992; Monarch Butterflies: Mysterious Travelers, 1992; A Gathering of Garter Snakes, 1993; Killer Bees, 1994; Tundra Swan, 1994.

DENNIS LEE

August 31, 1939–

AUTHOR OF *Alligator Pie*, etc.

Biographical sketch of Dennis Lee:

THE POET Dennis Lee was born in Toronto, Ontario. At the age of seven, he had his first poem published, in *Wee Wisdom* magazine. When he was in his twenties, he began to write seriously and to think he might become a writer. He received his B.A. degree from the University of Toronto in 1962, and earned an M.A. degree there in 1964. He became a teacher, lecturing in English at Victoria College of the University of Toronto from 1964 to 1967. He then helped to found Rochdale College in Toronto and worked there for two years, in an attempt to create an educational and housing cooperative that students would run. In 1967 he co-founded the House of Anansi Press, a still viable publisher of fiction, non-fiction, and poetry. He was an editor there until 1972.

Lee also worked as a freelance editor for Macmillan of Canada, and during the early 1980's he served as poetry editor for McClelland and Stewart. There he was the editor of *The New Canadian Poets 1970-1985*.

His first book of poetry for adults was *Kingdom of Absence*, published in 1967. His other adult work includes *Civil Elegies*, published in 1968, which in a revised and extended version won Lee a 1972 Governor General's Award from the Canada Council. He also writes essays and literary criticism, such as his book *Savage Fields*.

He first began writing for children when he read nursery rhymes to his three young children. "All we seemed to read about were jolly millers, pigs, and queens," he states. So he began writing for children poetry that reflected modern everyday Canadian life. His method of working includes reworking four-line poems as many as thirty times, and longer ones as many as fifty times. He worked on these poems for years, and fourteen of them were published in his *Wiggle to the Laundromat* in 1970. However, he kept working on the project. Eventually, the poems for younger children were published in his collection *Alligator Pie*, and the poems for older children appeared in *Nicholas Knock*.

Some of his work has not yet been published in the United States, including *Lizzy's Lion*. Lee is also a writer of song lyrics, and wrote the words for most on the songs in *Fraggle Rock*, which was co-produced by Jim Henson and the Canadian Broadcasting Corporation. Phil Balsam wrote the music. The team also wrote songs for the stage adaptation of *Jacob Two-Two Meets the Hooded Fang* and *Jacob Two-Two and the Dinosaur*, both based on children's books by Mordecai Richler. Lee has been a full-time writer for over fifteen years. He lives in Toronto with his wife.

A recording of *Alligator Pie and Other Poems* was produced by Caedmon in 1978.

Dennis Lee won the 1986 Vicky Metcalf Award, sponsored by the Canadian Authors Association, for the body of his work. In 1994 he received the Order of Canada Award.

Alligator Pie won the 1975 Canadian Library Association Book of the Year for Children Award 1975. It was included on the 1976 International Board on Books for Young People honor list and won the 1974 International Order of the Daughters of the Empire Best Children's Book of the Year Award. *Garbage Delight*, which was illustrated by Frank Newfeld, won the 1978 CLA Book of the Year Award, and was a runner-up in the 1978 Amelia Frances Howard-Gibbon Illustrator's Award. It was also on the 1978 IBBY honor list. *Jelly Belly* was a runner-up in the 1984 CLA Award.

Lizzy's Lion, which was illustrated by Marie-Louise Gay, received a 1984 Governor General's Literary Award from the Canada Council.

SELECTED WORKS: Alligator Pie, 1975; Nicholas Knock and Other People, 1977; Garbage Delight, 1978; Jelly Belly, 1985; The Ice Cream Store, 1992.

ABOUT: Canadian Children's Literature No. 4 1976; Contemporary Authors, (New Revision Series), Vol. 25-28; (New Revision Series), Vol. 11, 31; Contemporary Poets 1985; Descant Winter 1982; Dictionary of Literary Biography, Vol. 53; Kirkpatrick, D.L., ed. Twentieth-Century Children's Writers; Noyes, Stacey and Nancy Pearson, eds., Writing Stories, Making Pictures: Biographies of 150 Canadian Authors and Illustrators; Something About the Author, Vol. 14.

LOREEN LEEDY

June 15, 1959–

AUTHOR AND ILLUSTRATOR OF *Fraction Action*, etc.

Autobiographical sketch of Loreen Leedy:

AS A LITTLE GIRL, I regularly climbed onto Dad's lap with a book for him to read aloud to me. Found Mom's old primer with the alphabet, colors, simple words and sentences. Drew a picture of Rin-tin-tin for a contest on the local television station. We always had paper, crayons, glue, glitter, and scissors in the house, ready for the next burst of creativity.

When I told the first-grade teacher that I already knew how to read, she said, "That's not fair!" Followed the steps in an art instruction book entitled, *How to Draw the Big Cats*, and drew a picture of a lion. A classmate, Eddie, admired it and said, "You're a good artist."

Once, a teacher asked me to read a Thanksgiving story aloud to the class. I was so scared that I lost my voice entirely and had to tug on the teacher's skirt to get her attention. Skipped over fourth-grade reading. Started getting books from the "adult" section of the library. When I got desperate for reading material, I read the encyclopedia. (Mostly the captions under the pictures.)

The elementary art teacher awarded me a scholarship to weekly classes at the Delaware Art Museum. I continued to attend art lessons there until high school. A dynamic young teacher assigned creative writing projects throughout the sixth-grade year. There was that poem about a pencil sharpener, for example.

Sent a drawing of a horse to *American Girl* magazine and it was published! (I got paid $10.00.) Wrote poems in my eighth-grade English class and illustrated them around the margins. It was the last year they assigned any creative writing in school. Why? From then on, book reports and essay questions were the only writing the teachers wanted. It never occurred to me to write on my own time. I did draw and paint regularly, mostly animals.

Perhaps because of these early experiences, I ended up majoring in art in college. At the time, it was rather vague and fumbling—with no particular career goal in mind. Shortly after graduating, I decided to avoid getting a "job," and instead work for myself. I found a new type of clay that was available in bright colors and could be made into small items such as jewelry. Pig mermaids, cats in suspenders, and purple dragons were the results.

In 1984, I met an actual, live children's book author/illustrator named Olivier Dunrea, and saw his studio, a book plan, and illustrations in progress. "Maybe this is something *I* could do?" My frog earrings and pig chess pieces served as models for characters. The editor, Margery Cuyler of Holiday House, liked my sketches and asked, "Can you write?" I rummaged quickly through my memories of creative writing in school and replied in a confident tone, "Sure!" Actually, I had no idea.

A puzzle, a brain-teaser, a game, a recipe—that's how creating a picture book seems to me. Most of my books are informational, but with characters and settings to create a context. The basic ingredients of *Book Soup* are (in no particular order): character sketches, subject area, clothing, text, furniture, landscape, dialog, facial expressions, color combinations, page design, type, art technique, book plan, research, and dummy. Each element influences the others—add garlic and you may have to take out the cinnamon!

I love what I do, and plan to stay in my studio, blending words and art into my favorite confection, the picture book.

———

Loreen Leedy was born in Wilmington, Delaware. She attended Indiana University in Bloomington from 1978 to 1979. She majored in art at the University of Delaware, graduating with honors with a B.A. degree in 1981. Her first children's book was published in 1985, and shortly thereafter she relocated to the Orlando, Florida, area. She has had over twenty books published, and

has made author appearances at schools and conferences. She is a member of the Authors Guild and the Society of Children's Book Writers and Illustrators.

Tracks in the Sand was named an Outstanding Science Trade Book for Children by a joint committee of the National Science Teachers Association and the Children's Book Council. *The Furry News* and *Messages in the Mailbox* were Reading Rainbow Books. Four of her books have been named Junior Library Guild Books: *Blast Off to Earth, The Bunny Play, The Furry News,* and *Messages in the Mailbox.*

SELECTED WORKS WRITTEN AND ILLUSTRATED: A Number of Dragons, 1985; The Dragon ABC Hunt, 1986; The Dragon Halloween Party, 1986; The Bunny Play, 1988; The Furry News: How to Make a Newspaper, 1990; Blast Off to Earth!: A Look at Geography, 1992; Messages in the Mailbox: How to Write a Letter, 1991; Tracks in the Sand, 1993; Who's Who in My Family, 1995.

SELECTED WORKS ILLUSTRATED: The Dinosaur Princess and Other Prehistoric Riddles, by David Adler, 1988; Waiting for Baby, by Tom Birdseye, 1991.

ABOUT: Contemporary Authors, Vol. 122; Delaware Today October 1986; Something About the Author, Vol. 50, 54.

ELLEN W. LEROE

April 26, 1949–

AUTHOR OF *Ghost Dog,* etc.

Autobiographical sketch of Ellen Whitney Leroe:

I CAN STILL remember the day I learned to read. Suddenly those formerly mysterious black squiggles on the page coalesced into magical units I recognized as words. And the words—wonder of wonders!—told a story. I raced home from school in the rain, holding the copy of a Dick, Jane and Spot text in front of me like a banner out of the Crusades. I couldn't wait to tell my parents.

Reading led me to the library, which in turn led me down to the cellar.

Ellen W. Leroe

I grew up in East Orange, New Jersey, a suburb close to Newark, and houses there contained cavernous basements in which you could rollerskate, devise funny games or simply retreat for your own personal reasons. I chose to "go down the cellar" (as we called it) to concoct my own stories. My father was a mechanical engineer and had a big drafting table in one corner with just a tiny fluorescent lamp overhead for illumination. From my eight-year-old perspective, the cellar turned into a dungeon, but a snug and welcoming one. I loved sitting in the ghostly glow of that light, composing spooky fairytales that always revolved around evil wizards, talking ravens and spells of hideous natures.

To this day I delight in writing about all things ghostly and mysterious; the supernatural and the unexplained pique my interest. Many (I should say most) of my children's books feature robots, cupids, poltergeist pugs, warlock teenagers and even a spirit trapped in a peanut butter jar.

I wrote my very first story at the age of seven (*Jim and Johnny Build a Snowman*) and I still remember the excitement and thrill of achievement I experienced when I stapled the five pages into a "book." Here,

finally, was a tangible result of the joy of creating. What added to the allure of writing was the recognition I received from my family. Being the baby in a talkative, funny family of five, I had to struggle for people to notice or listen to me. My little stories captured their attention, and provided the fuel in later years to keep me going in my quest to get published.

I lived in New Jersey for twenty-five years, attending college in upstate New York and going into merchandising as a junior buyer at Hahne's in downtown Newark. During this period I stopped writing fiction, but the urge to create was not completely dormant. I wrote poetry, even managed to sell a few poems to small literary journals, and I filled up 300-page diaries with the details of my life.

It wasn't enough. When the pressures of retailing became too strong, I followed my sister Jane to Berkeley, California, in 1975, and took writing jobs in corporate public relations departments—editing newsletters, laying out in-house magazines. I was involved with words again, and getting paid for it. But the urge to create my own worlds, my own individualistic characters, became too strong to ignore. I wrote my first teen novel, *Confessions of a Teenage TV Addict*, in 1982, and when E. P. Dutton bought it, I became re-energized as a writer. I quit working for other people and became my own boss, churning out one, often two novels a year.

In the almost thirteen years I've been writing full-time, I've lived primarily in San Francisco, first on Russian Hill with fantastic views of the Bay and Alcatraz Prison, and then in North Beach, at the tip of Fisherman's Wharf. I have discovered that I do my best writing in a small, confined space, with nothing to distract me: music, people or views. I rely solely on my imagination to conjure up the colorful worlds in each of my books. This reinforces my strong belief that growing up in New Jersey proved to be the catalyst for my writing. Unlike the Bay Area, where you can leave your house and surround yourself with physical beauty within seconds, the nitty-gritty environs of New Jersey force you to go within yourself and create an appealing landscape, whether it be on canvas, music sheet or paper. Luckily for me, it was paper, and I still love making up stories.

———

Ellen Leroe was born in Newark. She received her B.A. degree from Elmira College in 1971 and studied further at the University of Leicester. She has been an editorial assistant at an engineering company as well as administrative manager of the San Francisco Junior Chamber of Commerce. She is a member of Media Alliance and the Society of Children's Book Writers and Illustrators.

Leroe has written poetry for adults and has been a contributor of poetry and articles to many magazines, including *Cosmopolitan*, *Travel*, and *Good Housekeeping*. She won first prize at the San Francisco Fair Poetry Competition in 1985. Her book *Personal Business* became the novelization of an ABC TV "After School Special." She also wrote the novelization of a New Line Cinema film released in 1994, *Monkey Trouble*.

SELECTED WORKS: Confessions of a Teenage TV Addict, 1983; Robot Romance, 1984; Have a Heart, Cupid Delaney, 1986; The Peanut Butter Poltergeist, 1986; Personal Business, 1986; H.O.W.L. High, 1989; Leap Frog Friday, 1991; Ghost Dog, 1994; Monkey Trouble, 1994; Ghost Dog Goes to the Races, 1995.

SELECTED WORKS EDITED: A Night to Remember, 1995.

ABOUT: Contemporary Authors, Vol. 116; (New Revision Series), Vol. 40; Something About the Author, Vol. 51; Vol. 61.

ELLEN LEVINE

March 9, 1939–

AUTHOR OF *Freedom's Children*, etc.

Autobiographical sketch of Ellen Levine:

Ellen Levine

AS A CHILD, I loved to curl up with a book, shut out the world around me, and travel to other times and places. As an adult, I still do. Several years ago I worked with an adult literacy volunteer program and felt a deep sadness that my students had never experienced the grand adventure of reading.

I grew up in a household of books. My mother was a constant reader—books, magazines, newspapers. Before I and my sisters were born, she was a columnist, writing book reviews and theater notes for two magazines, *Review of Reviews* and *The Golden Book*. There were two serious reading rules in the house: never read a classic comic ("read the book"); and never read a condensed book. The very idea of "condensing" a book provoked unbridled rage in my mother. "How dare someone edit what an author has written and published!" she would say, "Don't read the book if you don't want to, but leave it intact."

When I was old enough to write my name, my mother got a library card for me. Every week she and I would walk to the public library and take out books for the whole family. Five apiece for five people—we carried bags home. I didn't like to sit in the children's circle and be read to, so I roamed the shelves, adult and children, and made my discoveries. If a title intrigued me, I read the book.

I write out of the same sense of intrigue. I have to care about the subject, whether it's the civil rights movement, Anna Pavlova, the Underground Railroad, or the life of a veterinarian. And it's particularly important to me to show children that heroes are 'ordinary' people, like themselves, their parents, their friends, who take risks for what they believe in. In *Secret Missions*, for example, I wrote about four remarkable people few have heard of who engaged with history, thereby changing themselves and affecting those around them.

With *Freedom's Children*, I wanted both adults and children to realize how important young people were to the civil rights movement. No one has ever really told the stories of the thousands of elementary and high school kids who were the backbone of the movement. These young people found a joy in their struggle for justice, and they exercised a discipline few adults thought them capable of. A belief that the world can be a better place and that individuals can actively participate in change, is even more urgent today when the centers of power seem so far from our lives.

———

Ellen Levine was born in New York City. She received her B.A. degree in Politics in 1960 from Brandeis University, graduating magna cum laude. She earned an M.A. degree in political science from the University of Chicago in 1962 and a Juris Doctor degree from New York University School of Law in 1979. She has worked in film and television, for Consumers Union and CBS News, and has taught adults and immigrant teenagers in special education programs. A former staff attorney with a public interest law group, she now devotes her time entirely to writing, lecturing, and some wood carving.

Freedom's Children won the 1994 Jane Addams Children's Book Award. It was named a Best Book for Young Adults by the American Library Association and was named a Notable Children's Trade Book in the Field of Social Studies by a joint committee of the National Council on the Social Studies and the Children's Book Council.

I Hate English! was named an ALA Notable Book of the Year.

SELECTED WORKS: If You Traveled West in a Covered Wagon, 1986; If You Traveled on the Underground Railroad, 1988; Secret Missions: Four True-Life Stories, 1988; I Hate English!, 1989; Ready, Aim, Fire!: The Real Adventures of Annie Oakley, 1989; If You Lived at the Time of Martin Luther King, 1990; Freedom's Children: Young Civil Rights Activists Tell Their Own Stories, 1993; If Your Name Was Changed at Ellis Island, 1993; Anna Pavlova: Genius of the Dance, 1995; A Fence Away from Freedom: Japanese Americans and World War II, 1995; The Tree That Would Not Die, 1995.

ABOUT: Contemporary Authors, Vol. 69-72; (New Revision Series), Vol. 22.

TED LEWIN

May 6, 1935–

ILLUSTRATOR OF *Peppe the Lamplighter*, etc.

Autobiographical sketch of Ted Lewin:

I GREW UP in an old frame house in Buffalo, New York, with two brothers, one sister, two parents, a lion, an iguana, a chimpanzee, and an assortment of more conventional pets. The lion was given to my brother, Donn, while he was traveling as a professional wrestler, and he shipped it home. We kept Sheba in the basement fruit cellar until Donn returned and my mother convinced him to give it to the Buffalo zoo.

I always wanted to be an illustrator, and as a kid, I spent endless hours by myself drawing and copying the work of artists I admired: N.C. Wyeth, Winslow Homer, and John Singer Sargent. My whole family

encouraged what they saw as a gift. I was the only one in the family who could draw. I read every volume of my brother's first edition set of Edgar Rice Burroughs' *Tarzan* and copied those illustrations, too.

When it came time to earn money for art school, Pratt Institute, I followed in Donn's footsteps and took a summer job as a professional wrestler, the beginning of the fifteen year part-time career that eventually inspired my memoir, *I Was a Teenage Professional Wrestler.*

After art school I began freelancing, doing illustrations for adventure magazines. An agent, Elizabeth Armstrong, introduced me to children's books, and I did many illustrations for textbooks and book jackets.

I married, and with my wife, Betsy, also an illustrator, took our first trip, a trip to East Africa in 1970. It was a dream come true for both of us, and it set the tenor of our lives. I'm having more fun putting these experiences down in words and pictures than anything I've ever done before.

I wrote and illustrated a series of books for young readers that Dodd, Mead & Co. published. *World Within a World; Everglades, Baja;* and *Pribilofs* were my first attempts at this. The drawings were done in 4H pencil. In 1988 I was given a manuscript for a picture book, *Faithful Elephants.* The tragic, true tale moved me deeply, and I took on my first picture book. It gave me the chance not only to draw animals, but to make a strong statement about man's cruelty to them in certain circumstances. I realised then that the picture book was the best possible world for an illustrator, and I've devoted my full time to it ever since.

As well as writing and illustrating my own books, I enjoy illustrating the work of other authors. It gives me the chance to do things I might never have done on my own.

My studio is the entire top floor of our hundred-and-ten-year-old brownstone in the historic Clinton Hill section of Brooklyn, near Pratt Institute. I'm very disciplined and work almost every day from eight until one. Four times a week I work out in the gym for two hours to stay fit for our excursions into the bush. One of those excursions, a trip to India, produced *Tiger Trek* and *Sacred River*, which is my current project. A trip to Brazil inspired *Amazon Boy* and *When the Rivers Go Home.* A journey to Lapland produced *The Reindeer People*, and an upcoming book called *Market* draws on material gathered from all my travels. In the future I have two books set in Botswana, one about the Okavango Delta, the other about the bushmen of Kalahari. There is also *Nilo and the Tortoise*, set in the Galapagos Islands, *Billabong*, set in Australia's Northern Territory, and a relating of my encounters with wild creatures all over the world.

One day I was sketching a pair of lions in the Okavango Delta in Botswana, and thought, "This isn't such a great leap from that little kid surrounded by Tarzan books, sketching his big brother's lion cub."

———

Ted Lewin earned his B.F.A. degree from Pratt Institute in 1956. He had a one-man show at the Laboratory of Ornithology at Cornell University in 1978 and at the

Central Park 200 Gallery in New York City in 1994. He has illustrated more than one hundred books for children, and his work has appeared in such publications as *Boys' Life*, *Seventeen*, and *Reader's Digest*.

Peppe the Lamplighter was named an Honor Book in the 1994 Randolph Caldecott Awards given by the American Library Association. Both *Peppe* and *I Was a Professional Teenage Wrestler* were named Notable Books of the Year by the ALA. *Judy Scuppernong* won a 1991 *Boston Globe-Horn Book* Award.

SELECTED WORKS WRITTEN AND ILLUSTRATED: I Was a Teenage Professional Wrestler, 1993.

SELECTED WORKS ILLUSTRATED: Soup for President, by Robert Newton Peck, 1985; The Search for Grissi, by Mary Frances Shura, 1985; The Secret of the Indian, by Lynne Reid Banks, 1989; The Day of Ahmed's Secret, by Florence Perry Heide and Judith Heide Gilliland, 1990; Judy Scuppernong, by Brenda Seabrooke, 1990; Shanghai Passage, by Gregory Patent, 1990; A Brown Bird Singing, by Frances Wosmek, 1992; The Great Pumpkin Switch, by Megan McDonald, 1992; Peppe the Lamplighter, by Elisa Bartone, 1993.

ABOUT: Contemporary Authors, Vol. 69-72; (New Revision Series), Vol. 25; Something About the Author, Vol. 21, 76.

J. PATRICK LEWIS

May 5, 1942–

AUTHOR OF *The Moonbow of Mr. B. Bones*, etc.

Autobiographical sketch of J. Patrick Lewis:

MY PARENTS traveled equal distances—one came from Iowa, the other from Pennsylvania—and met working in the steel mills of Gary, Indiana. That's where I was born in 1942. I have two brothers, one of whom is my twin, my alter ego, my best friend. Our childhoods were ridiculously normal, lacking any mayhem or major misadventure, nor even the whisper of a scandal. Oh, I could mention my father, who

delighted in clacking his false teeth just to tease the bejabbers out of the neighborhood kids. Or my mother, who'd laugh herself silly at his antics. But my parents must have been too busy being who they were—salt-of-the-earth middle Americans doting on their kids—to create any kind of stir.

I finished college in 1964, married my high school sweetheart, and together we produced three children who, by some freak of fortune, happily ensconced themselves in California. In college I fell under the influence of social scientists rather than literature professors, and until fairly recently, that had made all the difference. I didn't publish my first children's book until I was forty-six. Until then, my writing—articles on economics—appeared exclusively in academic journals, magazines and newspapers.

A central event in our lives occurred in 1972-73 when my wife and I and our three young children spent the academic year in the former Soviet Union. I wrote my Ph.D. dissertation there on the Soviet economy and have taught college courses on Russia ever since. I've returned to Russia five times and continue to go back every two years or so to visit dear friends. Little wonder that my first children's book, *The Tsar and the Amazing Cow*, was set in Russia, a country for which I have a deep and abiding affection and many treasured memories.

My turn to children's books came in 1978 when my family and I visited Cumberland Falls, Kentucky, the site of a "moonbow," a white rainbow that appears only at certain times of the year and at only two places in the world. *The Moonbow of Mr. B. Bones* was actually the first story for children I had written, and it would eventually become my fifth book.

I like to say that when I grow up I want to be a poet for children. Without seeming too terribly earnest, I aim to write poetry worthy of the name—intelligent (not to say high-flown intellectual) poetry for children. And even intelligent *nonsense*, in the manner of the grand masters, Edward Lear and Lewis Carroll. I put it this way as a counterpoint to the embarrassing amount of doggerel that too often passes for children's poetry today, the treacly or forced rhyme that shames language and demeans the children who read it. The late John Ciardi called it verse that "sounds as if it were written with a sponge dipped in sugared milk."

Writing stories, and especially poetry for the young, has changed my life. I think of the books I've written as my imaginary children. If they should turn out half as splendidly as my real children have, that will be quite enough.

———

J. Patrick Lewis received a B.A. degree from St. Joseph's College in Rensselaer, Indiana, in 1964. He earned an M.A. degree from Indiana University in Bloomington in 1965. He earned his Ph.D. in Economics at Ohio State University in 1974 and has taught at Otterbein College in Westerville, Ohio, since then. He completed his doctoral dissertation as an International Research and Exchange Fellow. He has been published extensively in the field of economics. His articles and reviews have appeared in academic journals such as *The Nation, The Progressive*, and *Technology Review*. He has also written short stories and poetry for adults. In 1991 he was awarded an Ohio Arts Council Individual Arts Grant for his adult poetry. He is a contributor to magazines such as *Ms., Cricket, Ranger Rick*, and *Highlights for Children*.

The Moonbow of Mr. B. Bones was named a Notable Book of the Year by the American Library Association.

SELECTED WORKS: The Tsar & the Amazing Cow, 1988; A Hippopotamusn't, 1990; Two-Legged, Four-Legged, No-Legged Rhymes, 1991; Earth Verses and Water Rhymes, 1991; The Moonbow of Mr. B. Bones, 1992; One Dog Day, 1993; July Is a Mad Mosquito: A Book of Months, 1994; The Christmas of the Reddle Moon, 1994; The Fat-Cats at Sea, 1994; The Frog Princess, 1994; Black Swan/White Crow, 1995; Ridicholas Nicholas, 1995.

ABOUT: Contemporary Authors Vol. 138; Instructor January 1993; Language Arts April 1993; Ohio Reading Teacher Summer 1992; Something About the Author, Vol. 69.

RICHARD LEWIS

May 15, 1935–

AUTHOR OF *All of You Was Singing*, etc.

Autobiographical sketch of Richard Lewis:

JUST THE OTHER DAY I was sitting with a fourth-grade student who was having some trouble writing a poem. She couldn't get started—and was upset that her thoughts seemed to be everywhere, making it difficult for her to focus on what she really wanted to write. I suggested to her that if she could let one of her many thoughts stand still—and imagine it as something she could daydream on—it might free up that thought so she could begin to play with it—as she once played with her thoughts when she was younger. Well, it worked—and what she wanted to write about—gradually found its way on to paper.

As I watched her writing, I recalled the

importance of daydreaming in my own life. Even now I have a vivid memory of myself as a young child sitting at a living room window overlooking a crowded street in New York City. For hours (or at least it seemed that way) I would watch buses, cars, people, and trucks move in endlessly intricate patterns. It was like a great design coming to life right in front of me—and I could, as I watched, also travel into my own most secret thoughts. Unfortunately I got into trouble in school when I tried to daydream—and some of my teachers would tell me quite adamantly to stop dreaming and pay attention. It wasn't until I was older that I realized how much I was actually paying attention—not necessarily to what was being taught but to what I was personally thinking and feeling. Eventually it occurred to me that there was a vast landscape inside of me. If I patiently listened to it, I could learn a good deal about the nature of my own experience and perceptions.

I didn't have a name for this kind of listening when I was younger—but as I began to grow interested in music, or in reading books, or going to movies, it seemed that becoming absorbed in what someone else was attempting to say was also a kind of dream-ing. It seemed as if there was a language inside each of us that could communicate information you couldn't get at unless you let yourself daydream a little. Later I realized how this daydreaming was in large measure a quality of how we imagine—and that our imagination is a gift given to each of us so we might converse and play with those ideas and feelings that make up our sense of what it means to be alive.

My desire to make books was my way of sharing more about how we imagine and, in particular, how we make poetry from our imagining. I have always been interested in the fact that poetry—and knowing the world poetically—are basic human instincts that have been part of our ability to express ourselves. Many of the books I initially edited were gatherings of poetry that had been spoken, sung, and written by persons in a variety of cultures ranging from the ancient Greek to modern Spanish, to indigenous peoples throughout the world as well as individual poets from China, Japan and India. In addition I was very involved in collecting the poetry and prose written by children—and spent many years gathering examples of their work—which eventually I made into a series of books for both children and adults alike. Most recently I have published, in collaboration with the illustrator Ed Young, my renditions of ancient creation myths from Hawaii and Mexico.

Just as meaningful to me as creating books has been my working with young people and their teachers in schools in New York through an organization I began called The Touchstone Center—trying my best, in different classroom settings, to keep alive the importance of our imagination. And each time I have the pleasure of talking with children, helping them discover ways to use their imaginations, I'm confident that, in each of us, there is a unique window from which we can watch and participate in the shaping of the world around us. Like a large reflecting mirror, this same window can also bring us closer to the enormous richness of our imaginative selves—

speaking across time and cultures with each other.

Between writing and teaching I feel deeply fortunate to be still doing what I did so naturally as a child. In coming years I simply hope to continue this wondrous exploration.

———

Richard Lewis was born in New York City. He received his B.A. degree from Bard College in Music Composition in 1958. He also studied at the New School for Social Research, New York University, and Mannes College of Music from 1958 to 1961. In the 1963-1964 school year, he taught fifth grade at the Walden School in New York. He lectured at Wellington Training College in New Zealand the following year. Among other teaching posts, he taught at Bank Street College of Education and at North Adams State College in Massachusetts, and he was a lecturer at Fordham University in New York. He has been Adjunct Professor at many schools including Rutgers University from 1976 to 1978; Lesley College Graduate School in Massachusetts (where he was also Visiting Poet-in-Residence) from 1983 to 1984; and Queens College, City University of New York, in 1988.

Richard Lewis has pursued two major interests: creating books and developing the art of teaching. His books range from international collections of original writings by children, such as *Miracles*, *Journeys*, and *There Are Two Lives*, to anthologies of poetry of the Eskimo, such as *I Breathe a New Song*, to the myths he has retold for children.

In addition to his books, Lewis writes articles and essays, which have appeared in *Parnassus*, *Publishers Weekly*, *Elementary English*, *Childhood Education*, and *Parabola*. Lewis has created a number of theater pieces for children and adults that have been performed at places such as the American Museum of Natural History and the Hudson River Museum. He also writes

radio programs for young people on the origin and nature of poetry, and his work has been aired on National Public Radio.

The Touchstone Center for Children, founded in 1969, has been funded in part by the Rockefeller Foundation, Exxon Foundation, New York State Council on the Arts, and Con Edison. His work as a teacher was documented in a film, *The Journey Within*, produced by Renascence Films and winner of a 1991 Cine Golden Eagle Award.

Lewis is a member of PEN New York and Author's Guild. He is also on the editorial board of *Parabola Magazine*. He presents workshops and seminars for adults. He is married and has three children.

SELECTED WORKS EDITED: In a Spring Garden: A Selection of Haiku Poetry, 1965; Moon, for What Do You Wait?, by Rabindranath Tagore, 1967; Out of the Earth I Sing: Poetry and Song of Primitive Peoples of the World, 1968; Muse of the Round Sky: Greek Lyric Poetry, 1969; Of This World: A Poet's Life in Poetry, 1969; The Way of Silence: Prose and Poetry of Basho, 1970; The Luminous Landscape: Chinese Art and Poetry, 1981; Still Waters of the Air: Three Modern Spanish Poets, 1981.

SELECTED WORKS RETOLD: In the Night Still Dark: A Retelling of the Hawaiian Creation Chant, 1988; All of You Was Singing: A Retelling of an Aztec Myth, 1991.

ABOUT: Contemporary Authors (First Revision), Vol. 9-12; (New Revision Series), Vol. 5; Dictionary of Literary Biography, Vol. 24; Hopkins, Lee Bennett. Books Are By People; Something About the Author, Vol. 3.

REEVE LINDBERGH

AUTHOR OF *The Midnight Farm*, etc.

Biographical sketch of Reeve Lindbergh:

Reeve Lindbergh is the daughter of aviator Charles A. Lindbergh and Anne Morrow Lindbergh. She grew up in Connecticut. Her parents were both writers, and their house was filled with books. Her sister Anne also is a children's books writer.

Reeve Lindbergh writes the texts for children's books, often in rhyme. She frequently sets her stories on a farm, with its abundance of animals.

The Midnight Farm is a lullaby, in which a mother and child view a farm at night, when animals are sleeping. Lindbergh based the book on stories she told to her little girl to help her get over the fear of the dark. Susan Jeffers illustrated the book.

The Day the Goose Got Loose is a story in rhyme, depicting the chaos that occurs when a mischievous goose escapes its coop, sending all the barnyard animals into wild behavior. The book is illustrated by Steven Kellogg.

The barnyard theme continues in Lindbergh's *Benjamin's Barn*, illustrated by Susan Jeffers. A boy imagines what could fill the barn—a flock of pterodactyls, a rhinoceros—if it weren't home to the animals he knows so well.

Johnny Appleseed tells the legend of the folk hero, seen through the eyes of a pioneer family. The pioneer way of life is therefore depicted, as well as the story of John Chapman. Reviewer Mary M. Burns, writing in *The Horn Book Magazine*, calls it a "splendid production." It is illustrated by Kathy Jakobsen.

View from the Air is a book of aerial photographs by Richard Brown, who took them in the early 1970s when he flew with Charles Lindbergh. Reeve Lindbergh's text is, according to *The Horn Book Guide*, "a poetic statement intended to represent a plea for conservation by the author's father." The color photographs depict New England.

Reeve Lindbergh wrote *What Is the Sun?* when her son Ben was three years old and asking questions about the natural world. She composed a series of questions and answers between a boy and his grandmother, questions about the moon, the tides, the wind, and the rain. She composed the text from his questions and the true answers to them.

Grandfather's Lovesong was named a Notable Children's Trade Book in the Field of Social Studies by a joint committee of the Children's Book Council and the National Council on the Social Studies.

Lindbergh lives near St. Johnsbury, Vermont, with her husband and three children.

SELECTED WORKS: The Midnight Farm, 1986; Benjamin's Barn, 1990; The Day the Goose Got Loose, 1990; Johnny Appleseed, 1990; View from the Air: Charles Lindbergh's Earth and Sky, 1992; Grandfather's Lovesong, 1993; There's a Cow in the Road!, 1993; If I'd Known Then What I Know Now, 1994; What Is the Sun?, 1994.

ABOUT: People Weekly January 25, 1993.

PIJA LINDENBAUM

April 27, 1955–

AUTHOR AND ILLUSTRATOR OF *Boodil My Dog*, etc.

Biographical sketch of Pija Lindenbaum:

PIJA LINDENBAUM was born in Sundsvall in northern Sweden. Her father was a director, and her mother a teacher. After graduating from high school, she began her art education in Sundsvall in 1974. In 1975 she moved to Stockholm to study graphic design and illustration at Konstfackskolan. She finished this study in 1979. She then began a career as, first, a freelance graphic designer. Later, in the mid-eighties, she became an illustrator. She married Mikael Nilsson, an artist, in 1989.

Lindenbaum's first book was published in 1990. It is the story of a girl who has seven daddies, identical and all under two feet tall. In Sweden, *Else-Marie and Her Seven Daddies* was awarded three literary prizes and grants, and was dramatized for a production in Amsterdam. She won the Expressens Heffaklump Prize in 1990.

Boodil My Dog was named a Best Illustrated Book of 1992 by *The New York Times*. She won the Elsa Beskow Plaque in

PIJA LINDENBAUM

1992. She also won the UNICEF Illustrator of the Year Award in 1992, and was nominated to the August Strindberg Prize in 1993. Betsy Hearne wrote, in the *Chicago Bulletin of the Center for Children's Books*, "The artist has a talent for spacious simplicity activated by a few bold lines. Boodil's expressions . . . are all the wittier for a context of spare shapes and minimal color." Lindenbaum lives in Stockholm with her husband and daughter.

SELECTED WORKS WRITTEN AND ILLUSTRATED: (adapted by Gabrielle Charbonnet) Else-Marie and Her Seven Little Daddies, 1991; (retold by Gabrielle Charbonnet) Boodil My Dog, 1992.

SELECTED WORKS ILLUSTRATED: Louie, by Barbro Lindgren, 1994.

ABOUT: Something About the Author, Vol. 77.

CHRIS LYNCH

July 2, 1962–

AUTHOR OF *Shadow Boxer*, etc.

Autobiographical sketch of Chris Lynch:

I AM JUST LIKE many other authors

whose autobiographical sketches I've read. I knew early on what I wanted to do; I wanted to do nothing.

I left high school after my junior year, with no diploma, because I hated it there. I went to Boston University, where I had such a clear sense of direction that I majored in political science and minored in music. I washed out of the basic music theory class after one month because I had not a scintilla of a musical proclivity. The political science mistake lasted until sophomore year, until I wandered into my first journalism class and accidentally discovered that I liked writing about people doing things more than I liked being a person who did things.

So when I switched schools—to Suffolk University—I also switched majors and goals. Writing was clearly my focus now, and I set out to find where I fit. I took newswriting, features writing, public relations writing, copywriting, editing, and magazine writing courses. I found all kinds of subjects to write about, and discovered that I had a broad range of interests. I found different styles to write in, and found I could handle a broad range of assignments. No clear career path threw itself at me (which in those days was the only way I seemed to find anything), but one subtle development worked its way out: the more I wrote, the more I leaned in the direction of a more "creative," less structured brand of story-telling. I left school—this time with a diploma—reasonably sure that a job, and career, would present itself.

I drove a truck, delivering furniture. I painted houses. I did some proofreading. I painted houses again.

In the midst of all that, possibly in response to it, I created my first bona fide work of fiction: myself. Inexplicably, with nothing to back me up, I began to think of myself as a fiction writer. Even though I wrote very, very seldom, and very, very poorly, I believed a writer was what I was. But I didn't tell anybody.

In 1989, six years after leaving Suffolk, I entered the writing program at Emerson College. Still afraid to declare my intentions—my identity—as a fiction writer, I stressed the "professional," publishing-business aspect of the program. And just as I resisted exposing myself as an artist of some kind, I resisted, in my work, getting close to the bones of my own existence. Early on, I wrote stories that I believed *sounded* good, that I thought I could stylize into something good. And my work was failing because of it.

Only as I neared the end of my masters degree program, and once again heard the beating feet of the real world approaching, did I make the final, critical commitment. I took a children's writing course, and in looking back over my personal experiences, I realized that if I wanted to do work that was any good, if I wanted to get these stories *right*, I was going to have to cause myself some discomfort. If I tried to get around that, I wouldn't be telling the real story, I would be a fraud, and the work would fail.

So I made the decision to try, and still hardly a week goes by that I don't cause myself some profound discomfort. It's getting worse, too, as the longer I write, the more determined I am to get it real. But

writing, I've found, is the kind of work that pays you back several fold for the effort you put in.

And the bottom line is, whatever it takes, I *want* to write now. Which is many changes removed from when I wanted to do nothing.

———

Chris Lynch was born in Boston. He received his B.A. degree in Journalism from Suffolk University in 1983 and his M.A. in Writing and Publishing from Emerson College in Boston in 1991. He is married and has a daughter and a son. He is working on a trilogy of novels, called "Blue-Eyed Son."

Shadow Boxer, *Gypsy Davey*, and *Iceman* were all named Best Books for Young Adults by the American Library Association.

SELECTED WORKS: Shadow Boxer, 1993; Iceman, 1994; Gypsy Davey, 1995; Slot Machine, 1995.

GEORGE ELLA LYON

April 25, 1949–

AUTHOR OF *Come a Tide*, etc.

Autobiographical sketch of George Ella Lyon:

I HAD double vision until I was thirteen years old. Where you see this one book, I would see two, the second slightly higher and tilted to the left. Given this overlap of real objects with their doubles, I was a clumsy kid. It was a challenge to get in the reading circle, for instance. All those red and blue chairs, linked like a chain, all those classmates! But it was worth whatever chair-crashing and embarrassment it took me to get to the books. I loved what the ink-voice offered: colors, numbers, stories! And of course I read everything twice.

Like many difficulties, double vision brought with it certain gifts. It nourished my natural love of words both by requiring

George Ella Lyon

extra focus to read them and by making me a listener. When the physical world was crowded and unreliable—just how many steps were there and which ones were solid?—voices anchored me. The real teacher was the one the sound was coming from. The top of the steps was where a friend's voice stood.

I loved music as well as words and memorized easily, so between the radio, hymns, records, and my father's singing, I knew two hour's worth of songs by the time I was five. (I know this because two hours is how long it took to drive from Harlan, Kentucky, my hometown, to Knoxville, Tennessee, the big city. The story is that I could sing the whole way without repeating a song.)

When the flannelgraph missionaries came to our school, I memorized Bible verses too. Fifty verses got you a New Testament. That was harder than songs, but I figured I could do it. The words had a music of their own that held them together. I listened for that.

Along with songs and scripture rattling around in my head were the poems my parents read aloud at the table. I don't know how this got started or how often it hap-

pened, but I loved it. Poetry—that's what I needed! That made sense. Not that I could tell you exactly what it meant—that's not the purpose of poetry anyway—but that it reached through my senses and touched something real.

At the same time my inner library was being stocked with these written words, it was also being filled with words spoken around me. I come from a family, a community, a part of the country where storytelling is commonplace. It's how you share sad times and funny times, how you remember who you are. I could never have written *A Regular Rolling Noah* or *Borrowed Children* without family stories to draw on, stories told not just once but again and again. Part of my work is trying to hear the storytellers in my memory. The hard thing is getting quiet enough to listen when the rest of the world and my own life are so loud.

People often ask if I like being a writer. They might as well ask if I like being alive. Just as some days are hard and some are fun, some ask more than we can give and others offer more than we deserve, writing has its ups and downs. I may not *like* it at a given time, but it's where my heart is. I'm committed.

During eighth grade I had surgery to correct my double vision. The world felt a little empty, but I no longer ran into things. What a relief! And the lessons from double vision continue to be useful. After all, a lot of what our culture calls important is no more substantial than that ghost book I saw. It's up to us to figure out what's real and let the rest go.

———

George Ella Lyon earned a B.A. degree from Centre College in 1971, Phi Beta Kappa. She received her M.A. degree from the University of Arkansas in 1972, where she was a teaching fellow. She received her Ph.D. degree in English and Creative Writing from Indiana University in 1978. She was also a teaching fellow there. Her teaching experience includes a stint as Visiting Assistant Professor of English at the University of Kentucky; leading teaching and writing workshops in Ohio, North Carolina, and Georgia; and co-directing an institute for school administrators in 1987. She has made presentations to numerous organizations including the Folger Shakespeare Library in 1981; Carnegie Library of Pittsburgh in 1991; and the Missouri Whole Language Conference in 1992.

Lyon writes both picture-book texts and novels for children. She is a writer of stories, plays, poetry, and essays. She has had her plays produced and has been published in a wide variety of magazines and anthologies, including *California Quarterly, The American Voice, Appalachian Journal,* and *Kentucky Review.* She is a member of several professional organizations, including the Virginia Woolf Society, the Modern Language Association, and the Society of Children's Book Writers and Illustrators.

Borrowed Children won a 1989 Golden Kite Award from the Society of Children's Book Writers and Illustrators. *A B Cedar* was named an Oustanding Science Trade Book by a joint committee of the National Science Teachers Association and the Children's Book Council. *Come a Tide* was a Reading Rainbow Book.

SELECTED WORKS: Borrowed Children, 1988; A B Cedar: An Alphabet of Trees, 1989; Red Rover, Red Rover, 1989; Together, 1989; Come a Tide, 1990; Who Came Down That Road?, 1992; Dreamplace, 1993; Five Live Bongos, 1994; Here and Then, 1994; Mama Is a Miner, 1994.

ABOUT: Contemporary Authors, Vol. 120; Language Arts October 1990; Library Talk 1993; Poet's Market 1988; Something About the Author, Vol. 68.

MARY E. LYONS

November 28, 1947–

AUTHOR OF *Sorrow's Kitchen: The Life and Folklore of Zora Neale Hurston,* etc.

Biographical sketch of Mary Evelyn Lyons:

Mary E. Lyons

MARY E. LYONS considers herself to be a true child of the South. She was born in Macon, Georgia, the daughter of Joseph and Evelyn Lyons. She and her parents and three siblings moved a great deal; by the time Lyons was eleven years old, they had lived in five southern states and eight southern towns.

Moving from place to place can be hard for children, but Lyons writes that she always felt at home with books. She comes from a family of voracious readers, and her goal was to become "an authoress," but somewhere along the way, she decided to become a teacher instead. "Moving around a lot taught me not to be afraid to try something new," she says. Lyons completed her B. S. degree in Elementary Education in 1970 at Appalachian State University in North Carolina, and then in 1972, her M.S. in Reading Education. She also completed all the course work for a doctoral degree at the University of Virginia, but was diverted by teaching and writing children's books before she could finish.

For seventeen years, Lyons was a reading teacher in elementary and middle schools in North Carolina, near Chapel Hill, and in

Charlottesville, Virginia. Then, she became a school librarian and worked for seven years in elementary, middle, and high school libraries in Charlottesville. It was her work as a teacher that led her to write her first book. She found that her eighth graders enjoyed stories by African-American and women writers, especially Zora Neale Hurston's humorous folk tales. When she couldn't find a biography of Hurston in the school library, she decided to write one herself. *Sorrow's Kitchen: The Life and Folklore of Zora Neale Hurston*, which came out in 1990, won the Carter G. Woodson Book Award in 1991. It also was named a Best Book for Young Adults by the American Library Association.

Writing about Hurston taught Lyons to appreciate African-American history, and she continued to learn and write about the subject. Her interests include folklore, women's studies, and black studies, and these subjects inform much of her work. "People often do assume that I'm African-American," says Lyons, who is of Irish descent, "and I'm quite flattered when that happens because it means I'm an effective writer."

Lyons says that everything she has written about so far has come directly out of her teaching and librarianship. "One book leads to another," she says, and in this, her second year as a full-time writer, with ten books already under her belt, she is still using her "grab-bag of subject matter" collected during her years as a teacher and librarian. "I have so many ideas [for future books], they drive me crazy!" she claims.

Lyons wrote her first two books while working full-time. She began the research for her series on African-American Artists and Artisans during a year-long paid sabbatical in 1991-92, when she was the recipient of the National Endowment for the Humanities Teacher Scholar Award for Virginia. Four books in the series have been published to date, including *Stitching Stars: The Story Quilts of Harriet Powers* and *Starting Home: The Story of Horace Pip-*

pin, Painter. The latter book was named a 1993 ALA Notable Book and won the 1994 Carter G. Woodson Award. The series, intended for ages eight to eleven, will continue with *Painting Dreams: The Visionary Art of Minnie Evans* in the fall of 1995. In addition to the series, Lyons is the author of *Raw Head, Bloody Bones: African-American Tales of the Supernatural*, which was named a 1992 Notable Children's Trade Book in the Field of Social Studies by a joint committee of the National Council for the Social Studies and the Children's Book Council. *Stitching Stars* received the same award in 1994. Her *Letters from a Slave Girl: The Story of Harriet Jacobs* was named a 1993 Jane Addams Children's Book Award Honor Book and won the 1992 Golden Kite Award for fiction from the Society of Children's Book Writers and Illustrators. It was also named a Notable Book and as Best Book for Young Adults by the ALA. She is also preparing a book for young readers about the collected tales of Brer Rabbit, called *The Butter Tree: Tales of Bruh Rabbit*. In a departure from her usual emphasis on African-American history, her book *Keeping Secrets: The Girlhood Diaries of Seven Working Writers* shows how the diaries of seven girls helped them to develop their later voices as writers and activists.

Now that she is a full-time writer, Lyons still finds she is extremely busy. Her day is divided between writing and research, and often she will spend the evening doing revisions. She spends a lot of time travelling, attending conferences, making author appearances, and doing research. Lyons has received two Fellowships from the Virginia Foundation for the Humanities to sponsor her work. She usually works at home, and she admits to sometimes taking her laptop computer along with her on vacation, so she can continue to write. She is also very involved in the fight against censorship, and is concerned about the current passivity with which she feels people are dealing with this important issue. She is outspoken on a state and local level about the dangers of censorship, stating that "All writers should be very rigorous in fighting censorship."

Lyons lives in Charlottesville with her husband, Paul Collinge, who owns a used and rare bookstore, the source of many obscure reference sources for her writing. She feels lucky to be a children's book writer. She says, "Becoming a writer has added a whole new dimension to myself as a person—that's exciting." Lyons also encourages children to write, saying "Everyone is a writer at heart. Writing is a healthy thing to do. It helps you learn more about yourself."

In addition to being a writer, Lyons is also an amateur musician. She plays the Irish penny-whistle and banjo, and is part of a group, Virgil and the Chicken Heads, that plays traditional old-time and Irish music.

SELECTED WORKS: Sorrow's Kitchen: The Life and Folklore of Zora Neale Hurston, 1990; Raw Head, Bloody Bones: African-American Tales of the Supernatural, 1991; Letters from a Slave Girl: The Story of Harriet Jacobs, 1992; Starting Home: The Story of Horace Pippin, Painter, 1993; Stitching Stars: The Story Quilts of Harriet Powers, 1993; Master of Mahogany: Tom Day, Free Black Cabinetmaker, 1994; Deep Blues: Bill Traylor, Self-Taught Artist, 1994; The Butter Tree: Tales of Bruh Rabbit, 1995; Keeping Secrets: The Girlhood Diaries of Seven Women Writers, 1995.

HANA MACHOTKA

June 4, 1944–

AUTHOR OF *Breath-Taking Noses*, etc.

Autobiographical sketch of Hana Machotka:

I WAS BORN in troubled times in Prague, Czechoslovakia at the end of World War II. The country was still under Nazi occupation and my father was active in the resistance. He was gone for days at a time. It was a time of great fear and uncertainty. My father was involved in the interim government after the occupation, and when the communists staged a coup, they put him on

a death list. He fled the country immediately. My mother, brother, sister, and I fled later in two groups on foot, at night, across the mountains, in the cold of April. We arrived safely in Germany, and eventually we all reunited with my father. We came to America a few months later. My father had a job as a professor waiting for him.

I don't have any memory of those early years, but I think they had a profound effect on me. I found solace in nature and animals. The natural world is not a scary place to me. On the contrary, it is incredibly beautiful, and a source of peace and creativity.

When I was a child I had no interest in writing, despite the fact that my father wrote scholarly books about sociology. I loved animals and I was going to be a veterinarian. My love of animals started when we got our first cat. Cats have always been a very special part of my life. I soon expanded my interest to horses. In my spare time I drew a lot, mostly animals. On weekends and vacations, my father and brother liked to paint outdoors. You could call them Sunday painters. I liked to watch them and I sometimes joined in.

As a young adult I followed up with my

Machotka: *ma HOT ka*

interest in nature by joining a Naturalist club and learning all about plants, animals, and birding. I joined an Aquarium Society and learned about fish; a Hiking Club where I learned to plan trips, read maps, and take canoe and ski trips; I also joined a folk dance group and learned the dances of many countries. At about that time, I was sure I would become a naturalist, someone who traipses outdoors in the pursuit of rare and exotic animals. In college I majored in biology, but I soon realized that cutting up dead animals wasn't my way of appreciating nature.

I spent my junior year studying in France. That's where I got fired up about art. I took drawing courses and spent a great deal of time in museums and traveling. When I returned, I decided to go on in graduate studies in art, painting and sculpture. I studied in New York at the School of Visual Arts and City College. I painted, sculpted in stone, and photographed. I got married in 1976 and had two children.

I started to write stories for children. I also took lots of photographs. One day a photographer friend saw my photos and said, "You know, you should do something with them." So I did!

Another friend told me about a wonderful new circus with a terrific horse act. I went to see it and loved it. I contacted the trainer afterwards and asked if I could come watch her train and take some pictures. She agreed. From the pictures I wrote a story, which unfortunately was never published. But it got me my first contract for a book about the Big Apple Circus called *The Magic Ring.*

This book led to a series of photo books about animals. In these books I not only want to share my love of animals, but also I want to get children to look at nature; to think about shapes, forms, design, and how these help the animal survive in its world. I hope to help children understand the beauty of life and the natural world. I am very concerned by humankind's relationship to nature. In my small way I hope

through my books to help children develop a more loving relationship with our natural world.

At present I am writing a novel about prehistoric people. I am trying to recreate a time when people loved the earth and her creatures and lived a peaceful existence with one another.

For me writing is a way to keep exploring and learning about the world. It's also a wonderful way of sharing with others what I've found.

———

Hana Machotka received her B.A. degree from the State University of New York in 1965, majoring in biology. She studied drawing and painting in 1963 and 1964 at the Academie Julian in Paris, and received a Certificat de la Langue Practique from the Sorbonne in Paris in 1964. She received a Certificate of Fine Art from the School of Visual Arts in New York in 1967. She earned an M.A. degree in Fine Art from the City University of New York in 1970, and has taken education courses at Pratt Institute and the New School for Social Research.

Machotka was an intern in parent-child workshops held by the Metropolitan Museum of Art from 1991 to 1992. She has been an art teacher and conducted many workshops from 1971 through the present, including work with elementary school students in the Woodward School in Brooklyn in the YMCA, and in the Children's Museum of Arts. She taught photography to Bank Street School students in 1991-1992. She has done workshops in New York City public schools in 1992 and 1993. She worked with senior citizens in 1994 and with young mothers and fathers in the High School for Redirection in Brooklyn in 1994.

Breath-Taking Noses was named a 1992 Oustanding Science Trade Book for Children by a joint committee of the National Science Teachers' Association and The Children's Book Council. Hana Machotka is a member of Author's Guild.

Selected Works Written and Photographed: The Magic Ring: A Year with the Big Apple Circus, 1988; What Do You Do at a Petting Zoo?, 1989; What Neat Feet!, 1991; Breath-Taking Noses, 1992; Pasta Factory, 1992; Outstanding Outsides, 1993; Terrific Tails, 1994.

STEPHEN MANES

January 8, 1949–

Author of *Be a Perfect Person in Just Three Days!*, etc.

Autobiographical sketch of Stephen Manes:

I HAVE ALWAYS had an affinity for words. I somehow learned to read long before I began kindergarten. In second grade I gobbled up every book by Dr. Seuss that I could get my hands on. But I didn't begin to think of myself as a writer until the third grade, when I became a lowly roving reporter for the *Sunnyside Review*, our school newspaper. This fine publication was supervised by Miss Harris, the school librarian, who taught us the finer points of journalism, including respect for ink's staining powers both figurative and literal. Working on the paper was my favorite thing about school; to this day I remember with fondness the green keys and pica font of the typewriter, the cool metallic sheen of the mimeograph, the pungent smell of the ink.

By sixth grade I had risen through the ranks to become editor in chief. Although I produced my share of news articles, my first love was writing satire and humorous verse, for which I won a couple of statewide second prizes. They were to be the last literary awards I would receive for more than twenty-five years.

In high school I spearheaded an effort to develop a literary magazine, but a faculty censor managed to put us out of business before we published our first issue. I also became smitten with photography, set up a darkroom in the family basement, and had some of my pictures accepted for a show at

Pittsburgh's Three Rivers Arts Festival. When I arrived at the University of Chicago, I fell in with the thrillingly vociferous members of Doc Films, the nation's oldest film society. Soon I figured out a way to combine my interests in writing and photography: I would become a movie director.

Every film fanatic knew that the French New Wave directors like Godard, Truffaut and Chabrol had started out as film critics. With their example as a guide, friends and I founded a magazine called *focus!*, all lowercase to be arty, exclamation point to shout our position loud and clear. Our position was pretty much what the French called "politique des auteurs," the idea that a film's director is essentially its author (something I have since learned is not quite the whole truth). Like the French, we gave American directors particularly favorable scrutiny. The cover of the last issue I edited proclaimed the inferiority of pretentious poseurs like Michelangelo Antonioni to such clear-minded artists as Roger Corman, Otto Preminger, and Jerry Lewis.

Since Chicago didn't offer a cinema degree, I transferred to the film school of the University of Southern California, where I actually got to sit in on classes taught by Jerry Lewis but spent far more time watching old movies on TV and in seedy downtown theaters than I ever did attending class. During the summer after my junior year, a friend and I tried to raise funds to shoot a screenplay we had written. We didn't manage to produce either the money or the movie.

After college, I took a day job in the library of the American Film Institute and wrote screenplays in my spare time. Writing screenplays, I learned, is a miserable job. It's not just that they will be changed beyond recognition if they happen to turn into movies; more likely, they will never be filmed, doomed instead to sit on shelves forever. Either way, the frustration can be unbearable. But I also learned that I was cut out to be a writer, not a director.

The final break with Hollywood came when I saw a screenplay of mine transmogrified into a horror called *Mother, Jugs and Speed.* My name was on it, but not even the title was mine. At the time, my first wife worked as a children's librarian at the Santa Monica Public Library, and she had been bringing home books a lot more interesting than the movies I had been seeing, including "mine." I decided to try my hand at writing for kids because I figured they might get a kick out of my peculiar sense of humor. Besides, even if they didn't, I probably would.

What I discovered was that writing books is mostly a wonderful thing to do. You are your own boss. You get to say what you need to say precisely the way you want to say it. Editors may make suggestions, but ultimately the book is your handiwork, your creation. This is somehow extremely comforting in an era when increasingly we can't be sure who is speaking for whom, when politicians, corporate barons, movie stars, and even some very popular authors have ghostwriters.

Over the years I have written in just about every form and forum: fiction, nonfiction, biography, articles, interviews, essays; books, magazines, newspapers, movies, television, software, placemats. Each has its particular satisfactions and irritations, but I still keep coming back to books for their permanence and authorial control. Unlike newspapers, magazines, or the movies, books give you the time to get things right and the freedom to find the perfect tone to say them in. Writing for kids is especially gratifying, because kids can be the best audiences of all.

———

Stephen Manes was born in Pittsburgh, Pennsylvania. He attended the University of Chicago from 1965 to 1967 and received his A.B. degree from the University of Southern California in 1975. A freelance writer for most of his adult life, he has been writing for children since 1976 and covering computer topics since 1982. He is a council member of The Authors Guild and a member of the Writers Guild, PEN American Center, and Poets and Writers.

He has written about computers as a columnist for *The New York Times* and *Information Week* and has been a columnist and contributing editor for *PC Magazine, PC/Computing, PC Sources,* and *Pcjr.* In 1987, with Paul Somerson, he wrote Star-Fixer, a software enhancement for the WordStar word processing program. With co-author Paul Andrews, he wrote *Gates: How Microsoft's Mogul Reinvented an Industry—and Made Himself the Richest Man in America,* which was published in 1993. It was heralded by *Windows Magazine* as "The best biography of Bill Gates . . . the definitive work to date," and lauded by *Newsweek, The Wall Street Journal,* and many other publications. In addition to writing screenplays, he has written and co-produced a video documentary, *The Curse of Los Feliz.*

His first book, *Mule in the Mail,* was named a Book of the Year 1978 by the Child Study Children's Book Committee at Bank Street College. *Make Four Million Dollars by Next Thursday!* received the same award for 1991. *Pictures of Motion and Pictures that Move* was named a 1982 Outstanding Science Trade Book by a joint committee of the Children's Book Council and the National Science Teachers' Association. *Life Is No Fair!* was an International Reading Association Children's Choice Book in 1986. *Be a Perfect Person in Just Three Days!* was a 1982 Child Study Children's Book and received many state awards that are voted upon by children; it was also made into a Highgate Pictures film for television in 1984 and was adapted for stage and opera.

Stephen Manes was remarried in 1989 and lives in Seattle.

SELECTED WORKS: Hooples on the Highway, 1978; Mule in the Mail, 1978; The Boy Who Turned into a TV Set, 1979; Be a Perfect Person in Just Three Days!, 1982; Pictures of Motion and Pictures that Move: Eadweard Muybridge and the Photography of Motion, 1982; Life Is No Fair!, 1985; Chicken Trek, 1987; The Great Gerbil Roundup, 1988; The Obnoxious Jerks, 1988; It's New! It's Improved! It's Terrible!, 1989; Chocolate-Covered Ants, 1990; Some of the Adventures of Rhode Island Red, 1990; Make Four Million Dollars By Next Thursday!, 1991; Comedy High, 1992; An Almost Perfect Game, 1995.

ABOUT: Contemporary Authors, Vol. 97-100; Gallo, Donald R., Speaking for Ourselves, Too; Something About the Author, Vol. 40, 42.

FRED MARCELLINO

October 25, 1939–

ILLUSTRATOR OF *Puss in Boots*, etc.

Biographical sketch of Fred Marcellino:

FRED MARCELLINO was born in New York City. He decided at a very young age that he was interested in art. His older sister, Marie, who was also artistically inclined, paved the way for him, and he spent much of his time doing what she did: drawing. His early inspiration came from comic books and cartoons. It wasn't until he was in high school that he discovered more serious art—the paintings and sculptures he found in museums.

Marcellino went to Bayside High School in New York, where his talents were developed thanks to a strong art department and an excellent teacher who encouraged him to attend New York's Cooper Union. From there, he went on to Yale University to study painting, and received his B. F. A. degree in 1962. After graduating from Yale, Marcellino went to Venice for a year to paint and study on a Fulbright Fellowship. He returned to New York and continued to paint, but after a few years he turned to graphic design and illustration instead.

The majority of Marcellino's initial illustration assignments came from record companies; he designed pop album covers. But his heart was never really in it, and eventually he made the welcome switch from album covers to book covers. This was when his career really took off.

The cover Marcellino claims as his first to gain a lot of attention was the one he did for William Wharton's novel, *Birdy*, in 1979. It shows a bird cage with an open door, from the inside looking out. The book won Marcellino his first American Book Award for Best Cover Design (he subsequently won two more). Marcellino has designed and illustrated covers for many books, including

Tom Wolfe's *The Bonfire of the Vanities*, Judith Rossner's *August*, Mark Helprin's *Winter's Tale*, and Anne Tyler's *Dinner at the Homesick Restaurant*.

It was an editor at Farrar, Straus & Giroux, Michael di Capua, whom Marcellino approached with his first children's book idea. According to Marcellino, di Capua wasn't crazy about the text, but was interested enough in his work to start hiring him for book jacket designs, with the idea that an illustrated book was just a matter of time.

In fact, it wasn't until 1986 that Marcellino illustrated his first children's book, *A Rat's Tale*, by Tor Seidler, who, coincidentally, had been introduced to di Capua by Marcellino. It was the book Marcellino had been waiting for, and he convinced di Capua and the author to let him illustrate it. This novel is about the adventures of a community of rats living in New York. Marcellino's black-and-white illustrations emphasize the humor in the book, complementing but not overpowering the text. The book was well received, and Marcellino, proceeding slowly, went on to illustrate his first full-color picture book, *Puss in Boots*, which came out in 1990. In this tale, Marcellino found the perfect vehicle for his art. The illustrations, in colored pencils, are richly modulated and drawn from many arresting points of view. The artist includes a tip of the hat to Paul-Gustave Dore, who illustrated the tale in the nineteenth century. In one picture, a circle of peasants are bowing to Puss, much as Dore had drawn them. However, Marcellino rendered this particular illustration from a very low viewpoint, looking up. The result is an excellent view of the posteriors of several of the peasants, thus paying tribute to Dore's work, but with Marcellino's own humorous stamp!

Puss in Boots is also unusual in that the title and credits are not present on the front cover. This was an ingenious solution to a design problem, suggested by Marcellino's editor and skillfully realized by the artist. Reviewers hailed the book as "witty and skillful" and "richly detailed," calling it "an impressive debut." It was named a 1991 Caldecott Honor Book by the American Library Association.

Following the success of *Puss in Boots*, Marcellino designed and illustrated Hans Christian Andersen's *The Steadfast Tin Soldier*, a version retold by Tor Seidler. He travelled to Copenhagen, Denmark, in order to research the illustrations, which won an honorable mention for the Critici in Erba prize at the 1993 Bologna Book Fair. In 1993, he illustrated another book written by Tor Seidler, *The Wainscott Weasel*. The *New York Times* reviewer wrote that Marcellino's illustrations reflected "a warmth, a subtlety and a humor" that were in the text. The book was named an ALA Notable Book of the Year. His newest effort, to be published in 1995, is an illustrated collection of three tales by Edward Lear, *The Pelican Chorus: and Other Nonsense*.

Marcellino lives in New York. He married Jean Cunningham, an art director, in 1969, and they have a son, Nico.

SELECTED WORKS ILLUSTRATED: A Rat's Tale, by Tor Seidler, 1986; Puss in Boots, by Charles Perrault, translated by Malcolm Arthur, 1990; The Steadfast Tin Soldier, by Hans Christian Andersen, retold by Tor Seidler, 1992; The Wainscott Weasel, by Tor Seidler, 1993.

ABOUT: Eastern Review July 1984 (Newsday Magazine); Publishers Weekly July 17, 1995; Something About the Author, Vol. 68; U.S. News & World Report October 23, 1995.

JAN MARINO

AUTHOR OF *Eighty-eight Steps to September*, etc.

Autobiographical sketch of Jan Marino:

IN THE HOUSE where I grew up, there was a leather-bound set of the Harvard Classics.

At the age of seven or so, I decided to

JAN MARINO

read all fifty volumes. (I always had one foot in fantasy land.) The first five titles rather intimidated me and so I went on to Volume 6, "Poems and Songs" by Burns. Since I loved to sing and imagined myself a poet, this volume appeared to be the perfect beginning. But when I asked my mother over and over and over to explain what the poet Burns meant by—"Ha! whaur ye gaun, ye crowlin ferlie?" and " . . . Salalkali o'midge-tail clippings . . . "—my mother gently suggested I move on.

I did. To Volume 29, Darwin's "Voyage of the Beagle." I loved dogs, but when I learned on page one that the Beagle wasn't the four-legged variety, but "a ten-gun brig in her Majesty's Navy," and page two described "singular incrustations, atmospheric dust with infusoria, and the causes of a discoloured Sea," my interest vanished.

Discouraged, but not defeated, I followed my mother's not-so-gentle suggestions to move on to Volume 17: Aesop, Grimm, and Andersen's "Folklore and Fable."

I loved it from the start, even though it caused me considerable concern. I worried about Hansel and Grethel, Little Red Cap and all the rest. How could a father lead his children into the forest and leave them?

How could a mother let a little girl go off alone to visit her ailing grandmother? And what about Snow White? What was she thinking of when she neglected to invite the dwarfs to her wedding? I was so bitterly disappointed, I wrote my own endings. Hansel and Grethel's father sent the stepmother off into the forest. Little Red Cap took a taxi to Grandma's and she and Grandma ate sweet cakes and had a happy visit. And, at her wedding, Snow White danced the night away with the dwarfs. I was good at making up endings that pleased me. I could do that for any story. Except one.

When I was eight my brother, Bobbie, died. It was an awful time. I remember the sadness and the silence in our house. Nobody spoke of him. And so, I dreamt about him, wrote stories about him, but it wasn't until I wrote *Eighty-eight Steps to September* that I truly came to accept the loss of him.

So many scenes in *Eighty-eight Steps* are just the way they happened back then, especially the scene where Amy (Jan) is told by her father that Robbie (Bobbie) is dead. " 'He's gone, Amy', my father said. 'Robbie's gone. God damn it. He didn't make it'." My father never swore, but that morning he did.

And Amy (Jan) never cried in front of people, especially when other kids were present. I remember so clearly my teacher, Miss Farrell (Miss Alexander in *Eighty-eight Steps*) asking me to go into the cloak room with her. Nobody was asked to go into the cloakroom unless they had done something terrible. And I hadn't done anything at all. She asked me how I was doing and would I like to tell her about Bobbie. I remember shaking my head, determined not to cry. I looked up and kept my eyes on her nostrils, trying to count the little hairs I saw. I bit my lip and said nothing. I prayed I wouldn't cry, because all the kids were in the classroom, waiting for the three o'clock bell to ring.

While not all of my books are autobiographical, I suppose each one of them has a little bit of my past in them. *The Day that Elvis Came to Town* is set in a boarding house in Georgia. I've never lived in the South nor have I lived in a boarding house, but my aunt owned a boarding house of sorts in Cambridge, Massachusetts. Since Harvard was close by, my aunt had a wonderful assortment of boarders. One was a professor at Harvard. A Mr. Collins. He found his way into *Elvis*, as did my aunt.

The setting for *Like Some Kind of Hero* is really Oyster Bay, the town where I live. The butler, Bishopp, in *For the Love of Pete*, was a butler I once knew and loved. And Pa in *The Mona Lisa of Salem Street* is the grandfather I always wanted but never had.

As yet my grandmother hasn't found her way into my work. She found me terribly annoying as a child, always telling me how dramatic I was. How I daydreamed. How I never missed a trick. How I never forgot anything. How I stared at people and eavesdropped on their conversations. How she hoped one day I'd outgrow what she called my "character defects." I haven't yet and I hope I never do.

I love to write. To read (I've gone through most of my father's set of the Harvard Classics, but none pleases me as much as Volume 17). I love to imagine. To create my own characters. Yes, there are days of frustration. Days when I stare at the lifeless computer screen. Days when my characters refuse to talk to me. But give up? Never. I cajole. I plead. I beg until I hear their voices. And when my computer screen finally comes alive, I am beyond happy.

Jan Marino grew up in Boston, Massachusetts. As a child, she daydreamed and imagined stories but, she says, rarely put them to paper. She graduated from the two-year program at Katherine Gibbs School in Boston, then married a cartoonist and illustrator, Len Marino.

She made up stories for her three children, but found little time to write. Later, she wrote a monthly column for a local newspaper, and covered local events. When her youngest child was in junior high school, she decided to got back to school. She received encouragement to write while at Hofstra University, and committed herself to writing. *Eighty-eight Steps to September* began as several short stories, and is autobiographical.

Marino has been a scholar at Bread Loaf, Long Island University, and Bennington College. She teaches a course in Creative Writing at Long Island University (C. W. Post) campus. She also conducts workshops for adults and children.

Jan Marino is a member of the Society of Children's Book Writers and Illustrators, Poets and Writers, and the Authors Guild. She lives on the North Shore of Long Island.

SELECTED WORKS: Eighty-eight Steps to September, 1989; The Day that Elvis Came to Town, 1991; Like Some Kind of Hero, 1992; For the Love of Pete, 1993; The Mona Lisa of Salem Street, 1995.

ALBERT MARRIN

July 24, 1936–

AUTHOR OF *Cowboys, Indians, and Gunfighters*, etc.

Autobiographical sketch of Albert Marrin:

ONE OF MY most prized possessions is a copy of a painting by Charles M. Russell, America's "cowboy artist." It is called "The Story Teller" and depicts a scene inside an Indian tepee. The tepee is barren except for a quiver of arrows, a few blankets, and a small fire burning on the bare earth. Six children, ranging in age from about five to seventeen, are seated cross-legged on either side of an old, wrinkled man with long white braids. Their attention is total. They see only him with their eyes, hear only his word with their ears. He is the storyteller and, at least for now, the center of their world.

I don't know if it is considered a great

ALBERT MARRIN

painting. Yet it has always had a special meaning for me. In a sense, I am Russell's storyteller, and my readers—the youngsters around that fire.

Years ago, in my student days, I was counselor in a summer camp for boys from the Lower East Side of New York City. Somehow I found myself "volunteered" for story night. Once a week, I had to amuse a hundred and twenty red-blooded American boys around a campfire in a clearing in the middle of the woods. I began by resenting the job but ended by looking forward to it after a few sessions. At first, I made up the material as I went along. After a while, however, I took the "easy" way out. As a history major, I had a bottomless well of material. I decided to present some of this material not as lessons but as stories. Two of these stories stick in my mind: Custer's "last stand" and Sir Henry Morgan the buccaneer.

After graduate school, I became a college teacher. Professors, of course, are supposed to "publish or perish," that is, write books in their specialties or find work elsewhere. I had no intention of perishing. I wrote four scholarly books, all well received in the profession. That was nice, and I was pleased.

But I was not thrilled. I wanted to reach a larger audience, not as a scholar but as a storyteller. Actually, I wanted to go back to the woods, combining what I knew as a teacher with how I felt as a storyteller.

I began to write history for young adult audiences. I tried to write in the most interesting way I could, all the while remaining true to the facts. Now, more than twelve years and twenty-eight books later, I can say that it worked.

Readers sometimes ask, "How do you get your ideas?" That is a good question, because I do, literally, "get" an idea. It does not come from any deep thought—or at least not one that I am aware of. It simply comes. I know when to expect it, but little else. When I am about halfway through writing a book and the end is in sight, I become fidgety. I can sense something brewing deep down, below the level of consciousness. Then I go to a secondhand bookstore and wander the aisles. Or I visit the Columbia University Library, with its miles of bookshelves, and do the same. I take a book down here, thumb through another there, and before long, I have an armful of books on some general subject, like the Civil War or Indian tribes of the American Southwest. In my spare time, I read and scribble anything that comes to mind: facts, questions, a rough outline. By the time I finish my writing project, I already have a pretty good idea about what I want to do next. The rest is hard work, but I love it.

One thing is clear: All of my books deal with military subjects. Even my book on the Old West has a chapter on how the army broke the power of the Great Plains tribes to make way for the cattlemen.

Military history—the story of war—is not only exciting, but necessary. Next to the production of food, which sustains life, the family, which nurtures life, and religion, which hallows life and gives it meaning, no activity has so occupied people's thoughts and energies as war, which destroys life. In my books I try to deal with certain questions that are timeless: Why do people fight? How? What is it like to be a soldier, or a civilian caught up in a battle? In dealing with these questions, I stress that history is about real people in real, often terrible, situations. I think that if I can answer these questions for young people, they will have a better understanding of our world and how it got to be the way it is.

Receiving his B.A. degree from the City College of New York in 1958, Albert Marrin received an M.S. degree from Yeshiva University in 1959 and M.A. and PhD. degrees from Columbia University in 1961 and 1968. After teaching nine years in the high schools of the City of New York, he became Professor of History and Chairman of the History Department at Yeshiva University. His four scholarly books concern military history, religion, American higher education, and antiwar movements. He has also published articles on and lectured on propaganda, particularly as it relates to the graphic arts: prints, posters, and cartoons. A native New Yorker, he lives in the city with his wife, Yvette.

1812: The War Nobody Won was named a nonfiction honor book in the 1985 Boston Globe-Horn Book awards. *Unconditional Surrender* was also named a nonfiction honor book in the same awards, in 1994, and was named a Best Book for Young Adults by the American Library Association. *Cowboys, Indians, and Gunfighters* received the National Cowboy Hall of Fame's Western Heritage Award for Best Juvenile Non-Fiction Book, as well as the Western Writers of America's Spur Award for the Best Western Juvenile Nonfiction Book. Many of his books have been named Notable Children's Trade Books in the Field of Social Studies by a joint committee of the National Council for the Social Studies and the Children's Book Council. They include *1812: The War Nobody Won*; *Hitler*; *Aztecs and Spaniards*; *The Spanish-American War*; and *Cowboys, Indians, and Gunfighters*.

SELECTED WORKS: Overlord: D-Day and the Invasion of Europe, 1982; The Sea Rovers: Pirates, Privateers, and Buccaneers, 1984; 1812: The War Nobody Won, 1985; The Secret Armies: Spies, Counterspies, and Saboteurs in World War II, 1985; Aztecs and Spaniards: Cortes and the Conquest of Mexico, 1986; Hitler, 1987; Inca and Spaniard: Pizarro and the Conquest of Peru, 1989; The Spanish-American War, 1991; Cowboys, Indians, and Gunfighters: The Story of the Cattle Kingdom, 1993; Unconditional Surrender: U.S. Grant and the Civil War, 1994.

ABOUT: Contemporary Authors (First Revision), Vol. 49-52; (New Revision Series), Vol. 30; Something About the Author, Vol. 43, 53.

ANN M. MARTIN

August 12, 1955–

AUTHOR OF *Kristy's Great Idea*, etc.

Biographical sketch of Ann Matthews Martin:

ANN M. MARTIN was born in Princeton, New Jersey, in the middle of a hurricane. The daughter of Henry Read Martin, an artist and cartoonist for The *New Yorker* magazine, and Edith Martin, a former preschool teacher, Martin grew up surrounded by books. "Wherever we went, we found ourselves in a house full of books," she states. When she was a girl, she and her younger sister Jane even set up a lending library in her bedroom so that the neighborhood children could borrow books. Reading was an important aspect of life in the Martin household, and Martin and her sister were encouraged to be imaginative and creative. "I think reading is a gift," she writes. "It was a gift that was given to me as a child by many people, and now as an adult and a writer, I'm trying to give a little of it back to others. It's one of the greatest pleasures I know." Some of her favorite authors were Roald Dahl, Lewis Carroll, Beatrix Potter, E. B. White, and Astrid Lindgren.

A shy and quiet girl, prone to nightmares, Martin was a real observer, a good listener with a great attention span and an excellent

Ann M Martin

memory. Martin grew up in Princeton, then attended Smith College, intending to become an elementary school teacher. During the summers she worked as a therapist with autistic children (this experience provided some of the material for her book *Inside Out*). After graduating from Smith with honors in 1977, she co-taught a fourth-fifth-grade class in a Connecticut school. Then Martin went to work at a publishing company, where she also began her first book, *Bummer Summer*, about a girl coping with her widowed father's remarriage. Martin's first book took her three years to write; today, she completes two books a month. "I'm a very disciplined person, a trait I picked up from my father, a self-employed cartoonist," says Martin. "I usually work on two or three books at a time. If I get stuck—which does happen—I try to force myself to write. If I'm really stuck, I put it away and go back to it the next day."

The idea for Martin's Baby-sitters Club series came from an editor at Scholastic. It was originally planned as a four-book mini-series, published in 1986 and 1987. The books were wildly successful, so Martin continued the series. Today, the series has sold over a hundred million copies and contin-

ues to grow as new volumes are published each year. In addition, there are the Baby-sitters Club Little Sister series and the Baby-sitters Club Mysteries series. Martin is no longer the sole author of these books, although she is involved in the plotting and editing of all the books that bear her name.

Martin says that the clarity of her memory is a very important tool for her writing. Some of her work is based on vividly remembered incidents and situations from her childhood, and some of her characters are based on friends and family. The shy character in her Baby-sitters Club series, Mary Anne, is loosely based on Martin herself, and her best friend Beth McKeever is the model for the character Kristy. Martin says she babysat "nonstop" from about the age of nine until she was in college. The series features the friendship of seven girls who run a baby-sitting service. The Little Sister series is about the adventures of the younger stepsister of Kristy, one of the Baby-sitters Club characters. Martin's Baby-sitters Club books have been praised for the quality of the writing and characterization, and for plots that address some of the real concerns of pre-adolescent children.

In addition to these series, Martin is also the author of a number of other novels for middle-grade and young adult readers, as well as a picture book. The novels include *Yours Turly, Shirley*, about a ten-year-old girl with dyslexia; *Inside Out*, about Jonno and his autistic brother; and *With You and Without You*, which deals with death. In a lighter vein are her novels *Ma and Pa Dracula*, the story of fourth-grader Jonathan Primave and his unusual parents, which *Booklist* called "a fresh and funny story that strikes the right mix between the real and outrageous"; and *Ten Kids, No Pets*, about the persistent Rosso children and their quest for a pet. It has won three awards. *Bummer Summer* was named a 1984 Children's Choice Book by a joint committee of the Children's Book Council and the International Reading Association.

In 1990, The Ann M. Martin Foundation was created to "provide financial support to causes benefiting children, education and literacy programs, and homeless people and animals." Martin funds the foundation with the proceeds she receives from the sale of merchandise such as toys, clothes, and videos based on the Baby-sitters Club series.

Martin divides her time between her New York City apartment and a country house, where she finds time to pursue her other interests, which include sewing and needlework, gardening, and reading.

SELECTED WORKS: Bummer Summer, 1983; Inside Out, 1984; Me and Katie (the Pest), 1985; Kristy's Great Idea, 1986; Missing Since Monday, 1986; With You and Without You, 1986; Baby-sitters on Board!, 1988; Ten Kids, No Pets, 1988; Yours Turly, Shirley, 1988; Ma and Pa Dracula, 1989; Eleven Kids, One Summer, 1991; Rachel Parker, Kindergarten Show-off, 1992.

ABOUT: Contemporary Authors, Vol. 111; (New Revision Series), Vol. 32; Gallo, Donald R., Speaking for Ourselves, Too; People Weekly, August 21, 1989; Becker, R. Margot with Ann M. Martin, Ann M. Martin; Something About the Author, Vol. 41, 70.

RAFE MARTIN

January 22, 1946–

AUTHOR OF *The Rough-Face Girl*, etc.

Autobiographical sketch of Rafe Martin:

MY FONDEST childhood memories are of trees, rocks, and clouds. I spent a lot of my time in treetops, dreaming and watching. My mother read me fairy tales and told me Aesop's fables. I especially wanted to know what the world had been like when she was young, before I was born. She told me everything she remembered. I remember, too, lying in bed when she read fairy tales to me. In my mind I could see the great black raven, the prince riding through the dark forest, Rapunzel letting down her long long hair. When I feel asleep I could hear voices. I could never make out what they

were saying or the language they spoke, but words and stories filled my dreams.

At holidays my father's extended family would get together and reminisce about old times growing up in New York City's lower East Side. They were first-generation Russian Jews. Family, a sense of humor, and stories were what helped them face hardship. They often told hysterically funny stories but they told about tragedy, too. When they got together I never needed television to be entertained.

From my father, who had flown Intelligence and Rescue over the Himalayas in World War II, I heard different kinds of stories. Rescues in jungles, rogue elephants, tigers, cobras, headhunters, holy men, beggars, and words like "Calcutta" and "Bombay" were the stuff of his tales. I learned, too, how men may die or live by strange turns of fate or chance. My grandmothers, who had each left their families at sixteen to come alone to America, told me of their younger days in Russia, of revolution and turmoil and of the deep, mysterious snows of winters long gone by.

My family gave me what I wanted most—stories.

I loved to read. My favorite books were

Rafe: *Ray-F*

about King Arthur, the Knights of the Round Table, and Robin Hood. I loved any stories about animals, most especially Kipling's *The Jungle Books*.

In sixth grade I found Herman Melville's *Moby-Dick*. I devoured the abridged version first, then the unabridged, reading it over and over for many years. *Moby-Dick* was a seminal work for me. From it I learned about the deep mystery of animals and of the imagination. I learned too that a masterful storyteller can make you "see" in your mind and believe what might, at first, have seemed impossible.

I met my wife, Rose, at college. She had been born in Italy after World War II. Much of her family had been killed in the Holocaust, but her mother and father and her aunts escaped. Rose came to the United States when she was four. She spoke Italian, Polish, Yugoslavian, and Yiddish—but no English.

In college I majored in English literature. When I wrote my thesis on *Moby-Dick* I became the first student at Harpur College, (now the State University of New York at Binghamton), to receive Highest Honors in English. Rose and I got married when we graduated in 1966. I went to graduate school at the University of Toronto in literary criticism to study myth and story. After a time I felt that the power and joy I had found in stories couldn't be explained or understood by graduate study. It had to be experienced. In true sixties style (this was 1969), I walked out with only one in-class paper owing on a Masters degree. (I went back and finished the degree in 1983 taking a year's worth of classes over.)

My children, Jacob and Ariya, have helped me most to understand what stories are really about and why they've been told for so long. When Jake and Ayria were small, Rose and I read to them every night and sometimes I told stories. In those evenings I saw how stories, when told in voice, come *alive*. I decided I should tell stories to others, too.

So, after running a bookstore for a number of years, I began going into inner-city schools in Rochester, N.Y., where we live, and telling stories. I discovered that even children who don't enjoy reading or writing *love* to hear stories. In 1983 I won a national award for my storytelling (the Lucille Micheels Pannell Award from the Women's National Book Association) as "the bookseller in the United States and Canada who had been most creative and successful in bringing children and books together." I began telling stories throughout the United States. And my books began to be published in 1984.

I try to keep a voice alive in my books. When they're read aloud I want a reader to feel that a story is really being told. The stories I choose to turn into books are the ones that have spoken to my imagination. *The Rough-Face Girl* is from my geographic area. Native American people around here encouraged me to tell the story. After ten years of telling it I decided to make it a book. It's still one of my favorites.

I've now told stories in Japan, in Hawaii, and throughout the United States. I've been invited to perform in the Mideast and Africa, too. As a storyteller I've been featured at the National Storytelling Festival, where I've told stories to over three thousand people at a time.

Storytellers can only make sounds on the air—that's all spoken words are. A writer can only make squiggles on paper. Yet those who hear or read those words can see, can feel and live, a whole life in their minds. The imagination is not inside our skulls. No one knows where it really resides. Yet through stories, the most ancient technology of all, we can explore this deeply human, richly archetypal realm. I can think of nothing more amazing.

————

Rafe Martin has performed many of his stories on audio cassette tapes, such as "Animal Dreaming: Encounters in the Natural World," published by Yellow Moon Press. He is a contributor to such magazines as *Parabola, Enquiring Mind,* and *The Sun.*

Martin and his wife, Rose, live in Rochester, New York. Their children, Jacob and Ariya, are now twenty-five and twenty-one, respectively. Jacob is a graduate assistant in English and American Literature at UCLA and was named poet Laureate for 1994-5 of the University of California university system and its affiliated colleges. Ariya, a lover of the outdoors, is leaving for Montana, where she plans to continue her college education in the Rocky Mountains. Besides a focus on literature she is taking courses on wildlife and the environment.

Will's Mammoth was named a Notable Book of the Year by the American Library Association and appeared on their "Best of the Best for Children" book list. *Foolish Rabbit's Big Mistake* was also an ALA Notable Book. *The Boy Who Lived with the Seals* was named a Notable Children's Trade Book in the Field of Social Studies by a joint committee of the Children's Book Council and the National Council for the Social Studies.

SELECTED WORKS: Foolish Rabbit's Big Mistake, 1985; Will's Mammoth, 1989; The Rough-Face Girl, 1992; The Hungry Tigress: Buddhist Myths, Tales, and Legends, 1990; The Boy Who Lived with the Seals, 1993; Dear as Salt, 1993.

ABOUT: Martin, Rafe. A Storyteller's Story—A Writer's Autobiography.

CAROL MATAS

November 14, 1949–

AUTHOR OF *Lisa's War*, etc.

Autobiographical sketch of Carol Matas:

WHEN I WAS a child, I didn't want to be a writer. I wanted to be an actor—and that's what I did. I went to London, England, at the age of twenty to study acting and then I worked professionally in Toronto.

The friends I made while I lived in Toronto were interested in writing, and they

often read me their stories. I began to keep a journal. One day a friend read me a fantasy he'd written about a raindrop. It inspired me to try my first piece of fiction. As I sat at my kitchen table, staring at a white teapot with tiny blue flowers, I had an idea. What if some kids were playing, crashed into the teapot, and the magic of the teapot shrank them? I looked at the table by the window, which was covered in all sorts of different plants. What if the children ended up on the plant table and the plants came alive, and the children met a ferocious spider plant and a Professor Ivy? That was the beginning of my first story. When I finished it I shared it with my friends, and they liked it.

I continued to write, as a hobby, for the next few years. When I married and got pregnant, I suddenly had nine months during which I couldn't act. I decided to write my first full-length book, a fantasy called *Carstan and Kasper*. Again, I got a lot of encouragement from the people I showed it to.

I had a difficult time finding good care for my daughter Rebecca, so I ended up spending more and more time at home, writing stories involving a character named after my daughter. The second book I wrote was *The Fusion Factor*. I believe it was one of the first books in Canada to deal with the topic of nuclear war, and publishers were a bit afraid of the subject matter. In my files I have about twenty rejection slips for it. So I wrote *The DNA Dimension*, a book about genetic engineering in which Rebecca also appeared. That book was accepted by the first publisher I mailed it to, and I guess you could say my publishing career—as opposed to my writing career—was on its way. (*The Fusion Factor* was eventually accepted by Fifth House, and was published in 1986.)

Now I write or research full time, as both my children are in school. I also give talks to both children and adults about my writing.

For me, different books have begun in different ways, so the often asked question "Where do you get your ideas?" is not a simple one to answer. The idea for Lisa developed after I had already decided to do a book on the Danish resistance based on stories my husband told me about his father's and grandfather's exploits fighting the Nazis in Denmark. At that point a friend gave me a nonfiction book called *Rescue in Denmark* which chronicled how the Danish people managed to save almost their entire Jewish population. I never sat down and said "I want to write historical fiction." Rather I found a story, from the past, which I simply had to tell.

Ideas can come from many different quarters, and I always have at least three different ideas for new books circulating in my head.

Each book seems to have its own writing process and to take its own time. Often I will write four or five drafts. I have a very good professor friend who critiques my work, and sometimes very little is left of a book as it goes from the first to the second draft. *Lisa* on the other hand was written in three weeks and changed little from the beginning. However, I had been researching the book for two years, so when I sat down to write it, it almost wrote itself.

As for the rest of my life, I'm married, and have two children, Sam and Rebecca, and they take up most of the time I don't spend writing. I love to read, especially fantasy, science fiction and mysteries.

Even though I haven't acted for many years, I haven't left the theatre world totally behind; my husband Per Brask and I have adapted *Lisa* for the stage, and I have adapted *Sworn Enemies:*. Both plays have been produced with great success in Canada.

No matter what I'm working on, there has always been only one compelling reason for me to write—I love to tell a good story.

———

Carol Matas received her B. A. degree in English from the University of Western Ontario in 1969. She also spent two years in theater training at Actor's Lab in London, England. She has been a Creative Writing Instructor in the Continuing Education Division of The University of Winnipeg, and a Visiting Professor at Bemidji State University in Minnesota. She was a Writer-in-Residence in 1986 at Centennial Library in Winnipeg, Manitoba, where she lives.

Lisa, the play, was first produced by Prairie Theatre Exchange in 1991. *The Escape*, a play, was commissioned by the Winnipeg Jewish Theatre and produced in April 1993. *Sworn Enemies*, adapted from the novel, had a reading at the Jewish Repertory Theatre in New York in 1994. Her book *Daniel's Story* was commissioned by the U.S. Holocaust Memorial Museum in Washington, D.C.

Matas is a member of several writing and theatrical associations, including International P.E.N., Writers' Union of Canada, Canadian Actors' Equity Association, and Authors Guild of America.

Lisa, published in the U.S. as *Lisa's War*, was described by *Horn Book* reviewer Mary M. Burns as "not an adventure story with war as a backdrop but an account of events that irrevocably changed the lives of human beings." It won the 1988 Geoffrey Bilson Award for Historical Fiction in Canada. In the U.S., it was named an Honor Book in the 1989 Sydney Taylor Awards, given by the Association of Jewish Libraries. It was also named a 1990 Notable Children's Trade Book in the Field of Social Studies by a joint committee of the National Council for the Social Studies and the Children's Book Council.

Code Name Kris is the U.S. title of *Jesper*, the novel that continues the story of *Lisa's War*. It was a runner-up in the 1990 Young Adult Canadian Book awards, and in the U.S., was named a 1991 NCSS/CBC book.

The 1993 paperback edition of *Daniel's Story* was named a 1994 Notable Children's Trade Book in the Field of Social Studies by the NCSS/CBC. *Sworn Enemies* won a 1993 Sydney Taylor Book Award. It was also named a Notable Book by the Canadian Library Association in 1993, and was named a 1994 NCSS/CBC book. *The Fusion Factor* was reissued as *It's Up to Us* in Canada in 1991 and has not been published in the U.S. to date. Matas has had several other books published in Canada but not in the U.S., including *The Race*, which was named a Canadian Library Association Notable Book in 1992.

SELECTED WORKS: Lisa's War, 1989; Code Name Kris, 1990; Adventure in Legoland, 1991; Daniel's Story, 1993; Safari: Adventure in Legoland, 1993; Sworn Enemies, 1993; The Burning Time, 1994.

SELECTED WORKS WRITTEN WITH PERRY NODELMAN: Of Two Minds, 1995.

ABOUT: Emergency Librarian May/June 1989.

PETRA MATHERS

AUTHOR AND ILLUSTRATOR OF *Sophie and Lou*, etc.

Biographical sketch of Petra Mathers:

PETRA MATHERS was born in Germany,

PETRA MATHERS

in a small town in the Black Forest. Her parents lived there because they both had tuberculosis, and the climate was good for them there. As she told Anita Silvey in a *Horn Book* interview in 1991, Mathers grew up in the time after World War II, and had a very happy childhood despite that her family was very poor. The family returned to Stuttgart eventually, and when she was fourteen, they moved to a suburb of that city.

Mathers did not like school; she left as soon as she could. However, she always loved books. When she was a child, she put her books, rather than her dolls, to bed. She pursued her passion for books by becoming an apprentice in the book business. While attending school for the apprenticeship, she worked in a bookstore for three years. She also worked for Brockhaus, the largest encyclopedia company in Germany.

She married and had a son, born in 1965, and began painting around that time. In 1968, her husband accepted a job that took the family to the United States. There, Petra Mathers worked at odd jobs such as cook, hostess, and bookstore clerk. She painted in her spare time, and the first showing of her art was at the White Bird

Gallery in 1975. She had three more shows of her work there before she travelled to Singapore in 1980. She lived on a sailboat and was a deep-sea diver, searching for treasure in the South China Sea.

She returned to the United States in 1981. She had sent some photographs of her artwork to Harper & Row, now HarperCollins Children's Books, and editor Nina Ignatowicz encouraged her to bring her portfolio in to her. When Mathers was in New York, she did so, and was immediately given a manuscript to illustrate. The first two books she did were executed in black and white. They were the first of Miriam Chaikin's Yossi series.

Illustrating other people's books, Mathers says, is like visiting: "A certain politeness, consideration, and modesty are becoming." She feels differently about illustrating the books she writes herself, however. She will dress her characters, move their furniture, and "tell them when their time is up."

Mathers works out all the details of a picture-book story before she starts to paint. Her medium is watercolor, and she works on an "indestructible" watercolor paper upon which she can make changes and corrections. Critic Gertrude Herman, writing in her "A Picture Is Worth Several Hundred Words" column in the September 1987 *Horn Book Magazine*, compares the work of Petra Mathers to the naive art of folk painting. "[L]ike Henri Rousseau, the surrealists, and contemporary neorealists" she writes, Mathers "surpasses reality by imposing wit, fantasy, and sophisticated commentary upon subject and style."

Among the children's books Petra Mathers admires are William Steig's *Brave Irene* and *"More More More," Said the Baby* by Vera Williams. She has a collection, now, of both art books and children's books. She works at home, and she likes to stay there, avoiding errands and intrusions alike. While in her studio she listens to opera, and especially loves *Madama Butterfly*. She lives in Portland, Oregon, and she says she has now been in America long enough to

know and feel the language and to understand the humor and to call it home.

Sophie and Lou was named an honor book in the 1991 *Boston Globe-Horn Book* Awards and was a Reading Rainbow selection. *Molly's New Washing Machine* was named a Best Illustrated Book of 1986 by *The New York Times*. Mathers received the same honor for *I'm Flying!* in 1990 and for *Theodore and Mr. Balbini* in 1988. *Theodore . . .* was named a Notable Children's Trade Book in the Field of Social Studies by a joint committee of the Children's Book Council and the National Council on the Social Studies.

SELECTED WORKS WRITTEN AND ILLUSTRATED: Maria Theresa, 1985; Theodore and Mr. Balbini, 1988; Sophie and Lou, 1991; Victor and Christabel, 1993.

SELECTED WORKS ILLUSTRATED: How Yossi Beat the Evil Urge, by Miriam Chaikin, 1983; Molly's New Washing Machine, by Laura Geringer, 1986; Frannie's Fruits, by Leslie Kimmelman, 1989; The Block Book, by Susan Arkin Couture, 1990; I'm Flying!, by Alan Wade, 1990; Borreguita and the Coyote: A Tale from Ayulta, Mexico, by Verna Aardema, 1991; Little Love Song, by Richard Kennedy, 1992; When It Snowed That Night, by Norma Farber, 1993; Patchwork Island, by Karla Kuskin, 1994.

ABOUT: Horn Book March 1992.

MICHAEL McCURDY

February 17, 1942–

ILLUSTRATOR OF *Giants in the Land*, etc.

Autobiographical sketch of Michael McCurdy:

WHEN I WAS in junior and senior high school in Marblehead, Massachusetts, I was always drawing—and sometimes I drew more than I paid attention in class. My third-year high school English teacher apparently recognized something special in these sketches, as I was the only student allowed to doodle in her class. Even earlier, when I was in grammar school in New Rochelle, New York, and doing the usual

Michael McCurdy

drawings of battle scenes and funny creatures, I really had a love of printing. I wanted above all to print things. I wanted to set type, smell printers' ink, hear the clank of presses, and produce little newspapers. I wanted to put words together in a way that would please the eye.

My father was an illustrator in New York City. He did pictures for advertisements. He and my mother were also great readers, and there was always a warm connection in my home to writers and artists. I got the feeling that creative people like these were the most interesting people on earth.

It was only natural then that I would go to art school. In 1960, when I was eighteen years old, I enrolled at the School of the Museum of Fine Arts in Boston. I was a student in the graphic arts department, where everybody learned how to make prints. I made etchings, lithographs, woodcuts, and serigraphs. Then, one day, we were told we had to make a wood engraving. From that time on, I was hooked on this particular kind of printmaking process, and it's been one that I have used for years to illustrate books. My greatest hero was the illustrator and wood engraver Lynd Ward, whom I later got to know and work with. His art, to-

gether with the work of Fritz Eichenberg—also a wood engraver and illustrator of books—was to influence my direction a great deal.

When I was making my first book as a course assignment, something clicked. My old and almost forgotten passion for printing came back and joined forces with my love of making pictures. Now I knew what I was going to do with my life. I had forgotten that in the eighth grade I had written a term paper about what I wanted to be. Now it was coming to pass—I wanted to be a book illustrator!

Since 1965, when I had my first freelance assignment—a book jacket illustration for Harvard University Press—I have been making illustrations for many publishers. For some years I even had my very own publishing company, called the Penmaen Press. It produced limited editions by important writers and poets, and I designed, illustrated, and printed most of the books myself. It wasn't until 1983 that I illustrated my first children's book. Tony King's *The Very Best Christmas Tree* started out as a small edition that I printed on my own press. It later became available to a wider audience. Since then, I have illlustrated a good number of children's books in wood engravings and in scratchboard drawings. I have written a handful of books myself as well. I continue illustrating adult books and taking other commissions as I firmly believe that variety is a good thing. I have a good life, a creative life, of solitary work time in my old barn studio, balanced by collaborations with many writers, editors, and art directors. I wouldn't trade it for any other!

———

Michael McCurdy was born in New York City. He studied at the School of the Museum of Fine Arts, Boston. From Tufts University he received a B.F.A. in 1964 and an M.F.A in 1971. He has taught at the Museum School, Concord Academy, and Wellesley College. He is currently a Fellow at Simon's Rock of Bard College. His work has been commissioned by corporate clients, magazine editors, fine press publishers, and trade publishers for both adult and children's books. McCurdy has had numerous exhibitions, and he has lectured about his work throughout the country. He has illustrated fine editions for Yolla Bolly Press, including *My First Summer in the Sierra* by John Muir.

Giants in the Land was a New England Book Show winner and was named a Notable Book of the Year by the American Library Association. *The Owl-Scatterer* was named a *New York Times* Best Illustrated Book of the year. Both *American Tall Tales* and *Hannah's Farm* were named Notable Trade Books in the Field of Social Studies by a joint committee of the National Council on the Social Studies and the Children's Book Council.

SELECTED WORKS WRITTEN AND ILLUSTRATED: Devils Who Learned to Be Good, 1987; Hannah's Farm: The Seasons on an Early American Homestead, 1988; The Old Man and the Fiddle, 1992.

SELECTED WORKS EDITED AND ILLUSTRATED: Escape from Slavery: The Boyhood of Frederick Douglass in His Own Words, 1994.

SELECTED WORKS ILLUSTRATED: The Owl-Scatterer, by Howard Norman, 1986; How Glooskap Outwits the Ice Giants and Other Tales from the Maritime Indians, by Howard Norman, 1989; American Tall Tales, by Mary Pope Osborne, 1991; The Beasts of Bethlehem, by X. J. Kennedy, 1992; Giants in the Land, by Diana Appelbaum, 1993; Lucy's Christmas, by Donald Hall, 1994; Lucy's Summer, by Donald Hall, 1995; The Gettysburg Address, by Abraham Lincoln, 1995.

ABOUT: American Artist August 1984; Americana August 1986; Art New England, 1980; Contemporary Authors, Vol. 69-72; (New Revision Series), Vol. 25; Journal of the Print World Winter 1987; Kingman, Lee and others, comps. Illustrators of Children's Books; Something About the Author, Vol. 13; Vol. 82; Who's Who in American Art; Who's Who in America, 1996.

MEGAN McDONALD

February 28, 1959–

AUTHOR OF *Is This a House for Hermit Crab?*, etc.

Autobiographical sketch of Megan McDonald:

I GREW UP in a house stuffed with books in Pittsburgh, Pennsylvania, the youngest of five girls. My father, an ironworker, built bridges all across the city, including the Fort Duquesne Bridge (the real *Bridge to Nowhere*). Known among ironworkers as Little Johnny, he was a great storyteller. My mother, a social worker, was a very good listener.

Dinnertime took place around a large, round kitchen table, where we spun the lazy Susan, vying for ketchup or French Fries and a chance to talk or tell a story. My father could fashion a whole story just from the shape of peanut butter heaped on a Ritz cracker or imaginary "maps" created by ice-cream patterns stuck to the lid of the carton. He would call out, "Abba-no-potata-man" in the voice of the scary old one-eyed huckster who later became the inspiration for *The Potato Man* and *The Great Pumpkin Switch*.

With four older sisters, I couldn't get a word in edgewise during those dinnertime storytelling sessions. I'm told I began to stutter in elementary school. That's when I first started writing things down, in true Harriet-the-Spy fashion.

Older sisters inducted me into the world of books. They taught me to speed-read the end of a book first, and deem it worthy if it made me cry. After my bedtime, they secreted away the hardback book I received each Christmas and birthday, to read before I had a chance. They allowed me to tag along with them to the musty old green Bookmobile where I checked out the same worn biography of Virginia Dare every time.

Since the age of fourteen, I've worked in libraries. I like to think I've come a long

Megan McDonald [signature]

per, about a pencil sharpener. Told from the first-person point of view, it detailed a life of eating pencil shavings all day. Is that when I first became a writer?

Maybe it was in college when I took a creative writing class and my professor told me to go home and rip up all the poems I had ever written. The ripping up of the poems—is that what made me a writer? I think the most honest answer is that I am still becoming a writer. Still sharpening the pencil.

I remember a pottery teacher who once instructed me to take a wire and slice through the exact center of the first one hundred bowls I made, so that I could see the inside, and learn from it. Maybe that's what made me a writer. Always wanting to see the inside.

———

Megan McDonald received her B.A. degree from Oberlin College in 1981. She earned her M.L.S. degree from the University of Pittsburgh in 1986. She was a children's librarian at Carnegie Library in Pittsburgh from 1986 to 1990; at Minneapolis Public Library from 1990 to 1991; and at Adams Memorial Library in Latrobe, Pennsylvania, from 1991 to 1994. She now writes full-time, and lives in Sepastopol, California. She is a member of the American Library Association, the Society of Children's Book Writers and Illustrators, and the National Storytelling Association.

Is This a House for Hermit Crab? was named a Children's Choice Book by a joint committee of the International Reading Association and the Children's Book Council. It was also a Reading Rainbow Book. *The Potato Man* was named a Notable Children's Trade Book in the Field of Social Studies by a joint committee of the CBC and the National Council on the Social Studies.

SELECTED WORKS: Is This a House for Hermit Crab?, 1990; The Potato Man, 1991; The Great Pumpkin Switch, 1992; Whoo-oo Is It?, 1992; The Bridge to Nowhere, 1993; Insects Are My Life, 1995.

way in connecting children with books since my debut as a human piñata in a library Christmas play! I didn't know then that I would become a librarian or write books for children. What I did know was the enormous power of story. Whether I found myself working at a bookstore, a national park, a museum, or children's theater company over the years, I've carried inside me a strong connection to my own childhood, and to story.

Children are much closer to the unconscious than we are as adults. As a child, rivers can house mermaids, and bottles, genies. Eating a mustard seed can undoubtedly enable one to fly. In my book, *Is This a House for Hermit Crab?*, I invented a pricklepine fish to chase the hermit crab. I liked the image it conjured, as well as the sound of the word. Though imaginary, I have had many a child report sightings of pricklepine fish, from backyard creeks to the Hudson River or the San Francisco Bay. As a writer, I try to tell stories that will invite children to reestablish a connection with themselves and their own imagination.

My grade school teachers might be surprised to find me a writer, based on the first story I ever had published in the school pa-

ABOUT: Contemporary Authors, Vol. 135; Something About the Author, Vol. 67.

FREDRICK L. McKISSACK

August 12, 1939–

CO-AUTHOR OF *Sojourner Truth: Ain't I a Woman?*, etc.

Biographical sketch of Fredrick Lemuel McKissack:

Born in Nashville, Tennessee, Fredrick McKissack was the son of a writer. He served in the U.S. Marine Corps from 1957 to 1960. He graduated from the Tennessee Agricultural and Industrial State University in 1964, earning a B.S. degree. In 1964, he married Patricia C. McKissack, a graduate of the same school. He worked as a civil engineer from 1964 to 1974. He owned his own contracting company in St. Louis, Missouri, from 1974 to 1982. The McKissacks have three children.

Since they had first met, McKissack and his wife had in common a love of books. In addition to this bond, they both were idealistic, having grown up in the 1960's, during the Kennedy era. McKissack participated in a sit-in at a Woolworth store that had refused to serve black patrons. As segregation in restaurants began to crumble, he and his wife dined in all the local places where they would have been refused in the recent past.

He also shared with his wife an interest in black history, particularly biography. Fredrick McKissack became a writer in 1982, and most of his books are written with his wife. They are also co-owners of a company, All-Writing Services, and they live in St. Louis, Missouri.

McKissack is well known for his photo research; in the work he did for *A Long Hard Journey*, for example, he procured previously unpublished photographs from private collections. The book was honored by the Nashville *Banner* in 1993, and the paper named the McKissacks Tennessee Authors of the Year.

FREDRICK L. McKISSACK

One example of the McKissacks' work together on a book that is not biography is *Taking a Stand Against Racism*. According to critic Roger Sutton, writing in *The Bulletin of the Center for Children's Books*, he states that "the McKissacks have provided a cogent and provocative discussion of racism and civil rights from sociological, historical, legal, and personal perspectives." The *Horn Book Magazine* reviewer, Ellen Fader, calls *Sojourner Truth* a "fine contribution to the body of work about this remarkable and articulate activist." And their *Christmas in the Big House, Christmas in the Quarters* is a detailed look at the holiday as celebrated on a fictitious Virginia plantation in 1859, the last Christmas before the "Southern Rebellion." Notes and bibliography are included in the book, documenting the different lives of all who lived there.

In 1994, Fredrick and Patricia McKissack were honored by the National Association for the Advancement of Colored People with an Image Award for their work in children's literature; and in the same year, they were jointly presented with honorary doctorate degrees from the University of Missouri.

A Long Hard Journey was named a cowinner of a 1990 Coretta Scott King Award. It also won a 1990 Jane Addams Children's Book Award and was named a book of Outstanding Merit in the 1990 Carter G. Woodson Awards, given by the National Council for the Social Studies. *W.E.B. DuBois* was named a book of Outstanding Merit by the same organization in the 1991 Carter G. Woodson Awards.

McKissack won the 1993 *Boston Globe-Horn Book* Award for Nonfiction, for *Sojourner Truth: Ain't I a Woman?*, which he co-wrote with Patricia C. McKissack, and the book was also named an Honor Book in the 1993 Coretta Scott King Awards. It was also named a Notable Children's Trade Book in the Field of Social Studies by a joint committee of the Children's Book Council and the National Council on the Social Studies.

Christmas in the Big House, Christmas in the Quarters also won a Coretta Scott King Award, in 1995; and in the same year, the book won the National Council of Teachers of English Orbis Pictus Honor for Oustanding Nonfiction for Children.

The University of Missouri conferred honorary doctorate degrees on both McKissacks in 1994.

Selected Works Written with Patricia C. McKissack: A Long Hard Journey: The Story of the Pullman Porter, 1989; James Weldon Johnson: "Lift Every Voice and Sing," 1990; Taking a Stand Against Racism and Racial Discrimination, 1990; W.E.B. Dubois, 1990; Louis Armstrong: Jazz Musician, 1991; The Story of Booker T. Washington, 1991; Sojourner Truth: Ain't I a Woman?, 1992; Christmas in the Big House, Christmas in the Quarters, 1994.

About: Contemporary Authors, Vol. 120; Horn Book January 1994; Something About the Author, Vol. 53, 73.

PATRICIA C. McKISSACK

August 9, 1944–

Author of *The Dark-Thirty*, etc.

Biographical sketch of Patricia L'Ann Carwell McKissack:

Patricia C. McKissack

Patricia McKissack was born in Symrna, Tennessee, just outside Nashville. She grew up in the 1960's, and considers herself a "Kennedy product," that is, idealistic, a lover of the arts, and a believer in education. She has written and co-written nearly a hundred books for children, mainly biographies, historical fiction, and picture books. Her books reflect her deep interest in art, education, and the history of African Americans.

McKissack graduated from the Tennessee Agricultural and Industrial State University, earning a B.A. degree in English, in 1964. That same year, she married Fredrick L. McKissack, also a graduate of the school. They shared a love of books and have written many together. They have three adult children; Fred Jr. is a writer who co-authored *Black Diamond: The Story of the Negro Leagues Baseball Teams* with Patricia McKissack.

McKissack taught English to junior high school students in Kirkwood, Missouri, from 1968 to 1975. Her first books stemmed from that experience. She wanted to find a book about poet Paul Lawrence Dunbar for the class, but there was none; so she began a biography herself. In 1975, she earned an M.A. degree from Webster University in early childhood literature. She has taught at Forest Park College in St. Louis, Missouri, and has been a children's book editor at Concordia Publishing House, from 1976 to 1981. She has also been an instructor at the University of Missouri in St. Louis since 1978, and an author of radio and television scripts.

Lindenwood College in St. Charles, Missouri announced the opening of the McKissack Center for Black Children's Literature on September 27, 1987. The center houses McKissack's working papers, a collection of her writing, and a collection of books by, for, and about black Americans. She is a lecturer in conjunction with the Center and a board member of the National Storytelling Association.

She is a critic and has written for the *New York Times*. Presently she is co-owner with Fredrick McKissack of All-Writing Services. Together they lecture and serve as editorial consultants on minority literature. They live in St. Louis, Missouri.

In 1994, Fredrick and Patricia McKissack were honored by the National Association for the Advancement of Colored People with an Image Award for their work in children's literature; and in the same year, they were jointly presented with honorary doctorate degrees from the University of Missouri.

Flossie & the Fox was named a 1987 Fanfare Book by *The Horn Book Magazine*. *Mirandy and Brother Wind*, illustrated by Jerry Pinkney, was named a 1989 Caldecott Honor Book by the American Library Association and received a 1989 Coretta Scott King Award.

A Long Hard Journey was named a co-winner of a 1990 Coretta Scott King Award. It also won a 1990 Jane Addams Children's Book Award and was named a book of Outstanding Merit in the 1990 Carter G. Woodson Awards, given by the National Council for the Social Studies. *W.E.B. DuBois* was named a book of Outstanding Merit by the

same organization in the 1991 Carter G. Woodson Awards.

McKissack won the 1993 *Boston Globe-Horn Book* Award for Nonfiction, for *Sojourner Truth: Ain't I a Woman?*, which she co-wrote with Fredrick McKissack, and the book was also named an Honor Book in the 1993 Coretta Scott King Awards. It was also named a Notable Children's Trade Book in the Field of Social Studies by a joint committee of the Children's Book Council and the National Council on the Social Studies.

The Dark-Thirty: Southern Tales of the Supernatural also won a Coretta Scott King Award, in 1993; and it was named a 1993 Newbery Honor Book by the ALA. *Christmas in the Big House, Christmas in the Quarters* also won a Coretta Scott King Award, in 1995.

Black Diamond was named an Honor Book in the 1995 Coretta Scott King Awards and was named a Notable Children's Trade Book in the Field of Social Studies by a joint CBC/NCSS committee.

In 1995, the McKissacks received the National Council of Teachers of English Orbis Pictus Honor for Outstanding Nonfiction for Children, for *Christmas in the Big House, Christmas in the Quarters*.

SELECTED WORKS: Paul Lawrence Dunbar: A Poet to Remember, 1984; Flossie & the Fox, 1986; Mirandy and Brother Wind, 1988; Jesse Jackson: A Biography, 1989; Nettie Jo's Friends, 1989; The Dark-Thirty: Southern Tales of the Supernatural, 1992.

SELECTED WORKS WRITTEN WITH FREDRICK McKISSACK: A Long Hard Journey: The Story of the Pullman Porter, 1989; James Weldon Johnson: "Lift Every Voice and Sing," 1990; Taking a Stand Against Racism, 1990; W.E.B. Dubois, 1990; Sojourner Truth: Ain't I a Woman?, 1992; Christmas in the Big House, Christmas in the Quarters, 1994.

SELECTED WORKS WRITTEN WITH FREDRICK McKISSACK, JR.: Black Diamond: The Story of the Negro Leagues Baseball Teams, 1994.

ABOUT: Contemporary Authors, Vol. 118; (New Revision Series), Vol. 38; Horn Book January 1994; Language Arts January 1992; McElmeel, Sharron L. Bookpeople: A Multicultural Album; Something About the Author, Vol. 52, 73; Teaching PreK-8 May 1993.

SUSAN MEDDAUGH

October 4, 1944–

AUTHOR AND ILLUSTRATOR OF *Martha Speaks*, etc.

Autobiographical sketch of Susan Meddaugh:

MY FATHER views the world with a wry sense of humor. As a child, I thought he was both demanding and very funny. I also thought he made up some great bedtime stories.

My mother was given to pronouncements: I KNOW WHERE I WENT WRONG. I NEVER MADE YOU PICK UP YOUR SOCKS! Having delivered this statement (and others like it), to my brother and me, she would make a dramatic exit from the room. A wonderful line, and I remember it years later, but I still don't pick up my socks.

Aunts, uncles and grandparents lived nearby, and were consistently opinionated, often outrageous, and always loving. My brother, my cousins and I were spectators at the family drama, which had its highs and lows, but was certainly entertaining. It was a great family to grow up in.

Outside the family however, I was shy and unsure of myself. That is where art became so important to me. It was my area of expertise and my parents and teachers encouraged me. My mother saw no reason why I shouldn't be as great an artist as Degas or Renoir.

In elementary school, I entertained myself at boring moments by drawing adventure stories, tiny stick figures running across my blotter. I wanted to be a "commercial artist."

In high school the sky was the limit. I was encouraged by one art teacher to try everything from small still-life studies to huge backdrops for a school concert. I felt as though I could do anything. On the other hand, another art teacher revealed to me that the illustrated *Post* covers I so loved were not considered fine or great art. This was a blow. It took me a while to figure out

that while this might be true, it was only an indication that there are many different ways to be an artist.

I went to a liberal arts college where there was no major in studio art. An illogical step, a setback, you might think, but it wasn't. There were two wonderful artist/teachers who were in residence during my junior and senior years. And there were only three students who were interested in studio art. The result was what amounted to private lessons for the three of us. And, whereas high school had been a free-wheeling art experience, college offered timely and much-needed criticism. I got serious about painting.

After college, for some reason all my seriousness went right out the window, and I looked for a job that would be fun. In hindsight, I think this is probably a good approach to selecting a job. I couldn't type, and this protected me from most of the jobs available to young women in 1966. My first job was as a "girl Friday" for a small advertising firm in New York City. I loved New York but hated the job.

I drifted to Boston, where I eventually got a job as a book designer in the Juvenile Department at Houghton Mifflin. I didn't realize it then, but I had found my field. It was a wonderful place to work, and I stayed there for nearly ten years. But after so many years of thinking and talking about children's books, I decided I could no longer resist the urge to do my own.

So with a cheap apartment and only a beloved cat to support, I went free-lance, taking any art or design jobs I could find. My first book was *Too Short Fred.* Fred has been followed by seven more picture books of my own, and a bunch of books illustrated for other authors.

I met my husband, Harry Louis Foster, in 1982. He is an editor of natural history books (for adults). I rely on his response to my book ideas. If he says, "That's nice, sweetie" I know I have to rethink it. It's no good until I hear him laugh. it. It's no good until I hear him laugh.

Niko Foster was born in 1985. For a while, my brain seemed to shrink in direct proportion to his growth, or so it seemed at the time. But he eventually paid me back with some of the best ideas for books I ever had. When Niko was five, he asked me if witches had supermarkets. Where else would they get the unusual ingredients witches need for their cauldrons? When Niko was six, he jokingly said, "If Martha-Dog ate alphabet soup, would she be able to talk?" And so of course I must mention Martha, our dog, without whom, no Martha stories. Martha was a stray who joined our family when she was about eight months old. Now, in addition to Martha, we have another dog named Skits, two parakeets, two rats, three turtles, and the promise of more critters to come.

I think I have exactly the right job for me.

Although there were times in the past when I contemplated fine art, my lines on paper usually end up telling a story. I see the family influence creeping in everywhere, from my Father's humor to my Mother's whimsy. My family has given me ideas—on purpose and accidentally—and I hope to continue to grab those ideas and turn them into picture books.

———

Susan Meddaugh was born in Montclair, New Jersey. She graduated with majoring in French. She was a designer and art director of the trade division of the children's book department at Houghton Mifflin Company from 1968 to 1978. She has been a full-time writer and illustrator since 1978.

Martha Speaks was named a *New York Times* Best Illustrated Book of 1992.

Maude and Claude Go Abroad was named a Children's Choice Book by a joint committee of the International Reading Association and the Children's Book Council.

SELECTED WORKS WRITTEN AND ILLUSTRATED: Beast, 1981; Tree of Birds, 1990; The Witches' Supermarket, 1991; Martha Speaks, 1992; Martha Calling, 1994; Hog-Eye, 1995.

SELECTED WORKS ILLUSTRATED: Good Stones, by Anne Epstein, 1977; My Friend Bear, by Carol-Lynn Waugh, 1982; Red Sun Girl, by Jean and Claudio Marzollo, 1983; Bim Wili and the Zimwi, by Verna Aardema, 1985; No Nap, by Eve Bunting, 1989; In the Haunted House, by Eve Bunting, 1990; Amanda's Perfect Hair, by Linda Milstein, 1993; That Terrible Baby, by Jennifer Armstrong, 1994; Good Zap, Little Grog, by Sarah Wilson, 1995.

ABOUT: Contemporary Authors, Vol. 106; Something About the Author, Vol. 29.

CLAUDIA MILLS

August 21, 1954–

AUTHOR OF *Dynamite Dinah*, etc.

Autobiographical sketch of Claudia Jane Mills:

MY MOTHER was an elementary teacher who loved to write. When I was six years old she gave me a blank notebook and told me that this was to be my poetry book. So I began to write poetry. This was the beginning of my life as a writer.

I have one sister, one year younger than I am. She and I were (and are) extremely close, since we both loved reading and elaborate fantasy games. Together we dreamed up the magical kingdoms of Bladen (per-

fectly round), Maloone (shaped like a star), Socker (shaped like a sock), and Moo (shaped like a cow), ruled by princesses with names like Candleceina and Moonerette. So my sister helped me to become a writer, too.

I wrote dozens of poems in elementary school, as well as stories and plays. By the time I was in junior high school, I was writing love sonnets to one poor, persecuted boy I called "Apollo." My major literary effort in those years was a hundred-page-long autobiographical book about my eighth-grade year, called *T Is for Tarzan* (my nickname in those days was Tarzan). I still draw heavily from my own life in my books, but at least now I change the names. And I've learned that I can change the stories, too—to make them funnier, sadder, better, *truer*, to make them turn out the way things should have turned out, but didn't, in real life.

I began writing professionally when I left graduate school impulsively in mid-year to take a secretarial job at Four Winds Press in New York City. I had a two-hour commute each way by bus, and I used that time to write novels and picture books. I began submitting these to Four Winds Press, using

a fake name, so I could observe their fate undetected. On two occasions, I had the sad task of typing rejection letters to myself. But finally a story proved promising enough that the editor who was my boss asked me to read it for a second opinion. I took the challenge and wrote an objective, candid report on my own story, including suggestions for needed revisions. The editor then sent the author (me) a copy of my report and said that if the manuscript was revised as suggested, she would like to see it again and consider it for publication. And so I took all the advice that I had had the good sense to give myself and reworked my story accordingly. It became *At the Back of the Woods.*

I have always had another job while writing my books. In fact, I have two other "jobs" right now, because I am a philosophy professor and I am the mother of two small boys. This means that my writing never seems like a job to me. It is the special, secret work that I love best. I write early in the morning, while the rest of my family is still sound asleep. I lie on the couch upstairs, with a mug of Earl Grey tea or hot chocolate beside me, and scribble away with my favorite felt-tipped pen on a narrow-ruled pad, as I watch the rising sun cast a rosy glow on the Rocky Mountains beyond my house. It's a lovely way to start a day. And I love thinking that on some other couch far away, someone will someday be reading my stories and sharing with me the characters and worlds that I have created.

———

Claudia Mills was born in New York City. She received her B.A. degree from Wellesley College in 1976, her M.A. degree from Princeton University in 1979, and a Ph.D. in philosophy from Princeton University in 1991. She also received an M.L.S. degree from the University of Maryland in 1988. She worked as an editorial assistant at Four Winds Press from 1979 to 1980 and as an editor at the Institute for Philosophy and Public Policy at the University of Maryland from 1980 to 1989. Since 1991 she has taught philosophy, first as an assistant professor at the University of Maryland at Baltimore County, then as an assistant professor at the University of Colorado at Boulder. She was married to Richard W. Wahl, a natural resources economist, in 1985. They have two children, Christopher, born in 1988, and Gregory, born in 1991. She is a member of Phi Beta Kappa, the Author's Guild, the Society of Children's Book Writers and Illustrators, and the Children's Book Guild of Washington, D.C.

After Fifth Grade, the World! was published in a Spanish version in 1993. *Dinah for President* and *Cally's Enterprises*, and *Dinah Forever* were named Junior Library Guild selections. Both *Boardwalk with Hotel* and *All the Living* were named Notable Children's Trade Books in the Field of Social Studies by a joint committee of the Children's Book Council and the National Council on the Social Studies. Several of Mills' books have been nominated for several awards that are voted upon by children.

SELECTED WORKS: All the Living, 1983; The Secret Carousel, 1983; Boardwalk with Hotel, 1985; The One and Only Cynthia Jane Thornton, 1986; Cally's Enterprises, 1988; After Fifth Grade, the World!, 1989; Dynamite Dinah, 1990; Dinah for President, 1992; A Visit to Amy-Claire, 1992; Dinah Forever, 1995.

ABOUT: Contemporary Authors, Vol. 109; (New Revision Series), Vol. 27; Something About the Author, Vol. 41, 44.

BERNARD MOST

September 2, 1937–

AUTHOR AND ILLUSTRATOR OF *If the Dinosaurs Came Back*, etc.

Biographical sketch of Bernard Most:

BERNARD MOST was born and raised in New York City. From the age of four or five, he wanted to become an artist. He drew and painted all through school and attended the High School of Art and Design

in New York City. He won a scholarship to Pratt Institute in Brooklyn, New York, and graduated with a B.F.A. degree with honors in 1959.

He worked as art director and creative director at several advertising agencies since 1959. He was Senior Vice President and Creative Director at MCA Advertising, Inc. and also consulted for Bernie & Walter, Inc., a creative consulting company. He now is a full-time writer and illustrator of children's books.

Most was married in 1967 and he has two sons. He loved reading to them when they were little, and this reminded him of a desire he had to create children's books. He began his first published book for children in 1976, when he got the idea for it from his son Glenn. In doing the research for the book, he became "hooked on dinosaurs." And his interest in tropical freshwater fish led him to write *My Very Own Octopus* for his son Eric, who loves marine life.

He has won awards from the Art Directors Club and the American Institute of Graphic Arts, and has won a Clio Award for advertising. Several of his books have been named Children's Choice Books by a joint committee of the Children's Book Council and the International Reading Association. They include *If the Dinosaurs Came Back, Whatever Happened to the Dinosaurs?, My Very Own Octopus, The Littlest Dinosaurs,* and *There's an Ant in Anthony.* The latter was also named a Notable Book by the American Library Association. Reissued miniature versions of *Whatever Happened to the Dinosaurs?* and *If the Dinosaurs Came Back* were named Book-of-the-Month Club selections, along with *Dinosaur Questions.*

A video about Bernard Most was produced by Harcourt Brace Publishers in 1993, *Get to Know Bernard Most.* Now that their children are grown, Most lives in New York with his wife.

SELECTED WORKS WRITTEN AND ILLUSTRATED: If the Dinosaurs Came Back, 1978; My Very Own Octopus, 1980; There's an Ant in Anthony, 1980; Whatever Happened to the Dinosaurs?, 1984; The Littlest Dinosaurs, 1989; Dinosaur Cousins?, 1987; The Cow That Went OINK, 1990; Four and Twenty Dinosaurs, 1990; My Very Own Octopus (revised edition), 1990; Hippopotamus Hunt, 1994; Catbirds & Dogfish, 1995; Dinosaur Questions, 1995.

ABOUT: Contemporary Authors, Vol. 104; (New Revision Series), Vol. 27; Something About the Author Vol. 40, 48.

LYNN MUNSINGER

December 24, 1951–

ILLUSTRATOR OF *Howliday Inn*, etc.

Biographical sketch of Lynn Munsinger:

LYNN MUNSINGER was born in Greenfield, Massachusetts. She received a B. A. degree from Tufts University in 1974 and studied at the Rhode Island School of Design, majoring in illustration. She earned a B.F.A. degree in 1977. She has also studied art in London. After graduating, she began her career as a freelance illustrator. She has worked illustrating greeting cards and textbooks, and has been a contributor to *Cricket* magazine.

Lynn Munsinger's artwork often shows whimsical anthropomorphic animals. A *Publishers Weekly* reviewer remarked upon her portrayal of monsters in *Boris and the Monsters*: "At last, pictures of monsters that don't resemble the great Maurice Sendak's, nor do Munsinger's brightly colored, engaging pictures borrow from anyone else." *Horn Book* reviewer Mary M. Burns writes of *A Zooful of Animals*, an anthology of poems, "Lynn Munsinger's full-color illustrations contribute to making this book outstanding. She has a wonderfully expressive yet delicate line, the ability to be elegant and humorous at the same time, and a sure sense of the illustrator's role in such a collaboration. Her style captures the humor without resorting to slapstick; it is well suited to Cole's careful planning." Her artwork can also depict less boisterous moments. Vignettes for the best-selling chapter book, *Howliday Inn*, effectively convey a quiet mood. And the illustrations for *Hugh Pine* received the compliment from the *Children's Book Review Service* that "the pen-and-ink illustrations rival Garth Williams's illustrations for *Stuart Little.*"

Munsinger was married in 1981. She has lived in Vermont and Massachusetts, and now lives in New York City.

SELECTED WORKS ILLUSTRATED: An Arkful of Animals, edited by William Cole, 1978; Boris and the Monsters, by Elaine MacMann Willoughby, 1980; Hugh Pine, by Janwillem van de Wetering, 1980; Howliday Inn, by James Howe, 1982; My Mother Never Listens to Me, by Marjorie Weinman Sharmat, 1984; Hugh Pine and the Good Place, by Janwillem van de Wetering, 1986; A Porcupine Named Fluffy, by Helen Lester, 1986; Tacky the Penguin, by Helen Lester, 1988; Underwear!, by Mary Monsell, 1988; Me First, by Helen Lester, 1992; A Zooful of Animals, edited by William Cole, 1992; Three Cheers for Tacky, by Helen Lester, 1994.

ABOUT: Something About the Author, Vol. 33.

JIM MURPHY

September 25, 1947–

AUTHOR OF *The Boys' War*, etc.

Biographical sketch of Jim Murhpy:

JIM MURPHY was born in Newark, New Jersey and raised in nearby Kearny. It was a suburban town with a large population of Scots and Irish people, and he and his friends spent most of their time playing baseball and football, or exploring the then undeveloped New Jersey Meadowlands. They also made frequent trips, by bus or train, to Newark or New York, enjoying the contrast between big city life and their own quiet neighborhood.

Murphy wasn't much of a reader, that is until high school, when a teacher forbade him from reading Ernest Hemingway's *A Farewell to Arms*. He read it immediately, and began to read anything that might shock his teacher. He also began to write, mostly poetry, but also plays and stories. At the same time, he participated in sports, running track on a national championship team for the 440-yard and mile relays. He was the prep school state champion in the 60-, 100-, and 220-yard dashes and wound up in the top ten of high school sprinters.

He earned a B.A. degree in English at Rutgers University in 1970 and did graduate work at Radcliffe College in 1970. He married in 1970 and was later divorced. He went to work at Seabury Press (now Clarion Books) in 1970 as an editorial secretary. He had a shock at seeing his first paycheck, for $92.17. As a construction worker in 1969 and 1970, his take-home pay was often $700 a week after taxes and union dues.

Murphy stayed at Seabury for seven years, ending up as managing editor. He enjoyed helping authors shape ideas, and sometimes helped with the writing. He then realized that he would like to write himself. His first book was *Weird and Wacky Inventions*, in 1978.

Since then he has written both fiction and nonfiction titles. He became interested in

the idea of writing nonfiction history based on first-hand accounts, and began collecting journals, diaries, and letters—materials in which a person's "voice" told about past events. This eventually led to his writing *The Boys' War*, eyewitness accounts by boys sixteen years old and younger of life on the battlefield of the civil war.

Of his other books, *The Great Fire* presents first-hand accounts of the 1871 fire in Chicago; and *Across America on an Emigrant Train* chronicles an era by using Robert Louis Stevenson's own words to tell the story of Stevenson's 1879 train trip from New York to Monterey, California, combining a history of the emigrant experience with an examination of how arduous such a train trip was at that time. Reviewer Anita Silvey, writing in *The Horn Book Magazine*, states that, in writing his *The Long Road to Gettysburg*, Murphy "uses all of his fine skills as an information writer—clarity of detail, conciseness, understanding of his age group, and ability to find the drama appealing to readers—to frame a well-crafted account of a single battle in the war."

Two of Murphy's books were named nonfiction winners in the Golden Kite Awards presented by the Society of Children's Writers and Illustrators, *The Boys' War* in 1990 and *The Long Road to Gettysburg* in 1992. Both books were also named Best Books for Young Adults by the American Library Association. *Across America on an Emigrant Train* was named a Notable Children's Trade Book in the Field of Social Studies by a joint committee of the Children's Book Council and the National Council for the Social Studies. It was also named a Notable Book and a Best Book for Young Adults by the ALA. His novel *Death Run* was also named an ALA Notable Book. *The Call of the Wolves* was named an Outstanding Science Trade Book for Children by a joint committee of the CBC and the National Science Teachers Association. *Weird and Wacky Inventions* and *The Last Dinosaur* were named Children's Choice Books by a joint committee of the CBC the International Reading Association.

Jim Murphy was remarried 1987 and has a son. He lives in Maplewood, New Jersey.

SELECTED WORKS: Weird and Wacky Inventions, 1978; Death Run, 1982; The Last Dinosaur, 1988; The Call of the Wolves, 1989; The Boys' War: Confederate and Union Soldiers Talk About the Civil War, 1990; Dinosaur for a Day, 1992; The Long Road to Gettysburg, 1992; Across America on an Emigrant Train, 1993; Night Terrors, 1994; The Great Fire, 1995; Into the Deep Forest, 1995.

ABOUT: Contemporary Authors, Vol. 111; Something About the Author, Vol. 32, 37, 77.

BEVERLEY NAIDOO

May 21, 1943–

AUTHOR OF *Journey to Jo'burg*, etc.

Autobiographical sketch of Beverley Naidoo:

"ARE YOUR STORIES TRUE?" I am asked this question more than any other about my South African fiction. My reply challenges the usual definitions of 'nonfiction' and 'fiction' . . . 'true' and 'not

Naidoo: *NAY do*

true'. In the early 1980s I began to look at non-fiction books about South Africa written for young people in Britain, including some from the USA. I was horrified to find that most of them painted the kind of sanitised picture that I had grown up with as a white child in the 1950s in South Africa itself.

These books portrayed wonderful countryside, wild-life, gold mines, orange farms, sunny beaches and so on with little or no mention of apartheid—the system which preserved the 'good life' for whites only. The reader relying on these books for information would have no idea about the living hell which apartheid had created for the majority of people, black South Africans.

I was propelled into writing my first book, *Journey to Jo'burg*. It was a work of fiction, but I was determined that it would reflect the reality of apartheid and the terrible forced separation of children from parents under the 'pass laws'. As a white child, I always had, as it were, two mothers. I never questioned the fact that the black woman mothering me was separated from her own children, seeing them only when we went on holiday. I was brought up referring to her as a 'girl' and any black man—even someone old enough to be my grandfather—as a 'boy'.

Most fortunately, I was challenged about my racist ways of seeing when I went to university. The best friends are those who tell you when you are wrong. I had to learn to start seeing everything around me again—and it was a shock. It was a time of great political ferment. The African National Congress and other organisations had been banned. Nelson Mandela was working 'underground' before his arrest and sentence to life imprisonment. As a student I began to get politically involved and although I was only a 'small fish', I too ended up, like thousands of others, in solitary confinement in jail under the '90 day detention' law.

That was a great learning experience for me. After all, South Africa itself was a jail for most of its people. Although in my fiction I am frequently writing about experiences which are not directly my own, my South African writing has been fuelled by the anger I still feel about the damage racism does to everyone: those who practise it as well as those who experience it.

Writing *Chain of Fire* (the sequel to *Journey to Jo'burg*) was, in many ways, like undertaking historical fiction. Apartheid laws prevented me and my family living in South Africa. So I worked on evidence brought out of the country by journalists and others about forced removals and the 'ethnic cleansing' of nearly four million people. Writing the novel was a way to try and understand the experience myself, as well as giving it personal meaning for my readers.

Following South Africa's first democratic elections, I want to explore possibilities for children who still carry the legacy of the old society. In *No Turning Back*, set on the eve of the elections, my central character runs away from an abusive stepfather to the streets of Johannesburg. The problems he faces are those experienced by street children internationally. However they are also those of a child struggling to make sense of his world at a time of turbulent historical change. I have also collaborated on my first picture books—set in England!

———

Beverley Naidoo was born in Johannesburg, South Africa. She earned a B.A. degree from the University of Witwatersrand, S.A. She earned a B.A. degree with honors, in English and Education, from the University of York in 1967. She also has a P.G.C.E. degree in English from the University of York, which she received in 1968, and a Ph.D. from the University of Southampton in 1991. From 1969 to 1988 she was a teacher, starting with primary and secondary remedial classes in London, then taught children with severe literacy difficulties and did tutoring in Language and Literacy. She has been a part-time Advisory Teacher of Cultural Diversity and English in Dorset since 1988 and is also Visiting Fellow, School of Education, the University of Southampton, in addition to her writing.

Her writing for adults includes *Censoring Reality: An Examination of Non-Fiction Books on South Africa*, published in London in 1985; and *Through Whose Eyes? Exploring Racism: Reader, Text and Context*, published in England in 1992. She has been a contributor to many academic journals including *English in Education* and *Researching Language and Literature*. She also writes short stories and essays and is the editor of *Free As I Know*, an anthology published in London.

Beverley Naidoo delivers lectures and conducts workshops relating to anti-racist and multicultural education. She also conducts creative writing workshops. She has been a member of the British Defence and Aid Fund for Southern Africa's Education Committee since 1981. She is also a member of The Writers' Guild of Great Britain and the National Association for Teachers of English.

The Child Study Children's Book Committee of the Bank Street College of Education presented the Children's Book Award to *Journey to Jo'burg*. It was also named a Notable Children's Trade Book in the Field of Social Studies by a joint committee of the Children's Book Council and the National Council on the Social Studies.

Chain of Fire was named a Best Book for Young Adults by the American Library Association and Notable Children's Trade Book in the Field of Social Studies by the CBC/NCSS.

SELECTED WORKS: Chain of Fire, 1989; Journey to Jo'burg: A South African Story, 1985; Chain of Fire, 1990; No Turning Back, 1995.

ABOUT: Gallo, Donald R. Speaking for Ourselves, Too; School Library Journal May 1987; Something About the Author, Vol. 63.

LENSEY NAMIOKA

June 14 1929–

AUTHOR OF *April and the Dragon Lady*:

Autobiographical sketch of Lensey Namioka:

THE FIRST BOOK I ever wrote was a swashbuckler. The protagonist who swashed the buckle was a woman warrior called the Princess with a Bamboo Sword. I was eight at the time, and under the influence of the Chinese martial arts pulp novels.

Chinese readers, regardless of age, education, class or sex, love martial arts novels. While many of these books are hack work, some are great classics, such as *Shui Hu*. My mother and her friends bought stacks of them and traded with each other. I became an avid reader as soon as I learned enough Chinese characters. I also read Chinese translations of Western books. One was a collection of Sherlock Holmes stories, and another was *The Three Musketeers*.

Soon I decided to write my own pulp novel. I wrote the book (in Chinese) on pieces of scratch paper, stitched the pages together with thread, and voila, I had a book!

My career as a child novelist was cut short when our family emigrated to America. Speaking almost no English at first, I entered an American school and discovered that my best subject was mathematics. Math felt easier than other subjects since in China we used the same Arabic numerals. In high school I had a reputation as a math whiz because I liked story problems, which other students detested. When I entered college, it was natural for me to major in mathematics.

At the University of California at Berkeley, I received my Bachelor's and Master's degrees in math. I began working toward a doctoral degree, but stopped when I got married and moved to Ithaca, New York.

In Ithaca I taught math at Wells College, and then at Cornell Unversity. But I discovered that I had no real creativity for mathe-

matics, and after my two children were born I gave up my teaching job.

For a while I translated Chinese mathematical papers into English. The work dwindled when the Cultural Revolution broke out in China, and unversity professors had to stop research and devote themselves to political correctness.

Then I remembered my old love: writing swashbucklers. Since the political situation was uncertain in China, I didn't want to risk using a Chinese setting. Instead I wrote a book set in Japan, my husband's country. My father-in-law helped me to develop an interest in the Japanese samurai and feudalism, and the result was *White Serpent Castle*. Altogether, I've written six books about the adventures of my two samurai characters. The books show the influence of the Sherlock Holmes stories, *The Three Musketeers*, as well as the Chinese martial arts novels of my childhood. Later, when it seemed safe, I finally wrote an adventure novel set in China, about an outlaw band living in the mountains and fighting corruption.

At the urging of my editor and agent, I began writing books with a contemporary setting. The first, *Who's Hu?*, is about a

Chinese-American high school girl who is a whiz in mathematics. It is not completely autobiographical, since some of the episodes are from my daughter's experiences. My other contemporary books, *Yang the Youngest and His Terrible Ear*, *April and the Dragon Lady*, and *Yang the Third and Her Impossible Family*, all derive from the immigrant experience.

Whether writing a swashbuckler or social commentary, I work very hard to be entertaining. I want my readers to approach my books as a pleasure, not a duty.

———

Lensey Namioka was born in Beijing, China. Her family moved to the United States during the Second World War and lived for two years in New Haven, Connecticut, and for eight years in Cambridge, Massachusetts, before moving to Berkeley, California. She attended Radcliffe College for two years, then the University of California in Berkeley. She and her husband live in Seattle, Washington. She has two daughters. She is a contributor to the journal *The Lion and the Unicorn* and has written a book for adults, *Japan: A Traveler's Companion.*

Village of the Vampire Cat was a runner-up in the 1982 Edgar Allan Poe Award given by the Mystery Writers of America. It was named a Notable Book of the Year by the American Library Association, as was *Island of the Ogres.*

SELECTED WORKS: White Serpent Castle, 1976; Valley of the Broken Cherry Trees, 1980; Who's Hu, 1981; Village of the Vampire Cat, 1981; Island of Ogres, 1989; Yang the Youngest and His Terrible Ear, 1992; April and the Dragon Lady, 1994; The Loyal Cat, 1995; Yang the Third and Her Impossible Family, 1995.

ABOUT: Contemporary Authors, Vol 69-72; (New Revision Series), Vol. 11; Something About the Author, Vol. 27.

THERESA NELSON

August 15, 1948–

AUTHOR OF *And One for All*, etc.

Autobiographical sketch of Theresa Nelson:

MY MOTHER SAYS that when I was barely old enough to talk, I would sit glued to her side while she read to me—as close to the book as I could get. "Read!" I would command, tyrant that I was, nudging her frantically with my bony little elbow if she paused even for breath. "Read!"

I still remember those first stories—*Pinocchio, Uncle Wiggly, The Wind in the Willows*—not the exact words, so much, or the plots, but the physical sensations they gave me: the thrill in my stomach, the burning in the back of my neck, the feeling of being pulled right out of the "real" world—what's *real*, anyhow?—and into the tale itself. And if Mama stopped for a moment (which of course she had to do now and then; there were eleven of us children competing for her attention), I would feel something close to actual pain. It was like being torn from a wonderful dream or thrown from a speeding locomotive, and nothing could comfort me until she began again.

I never did learn to read—or to write, either—with anything like detachment. To this day I'm not really over Fodder-wing's death in *The Yearling*, any more than I'll ever be resigned to losing Wing in *And One for All*. And I suppose I'll always be half in love with *Jane Eyre*'s Mr. Rochester, just as I am with Cowboy in *The Beggars' Ride* and Old Tom in *Devil Storm*. I still read—and write, when it's going well—with that terrible/wonderful thrill and burn. I still ache when I come to the last page, and as often as not I turn back to the beginning and start all over again, just to ease the pain of parting.

There's an old saying that goes: "A dream is real for as long as it lasts." Dreaming, reading, writing—they're all just different paths into the same puzzle, so intertwined

shock to look up from my typewriter and see the real room around me. (I actually got out of bed one cold morning last winter and started to put on shorts, because it was May in *Earthshine*.)

Of course there's the sensible, rational part of me that's at least semi-aware of what I'm doing and that stands back and judges and tries to control that old speeding locomotive. Still, the farther I travel, the more it feels as if it's the characters, not I, who are really in charge. "Write!" they keep telling me, tyrants that they are, while I'm hanging on for dear life. "Write!"

---

in my brain that I hardly know where one leaves off and the other begins. Elvira's first memory in *The 25 Cent Miracle* is my first memory, too: a father killing snakes in the night to keep his little girl safe. But for Elvira the memory turns out to be a dream, after all, just as it did for me, though for both of us it was—and is—far more vivid than hundreds of "real" events. "Did it really happen?" readers often ask, and the answer is always *yes*—in a way. It did—and it didn't—in the crazy logic of dreams. And isn't it in dreams that we're supposed to uncover our deepest hopes and fears—the ones we keep so carefully guarded in real life?

For me the scariest and most frustrating part of writing is the groping at the beginning, the wandering blind when I know the story is out there, but I'm not sure how to find my way into it. Maybe that's why so many of my books begin—literally—in the dark. But if I don't panic, if I trust my instincts (as my wonderful editor, Richard Jackson, keeps trying to teach me) and mine my memories and take Winnie-the-Pooh's sage advice about "letting things come," eventually the characters and their world become so clear to me that sometimes it's a

Theresa Nelson was born in Beaumont, Texas. She earned a B.A. degree, magna cum laude, from the University of St. Thomas in Houston, Texas, in 1972. She was married in 1968 and has three children. She was an actress and teacher of creative dramatics at the Theatre Under the Stars in Houston from 1971 to 1980. She was Glee Club Director at St. Mary's School in Katonah, New York, from 1983 to 1990. She is a member of the Authors Guild, the Society of Children's Book Writers and Illustrators, the Golden Triangle Writers Guild, and the Southern California Council on Literature for Children and Young People.

Earthshine won the 1994 Child Study Children's Book Award given by the Child Study Book Committee at Bank Street College of Education. It was named an Honor Book in the 1995 *Boston Globe-Horn Book* Awards, and was named a Best Book for Young Adults by the American Library Association as well as an ALA Notable Book. *Devil Storm* was named a Notable Children's Trade Book in the Field of Social Studies by a joint committee of the National Council on the Social Studies and the Children's Book Council.

And One for All was also named a Notable NCSS/CBC book. Both *And One for All* and *The Beggars' Ride* were named ALA Notable Books of the Year and ALA Best Books for Young Adults.

SELECTED WORKS: The Twenty-Five Cent Miracle, 1986; Devil Storm, 1987; And One for All, 1989; The Beggars' Ride, 1992; Earthshine, 1994.

ABOUT: Something About the Author, Vol. 79.

LAURA NUMEROFF

July 14, 1953–

AUTHOR OF *If You Give a Mouse a Cookie*, etc.

Biographical sketch of Laura Numeroff, who wrote most of her first books under the name "Laura Joffe Numeroff":

Laura Joffe Numeroff was born in Brooklyn, New York. She grew up in a household where books were revered, and her favorites were *Stuart Little* by E.B. White and *Eloise* by Kay Thompson. She read six books every week. She loved to draw from an early age, and began to write stories, as well.

She studied art at Pratt Institute in Brooklyn, and took a course from author and illustrator Barbara Bottner, called "Writing and Illustrating for Children's Books." One of her homework assignments for school was a picture book, *Amy for Short.* She got a publishing contract for the book before she graduated. She earned her B.F.A. degree with honors in 1975. She created the art for her books with colored pencils and rapidograph pen.

After writing and illustrating nine books, she decided to stop illustrating and concentrate on writing, as she didn't feel that the illustrating was her strong point. She enjoys the fact that her two favorite childhood books were published by HarperCollins (*Stuart Little*) and Simon & Schuster (*Eloise*), which are now her two publishers.

Laura Numeroff has visited over a hundred schools, where she speaks to teachers, librarians, and children in kindergarten through grade six, on the subject of the process of writing. She also reads from her

works in progress. There was a Laura Joffe Numeroff Day in Sierra Oaks school in Sacramento, California. She gave a talk, and some students came dressed as characters in her books.

She is a collector of modern-day children's books, and specializes in autographed picture books. She also is very interested in film and likes documentaries especially. An avid hobby is horseback riding. She rides four times a week, is learning to jump, and wants her own horse very much. She says she "will probably sleep in the stall the first night" if she gets one.

She likes living in California because of the weather and the countryside, but misses the historical and architectural aspects of living in New York.

Numeroff is working on several picture books, including *If You Give a Pig a Pancake* and *If You Give a Cat a Cupcake.* She has also written a book of children's poetry, and is enthusiastic about having artist Lynn Munsinger illustrate another forthcoming book she is writing, which is about mothers and fathers.

Two of her books, *You Can't Put Braces on Spaces* and *The Ugliest Sweater*, have been made into filmstrips by the Westport Communications Group. *Emily's Bunch* has been anthologized in school textbooks.

Both *Beatrice Doesn't Want To* and *If You Give a Moose a Muffin* were named Children's Choice Books by a joint committee of the Children's Book Council and the International Reading Association. *If You Give a Mouse a Cookie* won many awards voted upon by children, and was a Book-of-the-Month Club selection.

SELECTED WORKS WRITTEN AND ILLUSTRATED: Amy for Short, 1976; Phoebe Dexter Has Harriet Peterson's Sniffles, 1977; Emily's Bunch, 1978; Does Grandma Have an Elmo Elephant Jungle Kit?, 1980; The Ugliest Sweater, 1980; Beatrice Doesn't Want to, 1982; Digger, 1983.

SELECTED WORKS WRITTEN WITH ALICE RICHTER AND ILLUSTRATED: Walter, 1978; You Can't Put Braces on Spaces, 1979.

Joffe: rhymes with *coffee*

SELECTED WORKS WRITTEN: If You Give a Mouse a Cookie, 1985; If You Give a Moose a Muffin, 1991; Dogs Don't Wear Sneakers, 1993; Chimps Don't Wear Glasses, 1995.

ABOUT: Contemporary Authors, Vol. 106; Something About the Author, Vol. 28.

NAOMI SHIHAB NYE

March 12, 1952–

AUTHOR OF *Sitti's Secrets*, etc.

Autobiographical sketch of Naomi Shihab Nye:

MY PARENTS met and married in Kansas, a place neither of them were from or really lived. Maybe this is why I have always thought it important that people travel. How can you ever tell what will *happen*?

Since my father was Palestinian, from Jerusalem, and my mother was American, our house in St. Louis held rich fragrances of cardamom, garlic, and olive oil. "Shihab" (pronounced She-hab) means shooting star in Arabic. I liked that. Languages danced together in our rooms and interesting people drifted through our doors. I used to think, "We're still waiting for a dull moment."

I did not learn Arabic as a child, which I have always regretted. Later I picked up bits and pieces, and also studied German, the language of my mother's grandparents, and Spanish. But I wasn't good in any of them. I would forget what I learned very quickly. Maybe I was just gaining a small sense of the wondrousness of human accents. I have always love to listen to people talking everywhere—their rhythms and word choices, their long drawn-out vowels or clipped syllables.

I wrote my first poem at age six, about visiting Chicago. I still remember the way the words felt coming out of my pencil, big and round and brave. My teacher at Central School let me hang it in the hall and a girl from an upper grade mentioned weeks later that she "knew what I meant." Boom—I was hooked. Words were magic wands. I felt powerful and satisfied when I used them. Somehow it felt even better using them on paper than just saying them. I could stand back and look at my life.

At seven I sent a poem about a cat named Cricket to *Wee Wisdom* magazine. They published it and our school principal let me read it over the intercom. He asked what "inspired" me. Well, obviously, that cat. But there were so many other possible answers. Our second-grade teacher, Harriet Barron Lane, loved poetry and urged us to write and memorize it. I remember walking home thinking, "The trees are inspiring, and the old houses losing their paint, the creek without a name, the ladies bending to rake their leaves, the laundry swinging from the lines, and the mean dogs too. You could write about any one of them and never feel through."

I had this sense of *abundance*. I still do. Our lives were short and we would only get to taste a small portion of the feast that was the world.

Writing helped me notice more, kept me tuned up like an instrument. You shaped the words, you plucked the chords. I studied violin, piano, and percussion, and especially loved to tune the tympani, or kettle drum. Its voice came from so deep in its throat. I attended three different high schools, the Friends School in Ramallah (now part of the West Bank), St. Tarkmanchatz Armenian School in the Old City of Jerusalem, and Robert E. Lee High School in San Antonio, Texas. These schools were about as different from one another as different planets are. But always I was writing, to keep myself steady. I edited student literary magazines and sent out letters to newspapers and looked for magazines that would publish works by young writers. And I read hungrily, voraciously, obsessively. It's the best thing you can do for yourself as a writer. Once my mother even found me in the car reading the car manual.

Now that I have written poems and stories and songs and essays and children's books, I can't say any one thing is my favorite. They're all related. I love the poetic elements of stories and I love the stories contained in poems. I also love the feeling of editing an anthology—the pleasurable task of picking out poems or stories you'd like to share with others. It makes me glad when one of my own pieces is chosen for an anthology because it becomes part of a new family there. No matter who we are or what job we claim, we're going to be talking to ourselves in our heads a lot of the time. Writing has helped me find the voices for doing that.

———

Naomi Shihab Nye was born in St. Louis, Missouri. She attended Trinity University in San Antonio, Texas, receiving her B.A. degree in World Religions and English in 1974. She has published four books of poems for adults, *Different Ways to Pray, Yellow Glove, Red Suitcase,* and *Hugging the Jukebox,* which was named a Notable Book by the American Library Association. She has also published a book of essays for adults, *Never in a Hurry: Essays on People and Places.* Her work appears in many jour-

nals, anthologies, and textbooks. *This Same Sky* was also named a Notable Book by the ALA.

For the past twenty years, Nye has worked as a writer-in-the-schools in such states as Texas, Oregon, Wyoming, Maine, conducting workshops with teachers and students of all ages. She has been Visiting Writer for the Texas Center for Writers, the University of Alaska at Fairbanks, the University of California at Berkeley, and the University of Hawaii at Manoa, among others. She has participated in three Arts America tours abroad, sponsored by the U.S. Information Agency. She has received the I.B. Lavan Award from the Academy of American Poets, and three Pushcart Prizes. She is married to the photographer Michael Nye and they have one son, Madison.

SELECTED WORKS WRITTEN: Benito's Dream Bottle, 1994; Sitti's Secrets, 1994.

SELECTED WORKS EDITED: This Same Sky: A Collection of Poems from Around the World, 1992; The Tree Is Older Than You Are: Bilingual Poems and Stories from Mexico, 1995.

ABOUT: Dictionary of Literary Biography, Vol. 120; New York Times September 26, 1994.

MATTIE LOU O'KELLEY

March 30, 1908–

AUTHOR AND ILLUSTRATOR OF *From the Hills of Georgia,* etc.

Biographical sketch of Emily Mattie Lou O'Kelley:

MATTIE LOU O'KELLEY was born in Maysville, Georgia, the daughter of Mary Bell Cox and Augustus Franklin O'Kelley. Her father and mother were farmers. O'Kelley was the seventh of eight children, all born in the family's farmhouse. She was the first to be born with a doctor in attendance. When her little brother was born, her mother took the baby out in the fields with the family while they worked, and hung up a quilt to shade him from the sun. Growing up on the farm is the subject of her book *From the Hills of Georgia: An Autobiography in Paintings.*

O'Kelley is a completely self-taught artist, whose interest in art began at a young age. She writes of her childhood passion in her autobiography, "I like to sit on the porch with my pencil and tablet, sketching chickens, roosters, horses, and other farm things, and painting portraits of people I've made up." She remembers the excitement of her sister Lillie's arrival from Atlanta, bringing "watercolor paints and pastels, specially for me."

It wasn't until O'Kelley was in her sixties that she started to devote all her time to painting. As she was in ill health and unable to work, she ordered supplies from the Sears, Roebuck catalogue and started to paint. She traded her artwork for goods. Through bartering, some of her paintings ended up in the museum shop of the Atlanta High Museum, where they were discovered by Robert Bishop, Director of the Museum of American Folk Art. Her work now hangs in permanent collections worldwide.

Bishop writes in his foreword to O'Kelley's autobiography, "In nearly every generation there are those who leave an indelible mark on America's history because of their significant contributions. The folk painter Mattie Lou O'Kelley is such a person." He describes her as a "memory painter," recalling her childhood in the rural South with "razor-sharp precision and vivid colors." *The Horn Book Magazine* reviewed the book, stating: "Words and wonderfully detailed pictures function in total harmony in an organically unified book." The magazine also named it a "Horn Book Graphic Gallery Book", honoring its design. The book was named a 1983 Notable Children's Trade Book in the Field of Social Studies by a joint committee of the National Council on the Social Studies and the Children's Book Council.

From the Hills of Georgia reproduces oil paintings on canvas that show such scenes from O'Kelley's childhood as harvesting cotton, picking apples, and killing hogs, along with scenes of playing games with her family on long winter nights: "we play our favorite games: Blindfold, Old Maid, Hide-and-Seek. Sometimes Papa plays Bear in the hall. Afterwards we pop corn in the fireplace." She shows nature in all her glory: spring blossoms, snowy winter days. The text reveals that O'Kelley's beloved little brother died suddenly when she was fifteen. She describes her mother dressing her about that time in a "beau-catching outfit," but says that her mother's plans for her to find romance "never struck flint." She wrote: "I'd much rather find a quiet place to curl up with a favorite book: *Beverly of Graustark*, Nathaniel Hawthorne's illustrated *Wonder Book*, or *Little Women.*"

Before publishing her autobiography, O'Kelley had some of her paintings grace *A Winter Place*, a picture book by Ruth Yaffe Rudin. Her pictures were compared to those of Grandma Moses in a review in *School Library Journal*, and the book was named a Reading Rainbow Book. It was also named a 1983 Children's Choice Book by a joint committee of the International Reading Association and the Children's Book Council. Since writing the text to illustrate her autobiography, she has also produced *Moving to Town* and *Circus!*, and her paintings have illustrated two calendars, *Celebration: The World of Mattie Lou O'Kelley* (published in 1985) and *The Mattie Lou O'Kelley Folk Art Calendar for 1987.*

SELECTED WORKS WRITTEN AND ILLUSTRATED: From the Hills of Georgia: An Autobiography in Pictures, 1983; Circus!, 1986; Moving to Town, 1991.

SELECTED WORKS ILLUSTRATED: A Winter Place, by Ruth Yaffe Radin, 1982.

ABOUT: Contemporary Authors, Vol. 116; Early Years October, 1984; Johnson, Jay and William C. Ketchum. American Folk Art of the Twentieth Century; Something About the Author, Vol. 36.

URI ORLEV

February 24, 1931–

AUTHOR OF *The Island on Bird Street*, etc.

Autobiographical sketch of Uri Orlev:

IN THE WALL of the house in Jerusalem in which I live, a small weed has planted itself in the handful of dirt between two stones, where it will not have an easy time surviving. It has no legs and can't find a better place. I can. When the sun gets too hot I can look for shade, and when I'm rained on I can open an umbrella. Yet the weed and I are alike. I was born in the 1930s in Warsaw, the capital of Poland, and there's no changing the time and place of my birth, my parents and family, or the culture I grew up in. I have no choice but to go on loving my first language and my first landscapes.

I was born in 1931. My father was a doctor. My first ambition was to be a streetcar driver. I wanted to lounge by the throttle and ring the tinkling bell that warned pedestrians, wagons, horse-drawn carriages, and automobiles of my approach by pressing an iron pedal with my foot. Until one day it struck me that the policeman who stopped and started traffic with a wave of his hand was even more powerful. From then on I wanted to be a policeman.

The Second World War broke out when I was eight and my brother was six. I was fourteen by the time it was over. The war accounted for a large part of my childhood.

I had read a lot of books before and during the war. Whenever I went to the library, or to a friend to borrow a book, there were two things I wanted to know. One was, did it have illustrations, and the other, was it scary. If the answer to both questions was yes, I took it out. My favorites were war and adventure books. I liked to read about heroic grown-ups or children who went through all kinds of ordeals until everything turned out all right. Books with sad endings left me feeling queasy long after I had finished reading them. Still, I never asked the

librarian how a book ended because I didn't want to spoil the suspense. I preferred to take my chances. The more I read, the more I envied the heroes I read about.

After a month of shelling following the outbreak of the war, my family found itself fleeing a building that had gone up in flames. You've probably seen scenes like it in the movies: fires shooting out of the windows, timbers cracking from the heat, walls crashing down, screaming people jumping from upper stories. We ran down the street, my mother holding our hands. The sparks flying through the air kept catching on my brother's jacket, and my aunt ran after him putting out the fire.

It was at that moment that I realized that now the hero was me. During the six years of the war I kept hoping that the book I was in would end happily.

My brother and I lived through the war in Warsaw and in the Warsaw Ghetto when we lost our mother and our whole family. After our mother was killed by the Nazis we were cared for by our Aunt Stefania, who fought for our survival. We were smuggled out of the ghetto and hidden by Polish families. In 1943 we were sent with our aunt to the concentration camp of Bergen-Belsen.

When I was fourteen, me and my little brother came alone to Palestine—most of which was soon to become the Jewish state of Israel.

I am living still in Israel, in Jerusalem. I'm married and have four children—two boys and two girls—and one granddaughter (at the present). My brother is living near New York. He is married too and has a daughter and a son.

I started to write when I was eleven, but poetry, not novels. Today I write only prose, perhaps because I lost my mother tongue and had to learn a new language. I wrote my first stories when I was twenty-three, and after writing three books for grown-ups I began in 1975 to write for children and adolescents. I am writing in Hebrew and I have had twenty books published for different age groups. I wrote also scripts for radio and television and translate children's and adult books from Polish into Hebrew. Some of my books are translated to other languages. My full autobiography is published by Gale Research in a volume of a series which includes autobiographies of authors and illustrators for children and young adults.

A woman called to speak to me about one of my books and asked: "Did writing this book enable you to finally put the Holocaust behind you?"

I answered her that I can no more put those years behind me than I can any other part of my childhood. Of course, there were many painful and freightening things about them, but there were others that were beautiful and exciting, as in my memories of my mother, surrounding us with her love in the most trying situations and treating us with great patience and sometimes with a spanking too. Many of these adventures I remember because of some strange place or strange object, the kinds of things one finds in the street only in wartime, like the barrel of a cannon which we exploded by mistake or a dead horse that opened its mouth and laughed.

My novels that have been translated into English till now for youth are: *The Island on Bird Street*, *The Man from the Other Side*, *Lydia, Queen of Palestine*, and *The Lady with the Hat*. All of them were published by Houghton Mifflin, but *The Man from the Other Side* and *Lydia, Queen of Palestine* by Puffin Books too.

———

Uri Orlev served in the Israeli Army from 1950 to 1952. He is a member of Hebrew Writers Association. He has received awards from the Israeli Broadcasting Authority for his radio scripts and has twice received the Prime Minister Prize for the body of his work. He also received the Ze-ev Prize from the Israel Ministry of Education in 1977 for *The Beast of Darkness*, his first book for children. The International Board on Books for Young People designated it an Honor Book in 1979.

The Island on Bird Street, translated by Hillel Halkin, was the winner of the 1985 Mildred L. Batchelder Award, awarded by the American Library Association. It was named an honor book in the 1985 Jane Addams Children's Book Awards and a runner-up in the 1985 Edgar Allan Poe Awards, which are presented by the Mystery Writers of America. It also won a 1985 Sydney Taylor Book Award. It received the Silver Pencil Prize in Holland in 1986 and was named an IBBY Honor Book. It was also named a Notable Book of the Year by the ALA.

The Man from the Other Side won the Batchelder Award in 1992. It also won an award in 1992 from the Jewish Book Council National Jewish Book Awards. Uri Orlev's books have been published in nine countries.

SELECTED WORKS: The Island on Bird Street, 1984; The Man from the Other Side, 1991; Lydia, Queen of Palestine, 1993; The Lady with the Hat, 1995.

ABOUT: Bookbird No. 31, 1993; Contemporary Authors, Vol. 101; (New Revision Series), Vol. 34; Something About the Author, Vol. 58.

KIT PEARSON

April 30, 1947–

AUTHOR OF *A Handful of Time*, etc.

Autobiographical sketch of Kathleen Margaret Pearson:

Kit Pearson

WHEN I WAS a child, growing up on the prairies and on the west coast of Canada, I ate books—literally! I became so absorbed in the story I was reading that I didn't notice that my hand was tearing off the corners of the pages, chewing them, and swallowing them. That's how voraciously I read; and I know that my passion for fiction is the main reason I became a writer. At age twelve I read—and digested!—a book which changed my life—*Emily of New Moon* by our most famous Canadian writer, Lucy Maud Montgomery. When I finished that book I decided that, like Emily, I would become a writer. From then on I kept a journal, but I didn't begin writing seriously until I was thirty-five. It's very easy to procrastinate about writing and I think I was too afraid of failure to risk trying it. Because books were still extremely important to me—although I no longer ate them—I got a degree in English followed by a degree in librarianship. Then I worked as a children's librarian in Ontario. Now my excuse was that I didn't have enough *time* to write! Interacting with children helped me realize that they were the audience I wanted to write for. I took time off from my career to attend the Simmons College Center for the Study of Children's Literature in Boston. That year and a half was a revelation—I met many children's writers, and besides studying children's literature, I took two inspiring writing courses. I left Simmons, moved back to Vancouver, and got a part-time job as a librarian, determined to finally start a novel.

My first two books are quite autobiographical: *The Daring Game* is based on a girls' boarding school I attended in Vancouver, and *A Handful of Time* takes place on the Alberta lake where my family had a

cottage for all of my childhood. The next three books, a trilogy, are set during World War II. Since I was born just after the war, I've always been fascinated by that time, and when I learned about the thousands of British children who were sent to Canada, I knew this would make a dramatic story.

I've tried many genres so far—a school story, a time travel fantasy, historical fiction—and now I'm writing a ghost story. However, the same themes seem to come up again and again in my work, such as children being uprooted, children feeling separate from adults, and children identifying with Canadian landscapes and with books—I'm always mentioning other children's book titles, because part of me is still a librarian!

I like to think that I'm on the kids' side in my fiction; perhaps that's because I have such strong memories of being nine to twelve years old. I know that the outer circumstances of children's lives have changed drastically since I was young, but I don't think their inner lives have. I'm confirmed in this by the fact that kids seem to identify strongly with my characters, even though some of my books are set fifty years ago.

I live with a lively cairn terrier in Vancouver, B. C., a great city to write in because it rains so much! And when it doesn't, there are lots of beaches and woods where I can walk and think of ideas. It's exciting to be a Canadian writer for children—our literature is just beginning to come of age, and I'm proud to be a part of it.

———

Kit Pearson was born in Edmonton, Alberta, and grew up there and in Vancouver, B.C. She received her B.A. degree from the University of Alberta, her M.L.S. from the University of British Columbia, and her M.A. from the Simmons College Center for the Study of Children's Literature in Boston. She worked for ten years as a children's librarian in Ontario and B.C., and occasionally teaches and writes articles on children's literature and writing for children.

The Sky Is Falling, Looking at the Moon, and *The Lights Go On Again* form a trilogy. *A Handful of Time* won the 1988 Canadian Library Association Book of the Year for Children Award. *Looking at the Moon* was a runner-up for the award in 1992. *The Sky Is Falling* also won the CLA award, in 1990, and it won both the 1990 Geoffrey Bilson Award for Historical Fiction and the 1989 Mr. Christie's Book Award Program. *The Lights Go On Again* won the 1994 Bilson Award and a National IODE Violet Downey Award.

SELECTED WORKS: The Daring Game, 1986; A Handful of Time, 1987; The Sky Is Falling, 1989; Looking at the Moon, 1991; The Lights Go On Again, 1994.

ABOUT: Canadian Children's Literature 1988, 1993; Emergency Librarian September 1989; Something About the Author, Vol. 77.

SUSAN PEARSON

December 21, 1946–

AUTHOR OF *Saturday I Ran Away*, etc.

Biographical sketch of Susan Pearson:

SUSAN PEARSON was born in Boston, Massachusetts. She and her parents lived in Auburndale, a Boston suburb, until she was nine. Because she was an only child and much younger than her youngest cousin, she enjoyed a lot of attention from her cousins and her other family. She had one uncle who lived on Cape Cod, Massachusetts, and another who lived in Portland, Maine, and she and her parents spent Christmases and vacation time with them.

For two years, she lived in Newport News, Virginia. She entered the fourth grade there and was "befuddled" by the racial segregation that existed there at the time—the separate drinking fountains, separate schools, and separate swimiming pools for white and black people.

Even as a child, Pearson was a writer. She was also a great reader, and her favorites were the novels of Lucy Maud Montgomery and Louisa May Alcott.

The family moved to Minnesota, where Pearson enjoyed learning from the excellent teachers she had in high school. She attended St. Olaf College in Northfield, Minnesota, receiving her B. A. degree in 1968. During college she was an English major, and despite the reluctance of her advisor in that subject, she obtained permission from the art department to write and illustrate a children's book. She was shown the basics of creating silk screen prints, and was left on her own. She created a concept book, which was enthusiastically received by her professor. He showed it to faculty in the education department and even sent the book to publishers in hopes of seeing it published.

After college, Pearson joined the Volunteers in Service to America (VISTA). She was sent to Columbia, South Carolina, where she lived from 1968 to 1969. She then worked for the Columbia Office of Economic Opportunity, writing programs to be funded by the federal government.

She returned to Minnesota and worked for a time as a sales representative of Quaker Oats. However, after she had saved enough money, she moved to New York City in order to become a writer. She tried to sell a children's book she had done, but she didn't succeed, and was running out of money. Finally she was offered a job as an assistant at Viking Press, where she worked from 1969 to 1971. She also worked at Dial Press, from 1972 to 1978, where she found Editor-in-Chief Phyllis Fogelman to be a great influence. Pearson's first book, *Izzy*, was published in 1975.

In 1978, Pearson became Editor-in-Chief of Carolrhoda Books in Minnesota. She worked there from 1978 to 1984. After a period of time as a freelance editor, she became Editor-in-Chief of Lothrop, Lee & Shepard in New York City.

Pearson has written over twenty books for children, with many titles in the "Eagle-Eye Ernie" series. Her *Saturday I Ran Away* was named a Children's Choice Book by a joint committee of the International Reading Association and the Children's Book Council.

SELECTED WORKS: Izzie, 1975; Monnie Hates Lydia, 1975; Saturday I Ran Away, 1981; The Day Porkchop Climbed the Christmas Tree, 1987; Happy Birthday, Grampie, 1987; My Favorite Time of Year 1988; The Campfire Ghosts, 1990; Eagle-Eye Ernie Comes to Town, 1990; The Tap Dance Mystery, 1990; Well, I Never!, 1990; The Green Magician Puzzle, 1991; The 1 2 3 Zoo Mystery, 1991; The Spooky Sleepover, 1991; The Spy Code Caper, 1991; Lenore's Big Break, 1992.

ABOUT: Contemporary Authors, Vol. 65-68; (New Revision Series), Vol. 14; Something About the Author, Vol. 27, 39.

TRACEY CAMPBELL PEARSON

December 29, 1956–

AUTHOR AND ILLUSTRATOR OF *The Howling Dog*, etc.

Biographical sketch of Tracey Campbell Pearson:

TRACEY CAMPBELL PEARSON was born in Norwalk, Connecticut, and raised in

TRACEY CAMPBELL PEARSON

a nearby town. As a child, she loved art in school, and had a book of paintings by El Greco, which she carried around with her. When she was in high school she loved snow skiing, and she and her friends would get up very early to drive to mountains in Massachusetts. They made as many ski runs as they could in a day.

When it came time to choose a college, she thought she would attend a good school near a mountain so that she could ski. Although she loved art, she didn't consider going to an art college, because she didn't think art as a career seemed practical. However, she was encouraged to study the subject, and since she had always made her own clothes and even was acquainted with a fashion illustrator, she went to Syracuse University in 1975 to study fashion illustration. She decided she would rather be in New York City, and transferred to the Parsons School of Design.

A class that she took at Parsons with author-artist Maurice Sendak and book designer Jane Bierhorst proved to be important to her career. She illustrated the dummy for a picture book, learning to design her artwork around a text. She began sketching people in public places in New

York, like the subway. She preferred this to drawing fashion models. She graduated from Parsons in 1978.

In 1979, she was married. She had a studio in Manhattan and began to create life-size soft sculptures of people. She talked to publishers about doing books at this time, but didn't feel ready. Her husband's career took her to Ohio for a while, and she worked there at American Greetings, a greeting-card company. She also did illustrations for magazines such as *Cleveland Magazine*. On her return to New York, she continued to do freelance illustration, but her goal was to have a book published. She landed a contract at Dial Books, and at that point, she and her husband decided to move to Vermont. Her husband had investigated a job opening there, and when they went to visit, they were delighted by the general store, the village green, and a little house that soon came up for sale.

Pearson had two children there, and her book *The Storekeeper* is a tribute to the little general store in their town. She enjoys putting members of her family, as well as their dog and cat, into the pictures of her books.

Pearson keeps a studio in nearby Burlington, Vermont, so that she can work normal business hours. She has no distractions there and can listen to music as she works. She created each book with specific music playing in the background. She carries sketchbooks wherever she goes.

She makes author appearances in schools, which she restricts to a size small enough so that she can participate in a classroom project.

As for her future work, she writes, "I will always consider myself a student of picture books. I try to learn with each book I work on. What do I consider wonderful? A book that sings—where the words and pictures move and grow together and play upon each other."

SELECTED WORKS WRITTEN OR ADAPTED AND ILLUSTRATED: We Wish You a Merry Christmas: A Traditional Christmas Carol, 1983; Old MacDonald Had a Farm, 1984; Sing a Song of Sixpence, 1985; The Storekeeper, 1988; The Howling Dog, 1991.

SELECTED WORKS ILLUSTRATED: Beats Me, Claude, by Joan Lowery Nixon, 1986; Fat Chance, Claude, by Joan Lowery Nixon, 1987; You Bet Your Britches, Claude, by Joan Lowery Nixon, 1989; The Missing Tarts, by B.G. Hennessey, 1990; School Days, by B.G. Hennessey, 1990; That's the Spirit, Claude, by Joan Lowery Nixon, 1992; There's a Cow in the Road!, by Reeve Lindbergh, 1993; No Dogs Allowed, by Jane Cutler, 1994.

ABOUT: Burlington Free Press April 25, 1984; Something About the Author, Vol. 64; Vermont Life Spring 1985.

TAMORA PIERCE

December 13, 1954–

AUTHOR OF *Alanna: The First Adventure*, etc.

Autobiographical sketch of Tamora Pierce:

I WAS A BOOKWORM as a child through necessity. Before and after my parents' divorce when I was twelve, we moved constantly. When I graduated high school, I had attended eleven schools. Books were my consistent friends. If I had to leave them behind, I found new copies in my new location. Even writing, which my father had started me on when I was eleven, failed me for five years; books never did. I can remember the tales that helped my imagination catch fire for each year of my childhood. Once I earned an income as an adult, I went back and bought my own copies of my favorites, and I read them at least once a year now.

My aim as a future published writer, however, was not children's literature, but adult fantasy and thrillers. After college, where I had recovered from that five-year case of writer's block, I wrote a fantasy novel for adults. Called *The Song of the Lioness*, it was 732 pages about a girl who achieves her knight's shield by disguising herself as a boy. During the writing, and re-

Tamora: *TAM a ra*

of mass-market media, plus a lone fantasy story. I edited essays and stories for an Idaho literary magazine, and letters for a men's magazine. I read and critiqued manuscripts for a formula romance publisher. In the eighties, I became head writer for a radio production company: my work ranged from sketch comedy to hour-long dramas. My exposure to actors, writers, singers, dancers and artists through the radio company was invaluable. It taught me two things: no matter what form creativity takes, it springs from the same place, and that, to keep the mind limber, a wide variety of input, from as many sources as possible, is necessary. Without input, the mind stiffens up, and the artist is finished.

I came to write for teens by accident, but I'll stick with it. Books made a vast difference in my childhood. From the mail I get, my books make that difference for other kids—girls and boys. The dreams in books carried me through hard times as a child. It means more than I can ever say that my book-dreams seem to be carrying other kids now.

———

Tamora Pierce was born in Connellsville, Pennsylvania. She received a B.A. degree from the University of Pennsylvania in 1976 and did graduate study in social work and education. She worked as a tax data collector and clerk in New York state from 1977 to 1978, and was a social worker and housemother at McAuley Home for Girls in Buhl, Idaho in 1978 and 1979. She worked as an assistant to a literary agent in New York before becoming Creative Director of ZPPR Productions, Inc., a radio production company. She lives in New York City with her husband, and their two cats.

The order of her two novel quartets is, in The Immortals quartet, *Wild Magic*, *Wolf-Speaker*, *The Emperor Mage*, and *The Realms of the Gods*, the last of which is a work in progress. The Song of the Lioness quartet consists of *Alanna: The First Adventure*, *In the Hand of the Goddess*,

writes, I moved to Idaho to live with my father and stepmother for a year. Out there, I actually found work of the kind I had trained for in college, as a live-in housemother in a group home for teenage girls.

Ours was a strict facility: staff could not allow sex or drugs to be discussed among the girls. Knowing I was a writer (with three publishing credits at that point, two true confession stories and an article for *The Christian Century*), the girls asked to see the novel I was then sending out. When the home's director heard that there was both sex and drugs in the manuscript, he ruled that they couldn't read it. Instead, I told the story (omitting the objectionable parts), every day after school, and every night before bedtime, at the girls' request. They would come running home each day, saying, "Pierce, Pierce, tell us more about Alanna!" A year later, when my new agent recommended that I turn the adult manuscript into a four-book fantasy series for teenagers, I realized that, in a sense, I already had.

As an adult writer, I turned my hand to whatever came my way. As a result, I've published (in addition to the credits given above) reviews of martial arts movies and

The Woman Who Rides Like a Man, and *Lioness Rampant*. Pierce has contributed short stories and articles to such varied magazines as *School Library Journal*, *Martial Arts Movies*, and *The Christian Century*. Her books are published in the U.S., Canada, the United Kingdom, and in German- and Danish-language translations.

Pierce has a permanent message-posting area in the computer bulletin-board service American On Line, in the Kids Only On Line area, as well as a weekly on-line chat on America On Line.

SELECTED WORKS: Alanna: The First Adventure, 1983; In the Hand of the Goddess, 1984; The Woman Who Rides Like a Man, 1986; Lioness Rampant, 1988; Wild Magic, 1992; Wolf-Speaker, 1994; The Emperor Mage, 1995.

ABOUT: Contemporary Authors, Vol. 118; Gallo, Donald R. Speaking for Ourselves, Too; Something About the Author, Vol. 49, 51.

DAV PILKEY

March 4, 1966–

AUTHOR AND ILLUSTRATOR OF *Dogzilla*, etc.

Autobiographical sketch of Dav Pilkey:

I KNOW this is a terrible thing to admit, but I always hated school. I hated being confined to desks arranged in lines, writing on lined paper, standing in lines, lining up, coloring *inside* the lines, putting my name on the dotted line. . . . There was never any room in school for creativity or spontaneity. It seemed like all they were teaching us was conformity and blind obedience.

Part of my problem was that I was extremely hyperactive, and everything in my body wanted to run and scream and laugh and, well, *explode!* But all I ever got to do in school was fill in the blank.

So I developed a sense of humor.

It all started out very crude. In the second grade I learned how to make the most glorious flatulence noises by pressing my hands firmly into my face and blowing really hard. Every time the teacher would bend over . . . "P-p-pbbbllltttt!" . . . the classroom would erupt with laughter.

Soon I graduated to more sophisticated forms of levity, like seeing how many crayons I could stick up my nose at one time, burping the alphabet, and playing "Onward Christian Soldiers" on my armpit (I went to parochial school).

As you might imagine, my little outbursts began getting me into a lot of trouble. At first, my teacher started sending me out into the hallway. After a while, I was spending so much time standing in the hallway that my teacher put a little desk out there for me. I was the only kid in school with my own desk in the hallway, and it was at this desk that I had my first experience creating books.

The desk itself was one of those flip-top desks, which was perfect for hiding stuff in. Every day before classes began I would make sure that my hallway desk was stocked full of paper, crayons, pencils, and magic markers. Then I would walk into the classroom just expecting to get into trouble, and *usually* my expectations came true.

Sometime during the day (often several

Dav: *DAVE*

times) I would do something really silly and disruptive, and get caught red-handed. My teacher would stop everything, look me straight in the eye, point a bony, wrinkled finger toward the door and shout, "Mr. Pilkey—OUT!"

And all at once I was free. No rows of desks, no lined paper, no worksheets, no math problems...no problems at all! Just a peaceful hallway with big white walls and the soothing hum of a nearby drinking fountain. It was my first real studio.

There in the hallway I would sit down at my desk, take out my drawing supplies, and start creating. In the beginning I only drew pictures, but as time went on (my hallway desk followed me through the end of fifth grade) I began making up stories, too. I used to staple sheets of paper together and make my own comic books. I invented a whole slew of incredible super-heroes, including "The Amazing Captain Underpants," who flew around the city giving "wedgies" to all the bad guys. These comic books were a real hit with my classmates, however they weren't too popular with my teachers.

I remember one teacher who, after furiously ripping up one of my stories, told me I'd better start taking life more seriously, because I couldn't spend the rest of my days making silly books.

Fortunately, I wasn't a very good listener.

I wrote my first children's book when I was nineteen years old, and entered the book into Landmark Edition's "National Written and Illustrated by . . . Awards Contest for Students". My book won first prize in my age category, and was published. Since then I have written and/or illustrated twenty other books, and have many more in the works.

Lots of people have asked me how I think up the stories for my books. Actually, I never *try* to think of a story, stories just *come* to me. I live a very simple life, and often spend several hours a day daydreaming (I don't plan to...it just ends up that way). I love to watch the sun set, listen to the rain, walk my dog, and sit in front of the fire. It is usually then, when I am quiet and at rest, that my ideas come to me.

I write the kinds of books that I liked to read when I was a kid. I've always loved funny stories and stories about animals, so the books I write are usually funny, and almost always about animals. I also liked stories with lots of pictures and very few words. I had a reading disability as a kid, and often found it difficult to read books with lots of words. I think because of that, I tend to tell my stories more with pictures than with words. The texts in my books are like skeletons, and the illustrations are the guts and the muscles and the skin and stuff. Basically I'm writing and illustrating for myself, or more accurately, for the *kid* in me.

It seemed like all I ever wanted to do as a child was draw pictures, write stories, and make other kids laugh. Even though I'm old now (I'll be thirty in a few years) I *still* love drawing pictures, writing stories, and making kids laugh. I feel really lucky to be able to make a living doing my favorite things.

———

Dav Pilkey was born in Cleveland, Ohio. He earned an Associate of Arts degree from Kent State University in 1987. He has lived in Northeast Ohio most of his life, and now lives in Eugene, Oregon. He is a full-time children's book writer and illustrator. His hobbies are watching movies, playing video games, cooking, and "wasting time."

Dogzilla and *Kat Kong* were named Best Books for Reluctant Young Readers by the American Library Association. *Dragon's Fat Cat* was named a Children's Choice Book by a joint committee of the Children's Book Council and the International Reading Association.

SELECTED WORKS WRITTEN AND ILLUSTRATED: 'Twas the Night Before Thanksgiving, 1990; A Friend for Dragon, 1991; Dragon's Fat Cat, 1992; When Cats Dream, 1992; Dogzilla, 1993; Kat Kong, 1993; Dog Breath: The Horrible Trouble with Hally Tosis, 1994; The Hallo-Weiner, 1995.

SELECTED WORKS ILLUSTRATED: Julius, by Angela Johnson, 1993; The Dumb Bunnies, by Sue Denim, 1994; The Dumb Bunnies' Easter, by Sue Denim, 1995.

ABOUT: Contemporary Authors, Vol. 136; Something About the Author, Vol. 68.

BRIAN PINKNEY

August 28, 1961–

ILLUSTRATOR OF *Sukey and the Mermaid*, etc.

Biographical sketch of Jerry Brian Pinkney, who has also done illustration under the name "J. Brian Pinkney":

BRIAN PINKNEY was born in Boston, Massachusetts. He grew up in an artistic family. His mother, Gloria Jean Pinkney, is a children's book writer, and his father is children's book illustrator Jerry Pinkney. He remembers that he and his two brothers and his sister played musical instruments, and were "always drawing, painting, or building things." He built cities of cardboard, wood, and other materials and fashioned little men out of pipe cleaners and colored wire, inventing elaborate adventure stories about them.

Pinkney always wanted to be an illustrator, because his father was an illustrator. When he came home from school, he could go into his father's studio and talk to him while he worked. He had a miniature version of his father's studio in a walk-in closet, complete with art supplies that his father could no longer use. In school, he was encouraged in his artistic talent, drawing posters for extra credit. He studied Leonardo da Vinci for a social studies project and admired him because da Vinci was an artist, a musician, an inventor—and left-handed, like Brian Pinkney. When Pinkney learned that da Vinci wrote his notes backward, Pinkney did, too, and had to read his notes for a school test by holding his notebook up to a mirror.

Pinkney attended the Philadelphia College of Art, studying pen and ink, watercolors, oil and acrylic paints, and printmaking. He received his B.F.A. degree in 1983. Pinkney later attended the School of Visual Arts in New York, where he was introduced to working with scratchboard, which he used in many of his illustrations for children's books. This technique consists of coating a white board with black ink; then the ink is scratched off with a sharp tool. He received his M.F.A. degree from the school in 1990, and had a one-person exhibition in the student galleries there. His work has also been exhibited in several Society of Illustrators "The Original Art" shows in New York City, and his illustrations have appeared in magazines such as *The New York Times Magazine, Women's Day,* and *Instructor.* He married Andrea Davis, an editor and writer, in 1991 and they live in Brooklyn.

In addition to being an illustrator, Pinkney has taught at the Children's Art Carnival in Harlem, New York, and at the School of Visual Arts. He is a member of the Society of Illustrators and the Society of Children's Book Writers and Illustrators. His hobbies include playing the drums.

253

POLACCO

Where Does the Trail Lead? describes a boy's adventures by the sea, and Pinkney was able to draw on memories of his childhood summers on Cape Cod for the illustrations. The book was named an Honor Book in the 1991 Golden Kite Awards presented by the Society of Children's Book Writers and Illustrators.

Cut from the Same Cloth and *The Ballad of Belle Dorcas* were both named Notable Children's Trade Books in the Field of Social Studies by a joint committee of the National Council on the Social Studies and the Children's Book Council. *Dear Benjamin Banneker*, a biography of the farmer, astronomer, and writer, was praised in a *Booklist* review: "The artwork, subtle shades of oil paints over scratchboard pictures, is handsome as well as distinctive. . . . Sweeping lines and repeated contours give the illustrations a feeling of energy and life." The book was a Book-of-the-Month Club selection.

Sukey and the Mermaid was based on a folk tale from the Sea Islands in South Carolina. It was named an Honor Book in the 1993 Coretta Scott King Awards. It was also named a Notable Book of the Year by the American Library Association. Both *Sukey and the Mermaid* and *The Dark-Thirty* were named Hungry Mind Review Children's Books of Distinction in 1993.

Max Found Two Sticks, the first book Pinkney wrote and illustrated, is about a boy who starts to play the drums. *JoJo's Flying Side Kick*, which he also wrote and illustrated, concerns a child who is preparing for a test in her Tae Kwon Do class. Pinkney draws upon his own experience for the book, as he holds a black belt in this Korean martial art.

SELECTED WORKS WRITTEN AND ILLUSTRATED: Max Found Two Sticks, 1993; JoJo's Flying Side Kick, 1995.

SELECTED WORKS ILLUSTRATED: (as J. Brian Pinkney) The Boy and the Ghost, by Robert D. San Souci, 1989; The Ballad of Belle Dorcas, by William H. Hooks, 1990; Where Does the Trail Lead?, by Burton Albert, 1991; The Dark-Thirty: Southern Tales of the Supernatural, by Patricia C. McKissack, 1992;

Sukey and the Mermaid, by Robert D. San Souci, 1992; Alvin Ailey, by Andrea Davis Pinkney, 1993; Cut from the Same Cloth: American Women of Myth, Legend, and Tall Tale, collected and retold by Robert San Souci, 1993; Seven Candles for Kwanzaa, by Andrea Davis Pinkney, 1993; Dear Benjamin Banneker, by Andrea Davis Pinkney, 1994; The Dream Keeper and Other Poems, by Langston Hughes, 1994; The Faithful Friend, by Robert D. San Souci, 1995.

ABOUT: McElmeel, Sharron L. Bookpeople: A Multicultural Album; Publishers Weekly December 22, 1989; Something About the Author, Vol. 74.

PATRICIA POLACCO

July 11, 1944–

AUTHOR AND ILLUSTRATOR OF *Chicken Sunday*, etc.

Biographical sketch of Patricia Polacco:

PATRICIA POLACCO was born Patricia Barber, in Lansing, Michigan. She lived in Michigan until she was six. After her grandmother died, her family moved to Coral Gables, Florida, and later to Oakland, California. However, they always returned to Michigan in the summers.

Polacco has a rich heritage: her great-grandparents emigrated from Soviet Georgia, and other family members were Irish and Jewish; in addition, she was brought up among people from other ethnic groups than her own, and with all of these influences, and with a tradition of family members as storytellers, poets, farmers, teachers, and artists, she has much to draw upon for the books she writes and illustrates.

As a child, holidays like Christmas and Epiphany were celebrated in the Russian tradition. *Uncle Vova's Tree* is a book that comes from that experience. And *The Keeping Quilt* is a story based upon a real quilt that has been passed down in her own family through generations.

Pink and Say is a true story of the Civil War that was passed down by Polacco's great-great-grandfather, who spent time in Andersonville Prison where he became friends with a black soldier.

PATRICIA POLACCO

Another family influence upon her writing was her relationship with her brother, which she recalled for her book *My Rotten Redheaded Older Brother*.

Some of her books, such as *Mrs. Katz and Tush* and *Chicken Sunday*, tell stories of friendships among people of different races. She feels it is important for children to learn and understand about other kinds of people and their ideas. In a featured *Booklist* review, Carolyn Phelan called *Chicken Sunday* a moving picture book in which "the hatred sometimes engendered by racial and religious differences is overpowered by the love of people who recognize their common humanity. In strident and divisive times, here is a quiet, confident voice of hope."

As a child, Polacco was dyslexic, and thus could not read very well, so it was hard for her to read in front of her class at school; but when she began to draw, people admired her drawing ability, which was especially welcome. When she was older, she received a scholarship to go to college, but she was married at eighteen, and after several semesters at California College of Arts and Crafts and Laney College, she left school and began working. After her son and daughter were born, she returned to school.

She earned her B.A. degree from Monash University in 1974, and later lived in Australia for five years. She attended graduate school there, and received first an M.A. degree and then a Ph.D. degree in art history from the University of Melbourne, in 1978. Polacco became a fellow of the Royal Australian Art Historians, and worked as a historical consultant to museums in Russian and Greek icons, which she paints and restores.

Over the years, she always made little books as gifts, and on the urging of a friend, she joined the Society of Children's Book Writers and Illustrators. After putting together a portfolio of her work, she visited sixteen New York publishers in one week in 1987.

At the age of forty-one, Polacco's first book, *Meteor!*, was published. It is based on a true story of when a meteor landed in on her family's property, and when she tells the story to groups she often brings a piece of the real meteor to show them. Polacco has a collection of rocking chairs, and she uses them to rock and dream about a story until it is finished in her mind. Then she works very hard to complete the book, breaking only to eat, and often working late into the night.

She is the Art Director of *Galleys*, a publication for writers and illustrators in the U.S., and has done illustrations for *Ladybug* magazine. Her work has appeared in New York Society of Illustrators exhibitions of original art from 1990 to the present. Her books have been adapted for audio, video, and in the case of *Thunder Cake* and *Rechenka's Eggs*, for CD-ROM computer format by Computer Curriculum Corporation.

Patricia Polacco reads her work in author appearances at schools and libraries, and she has been a speaker at conferences such as the Northern California Children's Booksellers Organization in 1991, the American Library Association, and the International Reading Association.

She is also a member of the Citizen's Exchange Council Program of the United States and the former USSR and has travelled to the Soviet Union for cultural exchange of authors and illustrators of children's books. In her spare time, Polacco enjoys running marathons and painting Ukranian eggs. She lives in Oakland, California.

Rechenka's Eggs won a 1989 International Reading Association Children's Book Award. It was a Reading Rainbow Book. It was also named a Notable Children's Trade Book in the Field of Social Studies by a joint committee of the Children's Book Council and the National Council on the Social Studies. *Uncle Vova's Tree* and *Babushka Baba Yaga* were also named NCSS/CBC Notable Books.

The Keeping Quilt won a 1989 Sydney Taylor Book Award given by the Association of Jewish Libraries. *Just Plain Fancy* was named a Notable Book of the Year by the American Library Association, as were *My Rotten Redheaded Older Brother* and *Pink and Say. Chicken Sunday* won a 1992 Golden Kite Award presented by the Society of Children's Book Writers and Illustrators.

Mrs. Katz and Tush was an honor book in the 1993 Jane Addams Children's Book Award. It was a Reading Rainbow Book, as was *Appelemando's Dreams. Pink and Say* won the 1995 Jefferson Cup Award, given by the Virginia Library Association.

SELECTED WORKS: Meteor!, 1987; The Keeping Quilt, 1988; Rechenka's Eggs, 1988; Uncle Vova's Tree, 1989; Babushka's Doll, 1990; Just Plain Fancy, 1990; Thunder Cake, 1990; Appelemando's Dreams, 1991; Chicken Sunday, 1992; Mrs. Katz and Tush, 1992; Babushka Baba Yaga, 1993; My Rotten Redheaded Older Brother, 1994; Pink and Say, 1994; Babushka's Mother Goose, 1995.

ABOUT: Instructor April 1993; Polacco, Patricia. Firetalking; Publishers Weekly February 15, 1993; Something About the Author, Vol. 74.

SUSAN PRICE

July 8, 1955–

AUTHOR OF *The Ghost Drum*, etc.

Biographical sketch of Susan Price:

SUSAN PRICE was born in Oldbury, an industrial town in Worcestershire, England, the daughter of Alan, an electrical motor technician, and Jessie Price. Her family was working class, and she attended state schools. At the age of eighteen, she left school to work briefly at a bakery—the job lasted only two weeks—then at a supermarket, a retail warehouse, and at an open-air museum as a guide. Since then, she has been a full-time writer and lecturer.

She writes, "An aunt recently told me that I'd informed her, when I was eight, that I was going to be a writer when I grew up. I can't remember that, but certainly I wanted to be a writer from an early age." She thinks she became a writer because "at the time I grew up, there was no such thing in England as a professional story-teller (there is now). As a child I was told stories by my parents—stories about their childhoods, and about my grandparents and my great-grandparents. I told stories myself—to my younger brother and sister, and to my schoolmates. Then I began to write them down, because I was taught to, at school."

Price took her writing very seriously, and worked hard at it from the age of fourteen, "with the serious intention of getting published one day, comparing my work with that of published writers and trying hard to improve." Her dream came true earlier than she could have imagined. Before her first novel was published, she won two major awards for short stories in a *Daily Mirror* competition. Then, at the age of sixteen, her novel *The Devil's Piper* won the *Daily Mirror* Children's Literary Competition. The book was published in Britain by Faber & Faber in 1973 and in the U.S. by Greenwillow in 1976. It is the story of an unconventional "luchorpan" (leprechaun) who kidnaps four children as well as the adults

S. Price [signature]

who come to rescue the children. *The Horn Book Magazine* stated: "There is much humor in the characterizations; the spectacle of the cunning luchorpan talking his way out of his punishment is very funny. A complex and extremely well-written fantasy. . . . " The *Glasgow Herald* called the book "authentic, often frightening, and sometimes beautiful."

The West Midlands, says Price, where she still lives, is "the place where the Industrial Revolution started. The very ground of the place is made of iron-ore, limestone, fireclay and coal—all the things you need for smelting iron. Within a few years the factories had moved in, and the little country villages had become a centre of heavy industry, with all the exploitation that implies, of land and people. This area and its history—the mix of country and industrial town, and the bitterness of British social history—constantly finds its way into my work, often through family stories. That past, and the way it hangs on, haunts me—which is perhaps why the supernatural figures in my writing so often."

Price not only writes about her surroundings, she also writes for the people she grew up with. "I write for working-class kids,"

she says. "I think their parents have been conned all their lives and they will be conned unless they start thinking for themselves."

Since the publication of *The Devil's Piper*, Price has continued to write. She also lectures, teaches creative writing, and tells traditional stories. She has published a number of books in England, including *Twopence a Tub*, which won Britain's 1975 Other Award, an alternative children's book award for "nonbiased books of literary merit." The first book in her fantasy series about shamans, witches, and evil czars is *Ghost Drum*. The book won the Carnegie Medal, administered by the British Library Association. *Ghost Song* and *Ghost Dance* followed. They are "set in an unnamed country which is a mixture of everything ever imagined about Tsarist Russia and Poland," says Price. The *Horn Book* said of *Ghost Song*, "the beauty of the descriptive language of this tragic tale adds to the folkloric quality of the story—which incorporates the Norse myth of the death of Balder—leaving a haunting memory for the reader."

SELECTED WORKS: The Devil's Piper, 1976; Ghost Drum, 1987; Ghost Song, 1992; Ghost Dance, 1995.

ABOUT: Contemporary Authors, Vol. 105; Kirkpatrick, D.L., ed. Twentieth-Century Children's Writers; Something About the Author, Vol. 25; The Writers Directory 1992-94.

JAMES E. RANSOME

September 25, 1961–

ILLUSTRATOR OF *Sweet Clara and the Freedom Quilt*, etc.

Autobiographical sketch of James E. Ransome:

ILLUSTRATION for me has always been a way to tell stories with pictures. Much more than color placed on canvas, over the years I have come to realize the effect im-

ages can have on an audience. Color becomes shape, shapes transform into figures and objects, which in turn trigger imaginations, rekindle memories and form emotional bonds between reader and image.

Design has always played a major role in my illustrations. Each book I illustrate demands its own voice and I attempt to let that voice be heard by placing each book in different settings and time frames. And within each book, each page possesses subtle intricacies that offer the reader more information than the text can provide. Bookcases, framed photos, quilts, freshly baked cookies are just some clues strategically placed to give the reader a revealing peek into the inner workings of each character.

Inspired by the need to provide young children with positive images such as strong family ties and a sense of history, I attempt to transcend the role of illustrator and enter into the realm of visual storyteller.

My interest in drawing began at a very early age. The grandmother who raised me was a woman who sharecropped all her life and was afraid for her grandson who loved to draw and said it was something for white folks, and that I could never get a job draw-

ing. She said this not because she was mean but because she knew that outside the loving walls of our North Carolina home was prejudice and hatred. She did not want me to dream of something that was not possible in the world in which she lived.

One of the reasons I so enjoyed illustrating *Aunt Flossie's Hats* is because it brought back memories of my grandmother. Like Aunt Flossie, my grandmother cherished family history and collected many remnants of her past such as photos and stories. I tried to convey the warmth of home and family through a generous use of earth tones.

After reading the manuscript for *Sweet Clara and the Freedom Quilt*, I realized I was uncomfortable with the subject of slavery because I'd had no formal study of that period in history. Yet I wanted to provide an accurate depiction. This desire led me to the library in search of research materials. Even after all of my reading I still felt a need to know more, so I visited first a plantation in North Carolina and finally Carter's Grove plantation in Colonial Williamsburg, which put everything in place. I viewed authentic slave cabins and learned about the everyday lives of slaves. All of this sparked an interest in my own past and prompted me to begin speaking to the elders in my own family. One of my discoveries was the Verona Plantation in North Carolina, home to the first Ransome descendant, Emma Ransome. The image of the road leading to the Verona Plantation is illustrated on the title page of *Sweet Clara*.

Coretta Scott King Honor Book *Uncle Jed's Barbershop* is my favorite book to date. As soon as I read the text, the illustrations easily came to me. I was amazed at how this story paralleled my own life. Based in the South, the story of pursuing dreams in the face of obstacles is one that touched me in a very special way. My own father worked as a part-time barber for over twenty years before he opened his own barbershop three years ago, the same year I read the manuscript for *Uncle Jed's Barbershop*. Several added elements such as the wood-burning stove, braided rug, patchwork quilt all placed in the blustery winds of a Southern fall convey the warmth and deep emotional ties I felt to this story.

More recently, I was faced with the unique task of illustrating James Weldon Johnson's *The Creation*. Not only did I have to illustrate a story previously illustrated, but creating images to accompany a poem about God's creation of the world proved to be my greatest challenge. Rather than attempting to illustrate God in the process of creating, I opted to illustrate a storyteller winding this tale to a group of children under the shade of a tree in a Southern field.

From slavery to the present, the stories I illustrate are, in a sense, a series of snapshots taken from the rich and varied pages of African-American life.

———

James Ransome was born in Rich Square, North Carolina. As a child, his first encounters with art came in the forms of television cartoons, superhero comic books, and *MAD* magazine. He began to write and illustrate his own stories. He was a teenager when his family moved to New Jersey. There he took filmmaking and photography classes in high school. This experience, he believes, influenced his illustration style, as he discovered the power that perspective, value, and cropping can have on an image. He produced several student films and began work in animation. His teacher, Charlie Bogasat, suggested he take a drawing and painting class, which rekindled his interest in illustration.

He earned a B.F.A. degree in illustration from Pratt Institute in 1987 and continued to study drawing and painting at the Art Students League in New York City. He considers among his influences Mary Cassatt, John Singer Sargent, Winslow Homer, and Edgar Degas, as well as his contemporaries, Bernie Fuchs, Robert Cunningham, Skip Leipke, and Jerry Pinkney. He has il-

lustrated textbooks for elementary and college students, including *Bonolo and the Peach Tree* and *Literature and the Child*, a retrospective of children's literature. He has illustrated many book jackets and has been a contributor to such magazines as *Esquire, Cricket,* and *Ladybug.*

Original artwork from his books have been exhibited in group and solo shows. His work is also in the permanent collection of children's book art of North Carolina's Charlotte Library. He is a member of the Society of Illustrators, and lives in New York state with his wife and two children.

The Creation won a 1995 Coretta Scott King Award. It was also named a Notable Book of the Year by the American Library Association. *Sweet Clara and the Freedom Quilt* was named a Notable Children's Trade Book in the Field of Social Studies by a joint committee of the National Council on the Social Studies and the Children's Book Council. It was also a Reading Rainbow Book. *Uncle Jed's Barbershop* was a Coretta Scott King Award winner in 1994 and an ALA Notable Book.

SELECTED WORKS ILLUSTRATED: Do Like Kyla, by Angela Johnson, 1990; Aunt Flossie's Hats (and Crab Cakes Later), by Elizabeth Fitzgerald Howard, 1991; How Many Stars in the Sky?, by Lenny Hort, 1991; The Girl Who Wore Snakes, by Angela Johnson, 1993; The Hummingbird Garden, by Christine Widman, 1993; Red Dancing Shoes, by Denise Lewis Patrick, 1993; Sweet Clara and the Freedom Quilt, by Deborah Hopkinson, 1993; Uncle Jed's Barbershop, by Margaree King Mitchell, 1993; The Creation, by James Weldon Johnson, 1994; My Best Shoes, by Marilee Robin Burton, 1994; Celie and the Harvest Fiddler, by Valerie and Vanessa Flournoy, 1995; Freedom's Fruit, by William H. Hooks, 1995; The Old Dog, by Charlotte Zolotow, 1995.

ABOUT: Something About the Author, Vol. 76.

DOREEN RAPPAPORT

October 31, 1939–

AUTHOR OF *American Women*, etc.

Autobiographical sketch of Doreen Rappaport:

I NEVER INTENDED to be a writer. I studied piano when I was six years old and majored in music at Brandeis University. Then I taught music and reading in junior high schools in New York City and in New Rochelle, New York. I loved teaching and being with children. During this time, the civil rights movement, then the antiwar movement, and then feminism were changing the world. I reexamined my life and beliefs. "It was harder and harder to focus on untangling a Bach fugue when there was so much work in the world to be done." I began to see that part of my work would be to write about history, to tell tales that others had forgotten, to help children separate fact from fiction.

When I was growing up, there were almost no books about American women in history. I read about the Founding Fathers, but not about women like Judith Sargeant Murray, Elizabeth Cady Stanton, and Ida B. Wells. Nor were there books about women pilots, lawyers, doctors, teachers, writers, artists or revolutionaries. I see my writing as part of my own personal struggle to fill in the gaps and undo the myths so power-

fully imposed on me as a child. I want to 'demythify' personal experience and historical events for young people. I'm interested in the untold stories in history. It's not that I don't love Jefferson and Lincoln—they were astounding human beings; but there are too many Mother Joneses and Zitkala-Sas out there, and relatively few have heard of them. Young women need role models like these women, and all young people need to learn that life is more of a struggle than what is usually presented on television or in many history books.

Ideas for books come from all kinds of places. The idea for *Be the Judge, Be the Jury* came to me when I was on jury duty and saw how incredibly complicated it was to be a juror—how complicated it was to determine whether someone was guilty or not guilty. I decided to write about women adventurers when I went hiking for the first time and found I wasn't as scared of heights as I had always believed. I realized that maybe if I had once read about women who lived dangerously, I might have had more courage about such things before.

Ideas for books come fast and furiously, but the research is much slower. Like a detective, you plod along, tracking down people and events. I remember the month my back ached from sitting over a microfilm reader five hours a day reading a local Pennsylvania newspaper that described how Mother Jones helped miners and their families during a long strike. It was grueling work of skimming over a hundred issues of a California historical magazine to find the first-person account of a nineteenth-century Hispanic woman, Maria Ascension Sepulveda y Avila. I can close my eyes and see the long stretches of South Dakota prairie that I drove through to get to the Yankton Reservation to talk with the eighty-three-year-old niece of Zitkala-Sa, a twentieth-century Yankton-Sioux reformer. Nor will I forget our two afternoons in which she shared her family's life with me. I still feel my ecstasy and see the shocked look on the other scholars' faces at the

Franklin Delano Roosevelt Library when I began to laugh uproariously while looking through letters and postcards and valentines sent to President Roosevelt's dog Fala, for I knew at that moment that I had the makings of an unusual book.

If you're lucky enough to find what you need, the next part is translating that research into writing. There are hours and hours and weeks and weeks of working and reworking a phrase, selecting the most appropriate words, and reordering your ideas. The most painful times are when you have to let go of a paragraph or a page or a chapter that you think is so wonderful, but you know detracts from the flow of the story.

I feel privileged and lucky to be a writer, to choose what to write about and to take a chance that my readers will agree that I've done a good job.

———

Doreen Rappaport was born in New York City, where she now lives. She graduated from Brandeis University in 1957 with a B.A. degree in Music History. She is divorced and is collaborating with a stepdaughter on several books. She is a member of the Authors Guild and the Society of Children's Book Writers and Illustrators.

Trouble at the Mines was an Honor Book in the 1988 Jane Addams Children's Book Awards. Three of Rappaport's books have been named Notable Children's Trade Books in the Field of Social Studies by a joint committee of the National Council on the Social Studies and the Children's Book Council: *Escape from Slavery, The Journey of Meng,* and *American Women.* The latter was also named a Best Book for Young Adults by the American Library Association.

SELECTED WORKS: The Boston Coffee Party, 1988; American Women: Their Lives in Their Words, 1990; Escape from Slavery, 1991; Living Dangerously: Women Who Risked Their Lives for Adventure, 1991; The Journey of Meng, 1991; The Lizzie Borden Trial, 1992; The Sacco-Vanzetti Trial, 1992; The Alger Hiss Trial, 1993; Tinker vs. Des Moines, 1993; The New King, 1995.

CHRIS RASCHKA

March 6, 1959–

AUTHOR AND ILLUSTRATOR OF *Yo! Yes?*, etc.

Autobiographical sketch of Christopher Raschka:

WHAT I'D LIKE to tell you about is my growing-up years, from when I was very small, from the time before I could read, up to when I left my home to go away to college. I have parents who come from two different countries. My father grew up in the United States and my mother grew up in Austria, which is a country in Europe. Because of this I grew up some in both places, in my mother's country and in my father's country. My parents met each other in a refugee camp after World War II, where they were both working to help find new homes for people whose old homes had been blown up by a bomb or burned in the fighting. This was in Austria. This was where my brother was born, too. After a few years my mother, father and brother moved, first to Philadelphia and then to Huntingdon, Pennsylvania, which is where I was born, on March 6, 1959. Huntingdon is a little town in the Appalachian Mountains where there is a small college, where my father was a teacher, but the biggest thing is the prison, which looks like a wide castle. All of this is from before I can remember, I only know about it because of things my parents have told me.

My family went back to Europe, this time to Germany. We didn't fly in an airplane, we traveled all the way across the Atlantic Ocean in an enormous boat, an ocean liner. This boat was so big that even though we lived on it for ten days, and my brother and I explored it every day, we never even saw all of the rooms. There were swimming pools. There was a movie theater, which my brother and I snuck into sometimes at night when my mother thought we were sleeping. On the last day of the trip, my parents, my brother and I walked from our cabin, which was way down deep in the ship, up many

Rascka: *RAH sh kah*

CHRIS RASCHKA

flights of stairs all the way to the bridge, where the captain and ship's pilots stand. While we were there the terrible, loud foghorn blew, right in our ears, even though it was a sunny day. Suddenly one of the ship's officers came running at us, wagging his finger at me, telling me not to do that! It was I who had blown the foghorn, with the little white switch I was flipping back and forth. I did something wrong without even knowing it.

That was when I was five. When we lived in Germany then, my sister was born. That year I went to school for the first time. I liked school, though sometimes it made me nervous, and there was a certain big girl who used to try to catch me on my way home, and if she did, she would slap me.

When we lived in the United States again, we lived in Chicago. While we lived in Germany I forgot how to speak English, but I remembered when I was with American friends again. My first teacher here would say, "Do you understand, Christopher?" I did. I had one teacher in that school whom I didn't like. My friend, Bryan, and I had long hair, which was kind of new and kind of cool then, but because we did, and because we were boys, the

teacher made everyone in the class call us Betty and Crissy until we got our hair cut. She also sent us to the principal. But we never did cut our hair.

My family lived in Germany again and the rest of the time in Chicago. I didn't get any more brothers or sisters. But we had two different dogs. Now I live in New York City with my wife, whose name is Lydie (Lie-dee), our baby boy Ingo, two cats and one turtle.

———

Chris Raschka received a B.A. degree from St. Olaf College in Northfield, Minnesota, in 1981. He was an art teacher in St. Croix, Virgin Islands, from 1985 to 1986. He lived in Ann Arbor, Michigan, for two years, working as an illustrator and freelance artist, before coming to New York City. A viola player, he has been a member of the Ann Arbor Symphony Orchestra and the Flint, Michigan, Symphony Orchestra. He had a one-person show at the Wittgensteiner Heimathaus in Bad Berleburg, Germany, in 1995. He is a member of the Society of Children's Book Writers and Illustrators, the Authors Guild, and PEN International.

Yo! Yes? was named an Honor Book in the 1994 Randolph Caldecott Medal Awards given by the American Library Association. It was the 1993 winner of the UNICEF-Ezra Jack Keats National Award for Children's Book Illustration. Its illustrations were included in a show of Caldecott Medal winners and Honor Books at the Chicago Art Institute. *Charlie Parker Played Be Bop* was included in the 1993 Bologna Book Fair Exhibition of children's books and was named an ALA Notable Book of the Year. Both *Charlie Parker* and *Yo! Yes?* are included in the VI Premi Internacional Catalònia D'Illustració. *Elizabeth Imagined an Iceberg* was included in the 1995 Bologna Book Fair Exhibition.

SELECTED WORKS: R and R: A Story of Two Alphabets, 1990; Charlie Parker Played Be Bop, 1992; Yo! Yes?, 1993; Elizabeth Imagined an Iceberg, 1994; Blushful Hippopotamus, 1995; Can't Sleep, 1995.

ABOUT: Something About the Author, Vol. 80.

JANE RAY

June 11, 1960–

ILLUSTRATOR OF *The Story of Christmas*, etc.

Biographical sketch of Jane Ray:

JANE RAY was born in London, England. She is the daughter of two teachers, and her father was also a musician. As a child she wrote and illustrated stories for herself. She studied ceramics in college, and graduated from Middlesex Polytechnic in 1972, receiving a B.A. degree with honors. In 1988, she married David Anthony Temple, a conductor. They have two children.

Ray has always wanted to draw and paint. She is an artist who has had her paintings shown in exhibits. She has a studio that she shares with a cartoonist and a fellow artist in a church in North London.

Ray has taught art on a part-time basis to children and adults in Special Education. In her spare time, she enjoys music, gardening, reading, and writing. She is an avid environmentalist, devoting her efforts to halt the greenhouse effect, the destruction of the rain forests, and the disappearance of species of plant and animal life. While working on her book *Noah's Ark*, she found parallels between her own "green politics" and the story of Noah, who must take charge of every beast, bird, and insect on the planet after God is disappointed with the state of the earth and its human beings. *Noah's Ark* is based on the Authorized King James version of the Bible.

In *The Story of Christmas*, which uses the text from the Gospels of Matthew and Luke, Ray's approach to the story was "fresh" and "unique," according to a review by Mary M. Burns in *The Horn Book Magazine*. "[T]he artist has incorporated ancient symbols of past and present and of many cultures," she writes, "The stylized

JANE RAY

figures are flattened in the manner of folk art, complementing the emphasis on homely details." Burns states that Ray inspires reverence while delighting the eye. There is also a version of *The Story of Christmas* in Spanish, *La Historia de Navidad.*

The Story of Creation was a runnerup in the 1992 British Book Awards, a prize organized by *Publishing News.* It was also published in a Spanish-language version, *La Historia de le Creacion: Segun el Genesis.* Ray has chosen to illustrate Bible stories, she says, because she thinks they are wonderful stories and an important part of her heritage.

Magical Tales from Many Lands includes fourteen stories from many cultures: Arabic, Native American, Japanese, and South African, for example, giving Ray the opportunity to depict a variety of peoples, costumes, and places.

SELECTED WORKS ADAPTED AND ILLUSTRATED: Noah's Ark, 1990; The Story of Christmas, 1991; The Story of the Creation: Words from Genesis, 1993.

SELECTED WORKS ILLUSTRATED: Island of the Children, compiled by Angela Huth, 1988; Casting a Spell, compiled by Angela Huth, 1991; Mother Gave a Shout: Poems by Women and Girls, edited by Susanna Steele and Morag Styles, 1991; Magical Tales from Many Lands, retold by Margaret Mayo, 1993.

ABOUT: Something About the Author, Vol. 72.

CAROLYN REEDER

November 16, 1937–

AUTHOR OF *Shades of Gray*, etc.

Autobiographical sketch of Carolyn Reeder:

UNTIL RECENTLY, my life was defined by the roles I played. First, the daughter growing up in Washington, D.C., next the student at American University, and then my longest-held trio of roles: teacher, wife, and mother.

I'm still a teacher, a wife, and a mother (an out-of-a-job mother now, with grown-up children), but I'm also a history buff, book lover, friend, hiker, cyclist, theatergoer, and writer.

Writing is an important part of my life—an end in itself. But at first, writing was just a sidelight to our family's favorite recreation: hiking in Virginia's Shenandoah National Park. We loved to follow faint trails through the forest to old homesites where we found cabin ruins and often discovered discarded tools or crockery. It wasn't long before we became curious about the people who had to leave their homes so the park could be created. My husband and I satisfied our curiosity by doing research and interviews that eventually led us to write three nonfiction books for adults.

When I began to write fiction for young people, I set my novels in or near the Blue Ridge Mountains where I had hiked for so many years. That made it easy for me to imagine what my characters were seeing. The research for the books I wrote with my husband provided much of the background information for *Grandpa's Mountain* and *Moonshiner's Son*.

The ideas for my stories grow out of thing that interest me rather than out of my experiences. But even though my early life doesn't influence what I write about, it was

a good preparation for writing. As an only child growing up in a neighborhood with no other children my age, most of my free time was spent reading. Through books, I met fascinating people and traveled all over the world—and into the past. Reading kept my imagination alive, and it gave me an "ear for language."

Now, I find that I like *writing* books as much as reading them. Writing is the most challenging thing I do. To take the spark of an idea and shape it into a story that develops into a book is a long and demanding process—but it's worth every bit of the time and effort.

———

Carolyn Reeder was born and grew up in Washington, D.C., and now lives in Glen Echo, Maryland. She received her B.A. degree from American University in 1959 and later returned for her M.Ed. degree, which she received in 1972. She has taught fourth through sixth grades at Georgetown Day School in Washington, where she now teaches reading to primary-grade children. She is married and has a grown son and daughter. With her husband, Jack Reeder, she has written three adult nonfiction books about Shenandoah National Park, including *Shenandoah Secrets: The Story of the Park's Hidden Past.* She is a member of the Children's Book Guild of Washington, D.C.

Shades of Gray won the 1989 Scott O'Dell Award for Historical Fiction. It was named an Honor Book in the 1990 Jane Addams Children's Book Awards and won the 1989 Child Study Children's Book Award, given by the Child Study Children's Book Committee at Bank Street College of Education. It was named a Notable Book of the Year by the American Library Association.

SELECTED WORKS: Shades of Gray, 1989; Grandpa's Mountain, 1991; Moonshiner's Son, 1993.

ABOUT: Contemporary Authors, Vol. 135; Something About the Author, Vol. 66.

FAITH RINGGOLD

October 8, 1930–

AUTHOR AND ILLUSTRATOR OF *Tar Beach*, etc.

Biographical sketch of Faith Ringgold:

FAITH RINGGOLD was born in New York City and grew up in Harlem during the Depression. As a child, she suffered from asthma. Because she was ill so often, she had a rather protected childhood, spending a lot of time at home while her siblings were in school. She recounts wonderful memories of this time, drawing and sewing at home with her mother, as well as visiting the museums of New York City, and seeing live performances of such greats as Duke Ellington and Count Basie. Ringgold also spent a lot of time with her father on his days off, an advantage her older siblings didn't have since they were in school.

When she wasn't ill, Ringgold led the life of an average New York City child, enjoying all the city had to offer. From early on, she drew and painted, and she was always the class artist. At the City College of the City University of New York, there was no

question that she would major in art. However, the lack of formal education about African-American art led her to pursue this interest on her own.

In 1950, Ringgold eloped with Robert Earl Wallace, a jazz pianist who was her childhood sweetheart. They had two daughters, Barbara and Michele, but the marriage did not last, and in 1956, they were divorced. In 1962, she married Burdette Ringgold.

Ringgold graduated with a B.S. in 1955 and an M.A. in 1959, both from CUNY. After graduating, she worked as an art teacher in the New York public schools. She continued working on her own art, but within a few years, she decided to become a full-time artist. In 1961, Ringgold took her children and her mother to Europe, and began to study art in France and Italy. When she returned, she began working on her political paintings, which she exhibited in her first one-person show at the Spectrum Gallery in 1967. The paintings explored the political issues of the day. She became more involved in the African-American arts community, and in 1966, she participated in the first African-American Exhibition in Harlem since the 1930s. She writes, "After I decided to be an artist, the first thing I had to believe was that I, a black woman, could be on the art scene without sacrificing one iota of my blackness, or my femaleness, or my humanity."

In 1972, she did her first "tankas"—paintings on canvas framed in fabric and quilted. She was inspired to work in this medium after seeing an exhibit of Tibetan Napalan tankas. The tankas were appealing to her for many reasons, but most of all because they could be so easily transported. She could simply roll them up and take them wherever she might have an audience for her work. Ringgold's mother helped her with the fabric frames and over the years these tankas developed into quilts.

Ringgold painted her first quilt in 1980, and in 1983 she made her first story quilt, the medium for which she is known today. These "picture story quilts," as she calls them, contain both pictures and words. When Crown editor Andrea Cascardi saw one, she approached Ringgold about making it into a children's book. *Tar Beach*, her first children's book, was the result.

Eight-year-old Cassie Louise Lightfoot dreams that she can fly in *Tar Beach*. As described in *Horn Book Magazine*, she leaves her Harlem rooftop (her "tar beach") to fly "over the city righting social wrongs and claiming parts of it—the Brooklyn Bridge, the ice-cream factory—for herself," The book, which is set in 1939, is reviewed by *The Horn Book Magazine* as a "stunningly beautiful book," an "allegorical tale [that sparkles with symbolic and historical references central to African-American culture."
Tar Beach was named an Honor Book in the 1992 Randolph Caldecott Awards, presented by the American Library Association 1992. It also won the 1992 Coretta Scott King Award for Illustration, and was named an ALA Notable Book of the Year. It was named a Hungry Mind Review Children's Book of Distinction, and a Best Illustrated Book of 1991 by *The New York Times*.

Ringgold won the Ezra Jack Keats New Writer Award, and the book was named a Notable Children's Trade Book in the Field of Social Studies by a joint committee of the National Council on the Social Studies and the Children's Book Council. It was also named a Reading Rainbow Book.

Aunt Harriet's Underground Railroad in the Sky, about Harriet Tubman, won a 1993 Jane Addams Children's Book Award. *Dinner at Aunt Connie's House*, which was also a story quilt, features quotations from twelve African-American women, such as Zora Neale Hurston and Rosa Parks, who have made important contributions to African-American history.

Both of Ringgold's picture books that are based upon story quilts end with a photograph of the original story quilt and notes on how the quilt was created. The *Tar Beach* story quilt has been exhibited in a number of shows, including at the Children's Museum of Manhattan.

Museums and galleries worldwide have had exhibitions of her work, and her art is in many public and private collections, including the Boston Museum of Fine Art, the Metropolitan Museum of Art and the Studio Museum in Harlem. From 1990 to 1993, an exhibition, "Faith Ringgold: A 25 Year Survey," toured nationally. Ringgold has continued to teach at the University of California, San Diego, and she has received numerous awards, including two National Endowment for the Arts Awards for painting and sculpture. She is a visiting lecturer and artist at art centers and universities, and has lectured at the Museum of Modern Art and the Museum of African American Art, among others.

The artist is also a writer, and has contributed articles and essays to such magazines and journals as *Artpaper*, *Arts Magazine*, and *Gallery Guide*. Her first book for adults, *We Flew Over the Bridge: The Memoirs of Faith Ringgold*, was published in 1995.

Ringgold's life as an artist is the subject of an award-winning video, "Faith Ringgold: The Last Story Quilt," created and produced by Linda Freeman. The video, distributed by L & S Video Enterprises, won the 1992 Cine Gold Eagle Award.

SELECTED WORKS WRITTEN AND ILLUSTRATED: Tar Beach, 1991; Aunt Harriet's Underground Railroad in the Sky, 1992; Dinner at Aunt Connie's House, 1993; My Dream of Martin Luther King, 1995.

ABOUT: Artweek February 13, 1992; Essence May 1990; Marks, Claude, ed. World Artists, 1980-1990; Miller, Lynn and Sally S. Swenson. Lives and Works; Publishers Weekly February 15, 1991; Ringgold, Faith. We Flew Over the Bridge: The Memoirs of Faith Ringgold; School Arts May 1989; Sills, Leslie. Inspirations: Stories About Women Artists; Something About the Author, Vol. 71; Teaching PreK-8 March 1993; Turner, Robyn Montana. Faith Ringgold.

HAZEL ROCHMAN

April 13, 1938–

EDITOR OF *Somehow Tenderness Survives*, etc.

Biographical sketch of Hazel Rochman:

HAZEL ROCHMAN calls herself a "Latvian Jewish South-African American . . . proud of every piece of that hyphenated identity." In a 1995 speech sponsored by the American Library Association and the Children's Book Council, she stated that she loves the title of the book *Kaleidoscope* by Rudine Sims Bishop, since the image "holds on to both the rich particulars of ethnic identity and their connectedness." "Them" and "us," she says, are words that shift their meaning all the time, and "they make a pattern together."

Rochman was born and raised in South Africa. Her relatives left eastern Europe at the turn of the century to escape racist persecution. Her grandparents and her father traveled steerage class in a boat to South Africa. She grew up, she says, in a "big extended Jewish immigrant family" in Johannesburg. She was a child there during World War II, at a time when there was a strong pro-Nazi movement in South Africa.

Her father made secret arrangements to have a Gentile family hide her, in the event that the anti-Semites gained power. "The Holocaust terror seemed very close," she states.

After the war, the pro-Nazis did become the South African government. They instituted apartheid, institutionalized racism. However, the people whom they persecuted were the black people, and not the Jewish people like herself.

Hazel Rochman lived in a place where she saw the white government invent countries, taking four fifths of the land for themselves, while they constituted only one fifth of the population. There was fierce censorship; even children were tortured, and one was forbidden to write about it. She read no books that showed blacks as people. Her home was "liberal," she says, and no one there made racist remarks. But she didn't know what was going on around her: "I was denied access to the stories and music of the world. Groups like Ladysmith Black Mambazo were making music right there and I couldn't hear them. I didn't know that in the streets of Soweto there were people like Nelson Mandela with a vision of a nonracial democracy that would change my life. I was ignorant and I didn't know I was ignorant."

Rochman married in 1959. She graduated with honors from the University of the Witwatersrand in Johannesburg in 1960. She worked as a journalist until she, her husband, and their three-year-old son left South Africa on one-way passports in 1963. Because of their active political resistance to apartheid, they weren't allowed back into South Africa until the 1990's. They were stateless. They lived in England for ten years. Their second son was born there, and she worked as an English teacher.

In 1972, she and her family moved to Chicago, where she earned her M.A.T. degree in Library Science at the University of Chicago in 1976. Each year she and her family had to line up at the Immigration Department to have their Certificates of Identity stamped; in 1982, she finally became a naturalized U.S. citizen. For eight years she was a school librarian at the University of Chicago Library Schools. When she began there, she says, "the kids and I were strangers. I had this prissy accent. I wasn't at all sure things were going to work out. But when I started going to classes to talk about books, we got to know each other. We discovered the fears and dreams we had in common. The books were a bond between us." Since 1984, Hazel Rochman has reviewed for the Books for Youth section at *Booklist*, where she is Assistant Editor.

Rochman believes that stories matter. "Stories have brought me close to all kinds of people who would otherwise have remained strangers. Stories are my work and my joy, and they have helped me find a home."

In 1988, when Nelson Mandela was still in prison and apartheid in South Africa was at its height, Rochman collected stories that showed what it was like to grow up under apartheid. "A black child sees his father dragged away by the police for not having his papers in order. For one white boy, growing up can mean breaking the best in himself so he can fit in with white

supremacy," she writes. "For a few whites, coming of age may be the opposite of acceptance. It may be the sudden realization that a black is a *person* or the slow dawning of the terrible knowledge that the moral universe you have always taken for granted is evil." The collection of stories that resulted is *Somehow Tenderness Survives.*

In 1995, Hazel Rochman visited Johannesburg and saw a quite different situation from the days when she had to learn the government language, Afrikaans, as a child. "It was wonderful to see all children going to school together and learning to speak each other's languages as well as their own."

Rochman has been an instructor at the 1988 and 1989 Children's Literature Institutes at the Columbia University School of Library Science in New York City. She speaks at schools and conferences across the country, including a presentation at "The World at Our Doorstep: Building Bridges of International Understanding Through Children's and Young Adult Books," the International Board on Book for Young People Conference in Georgia in 1995.

She is a contributor of reviews and articles to magazines such as *Horn Book*, the *New York Times Book Review*, and *School Library Journal.* She writes a monthly review column for *Sesame Street Parents' Magazine.*

In 1989 Hazel Rochman received the Children's Reading Round Table of Chicago Award, which honors a person "who has made an outstanding and long-term contribution in terms of quality and achievement in the field of children's books."

Against Borders: Promoting Books for a Multicultural World, a book for adults, won the 1994 ALA G.K. Hall Award for Library Literature. Her book *Tales of Love and Terror: Booktalking the Classics, Old and New* was produced as a video tape by the ALA.

Both *Somehow Tenderness Survives* and *Who Do You Think You Are?* were named Best Books for Young Adults by the American Library Association.

SELECTED WORKS EDITED: Somehow Tenderness Survives: Stories of Southern Africa, 1988.

SELECTED WORKS COMPILED WITH DARLENE Z. MCCAMPBELL: Who Do You Think You Are?: Stories of Friends and Enemies, 1993; Bearing Witness: Stories of the Holocaust, 1995.

ABOUT: Horn Book March 1995; Rochman, Hazel. Against Borders: Promoting Books for a Multicultural World.

"MISTER ROGERS"

March 20, 1928–

AUTHOR OF *Making Friends*, etc.

Biographical sketch of Fred McFeeley Rogers, who writes under the pen name "Mister Rogers":

FRED McFEELY ROGERS is a producer, writer, puppeteer, minister, and beloved performer on *Mister Rogers' Neighborhood*. He was born and grew up in 1928 in Latrobe, Pennsylvania. He was student council president and editor of the yearbook at Latrobe High School. He attended Dartmouth College, but transferred to Rollins College in Florida, studying music composition. He graduated magna cum laude in 1951 and went on to divinity school. He earned his degree from Pittsburgh Theological Seminary, magna cum laude, in 1962. He also studied child development at the University of Pittsburgh.

After graduating from Rollins College, he was hired by NBC in New York as an assistant producer and floor director of several television shows. In 1952, he married Joanne Byrd, a pianist whom he had met in college. In 1953, he became producer of and also appeared as a musician and a puppeteer on a daily children's television program on WQED, a public television station. In 1955, the show won the Sylvania Award for the best locally-produced children's program in the country.

In his spare time, he continued his

FRED McFEELEY ROGERS

studies. He was ordained as a Presbyterian minister in 1962, with a charge to continue his work with children and families through the media. He created the television show that became his career, *Mister Rogers' Neighborhood*, as a fifteen-minute show for Canadian Broadcasting Company in Toronto. He further developed a half-hour version of the show for the Eastern Educational Network, and in 1968 it was nationally distributed through WQED and the Public Broadcasting Service. The acclaimed show counts among its many honors a George Foster Peabody Award and two Emmy Awards (for performing and for writing) and is the longest-running children's program on public television. It is carried nationwide by more than three hundred stations of PBS, reaching approximately eight million households each week. There are over six hundred half-hour programs in the library of the television show.

The show itself depicts Mr. Rogers speaking directly to the camera, intending to offer child viewers a place where they can feel accepted, safe, and understood. As he relates to children, he explores feelings such as love, fear, sadness, jealousy, anger, and joy, and he sets out to affirm their feelings of self-worth. His tenets include encouraging children to feel good about themselves, respecting others, and helping them learn the skills needed for growing up. Many guests enhance the scope of the program, including marine botanist Sylvia Earle, chef Julia Child, cellist Yo-Yo Ma, and jazz enthusiast and musician Wynton Marsalis, to name a few.

The multitalented Rogers, a pianist and composer, also writes the music and song lyrics for the program. Rogers credits his thirty-year association with the late Dr. Margaret B. McFarland, a clinical psychologist and child development specialist, as being a crucial influence and important associate in working on the program. Fred Rogers has received numerous awards besides his broadcasting awards. For example, the International Meditation Society awarded him the 1980 Maharishi Award, for enhancing the quality of individual and family life, and the American Academy of Pediatrics presented him with a Certificate of Merit in 1980. Rogers has received many honorary degrees from colleges and universities, such as Yale University, Hobart and William Smith, Carnegie Mellon, and West Virginia University. He has contributed articles to magazines like *Redbook, Parents' Magazine*, and *Today's Health*. He has made many recordings for children, produced by Small World Entertainment. An audio cassette he recorded, "Bedtime," was released in 1992. He has also made videos and written books for children with cancer, funded and distributed by the American Cancer Society. He has made videotapes preparing children for being in the hospital, having an operation, and similar experiences. He has written books for parents, such as *Mister Rogers Talks with Parents*, which was published in 1983. His latest book for adults, *You Are Special: Words of Wisdom from America's Most Beloved Neighbor*, was published in 1994.

Rogers lives in Pittsburgh with his wife and spends summer vacations swimming and boating on Nantucket Island in Massa-chusetts. He and his wife have two grown sons and two grandchildren, one born in 1988 and one in 1993.

SELECTED WORKS: The New Baby, 1985; Going to the Doctor, 1986; Making Friends, 1987; Moving, 1987; Going to the Hospital, 1988; When a Pet Dies, 1988; Going on an Airplane, 1989; Going to the Dentist, 1989.

ABOUT: Broadcasting and Cable July 26, 1993; Contemporary Authors, Vol. 107; Current Biography 71; Ladies' Home Journal December 1988; Life November 1992; Newsweek May 12, 1969; People Weekly May 15, 1978; Something About the Author, Vol. 33; TV Guide March 23029, 1985; Who's Who in America, 1994.

PAT ROSS

February 4, 1943–

AUTHOR OF *Meet M and M*, etc.

Autobiographical sketch of Patricia Kienzle Ross:

SOME WRITERS can look back on their early years and immediately pinpoint all the factors that influenced them in becoming writers of children's books. I don't feel entirely confident about doing this.

During my early years, I had a passion for the how-to variety of children's books. My favorite book was a jumbo paperback—a serviceable grey cover with simple bold type—called *What Can I Do Now, Mommy?* (Obviously, asking Daddy this question in the late forties was out of the question!) As a first grader, I adored Dick and Jane and Baby Sally. To this day, "Run, Spot, Run" fills me with as much rapture as the theme song from "The Lone Ranger," which I was allowed to listen to over the radio in the dark after lights out.

During my hazy adolescent years, I became the resident expert in thin-spined selections for book reports, *Goodby Mr. Chips* and *A Bell for Adano* being my all-time favorite skinnys. My ninth-grade teacher, observing my fondness for slim offerings, gave

my reading life new weight with her suggestion of *The Forsythe Saga*. At first, I was as much hooked by her interest in me as I was by Mr. Galsworthy. In time, I became hooked on books of any length. Though I've often wondered if my early penchant for a short and satisfying read inevitably influenced my choice of writing short pithy books for children who, sad to say, might just be something like me.

It was through simple osmosis that I discovered I had a flair for writing children's books. As an editor of children's books, I grew so fond of working with other writers' words that I suppose it was inevitable that I'd eventually try out my own voice. Many claim that editors are simply frustrated writers, and I can cite many examples, past and present. But perhaps the truth lies in the simple and common affinity for words, images, characters, imagination. . . .

My first book was published by the parent company I worked for from the late sixties through the early eighties—Random House. During the awesome and tumultuous sixties, I was a vocal part of the newly emerging women's movement. I did underground photocopying after hours without blinking twice, considering it my employer's moral contribution to the cause! I went braless when I shouldn't have, and stirred up local consciousness as well as notice.

Then one day, a well-respected editor approached me about compiling an anthology for young women that could be used in response to the need for female role models in young adult books. We discussed this exciting new project at the Harvard Club in New York City where my editor, a Radcliffe graduate, enjoyed dining privileges. Ironically, however, Radcliffe women were required to dine separately from Harvard men! So the chanelling of future womanhood was decided in part in a small dining room hidden away from the mainstream of the male world.

There's a happy feminist ending to this story. The resulting book, *Young and Female*, enjoyed an exceptionally long and prosperous life, lasting through two editions and many printings. Eighteen years later, my own teenaged daughter checked her mother's book out of the high school library for a women's studies paper.

My books frequently focus on the spirit, vitality, and challenges of girls. I'd like to think I weave these elements into their characters, as opposed to hitting readers on the heads. Perhaps because I come from a family where the girls and women have always outnumbered the men, and perhaps because I have a daughter, feisty and motivated female characters prevail in my books. I only know that this has always mattered to me.

In *Molly and the Slow Teeth*, Molly's mother, the ubiquitous tooth fairy disguised in maternal garb, tells her frustrated daughter, "Trust me!" in a confidential mother/daughter moment. Mandy and Mimi, the friends who yearn to merge as best friends, pretend they are twins in the M and M beginning-reader series. Together, they have gotten into funny troubles in eight small volumes and have, in turn, discovered their separate identities. A more serious story for slightly older readers is *Hannah's Fancy Notion*, in which a 19th-century girl shoulders adult responsibilities as she learns to rely on her own cleverness. Daring and pluck get Gloria through a harrowing robbery by a soap-gun bandit in *Gloria and the Super Soaper*, and Gloria's father is the one who runs for cover. And so, over the past twentysome years, without any particular plot or plan, I've written stories about strong girls and young women.

For many years, I wrote as more of an avocation or second career than a primary career. During the time I worked full-time in publishing, I had to find odd hours to write. Some of my most inspired characters and plots have occurred on trains and planes, the motion lulling me into a state conducive to earlier memories. During the eight years when I ran my own business—a demanding little retail shop on Madison Avenue specializing in American crafts—I arranged the shop's staffing so that I could spend longed-for time in my home office writing. For the past three years, I have finally been able to write for children and adults full-time.

Now my days are filled with uninterrupted promise.

———

Pat Ross was born in Baltimore, Maryland, and was raised on the Eastern Shore. She received her B.A. degree from Hood College in Frederick, Maryland, in 1965. She began her career in publishing at *Humpty Dumpty's Magazine* in 1965, and also worked for publisher David White before joining Random House as an assistant in 1967. She worked there for fourteen years, serving as division vice president and editor-in-chief of the Knopf-Pantheon Books for Young Readers department at Random House from 1980 to 1983. In 1983 she opened a shop in New York City, selling the work of American artisans. In 1986, *Working Woman* magazine published an article about the business.

Pat Ross has written over twenty adult books, some on the subject of handcrafts and home design, such as *Formal Country*

and *Country Entertaining*, and some in a line of diminutive gift books featuring vintage artwork. She also wrote and illustrated, with photographs, *Remembering Main Street: An American Album*, which represents her interest in American Culture. In 1993, she was named Hood College Distinguished Alumna of the Year.

M and M and the Big Bag was named a Children's Choice Book by the International Reading Association and the Children's Book Council. Both *M and M and the Bad News Babies* and *M and M and the Mummy Mess* were named Junior Library Guild selections.

SELECTED WORKS: Young and Female, 1972; What Ever Happened to the Baxter Place?, 1974; M and M and the Haunted House Game, 1980; Meet M and M, 1980; Molly and the Slow Teeth, 1980; M and M and the Big Bag, 1981; Gloria and the Super Soaper, 1982; M and M and the Bad News Babies, 1983; M and M and the Mummy Mess, 1985; M and M and the Santa Secrets, 1985; M and M and the Super Child Afternoon, 1987; Hannah's Fancy Notions, 1988; M and M and the Halloween Monster, 1991.

ABOUT: Contemporary Authors, Vol. 128; Roginski, Jim. Behind the Covers; Something About the Author, Vol. 48, 53.

SUSAN L. ROTH

Feburary 29, 1944–

AUTHOR AND ILLUSTRATOR OF *The Story of Light*, etc.

Autobiographical sketch of Susan L. Roth:

I REMEMBER my grandfather sketching the Brooklyn Bridge and me sitting next to him, drawing with all his pencils. I was very young then, maybe two or three. He stood my pictures on the easel next to his.

I remember when I was five, when my father brought home a huge box of shiny foil paper samples in twenty colors. There were tinsels and ribbons with tiny holes in them and papers with little cuts which, if you pulled gently from both sides, became

Susan L. Roth

golden fences. The shiny paper was all for me, to make things. I decorated the house. Even now, when I see fancy foils, I still feel a splash of that amazement.

My father was a graphic designer. There were always art supplies in our house. I think we lived in a rather frugal way, but if one of us wanted something for a creative project, there were no limitations. The philosophy was that you could only do your best work if you used good papers, good paints, good tools—even for ten-year-old artists (me) or even four-year-old artists (my brother). I still believe that.

We were taught that a real present was one that was made with our own hands. No one ever laughed at the offerings. Both my brother and I were encouraged and appreciated. The windowsills in the kitchen were full with modeling-clay animals, cut-paper sculptures, drawings.

I remember creative writing classes in high school. I had an indulgent English teacher whose job it was to teach us to do expository writing. We were supposed to write succintly, clearly, intelligently on some given subject. I never could do the assignment properly. I usually came up with a strange format or no punctuation or a fan-

tasy instead of an essay, but this teacher encouraged me anyway. When she encouraged me, I felt like trying harder and writing more and more.

In college, while I was studying studio art, art history, and writing, I made three children's books. I wrote them, illustrated them with woodblock prints, hand set the type and printed limited editions of each on a small letterpress.

I completed my masters of arts degree concentrating in printmaking. I made woodcuts and printed on top of tissue paper collages.

But I still didn't think seriously about writing and illustrating for children, and it never occurred to me that collage was my medium. I didn't know what I wanted to do.

In 1968, I began teaching Head Start in Washington, D.C. Not from political dedication, which was especially chic at the time, but really because I liked the children.

Then I met my husband. We got married and started to travel. I loved travelling and I still do. We have three children and they love to travel with us.

When I was not traveling, I taught art classes—from preschool to college. I knew that I did not want to teach forever, but I still didn't know at all what it was that I really wanted to do.

In 1984, my friend Ruth Phang and I collaborated on our first book for children, *Patchwork Tales.* This was followed by *We Build a Climber* in 1986. Then I started to burn with passion inside to write and to illustrate children's books. I still feel this passion with every book I do.

By 1988, Ruth was already doing other things and I began to work alone. Although I still love woodcuts, I prefer to work in collage. I love to write, but I don't mind making collages for someone else's story—if I like the words.

With every new book that I do, I still feel the thrill of the first one. I hope I'll be writing and illustrating children's books forever.

Susan Roth received a B.A. degree in 1965 and an M.A. degree in 1968 from Mills College in Oakland, California. She has taught printmaking at the Smithsonian Institution. She is a member of the Children's Book Guild of Washington, D.C.

Fire Came to the Earth People was named a 1988 Best Illustrated Book of the Year by *The New York Times. The Story of Light* and *The Great Ball Game* were both named Notable Children's Trade Books in the Field of Social Studies by a joint committee of the Children's Book Council and the National Council on the Social Studies.

SELECTED WORKS WRITTEN AND ILLUSTRATED: Fire Came to the Earth People, 1988; We'll Ride Elephants Through Brooklyn, 1989; (retold) The Story of Light, 1990; Gypsy Bird Song, 1991; Another Christmas, 1992. Princess, 1993; Creak, Thump, Bonk, 1995.

SELECTED WORKS ILLUSTRATED: Ishi's Tale of Lizard, translated and edited by Leanne Hinton, 1992; The Great Ball Game: A Muskogee Story, retold by Joseph Bruchac, 1994; How the Sky's Housekeeper Wore Her Scarves, by Patricia Hooper, 1995; How Thunder and Lightning Came To Be, retold by Beatrice Harrell, 1995.

MARISABINA RUSSO

May 1, 1950–

AUTHOR AND ILLUSTRATOR OF *The Line Up Book*, etc.

Autobiographical sketch of Marisabina Russo:

I was the first person in my family born in the United States. Everyone else had immigrated after surviving the most brutal World War II experiences. My mother's family was German/Polish and I heard a lot of German and Yiddish growing up. My father was an Italian naval architect. He left before I was born. We communicated by mail and later in person when I visited him in Italy.

Marisabina: *ma REE sa BEE na*

My mother always worked. I had lots of different babysitters and started nursery school at the age of two. My two brothers were much older than I was and they babysat me (not always willingly). I remember spending a lot of time playing alone in the living room. When I could hold a pencil I began drawing pictures—at first on the furniture and later on pads of paper my mother brought home from her office. I loved to draw.

I was a very shy little girl. In first grade I attended a strict Catholic school. There were about fifty children in the class. I don't remember talking to any of them. We moved and I transferred to a public school, where the principal placed me in a class with mostly foreign students. Coming from a bilingual family there were certain English words that were not part of my vocabulary yet. But my second-grade teacher encouraged me to write and by the fourth grade I had moved into a special accelerated class.

When I was nine my mother remarried. That was a major trauma in my life. For about a year I kept a secret diary where I expressed my intense hatred of my stepfather. I eventually came to realize that he was a kind and gentle man, so I gave up the diary, but I learned that writing was a good way for me to express my feelings. At age twelve I began keeping a journal which I have continued to this day.

In high school and in college I always studied art, painting, drawing, printmaking. After graduation I freelanced for many different magazines and newspapers. I wanted to illustrate children's books and showed my portfolio to lots of publishers, but my first published books were cookbooks. I got married and had three children. When the youngest was still a baby I published my first picture book, *The Line Up Book*.

My children have inspired many of my books. But I also get ideas from my own childhood, situations and feelings I still remember so vividly. Before *The Line Up Book* I had a hard time writing stories. I was looking for some elusive original idea floating out there in the sky. It was only when I realized that the best stories come from the author's deepest feelings and experience that I was able to find my own voice.

I still like painting the pictures the best. Making up the characters, placing them in different scenes, choosing the colors, decorating and designing the pages are so much fun. Sometimes I feel as though I'm still six years old, because I get the same happy feeling I did when I was a kid drawing in a steno pad.

———

Marisabina Russo was born in New York City. In 1971 she received her B.A. degree from Mt. Holyoke College in Massachusetts. When she was a freelance illustrator, she had spot drawings in *The New Yorker* and did five covers for the magazine. She has also had her illustrations published in many other magazines. The cookbooks she illustrated are *More Classic Italian Cooking* by Marcella Hagan; *Classic Indian Cooking* by Julie Sahni, and *From My Mother's Kitchen* by Mimi Sheraton.

Her work has been exhibited at the Bien-

nale Illustrations Bratislava in 1989. It was also represented in a show, "Picture Books Edited by Susan Hirschman" in Tokyo, Shizuoka, and Hiroshima in 1990, and in the New York Society of Illustrators gallery in 1992 and 1993. *The Line Up Book* won a 1987 International Reading Association Children's Book Award.

SELECTED WORKS WRITTEN AND ILLUSTRATED: The Line Up Book, 1986; Why Do Grown-Ups Have All the Fun?, 1987; Only Six More Days, 1988; Waiting for Hannah, 1989; Where Is Ben?, 1990; A Visit to Oma, 1991; Time to Wake Up!, 1994; I Don't Want to Go Back to School, 1994.

SELECTED WORKS ILLUSTRATED: Big Fat Worm, by Nancy Van Laan, 1987; A Week of Lullabyes, by Helen Plotz, 1988; When Summer Ends, by Susi Gregg Fowler, 1989; It Begins with an A, by Stephanie Calmenson, 1993; Bear E. Bear, by Susan Straight, 1995; Goodbye, Curtis, by Kevin Henkes, 1995.

ABOUT: The Reading Teacher February 1988; Teaching Pre-K-8 March 1988.

LOUIS SACHAR

March 20, 1954–

AUTHOR OF *There's a Boy in the Girls' Bathroom*, etc.

Biographical sketch of Louis Sachar:

LOUIS SACHAR was born in East Meadow, New York. When he was nine years old his family moved to Tustin, California. He enjoyed school and was a good student, and played in the Little League. Some of his favorite books were those by E.B. White.

Sachar had started to attend Antioch College in Ohio when he received word of his father's sudden death. He returned to California to be near his mother, and took a semester off. He had a short career selling Fuller Brushes door-todoor, at which he had "surprising success." He returned to school in Berkeley, California, majoring in economics. He enjoyed reading, especially Russian literature; but he did not like analyzing books in English classes. His favorite

Sachar: *SACK er*

Louis Sachar

authors include Kurt Vonnegut, E.L. Doctorow, J. D. Salinger, Tolstoy, and Dostoevsky. He became a teacher's aide by a fluke. He thought it sounded easy: He got college credit for helping out in an elementary school, and he had no papers to write or homework to do. But it ended up becoming his favorite class in college, and inspired him to try writing children's books. He received his B.A. degree from the University of California in 1976.

After college, he worked for a while in a sweater warehouse in Norwalk, Connecticut, and wrote at night. Then he went to law school, and his first book, *Sideways Stories from Wayside School*, was accepted for publication during his first week of school. This began a long struggle over being a writer or a lawyer. He earned his J.D. degree from Hastings College of the Law in San Francisco, in 1980. He recalls waiting up all night to see if he and his friends passed the bar exam, allowing them to practice law. He was not as excited as the others when he learned he had passed. He realized he had to get a job. He kept putting off getting that job, as he continued to write children's books. He supported himself by doing parttime law work until he stopped

practicing altogether in 1989 to become a full-time writer.

Sachar says he needs to be alone when he writes. He doesn't talk about a book until it's finished. He starts with "a little idea," often just a character trait. One idea will lead to another until it "snowballs" into a strong story. Since his stories aren't planned or outlined beforehand—he usually doesn't know what's going to happen next—he needs to do several drafts. His first draft is very unorganized, he feels, with ideas at the end that don't fit the beginning. When he writes the second draft he can organize it better because he knows from the start who all the characters will be and what's going to happen to them. By the time he does his sixth and last rewrite, Sachar will "try to convince myself that the story is all true, and that I am simply telling it, not making it up."

Sachar gets a lot of fan letters and visits schools, which helps him to keep in touch with kids somewhat, but he feels the contact is mostly superficial. He never gets to know the kids, the way he did when he worked as a teacher's aide. Most of his ideas come from what he remembers doing and feeling and thinking as a child. Sachar was married in 1985, and his daughter was born in 1987. He gets some ideas from her. The boy in *The Boy Who Lost His Face* has a one-year-old sister, and Sachar's daughter was one at the time. When she was four, he wrote the Marvin Redpost books, in which Marvin's four-year-old sister was based on her. The main themes in the Marvin Redpost series play on children's fantasies, as Sachar sees it. The main character is in third grade and thinks he was kidnapped at birth. He's convinced he is really a prince. Sachar enjoyed writing those stories because he feels children like to wonder about such things.

Louis Sachar spoke at San Joaquin County Authors' Symposium in October of 1988. His *Sideways Stories from Wayside School* was named a 1979 Children's Choice Book by a joint committee of the International Reading Association and the Children's

Book Council. He has also won many state awards voted upon by children. Sachar is a member of the Society of Children's Book Writers and Illustrators and the Authors Guild.

SELECTED WORKS: Sideways Stories from Wayside School, 1978; Johnny's in the Basement, 1981; Someday Angeline, 1983; Sixth Grade Secrets, 1987; There's a Boy in the Girls' Bathroom, 1987; The Boy Who Lost His Face, 1989; Wayside School Is Falling Down, 1989; Dogs Don't Tell Jokes, 1991; Marvin Redpost: Kidnapped at Birth?, 1992; Marvin Redpost: Is He a Girl?, 1993; Marvin Redpost: Why Pick on Me?, 1993; Alone in His Teachers' House, 1994; Wayside School Gets a Little Stranger, 1995.

ABOUT: Contemporary Authors (First Revision), Vol. 81-84; (New Revision Series), Vol. 15, 33; Something About the Author, Vol. 50, 63.

BARBARA SAMUELS

September 28, 1946–

AUTHOR AND ILLUSTRATOR OF *Duncan and Dolores*, etc.

Biographical sketch of Barbara Samuels:

BARBARA SAMUELS was born on Long Island, New York, and spent her childhood in Great Neck. Her mother, Mildred, was a homemaker and her father, Julius, worked at a wholesale fish market that was a family business. She remembers that she didn't see a lot of her father since he had to get up at 1:30 every morning to go to work. "There aren't many fathers in my books," she says. "They're usually taking a nap!

"My family was all very musical," remembers Samuels; her mother played the cello, her father played the violin, and she played the flute. In addition, she and her two older sisters all liked to draw. "They were much better than I was because they were older, and now I do it for a living." Her artistic family was always very supportive of her talents.

After earning a B.A. degree from the University of Wisconsin at Madison in 1968

and an M.A. degree in Education at Columbia University in New York in 1970, Samuels taught for a few years. "It was what everyone was doing, but teaching wasn't for me," she says. She decided to go to art school. She graduated in 1976 with a B.F.A. from the School of Visual Arts in New York. Her first job was in an animation studio, painting watercolor backgrounds, and she also worked on a film, *Raggedy Ann*. In addition, she began doing freelance illustration work.

In 1980, her first book was published. It was a humor book for adults, called *Copycat*. This was followed by several more humor books, including several cat books, a genre that was popular at the time. "I got into the children's book thing gradually," she says. She was inspired by writers like Edward Gorey. "Black humor—I have a streak of that," says Samuels.

Her first two children's book were *Faye and Dolores* and *Duncan and Dolores*. "*Duncan and Dolores* is about the rivalry between two sisters," she says. "I always seem to write about sibling rivalry! I just can't seem to stop writing about it." She based the character Faye on a combination of her two sisters, Susie and Freya. Samuels notes that in addition to writing frequently about sibling rivalry, cats keep making appearances in her work. *Duncan and Dolores* won a 1987 Christopher Medal and was a Reading Rainbow Book. *Duncan and Dolores* and *Faye and Dolores* were both named Children's Choice Books by a joint committee of the Children's Book Council and the International Reading Association.

Two more Dolores books were published, *Happy Birthday, Dolores* and *What's So Great About Cindy Snappleby?* Samuels illustrated all four books. A fifth is in the works, about Dolores and Halloween.

Samuels says her family was the inspiration for much of her work. "I always wrote about girls because of my sisters," she says. Since the birth of her son, she has had a new source of inspiration for her books. "My son really has the truck thing, half the time he *is* a truck!" she says. "I've been trying to do a truck book, trying to make the transition from writing about my own experience to writing about my son."

In addition to her own books, Samuels has illustrated works by other writers. She illustrated two picture books for very young readers, *Baby Comes Home* and *The Baby House*.

Samuels works in her studio in the New York apartment she shares with her husband, Nicholas Stern, a psychotherapist, and thier son, Noah. Although she had to cut back her hours when her son was born, she has continued to work on her books and to pursue her illustration career; she has done illustrations for women's magazines and *The New York Times*, among others. Mostly she works in watercolor, sometimes with an ink line, but she keeps experimenting. "I like to surprise myself. . . . I try to keep in moving," she says.

SELECTED WORKS WRITTEN AND ILLUSTRATED: Faye and Dolores, 1985; Duncan and Dolores, 1986; Happy Birthday, Dolores, 1989; What's So Great About Cindy Snappleby?, 1992.

SELECTED WORKS ILLUSTRATED: Baby Comes Home, by Debbie Driscoll, 1993; The Baby House, by Norma Simon, 1995.

SCOTT RUSSELL SANDERS

October 26, 1945–

AUTHOR OF *Bad Man Ballad*, etc.

Autobiographical sketch of Scott Russell Sanders:

IN ONE OF my earliest memories, I am toddling beside a railroad track and singing "Chattanooga Choo-Choo," imagining that if I sing hard enough, a train will come chugging along. In another early memory, I look up from the barn doorway to see a skyful of green tickets fluttering down from an airplane; I rush out to snatch one, and discover that the green paper is covered with neat black marks—a wonderful gift, if only I could read.

The place would have been our farm outside of Memphis, my first home, and I would have been two or three years old. Learning new words every day, hearing the music in speech, I already felt the magical power of language. When I was four, my sister taught me to read, and suddenly those ink marks on paper set whole worlds moving inside me. Before I was able to print block letters with a fat pencil, that same patient sister wrote down the wild, rambling tales I dictated to her.

All these years later, after filling twenty books with my own ink marks, I still feel the miraculous power in language. How extraordinary, that a few sounds or a few squiggles can rouse up people and voices and landscapes in our minds! Like sunshine, like the urgency of spring, like bread, language is so familiar that we easily forget what an amazing gift it is.

A child tumbles words on the tongue, rhymes them and chimes them, stretches them, toys with them, flings them about. Realizing that, when I began to write books for children after writing novels and stories for adults, instead of feeling limited by a younger audience, I felt liberated. I knew that children would savor language, knew they could make leaps of imagination that grown-ups might be too stiff to follow. As

a father, I knew that children can detect any whiff of phoniness, and they will not sit still for a story out of duty, but only out of fascination or, on the best occasions, out of love.

When I was a boy staving off sleep on that Tennessee farm, or later in a creaky house on a military arsenal in Ohio, my father would often sing to me about the exploits of John Henry or Casey Jones, the adventures of Yankee Doodle or Mr. Frog who went a-courting, song after song. Lying in bed with my father's voice drawn over me like a comforter, I made up stories to fill out those sketchy lyrics, and the tales and music twined together. When my own children came along, I sang to them and told them the stories I had been hearing in folk songs, and those stories became my first book for young readers, *Hear the Wind Blow*.

Until I went away to college, I did all my schooling in Ohio. I spent much time in the woods spying on animals or learning the trees, digging in creekbeds for fossils, walking plowed fields, on the lookout for arrowheads. The past seemed to me close by, and wildness lurked beneath the tame surface. I wanted to know how the land had been

shaped. I wanted to know how people had lived here, from the early hunters and gatherers to the French and English explorers, from the settlers who came on horseback or foot over the mountains, right up to the recent immigrants who came by airplane or car.

That fascination with the Ohio Valley, the Midwest, and the great fertile interior of America stayed with me through my undergraduate years in New England and my graduate years in Old England. After finishing a Ph.D. in literature at Cambridge, I returned home to teach at Indiana University, in Bloomington, where my wife and I have lived now for twenty years. Through a series of books I have been trying to share with children my curiosity about the past and my feeling for the land.

The first of these books was *Bad Man Ballad*, a historical novel about a bizarre murder case set on the frontier during the War of 1812. Then I began addressing the youngest readers through a series of picture books: *Aurora Means Dawn* portrays a homesteading family; *Warm as Wool* tells of a pioneer woman who buys sheep and uses spinning wheel and loom to clothe her children; *Here Comes the Mystery Man* follows a peddler who brings news as well as goods to frontier settlements; *The Floating House* concerns a journey by flatboat down the Ohio River; and *A Place Called Freedom* tells of a black farming community founded in the North by freed slaves.

In all these books, I am trying to help children imagine history through the sharing of past lives, especially the lives of families who made their way from tame regions into the wild heart of the continent. Whether writing about past, present, or future, I am inviting children to dwell in language, as I do, with wonder and with delight.

———

Scott Russell Sanders was born in Memphis, Tennessee. He spent his early childhood in that state and his school years in Ohio. He studied physics and English at

Brown University, graduating first in his class in 1967. With the aid of a Marshall Scholarship and a Danforth Fellowship, he did graduate work at Cambridge University, where he completed his Ph.D. in English in 1971. Since 1971 he has taught at Indiana University, where he recently won its highest teaching award. He spent a year as writer-in-residence at Phillips Exeter Academy, and another year as visiting scholar at the Massachusetts Institute of Technology. He has received fellowships for writing from the National Endowment for the Arts, the Indiana Arts Commission, the Lilly Endowment, and the Guggenheim Foundation.

He served two years as literary editor of *The Cambridge Review* and four years as fiction editor of *The Minnesota Review*. He has been a columnist and has written fiction and essays for many publications, including *Omni, Harper's,* and *Georgia Review.* His writing for adults includes a book of personal essays, *The Paradise of Bombs,* which won the Associated Writing Programs Awards for Creative Nonfiction. He has won many honors for his work for adults.

Here Comes the Mystery Man was named a Notable Children's Trade Book in the Field of Social Studies by a joint committee of the National Council on the Social Studies and the Children's Book Council. *Bad Man Ballad* was named a Best Book for Young Adults by the American Library Association. *The Floating House* was a Junior Library Guild selection.

SELECTED WORKS: Wilderness Plots, 1983; Hear the Wind Blow, 1985; Bad Man Ballad, 1986; The Engineer of Beasts, 1988; Aurora Means Dawn, 1989; Warm as Wool, 1992; Here Comes the Mystery Man, 1993; The Floating House, 1995.

ABOUT: Contemporary Authors, Vol. 85-88; (New Revision Series), Vol. 15, 35; Something About the Author, Vol. 56; Utne Reader May 1991.

DANIEL SAN SOUCI

October 10, 1948–

AUTHOR AND ILLUSTRATOR OF *North Country Night,* etc.

Autobiographical sketch of Daniel San Souci:

There was real excitement about literature in my home. In the evenings my mother would read to me from the Scribner's Classics. I would spend hours poring over the illustrations by Howard Pyle, N.C. Wyeth and other fine illustrators. But the most exciting day I remember was when my father gave me Howard Pyle's *Book of Pirates.* This book was published in 1921 and was his childhood favorite. It was unlike all the other books. It seemed gigantic to me, and it was really heavy to carry. But the best thing about this book was the wonderful illustrations, full of detail and action. I loved that book so much that I used to tuck it underneath my mattress so no one would ever steal it. I remember coming home one day and discovering it was gone. I knew that some robber stole it because there was a picture of a treasure map inside and I'd never get it back. As it turned out, my grandmother had made my bed and set it on my shelf. I have always felt that this particular book was the seed of my passion for illustrating children's books.

When my father gave me this book, it was a symbolic "passing of the torch." He had a wonderful talent—the kind of person who could pick up a pencil and draw anything. But as much as he wanted to be a professional artist, it just didn't work out that way. I think he saw a lot of himself in me. The more artistic ability I showed, the more excited he became. We did a lot of drawing together and he taught me everything he had learned. He always made sure I had art materials and books for inspiration. When I was in junior high school, he encouraged me to take an oil painting class at the local night school. There must have been forty years' difference in age between me and

San Souci: *San Sue See*

the other students, but it turned out to be a wonderful experience and I did learn a lot about painting.

When I was in high school, I traveled across town to the California College of Arts and Crafts to take weekend classes. This was a new experience for me, being around so many gifted students. It was at this point in my life that I started to realize what kind of effort it takes to compete in the art world. I felt like a medium-sized fish in a very big pond.

During this time, my brother Robert, who is a writer of many award-winning books, and I worked together on the high school newspaper. We really enjoyed working with each other, my illustrations for his articles. Years later, after college, we decided it would be fun to pool our talents and collaborate on a children's book. Bob had visited the Blackfeet reservation in Browning, Montana, and came back home with the idea of The Legend of Scarface. I worked up some ideas for illustrations, hopped on a plane to New York, and left the proposal with an editor at a publishing house. Months later, it was accepted for publication. I'll never forget the day I received the news—it was a dream come true!

The first book received wonderful reviews and was selected as a New York Times Best Illustrated Book and was a Horn Book-Boston Globe Award Honor Book. But the highest honor came from the Blackfeet People themselves. A review for the Reservation newspaper said that every Blackfeet family should own a copy of the book and read it to their children. Since The Legend of Scarface, I have illustrated over thirty-five children's books, and written four of my own. Among the changes that have taken place over the years, the most important concerns my integrity regarding my work. I have developed a reputation for being reliable, meeting deadlines and having a "good eye" for what works when putting a book together. This is really important for an artist. When I first started in this business, there was the concern to please the art directors, editors, etc., who seemed to have so much more experience than I did. Now I please myself first, knowing that with my knowledge, research, and experience as an artist and writer, I usually have the best feel for what makes a good book.

The research I do for my books usually involves some travel and hours of research in some of the Bay Area's wonderful libraries. I feel that if I have a sound foundation in research, then everything else will eventually fall into place.

All the information I accumulate seems to trigger my imagination. Characters and enfolding drama appear in my mind and soon I capture it all in thumbnail sketches.

My family also serves as a source of inspiration for my books. I don't lose touch with my audience, because the audience is right in my own house. I have three children, and I love to hear what they are interested in. In a lot of ways, I see myself in them. They really care about the same things I cared about as a kid. Sometimes I sit and listen to them talk, and it takes me back to my youth, and when I'm creating my illustrations, I get a real feel for what should be on the page. I've always felt that the children's book illustrator's real calling is to bridge the gap between the words in the story and the child's imagination.

———

Daniel San Souci was born in San Francisco and grew up across the Bay in Berkeley, California. He was married in 1980. He studied at California College of Arts and Crafts in Oakland and graduated in 1972. He has taught illustration classes at the California College of Arts and Crafts and at the University of California, Berkeley. He is presently on the faculty at the Academy of Art College. He has lectured at many colleges and universities across the country.

He is a member of the Society of Children's Book Writers and Illustrators. He has illustrated many book covers, including the C.S. Lewis *Chronicles of Narnia.* In 1989 his work was included in the 24th Exhibition of Original Pictures of International Children's Books in Japan.

The Legend of Scarface was named a Best Illustrated Book of the Year 1978 by *The New York Times.* It was also named a Notable Children's Trade Book in the Field of Social Studies by a joint committee of the Children's Book Council and the National Council on the Social Studies.

Song of Sedna was named a Notable Book by the American Library Association. *Sedna, Ceremony in the Circle of Life,* and *The Legend of Sleepy Hollow* were named Notable Children's Trade Books in the Field of Social Studies by a joint committee of the Children's Book Council and the National Council on the Social Studies. *Sedna* was also named a Children's Choice Book by a joint committee of the CBC and the International Reading Association.

North Country Night was named an Outstanding Science Trade Book for Children by a joint committee of the National Science Teachers Association and the CBC. *Trapped in Sliprock Canyon* received the 1985 Western Writers of America Spur Award given by the Western Writers of America.

SELECTED WORKS WRITTEN AND ILLUSTRATED: North Country Night, 1990; Country Road, 1993.

SELECTED WORKS WRITTEN BY ROBERT D. SAN SOUCI AND ILLUSTRATED: The Legend of Scarface: A Blackfeet Indian Tale, 1978; Song of Sedna, 1981; The Six Swans, 1988; Feathertop, 1992.

SELECTED WORKS ILLUSTRATED: Ceremony in the Circle of Life, by White Tree of Autumn, 1983; Trapped in Sliprock Canyon, by Gloria Skurzynski, 1984; The Little Mermaid, by Freya Littledale, 1986; The Ugly Duckling, by Lillian Moore, 1987; The Golden Deer, by Margaret Hodges, 1992; Muir of the Woods, by W. Douglas, 1993.

ROBERT D. SAN SOUCI

October 10, 1946–

AUTHOR OF *The Legend of Scarface*, etc.

Autobiographical sketch of Robert D. San Souci:

I WAS BORN in San Francisco, but grew up and went to school on the Berkeley-Oakland side of the Bay. I always knew that I wanted to be a writer. Before I knew how to read or write, I would listen carefully to stories that were read to me, then I would retell them to my younger brothers and sister, or to friends. But I would add new bits or leave out those I didn't find so interesting—so the storytelling impulse was already at work in me. Many of the books I work on these days are retellings of traditional tales from all around the world, including several that I grew up enjoying. I love to take these old stories and bring them alive for a new audience of young readers, often working closely with my illustrators in the process.

I was lucky to have an artist/illustrator in the family: my brother Daniel, who, though younger, shares the same birthdate (October 10) as I do. He and I have collaborated on eight books together. While we also work with other writers and illustrators, we plan to continue working together on a variety of future projects. I was also fortunate in

San Souci: *San Sue See*

having parents who were both book lovers, and who both supported wholeheartedly my decision to become a writer. A variety of teachers along the way added their support to my early writing efforts.

I wrote for the school newspaper when I was in grammar school, and for my high school yearbook. The most exciting thing that happened to me in high school was to see an essay of mine printed in a paperback book entitled *T.V. as Art*, when I was a sophomore. In college, I took a variety of classes in creative writing and English and world literature. In graduate school, I began to focus more on studies of folklore, myth, and world religions. My interest in these areas grows stronger and stronger.

As a budding writer, I supported myself with a variety of jobs, working as a bookseller, copywriter for several publishers, and book editor. All the time, I was writing: newspaper articles, book and theatre reviews, stories for magazines—almost anywhere I could get myself into print. It wasn't until I was out of college that I realized my lifelong dream, and published (after a number of failed attempts) my first book, which was also my first collaboration with Daniel. That book, *The Legend of*

Scarface, adapted from the traditions of the Blackfeet people, was first printed in 1978, and has never been out of print.

Since then, I have gone on to retell stories from all over. Even when I create a story from my own imagination, you'll usually find some ideas and images that have come from world mythology. My fascination with fairytales, myths, and legends, has grown into passion for exploring and sharing with others the treasures of world literature. I particularly appreciate the way folk literature can "open a window" on other times, places, ways of living and looking at the world. These tales often remind us how alike we are—yet, at the same time, they affirm how wonderful it is that people have so many different, imaginative, and insightful ways of making sense of the world and celebrating its wonders.

While I have no talent for illustration, I am happy to help my illustrators by searching out art references to help them create their paintings. During the often lengthy process of researching and rewriting my stories, I assemble a file of photocopies of images that may help an artist complete an illustration. I've delightedly supplied artists with pictures of Japanese cricket cages, California Miwok burden baskets, a deadly Caribbean snake, or what-have-you. While I have been consistently gratified with the variety of illustrations that have graced my books, I have always insisted that the details be culturally and historically accurate. Beyond that, I stand aside and let the artist follow his or her own vision for the book.

In recent years, I have visited several hundred schools to talk about how I write my books and to encourage up-and-coming authors and illustrators. One of the questions I'm sometimes asked by students is, How many more books do I plan to write? I tell them that I plan to keep on writing until I run out of ideas or until people lose a love of hearing and reading and sharing stories. Since storytelling has been with us since the dawn of history, and since every day provides me a wealth of new ideas for stories, I like to think that this means I'll be able to share lots more stories in the future.

———

Robert D. San Souci was born in San Francisco. He received his B.A. degree from St. Mary's College in 1968 and did graduate study at California University at Hayward from 1968 to 1970. He has worked as a book buyer, a bookstore department manager, and a promotion coordinator at a publishing company. He has been a contributor to several children's magazines, including *Faces, Cobblestone*, and *Calliope*. He is also a story consultant for film studios that specialize in entertainment for younger viewers and families.

San Souci has conducted classes and workshops at San Francisco State University and California State University at Fresno. Has given speeches at meetings of such associations as the American Library Association (the International Reading Association, and The National Council of Teachers of English. He lives in San Francisco and enjoys travel and collecting old children's books.

The Talking Eggs was named an Honor Book in the 1990 Caldecott Awards given by the American Library Association, as well as an ALA Notable Book. It was also awarded the 1989 Irma Simonton Black and James H. Black Award given by Bank Street College of Education. It was named an Honor Book for Illustration in the 1990 Coretta Scott King Awards.

The Legend of Scarface was named a Best Illustrated Book of the Year 1978 by *The New York Times*. It was also named a Notable Children's Trade Book in the Field of Social Studies by a joint committee of the Children's Book Council and the National Council on the Social Studies. Several of his other books have been named Notable Children's Trade Books in the Field of Social Studies by the NCSS/CBC committee, including *Cut from the Same Cloth, Song of Sedna, The Enchanted Tapestry, The Legend of Sleepy Hollow*, and *The Samu-*

rai's Daughter. Song of Sedna was also named an ALA Notable Book.

Sukey and the Mermaid was named an Honor Book for Illustration in the 1993 Coretta Scott King Awards and an ALA Notable Book. *Short and Shivery, Young Merlin,* and *Song of Sedna* were named Children's Choice Books by a joint committee of the CBC and the International Reading Association. *Cut from the Same Cloth* was named cowinner of the 1993 Aesop Prize, conferred by the Children's Folklore Section of the American Folklore Society. The award honors the children's book or books that best incorporate folklore in text and illustration.

SELECTED WORKS: The Christmas Ark, 1991; N.C. Wyeth's Pilgrims, 1991.

SELECTED WORKS RETOLD: The Legend of Scarface: A Blackfeet Indian Tale, 1978; Song of Sedna, 1981; The Enchanted Tapestry: A Chinese Folktale, 1987; Short and Shivery: Thirty Chilling Tales, 1987; The Talking Eggs, 1989; The White Cat, 1990; Young Merlin, 1990; The Legend of Sleepy Hollow, 1991; The Samurai's Daughter, 1992; Sukey and the Mermaid, 1992; Cut From the Same Cloth: American Women of Myth, Legend, and Tall Tale, 1993; Sootface: An Ojibwa Cinderella Story, 1994; The Faithful Friend, 1995.

ABOUT: Contemporary Authors, Vol. 108; Something About the Author, Vol. 40, 81.

DEBORAH SAVAGE

December 15, 1955–

AUTHOR OF *A Rumour of Otters*, etc.

Biographical sketch of Deborah Savage:

DEBORAH SAVAGE was born in Northampton, Massachusetts. When she was a girl she lived out in the country and read a great deal. She loved to draw and paint, and she wrote many stories.

She earned a B.A. degree from the University of Massachusetts in 1987. She was a teacher in an arts program at Alderkill camp in Rhinebeck, New York, in 1975. She then worked as a teaching assistant in a creative writing course at the University of Massachusetts in Amherst in 1977.

She taught creative writing to elementary school students at Wildwood School in Amherst in 1978. In 1987, she taught art at The Hotchkiss School in Lakeville, Connecticut. From 1988 to 1991, she taught English and art at The Forman School in Litchfield, Connecticut.

She has taught workshops in woodcut printmaking in various places in Massachusetts and in New Zealand, and several of her novels are set in New Zealand. She was a guest author and workshop presenter in the Brookline, Massachusetts, schools from 1987 to 1988. She has presented talks at the Northwest Corner Coalition for Nuclear Disarmament, the Massachusetts Association for Educational Media, the Boston Public Library Creative Writing Workshop, and the International Federation of Teachers of English conference.

Her woodcuts and watercolors have been exhibited at museums such as The Berkshire Museum in Pittsfield, Massachusetts; The Pratt Museum of Natural History in Amherst, the Auckland Institute and Museum in New Zealand, and the White Memorial Conservation Area Museum in Litchfield, Connecticut. The American Museum Association presented her with an Award of Merit in 1984. She lives in Amherst.

Deborah Savage has had her poetry published in periodicals such as *Dark Horse*, *Spectrum*, and *Cross Currents*. She has also contributed illustrations to periodicals including *Planning Quarterly* and *Cross Currents*.

To Race a Dream, Savage's novel set in 1906 about a fifteen-year-old who longs to drive harness racing horses, is based upon her grandfather's horse, the world's fastest harness racer, called Dan Patch.

A Rumour of Otters was named a Notable Book of the Year by the American Library Association.

SELECTED WORKS: A Rumour of Otters, 1986; Flight of the Albatross, 1989; A Stranger Calls Me Home, 1992; To Race a Dream, 1994.

ABOUT: Contemporary Authors, Vol. 143; Something About the Author, Vol. 76.

RAFIK SCHAMI

June 23, 1946–

AUTHOR OF *A Hand Full of Stars*, etc.

Autobiographical sketch of Rafik Schami:

I CHOSE my own name. The way it happened is a long story. "Rafik" means friend, companion or comrade. "Scham" is a pet name for the city of Damaskus. Officially, the city's name is Dimaschk, in other words, Damaskus, but most Arabs call it Scham. Experts have long been fighting over the origins of this name. They suspect that it stems from the Aramaic language because the Aramaic people were once spread throughout the Orient. A much loved and less precise, but all the more poetic, explanation is that Scham means birthmark in Arabic. The Arabs gave Damaskus this name because the green gardens at the city's center looked like a birthmark in the middle of the bright Arabian desert. For Arabs the birthmark is a sign of beauty. Thus Schami simply means a resident of Damaskus, like a New Yorker or a Bostonian.

My parents are Christians. They came from the Christian-Aramaic village of Malula, only 60 kilometers from Damaskus. However, for generations we have lived in Damaskus. In the summer we would go into the mountains for three months to stay in Malula.

My lifestory is very short. I was supposed to be a baker, but didn't like the flour and early hours. I thought that I would rather be a chemist and discover a formula for immortality, but instead I discovered that only literature makes one live forever, so, after seventeen years (1965—1982), I gave up my work in chemistry. Since then I have been working on the immortality question. You see, I can't stand death.

Rafik Schami
رفيق شامي

My role models could fill a caravan, including those men and women who wrote the best book of all time, the Bible. Then Scheherazade, Sokrates, Abu Nuwas, Jarir, Gorki, Chaplin, Garcia Marquez, Heine, Lichtenberg, Marina Zwetajewa, Feiruz, Mozart, Calvino, Woody Allen, Cervantes and more than two hundred others, all immortal.

My experience as an author in a foreign language: First of all, I had already had experience as a writer before I came to Germany. Among the necessities that I brought in my suitcase (besides passport and underwear) were two thick folders. One held about three hundred pages of fairy tales, short stories, and aphorisms, and the other held the outline of a novel about the freeing of South Africa. The novel still lies dormant, but many of those original stories and tales gradually appeared in German. The folder was a treasure trove, a well of immature stories that I slowly reworked and published. I never dreamed that I would one day write literature in a foreign language. German was after Aramaic and Arabic (my two mother-tongues), French (six years), English (ten years) and Russian (three months), the sixth language that I learned.

My voyage into the German language was fairly easy. Because I am very curious, I quickly learned how to speak. The language school soon became too slow for my curiosity and so, after the third month, I started to read books at home. The first book was The Little Prince by Antoine de Saint-Exupery. I had a shabby German-Arabic dictionary and with it, in a hideously damp room near Heidelberg, I read every word and line of that wonderful story. It was arduous work, but every night I was excited to have learned a little more from the "Little Prince."

For four years I read like a madman. I read everything, I mean everything, that I could lay my hands on, and slowly I started to write bits and pieces in German. To my surprise they sounded pretty good. At the same time it became clear that I could no longer return to Syria. This bitter realization pushed me to write more in German, as both my field of experience and reading public depended upon that language. My life circumstances, my work in chemistry, and my financial need would not allow me to write longer works. Instead, I would write a short story and put it away for several months, then retell it spontaneously and, if it didn't seem to flow correctly, change its fundamental structure.

Why I tell stories and don't read them: Firstly, story-telling is a deeply rooted tradition in my society. I don't have to push myself at all to tell a story. Also, I enjoy speaking to people and see the transformation in their eyes as they listen. I begin and my listeners are still wrapped up in their own world. Then after a while I sense how they are leaving time and space to experience the adventure of my fictional time and space. This moment of magic fills me with a peculiar sort of happiness. It is the best sort of payment I have ever received and one which no financial office of the world can reduce by taxation.

Would I be offended if my tales or stories were labeled kiddy-business? No, I am of the same opinion. Even the most sophisticated stories are kiddy-business, but I have a special relationship to children. It is one of respect. Only the child in us likes to hear stories and lies. Only the child in us can get mixed up in the game of the fictional world and its creations. An adult, who has stifled the child within him, cannot hear stories.

Why do I write? As a youth I dreamed of the great effect that my writing would have upon society. As I grew older, my goals grew more modest, so that at forty I could say that the reason I wrote was "so that people don't forget how to read." Since then, my earlier ambitions have reemerged, and now I cannot be saved from my dreams. I simply want to outwit death for a few more years. But I have a trick. I try to write so well that my books and my voice will live for a long time. This will make Death absolutely furious.

Also I experience great pleasure when I hear good stories, or even more, when I myself tell one. At no other time do I laugh so heartily as when writing a new funny story or comical episode.

————

Rafik Schami was born in Damaskus, Syria. He was a journalist from 1965 to 1970 and emigrated to the German Federal Republic in 1971. He worked at odd jobs while studying chemistry from 1971 to 1979, when he received his doctorate degree. He has been a contributor to newspapers and anthologies, co-publisher and author of the series "Sudwind-Gast arbeiterdeutsch," and co-publisher and author of the series "Sudwind-Literatur." He is co-founder of the literary group "Sudwind" and the "PoLiKunst" group. He had a theater piece produced in Germany in 1987, and he has had many children's books published in Germany. Translations of his works have appeared in fifteen languages.

A Hand Full of Stars, won the 1991 Mildred L. Batchelder Award, presented by the American Library Association. Schami has won many awards in Germany, Switzerland, and Austria, including the 1993

Adelbert-von-Chamisso-Preis in Germany in 1993 and the Hermann-Hesse-Preis in 1994, both in Germany.

SELECTED WORKS: A Hand Full of Stars, translated by Rika Lesser, 1990.

ABOUT: Journal of Youth Services in Libraries Fall 1991.

S.D. SCHINDLER

September 27, 1952–

ILLUSTRATOR OF *Is This a House for Hermit Crab?*, etc.

Biographical sketch of Steven D. Schindler:

STEVEN SCHINDLER was born and raised in Kenosha, Wisconsin. He enjoyed drawing when he was very young, and especially enjoyed drawing animals. He was known as the class artist in grade school. He recalls as an early artistic influence the artwork in *MAD* magazine, which he first read in grade school. When he was in high school, he sold some botanical drawings he had done at a local art fair. As he was successful in selling his work, he continued to sell his artwork at art fairs in Kenosha and in Philadelphia to help earn money for college.

Even though art was his interest, he attended the University of Pennsylvania with the intention of becoming a doctor, which his parents considered a more practical course of study than art. However, he knew, during his junior year, that he wanted to be an artist. He graduated in 1974 with a degree in biology and went to New York City to begin his career as an artist.

While he was showing his art in New York at an outdoor exhibit, an agent saw it, and arranged for him to illustrate textbooks, which he did for two years. He then illustrated his first children's book. Schindler has illustrated over forty children's books, and works on several at a time. He also works in several different styles of illustra-

S.D. SCHINDLER

tion. He also occasionally executes botanical drawings, and offers them for sale. He is "not crazy about" the trademark, licensed-character books he sees selling in great numbers in bookstores.

His interest in science has led him to create several ponds near his home in Philadelphia. He created two formal ponds with lillies and goldfish near his house; and in a more wooded area nearby, he diverted a stream to make three small ponds, where he hopes that frogs and toads will thrive. He has obtained cocoons to repopulate the woods with Saturnid silk moths, a species that suffered when the area was sprayed to kill gypsy moths in the past. They are four to six inches wide with their wings spread. He also imported tadpoles of local species, which have hatched. His wife and fifteen-year-old stepdaughter don't share his enthusiasm for the amphibian propagation.

One of the books he recently illustrated, *If you Should Hear a Honey Guide*, concerns just this kind of subject matter, which Schindler enjoys: in it a bird brings a man to a bee hive, so that the man can have the honey and the bird can have the comb.

S. D. Schindler received the 1989 Carolyn W. Field Award, presented by the Youth Services Division of the Pennsylvania Library Association, for *Catwings. Is This a House for a Hermit Crab?* won a 1991 International Reading Association Children's Book Award.

Don't Fidget a Feather! was named a Notable Book of the Year by the American Library Association. *Is This a House for Hermit Crab?* was a Reading Rainbow selection.

Three of Schindler's books have been named Children's Choice Books by a joint committee of the IRA and the Children's Book Council: *Catwings, Catwings Return,* and *Not the Piano, Mrs. Medley!*

SELECTED WORKS ILLUSTRATED: The First Tulips in Holland, 1982; Every Living Thing, 1985; Children of Christmas: Stories for the Season, by Cynthia Rylant, 1987; Catwings, by Ursula K. Le Guin, 1988; Catwings Return, by Ursula K. Le Guin, 1989; The Three Little Pigs and the Fox, retold by William H. Hooks, 1989; Is This a House for Hermit Crab?, by Megan McDonald, 1990; Not the Piano, Mrs. Medley!, by Evan Levine, 1991; Whoo-oo Is It?, by Megan McDonald, 1992; Don't Fidget a Feather!, by Erica Silverman, 1994; Wonderful Alexander and the Catwings, by Ursula K. Le Guin, 1994; If You Should Hear a Honey-Guide by April Pulley Sayre, 1995; The Smash-Up Crash-Up Derby, by Tres Seymour, 1995.

ABOUT: Something About the Author, Vol. 50, 75.

ANN SCHWENINGER

August 1, 1951–

AUTHOR AND ILLUSTRATOR OF *Wintertime,* etc.

Autobiographical sketch of Ann Schweninger:

I HAVE ALWAYS loved to draw. One of my earliest memories is of drawing: I was very young and still in the scribbling stage as far as drawing anything goes. I didn't yet understand how to translate what I was seeing onto paper in a way that looked like anything that could be recognized. Then one day I was turning the pages of a magazine and saw an illustration of some flowers,

a tree, a house, and the sun, all drawn in the simplest childlike way. At once I saw how the visual world could be organized with simple lines. I began to draw, and not just scribble. I could express myself, and communicate that expression to other people. That experience was so important: I felt I had found a place in the world.

All through my childhood I drew just about every day. By the time I was in high school I knew that I wanted to illustrate children's books. The feel of a book, the turning of pages, the sequential unfolding of a story, had great appeal to me then, as they do now.

I grew up in Colorado and stayed there for several years after high school to major in art at the University of Colorado. Then I transferred to California Institute of the Arts and graduated in 1975. I moved to New York City to be near publishers and to study children's book illustration with Uri Shulevitz. He taught a workshop in Greenwich Village, and I found a secretarial job in an office to support myself, and took his workshop for four years. There was a small group of about twelve students, and he gave all of us a great foundation for illustrating children's books.

The first book that I wrote and illustrated, *A Dance for Three*, is a wordless picture book published by Dial Books for Young Readers in 1979. Since then I've done more than forty books, ten of which I have written myself.

Each book, whether I have written it, or it is by another author, begins with a sketch dummy: a mock-up of the book made by stapling paper together creating a spine and pages that turn. Using tracing paper, I draw fairly finished sketches. The tracing paper helps me to work out the composition. I draw a character or object on one piece of paper and move it around under another larger piece to arrange the various elements in each illustration. When the finished sketches are taped into the dummy the editor and art director look at it and suggest ways to clarify and improve. I revise, sometimes several times, and when the sketches are ready, I do sample watercolors to work out a color palette and submit those to the publisher too. Often there are suggestions that help me to improve the color of art. For me, a book is a cooperative project that I share with the editorial and art people at the publisher's. We put our experience and sensitivity together, always focusing on what is best for the book.

Finally, it is time to paint. I transfer the sketches onto watercolor paper by tracing with pencil on a lightbox. A lightbox is a wooden box several inches high with a piece of frosted plexiglass on top and florescent light tubes inside. It illuminates watercolor paper making it transparent enough that the sketch shows through. Once the tracing is done, I begin to paint, using a variety of watercolors. I also use graphite and colored pencils and perhaps pen and ink to define outlines.

Once I begin this final stage of creating the finished art, I am on my own. The publisher doesn't see the outgoing art until I deliver the finished book. The paintings take two, three, or four months of full-time work, depending on the complexity of the book.

———

Ann Schweninger was born in Boulder, Colorado. She, her two sisters and three brothers, and her parents lived in two small towns in the Colorado Rockies. When she was ten, the family moved to Boulder. Schweninger attended the University of Colorado from 1969 to 1972, majoring in art, then transferred to California Institute of the Arts, graduating with a B.F.A. degree in 1975. She moved to New York City where she studied with Uri Shulevitz and took painting lessons from Peter Hopkins, a painter. She and her husband have since moved to rural upstate New York, where she enjoys the room for work space and room to keep the animals she loves: cats, birds, and three tortoises.

SELECTED WORKS WRITTEN AND ILLUSTRATED: Christmas Secrets, 1984; Halloween Surprises, 1984; Valentine Friends, 1988; Wintertime, 1990; Autumn Days, 1991; Summertime, 1992; Springtime, 1993.

SELECTED WORKS ILLUSTRATED: Thump and Plunk, by Janice May Udry, 1981; The Read-Aloud Treasury, compiled by Joanna Cole and Stephanie Calmenson, 1988; Tales of Amanda Pig, by Jean Van Leeuwen, 1983; Oliver Pig at School, by Jean Van Leeuwen, 1990; Oliver and Amanda's Halloween, by Jean Van Leeuwen, 1992; The Make-Something Club, by Frances Zweifel, 1994.

ABOUT: Contemporary Authors, Vol. 107; Something About the Author, Vol. 29.

JON SCIESZKA

September 8, 1954–

AUTHOR OF *The Stinky Cheese Man and Other Fairly Stupid Tales*, etc.

Biographical sketch of Jon Scieszka:

JOHN SCIESZKA was born in Flint, Michigan. He graduated from Albion College with a B.A. degree in 1976. He had been studying a pre-medicine course and was accepted at Johns Hopkins Medical School, but he was also accepted at Columbia University for their School of the Arts graduate

Scieszka: *Shess Ka*

JON SCIESZKA

writing program. He and his wife, who is an art director, decided upon Columbia and he earned his M.F.A. degree in 1980.

He has had various jobs, such as painter and carpenter. He had originally intended to be a writer of novels. Then was "sidetracked," as he puts it, by teaching first and second grade. For many years he was an elementary school teacher at The Day School in New York City.

Scieszka came to write books for children by "hanging out with second graders," he told Stephanie Zvirin in a *Booklist* magazine interview. The children in his class wrote stories and read a lot, and after he met illustrator Lane Smith, he decided to take a year off from teaching and try to write his own books. He painted an apartment for a lawyer who, when he learned that Scieszka wanted to write, offered him an empty office to work in. For a year he used the office like an artist's studio in which to write.

During this year he wrote *The True Story of the Three Little Pigs*, and he and Smith collaborated on a dummy book, with the art and text roughly sketched in. Because of the unusual nature of the book, which was a parody of fairy tales, it was rejected by several houses, but he knew children would like it. "Turning something upside down or doing something wrong is the peak of what's funny to second graders," he told Zvirin.

Regina Hayes, an editor at Viking, knew and liked Lane Smith's artwork, but didn't have a story for the illustrations. Smith showed Scieszka's manuscript, and Viking published it. It sold out in the first few weeks. It offers an alternate, comic explanation of the story's familiar events, as told to Scieszka by "A. Wolf."

In *The Stinky Cheese Man*, also illustrated by Lane Smith, the table of contents falls and crushes everyone, and a title page is filled with the text of a discussion of assorted fairy tale characters, in different type fonts and sizes. The book was designed by Molly Leach. Critic Roger Sutton described the book as having a "new sensibility," stating in a review in *The Bulletin of the Center for Children's Books* that children can appreciate the parody of the tales. They can "cherish Cinderella," he writes. "The fondness for the first is the only thing that allows us to laugh at the second."

Jon Scieszka and Lane Smith collaborated on six other books, including the "Time Warp Trio" series, which includes *The Knights of the Kitchen Table, The Not-So-Jolly Roger, The Good, the Bad, and the Goofy, Your Mother Was a Neanderthal,* and *2095.*

Scieszka wrote another book that expands and distorts a fairy tale, *The Frog Prince, Continued.* It was illustrated by Steve Johnson. His *Math Curse*, illustrated by Lane Smith, was conceived as a way to write a funny book about math, and it was inspired, he says, by the way some of his "less accomplished" students viewed the world of mathematics.

The Stinky Cheese Man was named an Honor Book in the 1993 Randolph Caldecott Medal awards, given by the American Library Association. It was also named an ALA Notable Book of the Year, and a 1992 Best Illustrated Book of the Year by *The*

New York Times. The True Story of the Three Little Pigs won the Silver Medal from the New York Society of Illustrators. *The Book That Jack Wrote* and *Math Curse* were named Book-of-the-Month Club selections, as were three of the Time Warp Trio books.

SELECTED WORKS: The True Story of the Three Little Pigs, 1989; The Frog Prince, Continued, 1991; Knights of the Kitchen Table, 1991; The Not-So-Jolly Roger, 1991; The Good, the Bad, and the Goofy, 1992; The Stinky Cheese Man and Other Fairly Stupid Tales, 1992; Your Mother Was a Neanderthal, 1993; The Book That Jack Wrote, 1994; 2095, 1995; Math Curse, 1995.

ABOUT: Booklist September 1, 1992; Contemporary Authors, Vol. 135; Publishers Weekly July 26, 1991; Something About the Author, Vol. 68; Teaching PreK-8 May 1992.

BRENDA SEABROOKE

May 21, 1941–

AUTHOR OF *Judy Scuppernong*, etc.

Autobiographical sketch of Brenda Seabrooke:

AS A WRITER I have been influenced by a childhood spent exploring the woods near my house and listening to grown-ups' conversation and stories. I grew up during WW II in south Georgia, where people spent long hours talking on shady porches or in front of crackling fires. I can still hear the cadences of their voices, their personal expressions punctuated with the creaking of porch swings, gliders, and rocking chairs. I wrote about those times in *Judy Scuppernong* and its sequel *Under the Pear Tree.*

My mother and I were often alone at night while my father, a doctor, was away on housecalls. We didn't have TV and my mother didn't care much for radio, but she loved to read. Before I learned, she read to me. Sometimes when I took my book to her, she was engrossed in her own and didn't

Brenda Seabrooke

want to stop reading, so she put me in her lap and read hers aloud to me. I loved the sound of the words and still remember snatches of her books, *Sea of Grass*, *The Egg and I*, and *Green Dolphin Street*. On Sundays I sat in my father's lap and he read the colored comics to me. My favorite was, of course, "Brenda Starr, Reporter."

Parents were discouraged from teaching their children to read then in Fitzgerald, Georgia, because they might teach the wrong method. I desperately wanted to learn and memorized all of my books so that I could pretend to read them aloud. In the first grade I joyfully entered the world of Spot and Sally and Dick and Jane. I gulped books, all the comics, classics, horror, cowboy, Little Lulu, Wonder Woman, as well as encyclopedias and schoolbooks (which I always read the first day of school, except for math). Several times a week I rode my horse to the library and left him tied to the telephone pole in the alley. I could only check out four books at a time. I rode home with the books tucked under one arm and read them immediately unless I had to practice the piano or do homework.

I started writing stories when I was four, picture stories before I learned to write, po-

etry in the first grade. In high school I wrote for the school newspaper, the weekly *Fitzgerald Herald* and the *Atlanta Constitution*'s Saturday teen page, and I edited the high school yearbook. But I didn't start seriously writing stories until I was in my mid-thirties. I wrote on an old portable typewriter, sitting on the living room floor while my children, their friends, our dogs and cats, and half the neighborhood, it seemed, jumped over me on the way in and out of our house. I learned to concentrate on my stories while answering questions and directing traffic.

Perhaps because we moved so much, place is important, sometimes almost a character in my stories. My husband was in the Coast Guard so we lived around the perimeter of the country in houses as divergent as a twenty-three-foot travel trailer (two months) and an 18th century fort, on islands, a farm, and now on over two hundred acres of woods. Our last house in Virginia was the inspiration for *The Haunting of Holroyd Hill*.

When I was a child stories gave me insight and comfort, amused me and made me happy and allowed me to experience lives different from my own. I hope that my stories do that now for other children.

I wanted to be an explorer when I grew up. I think I am. Writing for me is an act of exploration.

———

Brenda Seabrooke was born in Mt. Dora, Florida, and grew up in Fitzgerald, Georgia. She received her B.A. degree from Newcomb College in New Orleans in 1963. She taught high school history and later substituted in "everything from Head Start to Mechanical Drawing".

Brenda Seabrooke is a 1994 recipient of a literary fellowship in fiction from the National Endowment for the Arts and the 1994 Sophie de Liedel fellowship from Emerson College—*Ploughshares*.

Her first book *The Best Burglar Alarm* was named a Children's Choice Book by a joint committee of the International Reading Association and the Children's Book Council. *Judy Scuppernong* was an Honor Book in the 1991 *Boston Globe-Horn Book Awards*. *The Bridges of Summer* was named a Notable Children's Trade Book in the Field of Social Studies by a joint committee of the CBC and the National Council on the Social Studies. It was also a Junior Library Guild selection.

SELECTED WORKS: The Best Burglar Alarm, 1978; Home Is Where They Take You In, 1980; Judy Scuppernong, 1990; Jerry on the Line, 1990; The Boy Who Saved the Town, 1990; The Chester Town Tea Party, 1991; The Dragon that Ate Summer, 1992; The Bridges of Summer, 1992; The Haunting of Holroyd Hill, 1995; Looking for Diamonds, 1995; The Swan's Gift, 1995.

ABOUT: Contemporary Authors, Vol. 107; Something About the Author, Vol. 30.

PAMELA F. SERVICE

October 8, 1945–

AUTHOR OF *The Reluctant God*, etc.

Autobiographical sketch of Pamela F. Service:

WHEN I was growing up in Berkeley, California, and adults asked the usual question, there were many exciting things I wanted to be when I grew up—none of which was a writer. What's more, I was a slow reader and a terrible speller (I still am), so a literary career seemed less than likely. Still, I loved making up stories just for fun or to tell my schoolmates. Teachers said I had an outrageous imagination. When I finally got my reading and writing act together, I enjoyed writing plays and stories to satisfy assignments. No straightforward subject would do, however. It had to be something weird—monsters, or UFOs or time travel, etc.

Just the same, I never thought of that sort of thing as a career option. I wanted to do neat stuff like politics or archaeology, and

eventually I got degrees in both subjects. But I still liked reading science fiction and fantasy, and ideas kept popping into my head for stories of my own. When I finally finished going to school (kindergarten through masters degree makes nineteen years!), I wrote some stories down. Then, being a goal-oriented sort, I decided to try to publish them.

Fortunately I am also stubborn. Eight years of rejection slips later, I sold my first short story to *Isaac Asimov's Science Fiction Magazine*. Six years and countless more rejection slips after that came the first book sale.

But still I wasn't thinking of writing as a career. I made use of those political science and archaeology degrees working in museums and on various campaigns. Then in 1978, the year of my first story sale, I became curator of the new history museum in Bloomington, Indiana, the town my husband, daughter and I had made home, and a year later I ran for and was elected to a seat on the city council. When I finally began publishing books fairly regularly, I found myself with three careers: politician, historian and writer. To this I added a fun but time-consuming involvement in amateur theater.

I now have fifteen books published, all science fiction and fantasy for young people (I still gravitate toward the weird). At the same time I am serving my fourth term on the city council, continuing as an historian, and am an enthusiastic if not particularly talented amateur actress. So, as much as I would like to spend more time writing, I would hardly call myself a full-time writer.

Nor do I think that I'd want to be. Some of my best ideas for books come from the other things I do with my life, as well as from that outrageous imagination my teachers alternately complained about and praised. Excavations in the Nile Valley, artifacts of the past, politics at home and in space, ghosts and murderers in theater, and the mysteries of ancient Britain—all have arisen from things I've done and places I've been, and have taken form in my stories.

I suppose I still don't know how to answer that question "what I want to be when I grow up". A little bit of a lot of things, I think. And if my writing can bring a glimpse of those exciting things to young readers, then I guess I *am* doing what I want.

———

Pamela Service was born in Berkeley. She received her B.A. degree in Political Science from the University of California at Berkeley in 1967 and her M.A. in African prehistory from the University of London in 1969. She has lived in England, Germany, and the Sudan, but has lived in Bloomington for twenty-five years. She met her husband during a political campaign in Berkeley, and he continues working professionally in campaigns. They have a daughter, Alex, who studies Vikings in England. Pam Service is a member of the Society of Children's Book Writers and Illustrators.

In addition to fiction, Service writes newspaper columns, magazine articles, brochures, and book chapters about local history and museum work. She has a short story anthologized in *Orphans of the Night*, a collection of stories based on creatures from the worlds of myth and folklore, edited by Josepha Sherman.

Her first book, *Winter of Magic's Return*, was published in 1985 and was named a Junior Library Guild selections, as were *Tomorrow's Magic*, *Stinker from Space*, and *The Reluctant God*. The latter was named an honor book in the 1988 Golden Kite Awards, given by the Society of Children's Book Writers and Illustrators.

SELECTED WORKS: Winter of Magic's Return, 1985; A Question of Destiny, 1986; Tomorrow's Magic, 1987; The Reluctant God, 1988; Stinker from Space, 1988; Under Alien Stars, 1990; Being of Two Minds, 1991; Weirdoes of the Universe, Unite!, 1992; All's Faire, 1993; Stinker's Return, 1993; Phantom Victory, 1994; Storm at the Edge of Time, 1994.

ABOUT: Contemporary Authors, Vol. 120; Something About the Author, Vol. 64.

NANCY SHAW

April 27, 1946–

AUTHOR OF *Sheep in a Jeep*, etc.

Autobiographical sketch of Nancy Shaw:

THE STORIES I WRITE about silly sheep start with woolgathering. When I daydream, I gather bits and pieces of ideas and put them together in new ways. The habit might go back to the ten-hour car trips our family made when I was growing up. I have two sisters and a brother. We'd fidget on the way to our grandparents' home in Rochester, New York. To pass the time, our family would play word games, including one where you rhymed two words and gave people clues to guess what your combination was—the sillier, the better. Often I get ideas for stories when I'm stuck somewhere—in a car, or at a meeting—and my mind starts to wander. At least one rhyme in a sheep book goes back to about fourth grade, when I was trying to amuse myself on a trip by drawing monsters. One monster fed himself by vacuuming up mustard custard. Over thirty years later when my sheep

NANCY SHAW

went to a restaurant, they put mustard on custard.

My family lived first in Pittsburgh; then in Midland, Michigan, where I remember climbing the pin-cherry trees in the nearby fields, playing outdoors in a neighborhood filled with starter homes and starter trees, sounding out words, and going to the library. My family's slogan was "Use your imagination." And we had to—we didn't own a television set until I finished third grade. I read Freddy the Pig books, *My Father's Dragon*, *Mrs. Piggle-Wiggle*, *The Good Master*, *Half Magic* and *Ellen Tebbits*. (I felt just like Ellen.) I loved Uncle Scrooge comics, which brought history, geography and mythology together with great jokes and impressive drawing.

In those days I wanted to be a ballet dancer or an artist. My grandfather was art director for a printing company, and a fine watercolorist. My grandmother sang in a rich voice while canning peaches and hooking rugs. My sister and I visited them in Rochester during the summers. Eventually Grandpa bought himself a Ben Franklin-style printing press, which he kept in the basement to print woodcuts; and a couple of times he helped us make our own prints.

They also took us to cottages, first on Lake Ontario, and later on Keuka Lake—an old house on a wooded hill, with rows of grapevines nearby. Sometimes we produced newspapers or home movies with our cousins while we hung around the lake. In junior high I wrote and drew comic strips.

My brother ended up as the artist in the family; I veered off toward words, sometime around high school, and went on to study English literature in college. I immersed myself in Shakespeare and Victorian novels.

A part-time job during college, shelving books at the Ann Arbor Public Library, renewed my interest in children's books. About that time I tried making up my first children's stories; but I never succeeded in writing one that was published until years later, after I had done some writing for newspapers and a radio show, and after I had children of my own, and made a habit of reading to them aloud. They loved silly stories.

In 1982 we were driving to visit my husband's parents, a four-hour trip, and I'd used up the stack of books I'd brought to read to our six-year-old and almost three-year-old. After reading animal rhymes aloud, I started to make up my own, and became so intrigued with the many rhymes for "sheep" that I challenged myself to see if I could make a story out of them. Eventually, I did. I took two and a half years, though, to find the exact wording for *Sheep in a Jeep*.

Sounds are always important when I make up a sheep story. If I start with the plot, and search for sounds to fit it, the process may not work. I like writing about the sheep because I get to be goofy with them—goofier than I get to be in my everyday life. If you worry about making mistakes, you can imagine somebody who makes sillier mistakes than you would. The sheep certainly do!

I enjoy talking with other writers and working with words. I visit schools and talk about writing. I still love to read—

mysteries, other novels, books about our society, newspapers, and of course, children's books.

———

Nancy Shaw was born in Pittsburgh, Pennsylvania. She received her A.B. degree from the University of Michigan in 1968 and her M.A.T. degree from Harvard University in 1970. She received the Jule and Avery Hopwood Award from the University of Michigan in 1968, which was awarded for a pair of essays she wrote. The honor is awarded to a writer who is a University of Michigan student.

She is a member of Authors Guild, the American Association of University Women, Phi Beta Kappa, and the Society of Children's Book Writers and Illustrators.

SELECTED WORKS: Sheep in a Jeep, 1986; Sheep on a Ship, 1989; Sheep in a Shop, 1991; Sheep Out to Eat, 1992; Sheep Take a Hike, 1994.

ABOUT: Something About the Author, Vol. 71.

NEAL SHUSTERMAN

November 12, 1962–

AUTHOR OF *What Daddy Did*, etc.

Autobiographical sketch of Neal Shusterman:

I am often asked why I write, and it's a hard question to answer. After a great deal of thought, I've come to the conclusion that writers are a lot like vampires. A vampire will never come into your house uninvited—and once you invite one in, he'll grab you by the throat, and won't let you go. A writer's much the same—feeding on the speed of your heart as it races; feeding on your tears and your sighs.

I suppose that's why I write—because I want to affect people—somehow change them for the better. I think most writers, deep down, have some hidden desire to change the world. They want to paint a pic-

ture of the possibilities—to show people the many things that are possible out in the world, or just within ourselves—both the good and the bad.

I've always felt that stories aimed at adolescents and teens are the most important stories that can be written, because it's adolescence that defines who we are going to be. That's the time when we choose paths for ourselves that are going to shape and define the rest of our lives.

Books played an important role in my life when I was growing up. I always loved reading. I remember a trick I would play for my friends; they'd blindfold me, then shove a book under my nose, and I could tell the name of the publisher by the smell of the paper and ink.

There were many books that had a powerful influence on the things I thought about, and how I made sense of the world. I distinctly remember when I was ten, waiting for my parents to pick me up after summer camp. Being the last kid there and with nothing else to do, I went back into the cabin, and climbed on the rafters, looking for trouble . . . but instead found a dust-covered copy of *Jonathan Livingston Seagull*, that appeared to have been there since the beginning of time. I opened the book, began reading, and was swept away by the story of the seagull in search of perfect flight. I read the book cover to cover, and the second I was done, my parents arrived—it was as if the book was left there just for me!

Around the same time, I read *Charlie and the Chocolate Factory*. I remember being awed by the fact that someone had actually thought of a story so clever. I remember wishing that I could create something as imaginative as *Charlie and the Chocolate Factory*, and as meaningful as *Jonathan Livingston Seagull*. In many ways that thought is still with me when I sit down to write.

A few summers later, I saw the movie *Jaws*, and decided that I was going to be Steven Spielberg, so I wrote a story about a seashore town that was attacked by shark-like man-eating sand-worms. It was terrible. But when I turned it in to my English teacher on the first day of eighth grade, she challenged me to write a story each month for extra credit. I rose to the occasion, and by the end of eighth grade I felt like a writer.

Things do come full circle, I suppose. When I was in college, I went back to that same summer camp I went to as a kid, this time as a counselor. I became known as the camp storyteller, and would make up tales to tell the kids at night. Some of those stories became books a few years later—*The Shadow Club*, and *The Eyes of Kid Midas*.

Being a bit too dramatic for my own good, on the day I left the camp for the last time, I took a copy of *Jonathan Livingston Seagull* and threw it up on the rafters. I wonder who found it.

———

Neal Shusterman was born and raised in the heart of Brooklyn, New York, where he began writing at an early age as a creative alternative to stickball.

When he was eight years old, he wrote to E. B. White, kindly suggesting that *Charlotte's Web* ought to have a sequel, and that Neal would be happy to help write it. White wrote back, sadly declining to collaborate on a sequel as he felt the story was complete as it stood. He advised Shusterman to keep on writing anyway, and he did.

After growing up in New York, Shusterman moved with his family to Mexico City, where he graduated from high school. He earned degrees in Psychology and Drama from the University of California in 1985. He lives in Southern California with his wife and two children.

The Shadow Club was named a Children's Choice Book by a joint committee of the International Reading Association and the Children's Book Council. *What Daddy Did* won the same honor, as well as being named a Notable Book of the Year by the American Library Association and winning many awards voted upon by young people.

SELECTED WORKS: The Shadow Club, 1988; Dissidents, 1989; Speeding Bullet, 1991; What Daddy Did, 1991; The Eyes of Kid Midas, 1992; Scorpion Shards, 1995.

ABOUT: Contemporary Authors, Vol. 133.

DIANE SIEBERT

March 18, 1948–

AUTHOR OF *Train Song*, etc.

Autobiograpical sketch of Diane Siebert:

I THINK I'll cut right to the chase. One afternoon in 1971 when I was twenty-one and six months out of nursing school, I realized that my unconventional childhood had left me totally unprepared to live a conventional life, and that I was becoming bored stupid in my attempt to do so.

Fortunately, my husband was feeling stuck in a rut of his own, so we hatched a plan: we would sell whatever possessions we could, buy two motorcycles, and set off to see America. And that's exactly what we did.

Diane Siebert

For the next ten years we travelled around the United States and Mexico on our trusty bikes, stopping to work whenever the money ran out and saving enough to get back on the road. We camped in the mountains, on beaches, beside rivers, in deserts, on the outskirts of big cities, and once, when the temperature dipped to below twenty degrees in Colorado, in a campground laundry room. We had close encounters with everything from bears and buffaloes (exciting!) to unfriendly cops in Louisiana (exciting, but in a completely different way . . .). We met hundreds of interesting people, gained a real appreciation for America's wildlife and natural resources, and fell off our motorcycles now and then. And each night I wrote in a journal. I wrote about what I was seeing and hearing and about all that was good and all that was bad. Some of it came out in prose, some in poetry, and some in song. Then one day in 1977, just for fun, I sent one of the poems to a little magazine called *American Candlemaker*. This poem, my first submission, was bought and published (just before the magazine folded), and the $2.00 I was paid inspired me to keep submitting.

By the end of the decade our journey be-

gan to wind down. Obsessed with the West and its wide open spaces, we settled, for a while, in the Mojave Desert. By this time I had become a fair long-distance runner, a mediocre classical guitarist, a rampant environmentalist, and a poet whose work was starting to get published in an assortment of magazines for children and adults.

In 1982 I turned my love of rhythm, rhyme, and road into a song about trucks. I sent it as a children's book to Harper & Row, went to Greece to run the Athens Marathon, and came back to find that the manuscript had been accepted for publication. The book *Mojave* was written next, the words coming to me one day as I sat with one of my dogs in the shade of a creosote bush beneath an endless stretch of blue sky. Soon, encroaching humanity pushed us north to a more remote area, where I continued to write poems and "songs" about the places and things I knew best. An old poem inspired by long training runs along the railroad tracks with my dogs was resurrected and became a book called *Train Song*. An environmental battle and threats from hostile neighbors resulted in *Sierra*.

I'm pleased that my work is getting published, but I'm sort of mystified, too. I've had no formal education in the field of writing and I feel out of my element in the "literary world." I have no children and have never written specifically for children. I just write. I write down what I hear and see and feel all around me and within me, whether I'm out at my tiny, remote cabin or running with my dogs on the trail or travelling down the highway on my motorcycle with the white lines streaking by. I try to capture on paper the songs that creep into my mind and hope that the music keeps on playing. And I hope the readers will feel the rhythms along with me and perhaps discover new ones of their own.

———

Diane Siebert was born in Chicago, Illinois. She is a registered nurse. Married in 1969, she and her husband now live in central Oregon with six dogs and their pet rats. They enjoy a "constant parade" of wildlife that visits the wildlife habitat they have created on their property. Siebert is passionate about running, playing the guitar, motorcycling, and the environment, and recently went skydiving for the first time.

Truck Song was named a Notable Book of the Year by the American Library Association, a Reading Rainbow Book, and a Notable Children's Trade Book in the Field of Social Studies by a joint committee of the National Council on the Social Studies and the Children's Book Council. *Mojave*, *Heartland*, *Train Song*, and *Sierra* were also named NCSS/CBC Notable Books. *Train Song* was named an ALA Notable Book.

Train Song, *Sierra*, and *Plane Song* were all named Outstanding Science Trade Books by a joint committee of the CBC and the National Science Teachers Association.

SELECTED WORKS: Truck Song, 1984; Mojave, 1988; Heartland, 1989; Train Song, 1990; Sierra, 1991; Plane Song, 1993.

ABOUT: Who's Who in America, 48th ed.

JANICE LEE SMITH

JANICE LEE SMITH

May 12, 1949–

AUTHOR OF *The Kid Next Door and Other Headaches*, etc.

Autobiographical sketch of Janice Lee Smith:

I HAD the great good sense to be born into a wonderful town of storytellers, liars, eccentrics, and scoundrels. Minneola, Kansas, population 700, was neighbor to Dodge City and was steeped in the lore and character of the Old West. When I was a child, there were still lots of those around who claimed to have fought the battles of settling the high prairie, known the famous and infamous, and been eyewitnesses to astounding things. It was folklore at its funniest and most outrageous, and our daily lives were filled with stories, legends, and amazing lies.

Naturally, I started telling great whopping stories myself when I was very young. Unable to find a satisfactory audience who would sit still and listen for hours, I would wage kidnapping campaigns, luring or dragging every dog, cat, and small child within range into my playhouse to serve as a captive audience. I would then sit on them to improve their listening skills.

My favorite scoundrel was my best friend, Jimmy, the proverbial kid next door. Two years older than I, he had a scientific mind, a kind heart, and a wicked sense of humor, all reasons we were often in trouble. When I was four, after a day of listening to me grumble about the fact that my long curly hair wouldn't fit beneath my cowboy hat, he neatly solved the problem by cutting it all off for me. I was absolutely delighted at the fit of my hat and, forgetting reality, strutted in to show my mother. When I finally made it out of the house again, I went looking for Jimmy to share a little reality. I got revenge by sitting on him and making him eat a box of dog biscuits. I got even better revenge by marrying him when we grew up.

Married at nineteen to an up-and-coming corporate whiz kid meant a lot of moves, so it took me eight years, two babies, and four colleges to get my degree. I graduated from Douglass College of Rutgers University in 1977. I won a *Mademoiselle* magazine Guest Editorship the same year, and spent a wonderful month in New York, being introduced to the literary scene. Sylvia Plath had recorded the same experience in *The Bell Jar*. She didn't have as much fun, but then she wasn't on a vacation from two pre-schoolers. A lovely result of the month was a first book about a boy named Adam Joshua signed with HarperCollins, and the editorial mentoring of Charlotte Zolotow.

Our two children, Bryan and Jaymi, take after their father and are nicely eccentric. They became hilarious inspirations for my books, and I found I never even had to leave my house to come up with ideas that delighted me. After walking by the bathroom door and seeing Jaymi, age four, in the bathtub with her boots on, I put Nelson in the bathtub wearing boots. After weeks of chuckling through Bryan's Superman phase, I wrote a story called *The Superman Kid*. While no one character is modeled on a particular child, personality quirks and traits from each member of our family show up in all my book people.

I loved having a way to chronicle my children's lives as they grew, and they gleefully endured having a mother who laughed and took notes about their escapades rather than yelling. With Bryan and Jaymi grown now, I rely on my notes about them to get a funny perspective on the world for my books. I am also waiting, as patiently as possible, for nicely eccentric grandchildren.

———

Janice Lee Smith graduated magna cum laude from Rutgers. She has been writing since 1978. She has also worked in Lee-Smith Enterprises, a land development company, since 1988. She is a member of the Society of Children's Book Writers and Illustrators. She received a Bread Loaf Conference Scholarship in 1981 for children's writing and a Bread Loaf Fellowship in 1982. She received a Master Fellowship Grant from the Indiana Arts Commission and the National Endowment for the Arts in 1984, for *The Show-and-Tell War*.

The Show-and-Tell War and *The Kid Next Door* were both named Children's Choice Books by a joint committee of the Children's Book Council and the International Reading Association.

SELECTED WORKS: The Monster in the Third Dresser Drawer and Other Stories About Adam Joshua, 1981; The Kid Next Door and Other Headaches: More Stories About Adam Joshua, 1984; The Show-and-Tell War and Other Stories About Adam Joshua, 1988; It's Not Easy Being George: Stories About Adam Joshua (And His Dog), 1989; The Turkeys' Side of It: Adam Joshua's Thanksgiving, 1990; There's a Ghost in the Coatroom: Adam Joshua's Christmas, 1991; Nelson in Love: An Adam Joshua Valentine's Day Story, 1992; Serious Science: An Adam Joshua Story, 1993; The Baby Blues, 1994; Wizard and Wart, 1994; Wizard and Wart at Sea, 1995.

ABOUT: Indianapolis News August 7, 1984; Something About the Author, Vol. 54.

LANE SMITH

August 25, 1959–

ILLUSTRATOR OF *The Stinky Cheese Man and Other Fairly Stupid Tales*, etc.

Biographical sketch of Lane Smith:

LANE SMITH has always loved the more macabre side of things, probably, he says, because he had such a well-adjusted childhood. Halloween was his favorite time of the year. "I must have been the only kid in elementary school who collected tapes of old-time radio shows like *The Shadow*," he writes in a 1993 *Horn Book Magazine* article. "I loved that whole theater of the mind."

Drawing was always Smith's talent in school. Although he was born in Tulsa, Oklahoma, most of his childhood was spent

in the foothills of Corona, California, with his parents and his brother Shane. In junior high school, because of his affinity for superheroes in comic books, he thought that he would be a cartoonist. He recounts many influences for his work. Both he and his frequent collaborator, Jon Scieszka, credit the British television show, "Monty Python's Flying Circus," as well as *MAD* magazine. And among Smith's other influences are Disney films such as *Snow White* and the 1967 animated version of *The Jungle Book*; the animation director Tex Avery, famous for having his cartoon characters' eyeballs pop out of their heads; Buster Keaton; and Robert Benchley.

Smith graduated from the California Art Center, College of Design. He was interested in Pop Art and the European aesthetic, but advertising art was taught at the school. When influences from European art and from art of the 1940's and 1950's came out in his work, his instructors warned him that he would not find work in America. But by then the "punk/new-wave" artistic movement had arrived, and his work, he said, "fit acceptably into that category." Smith graduated with a B.F.A. degree in 1983.

He moved to New York in 1984 and had a portfolio of illustrations to take around to magazine art directors. He did illustration by day, and at night, he learned to paint by creating paintings of the alphabet with a Halloween theme. He took them to the Macmillan Children's Book Department, and Eve Merriam wrote verse to go with the illustrations. The book, *Halloween ABC*, was published in 1987. Unfortunately, Smith states, it was immediately banned and even labelled 'satanic.' There *is* a definite dark side to my work," he writes, "But there are certainly antecedents for it: N. C. Wyeth was really dark, as was Arthur Rackham." The book prompted debate, and his work was defended in magazine editorials.

Smith met Jon Scieszka through Molly Leach, a book designer and art director. The two of them collaborated on a dummy book, in which the art and text are roughly sketched in. It was rejected by "everybody," he says, until editors at Viking Press saw it. This book—*The True Story of the Three Little Pigs*—sold out in the first few weeks. A parody of the famous story, it offers an alternate, comic explanation of events, as told to Scieszka by "A. Wolf."

In *The Stinky Cheese Man*, also written by Scieszka, the table of contents falls and crushes everyone, and a title page is filled with the text of a discussion of assorted fairy tale characters, in different sizes and type fonts. The book was designed by Molly Leach. Critic Roger Sutton, writing in *The Bulletin of the Center for Children's Books*, described a "new sensibility" in the book, a new kind of storytelling. Kids, he wrote, don't need to be cynical to understand the book. They can "cherish Cinderella" as well as appreciate its parody. "The fondness for the first is the only thing that allows us to laugh at the second. It's cultural literacy with the ante upped. . . . "

Scieszka and Smith went on to collaborate on six other books, including the "Time Warp Trio" series, which includes *The Knights of the Kitchen Table*, *The Not-So-Jolly Roger*, *The Good, the Bad, and the*

Goofy, Your Mother Was a Neanderthal, and *2095.*

Lane Smith works in oil on illustration board. He obtains a textured effect by acrylic paints or sprays. Sometimes, if the painting gets very thick, he sands down areas to another layer. He believes that the collage he sometimes adds is a natural extension of his affinity for texture.

He still considers himself an illustrator, not only a children's book illustrator. He still works for magazines, and does animation. Lane Smith lives in New York City.

The Stinky Cheese Man was named an Honor Book in the 1993 Randolph Caldecott Medal awards, given by the American Library Association. It was also named an ALA Notable Book of the Year, and a 1992 Best Illustrated Book of the Year by *The New York Times. Halloween ABC* was also named a *New York Times* Best Illustrated Book of the Year, in 1987.

The Big Pets was awarded a 1991 Golden Apple Award by the Biennale of Illustrations Bratislava. Both *The Big Pets* and *The True Story of The Three Little Pigs* won the Silver Medal from the New York Society of Illustrators.

Glasses (Who Needs 'Em?) was named an ALA Notable Book. *Math Curse* was named a Book-of-the-Month Club selection.

SELECTED WORKS WRITTEN AND ILLUSTRATED: Flying Jake, 1989; The Big Pets, 1990; Glasses (Who Needs 'Em?), 1991; The Happy Hocky Family!, 1993.

SELECTED WORKS WRITTEN BY JON SCIESZKA AND ILLUSTRATED: The True Story of the Three Little Pigs, 1989; Knights of the Kitchen Table, 1991; The Not-So-Jolly Roger, 1991; The Good, the Bad, and the Goofy, 1992; The Stinky Cheese Man and Other Fairly Stupid Tales, 1992; Your Mother Was a Neanderthal, 1993; 2095, 1995; Math Curse, 1995.

ABOUT: Booklist September 1, 1992; Bulletin of the Center for Children's Books October 1992; Cummings, Pat, comp. and ed. Talking with Artists; Horn Book January 1993; Publishers Weekly July 26, 1991; Something About the Author, Vol. 76.

VIRGINIA DRIVING HAWK SNEVE

February 21, 1933–

AUTHOR OF *Betrayed*, etc.

Autobiographical sketch of Virginia Driving Hawk Sneve:

I WAS BORN and raised on the Rosebud Sioux reservation in South Dakota. Storytelling was part of my American Indian culture, and it was an easy step to begin writing the stories I heard as a child. But I didn't think of writing for children until my daughter, in elementary school, became enchanted with Laura Ingalls Wilder's "Little House" books and excited about their South Dakota setting in Desmet, not too far from where her father grew up. She asked questions about the locale and the early settlers, "Was this the way the Sneve homesteaders lived?"

In order to answer her, I read the books. Always interested in history, I enjoyed them. But the reference to Indians in *Little House on the Prairie*—"The naked wild man stood by the fireplace . . . Laura smelled a horrible bad smell . . . Their faces were bold and fierce."—made me wonder what ideas my daughter was acquiring about Indians in the fiction she read. Then I began to wonder how my children viewed their own Native American relatives in South Dakota.

At that time we lived in Iowa, and our visits to family on the Dakota reservations were only a few days in the summer— usually during a Pow Wow or Sun Dance time. We'd make a brief stop to see my Grandma Driving Hawk, then went on to Uncle Harvey's in Pine Ridge. My son, Paul, was fascinated with Uncle Harvey, who took him fishing and horseback riding, and told him stories. Back at home, unbeknownst to me, Paul told his pals that Harvey hunted buffalo from a horse, and was a fierce warrior.

Uncle Harvey was coming to visit us, and Paul eagerly anticipated their arrival. He and several of his buddies camped on the

Sneve: rhymes with *navy*

VIRGINIA DRIVING HAWK SNEVE

edge of our driveway to welcome Harvey, who came riding up in an air-conditioned automobile, and was wearing sports shirt, slacks, and shoes.

Later, a mother of one of Paul's friends said that they had been furious with Paul. Harvey wasn't an Indian; he looked just like anybody's uncle.

I was amused, yet dismayed. I wanted my children to have positive and accurate information about their American Indian heritage. I knew that they wouldn't learn much about them in school. I had taught from the same texts that either ignored the Indians' place in the United States, or briefly mentioned the wars with savages that hindered western movement. I began to read children's literature and found that Indians were a popular theme, but always of the past—brave boy warriors and noble princesses who often saved white settlers from other Indians, who were brutal savages.

Up to this time (the 1970s) I had been writing for adults, but when I found that my children were getting wrong facts and false images about American Indians, I began writing for them and for all children.

All of my adult life I have been involved in education from kindergarten through college. My writing is an extension of being an educator because I strive to be honest and accurate about the Native American experience portrayed in my work. In so doing, I hope to dispel stereotypes and to show my reading audience that Native Americans have a proud past, a viable present, and a hopeful future.

———

Virginia Driving Hawk Sneve was born and raised on the Rosebud Reservation, South Dakota, and is an enrolled member of the Rosebud Sioux tribe. She attended Bureau of Indian Affairs day schools on the reservation and graduated from St. Mary's High School for Indian Girls, Springfield, South Dakota, in 1950. She received a B.S. degree in 1954 and an M.Ed. degree in 1969 from South Dakota State University in Brookings.

She taught music and English at White Public High School and in Pierre Junior High; and English, speech, and drama at the Flandreau Indian School. She later served as a guidance counselor there. She has worked as a consultant producer-writer for South Public TV, and as an editor for Brevet Press in Sioux Falls. She was also a counselor at Rapid City Central High School and an associate instructor in English for Ogalala Lakota College Rapid City Extension. She has written several books for adults, including *South Dakota Geographic Names* and *They Led a Nation*. Her short stories have been published in magazines and anthologies.

She is married to Vance M. Sneve, retired from the Bureau of Indian Affairs. The Sneves have three children and four grandchildren.

Betrayed won the 1994 Western Writers of America Spur Award for fiction.

SELECTED WORKS: High Elk's Treasure, 1972; Jimmy Yellow Hawk, 1972; Betrayed, 1974; When Thunders Spoke, 1974; The Chichi HooHoo Bogeyman, 1975; The Navajos: A First Americans Book, 1993; The Sioux: A First Americans Book, 1993; The Seminoles:

A First Americans Book, 1994; The Iroquois: A First Americans Book, 1995.

SELECTED WORKS EDITED: Dancing Teepees: Poems of American Indian Youth, 1989.

ABOUT: Contemporary Authors, Vol. 49-52; (New Revision Series), Vol. 3; McElmeel, Sharron L. Bookpeople: A Multicultural Album; Something About the Author, Vol. 8.

GARY SOTO

April 12, 1952–

AUTHOR OF *Baseball in April*, etc.

Biographical sketch of Gary Soto:

GARY SOTO

GARY SOTO is a poet, essayist, fiction writer, and film producer. He was born in Fresno, California, the son of Mexican-American parents. His whole family worked as farm laborers around Fresno, or took such jobs as working in the packing houses of raisin companies. Soon after a move to a new house when he was five, Soto's father died in a factory accident at the age of twenty-seven. Soto and his brother and sister were raised by his mother and grandparents.

The neighborhood they lived in was an urban Latino one. Soto did not have books at home, and he was not much interested in schoolwork. He graduated from high school in 1970, and, faced with the prospect of making $1.65 per hour, he applied to Fresno City College, where he began to study geography. He received an A.A. degree from the institution in 1972.

While in school, he encountered a poem that had a great effect upon him: "Unwanted," by Edward Field. The poem made clear to him that alienation was not unique to himself but was common to humanity. He also realized that he wanted to express himself as a writer. He read a collection of poems called *The New American Poetry*, edited by Donald Allen. The book influenced him to begin writing his own po-

etry, and besides Edward Field, he admired the poets Gregory Corso, Kenneth Koch, Theodore Roethke, and Gabriel Garcia Marquez. He attended California State University in Fresno, where he studied with the poet Philip Levine. He earned his B.A. degree in English, magna cum laude, from the University in 1974. He was married in 1975.

Soto received the Discovery-*Nation* Prize in 1975. He received his M.F.A. degree in Creative Writing from the University of California in 1976. He was named 1976 Graduate Student of the Year in Humanities at the University, and in 1976 won the U.S. Award of the International Poetry Forum. In 1977, his first book of poetry, *The Elements of San Joaquin*, was published. It was followed by *The Tale of Sunlight* in 1978. The same year, he received the Bess Hokin Prize from *Poetry* magazine. He twice won National Endowment for the Arts Fellowships for Creative Writing, and he was awarded a Guggenheim Fellowship in 1979.

From 1979 to 1985 Gary Soto was Assistant Professor of English and Ethnic Studies. He then became Associate Professor from 1985 to 1992. Since 1992, he has been a half-time Senior Lecturer in the English Department there. Soto continued to write poetry, but also began to publish prose. His *Living up the Street: Narrative Recollections*, for adults, came out in 1985. After he wrote it, he received mail from his readers, which allowed him to feel a kinship to them. The book was reissued in 1992. His book of memoirs, *Small Faces*, was published in 1986. A collection of autobiographical essays about his childhood, *Lesser Evils: Ten Quartets* was published in 1988, and he had a novel for adults published in 1994, *Jesse*. He won a National Book Award in 1995.

Baseball in April is the first of Soto's books to be published for children. It was named a Best Book for Young Adults by the American Library Association. He followed it with *Taking Sides* in 1991, and its sequel, *Pacific Crossing*, in 1992. He then began to publish poetry for young readers: *A Fire in My Hands* and *Neighborhood Odes*, which was named a *Hungry Mind Review* Children's Book of Distinction. He has also written a picture book, *Too Many Tamales*, which was named a Notable Children's Trade Book in the Field of Social Studies by a joint committee of the National Council on the Social Studies and the Children's Book Council.

Soto continues to write for adults and children, and he produces short 16mm films. He has been a speaker at conferences, such as the Shenandoah University-sponsored "Using Literature from Many Cultures" in 1995 and the Northern California Children's Booksellers Association in 1991, on the topic "Publishing Multicultural Books for Children and Young Adults in the 1990's." His poetry appears in many anthologies, including *Modern Poems: A Norton Anthology*, and in magazines like *Poetry, The Nation*, and *Ontario Review*. He has served as a juror in many literary awards competitions and contributes articles and short stories to many publications.

Soto lives in Berkeley, California, with his wife and daughter.

SELECTED WORKS: Baseball in April and Other Stories, 1990; Taking Sides, 1991; A Fire in My Hands: A Book of Poems, 1992; Pacific Crossing, 1992; The Skirt, 1992; Neighborhood Odes, 1992; Too Many Tamales, 1993; Boys at Work, 1995; Canto Familiar, 1995; Chato's Kitchen, 1995; Summer on Wheels, 1995.

ABOUT: Acevedo, Maria, ed. The Illustrated Hispanic American Profiles; Contemporary Authors, Vol. 119, 125; Copeland, Jeffrey S. Speaking of Poets; Gallo, Donald R. Speaking for Ourselves, Too; Hungry Mind Review Fall 1992; Reading Teacher November 1992; Something About the Author, Vol. 80.

GENNADY SPIRIN

December 25, 1948–

ILLUSTRATOR OF *The Fool and the Fish*, etc.

Autobiographical sketch of Gennady Spirin:

THE FIRST TIME I saw a real artist's studio I was enraptured by the sight: statues of mythological gods, torsos and capitals, beautiful still lifes, easels and canvasses, paint boxes with beautiful paints and brushes—all of this cast the magical spell of art on my soul and the overwhelming desire to be there. It turned out that students were accepted into the studio from the age of eight. I was only six at the time, but completely unexpectedly they made an exception for me, this to my great joy and the joy of my grandmother who had brought me there at my request and who played a key role in my becoming an artist, although she herself had no relation to art and probably understood little about it, but who loved her grandson very much. The other extraordinary circumstance was that the people studying at the studio were my father's age and older. In this exceptional situation I was warmly accepted like a son by these adults who watched over me from the very first moment of my studies.

I was born and lived in Orekhovo-Zuevo, a small textile-producing town outside Moscow. The entire studio consisted of workers

from the textile factories who came to study art after working hours and on free days. The atmosphere of love for art, the talent of these people, and, finally, the director whom I took to be nothing less than a magician—all of this made the world of art my life—in spite of my enthusiasm for soccer, and the disappointment of my father who now assumed a secondary role in my development.

The choice was made. At the age of eleven I entered the school of my childhood dreams—the Moscow Art School at the Academy of Arts. In spite of the tremendous competition (the admission rate was approximately 10 to 1), I successfully completed the examinations in drawing, painting, and composition, and was admitted into the first level. I remained at this school, which is located directly across the street from the renowned Tretiakov Gallery, for seven unforgettable years. The level of education I received there was such that although I was in competition with students of the best art institutes, I experienced no difficulty gaining admission into an art establishment of higher education.

In order to study and live in Moscow I needed money and my grandmother gave

her entire pension for my education. I now recognize this to have been unquestionably an act of heroism. Art school was the major school of my life. I lived in a dormitory together with tens of children from the entire country: Siberians, Asiatics, people from the Caucuses. I had many friends. We learned from each other and were guided by outstanding pedagogues.

I envisioned myself as a painter and this raised no doubts in anyone, but unexpectedly in my final year I developed an allergy to oil paint. I switched to tempera and watercolor, and studied graphics for the first time in earnest. This circumstance determined my selection of a higher education establishment. This became the "Stroganovka" as we called it. The "Stroganovka" was attractive because of the variety of its departments and faculty: monumental painting, graphics, ceramics, glass, metal, wood, architecture. I wanted to devour everything at once.

The five years at the "Stroganovka" flew by imperceptibly, with "excursion-like" ease without augmenting my professional skills but significantly expanding my knowledge of various technologies. This was interesting and at times absorbing, but as they say, this was no longer my first love.

Having received my diploma as a freelance artist, this is what I remained until the end of the seventies when I suddenly decided to try my hand at illustration. This is what I continue to do with great pleasure to this very day, having become firmly established as an illustrator, specifically of children's books.

I illustrated several books for the Moscow publishing houses "Children's Literature" and "Book," most of which have been reprinted in Europe and the United States. One of my books of the "Moscow period" received the Golden Apple Prize in 1983 in Bratislava. From 1984 on I have worked only with Western publishers, principal among which have been New York-based Dial Books and Philomel Books. Thanks to their taking part in my fate I now live and work in Princeton, New Jersey. I have come to love America, where I can work peacefully and productively, and its people. The son who was born here is already an American, a symbol of my new life.

———

Gennady Spirin was born in the small town of Orekhovo-Zuevo near Moscow. From 1960 to 1967 he studied at the Moscow Art School at the Academy of Arts. From 1967 to 1972 he studied in the Moscow Stroganov Institute. Since 1979 he has illustrated children's books. His first book was published in 1979 in Moscow. He won the Golden Apple Award at the Biennale of Illustration in Bratislava in 1983 for the book *Marissa and the Gnomes*.

The Fool and the Fish was named a Best Illustrated Book of the Year by the *New York Times*. *Gulliver's Adventures in Lilliput* later received the same honor.

In 1991 Spirin received the honor of Fiera Di Bologna for his book *Sorotchintzy Fair*. He was awarded th VI Premio Internacional Catalonia d'Il.lustració de Llibres per a Infants, deliberated upon by a seven-member international jury, for *Kashtunka*. The New York Society of Illustrators awarded him a gold medal for *Boots and the Glass Mountain* in 1992. He received the same honor for *The Children of Lir*. *Once There Was a Tree* was also named an Outstanding Science Trade Book for Children by a joint committee of the National Science Teachers Association and the Children's Book Council.

Gennady Spirin lives in Princeton, New Jersey, with his wife and three children.

SELECTED WORKS ILLUSTRATED: Once There Was a Tree, by Natalia Romanova, 1985; The Tale of the Unicorn, by Otfried Preussler, 1989; The Fool and the Fish: A Tale from Russia, by Alexander Nikolayevich Afanasyev, retold by Lenny Hort, 1990; The White Cat, retold by Robert D. San Souci, 1990; Rumpelstiltskin, by Jacob and Wilhelm Grimm, retold by Alison Sage, 1991; (as Gennadij Spirin) Sorotchintzy Fair, by Nikolai Gogol, adapted by Sybil Schoenfeldt, 1991; Snow White and Rose Red, by Jacob and Wilhelm Grimm, 1992; Boots and the Glass Mountain, retold by

Claire Martin, 1992; The Children of Lir, by Sheila MacGill-Callahan, 1993; Gulliver's Adventures in Lilliput, by Johnathan Swift, retold by Ann Keay Beneduce, 1993; Kashtanka, by Anton Chekhov, 1995.

JERRY STANLEY

July 18, 1941–

AUTHOR OF *Children of the Dust Bowl*, etc.

Autobiographical sketch of Jerry Stanley:

IF THERE IS such a thing as a typical writer, I'm not it. I can't remember writing anything in grade school or reading any books. All I remember about high school is that I hated it and I regularly cut classes to go swimming in a gravel pit with my friends. Woodshop and gym were the only classes I passed, and I was finally expelled for fighting, which was fine with me. My great regret about these years is that I must have been a disappointment to my mother and father, but they never showed it. I think they knew I was one of those kids who just wasn't ready for school, and I wasn't.

The Air Force made me grow up fast and assume responsibility for my own life. I had to wash my own socks, work, and save my own money if I wanted a car, a girlfriend and a set of drums. I managed to get all these things and one day started thinking about what I wanted to do after the Air Force. I never did figure it out, and the test the Air Force gave me didn't help at all; it said I would make a great mortician. I knew I didn't want to do that or operate bulldozers, which was an O.K. job in the Air Force, but not for the rest of my life. The only thing I knew is what I didn't want to be; I didn't want to be like the civilians on the base. They were old men with crumbled faces and blistered hands, and I could see they had worked all their life for little more than food and clothing, and none of them were happy. After the Air Force, I enrolled in a junior college because I knew what I didn't want to do.

Jerry Stanley

Now I was ready for school. I loved every subject and wanted to be a biologist, mathematician, sociologist and psychologist all in one person. But I was drawn to history more and more because the history teachers I had seemed to know more about more things than anyone else. Of all the subjects in high school, I held history in the greatest contempt for being the most boring and irrelevant to my life. Now I found it exciting and important in explaining things in my world that I didn't understand. Finally I found something I liked to do, and I did it with such passion that one day the university gave me a Ph.D. and kicked me out because there was nothing to earn beyond that degree. I became a Professor of History without ever having that as a goal, and I discovered I liked being a Professor of History.

At the same time, I liked writing about history, but only if I could do it as dramatic story telling. As an author of children's books, what I'm most concerned about is truth in history and how children can learn from it to make the world a better place to live. My books are aimed at the heart of the ignorance and intolerance in our world, and if I could, I would fashion them into stakes and drive them in. I wish everyone could be made to experience prejudice and discrimination from their looking different or having a different culture. I wish everyone understood that all cultures have value because all human beings have value. I wish everyone could learn to appreciate another culture, or if not that, learn at least to tolerate the existence of other ways of living. I make no apology for feeling so passionately about history as a tool for teaching tolerance and understanding. The best way to deal with the present is to face the past, as unpleasant as that sometimes may be.

———

Jerry Stanley was born in Highland Park, Michigan. He served in the Air Force from 1958 to 1962. He received an A.A. degree with honors from Yuba College in 1965 and a B.A. degree with honors from the California State University at Chico in 1967. He went on to earn an M.A. degree in 1969 and a Ph.D. in 1973 from the University of Arizona. Among the organizations he belongs to are Phi Beta Kappa and Phi Kappa Phi. He is a teacher in the field of the American West, the American Indian, and California History, and has taught at California State University at Bakersfield since 1973. He has been Professor of History since 1981.

Stanley has presented papers at conferences, has reviewed books for such publications as *Choice* and *American Historical Review*, and has contributed articles to journals such as *Pacific Historical Review* and *Southern California Quarterly*. He is married, he has two children, and he lives in Bakersfield, California, where he is preparing a book on the fate of the California Indians.

Children of the Dust Bowl won the 1993 John and Patricia Beatty Award sponsored by the California Library Association. It won the 1993 Jefferson Cup Award given by the Children's and Young Adult Round Table of the Virginia Library Association. It was named a Notable Book of the Year by the American Library Association and a

Notable Children's Trade Book in the Field of Social Studies by a joint committee of the Children's Book Council and the National Council on the Social Studies. It also won the 1993 Spur Award from the Western Writers of America.

I Am an American was named a Notable Book for Children by the ALA and an NCSS/CBC Notable Children's Trade Book in the Field of Social Studies. Both books were named Children's Books of Distinction by *The Hungry Mind Review*.

SELECTED WORKS: Children of the Dust Bowl: The True Story of the School at Weedpatch Camp, 1992; I Am an American: A True Story of Japanese Internment, 1994.

ABOUT: Dictionary of American Scholars, Vol. 4; Something About the Author, Vol. 79.

Suzanne Fisher Staples

SUZANNE FISHER STAPLES

August 27, 1945–

AUTHOR OF *Shabanu: Daughter of the Wind*, etc.

Autobiographical sketch of Suzanne Fisher Staples:

WHATEVER MAKES US into writers is a mystery to me. I like to think there's magic involved—magic, and of course, family.

My father and brother are engineers—they know how things work. When my brother won the Soap Box Derby on the hill on Franklin Street beside our house in Jermyn, Pennsylvania, I was sure our family had reached its pinnacle of fame.

My mother, who acts and speaks without pretense or subtlety, is brave and intuitive. When I was ten, Carlie Fron, our school bus driver, told me she was a wonderful mother. I stood there a moment, breathing in the silage smell of the bus (Charlie kept it in his barn when it was cold) and thought my heart would burst with pride.

My father's mother, Mema Fisher, was gentle and lovely—she knew about color

and texture and mood. She had a chaotic garden that was always in bloom, and I loved listening to our favorite songs (including "Mockingbird Hill") on her record player.

Mema Brittain, my other grandmother, and my aunt Elaine were delicate and feminine. I was a flower girl at Aunt Elaine's wedding, and I treasured the weeks of preparation, during which the two of them introduced me to the mysteries of face creams and perfume and silk slips.

Until I discovered boys I lived to fish. I got up before dawn and spent every day on the dock in front of our house on Chapman Lake with a line in the water, daydreaming about all the exotic places I'd ever heard of. My sister Karen, who had the family sense of humor, thought I was a hopeless tomboy. She and her friends painted their toenails! (But that's another story.)

After college I had various jobs, all having to do with writing. Eventually I landed in Hong Kong, where I became a reporter for United Press International. For six years I learned the ropes and pursued the China story, sailed on the South China Sea, ate Suchow food in back alleys, and sometimes talked until dawn in cafes with triad members, communists, and other characters who would have made my mother's hair stand on end. (Yet another story!)

When UPI offered me my own bureau in South Asia, my mother said, "Come home. Quit this Mata Hari life and marry a nice man, have some children." But I went to India instead and covered all the following stories: In Pakistan, Prime Minister Zulfikar Ali Bhutto was hanged. Islamic fundamentalists burned the Amerian Embassy with ninety people inside. Six people died. In India, Indira Gandhi returned to power and the most violent era since independence from British rule began. Soviet troops entered Afghanistan, to remain for ten bloody years.

It was the most adventurous phase of my life. I traveled with Mrs. Gandhi as she campaigned. We talked early in the morning over tea and late at night over warm milk. I shot the first photographs of Soviet troops in Afghanistan as they marched across the tarmac at Kabul airport Christmas eve of 1979. Among their ranks a young man carried a yule tree on his shoulder. Our Afghan colleagues began to disappear. Fear was as thick as dust in the air.

I returned to Pakistan in 1985 and worked under contract with the U.S. government to study poor rural women. I met an extraordinary girl in the Cholistan Desert, the daughter of camel herders, whose story became the basis for *Shabanu*.

If there is anything special at all about us odd ducks who write, perhaps it's our passion for stories. I used to worry that I'd run out of stories, but so far I haven't. If I ever do, I plan to take up fishing again.

———

Suzanne Fisher Staples was born in Philadelphia, Pennsylvania. She received her A.A. degree from Keystone Junior College in LaPlume, Pennsylvania, in 1965, and her B.A. degree from Cedar Crest College in Allentown, Pennsylvania, in 1967. She lives in Florida with her husband, Wayne Harley, where she is at work on another story.

She is a member of Authors Guild and the Asia Society.

Her first book, *Shabanu: Daughter of the Wind*, was named an Honor Book in the 1990 John Newbery Medal Awards, presented by the American Library Association. The ALA also named it a Notable Book of the Year and a Best Book for Young Adults. It was placed on the 1992 International Board on Books for Young People Honour List. It was named Notable Children's Trade Book in the Field of Social Studies by a joint committee of the National Council on the Social Studies and the Children's Book Council.

Haveli, the sequel to *Shabanu*, was named an ALA Best Book for Young Adults.

SELECTED WORKS: Shabanu: Daughter of the Wind, 1989; Haveli: A Young Woman's Courageous Struggle for Freedom in Present-Day Pakistan, 1993; Dangerous Skies, 1995.

ABOUT: California Media and Library Educators Association Journal Spring 1993; Contemporary Authors, Vol. 132; The New Advocate Summer 1993; Something About the Author, Vol. 70; Teaching PreK-8 March 1984.

R. L. STINE

October 8, 1943–

AUTHOR OF *Blind Date*, etc.

Biographical sketch of Robert Lawrence Stine, who also writes under the names "Eric Affabee," "Zachary Blue," and "Jovial Bob Stine":

BORN IN Columbus, Ohio, R. L. Stine was a writer from the time he was a child. He discovered an old typewriter when he was nine years old, and began typing up joke books. He always knew he would go to New York, because he knew that was where writers lived. He even tuned in New York radio stations at night with a powerful radio, listening to Jean Shepherd tell stories on the air.

R. L. STINE

As a child, he was influenced by Ernie Kovacs, Bob & Ray, Max Shulman, and Sid Caesar. He discovered *MAD Magazine*, and he wanted to someday have his own humor magazine. He also liked ghost stories and science fiction.

Stine attended Ohio State University, receiving his B.A. degree in 1965. He taught social studies at a junior high school in Columbus from 1965 to 1966. He then went to New York City, where he took some graduate courses at New York University from 1966 to 1967, and he began working as a magazine writer. He worked on *Junior Scholastic* in 1968, writing news and history articles. He later became editor for a new magazine, *Search*, which he worked on for three years. In 1975, he created *Bananas*, for teenagers. He had then achieved his ambition of editing a humor magazine. In 1984, he created *Maniac*, a magazine he edited for a year.

Stine made a change in his genre of writing, from humor to horror. Jean Feiwel, Editorial Director at Scholastic, asked if he would write a scary novel for children. His first attempt, *Blind Date*, was a big seller, and with the growth of the horror genre for teenagers that he helped create, he became

a best-selling children's author, with over a hundred books published. He created a series, *Fear Street*, in which the books come out about once a month. More than twenty million copies of the series book are in print. He has since created several other series, including *Goosebumps*, a scary series for younger readers.

In an interview with Jim Roginski, Stine talked about the kinds of fiction he writes: "Adults have their right to pick out a book that's just for entertainment, nothing else. But many adults seem to feel that every children's book has to teach them something, has to be uplifting in some way. My theory is a children's book doesn't have to teach them anything. It can be just for fun."

Stine is head writer for *Eureeka's Castle* a television show on the Nickelodeon cable network. He is married and has one son, and he enjoys watching old classic movies and reading. He is a member of the Mystery Writers of America. *The Sick of Being Sick Book* was named a Children's Choice Book by a joint committee of the Children's Book Council and the International Reading Association.

SELECTED WORKS AS JOVIAL BOB STINE: How to Be Funny: An Extremely Silly Guidebook, 1978; The Sick of Being Sick Book, 1980; Bananas Looks at TV, 1981.

SELECTED WORKS: Blind Date, 1986; Twisted, 1987; The Baby-sitter, 1989; Beach Party, 1990; Lights Out, 1991; The Prom Queen, 1992; The Baby-sitter IV, 1995.

SELECTED WORKS WRITTEN WITH JANE STINE: The Sick of Being Sick Book, 1980; The Cool Kids' Guide to Summer Camp, 1981.

ABOUT: Biography Today April 1994; Contemporary Authors, Vol. 105; (New Revision Series), Vol. 22; Gallo, Donald R. Speaking for Ourselves, Too; The New York Times September 7, 1995; Roginski, Jim. Behind the Covers; Something About the Author, Vol. 3l, 76.

CATHERINE STOCK

November 26, 1952–

ILLUSTRATOR OF *Galimoto*, etc.

Autobiographical sketch of Catherine Julia Stock:

MY FATHER was a diplomat, so when I was young I lived in many interesting cities—Stockholm, Paris, Pretoria, New Orleans, San Francisco, Cape Town, Hong Kong, London and New York. I changed schools often, leaving friends behind and sometimes having to learn new languages, so I was a little shy.

My mother was a painter and I was always given paper and paints for my birthday. I loved drawing—I suppose I created a safe, private world in my pictures. So after graduating from high school, I went to art school in Cape Town.

It was a bit of a shock because in those days everyone was doing very serious and political conceptual art. Their *ideas* for the projects were so important that sometimes students didn't even bother to enact them. I was different—I would just sit down in front of a white piece of paper or canvas and start work. I usually had no idea how a picture would look in three days or even three hours. My hands and eyes just got on with it while sometimes my mind seemed to drift miles away. One older teacher, who had illustrated many children's books, took an interest in me. She taught me printmaking—etching, lithography, woodcuts and typesetting. It was a wonderful four years, but soon I had to think about earning a living, so I went to London University and got a teaching diploma.

I taught a little while and then came to New York on holiday. I *loved* New York—the energy, the color, the people from all over the world! I visited some art schools with my portfolio, but they were very similar to my old art school. No one could take my pictures seriously. Then I went to Pratt and the professor looked at my pictures and exclaimed, "But these are wonderful!" My heart soared. My drawings at last meant something to somebody.

I enrolled at Pratt to do a graduate degree in design and met many talented designers and illustrators, and a year later I signed a contract with Scribners to do my first book. I have never looked back.

It's not always an easy life. I am not sure that I have the temperament to be a freelance artist, never quite knowing how I will be paying next month's rent, but one year has led to the next and I still feel challenged and excited by my work. My studies in fine art, education and graphic design all came together in children's books, and I still get to travel all over the world to research my books in places like South Africa, Malawi, Trinidad and Tobago, Zimbabwe, Haiti and Greece.

———

Catherine Stock was born in Stockholm, Sweden. She graduated from high school in San Francisco in 1970. She earned her B. F.A. degree from the University of Cape Town in South Africa in 1974. She received a Postgraduate Certificate in Education in 1976 from the University of London, and earned an M.A. degree from Pratt Institute in Brooklyn, New York, in 1978.

She was a lecturer in drawing and art history at Hewat Teacher's Training College in Cape Town in 1975. She became Art Director at the Putnam Publishing Group from 1978 to 1981. She then lectured for a year in children's book writing, illustrating, and design at the University of Cape Town. She has also held positions at other publishing companies.

Catherine Stock's work has been shown at the Irma Stern Museum, Cape Town, the Master Eagle Gallery and the Society of Illustrators in New York, and the South African National Gallery.

Justin and the Best Biscuits in the World won a 1987 Coretta Scott King Award. *Posy* won a 1984 Christopher Award. *Emma's Dragon Hunt* and *Galimoto* were Reading Rainbow featured selections. Several of her books were named Notable Children's Trade Books in the Field of Social Studies by a joint committee of the Children's Book Council and the National Council on the

Social Studies. They include *Galimoto, Armien's Fishing Trip*, and *An Island Christmas*.

Midnight Snowman was named a Children's Choice Book by a joint committee of the CBC and the International Reading Association. *Secret Valentine, Mara in the Morning*, and *Tap-Tap* were named a Junior Literary Guild selections. *Secret Valentine* is one of six holiday books Stock wrote and illustrated.

SELECTED WORKS WRITTEN AND ILLUSTRATED: Emma's Dragon Hunt, 1984; Armien's Fishing Trip, 1990; Secret Valentine, 1991; Where Are You Going, Manyoni?, 1993.

SELECTED WORKS ILLUSTRATED: Posy, by Charlotte Pomerantz, 1983; Justin and the Best Biscuits in the World, by Mildred Pitts Walter, 1986; Midnight Snowman, by Caroline Bauer, 1987; Galimoto, by Karen Lynn Williams, 1990; Mara in the Morning, by C.B. Christiansen, 1991; An Island Christmas, by Lynn Joseph, 1992; Tap-Tap, by Karen Lynn Williams, 1994; By the Dawn's Early Light, by Karen Ackerman, 1994; Too Far Away to Touch, by Lesléa Newman, 1995; A Very Important Day, by Maggie Rugg Herold, 1995.

ABOUT: Contemporary Authors, Vol. 119; Something About the Author, Vol. 65.

LYNN SWEAT

May 27, 1934–

ILLUSTRATOR OF *Good Work, Amelia Bedelia*, etc.

Autobiographical sketch of Lynn Sweat:

I GREW UP in Nederland, Texas, a small town that had quite a few Dutch families. They had founded the town many years before. Some of my early school memories were . . . making crepe-paper tulips for some of the Dutch holiday celebrations . . . drawing a fire prevention poster that won a prize in fourth grade . . . catching dragonflies by the tail off my mother's clothesline.

I always had a love of color and drawing. Books were important at an early age. I re-

LYNN SWEAT

member how exciting it was to get my very own library card. My grandmother encouraged my love of art and reading. My very first large set of crayons that actually had silver and gold colors was a proud and memorable moment.

When I graduated from high school, I knew being an artist would be my career. I was not so sure that I would be able to earn enough to make a living. As I went through Lamar College in Beaumont, Texas, I got a part-time job as cameraman and artist at a local TV station. After graduation I worked for several newspapers as a graphic artist. At this time I married my wife Elynor, and we built a small house together.

Painting pictures occupied all of my spare time during these years. I had many exhibits and entered every show that I could. My first museum show was a complete sell out, mainly because the prices on the paintings were very low. Painting is still my major focus, even now. What makes painting so enjoyable is that you, the artist, are in total control. If you are a commercial illustrator, that is not always the case, and is sometimes frustrating.

In 1963 I came to New York City. My first jobs in the city were with fashion agen-

Sweat: like *"sweat of the brow"*

cies and art studios. After two years I had enough experience and contacts to become a freelance illustrator and have remained so ever since. My first children's book came about through a mailer that I had created on my own for promotional purposes. It won an award in the New York Society of Illustrators show and led to my first meeting with Susan Hirschman, who at that time worked as editor-in-chief at Macmillan Publishing Co., Inc. She encouraged my first efforts in writing and illustrating children's books.

Some years later I did a few "how to do" books with Peggy Parish, and when the chance came to work on the Amelia Bedelia series with her, I did my first Amelia title called *Good Work, Amelia Bedelia*. In the years to follow we did nine books together.

It has been nine years since I have done an Amelia book. In 1995 there was a new title called *Good Driving, Amelia Bedelia*.

One of the most satisfying things about being an author-illustrator is the sense of permanence that doing a book gives. You can walk into a library twenty years after doing a book and it is still there on the shelf, being enjoyed by a whole new generation.

———

Lynn Sweat was born in Alexandria, Louisiana. He moved to Texas at an early age and grew up in Nederland, Texas. He earned his B.S. degree at Lamar College in Beaumont, Texas. He married in 1956, and he and his wife have four children. He has illustrated over fifty books, and is best known as the illustrator of the beloved Amelia Bedelia series. He lives and works in Connecticut. A large part of his artistic output is in the area of painting. He has shown at the Roko Galleries in New York and is currently represented by two galleries in Connecticut. Lynn Sweat received an Award of Excellence from the Society of Illustrators in 1970 for a promotional book, *Birds Without Words*.

Several of the Amelia Bedelia easy-to-read series have been named Children's Choice Books by a joint committee of the International Reading Association and the Children's Book Council, including *Good Work, Amelia Bedelia, Amelia Bedelia and the Baby*, and *Amelia Bedelia's Family Album. The Cats' Burglar* received the same honor. Many of the books Sweat illustrated won Child Study Children's Book Awards, given by the Child Study Children's Book Committee at Bank Street College of Education, including *Let's Celebrate: Holiday Decorations You Can Make*, and *Good Work, Amelia Bedelia*.

SELECTED WORKS WRITTEN AND ILLUSTRATED: (with Louis Phillips) The Smallest Stegosaurous, 1993.

SELECTED WORKS ILLUSTRATED: Good Work, Amelia Bedelia, by Peggy Parish, 1976; Let's Celebrate: Holiday Decorations You Can Make, by Peggy Parish, 1976; Teach Us, Amelia Bedelia, by Peggy Parish, 1977; Amelia Bedelia Helps Out, by Peggy Parish, 1979; Amelia Bedelia and the Baby, by Peggy Parish, 1981; The Cats' Burglar, by Peggy Parish, 1983; Amelia Bedelia Goes Camping, by Peggy Parish, 1985; Merry Christmas, Amelia Bedelia, by Peggy Parish, 1986; Amelia Bedelia's Family Album, by Peggy Parish, 1988; One Good Horse: A Cowpuncher's Counting Book, by Ann Herbert Scott, 1990; Wake Up, Baby!, by Joanne Oppenheim, 1991; Good Driving, Amelia Bedelia, 1995.

ABOUT: Something About the Author, Vol 57.

MARC TALBERT

July 21, 1953–

AUTHOR OF *Dead Birds Singing*, etc.

Autobiographical sketch of Marc Talbert:

I'VE ALWAYS KNOWN I was a writer. It seems to me that writing is not something one chooses to do—writing does the choosing. For as long as I can remember, I've felt compelled to read and write—a curious thing for a boy who read painfully slowly and couldn't spell correctly. I still feel compelled to read and write—and I still read painfully slowly and find it very difficult to spell correctly. Why do I feel so compelled?

Perhaps reading is a way of feeding my appetite for living many lives—who wouldn't like to transcend the limitations of a single, ordinary life? Perhaps writing is a way for me to understand myself and my place in the world.

Whatever. I began writing, at the age of seven or eight, by inventing words. Soon I began putting those words and other, more conventional words together into poetry. Not long after, I began to write short stories. And then columns for the editorial pages of several newspapers—which I did through college and all the time I taught fifth grade (several years in one of the schools I went to as a child). When I moved from Iowa to New Mexico, I worked as a writer at a national laboratory, making science understandable to a general audience. For a year I worked as a speech writer in Washington, D.C., for a friend who was Director of the National Science Foundation.

All these things helped when I decided to write my first novel—inspired by the death of one of my students the last year I taught fifth grade. An appreciation for the playfulness of words, and a love of their sounds, came from inventing words—and trying to figure out how they were spelled. Not shy-

ing away from personal feelings came from writing poems and short stories—very few of them ever shown to other people. The columns gave me discipline (there were deadlines) and helped me mature—twice a week some of my students would bring my columns to class and hold me accountable for what I'd written; there is nothing like looking foolish in yesterday's column to make you work harder on tomorrow's. Writing about science made me realize I loved writing, even about things I wasn't naturally fond of. And of course writing speeches was a great way to hone skills at dialogue as well as fiction (fiction is, after all, the art of making sense where nonsense prevails, giving structure to mush—and Washington, D.C., is the capital of nonsense and mush).

I love what I do, but my books are never easy to write. Too often they push me up against the limits of my talent as well as limits of personal comfort. Why do I write about death and sexual abuse and human sacrifice and pilgrimages and divorced parents and Vietnam and magical uncles who die of AIDS? These things, by and large, have never happened to me—I've never died or been sexually abused or gone to Vietnam. I haven't done or experienced a lot of things I write about.

Perhaps I write about them because they haven't happened to me. I find myself wanting to explore, through my writing, those parts of me that need to grow up. Too often we hear: "Write what you know." I find myself writing about things I don't know, using writing as a tool of discovery. While writing about science, I learned that a good scientist doesn't do experiments to prove something he or she already knows to be true, but to challenge (one hopes, in a playful way) an hypothesis or model of reality. Most scientists are delighted by whatever results they get—as long as the results are honest. I've worked around good scientists long enough (my father is a nuclear physicist) to know the tremendous value of not knowing—the value of being open to all possibilities. I've started many books thinking I knew more than I did about what I was writing, and then been honored by characters who patiently taught me the many important things I needed to know.

In fact, I write for my characters more than I write for my readers or myself. I hope to do my characters justice—to present their lives honestly and well, to bring their struggles and joys to the attention of a wide audience. If I have any regrets as a writer, it is that I was not good enough in the portrayal of my characters' lives. My greatest joy as a writer is learning that someone has connected emotionally with one of my characters—invited that character to be life-long companion.

If my characters are so alive you can *smell* them, I've done a sufficient job. If my characters make a lasting impression on you—help you forever after see yourself or the world differently—I might even allow myself to feel proud of the job I've done.

Marc Talbert was born in Boulder, Colorado. He attended Grinnell College from 1971 to 1973 and received his B.S. degree from Iowa State University in 1976. He has been a teacher in public schools, in Marshalltown, Iowa from 1976 to 1977, and in Ames, Iowa from 1977 to 1981. He was a columnist for the Ames, Iowa *Daily Tribune* and the Vinton, Iowa *Cedar Valley Times* and a writer and editor at Los Alamos National Laboratory in New Mexico from 1981 to 1986. He was a speech writer for National Science Foundation from 1984 to 1985, and he is an occasional instructor in children's literature at the University of New Mexico.

Talbert was the sponsor of a conference in Santa Fe, New Mexico, entitled "The Courage to Write for Children" from 1988 to 1991. He is a member of PEN, The Society of Children's Book Writers and Illustrators, and Authors Guild. He is married and has two daughters.

Dead Birds Singing was named a Best Book for Young Adults by the American Library Association. *Toby* was named a Notable Children's Trade Book in the Field of Social Studies by a joint committee of the Children's Book Council and the National Council on the Social Studies.

SELECTED WORKS: Dead Birds Singing, 1985; Thin Ice, 1986; Toby, 1987; The Paper Knife, 1988; Rabbit in the Rock, 1989; Double or Nothing, 1990; Pillow of Clouds, 1991; The Purple Heart, 1992; Heart of a Jaguar, 1995; A Sunburned Prayer, 1995.

ABOUT: Contemporary Authors, Vol. 136; Something About the Author, Vol. 68.

ELEANORA E. TATE

April 16, 1948–

AUTHOR OF *Just an Overnight Guest*, etc.

Biographical sketch of Eleanora Elaine Tate:

ELEANORA TATE is an author of books for both adults and children. She was born in Canton, Missouri, the daughter of Clifford and Lillian Douglas Tate. She was raised by a grandmother and had a happy childhood.

She was married in 1972 and graduated from Drake University in Des Moines, Iowa, with a B.A. degree in 1973. Beginning her career in the newspaper business, she was a news editor of the *Iowa Bystander* in West Des Moines from 1966 to 1968. She then became a reporter for the *Des Moines Register* and the evening version of the paper, the *Des Moines Tribune*, a job she held from 1969 to 1976. During this time, she participated in black history and black culture workshops in Des Moines. She also won the Unity Award from Lincoln University in 1974 for educational reporting.

She moved to Tennessee, working as a staff writer for the *Jackson Sun* for a year. She also wrote for the *Memphis Tri-State Defender* in 1977, and won the Community Lifestyles Award from the Tennessee Press

Association in 1977. In 1979, she was a writer for the company Kreative Koncepts, Inc. in Myrtle Beach, South Carolina. She became a freelance writer in 1982, started her own company, Positive Images, Inc., in Myrtle Beach in 1983.

A poet and writer of fiction and nonfiction, Tate presented poetry at the Iowa Arts Council Writers in the Schools program from 1969 to 1976 and at Grinnell College in 1975. Tate was co-editor, with her husband Zack E. Hamlett III, of *Wanjiru: A Collection of Blackwomanworth*, which was published in 1976. She was also a contributor to the collection. She had several books for adults published, including *Sprays of Rubies*, an anthology, in 1975, and *Vallhalla Four* in 1977. She is a contributor of poetry and fiction to periodicals such as *Journal of Black Poetry* and *Des Moines Register Picture Magazine*. She was awarded a fellowship in children's fiction for the 1981 Bread Loaf writers conference.

Gradually, Tate became more interested in writing for children than for adults. She was a guest author in the School Libraries Association Conference in 1981 and 1982. One of her books for children, *Just an Overnight Guest*, is the story of nine-year-old Margie, whose mother allows a "trashy little kid," a four-year-old, to stay with them for several weeks, a time period that threatens to last much longer and tries Margie's patience until she comes to understand the reasons behind the visitor's presence. The book was made into a movie by Phoenix/B. F.A. Film & Video in 1983. Tate's most recent fiction is a collection of short stories for children.

Eleanora Tate lives in South Carolina. She and her husband have one daughter.

SELECTED WORKS: Impossible?, 1972; Communications, 1973; Off-Beat, 1974; Just an Overnight Guest, 1980; Secret of Gumbo Grove, 1987; Thank You, Dr. Martin Luther King, Jr.!, 1990; Front Porch Stories at the One-Room School, 1992.

ABOUT: Contemporary Authors, Vol. 105; (New Revision Series), Vol. 25; Rollock, Barbara. Black Authors and Illustrators of Children's Books; Something About the Author, Vol. 38; Who's Who Among Black Americans, 8th ed.

WILLIAM TAYLOR

October 11, 1938–

AUTHOR OF *Agnes the Sheep*, etc.

Autobiographical sketch of William Taylor:

I HAVE no memories of writing or of wanting to write when I was a child. One piece of my fairly early writing stands out in my memory. At around age ten I wrote a story about gypsies. It was given a very good grade indeed. Why do I remember it? Well, I must now confess. It was not my own work at all; my mother wrote it for me! I have suffered very slight pangs of guilt ever since.

As a child growing up for the most part in rural New Zealand, I was very much a loner. I read and I read and I read. I read everything I could lay my hands on. I have my parents to thank for this. Avid readers themselves, they instilled a love of reading in all their children.

Not remarkably successful academically, I left school at age sixteen and worked in a bank for two years before deciding to take up teaching as a career, training in Christchurch, New Zealand. For the next twenty or more years I taught in primary (elementary) and intermediate (junior high) schools in the North Island of our country. I loved my job and I loved kids. It is not an accident that the prime audience for whom I write today, eleven to thirteen year olds, is the age group I taught for many years.

I started writing in 1968 and over the next five years wrote half a dozen novels for adults. All were published, although they were not remarkably good! I now look upon this period as the apprenticeship for what I do now. In 1981 my first novel for older children, *Pack Up Pick Up & Off* was published, and on being awarded a literary bursary for children's writers in 1984, I decided

to leave teaching and to write fulltime. In the decade since, I have written almost a score of novels for children and young adults. Some of my titles such as *Paradise Lane* and *Agnes the Sheep* are published in the U.S.A. or in Britain or, in translation, in various European countries. Others are more Kiwi (N.Z.) in flavour and are found only in New Zealand or Australia.

I guess New Zealand is one of the most isolated countries in the world. We are a long way from just about anywhere. I choose to live in an isolated corner of our isolated country—a very beautiful spot in the central high country of the North Island. It is an area I know and love well. I enjoy skiing, the outdoors and my garden. Most of all I enjoy the time I am able to spend with family and friends who often stay with me here.

I suppose that primarily I am a storyteller and entertainer who has chosen the written word as his medium. My greatest wish in writing my books is that I am able to capture a little bit of what it is like to be young and to express the hopes and fears, the joys and occasionally the pains of growing up. As long as I am able to do this I will go on writing.

———

William Taylor was born in Lower Hutt in New Zealand and educated at Christchurch Teachers' College in 1957 and 1958. He taught one year in London. He received the Choysa Bursary for Children's Writers in 1985. He was mayor of the borough of Ohakune from 1981 to 1988. He was Writer in Residence at Palmerston North College of Education in 1992. He is divorced, and has two sons.

Some of the books he has had published in New Zealand include *S.W.A.T.* in 1993 and *The Blue Lawn* in 1994. *Paradise Lane* was published in New Zealand as *Possum Perkins*. *The Blue Lawn* won a New Zealand AIM Children's Book Award for senior fiction in 1995.

Agnes the Sheep won the 1991 Esther Glen Award from the New Zealand Library Association. The award honors the author whose literature is considered the most distinguished of the year. *Agnes the Sheep* and *Knitwits* were both named Notable Books of the Year by the American Library Association.

SELECTED WORKS: Paradise Lane, 1987; Agnes the Sheep, 1990; Knitwits, 1992; Numbskulls, 1995.

ABOUT: Fitzgibbon, Ashton. Beneath Southern Skies; Contemporary Authors, Vol. 146; Something About the Author, Vol. 78; Who's Who in New Zealand, 12th ed.

KEIZABURO TEJIMA

1935–

AUTHOR AND ILLUSTRATOR OF *Fox's Dream*, etc.

Autobiographical sketch of Keizaburo Tejima, who also writes under the name "Tejima":

I WAS BORN in a little fishing village, within the jurisdiction of Abashiri, Hokkaido, in 1935. My father was a railway worker, so my family changed our address from village to village along the railway many

times. Every village where I lived was small; some depended on fishing, others on agriculture, and some were just hamlets, too small even to be called a village. So I've never lived in the prosperous city. This has had a big influence on my character. I mean, I used to have an inferiority complex as a 'country boy'. But now, as a painter, I'm aware of the positive side of country life.

I can recall my childhood, in a village near the Ohotsuku ocean, which was covered with drift ice in winter, giving me the feeling that this was the end of the earth. It was a really dreary view. But it gave me the patience and imagination to change a dreary world into a varied world.

Living near a station in the countryside in the mountains, I got accustomed to being alone and became familiar with nature through play, which fostered my interest and knowledge in animals, plants, and insects.

At the age of three or four, I liked to play by myself at home all the day, drawing and making handicrafts. When I came to enter elementary school, every morning I cried, "I don't want to go to school." My mother was very upset, and I was forced to go to school with my two brothers and my sister. Though I am now nearly sixty years old, even now I still feel the same; if I am able to work in my atalier all day, I am satisfied.

But it was a very long time before I could finally earn enough to get along as a painter independently, in 1977. (When I was forty-two years old.)

Graduating from Hokkaido Liberal Arts University in 1957, I taught art at a junior high school, while continuing my creative activities. I experienced a lot of difficulties and frustration. I think the following reasons contributed to my success.

Firstly, choosing wood block prints as my medium of expression.

Secondly, choosing the nature and animals of Hokkaido as the theme of my works.

Thirdly, growing up watching the drift ice helped me to develop the quality of patience.

Ainu, who are the former inhabitants in Hokkaido, worshipped the shimafukuro (the biggest kind of fish-owl) as the guardian god of their villages. This owl is mysterious enough to be called a 'god'. It has the countenance of an old man, and its hoot is low and resounding.

Nowadays, Hokkaido is developed, and there are few primitive areas where the shimafukuro can live. It is believed that only about 100 shimafukuro survive now. A hundred years ago, you could see them everywhere. I have chosen the shimafukuro for the theme of my works partly because I feel nostalgia for how Hokkaido was before it was developed, partly because I have affection for nature which was implanted in my mind since boyhood in the countryside, and partly because the simplicity and strength of wood block prints is an effective means of expression for the shimafukuro.

In 1981 I presented one of my works at an exhibition of the Japan Print Association, which depicted a scene of an owl fishing in a lake at night. This work caught a leading publisher's eye. That publisher was Fukutake Publishing Co., Ltd. (now Benesse Corporation). I was asked to illustrate a picture book, and in this way, my first book, *Shimafukuro no Mizuumi (Owl Lake)* came to be published. This book won the Japan Picture Book Award in 1982 and, happily, has been selling for over twelve years. I published five books consecutively in the "Northern Animal Picture Book Series". *Oohakucho no Sora (Swan Sky)*, *Kitakitsune no Yume (Fox's Dream)*, etc. Next, I published five books in the "Kamay yukara" series, which is the traditional literature of Ainu, and a fantasy series. Thanks to excellent publishers, my books were translated and published in many overseas countries. And today, I can thank my parents and everything implanted in my mind during my childhood in the countryside of Hokkaido. All of my works reflect the nature and animals of the area where I have lived for such a long time.

The theme of nature and animals is readily accepted in overseas countries, as it is common to all cultures. And wood block prints are more admired for their beauty overseas than in Japan. I feel very fortunate.

Keizaburo Tejima studied art at Hokkaido Liberal Arts University from 1953 until his graduation in 1957. In 1992, he was commissioned by the United Nations to create a poster for Earth Summit. He is a member of the Japanese Woodcut Society.

Fox's Dream was praised by the *New York Times Book Review*: "*Fox's Dream* is an astonishing work, a near-perfect picture book. Like the fox's run through the snow, like the air in those frosty mountain valleys, it will take your breath away."

Barbara Elleman wrote in *Booklist*, "The contrasts of color that Tejima achieves in his woodcuts are exemplary and heighten the story's drama as do the sure, bold lines that effectively form the figures and emphasize the action." And Betsy Hearne, writing in *The Bulletin of the Center for Children's Books*, called *Swan Sky* "a stunning picture book."

In 1986, *Fox's Dream* was awarded the Graphic Prize at the Bologna International Book Fair in Italy. It was also named a Best Illustrated Children's Book of the Year 1987 by the *New York Times. Swan Sky* received the same honor in 1988.

Two of his books were named Notable Books of the Year by the American Library Association: *Fox's Dream* and *Owl Lake*.

Tejima's books have been published in France, the Netherlands, Spain, Italy, Belgium, and Bangladesh, in addition to Japan and America.

SELECTED WORKS WRITTEN AND ILLUSTRATED: The Bears' Autumn, 1986; Fox's Dream, 1987; Owl Lake, 1987; Swan Sky, 1988; Woodpecker Forest, 1989; Holimlim: A Rabbit Tale from Japan, translated by Cathy Hirano, 1990.

ABOUT: Children's Literature Review, Vol. 20; Horn Book March 1989.

FRANCES TEMPLE

August 15, 1945–July 5, 1995

AUTHOR OF *Taste of Salt*, etc.

Autobiographical sketch of Frances Temple:

WHEN MY THREE SISTERS and I were very young, we lived on a farm in Virginia and spent our days in make-believe. Stories happened to us. I couldn't write yet, but I remember lying underwater in a swamp, breathing through a reed while the Enemy passed on horseback, searching for me. . . .

My sisters and I slept four in the same room and took turns making up stories to tell at night. My older sister kept us riveted and awake. I planned to be a firefighter when I grew up.

When I was nine, we moved away from our farm to a hotel in Paris, France, abruptly expected to wear dresses and speak French. At school, we were not allowed to say anything unless we raised a hand first,

FRANCES TEMPLE

were given permission, and then stood to speak. My best friend in France lived in a half-ruined castle. Her mother was paralysed; we carried her in a litter through long hallways and up staircases hung in tapestries, pretending she was the Queen.

When I was fourteen my family moved to Vietnam. Our Vietnamese school was damaged by a bomb; the nuns sent us to help in an orphanage. When school reopened I kept working because I liked being with the children and there was much to do; mopping, feeding, playing, sometimes just holding a baby while it died. This is like saying good-bye for the whole world.

My best friend in Saigon played Chopin on the piano to break your heart. Her brother had a fighting cock who ate rice at the family table, with parents, eight children, three grandmothers, and for a while, me.

My first job after high-school was in West Africa, with a midwife: we walked footpaths through bushy woods, from one village to another. At each village we met with the women who were pregnant and admired all the new babies, checking for health problems. At night we sat around and exchanged gossip and stories. The midwife, Jeneba, gave women advice. I helped

carry her gear and gifts: vitamins, scissors, live chickens.

Back in the U.S. for college, never having met a card catalog, I sat in the stacks of the library leafing through any book on the shelf that looked interesting. Finally, as assistant to an African studies professor, I learned how to use a library and how to type. My first literary job was to read and recommend Black French-speaking poets and novelists, some Haitian, some West African, for the French literature curriculm at University of North Carolina.

After college, I moved with my husband to a farm in Virginia, did some local organizing, and began teaching school and writing books. Organizing work depends almost entirely on other people, and teaching is a two-way street, but writing is something you can do alone, and sometimes that is a blessing.

When our children were little, I told them stories at night. Sitting on the floor in the dark, listening to them breathe, I found out that there are just two hard parts to making up stories: the first is getting started, the second is stopping.
Bare facts:
I was born in Washington, D.C. on the last day of World War II. I live with my husband, who is a teacher, musician, and writer, our three children and their friends, and a dog.
I teach first and second grade.
I like to make music, draw pictures, take walks, and read.

———

Frances Temple died on July 5, 1995 of a heart attack, about one year after she wrote the above autobiographical piece for this book. She was the author of four novels and an illustrated picture book, *Tiger Soup*. She also co-wrote books about teachers and children learning together. They are *Classroom Strategies that Work: An Elementary Teacher's Guide to the Writing Process*, published in 1989, and *The Beginnings of Writing*, the third editon of which was published in 1992.

Of her first book, *Taste of Salt*, Betsy Hearne wrote, in *The Bulletin of the Center for Children's Books*: "Temple handles, with unobtrusive ease, the intricacies of changing and emerging viewpoints, the juxtaposition of past and present, the blend of political and personal, the balance of romance and violence."

Taste of Salt won the 1993 Jane Addams Children's Book Award. *The Ramsay Scallop* was named a Best Book of the Year for Young Adults by the American Library Association.

SELECTED WORKS: Taste of Salt: A Story of Modern Haiti, 1992; Grab Hands and Run, 1993; The Ramsay Scallop, 1994; Tiger Soup, 1994; Tonight, by Sea, 1995.

ABOUT: Publishers Weekly December 28, 1992.

FULVIO TESTA

April 6, 1947–

AUTHOR AND ILLUSTRATOR OF *If You Take a Pencil*, etc.

Autobiographical sketch by Fulvio Testa:

THERE IS a photograph by Eugene Smith, two children hand-in-hand, coming out of a cave. They are alone in front of the universe. What an experience! How beautiful, how scary! To approach life, the world, we need friends; maybe just one. Children's books are children's friends: pages open, they introduce and lead us into a mysterious world. When I was a child, growing up in Italy, I was not surrounded by children's books. I grew up with *Brother's Grimm Tales*, *Aesop's Fables*, and *Pinocchio*. That's all.

I never thought then, or dreamed that I would later create children's books. I grew up liking painting and architecture. Strangely enough, I didn't study art. I never finished my studies in architecture. I became a painter. I was introduced to the world of children's books in 1970 when I met Stepan Zavrel, a Czech artist, a door

suddenly opened onto a new horizon. *Grimm's Tales*, *Aesop's Fables*, and *Pinocchio* were still alive in me. Little by little my own voice felt at ease; I started illustrating a story written by H. C. Andersen, "The Nightingale," and later I started to develop my own ideas and texts. I illustrated, also, texts by contemporary writers, Gianni Rodari and Anthony Burgess.

In making books for children I have learned a lot from the child's voice in me. I must say I have had a lot of fun. There have been, and there are, struggles—it happens that an illustration has to be redone because of a dissatisfaction; or it can take a long time to realize that something is wrong. But I have never seen my work as a job, I have always felt lucky to have the chance to create. I don't make many books; painting, now, comes first. I feel part of an extended family. Still, I hear the voice in me of that child of forty years ago, the child who desires to communicate with all the other children.

———

Fulvio Testa was born in Verona. He studied architecture at the University of Florence and Venice from 1968 to 1972. Since 1972 he has done twenty picture books and several other books, published in over twenty countries and translated into fifteen languages. His books have received awards in Germany, Switzerland, France, and the U.S.

Since 1980 he has been working mainly as a painter. He has had exhibitions in the U.S. and abroad. His work is represented in public collections such as the Art Institute of Chicago and the Philadelphia Museum of Art. He lives in Verona and New York City.

A review of *If You Look Around You*, in *The Horn Book Magazine*, stated: "The carefully composed, brilliantly colored illustrations arouse curiosity and create tension by combining the expected and the unexpected, realism and surrealism, naivete and sophistication, order and disorder. . . .

the author extends thought and suggests that geometry is an interesting but limited tool in describing a world that remains mysterious and enigmatic."

If You Look Around You received a Child Study Children's Book Award given by the Child Study Children's Book Committee at Bank Street College of Education. It was represented in The *Horn Book* Graphic Gallery, an article about outstanding information books published from 1983-1987. *If You Take a Pencil* was a Reading Rainbow Selection.

SELECTED WORKS: If You Take a Pencil, 1982; If You Look Around You, 1983; If You Take a Paintbrush: A Book of Colors, 1983; If You Seek Adventure, 1984; The Ideal Home, 1986; Wolf's Favor, 1986; Never Satisfied, 1982; Aesop's Fables, 1989; Time to Get Out, 1993.

SELECTED WORKS ILLUSTRATED: The Paper Airplane, by Kurt Baumann, 1982; Aesop's Fables, 1989; Things That Go: A Traveling Alphabet, by Seymour Reit, 1990.

JEAN THESMAN

AUTHOR OF *Rachel Chance*, etc.

Biographical sketch of Jean Thesman:

JEAN THESMAN's mother taught her to read before she went to school. She believed it was an endeavor "too important to leave to strangers." Thesman read a great deal while growing up, and had a poem published in the newspaper when she was in the first grade.

Thesman heard a great deal of storytelling in her house. Her mother and her friends told stories over the kitchen table. The stories they told were not only about their own lives, but, as Jean Thesman describes them, those of their mothers, grandmothers, and great-grandmothers. When Thesman was fourteen and considered old enough to understand the conversation, she was invited to join the ladies; however, she

JEAN THESMAN

had already been listening from nearby rooms for a long time.

Her father, too, was a storyteller. He had traveled a great deal, and told stories of his adventures. He described shipwrecks, battles, encounters with Chinese warlords, and even beheadings. He took photographs on his travels and was able to illustrate his stories with the pictures. Thesman found his stories fascinating as well as horrifying.

Considering her heritage, Thesman believes she has storytelling in her blood, and she prefers the term storyteller to author. She lives in Washington State. She and her husband have two daughters and a son.

The novels of Jean Thesman are often set in Washington. They feature unusual tales of independent and resourceful young women. The protagonist of *Rachel Chance*, for example, schemes to rescue her illegitimate baby brother from the traveling band of revivalists that has kidnapped him. The novel is set in the 1940's. A *Horn Book* reviewer called it a satisfying story of "rugged individualism against the immovable nature of local mores."

When the Road Ends depicts a small group of foster children who are shifted off to a lakeside cottage for the summer, to be cared for by an irresponsible baby sitter who leaves them alone. Their struggles and plans to stay together and be independent emphasize Thesman's theme of, as a *Horn Book Magazine* reviewer stated, "children forced before their time to behave like adults."

The plot of *Molly Donnelly* is quite different from books like *When the Road Ends*. It is set in 1941, when the Japanese bombing of Pearl Harbor is seen through the eyes of a twelve-year-old girl. Molly lives on Puget Sound, and one of her friends is Japanese. The friend's family is sent to an internment camp, and many other consequences and conditions of wartime are reflected in Molly's experiences as she comes of age.

The Cattail Moon describes a protagonist who decides to live with her father in a small town in the Cascade Mountains. The story contains an element of the supernatural as well as a romance, all in contemporary times.

The Rain Catchers won a 1991 Golden Kite Award from the Society of Children's Book Writers and Illustrators. It was also named a Notable Book of the Year by the American Library Association, as were her books *Rachel Chance* and *When the Road Ends*. *Rachel Chance* was also named a Best Book for Young Adults by the ALA. *Appointment with a Stranger* and *The Last April Dancers* were named Young Adult's Choice Books by a joint committee of the Children's Book Council and the International Reading Association.

She has written two series, the "Whitney Cousins" series, which includes *Heather* and *Amelia*; and the "Birthday Girls" series, which consists of *I'm Not Telling, Mirror, Mirror*, and *Who Am I, Anyway?*.

SELECTED WORKS: The Last April Dancers, 1987; Appointment with a Stranger, 1989; Amelia, 1990; Heather, 1990; Rachel Chance, 1990; The Rain Catchers, 1991; I'm Not Telling, 1992; Mirror, Mirror, 1992; When the Road Ends, 1992; Who Am I, Anyway?, 1992; Molly Donnelly, 1993; The Cattail Moon, 1994; Summerspell, 1995.

ABOUT: Something About the Author, Vol. 74.

RACHEL VAIL

July 25, 1966–

AUTHOR OF *Wonder*, etc.

Autobiographical sketch of Rachel Vail:

I NEVER THOUGHT I wanted to be a writer. I never wanted to write the Great American Novel or hang out smoking a cigarette and drinking Scotch in a cafe in Paris. Scotch and cigarettes both made me feel like throwing up and although I liked Paris when I went there in tenth grade, my French wasn't great and I missed my parents. Besides, I thought writers were much moodier and deeper than I. I went out with a writer in high school. He wrote poems I didn't understand in which I appeared as either smoke or a grey cat, and left them in my locker before lunch period. He spent a lot of time clutching his hair and listening to Mahler. I just liked to make things up.

In some ways, I guess my younger brother, Jon, taught me to be a writer. He was my first audience and always wanted me to make up stories to act out with him. We traveled through the centuries by pressing the pedal of our time machine (a stake that held up a wobbly tree in the back yard), went to magic school at night (while we slept), explored the terrifying Way Back (of the basement, where the water heater was).

I wanted to create characters, so I auditioned for plays. I was an old woman when I was ten, a middle-aged man at eleven, a murderer at twenty-one. It was important to figure out how each character walked and breathed, whether she slept on her back, if he believed in God, what she carried in her purse—because I needed to know everything in order to become the character. It was fun. But I must admit I learned everybody's lines. I wanted to play all the parts, and direct, maybe write the betrayal scene that took place off-stage. So I kept making up my own stories. But I didn't want to be a writer! Writers are so solemn.

Some of my teachers, luckily, made writ-

ing seem really exciting. Mrs. Sudak helped me through the traumatic loss of my first tooth down the garbage disposal by getting me to turn it into fiction. Mrs. T., shorter than I in fifth and sixth grade but tougher than a middle linebacker, was never satisfied, always demanded more, more revelations, more truth. Ms. Carozi found me incredibly frustrating in my lack of desire to be a writer, when she had decided that was my future. "You'll never be a writer with that attitude," she insisted in her weird falsetto. Mr. Hubscher, in his Hush Puppies, forced me to argue logically and to figure out what I believed. Professor Glavin threw a manuscript at me in passionate frustration because we disagreed about what a character would say at a pivotal moment. And cross-eyed Doc Murphy, who told me to "astonish" him, taught me that character, and thus everything, is revealed in the details. I learned, slowly, that writing could be thrilling, fun, joyous.

And now I am a writer. I sit around all day and ask myself questions like what does she have in her pockets and what is she afraid of and if he could change one thing about himself what would it be and what kind of sheets does she sleep on. There is no job I would rather have. Even though Scotch and cigarettes still make me feel like throwing up.

————

Rachel Vail was born in Manhattan in 1966. She grew up in New Rochelle, New York, with her parents and her younger brother. She graduated from Georgetown University in Washington, D.C., in 1988 with a major in English and theater. She is a member of the Authors Guild. Vail lives in Cambridge, Massachusetts, with her husband, Mitchell, and their new baby boy, Zachary.

SELECTED WORKS: Wonder, 1991; Do-Over, 1992; Ever After, 1994.

ABOUT: Horn Book May 1994; Publishers Weekly December 20, 1991.

PIERO VENTURA

December 3, 1937–

AUTHOR AND ILLUSTRATOR OF *Piero Ventura's Book of Cities*, etc.

Biographical sketch of Piero Luigi Ventura:

PIERO VENTURA was born in Milan, Italy. He attended the Art School of Castello Sforzesco from 1956 to 1957. He also attended Architecture University in 1958. He married in 1962 and has three children.

Ventura worked for several advertising agencies from 1959 to 1978, ending up as art director of P & T of Milan. Since then, he has been an author and illustrator of children's books and a freelance illustrator.

His first book, *Piero Ventura's Book of Cities*, was recognized with many awards. It won the Award of Excellence from the Society of Illustrators, to which he belongs. It was named Book of the Year by the American Institute of Graphic Arts, and it received an Art Books for Children citation from the Brooklyn Musuem and the Brooklyn Public Library.

His work concentrates on portraying society and the arts in historical periods. In *Great Painters: Art Masterpieces Throughout History* works of art are reproduced in the environments in which they were created. The day-to-day life, art techniques, and social and political conditions of the time are portrayed, lending perspective on the creation of over seventy well-known works of art. *Michelangelo's World* shows the artist's work against a backdrop of what the cities, the courts, and the artistic community of the sixteenth century were like.

Turning to the lives of ordinary people, Ventura presents in *There Was Once a Time* the ways that people lived in various historical periods, offering information on work, clothing, social interaction, as well as streets, houses, and marketplaces. Ventura's interest in cities and architecture also led him to create *Grand Constructions*, which portrays great creations of mankind such as Stonehenge, the pyramid of Cheops, and Machu Picchu. Ventura has also worked on several books on historical subjects. His book *Christopher Columbus* won the Prix de Treize from the Office Chretien du Livre in 1979 and an award from the Ministero Spagnolo della Cultura in 1980. His illustrations for *The Voyages to the North Pole*, published in Italy, won an Art Citation from the Fiera of Bologna. *La scoperta di un mondo: Pompei*, published in Italy, garnered an Honorable Mention at the Biennale of Illustration in Bratislava in 1983.

Ventura also won the Pier Paolo Vergerio Honor in 1989 for *Venice: Birth of a City*. A *Horn Book Magazine* reviewer called the book a "beautifully organized and illustrated look at the rich history of the ancient, intriguing city." The book was also named a Notable Children's Trade Book in the Field of Social Studies by a joint committee of the Children's Book Council and the National Council on the Social Studies.

Piero Ventura is a member of the Illustrators Society of Italy and lives in Milan.

SELECTED WORKS WRITTEN AND ILLUSTRATED: Piero Ventura's Book of Cities, 1975; Grand Constructions, 1983; Great Painters, 1984; There Was Once a Time, 1987; Venice: Birth of a City, 1988; Great Composers, 1989; Michelangelo's World, 1989; 1492: The Year of the New World, 1992; Communication: Means and Technologies for Exchanging Information, 1994; Darwin: Nature Reinterpreted, 1995.

SELECTED WORKS ILLUSTRATED: Christopher Columbus, by Gian Paolo Ceserani, 1978; Marco Polo, by Gian Paolo Ceserani, 1982; In Search of Ancient Crete, by Gian Paolo Ceserani, 1985.

ABOUT: Bookbird No. 2, 1986; Contemporary Authors, Vol. 103; (New Revision Series), Vol. 39; Something About the Author, Vol. 43, 61.

JUDITH VIGNA

April 27, 1936–

AUTHOR OF *Nobody Wants a Nuclear War*, etc.

Autobiographical sketch of Judith Vigna:

I HAD A PROPER English upbringing: born in a manor house, tended by nannies, and packed off at twelve to boarding school. My father was a doctor, but not a rich one. In the thirties and forties old country houses were there for the fixing, and domestic help came cheap.

My sister, brother and I were rich—in books. Birthdays and Christmasses brought book tokens, which were happily exchanged for tales by authors like Beatrix Potter, A. A. Milne and Kenneth Grahame.

I wrote my first poem at six, at my father's knee. He often wrote for medical journals, and when my siblings and I were away at school he sent us letters composed entirely of rhyming couplets. Before she married, my mother sang with an amateur operetta group, and an uncle was an artist. So whatever gifts I had were nurtured. My outlets were work for school magazines, and later my first job as a cub reporter for a local newspaper, where I often illustrated my own articles.

Judith Vigna

After my parents' divorce I joined a public relations firm in London, studying in my free time at St. Martin's School of Art. But my feet were itchy. In March 1957, just before my twenty-first birthday, I boarded the ocean liner Sylvania for Montreal, Canada. Holed up in a Bohemian apartment, I wrote a soapy saga of adolescence—mercifully unpublished. Too practical to risk starvation, I took a job in the advertising department of a retail store. Ten months later I emigrated to New York, where I continued copywriting, this time for a large Madison Avenue agency. I felt creatively stifled, but the discipline drilled into me stayed.

My ambitions were further detoured by marriage. He was a family physician, and I loved working with his patients. But the long hours left little time for eating, much less writing the great American novel.

Then fate intervened. Surgery prevented me from having my own children, and I found myself inventing them. *The Little Boy Who Loved Dirt and Almost Became a Superslob* caught the spirit of my near-perfect childhood.

With my divorce, I resumed my studies, at Queens College, New York. An interest in psychology and art therapy forced me to re-examine my early life. Was it as perfect as I had imagined? So many children's books told only of the sunny side of childhood. But what of children growing up in dysfunctional families? *She's Not My Real Mother* emerged, followed by other books about troubled homes. It has always been difficult for me to write for young kids about subjects like nuclear war, racism, substance abuse, or a parent's death. I'm afraid I might disturb the very children I'm trying to reassure. But when I dig into the research, and listen to children and their adults, I relax. So many tell me they feel less alone. Cushioned by hope, truth can be comforting. The imagined is often far scarier.

Uncle Alfredo's Zoo was a joy to write and illustrate—a story inspired by a recent trip to Italy with my fiance. But from time to time frustration over human rights violations pulls me to thornier topics. I hope to keep this kind of balance in my writing.

———

Judith Vigna was born in Gedney, England. In 1957 she emigrated to Canada, and the following year to New York City, where she still lives. She studied art at the St. Martin's School of Art in London in 1956; at the School for Visual Arts in New York City in 1960; and at Queens College of the City University of New York in 1973. She is a member of PEN and the Authors League of America.

Nobody Wants a Nuclear War won the 1987 Jane Addams Children's Book Award.

SELECTED WORKS WRITTEN AND ILLUSTRATED: She's Not My Real Mother, 1980; Grandma Without Me, 1984; Nobody Wants a Nuclear War, 1986; Mommy and Me By Ourselves Again, 1987; I Wish Daddy Didn't Drink So Much, 1988; My Big Sister Takes Drugs, 1990; Saying Goodbye to Daddy, 1991; Black Like Kyra, White Like Me, 1992; When Eric's Mom Fought Cancer, 1993; Uncle Alfredo's Zoo, 1994; My Two Uncles, 1995.

ABOUT: Contemporary Authors, Vol. 77-80; (New Revision Series), Vol. 13, 29; Something About the Author, Vol. 15. Pronunciation: VEEN-ya

JULIE VIVAS

1947–

ILLUSTRATOR OF *Possum Magic*, etc.

Biographical sketch of Julie Vivas:

JULIE VIVAS was born in Adelaide, South
Australia, and grew up in Melbourne and
Sydney. In 1965, she graduated from a
three-year diploma course in Interior Design at East Sydney Technical College. After college, Vivas worked as a color mixer
and a cel painter at the Artransa animation
studio. In 1967, she was an assistant anima-
tor at Air Programs International.

Vivas moved to Spain in 1968. She lived
first in Madrid, and then in Jerez de la
Frontera, where she began a series of portraits. She returned to Madrid in 1970, and
in 1972 she moved back to Australia, where
she had her first art exhibit. She had exhibitions in Sydney and New Castle, New South
Wales, showing her work based on her
Spanish drawings, as well as work depicting
Australian lizards with nudes, an anthropomorphic lion in a suburban garden setting,
and a series of visual comments on being a
young mother in the suburbs.

It wasn't until 1978 that Vivas was first
offered a picture-book text to illustrate. It
was called *Hush the Invisible Mouse*, written by the Australian writer Mem Fox, and
it was the forerunner of Fox's book *Possum
Magic*.

The first published book by Vivas was
The Tram to Bondi Beach, written by Eliz-
abeth Hathorn and published in Australia
in 1981. Her watercolor illustrations depict
Sydney in the 1930's, and the story is about
a young boy who longs to get a job selling
newspapers to the passengers on the tram.
The Tram to Bondi Beach was named a
Highly Commended Picture Book of the
Year 1982 by the Australian Children's
Book Council.

Possum Magic was published in Australia
in 1983. It was also named a Highly Commended Picture Book of the Year (for 1984)
by the Australian Children's Book Council.

JULIE VIVAS

It received an International Board on Books
for Young People Honor Diploma for Illustration in 1986 and was named Best Children's Book of 1984 by the Australia New
South Wales Premier's Literary Awards. It
also received the Australian Koala Award in
1987. Vivas illustrated another book by
Mem Fox, *Wilfrid Gordon McDonald
Partridge*, which was named an American
Library Association Notable Book in 1985.
Weston Woods produced a film version of
the book, which was named a Notable
Filmstrip for 1988 by the ALA.

In 1988, Vivas adapted a King James Bible story. *The Nativity* was named an Hon-
or Book in the picture-book category of the
1989 *Boston Globe-Horn Book* awards. It
won the Italy Bologna Children's Book Fair
1987 Commendation Premio Grafico
Award, and was an ALA Notable Book of
the Year.

The Very Best of Friends was named Picture Book of the Year 1990 by the Children's Book Council of Australia and an
ALA Notable Book. She also illustrated *Let
the Celebrations Begin!*, a book based on a
true incident that occurred during the
Holocaust. On the eve of liberation from a
concentration camp, several mothers made

a celebration for their children, and made stuffed toys for them from scraps of cloth. Barbara Marinak, a reading consultant writing in *The Horn Book Magazine*, described its powerful effect when she read it to a class of adolescent children. She found it to be a fine introduction to novels written about the subject.

Other books she has illustrated include *Our Granny* by Margaret Wild, which was named an ALA Notable Book of the Year.

Vivas has stated that the way she experiences life is "primarily visual," and that she chooses stories that draw on her "visual sense." She works first in pencil and does the final artwork in watercolor paint. "I enjoy the wet paint melting into the wet paper," she states.

Critic Karen Jameyson, in her *Horn Book* column "News from Down Under," writes that "Julie Vivas's illustrations . . . are as familiar and pleasing to Australian children as Vegemite on toast. Her distinctive watercolors, dominated by circular shapes and by unpretentiousness, make dexterous use of line and color, leading viewers through comfortably rounded images from page to page."

In addition to doing illustration and painting, Vivas has also given talks on writing and illustrating for children, and she was a participant in the Australian Children's Book Council delegation to China in 1987. In 1992, she was awarded the Dromkeen Medal for contribution to the appreciation of children's literature.

Vivas makes her home in inner-city Sydney, where she lives with her two daughters.

SELECTED WORKS RETOLD AND ILLUSTRATED: The Nativity, 1988.

SELECTED WORKS ILLUSTRATED: Possum Magic, by Mem Fox, 1987; The Tram to Bondi Beach, by Elizabeth Hathorn, 1989; I Went Walking, by Sue Williams, 1990; Stories from Our Street, by Richard Tulloch, 1990; The Very Best of Friends, by Margaret Wild, 1990; Nurse Lugton's Curtain, by Virginia Woolf, 1991; Let the Celebrations Begin!, by Margaret Wild, 1991; Our Granny, by Margaret Wild, 1994.

ABOUT: Horn Book May 1993.

CHARLOTTE VOAKE

1957–

AUTHOR AND ILLLUSTRATOR OF *Over the Moon: A Book of Nursery Rhymes*, etc.

Biographical sketch of Charlotte Voake:

CHARLOTTE VOAKE was born in Wales and grew up in Chepstow and Wirral, England, where her father was a theater critic. Her father used to tell her stories that he had made up, some with gruesome and exciting details. She always wanted to be an illustrator, and at the age of twelve, she won a European Schools poster competition. By the time she was seventeen she had designed a number of other posters, including one for a conservation society and one for the Liverpool Grand Opera.

She did not go to art school, but she had a good art course at Birkenhead High School. She later studied art history, obtaining a degree at London University. Her first book, *The New Red Bike*, was published while she was still at the university.

After she graduated, she worked at a gallery in Liverpool, England, for a short time. Since then, she has worked full-time, first as an illustrator, then as an author-illustrator.

After she illustrated several books written by others, her publishers asked her to create her major work *Over the Moon: A Book of Nursery Rhymes*, a 128-page collection that was first published in England in 1985. Critic Anne Wood stated about the book, "Never since Harold Jones's classic nursery collection, *Lavender Blue*, has there been such a versatile use of pen and ink drawings and watercolour to suggest a whole new world."

She wrote and illustrated a book for beginning readers, *Tom's Cat*, and illustrated another written by Jan Mark, called *Fur*. Both were published in England in 1986.

The London *Observer* reviewed *The Ridiculous Story of Gammer Gurton's Needle*, an adaptation of a Tudor comedy, mentioning the "fine light summery pictures." A review in *The Bookseller* stated that David Lloyd's text "gains a classic quality from Charlotte Voake's folksy illustrations."

She also created a book for very young children, *First Things First*, that reviewer Ann A. Flowers, writing in *The Horn Book Magazine*, calls "[as] alluring a compendium for the very young as one is likely to find." Lists of verbs, rhymes, pictures of animals, fruits, vegetables, and other common objects that babies see around them are shown, making the book an "absolute winner for the very youngest child," according to Flowers.

Reading aloud to her own daughter gave Voake the idea to retell and illustrate her collection *The Three Little Pigs and Other Favourite Nursery Stories*, which was published in England in 1991.

Voake and her husband and daughter live in Surrey, England, and enjoy recreational time on their boat.

The Mighty Slide won Second Prize in the 1989 W.H. Smith Illustration Awards organized by the Victoria and Albert Museum in London. *The Best of Aesop's Fables* was shortlisted for the 1990 Kurt Maschler Award administered by the British Book Trust.

SELECTED WORKS WRITTEN AND ILLUSTRATED: First Things First, 1988; Mrs. Goose's Baby, 1989.

SELECTED WORKS RETOLD AND ILLUSTRATED: Over the Moon: A Book of Nursery Rhymes, 1992; The Three Little Pigs and Other Favourite Nursery Stories, 1992.

SELECTED WORKS ILLUSTRATED: The Mighty Slide, by Allan Ahlberg, 1988; The Ridiculous Story of Gammer Gurton's Needle, by David Lloyd, 1987; The Way to Sattin Shore, by Philippa Pearce, 1984; Amy Said, by Martin Waddell, 1990; The Best of Aesop's Fables, retold by Margaret Clark, 1990; Caterpillar, Caterpillar, by Vivian French, 1993.

ABOUT: Liverpool Daily Post November 14, 1985.

MARTIN WADDELL

April 10, 1941–

AUTHOR OF *Can't You Sleep, Little Bear?*, etc.

Autobiographical sketch of Martin Waddell, who also writes under the pen name "Catherine Sefton":

I WAS BORN on a night when the Luftwaffe were bombing Belfast. The next day my father brought my mother and myself to the quiet countryside of County Down, to the seaside town of Newcastle at the foot of the Mountains of Mourne.

We lived on the coast road, in Rock Cottage, an old stone cottage that had once been a tollhouse. Later on, when we were doing renovations, we discovered a secret staircase that led to a hiding place under the roof. There were old clothes and rifles lying there—just the sort of thing to start the imagination going.

Behind the cottage there were the woods and the mountains. I spent hours there and I could believe that the stories of Andersen and Grimm and the Norse sagas were around me. I was an only child and I read voraciously. The house was full of books, books of all sorts: Enid Blyton, Jung, G. K. Chesterton, E. Nesbit. I read them all.

Other hours I spent on the beach in front of the cottage and at the Rock swimming pool. We were taught to swim by a man who tied a rope round our middles and then towed us from the side—most definitely not a method I recommend. And there was football, soccer, which I've always loved and which I would still love to play, although I know that I can't. When I wrote the Napper football stories I put in full match descriptions, training sessions, team tactics—kids love it: adults think there's too much football!

I left school early, which was a bad mistake, and went to work on the local newspaper where I was all right as a cub reporter because I was always happy with putting words together, and where I was disastrous as a printer's apprentice.

Football came to the rescue. I asked for a trial at Fulham Football Club in London and they took me! Sadly, several months later it was clear that I was not going to be a professional footballer.

A variety of jobs in London followed, none of them very wonderful as I had escaped from school without any qualifications. Football as a career was definitely out. The job was dull. I started to write. The world of books and story was there and I come from a family that had writers in several generations. I wrote and I wrote, and eight years and thirty rejected manuscripts later I had my first book published. *Otley*, a comedy spy thriller, was made into a film with Tom Courtney and Romy Schneider, and I made some money. Back to Ireland!

I got married in 1969 and Rosaleen and I settled in Donaghadee, a small seaside town, where I wrote my first book for children: *In a Blue Velvet Dress*. I was published under the name Catherine Sefton, as the name of Martin Waddell was associated with adult thrillers and I thought that this book for children would be a one-off. The next hundred or so books, some written as Catherine Sefton and some as Martin Waddell, have all been for children and young people: picture books for babies and bigger; beginner books; football stories; adventure stories; ghost stories; teenage stories, several of which are Northern Ireland stories.

Writing about Northern Ireland was almost inevitable. We live there after all and the violence affected our own lives directly—I was injured in a bomb explosion in 1972 and writing all but stopped for several years. As our three boys grew up there were all sorts of questions and discussions, and these made their way into books showing the effects of the Troubles on teenagers, the shadowing of their lives.

———

Martin Waddell writes fiction for adults and is also the author of a play for radio, *The Fleas and Mr. Morgan*, which was broadcast in 1969. He is a member of the Society of Authors in London, the Irish Writers Union of Dublin and the Children's Literature Association of Ireland.

Waddell's books have won many awards in England and in Europe. *Can't You Sleep, Little Bear?* won the 1988 Kate Greenaway Medal, awarded by the British Library Association, for the illustrations by Barbara Firth. *Farmer Duck* was named a Highly Commended Book in the same awards in 1991, as was *The Pig in the Pond* in 1992.

Can't You Sleep, Little Bear? won the Sheffield Book Award and the Prix de critiques de Livres pour Enfants de la Communaute Francaise de Belgique.

The Park in the Dark won the 1989 Emil /Kurt Maschler Award given by the Book Trust in Britain.

Island of the Strangers was nominated for a 1984 Carnegie Medal, which is awarded by the British Library Association.

SELECTED WORKS: Amy Said, 1990; The Hidden House, 1990; The Pig in the Pond, 1991; Sam Vole and His Brothers, 1991; Can't You Sleep, Little Bear?, 1992; Farmer Duck, 1992; Little Dracula Goes to School, 1992; Sailor Bear, 1992; Stories from the Bible: Old Testament Stories Retold, 1993; John Joe and the Big Hen, 1995; Tango's Baby, 1995.

SELECTED WORKS AS CATHERINE SEFTON: In a Blue

Velvet Dress, 1973; The Haunting of Ellen: A Story of Suspense, 1975; Island of the Strangers, 1985.

ABOUT: Books for Keeps May 1991; Contemporary Authors, Vol. 113; (New Revision Series), Vol. 34; ; Kirkpatrick, D.L. Twentieth-Century Children's Writers, 2nd ed.; Something About the Author, Vol. 43; 81; Something About the Author Autobiography Series, Vol. 15.

BILL WALLACE

August 1, 1947–

AUTHOR OF *True Friends*, etc.

Autobiographical sketch of William Keith Wallace:

I'M FORTY-SEVEN years old and still trying to decide what I want to be when I grow up.

Raised by my grandmother, parents and an older sister, there were some things I *didn't* want to be. I didn't want to be an older sister because they're too bossy. Being a "baby brother" wasn't too hot, either. They get pushed around a lot.

A cowboy or a fireman sounded a lot more exciting. But someday I wanted to be rich and famous, and there aren't many rich and famous firemen. My best friend taught me how to hunt and fish. I loved it. Maybe I would become a professional hunter. Then again, there aren't too many rich and famous hunters or fishermen, either.

In high school, I met this really cute girl named Carol. When we graduated, I finally decided on something I did want to be—a husband. A year later we had a baby. I didn't decide I wanted to be a daddy, but since there was no way to send it back . . . Besides, I loved being a husband and a father.

After hauling hay, running jackhammer, working as a salesman at a hardware store, being an orderly in a hospital, and various other jobs, I also decided that I wanted to be a college graduate!

I liked studying about animals. Only it

seemed as though the college teachers were always wanting to dissect them. I liked animals—intact—not cut up into little pieces. English wasn't too bad, until I took a writing course. My teacher suggested that I "please leave the English Department." She told me that my usage was terrible and my spelling was "the most creative" she had ever seen. Then she smiled. "But what you say and the way you say it is very special. There's a man in Journalism who teaches professional writing. I want you to meet. . . . "

William Foster-Harris didn't help much with my spelling or my usage. He gave me a love for writing. He let me feel the excitement of weaving stories and painting pictures with my words. He showed me the "rush" of using my imagination to go anyplace and be anything I wanted to be. He loved writing. I loved him. I finally knew what I was going to be when I grew up.

Daddy said that being a writer was, "Great! Only get a real job!"

I went to work as a reporter on a newspaper. But I'd been brought up to feel that if someone didn't want to tell me something . . . well, it was their business and I shouldn't bother them. (Not a very good attitude for an investigative reporter.) I *didn't* want to be a newspaper reporter. So at the encouragement of my mother, who was a teacher; my sister, who was a teacher; and my wife—(come to think of it, ALL of them were teachers)—I went back to school, because I was grown up now and I knew what I was going to be.

Suddenly, I found myself trapped in a classroom with twenty-five "screaming" fourth graders. Well maybe not screaming, but they were full of energy and life. Besides, they seemed to know a whole lot more about fourth grade than I did. It was scary!

But my girls took care of me. They helped with "lunch count", reminded me when it was time for recess and P.E., and talked me into reading. The boys and girls both loved *Old Yeller*, but when I tried to find other books, we couldn't find one they liked. One student, Terry, talked me into telling stories about when I was growing up and when I ran out, another student, Mary Ann, suggested that I "make up" stories. I wrote the stories down so I wouldn't forget. My kids liked listening, but they wanted to read the stories, too. So one of the boys suggested that I find someone who would make "real books" for us.

I loved teaching fourth grade! I guess that's why the school people made me a principal???

I write stories full time and go around talking to students at schools. Although I never planned on being an author, I guess that's what I am. Now, I write books.

Wonder what I'll be when I grow up?

———

Bill Wallace was born in Chickasha, Oklahoma. He studied writing at the University of Oklahoma. He received his B.S. degree in Elementary Education from the University of Science and Arts of Oklahoma in 1971 and an M.S. degree in Elementary Administration from Southern Western State University in 1974. He was principal at West Elementary in Chickasha from 1977 to 1988.

He is a speaker at such conferences as the 1984 School of Library Science spring festival at Sam Houston State University in Texas, and has appeared at many schools and universities. He is also a short story contributor to such magazines as *Western Horseman* and *Hunting Dog*. He is a member of the Authors Guild and the Society of Children's Book Writers and Illustrators.

Beauty won the 1991 William Allen White Award. *Ferret in the Bedroom, Lizards in the Fridge* was named a Children's Choice Book by a joint committee of the International Reading Association and the Children's Book Council. Wallace's books have won many state awards voted upon by children.

SELECTED WORKS: A Dog Called Kitty, 1980; Trapped in Death Cave, 1984; Shadow on the Snow, 1985; Ferret in the Bedroom, Lizards in the Fridge, 1986; Danger on Panther Peak, 1987; Red Dog, 1987; Beauty, 1988; Danger in Quicksand Swamp, 1989; Snot Stew, 1989; The Christian Spurs, 1990; Totally Disgusting, 1991; The Biggest Klutz in Fifth Grade, 1992; Buffalo Gal, 1992; Never Say Quit, 1993; Blackwater Swamp, 1994; True Friends, 1994; Watchdog and the Coyotes, 1995.

ABOUT: Contemporary Authors, Vol. 124; Something About the Author, Vol. 47, 53.

BERNADETTE WATTS

May 13, 1942–

ILLUSTRATOR OF *Rumpelstiltskin*, etc.

Autobiographical sketch of Anna Bernadette Watts, who also does illustration under the name "Bernadette":

I MUST HAVE BEEN about eight years old when I was taken to the cinema—a rare treat with gold-braided commissioners standing at the door—to see Walt Disney's *Pinocchio*. When the first sequence went up, the starry deep blue night sky with twinkling stars, the sleepy village below with cosy candle-lit windows, my fate was sealed. I wanted only to go to Hollywood and paint backgrounds for Walt Disney.

I was a "war-baby" and treats were rare, but my father always managed to get paper and pencils and pens for my use. Every brown paper bag was also saved which my mother rationed out to me for drawing. I had a younger brother, but luckily he was not art-oriented, so I did not have to share the paper! He made miniature models from match sticks and scraps of balsa wood. He later became a civil engineer and designed bridges over motorways. My mother had also graduated from art school and also encouraged my talents—especially when I neglected them.

My parents were great readers. Every Christmas morning I would find a mile high pile of second-hand books by my bed—picture books by Edmund Dulac and Anne Anderson, books on the history of architecture, books on Kierkegaard and Jung—the philosophy and heavy literature started coming along when I was about thirteen. The supply of illustrated classic children's books, collections of fairy tales and girls school stories has never ceased. My father, now in his eighties, still buys me anything to do with the history of illustration.

There was never any discussion as to my future—I was going to be a novelist of the highest order and an artist. Well, I didn't get off that ladder, but as time went by I found which rung suited me, and it wasn't the topmost! Last year I did write a novel—still unpublished! My art college was very supportive of my ambition. The college was in a grubby but lively town. I travelled daily from my parental home—a crumbling old Victorian Gothic monstrosity deep in the Kentish countryside.

Living in the countryside most of my life, I have always loved nature. I feel very close to the wild animals, shy rabbits and hedgehogs, birds, even foxes. They are nicer than human beings and don't argue or try to organize your life for you. When I was a teenager I did become very knowledgeable about plant life and looking back now I realize I could very happily have become a biologist. Side interests developed—I spent a summer meticulously drawing various cloud formations and studying clouds scientifically. On a trip to Denmark I collected lots of pebbles on the shore as they are very special there. I think I was very lonely and solitary, loving books and animals and my own company, until I left home and threw up my job, and went to London.

I loved living in London in the 1960's, until I left in 1973 to live an entirely opposite way of life in Wales. In London I started working for many publishers, eventually settling down with Nord-Süd-Verlag in Zurich. Since then they have become world wide (North-South Books in the U.S.A.). My life in London with all my new friends, parties, mini-skirts, Hirondelle wine, Saturday mornings doing the rounds of the art galleries, and listening to the 1960's pop groups at gigs and on radio was regularly punctuated by trips, to almost every European country. I am glad I did that, as Europe has now sadly changed and is all much of a muchness, also very expensive.

In North Wales I rented a tiny stone cottage built in 1372 and mentioned in history books. It stood all alone, crouching close to the ground, on the foothills of Snowdon. I was very happy there, I became very interested in trees and mountains. I met a potter who was also a naturalist and we had a son, Bernard, in 1975. We parted company within a few months of his birth due to sad circumstances. By 1982, by which time I had returned to Kent, I had my own home, a mortgage, had learnt to drive a car, and my son had started at the Rudolph Steiner School. A few years later I won the Japanese "Owl Prize."

At present my son and I live in a huge decrepit Victorian seaside home. My son has a music room with posters of Fleetwood Mac and The Who stuck on the walls. He has a rock and roll band which works locally—they play all the songs I loved in the sixties. I have a studio on the first floor which opens out onto a balcony full of potted plants. I won't have central heating, we have a wood burning stove, and an open fire. I won't have a micro-wave or a food processor, nor will I buy fast food or convenience food. People imagine I have "technophobia"—I still refer to wirelesses and record-players. In truth my heart is still in the Welsh Mountains.

————

Bernadette Watts was born in Northampton, England. Her family moved to Kent when she was four. She attended Ashford Grammar School and at age eighteen she left to work briefly in the County Library. She studied book production for three years at Maidstone College of Art, and studied one year of painting. She worked as assistant in the Liberal Studies Department of the college. When she moved to London at the age of twenty-four she began travelling. She attended the Frankfurt Book Fair in 1967, where she discoverd Nord-Süd-Verlag, then a small publisher, and she has since published two picture books a year with them. She has also travelled in South Africa. Her interests are work, cooking, and gardening, and she also likes driving, reading, and difficult crossword puzzles.

Das Kleine Madchen mit den

Schwefelholzchen, which was published by Nord-Sud in 1983, won the 1986 Owl Prize of Japan, for the best illustrated book in an exhibition of International Children's Books. She also won the Premio Graphico prize at the Bologna Book Fair in 1970.

SELECTED WORKS RETOLD AND ILLUSTRATED: The Wind and the Sun: An Aesop Fable, 1992.

SELECTED WORKS ILLUSTRATED: Mother Holly, by Jacob and Wilhelm Grimm, 1972; Rapunzel, by Jacob and Wilhelm Grimm, 1975; The Ragamuffins, by Jacob and Wilhelm Grimm, 1989; The Bremen Town Musicians, by Jacob and Wilhelm Grimm, 1992; Rumpelstiltskin, by Jacob and Wilhelm Grimm, 1993; The Fir Tree, by Hans Christian Andersen, 1995; The Wolf and the Seven Little Kids, by Jacob and Wilhelm Grimm, 1995.

ABOUT: Contemporary Authors (First Revision), Vol. 29-32; (New Revision Series), Vol. 31; Peppin, Brigid and Lucy Micklethwait. Book Illustrators of the Twentieth Century; Something About the Author, Vol. 4.

JEROME WEXLER

February 6, 1923–

PHOTOGRAPHER OF *A Frog's Body*, etc.

Autobiographical sketch of Jerome LeRoy Wexler, who has also published photographs under the pseudonym "Roy Delmar":

SOME PEOPLE, even when quite young, know what they want to be and do as adults. I admire them. Having a goal and working towards that goal must make life a lot simpler.

In my case I sort of backed into being a photographer and author. A series of unrelated events, many occurring years apart, plus a varied background and a few snap decisions brought me to where I am today.

I was introduced to photography by my ninth-grade science teacher who started an after-school photography club. By the time I graduated high school, I was a pretty good photographer.

After graduating I served a 4,800-hour apprenticeship as a toolmaker. Upon completing my apprenticeship I was drafted and sent to Europe, and fought in the Battle of the Bulge as an infantryman.

After the war I took my discharge in England and went to work for the State Department as one of two American civilian photographers in charge of a small photo department.

Many of my photographic assignments required me to travel to various parts of Europe. I didn't realize it then but these trips were to lead to my becoming, eventually, a writer/illustrator of children's books.

Returning to the States I decided I wanted to be a teacher. While driving to school for the opening session I chose to take the country back roads instead of the highway. As I traveled I kept passing farms that looked very unlike those I saw in France and Germany. A few of the European farms looked up-to-date but many looked like photos one sees in old textbooks. I kept thinking if I become a teacher I could affect perhaps thirty or forty lives a year. If I used my photographic skills to teach better farming methods I could influence the lives of thousands. I never did reach the school.

Returning home I started a one-man business called "The Agricultural Photo Library." Over the years thousands of my photos were published both here and in Europe. They were used editorially in farm papers and farm magazines, textbooks, manuals, posters, etc. and, of course, for advertising purposes.

Like most professional photographers back in the 50's and 60's I used a 4x5 Crown Graphic and a 6x6cm Rollei. Both are nothing more than boxes fitted with lenses. They're OK for general photography but not for close-up photography. In other words, with those cameras I was able to photograph a field of wheat, but not the flowers on a single plant.

About 1963 I purchased a 35mm single lens reflex camera that was built modularly somewhat like Nikon's F2's and F3's. Everything on the camera was removable and replaceable—the lens, the pentaprism, the viewing screen, etc. Here was an ideal camera body for close-up photography. (Generally meaning photography where the *image* on the film can vary from 1/10 lifesize to 10 or even 20 times life-size.)

Today if one wants to do close-up photography all one has to do is go to the store and buy the equipment. Back then there was no such equipment to buy. Drawing upon my toolmaking background I designed and built all of my own—much of which I still use today.

Some problems are unique to close-up photography. When the image of a subject is enlarged ten times everything else is also enlarged ten times. A truck passing in the street may cause a camera on a tripod to vibrate one thousandth of an inch. This would be invisible in normal photography but in this case its effect is enlarged ten times on the slide. For use in books 35mm slides are always enlarged five to ten times. This means that the effect of the vibration is also increased. The original one thousandth of an inch vibration movement would now reproduce as a blur of almost an eighth of an inch.

Another problem unique to this kind of photography is light fall-off. A 35mm slide is approximately 1 x 1.5 inches. At ten times life-size the light that would normally fall on this small area is, in effect, falling on an area 10 x 15 inches. To compensate one must change the speed rating of the film from, say, 100 to 0.75 or increase greatly the amount of light that is used on the subject.

To overcome this, and other problems, special equipment must be designed and built and special photographic techniques must be developed.

As an agricultural photographer I already had a good knowledge of plants, animals, and insects so it was very easy to do photograpic life history studies of these subjects. My first study was of a milkweed plant, and it became my first book. The text was done by Millicent Selsam. As a team Millicent and I produced more than two dozen books. I also did many studies of animals. Joanna Cole did the texts for those. Another famous author I worked with was Patricia Lauber. We did three books together, and to date I've had nine books published where I did both texts and illustrations.

I think my books are successful for a number of reasons: for me to photograph a life history of a plant or animal I must actually raise/grow it through its complete life cycle. This firsthand information produces a book that is quite different from one where an author does his or her research in a library and then rewrites what others have written.

Also, in most books the text/story is told using words and illustrated with photos or drawings. In my books the text/story is told using photographs and illustrated with words! Even children with poor reading skills can 'read' my books.

———

Jerome Wexler was born in New York City, served in the U.S. Army from 1943 to 1946, is a self-taught photographer, and operated his agricultural photography business from 1950 to 1958. He lives in Connecticut, has two children and one grandchild, and has been writer and photographer exclusively since 1974.

Seeds was nominated for an American Book Award for the best nonfiction children's book on 1982. The New York Academy of Science has given two of Wexler's books honorable mentions in their Children's Book Science Awards: *Flower to Flower* and *A Snake's Body.*

Many of Wexler's books have been named as Outstanding Science Trade Books for Children by a joint committee of the National Science Teachers Association and the Children's Book Council. They include *A Frog's Body, A Chick Hatches, Seeds: Pop-Stick-Glide* and *Jack-in-the-Pulpit,* which he both wrote and illustrated, and many others.

The American Library Association has also honored many of his books, by naming them Notable Books of the Year. These include *Peanut* and *The Harlequin Moth, A Chick Hatches,* and *A Frog's Body.*

SELECTED WORKS WRITTEN AND ILLUSTRATED: Pet Hamsters, 1992; Wonderful Pussy Willows, 1992; Jack-in-the-Pulpit, 1993; Queen Anne's Lace, 1994.

SELECTED WORKS ILLUSTRATED: Peanut, by Millicent Selsam, 1969; The Harlequin Moth: Its Life Story, by Millicent Selsam, 1975; A Chick Hatches, by Joanna Cole, 1976; A Frog's Body, by Joanna Cole, 1980; Seeds: Pop-Stick-Glide, by Patricia Lauber, 1981; A Snake's Body, by Joanna Cole, 1981; From Flower to Flower: Animals and Pollination, by Patricia Lauber, 1987.

ABOUT: Bader, Barbara. American Picturebooks from Noah's Ark to the Beast Within; Contemporary Authors, Vol. 73-76; Something About the Author, Vol. 14.

RUTH WHITE

March 15, 1942–

AUTHOR OF *Sweet Creek Holler*, etc.

Autobiographical sketch of Ruth White:

Ruth White

I GREW UP in the small mining town of Grundy, Virginia, in the Appalachian Mountains, and received an excellent basic education there in the public schools. My father, a coal miner, was killed in a late-night brawl in 1948. He and my mother were only thirty years old at the time, and she was left to care for four young girls, a job which she handled bravely, magnificently. Her story is told in *Sweet Creek Holler*, which is more a memory than a story, but somewhat dressed up.

As poor as we were, there were always books in our house which we were encouraged to read. In school I met the first great loves of my life—music and writing. After college at Montreat-Anderson and Pfeiffer, both in North Carolina, I let the music slip away from me, and I didn't find it again until twenty-six years later when I joined a choir and began piano lessons. It was like finding a part of myself that had been lost. But all through the years I pursued my writing in journals and short stories, until in 1977 I published *The City Rose*, a story of a black child who moved from a Northern ciy to a small Southern town. It was loosely based on my teaching experiences in North Carolina.

Weeping Willow, my personal favorite, was based on memories of my high school days in the mountains of Virginia. The main character, Tiny Lambert, is more like me than any other character I have created. She, too, loved music. She was a dreamer who longed for a better life, and in the end she managed, against all odds, to go away to college just as I did.

My upcoming novel, to be published in 1996, *Belle Prater's Boy*, is a story about attaching too much importance to superficial appearances, thereby creating pain for ourselves, and sometimes others.

Today I live near the ocean in Virginia Beach, and work in the large metaphysical library of the Association for Research and Enlightenment. Here I meet the most wonderful and interesting people and books in the world.

The greatest love of my life today is my daughter, Dee Olivia, who is vibrant, bright, happy and more successful at enjoying life than anybody I have ever known.

As much as I want young people to read and enjoy the books I have written, I also recommend to them my own personal favorite books of all time—*To Kill a Mockingbird* by Harper Lee and *The Education of Little Tree* by Forrest Carter. Great reads!

———

Ruth White was born in Whitewood, Virginia. She earned her A.A. degree from Montreat-Anderson College near Asheville, North Carolina, in 1962 and her A.B. degree from Pfeiffer College, near Albemarle, N.C., in 1966. She earned a degree from Queens College in Charlotte, N.C., in 1976 as a Library Media Specialist. She taught school from 1966 to 1977 and has been a librarian since 1977.

SELECTED WORKS: Sweet Creek Holler, 1988; Weeping Willow, 1992.

SELECTED WORKS AS RUTH WHITE MILLER: The City Rose, 1977.

ABOUT: Contemporary Authors, Vol. 111; Something About the Author, Vol. 39.

DAVID WIESNER

February 5, 1956–

AUTHOR AND ILLUSTRATOR OF *Tuesday*, etc.

Biographical sketch of David Wiesner:

DAVID WIESNER was born and grew up in Bridgewater, New Jersey. He was raised in a family that encouraged an interest in art and music, and his older brother and sister, who also enjoyed drawing, gave him art supplies. He remembers visits to a paint and wallpaper store, because there was a small section that displayed art supplies. He also taught drawing to himself by completing workbooks and following the televised lessons of Jon Gnagy, who demonstrated techniques on a Saturday morning television show.

He went to the library to look at art books, especially "the great draftsmen": Da Vinci, Michelangelo, Albrecht Durer, and Pieter Breughel the Elder. He was also fascinated by the surrealists Dali, Magritte, and de Chirico.

He went on, in high school, to create his own comics, "Slop the Wonder Pig." He has stated that in comics, a single movement can be broken down into a dozen separate pictures; this is the equivalent of slow motion in film, he says, and he has used the technique in *Tuesday*. He and his friends produced a vampire movie called *The Saga of Butchula*. The art teacher at Bridgewater Raritan High School was the first teacher who influenced David Wiesner. He taught printmaking, photo silk screening, and watercolor painting, and invited an art student from the Rhode Island School of Design to visit class, which gave Wiesner the idea of going to that particular art school. At the school, he tried oil painting, but returned to watercolor as his primary medium. He later dedicated his book *Tuesday* to his art professor, Tom Sgouros.

Wiesner designed his first children's book in art school, after being impressed by a Lynd Ward wordless picture book. He graduated from the school with a B.F.A. degree in 1978. While at RISD, he was asked to do a *Cricket* magazine cover. In 1989, he did his second *Cricket* cover with the subject of frogs. The assignment led him to create his picture book *Tuesday*. He made a clay model of a frog so that he could pick it up and see perspectives around it, and he has used that technique of model building in the creation of other books.

The artwork of David Wiesner has been exhibited at the Metropolitan Museum of Art in 1982; at the Academy of Natural Sciences in Philadelphia in 1986; and at the Society of Illustrators in New York City in 1991 and 1992. He is a frequent speaker at such gatherings as a symposium on books for young readers sponsored by Brigham Young University in Provo, Utah, in 1995. Wiesner lives in Philadelphia, Pennsylvania, with his wife and son.

Tuesday was the winner of the 1992 Randolph Caldecott Medal, presented by the American Library Association. *Free Fall* was named a Caldecott Honor Book in 1989, and they were both named ALA No-

Wiesner: *WEEZ ner*

table Books of the Year, as was *June 29, 1999.*

SELECTED WORKS WRITTEN AND ILLUSTRATED: Hurricane, 1990; Tuesday, 1991; June 29, 1999, 1992.

SELECTED WORKS RETOLD AND ILLUSTRATED WITH KIM KAHNG: Loathsome Dragon, 1987.

SELECTED WORKS ILLUSTRATED: Honest Andrew, by Gloria Skurzynski, 1980; Man from the Sky, by Avi, 1981; Neptune Rising, by Jane Yolen, 1982; Owly, by Mike Thaler, 1982; The Kite Flier, by Dennis Haseley, 1986; Firebrat, by Nancy Willard, 1988; The Rainbow People, by Laurence Yep, 1989; Night of the Gargoyles, by Eve Bunting, 1994.

ABOUT: Clarionews No. 5; Cummings, Pat, comp. and ed. Talking With Artists; Horn Book July 1992; The Reading Teacher December 1992; Something About the Author, Vol. 72.

MARGARET WILLEY

November 5, 1950–

AUTHOR OF *Saving Lenny*, etc.

Autobiographical sketch of Margaret Willey:

I WAS BORN in Chicago, the eldest daughter in a family of eleven children. In 1955, my family moved to St. Joseph, Michigan, a small town on the Lake Michigan shoreline, the St. Martins of my early novels. As a teenager, I discovered the novels of J.D. Salinger, Carson McCullers and Rumer Godden; these books helped me to cope with my own difficult adolescence, making it at once more manageable and more mythic. I feel that my early love for these classic coming-of-age novels, and my general fascination with an adolescent perspective on the contemporary world, inspired me to eventually write my own young adult novels. I wrote *The Bigger Book of Lydia*, my first young adult novel, out of an artistic and personal need to revisit those years, which had been overly full of maternal responsibility because I had so many younger siblings.

Margaret Willey

I left home at seventeen to attend Michigan State University, where I stayed for two years and then dropped out, drifting through jobs and feeling generally unclear about my future. In 1972, I went back to school and graduated with a teaching certificate from Grand Valley State University in Michigan. However, I quickly decided that classroom teaching was not for me and it was at this point in my life that I began writing more seriously and submitting work to editors and publishers, while supporting myself with clerical jobs. At the advice of a past college professor, I enrolled in a creative writing program at Bowling Green State University in Ohio, where I earned an M.F.A. in Fiction in 1980. After earning this degree, I married, had a daughter in 1981 and began composing *The Bigger Book of Lydia* in the Michigan farmhouse where we were all living at the time.

Looking back, I see that my need to be a writer came late in life—not until I was in my late twenties did I realize that writing was exactly what I wanted to do professionally. At that point, and especially through my first two novels, I was able to unravel some of the mysteries of my own adolescence in a much more coherent and mean-

Willey: *WILL ee*

ingful way that I had been able to do while living through those years. This, I believe, is the greatest gift of the young adult novel to its readers—a chance to sort out carefully, through the novel form, the chaos and confusion of coming-of-age.

People often ask me what the "message" behind my novels is. I see the characters themselves as a kind of message. I write about strong-willed, sensitive teenagers, mostly girls, who possess great integrity and courage. My characters yearn and struggle for resolution in a confusing world. As they confront obstacles to their own becoming— familial, social and psychological obstacles—they persevere, sometimes alone, relying on inner strength and creativity, and sometimes with help from an unlikely friendship, someone outside the circle of peers.

I also write fiction and essays for adults, and I have written many short stories. In 1995, I received my third Creative Artist Grant from the Michigan Council for the Arts, this one to create a short-story collection on the theme of adults and teenagers in confrontation. It is a subject I am lately very interested in, because I have my own teenage daughter now and because I have noticed that often when adults and teenagers meet in anger, it is difficult to tell which person is the true adult.

———

Margaret Willey received B.Ph. and B.A. degrees in 1975 from Grand Valley State College.

Her fiction for adults has been published in such publications as *Redbook*, *Sou'wester*, and *Good Housekeeping*. She is a member of the Authors Guild and the Children's Reading Round Table.

Margaret Willey received three Michigan Council of the Arts Grants, in 1984, 1988, and 1995.

Three of her novels were named Best Books for Young Adults by the American Library Association. They are *The Bigger Book of Lydia*, *Saving Lenny*, and *Finding*

David Dolores. Finding David Dolores was also voted a "Best of the Best" book by the ALA in 1993. Both *Saving Lenny* and *Finding David Dolores* were also named Children's Choice Books for Young Adults by a joint committee of the Children's Book Council and the International Reading Association.

SELECTED WORKS: The Bigger Book of Lydia, 1983; Finding David Dolores, 1986; If Not for You, 1988; Saving Lenny, 1991; The Melinda Zone, 1993.

ABOUT: Contemporary Authors, Vol. 117; (New Revision Series), Vol. 40; Gallo, Donald R. Speaking for Ourselves, Too.

SHERLEY ANNE WILLIAMS

August 25, 1944–

AUTHOR OF *Working Cotton*.

Biographical sketch of Sherley Anne Williams:

SHERLEY ANNE WILLIAMS is a poet, novelist, critic, and teacher. She was born in Bakersfield, California, the third of four girls in her family. In order to find work, the family followed the crops, and Williams later wrote about this experience of moving from town to town, and feeling dispossessed, in her poetry. Her two older sisters had left home by the time she was sixteen, when her mother died. Her older sister Ruby became her guardian, and with her friends, Ruby provided role models for her younger sister's upbringing.

Williams graduated with a B.A. degree from California State University in Fresno in 1966. She began writing short stories at that time, and specifically wanted to write about the lower-income black women who had been important in her own life. Her first story was published in *Massachusetts Review* in 1967. She did graduate work at Howard University in Washington, D.C. from 1966 to 1967. She was a lecturer in the Ethnic Studies Program at California State

from 1969 to 1970. She earned her M.A. degree from Brown University in Providence, Rhode Island, in 1972. She also taught there, in the Black Studies Program.

She was Associate Professor at California State at Fresno for a year, then moved to California State at San Diego. She was Assistant Professor from 1973 to 1975; Associate Professor until 1982; and since then she has been Professor in the Department of Literature. She has taught fiction and poetry writing, Afro-American literature, Pan-African literatures in English, and American Women's Literature.

Williams has been Advisory Editor for publications such as *Langston Hughes Review* and *Callaloo*; has been a judge in fiction and poetry writing competitions, and has been Co-ordinator of the Writing Program at the University's Department of Literature. She is the author of a novel for adults, *Dessa Rose*, and wrote a book of criticism, *Give Birth to Brightness: A Thematic Study in Neo-Black Literature.*

Though Williams is the author of an award-winning children's book, she is probably best known as a poet. *The Peacock Poems*, published in 1975 as part of the Wesleyan Poetry series, was nominated in

1976 for a National Book Award. She also wrote *Some One Sweet Angel Chile*, a book of poetry that pays homage to the blues singer Bessie Smith. Williams won a Regional Emmy Award for a television performance of poems from the book. She also had a play, *Letters from a New England Negro*, produced at the National Black Theater Festival in 1991.

In addition to holding many lectureships, such as a Senior Fulbright Lectureship at the University of Ghana in 1984, and visiting professorship positions at various universities, Williams is also a featured reader at jazz and poetry festivals around the country.

Working Cotton, her book for children, is a child's story of the day's work as a family picks cotton as migrant farm workers in California. Critic Betsy Hearne, writing in the *Bulletin of the Center for Children's Books*, writes: "[I]t's a slice of life that's presented without judgment or story, but the arresting art and brief text . . . will bring home an organic experience of work that few children have known or imagined." The book, with illustrations by Carole Byard, was named an Honor Book in the 1993 Randolph Caldecott Medal awards given by the American Library Association. It was also named an Honor Book in the 1993 Coretta Scott King Awards and was named an ALA Notable Book of the Year.

SELECTED WORKS: Working Cotton, 1992.

ABOUT: Dictionary of Literary Biography, Vol. 41; Contemporary Authors, Vol. 73-76; (New Revision Series), Vol. 25; Essence December 1986; Jordan, Shirley Marie, ed. Broken Silences: Interviews with Black and White Women Writers; Los Angeles Times July 4, 1982; Something About the Author, Vol. 78; Walker, Alice. Interviews with Black Writers.

BUDGE WILSON

May 2, 1927–

AUTHOR OF *The Leaving*, etc.

Autobiographical sketch of Budge Wilson:

Budge Wilson

WHEN I WAS eleven years old, I wrote a lot of poems and stories, but I felt that a real author shouldn't really start writing till he or she was at least thirty-five—to make sure of having lots of interesting things to write about. Ironically, when I finally started writing full-time at age fifty-six, it was for children that I wrote. Even in my adult short stories, I often still write about children, particularly about adolescents. Perhaps for that reason, certain of my adult collections of short stories are being targeted to a teen-aged market. In *The Leaving*, published in the U.S. by Philomel (and in mass market paperback by Scholastic), most of the stories center around the difficult movement from childhood into adulthood. In *The Dandelion Garden*, published by Philomel, the stories are also for young adults.

In the last eleven years, I've published fifteen books, but before that, I did many things that I may or may not find useful in my writing. I married, brought up two daughters, taught school, worked as a second-rate commercial artist, was a professional photographer, and enjoyed being a fitness instructor for over twenty years. Only when a foot injury affected my fitness

teaching and when eye problems made me start taking inferior pictures, did I turn to writing.

It's been fun starting a whole new career in late middle age. I've enjoyed reconnecting with children through school visits and correspondence, and I'm very comfortable with them. This is probably because in some ways I feel that I'm not yet entirely grown up. Certainly there's a child inside me who is very much alive—feeling things as intensely as a ten-year-old, reacting very strongly to what happens to me. It's good to be able to put these hot emotions into fiction, letting my characters express the rage, sorrow and wild joy that I have often felt.

Writing for children has also led to pleasurable and extensive travelling—all over my own country, from coast to coast, and in the very far north. I've enjoyed riding on snowmobiles over the frozen sea, and travelling in planes which are so small that they have to stuff your luggage in the nose and wings, travelling very low over spectacular mountains and fjords and rocky islands.

I've also enjoyed meeting many Native children during school visits—Indian students and the Inuit of northern Canada (who used to be called Eskimos). I've found that many important things can be learned from Native peoples—their deep respect for the value and beauty of nature, their spirituality, their readiness to cooperate with and help one another, their understanding of the value of silence. It's been a great privilege to meet so many of them.

When I'm at home, I live in a fishing village in Nova Scotia, on Canada's east coast. I write in a tiny cabin which my husband built for me on the edge of a cliff overlooking the sea. This is a wonderful place in which to concentrate and to write.

Children's writers are usually very busy people. They also tend to be happy ones.

———

Budge Wilson was born in Halifax, Nova Scotia, Canada. She received her B.A. degree in Psychology and Philosophy in 1953 and her Dip. Ed. in 1954 from Dalhousie University in Halifax. Between those years, she also studied English Literature in the Graduate School of University of Toronto and taught school. She was married to Alan Wilson in 1953, moving to Ontario for most of the next thirty-five years. They returned home in 1988. During the 1950s and 1960s, she worked at the University of Toronto's Institute of Child Study, editing, and writing for the Toronto *Globe and Mail.* She illustrated three books for University of Toronto Press. Her stories have also been published in the U.S., Denmark, Finland, Australia, and New Zealand, and will soon be published in Italy. She received the Canadian Broadcasting Corporation's Short Fiction Prize in 1981.

The Leaving won the Young Adult Canadian Book Award from the Canadian Library Association in 1991 and the 1991 City of Dartmouth Fiction Award. Also in 1991, was named a Best Book for Young Adults and a Notable Book of the Year by the American Library Association, was placed on an ALA list of "75 Best Books of the Last 25 Years" in 1994. Some of her titles not yet published in the U.S. include *Breakdown, Oliver's Wars,* and *Lorinda's Diary.*

SELECTED WORKS: Thirteen Never Changes, 1991; The Leaving, 1992; The Dandelion Garden, 1995.

ABOUT: Atlantic Books Today Fall 1994; Canadian Materials for Young People November 1991; Children's Book News Spring 1991; Contemporary Authors, Vol. 121; Quill & Quire October 1991; Something About the Author, Vol. 51, 55.

JEANETTE WINTER

October 6, 1939–

AUTHOR AND ILLUSTRATOR OF *Diego*, etc.

Autobiographical sketch of Jeanette Winter:

I CAN'T REMEMBER a time when I didn't love to draw. In elementary school in

Chicago, I remember the feel of the rough oatmeal paper I drew on with my deluxe 64-color box of Crayolas. And at home if paper wasn't available, I drew on the cardboard from laundered shirts, and even on endpapers in books. I loved the smell and look of the crayons with their striped wrappers.

There weren't many books in my house as I was growing up, but I remember the books of the d'Aulaires, Marguerite de Angeli, Elizabeth Orton Jones, and Robert Lawson from the library. And the stacks of comic books that my friends and I read and traded. I treasured my collection of *Saturday Evening Post* covers by Norman Rockwell, whose pictures were magical to me.

During high school, all my free time on Saturdays and during the summer was spent in art classes at the Art Institute of Chicago. Because of a special teacher there, Mr. Jacobson, those years were important in helping me become an artist.

I went to college in Iowa, enjoying small-town life after growing up in a large city. I married, lived in New York City briefly, then moved to Texas, where our two sons were born and raised. Living in rural Maine is a new experience, and has begun to make its way into my books, as have all the years in Texas, and my childhood in Chicago.

I always knew I wanted to make pictures that told a story. Except for a brief time when, at age ten, I was sure that what I really wanted to be was a ballet dancer.

The most important thing in my childhood books were the pictures. I loved the kind of details and information they gave me. The rectangle of the pictures was like a window into another world. Now I try to make the kind of pictures I would have liked as a child.

Doing research is one of the best parts of making a book. My drawing table is usually surrounded by books on the subject of whatever I'm working on.

Photographs are also a research resource. I always carry a camera with me, to record specific things for a book, or simply to have a record of things I see that I want to remember. I often find myself going back to pictures I took years ago as a reference for a current book.

I listen to music while I work, and if possible, music that fits the theme of the book—Mexican mariachi and accordian music for *Diego*, African-American spirituals and work songs for *Follow the Drinking Gourd*, Swedish fiddle music for *Klara's New World*, Christmas music (in the spring!) for *The Christmas Tree Ship*, and cowboy songs for *Cowboy Charlie*.

Sometimes I make wood carvings. My favorite is of a big black crow, like the crows in the field outside my studio window.

One of the rewards of being an illustrator is that I keep learning about new things. It's often sad to finish a book, and leave a place that I had grown close to and learned so much about. But then I begin a new book, and I'm on a new adventure into a new world.

Jeannette Winter was born in Chicago. She attended the Art Institute of Chicago and received her B.F.A. degree from the Unversity of Iowa. She was married in 1960 and has two children.

Witch, Goblin, and Ghost in the Haunted Woods was named a Children's Choice Book by a joint committee of the International Reading Association and the Children's Book Council.

Three of her books have been named Notable Children's Trade Books in the Field of Social Studies by a joint committee of the CBC and the National Council on the Social Studies: *Shaker Boy*, *Diego*, and *Follow the Drinking Gourd*. *Diego* was also a Reading Rainbow Book and was named a Best Illustrated Book of the Year by the *New York Times*.

Follow the Drinking Gourd was named a Notable Book of the Year by the American Library Association and was a Reading Rainbow Book.

The Christmas Visitors, *Hush Little Baby*, and *Cotton Mill Town* were all included in American Institute of Graphic Arts shows. *Hinny Winny Bunco* was named an ALA Notable Book of the Year. *A Fruit and Vegetable Man* was named the 1993 Children's Book of Distinction by the *Hungry Mind Review*.

SELECTED WORKS WRITTEN AND ILLUSTRATED: The Christmas Visitors, 1968; Hush, Little Baby, 1984; Follow the Drinking Gourd, 1988; Diego, 1991; Klara's New World, 1992; The Christmas Tree Ship, 1994; Cowboy Charlie: The Story of Charles M. Russell, 1995.

SELECTED WORKS ILLUSTRATED: Witch, Goblin, and Ghost in the Haunted Woods, by Sue Alexander, 1981; Hinny Winny Bunco, by Carol Greene, 1982; The World's Birthday, by Barbara Goldin, 1990; Eight Hands Round, by Ann Whitford Paul, 1991; A Fruit and Vegetable Man, by Roni Schotter, 1993; Shaker Boy, by Mary Lyn Ray, 1994; Snow, by Steve Sanfield, 1995.

G. CLIFTON WISLER

May 15, 1950–

AUTHOR OF *Winter of the Wolf*, etc.

Autobiographical sketch of Gary Clifton Wisler, who also writes under the pen name "Will McLennan":

I THINK I first imagined myself a writer when I was in junior high school, but I began a lifetime of telling stories long before that. When I was a boy, there were no video games or cable networks. Television itself was fairly new, and totally unexciting most days. This was also the era before air-conditioned houses, and in Texas, boys simply didn't stay indoors if they were healthy. My friends and I escaped on our bicycles to the neighborhood park or the empty field at the end of my street. There we pretended we were heroes of the Alamo, knights in shining armor, or space adventurers visiting distant galaxies. Sometimes we would put on puppet plays for younger kids in a garage across the street. Our minds were personal time machines, and they took us anywhere we wanted to go—so long as we were home by supper time.

A creative mind wasn't always an advantage, though. It often interfered with my schoolwork. I was neither a very strong speller nor a good grammar student, and my grades were not always the best. In fourth grade I discovered that teachers gave "extra credit" for writing stories or entering school essay contests. I needed all the points I could muster, so I wrote a lot of bonus stories and essays.

When I was eleven, I joined the Boy Scouts (I've been with them ever since). In the evenings, around the dying embers of campfires, I began sharing stories with my friends and fellow Scouts. By age thirteen I was the unofficial troop storyteller. Some of those stories, such as the phantom silver wolf of Comanche legend and the story of the white boy, Metaha, adopted by Indians, grew into *Winter of the Wolf* and *Spirit Warrior*. I still enjoy trying out ideas on the Scouts, and so far they haven't complained.

I took my first serious step toward becoming a *writer* in high school. I was fortunate to attend Hillcrest High School in Dallas, where Mrs. Julia Jeffress taught journalism. My senior year I served on the *Hurricane*, our school paper, writing sports stories and editorials. (My favorite story was covering the brutal "Powder Puff" football game between the senior and junior *girls!*) Mrs. J spotted a lot of my problems, particularly how to start off a story. She also insisted that writers should write well and often, and the more I practiced what she preached, the better I got. Later, after I graduated, Mrs. J invited me back to Hillcrest to talk about writing to her students, and she always considered *Winter of the Wolf*, which I dedicated to her, our book. I would never have had the courage to attempt a book without her encouragement. It was because of her example that I entered the classroom myself after college.

I enjoyed my years of teaching, and I relish the rare chances I now have to share time with students during "guest author" visits. My sixth grade students at Jackson Middle School in the 1970s and 1980s were my first audiences, and their support and enthusiasm led me to write my first novel, *My Brother, the Wind*, in 1977. It might still be gathering dust if Margaret Weiss, then editor of a small press in Missouri, had not suggested sending it to Ray Puechner. Ray liked the book, sold it to Doubleday, and became my agent, friend, and mentor. Following his untimely and premature death, his wife Barbara has filled his shoes.

_____

Gary Clifton Wisler was born in Oklahoma City, Oklahoma. Soon afterward, his family moved to Texas. He attended high school in Dallas. He was a journalism major at Southern Methodist University, where he received his B.F.A. degree in 1972. While at school, he worked part-time for the *Dallas Morning News.* He taught high-school journalism before returning to SMU for his M.A. degree, which he received in 1974.

Wisler taught school for ten years in Garland, Texas, and left teaching to write full-time in 1984. He also speaks to school and writing groups. As of January 1995 he had published sixty-three novels, mostly for adults. His books have been translated into five foreign languages.

Wisler's many historical novels reflect his lifelong interest in history. He undertook doctoral studies in history at the University of North Texas in 1993, with his planned dissertation topic a history of the Ninth Texas Infantry Regiment in the Civil War. Mr. Wisler remains active in Boy Scouting, having received several awards recognizing his service. He remains an avid hiker and camper. He is an active member of Western Writers of America and the Author's Guild, and has written short stories and contributed an article on writing young adult westerns to *The Western Writers Handbook.* Some of Wisler's books, such as *The Antrian Messenger,* are science fiction novels.

My Brother, the Wind, a book for adults and Wisler's first novel, was a 1980 American Book Award nominee. *Thunder on the Tennessee* won the 1984 Western Writers of America Spur Award for Best Western Juvenile Book of 1983 in the fiction category. *The Antrian Messenger* was named a 1987 Children's Choice Book by a joint committee of the Children's Book Council and the International Reading Association. Its sequel is *The Seer. The Wolf's Tooth* was named a 1988 Notable Children's Book in the Field of Social Studies by a joint committee of the National Council on the Social Studies and the CBC. *Red Cap* was also a NCSS/CBC choice, in 1992, and it was named a Best Book for Young Adults by the American Library Association. Several of his books have won state awards chosen by children.

SELECTED WORKS: Winter of the Wolf, 1981; Thunder on the Tennessee, 1983; Buffalo Moon, 1984; The Raid, 1985; The Antrian Messenger, 1986; The Wolf's Tooth, 1987; The Seer, 1989; Red Cap, 1991; Jericho's Journey, 1993.

ABOUT: Contemporary Authors, Vol. 129; Something About the Author, Vol. 46, 58.

DAVID WISNIEWSKI

March 21, 1953–

AUTHOR AND ILLUSTRATOR OF *Elfwyn's Saga,* etc.

Autobiographical sketch of David Wisniewski:

BORN IN ENGLAND to a U.S. Air Force Dad and a British Mum, my two younger brothers and I traveled often, stationed stateside (Nebraska, Alabama, Texas and Maryland) and overseas (England and Germany).

Mum gave me a penchant for art, teaching me how to draw jointed human figures out of ovals and circles. I doodled these "bubble men" all the time, especially in dramatic underwater scenes of men fighting off sharks with spearguns. After I learned to read, my drawing skills improved through constant freehand copying of superheroes from D.C. and Marvel comic books. By the time I was in fourth grade, I was "the kid who could draw." I also became an avid reader, eventually leaving

Wisniewski: *wiz NESS key*

comic books for the science fiction and fantasy of Ray Bradbury, Robert Heinlein, Andre Norton and H.P. Lovecraft.

In high school, I kept up with art, but also became interested in theatre and speech. Theatre broadened my reading to include plays and poetry. Speech gave me the opportunity to research and write oratory. Both required presentation, and I became acclimated to performing in public.

After graduation, we were stationed at Andrews Air Force Base outside Washington, D.C. I worked at a gas station to earn enough money for an initial semester in the drama department at the University of Maryland. There, the public relations clown for Ringling Brothers and Barnum & Bailey Circus, Leon McBride, visited to talk about the Ringling Clown College. I filled out an application, had an interview in New York City with its dean, Bill Ballantine, and was accepted for the 1972 class. After an eight-week training course (including unicycling, juggling, mime and acrobatics) and a successful audition/performance, I was hired.

The two years at Ringling were hard work, but I certainly learned a lot. Older clowns like Lou Jacobs and Bobby Kay of-

fered their expertise and training. Watching them perform taught me much about timing and showmanship. Also, twelve to fourteen performances a week (with up to twelve appearances in each show) assured plenty of chances to try out my own routines and polish them. A third year of clowning followed at Circus Vargas, a California tent circus. But life on the road with few friends and no family began to pall, so I returned home.

After a brief interlude of freelancing as an actor, mime and prop-maker for local theatre and opera companies, I interviewed for a puppeteer's position with a local parks department. Although I hadn't done much puppetry, I was good at making props, and it was on that basis that Donna Harris hired me. Six months later, we got married.

We produced conventional hand puppet and rod puppet shows for a while, but eventually became interested in shadow puppetry. This form of puppetry began in India and China about two thousand years ago and requires three elements: a light, a screen, and flat, jointed figures operated behind the screen to cast shadows. Our first shadowplay was Rudyard Kipling's *Rikki Tikki Tavi*. It was a big hit with school audiences, so we began to specialize in the art.

In 1980, we began our own touring company, Clarion Shadow Theatre. Although I couldn't know it at the time, my work as a shadow puppeteer prepared me to author and illustrate picture books later on. We used overhead projectors to project transparent colored scenery for the shadow puppets to act against. It was the planning and construction of this projected scenery that gave me an eye for composition and the cutting skills necessary to do cut-paper illustration later on. The search for myths, legends and classic stories to turn into shadowplays familiarized me with the tales of cultures of many different lands. Transforming these stories into scripts afforded me lots of practice in the mechanics of effective writing: concise plot development, motivated characters, and interesting dialogue.

But with the arrival of our children (Ariana in 1981 and Alexander in 1985), touring gradually became impossible. We decided that Clarion Shadow Theatre had to take a back seat for a time. As Donna had a college education in graphic design, we started Clarion Graphics and began producing logos and brochures for our friends in the performing arts and education fields. As with puppetry, Donna taught me the basics of the profession; art preparation techniques and the jargon necessary to talk with printers.

But projects were few and far between. Then, for the first time, I transferred the cutting skills learned from shadow puppetry to silhouettes. A friend, Carolyn Miller, suggested that I prepare a portfolio and show it to art directors of newspapers and magazines. Taking her advice, I wore out a pair of shoes walking around Baltimore and Washington, but I finally landed some assignments.

At first, my work was simple black silhouette on a white background. Then I started adding color. I discovered that more shadows could be achieved by slipping pieces of matboard or Fomecore behind sections of my art to "bump" it forward.

About this time, Carolyn told me about a children's book seminar conducted by The Children's Book Guild of Washington. I attended it and met an editor who really liked my portfolio. She suggested that I bring my work to the attention of some publishers in New York City, but cautioned that I should go with a story. That way, I would be an illustrator with a definite project in mind.

I came up with *The Warrior and the Wise Man*, prepared the manuscript and two prototype illustrations. Then I went to my first appointment at Lothrop, Lee & Shepard Books. The editor enjoyed my portfolio and asked if I had a story. After hearing it, she said, "You just sold yourself a book!"

That's how I got started. Now that I look back on my life, I see how each step pre-pared me to do something new later on. Maybe these picture books are the end result; perhaps they're yet another step. I don't know just yet, but it's fun and worthwhile.

———

David Wisniewski was born in Middlesex, England. His work was represented in the 1995 Dreamweavers Exhibit, a travelling exhibit of illustrations from children's literature in the fantasy genre. *The Wave of the Sea-Wolf* was named a Best Illustrated Book of the Year by *The New York Times. Elfwyn's Saga* was named a Notable Children's Trade Book in the Field of Social Studies by a joint committee of the National Council on the Social Studies and the Children's Book Council.

SELECTED WORKS: The Warrior and the Wise Man, 1989; Elfwyn's Saga, 1990; Rain Player, 1991; Sundiata: Lion King of Mali, 1992; The Wave of the Sea-Wolf, 1994.

ABOUT: Contemporary Authors, Vol. 132; School Library Media Activities Monthly February 1994.

VIRGINIA EUWER WOLFF

August 25, 1937–

AUTHOR OF *Make Lemonade*, etc.

Autobiographical sketch of Virginia Euwer Wolff:

I'M A NATIVE OREGONIAN. Although I've lived in a lot of different places—from the silence of rural, unelectrified Oregon to the noisy middle of Manhattan—I feel most at home among the forests, rivers, and mountains of the Northwest.

My father died when I was five; this loss may have been the chief shaping event of my life.

I wanted to be a writer from childhood on, but didn't begin to write until I was nearly forty.

During my 1940's girlhood, I weeded the

Virginia Euwer Wolff

family Victory Garden, joined the Camp Fire Girls and went to summer camp, began violin lessons at age eight, did 4-H cooking and sewing projects, drank milk from the family cow, learned to swim in a mountain lake, picked strawberries in the summertime to earn money, and celebrated the end of World War II. I read comic books, the Betsy-Tacy books, Nancy Drew, and *Jane Eyre*, and went to the movies.

As a teenager I meandered through classes, reluctantly did homework, sporadically practiced the violin, read *Mad* magazine and J. D. Salinger, exasperated my mother, frustrated my teachers, and went to the movies.

When I was sixteen, my mother gave me a brisk waking-up by sending me to boarding school. Two years later my violin and I ended up at Smith College; I was a geographical distribution student, mystified by the plethora of exotic names, buildings, books, accents, experiences, and ideas. I majored in English without even realizing that I was probably a born English major. Playing the violin was the one constant in my life.

I graduated, married, taught school, and had children. We lived in Philadelphia,

New York City, Long Island, Washington, D. C., Ohio, and Connecticut. I hardly ever played the violin.

When my son and daughter were teenagers I began to try writing. More than a decade later, after being single for several years, after teaching a lot of high school English and making several false starts in writing, I decided to try books for young readers. And I got out my violin again.

My fictional characters confront experiences that confuse and often disorient them. Their hard-won, partial victories evolve through much faltering and soul-searching. The protagonist of *Probably Still Nick Swansen* is learning-disabled; in my life I've had agonizing moments of not "getting" what everyone else seemed to catch onto easily. Allegra Shapiro in *The Mozart Season* is a gifted violinist; I've known many of these, and she has my personal, passionate love of music. The young women in *Make Lemonade* live in a world that pretends to be sensitive to their dilemma but behaves with appalling indifference. I've never been as economically deprived as they are, but I have been poor in spirit, and I love to see victims stop being victims; that love kept me going in writing their story.

I write very slowly. Each book pushes me farther out on an intellectual and emotional limb. Uncomfortable as that is, I wouldn't have it any other way. My fascination with what we humans do when we learn the consequences of our own behavior keeps me writing.

These days I play the violin more than ever, and I listen to classical music while I write. I teach English at Mt. Hood Academy, a private school for skiers in Oregon. I hike, swim, cross-country ski, garden, and I still love going to the movies.

My son Anthony is a jazz guitarist with a degree in religious studies. My English-major daughter Juliet is a psychotherapist who is married with a child of her own, my grandson Max.

Virginia Euwer Wolff was born in Port-land, Oregon. She graduated from Smith College in 1959. She taught elementary school for eleven years in Philadelphia and on Long Island, New York. She has also taught at Hood River Valley High School in Oregon.

Her first foray into writing fiction result-ed in a novel for adults, *Rated PG*, which was published in 1980. She has also had a short story appear in the 1995 book *Ultimate Sports: Short Stories by Outstand-ing Writers for Young Adults*, edited by Donald R. Gallo. In addition to her writing, she is a frequent speaker at children's book conferences, such as the 1993 International Reading Association Conference in San An-tonio, Texas, and a 1989 American Library Association Conference.

Make Lemonade won the 1994 Golden Kite Award for fiction from the Society of Children's Book Writers and Illustrators. It also won a 1993 Child Study Children's Book Award, given by the Child Study Children's Book Committee at Bank Street College of Education. It was named a Nota-ble Book and a Best Book for Young Adults by the American Library Association.

Mozart Season was named a Notable Book of the Year and a Best Book for Young Adults by the American Library Associa-tion. It was also a Junior Library Guild se-lection. *Probably Still Nick Swansen* won a 1989 International Reading Association Children's Book Award in the older catego-ry, as well as an International PEN Chil-dren's Book Award from the U.S.A. Center West. It was also named an ALA Best Book for Young Adults, and was a Junior Library Guild selection.

Virginia Euwer Wolff is a member of The Society of Children's Book Writers and Illustrators and The Chamber Music Soci-ety of Oregon.

SELECTED WORKS: Probably Still Nick Swansen, 1988; The Mozart Season, 1991; Make Lemonade, 1993.

ABOUT: Book Links November 1991; Booklist March 1, 1994; Brown, Jean E. and Elaine C. Stephens. Teaching Young Adult Literature: Sharing the Con-nection; Contemporary Authors, Vol. 107; Gallo, Don-ald R. Speaking for Ourselves, Too; Something About the Author, Vol. 78.

PATRICIA C. WREDE

March 27, 1953–

AUTHOR OF *Searching for Dragons*, etc.

Biographical sketch of Patricia Collins Wrede:

PATRICIA C. WREDE was born in Chica-go, Illinois, the oldest of five children. She was an avid reader, and enjoyed the Oz books, Walter Farley's horse novels, Robert Lawson's animal stories, and books like the Narnia Chronicles and *The Borrowers*. She began writing her first novel when she was in the seventh grade. She wrote it during class, and brought the pages home, where her mother typed them for her. For a long time, though, she thought of her writing as only a hobby.

She attended Carleton College, in Minne-sota, earning an A.B. degree in 1974. Then she had to decide whether to do more study in science, which she liked, or business, which was more practical for her. She worked as a secretary for a year and took night school classes, aiming for business school. She then earned her M.B.A. degree from the University of Minnesota in 1977.

Wrede went to work as a rate review ana-lyst at Minnesota Hospital Association in Minneapolis, then became a financial ana-lyst at B. Dalton Bookseller, and later at Dayton-Hudson Corporation. She was se-nior financial analyst there and then be-came senior accountant from 1983 to 1985. She has been a full-time writer since then.

After graduation, she began work on *Shadow Magic*; it took her five years to fin-ish it. This was the first book in the "Lyra" series. Most of her books are published for adults, but are widely read by young adults.

Wrede: *REED y*

Her book *Talking to Dragons* started out as one book. However, Wrede often thought about doing a prequel or sequel to it, and editor Jane Yolen asked her to contribute a story to an anthology Yolen was working on. "The Improper Princess" was the result, and it also became the beginning of another novel in the series of, now, four books.

Most of Wrede's books are in series, such as the Lyra series and the Chronicles of the Enchanted Forest, which includes, in order, *Dealing with Dragons, Searching for Dragons, Calling on Dragons,* and *Talking to Dragons.* The short stories relating to Enchanted Forest chronicles are published in anthologies, such as *Spaceships and Spells* and *The Unicorn Treasury.* Some of the fiction published for adults includes *Mairelon the Magician* and *The Seven Towers.*

Wrede balances highly productive days at the computer with catch-up days of errands or chores. As her brother David and sister Carol are science fiction readers, they are eager to read her work, and her brother offers help with plot points.

Patricia Wrede lives in Minneapolis, Minnesota.

Dealing with Dragons was named a Best Book of the Year for Young Adults by the American Library Association. *Searching for Dragons* was named an ALA Notable Book of the Year.

SELECTED WORKS: Talking to Dragons, 1985; (new ed., 1993); Dealing with Dragons, 1990; Searching for Dragons, 1991; Calling on Dragons, 1993.

ABOUT: Contemporary Authors, Vol. 134; Something About the Author, Vol. 67.

CAMILLE YARBROUGH

1938–

AUTHOR OF *Cornrows*, etc.

Biographical sketch of Camille Yarbrough:

CAMILLE YARBROUGH was born in Chicago, Illinois. She studied acting and voice and, in addition to her writing for children, she is a dancer, a singer, a songwriter, and a poet.

She appeared in plays such as *To Be Young, Gifted, and Black, Trumpets of the Lord,* and *Critics in Bezique.* She has also performed on television and in film, such as her appearance in *Shaft.*

She danced in the Katherine Dunham dance company and was an instructor at the Performing Artists Training Center at Southern Illinois University in East St. Louis, Missouri. She conducted drama workshops in New York high schools. She has also worked as a drama teacher. She has toured as a singer in the United States, Canada, and South America.

She currently works in the tradition of a griot, or a traditional West African musician and storyteller who preserves and teaches tribal history and values. She describes the griot as an "oral historian, preacher, teacher, and social catalyst." In 1975, she was honored by the Griot Society of New York as Griot of the Year.

A program of poetry and songs she wrote was performed by Nina Simone at Philharmonic Hall in 1972.

Yarbrough's children's stories are written

for late elementary and middle grade readers. *Cornrows*, which was illustrated by Carole Byard, tells the story of two children who learn about their black heritage and of important ancestral life in Africa and of African-American historical figures from their mother and great-grandmother. Martin Luther King, W.E.B. Du Bois, Harriet Tubman, Rosa Parks, Richard Wright, Langston Hughes, and others are discussed. The title signifies the braids were named after the planting of rows of corn in the fields, and the children are told that in Africa, one could determine whether someone came from a certain village by the style of hair they wore. The book won a 1980 Coretta Scott King Award for Illustration and was named a Notable Children's Trade Book in the Field of Social Studies by a joint committee of the Children's Book Council and the National Council on the Social Studies.

In *Shimmershine Queens*, Angie, who is ten years old, attends an inner-city school that is beset with problems. She wins the lead in a school play, but she is nervous and has to overcome being made to feel ashamed because of her black skin. Her cousin encourages her, and going through the experience changes and matures her. African traditions and proverbs are represented in the story, and there is a message to respect education and respect one's self. A reviewer in *Booklist* magazine called it a "brave book."

Camille Yarbrough lives in New York City.

SELECTED WORKS: Cornrows, 1979; The Shimmershine Queens, 1989.

ABOUT: Children's Literature Review, Vol. 29; Contemporary Authors, Vol. 125; Rollock, Barbara. Black Authors and Illustrators of Children's Books; Something About the Author, Vol. 79.

PAUL RICHARD YEE

October 1, 1956–

AUTHOR OF *Tales from Gold Mountain*, etc.

Autobiographical sketch of Paul Richard Yee:

WHEN I WAS a child, I never thought that one day I would write books. When grown-ups asked what I wanted to become, I replied, "A teacher" because that was the only kind of professional adult I saw regularly.

I was raised by an elderly aunt and uncle. There was no television at home and I did not have many friends. My aunt spoke fluent English herself, but she insisted that we speak only Cantonese at home. That way, she thought, I would be sure to learn my ancestral tongue.

I grew up in Vancouver's Chinatown, and went to an elementary school where 95 percent of the students were Canadians of Chinese descent. Every day, after the school buzzer sounded, I also went to Chinese language school. I went from the time I was in kindergarten until I was in grade eight. I learned to read and write in Chinese. At first I really liked it because there wasn't any arithmetic, which was my worst subject at regular school. Then I got lazy and careless and wanted to quit. But my aunt wouldn't let me.

Growing up surrounded by a Chinese-

Canadian community meant I never had to think about what it meant to be Chinese. In fact, most of the families that lived around Chinatown wanted to move away, to the better neighbourhoods of the city. By the time I finished high school, only a handful of my school-mates still lived near Chinatown. Even my family had moved away.

Ironically, it was at that same time that I became involved in community projects in Chinatown. I worked on street festivals, helping to build a Chinese Cultural Centre. I taught English to recent immigrants. I helped produce an English-language Chinese-Canadian radio program. I worked on several public exhibitions that told the story of the Chinese in Vancouver in historic photographs and museum artifacts.

Young Chinese-Canadians were getting involved in their own community, and these were exciting times. Part of that excitement came from doing something our parents had not expected. When we were growing up, we were ordered to "Study hard, get good marks, go to university, and find a well-paying job." Doing volunteer work had not been part of their plans. What we were doing in Chinatown sounded like too much fun!

At university, I majored in history. I felt strongly that Chinese-Canadians did not know enough about their past in this country. Without that knowledge, I felt they were rootless and without pride. A lot of history had been already forgotten or lost, so I wanted to do research and to help preserve old photos and documents.

This led me to do a masters degree in Canadian history, with a focus on Chinese-Canadians. Then I started working at the City of Vancouver Archives, which held very important collections of historic documents.

I became a writer of children's books by accident. A publisher came to Vancouver, looking for someone to write a book about kids growing up in Chinatown. They found out about me through my volunteer work and looked at some short stories I had written at university. So they asked me to write four stories, which became the book *Teach Me to Fly, Skyfighter*. For that book, I went back and visited my old elementary school to get a sense of neighborhood children in the 1980s.

My second book *Curses of Third Uncle* is based on the stories my aunt told me about her childhood in Vancouver during the 1900s. *Saltwater City*, my third book, is an account of the Chinese in Vancouver with photos and oral history.

Tales from Gold Mountain allowed me to link my fascination with history to fiction. Not everyone is interested in the past, but almost everyone likes a good story, especially when there are ghosts or lovers or revenge. *Roses Sing on New Snow* was originally written as one of the stories for *Tales*, but the publisher decided to make it into a picture book on its own.

All my writing to date deals with Chinese people in North America. These are the people I know best, these are the people who will find a part of themselves reflected in my words.

———

Paul Yee receeived his B.A. degree from the University of British Columbia in 1978. He was awarded the Southcott Prize for Research in B.C. history. He earned a Master of Arts History degree from the university in 1983, and was awarded a graduate fellowship of $5,000. He worked as an assistant city archivist at the City of Vancouver Archives from 1980 to 1987. He was Portfolio Manager at the Archives of Ontario, Ontario Ministry of Culture and Communications, from 1988 to 1991. He has been a Policy Analyst at the Social and Economic Policy Unit of the Policy and Research Branch, Ontario Ministry of Citizenship, since 1991. He has been a teacher from 1975 to 1989, in elementary schools, universities, and museums. He has curated exhibits such as an exhibit of historic photographs at the Vancouver Art Gallery in 1984 and 1985. He has had many articles published, especially on the Chinese Canadian community, in such journals as *B.C. Studies* and *West Coast Review*. He also has presented papers at workshops, writers' conferences, and booksellers' and archivists' conferences.

Yee won the Outstanding Young Alumni Award from the University of B.C. in 1989. He won a Community Service Award from the Chinese Benevolent Association in 1987. He is a member of Writers Union of Canada, and the Canadian Society of Children's Authors, Illustrators and Performers. His books have won many Canadian book awards.

Tales from Gold Mountain won the 1980 Sheila A. Egoff Award presented by the West Coast Book Prizes Society. It was a runner-up in the 1990 Canadian Library Association Book of the Year for Children Awards. It also won the 1990 National Chapter of Canada IODE Violet Downey Book Award. *Saltwater City: An Illustrated History of the Chinese in Vancouver* is a book for adults published in the U.S. in 1988.

SELECTED WORKS: Roses Sing on New Snow: A Delicious Tale, 1992; Tales from Gold Mountain: Stories of the Chinese in the New World, 1990.

ABOUT: Contemporary Authors, Vol. 135; Something About the Author, Vol. 67.

HARRIET ZIEFERT

HARRIET ZIEFERT

July 7, 1941–

AUTHOR OF *Let's Get a Pet*, etc.

Biographical sketch of Harriet Ziefert:

HARRIET ZIEFERT was born in New Jersey. She grew up in North Bergen, New Jersey, where she attended the local schools. She graduated from Smith College, then received a Masters degree in Education from New York University.

For many years, Ziefert was an elementary school teacher. She taught most grades from kindergarten to fifth grade. "I liked it," she said, but she stopped teaching when she had her own sons. When her children were older, Ziefert wanted "a bigger arena" for her work. She went to work at a publishing company, Scholastic in New York City, developing materials for teacher's guides for kindergarten language arts and social studies programs.

"About twelve years ago," says Ziefert in a 1995 interview, "I tried to get a job as an editor, but no one would hire me as a trade editor. So I decided to write my own books." Since then, she has written several hundred books, mostly picture books and easy-to-read books. "I write books very quickly," she says, "in about twelve hours. I rewrite them three times over three days, and then they're done." She writes about twenty books a year.

Ziefert's picture book, *A New Coat for Anna*, is about a girl in a bombed-out European city during the months just after World War II. Anna has outgrown her old coat, and her mother trades her few surviving treasures—a watch, a lamp, a necklace, and a porcelain teapot—in order to obtain wool and have it spun, woven, and finally sewn into a fine red coat for Anna. A *Horn*

Outstanding Science Trade Book for Children by a joint committee of the National Science Teachers Association and the Children's Book Council.

The reason Ziefert began writing easy-to-read books was that she felt "they were getting too hard for kids to read in the first grade." She says that she wrote easy-to-read books with seventy-five or fewer words, even ones with fifty or fewer words, "to see how much of a story" she could produce with that limit. She enjoyed the challenge, and cites her book *Sleepy Dog* as an example. "*Sleepy Dog* is the most successful book I've ever done, in terms of number of books sold." She's also been working on a developmental program with publisher Dorling Kindersley, made up of books for babies, toddlers, and preschoolers.

"I happen to like to have control over my work," says Ziefert. She is a book packager, writing all the text, finding the illustrator, designer, and printer and then delivering the completed package to the publisher for distribution. "I very much like to work directly with illustrators," she says, noting that this is the main reason she chooses to work as a book packager, rather than through a publisher. "I'm very visual. I do a very loose text and try to develop it with an illustrator," she says. "I work with artists and turn them into illustrators. I like finding new artists and watching them grow."

Her book *Pete's Chicken*, which was illustrated by Laura Rader, was reviewed in the *New York Times Book Review* as "a simple, sweet 'Song of Myself' for children . . . [which] applauds the specialness of every child as it reminds parents of the healing power of just being there for children." Among her other books is a series of easy-to-read books, such as *Trip Day* and *Worm Day*, about an inventive science teacher and his rambunctious class of students. Ziefert's book *Let's Get a Pet* was named an Outstanding Science Trade Book for Children by a joint committee of the National Science Teachers Association and the Children's Book Council.

SELECTED WORKS: A New Coat for Anna, 1986; I Won't Go to Bed!, 1987; Pet Day, 1987; Trip Day, 1987; Worm Day, 1987; Before I was Born, 1989; With Love from Grandma,1989; Henry's Wrong Turn, 1989; Getting Ready for New Baby, 1990; Parade, 1990; Who Can Boo the Loudest?, 1990; Bigger than Baby, 1991; Harry Gets Ready for School, 1991; When Daddy Had the Chicken Pox, 1991; Bob and Shirley: A Tale of Two Lobsters, 1991; Halloween Parade, Viking 1992; Clown Games, 1993; Let's Get a Pet, 1993; Pete's Chicken, 1994; Little Mouse Meets Santa, 1995.

SELECTED WORKS WITH MARTIN SILVERMAN: Where Babies Come From: Stories to Help Parents Answer Preschoolers' Questions About Sex, 1989.

Authors and Illustrators Included in This Series

The following list indicates the volume in which each individual may be found:

J—THE JUNIOR BOOK OF AUTHORS, second edition (1951)

M—MORE JUNIOR AUTHORS (1963)

3—THIRD BOOK OF JUNIOR AUTHORS (1972)

4—FOURTH BOOK OF JUNIOR AUTHORS AND ILLUSTRATORS (1978)

5—FIFTH BOOK OF JUNIOR AUTHORS AND ILLUSTRATORS (1983)

6—SIXTH BOOK OF JUNIOR AUTHORS AND ILLUSTRATORS (1989)

7—SEVENTH BOOK OF JUNIOR AUTHORS AND ILLUSTRATORS (1996)

Bridgers, Sue Ellen—5
Bridwell, Norman R(ay)–7
Brier, Howard, M.—M
Briggs, K(atherine) M(ary)—5
Briggs, Raymond—3
Bright, Robert—M
Brindze, Ruth—M
Brink, Carol—J
Brinsmead, Hesba Fay—4
Brittain, Bill (William)—5
Bro, Margueritte—M
Brock, C. E.—J
Brock, Emma L.—J
Brock, H. M. See Brock, C. E.—J
Brodsky, Beverly (Beverly Brodsky
  McDermott)—5
Bromhall, Winifred—M
"Bronson, Lynn." See Lampman,
  Evelyn Sibley—M
Bronson, Wilfrid S.—J
Brooke, L. Leslie—J
Brooks, Bruce—6
Brooks, Gwendolyn (Gwendolyn
  Elizabeth Brooks Blakely)—4
Brooks, Martha—7
Brooks, Polly Schoyer–7
Brooks, Walter R.—J
Broster, D. K.—J
Brown, Marc (Tolon)—5
Brown, Edna A.—J
Brown, Marcia—M
Brown, Margaret Wise ("Golden
  MacDonald")—J
Brown, Palmer—5
Brown, Paul—J
Brown, Roy—4
Browne, Anthony—6
Bruckner, Karl—4
Bruna, Dick—5
Brunhoff, Jean de—J
Brunhoff, Laurent de—M
Bryan, Ashley (F.)—5
Bryson, Bernarda—3
Buehr, Walter—3
Buff, Conrad—J
Buff, Mary Marsh—J
Bulla, Clyde Robert—M
"Bunting, A. E." See "Bunting,
  Eve"—5
Bunting, Anne Evelyn. See
  "Bunting, Eve"—5
"Bunting, Eve" ("A. E. Bunting,"
  Anne Evelyn Bunting, "Evelyn
  Bolton")—5
Burbank, Addison. See Newcomb,
  Covelle—J
Burch, Robert—3
Burchard, Peter—3
Burgess, Thornton W.—J
Burglon, Nora—J
Burkert, Nancy Ekholm—3
"Burnford, S. D." See Burnford,
  Sheila—4
Burleigh, Robert–7
Burnford, Sheila ("S. D. Burnford,"
  "Philip Cochrane Every")—4

Burningham, Helen Oxenbury. See
  Oxenbury, Helen—3
Burningham, John—3
Burton, Hester—3
Burton, Virginia Lee—J
Busoni, Rafaello—J
Butler, Beverly (Beverly Kathleen
  Butler, "Kathleen Victor")—6
Butterworth, Oliver—4
Butterworth, W(illiam) E(dmond)
  ("William Edward Butterworth
  III," "Webb Beach," "Walker E.
  Blake," "James McM. Douglas,"
  "Eden Hughes," "Edmund O.
  Scholefield," "Patrick J.
  Williams")—5
"Buxton, Ralph." See Silverstein,
  Virginia B.—5
Byard, Carole (Marie)–7
Byars, Betsy—3

Caldecott, Randolph—J
Calhoun, Mary (Mary Huiskamp
  Calhoun Wilkins)—3
Callen, Larry (Lawrence Willard
  Callen Jr.)—5
Calvert, Patricia ("Peter J.
  Freedman")—6
Cameron, Ann–7
Cameron, Eleanor—3
Cameron, Polly—4
Camp, Walter—J
"Campbell, Bruce." See Epstein,
  Samuel—M
Carigiet, Alois—3
Carle, Eric—4
Carlson, Natalie Savage—M
Carlstrom, Nancy White—6
Carpenter, Frances—M
Carr, Harriett H.—M
Carr, Mary Jane—J
Carrick, Carol—4
Carrick, Donald—4
Carrick, Valery—J
Carris, Joan (Davenport)–7
Carroll, Latrobe—M
Carroll, Ruth—M
Carter, Alden (Richardson)–7
Carter, Helene—M
Caseley, Judith–7
Cassedy, Sylvia—6
Casserley, Anne—J
Catalanotto, Peter–7
Caudill, Rebecca—M
Cauley, Lorinda Bryan—6
Cavanah, Frances—M
Cavanna, Betty (Elizabeth
  Headley)—M
Cavoukian, Raffi. See Raffi—6
Cazet, Denys–7
Chaikin, Miriam—6
Chalmers, Mary—3
Chambers, Aidan ("Malcolm
  Blacklin")—6

"Chambers, Catherine E." See
  Johnston, Norma—5
"Chance, Stephen." See Turner,
  Philip—4
"Chapman, Walker." See Silver-
  berg, Robert—3
Chappell, Warren—3
"Charles, Nicholas." See Kuskin,
  Karla—3
Charlip, Remy—3
Charlot, Jean—M
"Chase, Alice Elizabeth." See
  McHargue, Georgess—5
Chase, Mary Ellen—4
Chase, Richard—M
Chastain, Madye Lee—M
Chauncy, Nan—3
Chen, Tony (Anthony Young
  Chen)—5
Cherry, Lynne–7
Chess, Victoria (Dickerson)—6
Chetwin, Grace–7
Chew, Ruth (Ruth Silver)—6
Childress, Alice—5
Chipperfield, Joseph E.—M
Chönz, Selina—3
Chorao, Kay (Ann McKay Sproat
  Chorao)—4
Chrisman, Arthur Bowie—J
Christelow, Eileen–7
"Christopher, John" (Samuel
  Youd)—4
Christopher, Matt(hew F.)
  ("Fredric Martin")—5
Church, Alfred J.—J
Church, Richard—M
Chute, B. J.—M
Chute, Marchette—M
Chwast, Jacqueline—4
Chwast, Seymour—4
Ciardi, John—3
Clapp, Patricia—5
"Clare, Helen." See Clarke,
  Pauline—3
Clark, Ann Nolan—J
Clark, Emma (Chichester)–7
Clark, Mavis Thorpe (Mavis Thor-
  pe Clark Latham)—4
Clarke, Arthur C.—4
Clarke, Pauline ("Helen Clare")
  —3
Cleary, Beverly—M
Cleaver, Bill—4
Cleaver, Elizabeth—4
Cleaver, Vera—4
Clements, Bruce—5
Clifford, Eth ("Ruth Bonn Penn,"
  "Ethel Rosenberg")—6
Clifton, Lucille (Sayles)—5
Climo, Shirley–7
Clymer, Eleanor ("Elizabeth
  Kinsey")—4
Coatsworth, Elizabeth—J
Cobb, Vicki—5
Cober, Alan E.—4
Coblentz, Catherine Cate—J

Duggan, Alfred—4
Dulac, Edmund—J
Duncan, Norman—J
"Duncan, Lois" (Lois Steinmetz Arquette)—5
Dunlop, Agnes Mary Robertson. See "Kyle, Elisabeth"—M
Dunlop, Eileen (Rhona)—6
Dunrea, Olivier (Jean-Paul Dominique)-7
Duval, Colette. See "Vivier, Colette"—4
Duvoisin, Roger—J
Dyer, Jane-7
Dygard, Thomas J.—6

Eager, Edward—M
Earle, Olive L.—M
Eastman, Charles A.—J
Eaton, Jeanette—J
Eberle, Irmengarde—J
Eckert, Allan W.—4
Eckert, Horst. See "Janosch"—4
Edmonds, Walter Dumaux—M
Egielski, Richard—6
Ehlert, Lois (Jane)-7
Ehrlich, Amy-7
Ehrlich, Bettina. See "Bettina"—M
Eichenberg, Fritz—M
Eipper, Paul—J
Elkin, Benjamin—4
Ellis, Ella (Thorp)—5
Ellis, Sarah-7
Ellsberg, Commander Edward —J
Elting, Mary ("Campbell Tatham")—M
Emberley, Barbara—3
Emberley, Ed—3
Emery, Ann—M
Engdahl, Sylvia Louise—4
Enright, Elizabeth—J
Epstein, Beryl Williams—M
Epstein, Samuel ("Adam Allen," "Bruce Campbell")—M
Erdman, Loula Grace—M
Ernst, Lisa Campbell-7
Estes, Eleanor—J
"Estoril, Jean." See Allen, Mabel Esther—6
Ets, Marie Hall—J
Evans, Eva Knox—M
"Every, Philip Cochrane." See Burnford, Sheila—4
Eyerly, Jeannette (Hyde) ("Jeannette Griffith")—5
Eyre, Katherine Wigmore—M

Fabre, Jean-Henri—J
"Fall, Thomas" (Donald Clifford Snow)—4
Falls, C. B.—J
Farber, Norma—5

Farjeon, Eleanor—J
Farley, Carol ("Carol McDole")—5
Farley, Walter—J
Farmer, Nancy (Forsythe)-7
Farmer, Penelope (Penelope Farmer Mockridge)—4
Fatio, Louise—M
Faulkner, Nancy (Anne Irvin Faulkner)—4
Feagles, Anita MacRae—4
Feelings, Muriel—4
Feelings, Tom—3
Felsen, Gregor—J
Felton, Harold W.—M
Fenton, Carroll Lane—M
Fenton, Edward—3
Fenton, Mildred Adams—M
Ferris, Helen—J
"Feydy, Anne Lindbergh." See Lindbergh, Anne—6
Field, Rachel—J
Fife, Dale—4
Fillmore, Parker—J
Fine, Anne-7
Fischer, Hans Erich—M
Fischtrom, Harvey and Margot Zemach. See Zemach, Harve and Margot—3
Fisher, Aileen—M
Fisher, Leonard Everett—3
Fitch, Florence Mary—M
"Fitzgerald, Captain Hugh." See Baum, L. Frank—3
Fitzgerald, John D(ennis)—5
Fitzhardinge, Joan Margaret. See "Phipson, Joan"— 3
Fitzhugh, Louise—3
Flack, Marjorie—J
Fleischman, Paul (Taylor)—5
Fleischman, Sid—3
Fleming, Denise-7
Fleming, Ian (Lancaster)—5
Floethe, Richard—M
Floherty, John J.—J
Flora, James—3
Florian, Douglas—6
Folon, Colette Portal. See Portal, Colette—4
Forberg, Ati (Beate Gropius Forberg)—4
Forbes, Esther—M
Foreman, Michael—6
Forman, James—3
Fortnum, Peggy (Margaret Emily Noel Nuttall-Smith)—4
Foster, Genevieve—J
Foster, Marian Curtis. See "Mariana"—3
Fox, Mem (Marion Francis)—6
Fox, Paula (Paula Fox Greenberg)—4
"Francis, Dee." See Haas, Dorothy—6
François, André—3
"Françoise" (Françoise Seignobosc)—M

Franchere, Ruth—4
Franklin, George Cory—M
Franklin, Madeleine. See "L'Engle, Madeleine"—M
Frascino, Edward—5
Frasconi, Antonio—3
Fraser, Claud Lovat—J
Freedman, Russell—6
"Freedman, Peter J." See Calvert, Patricia—6
Freeman, Don—M
Freeman, Ira Maximilian—M
Freeman, Lydia—M
Freeman, Mae Blacker—M
French, Allen—J
French, Fiona-7
"French, Paul." See Asimov, Isaac—3
Freschet, Berniece—4
Friedman, Frieda—M
Friermood, Elisabeth Hamilton —M
"Friis, Babbis." See Friis-Baastad, Babbis—3
Friis-Baastad, Babbis ("Eleanor Babbis," "Babbis Friis")—3
Fritz, Jean—3
Froman, Robert—4
Frost, Frances—M
Fry, Rosalie K.—3
Fuchs, Erich—4
Fujikawa, Gyo—4
Fyleman, Rose—J

Gackenbach, Dick—5
Gaer, Joseph—M
Gág, Flavia—M
Gág, Wanda—J
"Gage, Wilson" (Mary Q. Steele)—3
Galdone, Paul—3
Gall, Alice Crew—J
Gallant, Roy A(rthur)—5
Galt, Tom—M
Gammell, Stephen—5
Gannett, Ruth Chrisman—M
Gannett, Ruth Stiles (Ruth Stiles Gannett Kahn)—4
Gans, Roma—5
Gantos, John (Bryan)—5
Gardam, Jane—5
Garden, Nancy—5
Gardiner, John Reynolds—6
Gardner, Beau—6
Gardner, John (Champlin)—5
Garfield, Leon—4
Garland, Sherry-7
Garner, Alan—3
Garnett, Eve (C. R.)—5
Garrett, Randall. See Silverberg, Robert—3
Garrigue, Sheila—6
Garst, Shannon—J
Gates, Doris—J
Gatti, Attilio—J

"Kendall, Lace." *See* Stoutenburg, Adrien—3
Kennaway, Adrienne–7
Kennedy, Joseph Charles. *See* Kennedy, X. J.—6
Kennedy, Richard—5
Kennedy, X. J. (Joseph Charles Kennedy)—6
Kent, Jack (John Wellington)—5
Kent, Louise Andrews—J
Kepes, Juliet—3
Ker Wilson, Barbara (Barbara Ker Wilson Tahourdin)—4
Kerr, Judith (Anne)—5
"Kerr, M. E." (Marijane Meaker) —4
"Kerry, Lois," *See* "Duncan, Lois"—5
Kessler, Ethel—5
Kessler, Leonard (P.)—5
Kettelkamp, Larry—3
Khalsa, Dayal Kaur–7
Kherdian, David—5
Kimmel, Eric A.-7
King-Smith, Dick—6
"Kinsey, Elizabeth." *See* Clymer, Eleanor—4
"Kirtland, G. B." *See* Hine, Al and Joslin, Sesyle—3
Kingman, Lee—M
Kitchen, Bert (Herbert Thomas Kitchen)-7
Kjelgaard, Jim—J
Klause, Annette Curtis-7
Klein, Norma—5
Kleven, Elisa ("Elisa Schneider")-7
Kline, Suzy-7
Knight, Eric—4
Knight, Hilary—4
Knight, Kathryn Lasky. *See* Lasky, Kathryn—6
Knight, Ruth Adams—M
Knipe, Alden Arthur—J
Knipe, Emilie Benson—J
"Knox, Calvin M." *See* Silverberg, Robert—3
Knox, Rose B.—J
Knudson, R. R. (Rozanne Ruth)—6
Kobayashi, Masako Matsuno. *See* Matsuno, Masako—4
Koehn, Ilse (Ilse Koehn Van Zwienen)—5
Koering, Ursula—M
Koertge, Ron-7
Koffler, Camilla. *See* "Ylla"—M
Kogan, Deborah Raphaela. *See* Ray, Deborah Kogan—6
Konigsburg, E. L.—3
Korman, Gordon (Richard)-7
Krahn, Fernando—4
Krasilovsky, Phyllis—M
Kraus, Robert ("Eugene H. Hippopotamus")—3
Krauss, Ruth—M
Kredel, Fritz—M
Krementz, Jill—5

Krensky, Stephen—6
Kroll, Steven—5
Krull, Kathleen-7
Krumgold, Joseph—M
Krush, Beth—M
Krush, Joe—M
Krüss, James—3
Kuklin, Susan-7
Kullman, Harry—5
Kurelek, William—5
Kuskin, Karla ("Nicholas Charles")—3
Kyle, Anne D.—J
"Kyle, Elisabeth" (Agnes Mary Robertson Dunlop)—M

Laboulaye, Édouard—J
La Mare, Walter De. *See* De La Mare, Walter—J
Lamb, Harold—J
Lambert, Janet—3
Lamorisse, Albert—4
Lampman, Evelyn Sibley ("Lynn Bronson")—M
Lamprey, Louise—J
Lane, Sheena Porter. *See* Porter, Sheena—3
Langstaff, John—3
Langton, Jane (Gillson)—5
Lansing, Marion Florence—J
Lasker, Joe (Joseph Leon)—5
Laskowski, Janina Domanska. *See* Domanska, Janina—3
Laskowski, Jerzy—3
Lasky, Kathryn (Kathryn Lasky Knight)—6
Latham, Jean Lee—M
Latham, Mavis Thorpe Clark. *See* Clark, Mavis Thorpe—4
Lathrop, Dorothy P.—J
Lattany, Kristin Elaine Eggleston Hunter. *See* Hunter, Kristin—4
Lattimore, Deborah Nourse-7
Lattimore, Eleanor Frances—J
Lauber, Patricia—3
Laut, Agnes C.—J
Lavies, Bianca-7
Lawrence, Jacob—4
Lawrence, Louise (Elizabeth Rhoda Holden)—6
Lawrence, Mildred—M
Lawson, Don (Donald Elmer)—6
Lawson, Marie Abrams. *See* Lawson, Robert—J
Lawson, Robert—J
Le Cain, Errol (John)—6
Le Guin, Ursula K.—4
Le Sueur, Meridel—M
Le Tord, Bijou—6
Leach, Maria (Alice Mary Doane Leach)—4
Leaf, Munro—J
Lee, Dennis-7
Lee, Manning de V.—M

Lee, Mildred (Mildred Lee Scudder)—3
Lee, Tina—M
Leedy, Loreen-7
Leeming, Joseph—J
Leeuw, Adèle de. *See* de Leeuw, Adèle—J
"Le Grand" (Le Grand Henderson)—J
Leighton, Margaret—M
Leisk, David Johnson. *See* "Johnson, Crockett"—3
"L'Engle, Madeleine" (Madeleine Franklin)—M
Lenski, Lois—J
Lent, Blair ("Ernest Small")—3
Lent, Henry B.—J
"Leodhas, Sorche Nic." *See* "Nic Leodhas, Sorche"—3
Lerner, Carol—3
Leroe, Ellen W(hitney)-7
Lester, Julius—4
Levin, Betty—6
Levine, Ellen-7
Levinson, Riki—6
Levitin, Sonia ("Sonia Wolff")—5
Levoy, Myron—5
Levy, Elizabeth—5
Lewellen, John—M
Lewin, Ted-7
Lewis, C. S.—M
Lewis, Elizabeth Foreman—J
Lewis, J. Patrick-7
Lewis, Richard-7
Lewiton, Mina—M
Lexau, Joan M. ("Joan L. Nodset")—4
Ley, Willy—3
Lifton, Betty Jean—3
Lindbergh, Anne ("Anne Lindbergh Feydy")—6
Lindbergh, Reeve-7
Linde, Gunnel—4
Lindenbaum, Pija-7
Linderman, Frank B.—J
Lindgren, Astrid—M
Lindgren, Barbro—6
Lindman, Maj—J
Lindquist, Jennie D.—M
Lindquist, Willis—M
Lingard, Joan—5
Lionni, Leo—3
Lipkind, William—M
Lippincott, Joseph Wharton—M
Lipsyte, Robert—5
Lisle, Janet Taylor—6
Little, Jean—4
Lively, Penelope—4
Livingston, Myra Cohn—4
Lobel, Anita—3
Lobel, Arnold—3
Locke, Robert. *See* Bess, Clayton—6
Locker, Thomas—6
Löfgren, Ulf—4
Lofting, Hugh—J

Picture Credits

Arthur Arnold, Caroline Arnold; *Aliza Aurbach*, Uri Orlev; *Merrilee Brand*, Michael Bedard; *Paul Brewer*, Kathleen Krull; *Dwight Carter*, Brian Pinkney; *Hugh Cunningham*, Susan Price; *Das Anudas*, Ann Cameron; *deKun*, Carolyn Reeder; *Ruth DeMauro*, Susan Meddaugh; *Dewey Neild Photography*, Minfong Ho; *Louise Erdrich*, Michael Dorris; *Irene Ferguson*, Alexandra Day; *Murray Forbes*, Budge Wilson; *Clyde Garland*, Sherry Garland; *Jose Gaytan*, Pat Ross; *John Griffith*, Helen Griffith; *Al Guiteras*, Patricia Polacco; *J. Heinrichs*, Ron Koertge; *Jane Hill*, Marc Talbert; *Ross Hipwell, Courtesy of News Limited*, Graeme Base; *James Ho Lim*, Paul Richard Yee; © *Holman's Photography Studio*, Ruth White; *Len Irish*, David Wiesner; *Jules*, Bruce Coville; *Diane Kaufmann*, Claudia Mills; *Russell Kelly*, Kit Pearson; *Lawrence J. Kennedy*, William Jasperson; © *Bill Kontzias*, Ted Lewin; *Root Leeb*, Rafik Schami; *Jodi Levinson*, Gennady Spirin; *Carol Grocki Lewis*, Richard Lewis; *Bjorn Lindenbaum*, Pija Lindenbaum; © *Mark Lovewell*, Norman Bridwell; *Keith Maillard*, Sarah Ellis; *Gerald Malanga*, Michael McCurdy; *George Marsden*, Shonto Begay; © *Pierre Masure*, Juanita Havill; *Michele McDonald*, Megan McDonald; *Glenn Most*, Bernard Most; *Michael Nye*, Naomi Shihab Nye; *Julie Offutt*, Jane Dyer; *Ann W. Olson*, George Ella Lyon; *Marla Paraskevas*, Loreen Leedy; *Peter Pate*, Carole Byard; *Don Perkins*, Lensey Namioka; *Susan Perly*, Dennis Lee; © *1994 Vicki Reed*, Barbara M. Joose; *Eva Sanders*, Scott Russell Sanders; *Marilyn Sanders*, Deborah Nourse Lattimore; *J. Brough Schamp*, Jane Leslie Conly; *Lillian Schultz*, Lois Ehlert; *Kevin Seabrooke*, Brenda Seabrooke; *Matthew Self*, Sharon Creech; *Ken Shung*, Fred Marcellino; *Elaine Shusterman*, Neal Shusterman; *Brian Smale*, Jon Scieszka; *Brian Smale*, Lane Smith; *James F. Smith*, Janice Lee Smith; *Carolyn Soto*, Gary Soto; *Alison Speckman*, Joan Carris; © *Natalie Stultz*, Lyll de Becerra Jenkins; *Bob Talbot*, Pamela Service; *Julie Betts Testwuide*, Marisabina Russo; ©*1994 Jeff Thiebauth*, Chris Lynch; © *Thomas Victor*, Sherley Anne Williams; *Tim Wainright*, Jane Ray; *Howard Wallach*, Mel Glenn; *Bee Weber*, Sheila Gordon; *Warren Welch*, Linda Crew; ©*1994 Jerome Wexler*, Jerome Wexler; *Rosemary Willey*, Margaret Wiley; *Cecelia Diaz Zieba*, David Diaz.